Creating Safe and Supportive S
Fostering Students' Mental Hea....

Creating Safe and Supportive Schools and Fostering Students' Mental Health provides pre- and in-service educators with the tools they need to prevent, pre-empt, handle, and recover from threats to students' mental health. School safety and fostering a supportive learning environment have always been issues fundamental to educators. Over the last decade, teachers and administrators have been called on more than ever to cope with bullying, suicide, and violence in their schools. Handling every stage of this diverse set of obstacles can be unwieldy for teachers and administrators alike. Framed with interviews from experts on each of the topics, and including practical and applicable examples, this volume draws together the work of top-tier school psychologists into a text designed to work with existing school structures and curricula to make schools safer.

A comprehensive and multi-faceted resource, this book integrates leading research with the well-respected Framework for Safe and Successful Schools to help educators support school safety, crisis management, and students' mental health.

Featuring interviews with:

Dewey G. Cornell, Frank DeAngelis, Beth Doll, Kevin Dwyer, Katie Eklund, Maurice J. Elias, Michele Gay, Ross W. Greene, Rob Horner, Jane Lazarus, Richard Lieberman, Troy Loker, Melissa A. Louvar-Reeves, Terry Molony, Shamika Patton, Donna Poland, Scott Poland, Eric Rossen, Susan M. Swearer, Ken Trump, and Frank Zenere.

Michael L. Sulkowski is Assistant Professor in the School Psychology Program and Clinical Assistant Professor in the Department of Psychiatry at the University of Arizona, USA.

Philip J. Lazarus is a past-President of the National Association of School Psychologists and Associate Professor and Director of the School Psychology Training Program at Florida International University, USA.

J.H. Schlegel

Creating Safe and Supportive Schools and Fostering Students' Mental Health

Michael L. Sulkowski and Philip J. Lazarus

Routledge
Taylor & Francis Group

NEW YORK AND LONDON

First published 2017
by Routledge
711 Third Avenue, New York, NY 10017

and by Routledge
2 Park Square, Milton Park, Abingdon, Oxon, OX14 4RN

Routledge is an imprint of the Taylor & Francis Group, an informa business

Library of Congress Cataloging in Publication Data
Names: Lazarus, Philip J., author. | Sulkowski, Michael L., author.
Title: Creating safe and supportive schools and fostering students mental health / Philip J. Lazarus and Michael Sulkowski.
Description: New York : Routledge is an imprint of the Taylor & Francis Group, an Informa Business, [2017]
Identifiers: LCCN 2016010396| ISBN 9780415736992 (hardback) |
    ISBN 9780415737005 (pbk.) | ISBN 9781315818221 (e-book)
Subjects: LCSH: School mental health services. | Students—Mental health. | Behavior modification. | School violence—Prevention. | Schools—Safety measures.
Classification: LCC LB3430 .L39 2017 | DDC 371.7/13—dc23
LC record available at https://lccn.loc.gov/2016010396

ISBN: 978-0-415-73699-2 (hbk)
ISBN: 978-0-415-73700-5 (pbk)
ISBN: 978-1-315-81822-1 (ebk)

Typeset in Times New Roman
by Swales & Willis Ltd., Exeter, Devon, UK

Printed and bound in the United States of America by
Edwards Brothers Malloy on sustainably sourced paper

This book is dedicated to the late Dr. Thomas "Tom" Oakland. He was singular in his ability to support students and be kind to everyone; he lived his life with the end in mind. Tom's legacy continues to live in the hearts and minds of an incalculable number of former students, friends, and others whose life he touched. He was a consonant educator, mentor, and friend—a true man in full. Although I miss him deeply, it brings me great joy to know that countless students around the world live richer lives because of Tom's indelible influence. MLS.

This book is dedicated to all the students and school personnel who were seriously injured or lost their lives due to school violence. It is also dedicated to all educators who have risked their lives to protect children from threats. One person who exemplifies this courage is Jon Lane, a math and physical education teacher at Frontier Middle School in Moses Lake, WA, who risked his life to enter a classroom where a school shooter had killed a teacher and left two students in his algebra class dead. Jon charged the perpetrator and subdued him while he was holding the class hostage. While I was consulting with the FBI on the *School Shooter: A Threat Assessment Perspective*, Jon told me, "Although I have been honored for bravery, I was just doing my job as a teacher to protect my students." Jon is an exemplar of all the heroes who represent the better angels of our profession. PJL.

Contents

Preface

The Origin of This Book

On April 19, 1995, two domestic terrorists bombed the Alfred P. Murrah Federal Building in downtown Oklahoma City, which killed more than 168 people and injured more than 680 others. In the immediate aftermath of this horrific act, members of the National Association of School Psychologists (NASP) responded to help children and schools who were impacted by this national tragedy. NASP leaders realized that there was no formal structure or task force within the association that could officially respond to events of this magnitude and support the mental health needs of impacted students. Consequently, NASP proposed the development of a team of crisis responders that could respond to large-scale tragedies. Because I, Philip J. Lazarus, had experience in Florida leading crisis response teams in the aftermath of hurricanes and tornadoes, I was asked to serve as one of the five members of this team, which was later named the National Emergency Assistance Team (NEAT). Most of our members were selected because they had responded to floods, fires, earthquakes, and other natural disasters as well as suicides.

Shortly after the NEAT team convened, a series of rampage school shootings occurred in the United States. As a result of these unprecedented attacks, the NEAT team was contacted by local school districts to offer crisis intervention services. In our first few years, we responded on site to fatal tragedies in Pearl, MS, West Paducah, KY, Jonesboro, AK, Edinboro, PA, Springfield, OR, Littleton, CO, Lake Worth, FL, Flint, MI, Red Lake, MN, Santee, CA, and El Cajon, CA, among other communities.

When our team was first developed, never in our wildest imagination did we expect to respond to tragedies in which students took loaded weapons to school with the intent of killing their classmates and school staff. Our country and our schools were changing rapidly, and what had first appeared shocking and unthinkable, was soon becoming the new normal.

In the aftermath of three school shootings within a two-week period, I was called on to do media interviews. Before one of these interviews for the Glenn Beck show, I was trying to think of the most important message to get across to the public. In an effort to reassure parents and mitigate panic, the one message I came up with was: "Children are safe in school. The actual chance of being killed at school is less than one in a million. Send your children to school." During the first part of the interview, Glenn Beck asked me predictable questions. I provided facts, warning signs, advice for parents, and statistics such as we are losing 25 students every three days to violence in America, the equivalent of losing a classroom of children. Then Mr. Beck asks, "So, Dr. Lazarus, what's going on with our society? Why all this violence? Are we like the Romans, feeding our kids to the lions?"

Wow! How do you answer a question like that? For a moment I felt like a deer in the headlights but eventually I talked about how we as a society glorify violence. By the time a typical child graduates from elementary school, he or she has already witnessed more than 100,000 violent events on television. Moreover, children often cannot tell the difference between the bad guys and the good guys.

During the course of the interview, I explained how it used to take the army weeks or months to train soldiers to kill an enemy combatant during World War I and World War II. However, with the advent of point-and-shoot video games, many students already have simulated practice with killing people before they even attend middle school. In fact, the average age of a targeted school shooter is 14.5 years old, the age range of a middle school student.

The day after the interview, I could not get Glenn Beck's question out of my mind. I wished I had said: "The reason this all is happening is because our society is out of whack. We have neglected the emotional well-being of our nation's youth. We can do better. We must do a lot better." My co-author, Michael L. Sulkowski, agrees with this point, and this perspective helped galvanize the creation of this book.

Collectively, we need to see school shooters as the canary in the coal mine. Canaries warn miners of the presence of a toxic leak. Essentially, when the canaries die, the miners get out of the mine. Similarly, school shooters inform us that something is wrong—desperately wrong. Get out. Go in a new direction. We believe, as all concerned educators believe, that this new normal can no longer continue.

From experience gleaned from responding to one senseless tragedy after another and listening to the countless cries of students, parents, and educators, the message became clear that we all must become stronger advocates for the mental health needs of students. With this in mind, I decided to run for President of the National Association of School Psychologists. After I was elected, I spoke across the country and asked audiences of school psychologists if they believed that we, as a society, had done a good job of nurturing the emotional well-being of our nation's youth and to raise their hand if they thought so. As I scanned rooms filled with hundreds of school psychologists from different parts of the country, I noted that no one was raising their hand. That is, school psychologists who are in the schools every day clearly understood that we are not doing a good job supporting our youth. They understood that we needed to go in a new direction. Unfortunately, however, I also realized that I was preaching to the choir, and—for meaningful change to occur—it was necessary to engage all educators and school personnel (not just school psychologists).

In 2011, the two authors of this book connected and began writing articles together on issues related to preventative mental health; however, the primary audience for our work was mental health professionals. In an effort to inspire foundational change, we then decided to write this book to help not just mental health professionals, but all school personnel create safe and supportive schools and address the mental health needs of children. Our intention is to equip all educators—not with firearms—but with the requisite knowledge on how to execute this important task.

Fortunately, during the past two decades, literature on creating safe and supportive schools and fostering students' mental health has expanded considerably This is especially true for topics such as environmental design for safe schools, bullying prevention, suicide prevention, school climate, school connectedness, and school-wide positive behavioral interventions and supports (SWPBIS). Moreover, new areas of inquiry have emerged such as social-emotional learning (SEL), positive psychology, student threat assessment, trauma-sensitive schools, and creating safe learning environments for lesbian, gay, bisexual, transgender, and questioning (LGBTQ) students. In addition, most recently, my co-author, Michael Sulkowski, and a team of researchers at the University of Arizona, were awarded a multi-year, multimillion dollar research grant by the National Institute of Justice to study efforts to create safe schools. They are partnered with the Arizona Department of Education and are working in about 50 schools across the state. Other teams of scholars and practitioners world-wide are researching and developing new approaches to bolstering students' mental health. Essentially, through concerted effort, knowledge is expanding and we are moving into a new paradigm.

Through our work with educators, including administrators and school support personnel, we have learned that they have rarely or never received training on the aforementioned topics.

However, these professionals have told us that they desperately need information on how they can create safe schools and support students' mental health. Through this work, we learned that current and future educators want answers to questions such as:

- How do I stop students from bullying each other?
- What should I do if a student tells me he wants to kill himself?
- I have a homeless student in my class and want to help. What can I do?
- Is it possible to identify a student who could be a school shooter?
- I have a student in my class who often seems so sad. How can I help?
- The father of one of my students was just arrested and I want to reach out to her, but without letting the other students know. What should I do?
- I have heard that we can help children do better in school by teaching them mindfulness. Is that true?
- Can we teach children how to be more resilient?
- A girl in my second grade class lost her mother in a car accident. She seems to have lost all interest in school. I know she is grieving and I want to help. What advice do you have?
- My brother had mental health problems all through childhood and had no friends in school. I want to set up my class so that students don't ignore or pick on each other. What can I do to help students in my class establish friendships?
- My cousin is gay and he often got tormented in school. I am a sixth grade teacher and want to do something in my school to support gay students. There are other teachers that have the same concern. Any advice?
- I noticed a student had cut marks on her arms that I had never seen before. She told me she cut herself whenever she felt sad or angry. She asked me not to tell anyone and said she would stop. I agreed in order to keep her trust, but now I think I made the wrong decision. What do you recommend I do now?

As illustrated by these thoughtful questions, educators are on the front lines when it comes to addressing the basic safety and mental health needs of students. Concerned educators deal with much more than teaching students academics and getting them ready for standardized tests. They grapple with the best ways to educate the whole child—in mind, body, and spirit. They often serve as unofficial social workers and counselors; they advise and mentor their students; they teach them social and emotional skills; and they help students cope in midst of hardship. And though it is not in their job description, teachers often are first responders who address the immediate mental health needs of their students. In essence, educators protect the future security of our country. This idea is best exemplified by the words of Marian Wright Edelman, the founder of the Children's Defense Fund who said, "The greatest threat to America's national security comes from no enemy without but from our failure to protect, invest in, and educate all our children who make up all our futures."

In our book, we address the aforementioned questions so that you are prepared to manage the scenarios behind these questions. Our intention is to help you in your role (e.g. teacher, principal, counselor, special education professional, social worker, school resource officer, coach, school psychologist, school nurse) to foster the emotional well-being of our youth and to ensure that future generations are equipped with the knowledge, skills, and dispositions that are needed to lead successful and fulfilling lives. However, we also challenge you as a reader of this book to develop new questions about the best ways to create safe and supportive schools and support students' mental health. With the publication of this book, we hope to educate, yet we also value your thoughts and feedback. We wish to learn from you regarding your successes and your challenges. Please write to us! We can be reached at lazarusp@fiu.edu (Philip J. Lazarus) and sulkowski@email.arizona.edu (Michael L. Sulkowski).

Although school safety and security have been compromised by egregious acts of violence, we do not have to accept this as "our new normal." As any able sailor knows, a subtle shift in direction can create a sea change in momentum. With this metaphor in mind, we believe that, in uncertain waters, concerned educators can help bring about this sea change and create better futures for all students. The words of Franklin D. Roosevelt are most fitting in this regard: "To reach a port, we must sail—sail, not tie at anchor—sail, not drift." In the spirit of these words, let us be steadfast in our efforts to create safe and supportive schools and to foster the mental health of all students. We welcome you to sail with us to usher in a sea of change.

Acknowledgments

We would especially like to thank Philip Lazarus' wife, Jane Lazarus, for reading over the drafts of the manuscript and for her helpful editing and insight. We also appreciate her practical suggestions based on over 30 years of experience as a school psychologist for Broward County Public Schools. When she asked, "What are we doing this weekend?" and I (PJL) replied, "working on the book" she was both understanding and patient. We also wish to thank all the interviewees who contributed their time and expertise to help provide useful suggestions to educators, administrators, and school-based mental health professionals. We are indebted to their contribution. They all made this a much better work. We would like to thank Caitlyn Francis, a doctoral student at the University of Arizona, for her help with compiling references and checking citations. Additionally, we are grateful to Annela Costa, school psychologist and doctoral student in special education at Florida International University, who was especially important in writing this book. She provided research in the areas of positive psychology, mindsets, resilience, and trauma-informed schools. She could always be counted on to be timely and thorough. Thanks also go out to Munirah McNeely who double checked all the websites and links to see if they were still viable. I (PJL) would also like to thank my 93 year old dad, Morris Lazarus, for permitting us to use his art work on the cover. We also appreciate Rebecca Novack, our first editor at Routledge. When we told her that we needed to expand the coverage of our text in order to provide more breadth and depth to our readership, she had our backs and helped convince the publisher that this was the right way to go.

PJL & MLS

Part I

Creating Safe and Emotionally Healthy Schools

1   The Evolving Role of Educators

The story of Keyshawn. "I'm not going to talk to you" were the first words that Keyshawn said to the school psychologist who was assigned to work with him. Keyshawn was nine years old. He had an extensive history of trauma and abuse. In a fit of rage, he turned over an entire classroom. He caused thousands of dollars in damage and he had to be restrained by a school resource officer while he was using a chair to smash school windows. Fortunately, the school psychologist gave Keyshawn the time and space he needed to feel comfortable and open up. She met with him outside the classroom and offered him tissues and water, which he reluctantly took. Then she asked him to take her to his favorite place in the school and they proceeded to go to a large oak tree where students gather for recess. She also validated his frustrations and provided him with emotional support. Keyshawn then melted. He began crying loudly, shaking, and profusely apologizing; he wrapped his arms around the school psychologist while he wept. Keyshawn and the school psychologist began therapy the next day and worked with his teacher to develop a trauma-sensitive classroom.

The story of Chloe. Chloe did not fit in. According to her own words, she "was not like the other girls." Chloe was feeing increasingly more attracted to her female peers. However, her family ascribed to traditional values and they did not accept non-heterosexual relationships. Therefore, Chloe was very worried that her family might find out about her sexual interest in other girls. Because of pain associated with living "in the closet," Chloe began cutting herself with razors, glass, and other sharp objects. Her family members were confused by her behavior. They wondered why she would deliberately hurt herself when she had everything: beauty, intelligence—and she was making good grades. Fortunately, the cuts on Chloe's arm were noticed by a concerned teacher. Her teacher then encouraged Chloe to start seeing a counselor who helped her immensely. She and her counselor worked together on problem-solving and developed strategies to reduce Chloe's emotional distress. They saw each other twice a week for a semester. Chloe is now in college and she is doing well.

The story of Jared. It was the first week of school, a week that often sets the tone for the rest of the year, and Jared had already gotten in a fight with another student. He was suspended for fighting but the other student was not. This enraged Jared and he vowed revenge. Jared told a friend that he was going to bring a gun to school and shoot the student that he fought, as well as the school's assistant principal whom he blamed for his suspension. Fortunately, Jared's friend took this threat seriously and he told his mother who then called a teacher she knew at Jared's school. Immediately, consistent with the school's established safety plan, local authorities were contacted and the police searched Jared and his possessions. They found a gun in his backpack and a suicide note. Upon expulsion, Jared was sent to a residential treatment center where he and his family received intensive therapy.

What is common in these stories is that concerned educators, as well as school-based mental health professionals, students, parents, administrators, and local police officers, all stepped in to support students' mental health and ensure school safety. In the first story, a school psychologist had the forbearance to look past the student's abusive words and the equanimity to provide emotional support. In the second story, a teacher noticed that a student was in distress and had the foresight to refer her for counseling. Lastly, in the third story, a range of educators and others from the community acted to avert a potential tragedy while providing a highly distraught student with the support that he needed. Overall, these stories underscore how creating safe and supportive schools and fostering students' mental health is a job for all members of school communities—not just for school-based mental health professionals, administrators, and school resources officers (SROs). Moreover, to maximize these efforts, all educators such as teachers, administrators, teachers' aides, school-based mental health professionals, and other key adults at school must come together and work collaboratively.

Creating Safe Schools and Fostering Students' Mental Health

Educators are well positioned to help create safe and supportive schools and to foster students' mental health. In fact, they are on the front line with these efforts as they influence the way that students feel at school. In addition, they frequently encounter students with mental health problems. In support of the former, educators typically spend almost eight hours per day with the students they teach and support in varying capacities. Moreover, many students report that educators are among the most important adults in their lives (Sulkowski, Demaray, & Lazarus, 2012; Woolley & Bowen, 2007). Further, regarding the role of educators in supporting students' mental health, one study found that approximately three-quarters of educators report having worked with or encountered a student with a serious mental health problem during the past year (Reinke, Stormont, Herman, Puri, & Goel, 2011). Thus, educators have tremendous power to influence learning environments and impact the lives of the students they serve. To help in this regard, Chapter 2 discusses strategies for creating safe and supportive schools.

But isn't the role of educators to teach? Although it is true that delivering rich instruction remains the central role for educators, thousands of educators across the U.S. and beyond are now also helping to foster students' emotional well-being. Research suggests that educators are becoming increasingly open to supporting students' mental health. Specifically, results from a study by Reinke et al. (2011) indicate that the overwhelming majority of teachers (94 percent) report that schools should be involved in the delivery of mental health services to students, which indicates that the majority of educators view their role as being broader than just delivering instruction. Unfortunately, however, in the same study, 66 percent of teachers reported that they lacked the skills necessary to support students with mental health problems. Therefore, an obvious need exists for providing educators with the knowledge and skills they can use to support students' complex and multifaceted mental health needs. Chapters 3, 4, 5, and 6 discuss individual and whole-school efforts to foster students' mental health.

The Evolving Role of Educators in Public Education

Schools have not always been democratic institutions in the U.S. Prior to compulsory school acts—first in Massachusetts in 1852 and last in Mississippi in 1917—education largely was reserved for the wealthy (Jeynes, 2007; Rothbard, 1999). Schools enrolled children from affluent families and these students were taught skills that would enable them to navigate the upper echelons of society successfully. However, U.S. education has become increasingly more egalitarian in that its role has changed from being a vehicle for propagating the status quo to a mechanism for social advancement, cohesion, and justice (Boli, Ramirez, & Meyer, 1985).

As a general trend, public education has become increasingly more inclusive throughout the twentieth century. Following the landmark U.S. Supreme Court case *Brown v. Board of*

Education of Topeka (347 U.S. 483) in 1954 that established that separate public schools for black and white students were unconstitutional, great strides have been made toward opening the doors of education to all students, regardless of their race, ethnicity, background, or beliefs (see Kluger [2011] for review). However, as schools became more inclusive of students from culturally diverse backgrounds, students with disabilities were often still prohibited from benefiting from public education (Sulkowski & Joyce-Beaulieu, 2014). In fact, it was not until the passage of the Rehabilitation Act of 1973 (29 U.S.C. 794; 34 C.F.R. 300.1 et. seq.) that Federal programs could no longer discriminate against individuals on the basis of their disability.

To provide protections to students with disabilities, President Gerald Ford signed into law the Education for All Handicapped Children Act of 1975 (Public Law [PL] 94-142). This major piece of legislation has been aptly described as the "Bill of Rights for Handicapped Children." The implementation of PL 94-142 had a profound effect on exceptional student education. Children with disabilities who were not previously served in schools were afforded a free and appropriate public education (FAPE) centering on special education and related services (Strichart & Lazarus, 1986). The law provided handicapped students with rights, including the right to due process, nondiscriminatory assessment, confidential handling of personal records and information, and the opportunity for caregivers to examine all records pertaining to the evaluation, placement, and educational programming of their child. Furthermore, caregivers were given the right to challenge the contents of records and to obtain an independent evaluation of their child.

Public Law 94-142 was later re-authorized as the Individuals with Disabilities Education Act (IDEA) in 1990 with additional provisions. Basically, PL-94-142 and IDEA aimed to level the playing field and mandated that every student with a disability be provided with an individualized educational plan (IEP) that allows them to participate fully in their education in the least restrictive environment possible (Sulkowski, Joyce, & Storch, 2012). This act was re-authorized in 2004 as the Individuals with Disabilities Education Improvement Act (IDEIA; PL 108-446) and under the McKinney–Vento Homeless Assistance Act (McK-V Act; Pub. L. 100-77), which was incorporated under IDEIA, it provided additional protections to some highly at-risk or vulnerable student populations such as homeless students. In addition to providing other protections, the McK-V Act ensures the immediate enrollment of students who lack a fixed, regular, and adequate night-time residence (Sulkowski & Joyce-Beaulieu, 2014; Sulkowski & Michael, 2014). Therefore, the act protects students who are homeless or seriously economically disenfranchised. To help address the needs of students who often are overlooked, Chapter 14 discusses helping highly vulnerable student populations such as homeless students.

As a general trend, U.S. schools have become increasingly more inclusive of students who are racially, ethnically, and economically diverse as well as supportive of students with classifiable disabilities. However, despite this progress, considerable room for improvement still exists to support all students. Currently, consistent with the school mental health movement, which began roughly in the 1990s, thousands of schools appear to be in the process of becoming more inclusive and supportive of the needs of another group of students—those who have mental health needs—who traditionally have been neglected (Flaherty, Weist, & Warner, 1996; Sulkowski et al., 2012). Therefore, as recent trends suggest, the evolving role for educators likely will involve supporting students' mental health and emotional well-being.

School-based Mental Health

One out of every five students is suffering with a serious mental health problem according to estimates by the office of the U.S. Surgeon General (Department of Health and Human Services [DHHS], 2000). The prevalence of mental illness among children has increased (Perou et al., 2010) and almost half of adolescents ages 13 to 18 have had a mental disorder (Merikangas et al., 2010; see Chapter 3 for further discussion on the impact of mental illness). Moreover, from

2007 to 2010 there was an increase of 24 percent in inpatient mental health and substance abuse admissions according to the Health Care Cost Institute (2012).

Mental illness places a huge burden on U.S. students, schools, and society. As noted by Dr. Stephen Brock, the Past President of the National Association of School Psychologists (NASP), experiencing mental illness causes significant pain and impairs healthy functioning (2015). In a NASP Presidential Address, Brock argues forcefully that all stakeholders in schools should support efforts to provide access to school mental health services. Failure to do so can result in the loss of life. For example, research indicates that suicide is the second leading cause of death among young people ages 15 to 19 and that than 9 out of every 10 completed suicides are related to some type of mental illness, most frequently depression (Erbacher, Singer, & Poland, 2015; Miller, 2011; Shaffer & Craft, 1999). Moreover, more youth have died by suicide than by cancer, heart disease, birth defects, pneumonia, influenza, cerebrovascular disease, pregnancy and childbirth complications, and chronic lung disease *combined* (Brock, 2015; Hoyert & Xu, 2012; Kalafat & Lazarus, 2002). Because of the importance of this topic, Chapter 16 discusses suicide assessment, prevention, and intervention.

Student Access to Service

As previously noted, millions of students display mental health needs. Unfortunately, however, most of these students do not receive mental health services to address these needs (Farmer, Burns, Phillips, Angold, & Costello, 2003). In fact, according to the U.S. Public Health Service (2000), in any given year only 20 percent of children and adolescents with mental disorders receive mental health care. Yet, for students who do receive mental health support, over 60 percent of these individuals receive it in public school settings. Therefore, school is the entry point for the delivery of mental health services for a majority of our nation's youth (Farmer et al., 2003). In light of this, in addition to their traditional goal of teaching academic skills, U.S. public schools have become key institutions that also support students' mental health. Further, a great capacity exists for these institutions to expand the provision of school-based mental health services to support students who experience barriers to access treatment in clinical or community mental health centers—that is, the rest of the students who need mental health care—yet do not receive these supports (Sulkowski et al., 2012; Sulkowski, Wingfield, Jones, & Coulter, 2011).

Providing further support for the provision of school-based mental health support, Brock (2015) argues the following: (a) at some point in their lives, the great majority of youth will attend public school; (b) youth are 21 times more likely to visit a school-based clinic for their mental health care than they are to visit a community-based clinic (Juszczak, Melinkovitch, and Kaplan, 2003); and (c) half of all lifetime cases of mental illness have their onset prior to age 14. Moreover, Brock (2015) points out the significant burden that mental illness places on society. Approximately half of students aged 14 or older who are living with mental illness drop out of school according to the U.S. Department of Education (2001). This is the highest dropout rate of any established disability group.

Not only would the provision of mental health supports by schools help reduce the pain and suffering of so many of our youth, but it could also have long-term economic and health benefits for our nation. In support of this position, the National Research Council & Institute of Medicine (2007) has noted that mental disorders in children—especially those untreated—are associated with an increased risk for mental disorders in adulthood. In the U.S. alone, the estimated cost of mental disorders (which includes health care, juvenile justice, the use of special education services, and decreased productivity) in any given year has been estimated to be 2.5 billion dollars.

Further supporting the need for school-based mental health services, a study by Cummings, Ponce, and Mays (2010) found that providing these services in schools helps reduce disparities in service delivery, particularity among racial and/or ethnic minority students. Students often view schools as trustworthy institutions and centerpieces in communities across the U.S., which makes some students more willing to access mental health services in these familiar and trusted settings (Sulkowski & Joyce-Beaulieu, 2014; Sulkowski et al., 2013). In addition, schools also have a precedent for delivering services to highly at-risk, vulnerable, underserved, victimized, and stigmatized students (Sulkowski & Michael, 2014). In light of this, increasing numbers of educators and members of related disciplines are advocating for the provision of mental health services at school (Brock, 2015; Kutash, Duchnowski, & Lynn, 2006). Thus, consistent with a trend to support all students, many schools across the U.S. are increasing their capacity to address the needs of students with mental health problems.

School Safety and Violence Prevention

In addition to supporting students' mental health, educators are now also taking on roles to increase school safety and prevent violence. School safety has become a salient issue for legislators and policy makers who develop and enforce educational standards and guidelines. To address problems with student drug use and school violence, the Clinton administration promoted the Goals 2000: Educate America Act (U.S. Department of Education [COE], 1994) in 1993. A key goal of this act focused on enhancing school safety by stating that: "by the year 2000, every school in America will be free of drugs and violence and will offer a disciplined environment conducive to learning, by ensuring that all schools are safe and free of violence" (U.S. DOE, 1994, p. 2).

In the following year, the Gun-Free Schools Act was passed to specify how disciplinary actions would be carried out for students in possession of guns while on school grounds. In general, this act stated that schools receiving federal funding are required to expel offending students for a minimum of one year. However, despite these efforts, President Clinton formally requested that the U.S. Department of Education (DOE) draft guidelines to address school violence and support students with serious mental health problems. The guidelines were written because of a series of highly publicized rampage school shootings that occurred in the mid to late 1990s and the inability of the previous efforts to prevent these tragedies. The goal for developing school violence prevention and intervention guidelines was to help educators and parents more effectively identify warning signs when students were displaying signs of serious emotional disturbance or violent potential. Ultimately, the U.S. DOE's guidelines were crafted into the publication entitled *Early warning, timely response: A guide to safe schools* (Dwyer, Osher, & Warger, 1998). Expert Interview 1.1 by Kevin Dwyer, co-author of the *Early warning guide*, discusses how education has changed over the past half century and the impact of this document on school violence.

Expert Interview 1.1 with Kevin Dwyer

Past President, National Association of School Psychologists

PJL. You have worked as a school psychologist for more than 50 years. Have the conditions in schools gotten better, worse or remained about the same? Are we making progress since the publication of the text you co-wrote: Early warning, timely response: A guide to safe schools?

KD. Public education has improved over the half century. Previously, many more youth did not graduate. In my earliest years (starting in 1962), all schools in my district were still segregated. Children with disabilities such as Down's syndrome were placed in restrictive institutions rather than in public schools. Some children with IQs of 79, then called retarded, had their education terminated in eighth grade where they could stay in special education classes until age 16; they could not even enter vocational high schools. Supports for children with learning disabilities were non-existent and the recognition of poverty as a barrier to learning was close to zero. Moreover, in 1992 data from CDC and elsewhere were quite depressing. Rates of homicide and suicide were at an all-time high, as well as rates of drug use and teen pregnancy. Further, a lot more students reported carrying weapons at school. However, measures undertaken by the U.S. Courts and initiatives from presidents such as Lyndon Johnson have changed this and things have gotten better. On all the previous metrics, levels of danger and lethality are down and graduation rates are higher. Since Columbine, more students have gotten the message that they need to tell an adult when they have heard that a fellow classmate has threatened violence. But most importantly, students are much more likely to inform an adult when they perceive the school culture as positive; that is, when they trust that adults at the school will take positive action and when they view the school faculty as respectful and caring. Positive relationships between students and staff matter.

More recently, following the tragic shooting that occurred at Sandy Hook Elementary in CT, the American School Counselor Association (ASCA), the National Association of Elementary School Principals (NAESP), the National Association of Secondary School Principals (NASSP), the National Association of School Resource Officers (NASRO), the School Social Work Association of America (SSWAA), and the National Association of School Psychologists (NASP) drafted the *Framework for safe and successful schools* document (Cowan, Vaillancourt, Rossen, & Pollitt, 2013). This document provides a framework that aims to improve school safety and increase access to mental health supports for students. In the document, efforts to improve school climate and safety are described as being overlapping initiatives that complement each other. Ultimately, in order to create safe and supportive schools, schools must work toward integrating the services they provide (e.g., academic, behavioral, social, emotional, mental health). Table 1.1 lists key best practices from the *Framework* on how to create safe and successful schools. In addition, Expert Interview 1.2, with Eric Rossen, one of the authors of the NASP Framework, discusses the development and the implementation of the *Framework* and actions that all educators can take to help ensure the physical and psychological safety of all students.

Table 1.1 Key points from the *Framework* on how to create safe and successful schools

1.   Integrate services through collaboration
2.   Implement multi-tiered systems of support
3.   Improve access to school-based mental health supports
4.   Integrate school safety, crisis/emergency prevention, preparedness, response, and recovery
5.   Balance physical and psychological safety
6.   Employ effective, positive school discipline
7.   Allow for consideration of context
8.   Acknowledge that sustainable and effective improvement takes patience and commitment

Expert Interview 1.2 with Eric Rossen

National Association of School Psychologists

PJL. What is the Framework for safe and successful schools *and why was it developed?*

ER. The *Framework for safe and successful schools* constitutes a joint statement from school principals and organizations that represent the professionals and community partners who work day in and day out to keep our children safe, ensure their well-being, and promote learning. The partnership between our organizations seeks to reinforce the interdisciplinary, collaborative, and cohesive approach that is required within each school building to create and sustain genuinely safe, supportive environments that meet the needs of the whole child. The Framework is available at http://www.nasponline.org/Documents/Research%20and%20Policy/Advocacy%20 Resources/Framework_for_Safe_and_Successful_School_Environments.pdf.

The Framework outlines evidence-based policies and practices for improving school safety and increasing access to mental health supports for children and youth. Efforts to improve school climate, safety, and learning are not separate endeavors and must be designed, funded, and implemented as a comprehensive school-wide approach. The statement is intended, in part, to guide policy leaders in shaping meaningful policies that will genuinely equip America's schools to educate and safeguard our children over the long term.

Despite growing consensus in recent years among educators (administrators, mental health professionals, and security personnel) regarding best practices to improve and sustain school safety, there has been little commonality in public policy discussions or proposals. This disconnect became glaringly apparent in the wake of the Sandy Hook shootings. Almost every company/ organization/advocacy group had an opinion about the best way to safeguard schools (e.g., bulletproof whiteboards and backpacks; arming every teacher; installing bulletproof doors). The Obama administration took a proactive role in generating a set of executive actions, (found within the Now Is the Time plan: www.whitehouse.gov/issues/preventing-gun-violence).

Despite attempts to gather ideas and recommendations from a variety of stakeholder groups, these executive actions lacked specific guidance on scientifically proven approaches to improve school safety. When combined with the call by some vocal groups to arm educators as a primary solution, the core Framework group came together and unanimously agreed on the need for a collaborative, unified document providing specific policy and practice guidance on maintaining physical and psychological safety in schools, and to seek endorsement from other education and mental health groups. We needed one voice making clear, evidence-based recommendations from the professions charged with this work to cut through the din of often misdirected and potentially harmful ideas. The Framework provided that voice.

PJL. What are the major actions that schools can take to ensure the physical safety of students?

ER. As described in the Framework, the degree of physical violence in a school is significantly impacted by the attention to school culture, connectedness, and psychological safety. Schools that encourage positive behavior supports, restorative justice, and appropriate discipline policies, and create an improved sense of school community tend to notice reductions in violence.

Additionally, the Framework describes the importance of evidence-based, sustainable emergency and crisis preparedness, response, and recovery planning and training, along with multi-tiered systems of supports.

The following excerpt from the Framework best answers this question:

> Any effort to address school safety should balance building security/physical safety with psychological safety. Relying on highly restrictive physical safety measures alone, such as increasing armed security or imposing metal detectors, typically does not objectively improve school safety. In fact, such measures may cause students to feel less safe and more fearful at school, and could undermine the learning environment. In contrast, combining reasonable physical security measures with efforts to enhance school climate more fully promotes overall school safety. Effectively balancing physical and psychological safety entails:
>
> - Assessing the physical security features of the campus, such as access points to the school grounds, parking lots and buildings, and the lighting and adult supervision in lobbies, hallways, parking lots, and open spaces.
> - Employing environmental design techniques, such as ensuring that playgrounds and sports fields are surrounded by fences or other natural barriers, to limit visual and physical access by non-school personnel.

- Evaluating policies and practices to ensure that students are well monitored, school guests are appropriately identified and escorted, and potential risks and threats are addressed quickly.
- Building trusting, respectful relationships among students, staff, and families.
- Providing access to school mental health services and educating students and staff on how and when to seek help.
- Providing a confidential way for students and other members of the school community to report potential threats, because educating students on "breaking the code of silence" is one of our most effective safety measures.

PJL. What are the major actions that schools can take to ensure the emotional safety of students?

ER. This question is even more complex than the last, and the entire Framework is dedicated to answering that question. If it had to be boiled down to a few short sentences, it would likely require a dedicated, comprehensive, and integrated approach to addressing the mental health needs of all students through multi-tiered systems of support (MTSS); ensuring appropriate staffing of school-employed mental health professionals (school psychologists, school counselors, and school social workers); and improving school climate and connectedness so that students never question whether they will be cared for or accepted as part of the school community.

PJL. What is the connection between physical/emotional safety and academic achievement in children?

ER. They are deeply integrated, such that you likely won't find one without the other. Ensuring physical and emotional safety is a prerequisite to learning. In simple terms, the brain does not attend to learning under stress, even if that stress is a dull yet chronic sense of fear and isolation. This document summarizes the research regarding mental health and academic achievement: www.nasponline.org/advocacy/Academic-MentalHealthLinks.pdf.

PJL. What are the major actions that principals can take to create safe and successful schools?

ER. Principals should consult and collaborate with their school psychologist and professionals in the building to help determine what would work best for their school. The Framework provides some more specific recommendations for systemic change:

1. Fully integrate learning supports (e.g., behavioral, mental health, and social services), instruction, and school management within a comprehensive, cohesive approach that facilitates multidisciplinary collaboration.
2. Implement MTSS that encompass prevention, wellness promotion, and interventions that increase with intensity based on student need, and that promote close school–community collaboration.
3. Improve access to school-based mental health supports by ensuring adequate staffing levels in terms of school-employed mental health professionals who are trained to infuse prevention and intervention services into the learning process and to help integrate services provided through school–community partnerships into existing school initiatives.
4. Integrate ongoing positive climate and safety efforts with crisis prevention, preparedness, response, and recovery to ensure that crisis training and plans: (a) are relevant to the school context, (b) reinforce learning, (c) make maximum use of existing staff resources, (d) facilitate effective threat assessment, and (e) are consistently reviewed and practiced.
5. Balance physical and psychological safety to avoid overly restrictive measures (e.g., armed guards and metal detectors) that can undermine the learning environment and

instead combine reasonable physical security measures (e.g., locked doors and moni-tored public spaces) with efforts to enhance school climate, build trusting relationships, and encourage students and adults to report potential threats. If a school determines the need for armed security, properly trained school resource officers (SROs) are the only school personnel of any type who should be armed.

6. Employ effective, positive school discipline that: (a) functions in concert with efforts to address school safety and climate; (b) is not simply punitive (e.g., zero tolerance); (c) is clear, consistent, and equitable; and (d) reinforces positive behaviors. Using secu-rity personnel or SROs primarily as a substitute for effective discipline policies does not contribute to school safety and can perpetuate the school-to-prison pipeline.

PJL. What are some of the actions that legislators can take to help ensure that our schools are safe and successful?

ER. From the Framework:

Policy Recommendations to Support Effective School Safety

1. Allow for blended, flexible use of funding streams in education and mental health services.
2. Improve staffing ratios to allow for the delivery of a full range of services and effective school–community partnerships.
3. Develop evidence-based standards for district-level policies to promote effective school discipline and positive behavior.
4. Fund continuous and sustainable crisis and emergency preparedness, response, and recovery planning and training that uses evidence-based models.
5. Provide incentives for intra- and interagency collaboration.
6. Support MTSS.

PJL. How might all educators get more involved to help make schools a nurturing and supportive environment?

ER.

- Contribute to a positive school climate by making sure that every student has a trusted adult in the building to whom they can turn and by actively working to prevent negative behaviors such as bullying, instead of ignoring them.
- Know the risk factors and signs of students at risk for a mental health problem or unsafe behaviors. Know what to do and how to get help.
- Reach out and engage families to make them genuine partners in their child's school and education.
- Understand the importance of mental health and well-being to both safety and learning and commit to meeting the social-emotional needs of students as well as their academic knowledge base.
- Insist on and help implement a MTSS model for academics, behavior, and mental health.
- Model positive behavior in interactions with students and other staff.
- Engage in positive discipline practices that focus on underlying issues and teaching appropriate skills rather than simple punishment.
- Use data to identify and address school-wide risk factors for unsafe or negative behaviors.
- Incorporate school psychologists and other school mental health professionals into school leadership teams.
- Advocate with local, state, and federal policy makers for the policies outlined in the Framework to improve the funding, objectives, and structures aimed at improving school safety.

PJL. What are some of the best resources that NASP provides for creating safe schools and fostering students' mental health?

ER. The best resources NASP "provides" are our members, the school psychologists who promote student well-being and support those students with risk factors every day. School psychologists work with teachers, school crisis teams, and administrators to improve the school climate, prevent and respond to safety issues, and help educators and families link mental health to learning and behavior to improve student outcomes in school and life. Professional development and knowledge of research-based practices are important, but they are not a substitute for our most valuable resource—the school psychologist.

NASP also developed the PREPaRE School Crisis Prevention and Intervention Training Curriculum in 2006 as part of NASP's decade-long leadership in providing evidence-based resources and consultation related to school crisis prevention and response. PREPaRE training is ideal for schools committed to improving and strengthening their school safety and crisis management plans, teams and emergency response. See http://www.nasponline.org/professional-development/prepare-training-curriculum.

In terms of other resources, NASP provides publically available free information related to supporting children's mental health and safety; see:

- Framework for School-wide Bullying Prevention and Safety: https://www.nasponline.org/Documents/Research%20and%20Policy/Advocacy%20 Resources/Bullying_Brief_12.pdf.
- Relevant professional development for school psychologists and other school mental health professionals relating to crisis. http://www.nasponline.org/professional-development/prepare-training-curriculum.
- Publications and research; and advocacy for effective policies and funding: http://www.nasponline.org/Documents/Research%20and%20Policy/Advocacy%20 Resources/School_Discipline_Congressional_Briefing.pdf.

School Violence and School Shootings

Although tragedies can inform improvements in practice and policy related to school safety, considerable misinformation and questionable practices also can abound in their wake. For example, a veritable cottage industry has sprung up to offer dubious technologies and unsubstantiated strategies for reducing school violence and increasing student safety in the aftermath of the Sandy Hook shootings. Some companies now offer bulletproof backpacks and sleeping mats, while others have proposed arming teachers with firearms (Siebold, 2013). Ultimately, however, violent school attacks are exceedingly rare. Contrary to public perception, less than 1 percent of annual homicides among youth between the ages of 5 and 18 in the U.S. occur in schools (Modzeleski et al., 2008).

According to an analysis of FBI data, Cornell (2015) has noted that for school-age youth for the time frame from 2005 to 2010, there were 9,847 homicides that occurred in a residence, 4,455 on a street, 1,209 in a parking lot, 522 in a bar or restaurant, 492 in a store or gas station, 288 in a public building or business, and 211 in a motel or hotel. In comparison, there were 49 homicides that occurred in a school. Certainly, based on this data, our young people are much safer in schools than in homes or on the street. Lastly, providing further support that schools are generally safe places for students, research by Cornell and Nekvasil (2012) indicates that the average school could expect to experience a student homicide about once every 6,000 years at the current rates. Thus, in light of the aforementioned statistics, it is hard to justify the high costs associated with untested and dubious security technologies (e.g., bulletproof backpacks) coupled with inflating risks associated with increasing the presence of weapons in schools (e.g., arming teachers). This is especially true because effective school violence prevention and intervention approaches exist.

Even though extreme acts of school violence such as school shootings are rare, threats of violence are common in schools. According to the National Center for Education Statistics (Neiman & De Voe, 2009), approximately 48 percent of schools experienced a student threat of physical harm without a weapon during the 2007–2008 academic year and middle schools accounted for the highest rate of student threats, at close to 15 per 1,000 students. Also concerning, Roberts, Zhang, and Truman (2010) found that threats with weapons among high school students during the 2008–2009 academic year ranged from 5 percent of twelfth graders to 9 percent of ninth graders. In another survey of 4,400 high school students, Nekvasil and Cornell (2012) found that approximately 14 percent of students reported being threatened by another student in the past 30 days, and among the 163 students who believed the threat was serious, only 22 percent informed a teacher or other staff member. For more information on school violence, Chapter 15 covers threat assessment and school violence prevention.

The Role of Educators

As illustrated in this chapter, efforts to create safe and supportive schools and foster students' mental health have continued to evolve in light of the challenges that schools and students encounter. Although it is impossible to predict the future, it is safe to assume that increased progress in supporting the needs of all students will result from innovations in research and educators' practice. Thus, if emerging themes from the past reliably predict the future, the ways that educators serve students and school communities likely will continue to advance. In this regard, in addition to educating the minds of students or supporting their academic development, educators likely will also increase the amount of energy they invest in supporting "the whole student" and the environment in which students learn.

Supporting the whole student involves prioritizing the emotional well-being, mental health, safety, and security of all students. Similarly, ensuring that school environments are safe, secure, and healthy, involves implementing academic, behavioral, and social supports for all members of school communities. These goals build on what educators already do—and do well. In other words, they complement efforts to teach students the skills they need to be successful in school and in life more generally. Similar to how students need adequate nutrition to learn optimally, they also need emotional nourishment to feel safe and mentally strong, which then allows them to do their best in school. Thus, the overlapping goals of supporting the whole student and fostering healthy learning environments are foundational for maximizing student success. Consistent with these goals, Chapters 7, 8, and 9 discuss strategies for creating nurturing learning environments. Collectively, these chapters are integral for supporting the whole student.

Doing More with Less

A common theme impacting U.S. public education is that educators are being asked to do more with less. Almost across the entire country, budgets for state departments of education (DOEs), state educational agencies (SEAs), and local education agencies (LEAs), have been cut. This, in turn, is resulting in the closure of schools, classroom and school overcrowding, and unacceptably high ratios of students to school-based mental health professionals as well as other support personnel. Because of this difficult reality, it is reasonable to wonder how educators will be able to find the time and resources to do more for their students with less. In fact, in an era of aggressive accountability standards, high stakes testing, and administrative pressures for teachers to "teach to the test," it is reasonable to wonder how educators will continue to do what they already do well for their students.

However, efforts to support the whole student and to foster healthy schools do not need to overburden already busy educators. Instead, educational priorities must be shifted. For example, when a school prioritizes school efforts to reduce bullying, the entire learning environment can change (Espelage, Low, Polanin, & Brown, 2015). Research indicates that most often it takes three years to make this shift (Cohen, McCabe, Michelli, & Pickeral, 2009), yet once the school climate changes and all students feel physically and emotionally safe, learning becomes optimized and students and members of school communities work together to help keep it that way. This same dynamic is also true for schools that have implemented school-wide positive-behavior supports (SWPBS; Horner et al., 2009; Horner, Sugai, & Anderson, 2010). It takes a great deal of effort up front to make the shift, but, if sustained, the benefits are reaped for years to come and as a result, it makes it easier and more rewarding for educators to teach (see Chapter 10 on SWPBS).

Enlightened educators understand the importance of making each and every student feel safe, valued, and supported and that children cannot optimize their learning unless their mental health needs are met. Thus, the major aim of this book is to build on what educators already know and already do well by providing practical information on creating safe and supportive schools and fostering students' mental health so they integrate this knowledge into their current practices. To help in this regard, this book sets forth an integrated and comprehensive framework to help all educators, administrators, and school-based mental health professionals promote school safety, and provide the requisite knowledge, skills, and strategies to enhance the emotional well-being of all their students.

It is worth noting that this book does not advocate for educators to abandon their instructional or administrative roles. Similar to how efforts to help improve children's physical health at school such as reducing the spread of germs do not require expert medical knowledge, efforts to create safe and supportive schools and foster student mental health do not require expert knowledge of psychology or criminal justice. However, what is needed is a willingness to learn and intervene in one's own school or classroom. To date, the most comprehensive review of research on supporting the educational and emotional well-being of students found that educators are more than capable of accomplishing these goals. In a meta-analysis that involved analyzed data from 270,034 students who participated in 213 school-based, social-emotional learning (SEL) studies, Durlak, Weissberg, Dymnicki, Taylor & Schellinger (2011) found that educators were capable of effectively implementing SEL without additional personnel or expert help. In addition, results of this investigation indicated that, students who participated in programs designed to improve their social-emotional competence displayed an 11-percentile-point gain in academic achievement as well as improvements in their social-emotional skills, attitudes about school, and overall school behavior when compared to students who were not exposed to SEL. Thus, in addition to underscoring the capacity of educators to help support safe schools and foster students' mental health, results of the aforementioned study also highlight that future efforts to improve students' academic success can be bolstered by improving their social and emotional competencies (see Chapter 4 for discussion of SEL).

Transforming School Communities and Engaging Every Educator

The Story of East Feliciana Middle School

East Feliciana Middle School, located about an hour north of Baton Rouge in rural Louisiana, struggled with school-wide behavioral problems. During transition time, the halls roared with noise; fights between students happened on a regular basis and many students skipped school because they were afraid of being bullied. The behavioral problems impacted everyone in the school. Teachers felt as if the students were in control; administrators felt like they were reacting to behavioral problems and could not get ahead on school discipline; students were struggling to learn in a chaotic environment; and caregivers were thinking of pulling their children out of the school.

Fortunately, East Feliciana Middle School had a dedicated group of educators, many of whom were new to teaching and working in schools. Collectively, the school formed a school-wide positive-behavior support (SWPBS) team and this team began planning school-wide initiatives to improve student behavior and the school climate more generally. With buy-in from all educators and support personnel, the SWPBS team helped to get positive behavior supports and interventions in place across multiple tiers of service delivery. Then, once these supports were in place, the school climate began to improve. By the end of the school year, many of the behavior problems that had plagued the school had been reduced and parents often commented on how much happier their children were at school. The year after East Feliciana Middle School implemented their SWPBS program, student enrollment went up by about 20 percent.

The Story of Lincoln High School

Students at Lincoln High School in Portland, Oregon, were concerned about the level of bullying and cyberbullying they experienced in their school. Students also found the social and academic pressures at the school to be overwhelming at times, which may have contributed to suicidal behavior. Consequently, students in the Leadership Class got organized and asked for help from the counseling center. The school psychologist showed them data from years of formal and informal surveys regarding bullying at Lincoln. With the help of their school psychologist, they researched the literature on student-led, anti-bullying efforts and set goals for making the school a safer and friendlier place. The students then created a PowerPoint presentation with student-made movie clips, motivational messages, and information regarding the impact of bullying on students' lives. In groups of four, they presented to every ninth grade English class and also taught the students how to respond when they heard intolerant statements. Every year, the Leadership Class updated and improved their presentation, and chose successors to carry on this project. As a result of this initiative, students felt more connected to the school and empowered to help create a culture of respect where harassment and bullying were not tolerated. According to the school psychologist, this project, which is now in its seventh year, has reduced discipline referrals by 75 percent, increased students speaking up when they hear intolerant comments from 20 percent to over 50 percent, reduced student reported instances of bullying by two-thirds, and youth suicide has been reduced to zero (J. Hanson, May 15, 2015, personal communication). Now when students walk into Lincoln, they immediately see an entire wall covered by hundreds of anti-bullying pledges and the biggest trophy in the school is the annual award for the person(s) who contributed the most to the anti-bullying campaign.

The Story of Santana High School

In the aftermath of a tragic school shooting in Santee, California, in which two students were killed and 13 injured, the National Association of School Psychologists' National Emergency Assistance Team (NEAT) provided crisis intervention to Santana High School and the community. Based on the suggestion of this national crisis response team, the principal wrote a letter to all the students in the school in which she expressed her own thoughts and feelings and gave students permission to express a wide range of emotions. In addition, she informed them that a wide variety of activities would be provided to let them express their feelings including talking, writing, music, artwork, projects, ceremonies, and rituals. With the help of their teachers, students were asked to respond to a number of questions such as "What are you experiencing now and what are you worried about?" and "What would make you feel safer at school and what do you need in your life to help you cope?" Within two weeks, the principal commented that almost every student in the school had responded and, as noted by Poland and Gorin (2002), "the resounding message was that students wanted adults more involved in their lives" (p. xvi.).

Moreover, in surveying students the principal found that there were a number (between 20 and 25 percent) who had no adult in school with whom they felt emotionally connected enough to discuss school-related or personal problems. As a result of this survey, a major project was undertaken to ensure that every student was connected to a significant adult in school, such as an athletic coach, resource teacher, cafeteria worker, school secretary, reading coach, assistant principal, guidance counselor, volunteer, etc.

These three vignettes illustrate that creating a safe and supportive school is not just about providing psychological services to those most in need of mental health intervention. It is also about creating a culture of caring, respect, tolerance, order, and fairness; listening to and establishing emotional connections with all students; and providing the necessary social supports to every student in the school. It is about preventing problems and promoting wellness, not just ameliorating or repairing psychological disturbance or psychic pain. Furthermore, any or all concerned members of the school community including educators, administrators, and even students, can take the lead to make this happen.

The previous stories also highlight the importance of transforming entire school communities as a way to support safe schools and foster student mental health. The story of East Feliciana Middle School discusses the implementation of a SWPBS program to improve overall school behavior. In this story, a concerned group of educators worked together to get buy-in from their colleagues and address student behavior across multiple tiers of support. In addition they focused on increasing positive behavior in students—not just eliminating negative behaviors. With this aim in mind, Chapter 10 discusses implementing SWPBS and Chapter 11 covers the use of effective behavior management strategies.

The story of Lincoln High School illustrates how a group of concerned students helped create a safer and more emotionally healthy school climate for their school. This story underscores the point that when the entire school community saw the benefits of any successful program to create safe and supportive schools, the project became sustainable. To address problems such as bullying, Chapter 12 covers bullying prevention and intervention and Chapter 16 reviews suicide assessment, prevention, and intervention. These chapters also discuss effective strategies to prevent these concerning problems.

Lastly, the story of Santana High School describes how a school community began to recover from a tragedy. In this story, a concerned administrator worked with other educators to reach out to students so that they could support the individual needs of students who were coping with distress and trauma in the wake of a school shooting. Additionally, other members of the school community worked together to reach out to a national organization to help navigate the crisis as it unfolded and to help to facilitate healthy coping. To help schools prevent and prepare for crises, Chapter 17 covers crisis prevention; to help schools respond to these events, Chapter 18 discusses crisis intervention.

Working Together: Educators and Mental Health Professionals

The need to engage educators in efforts to support school safety and students' mental health is critical in order to ensure the success of *all* students. Unfortunately, far too many students need help than can be addressed by extant providers. In fact, most professional associations for school-based mental health professionals report that the ratios between these individuals and students are far too high and National Education Association (NEA) agrees. As noted by Dennis Van Roekel, a Past President of the NEA: "We must dramatically expand our investments in mental health services. Proper diagnosis can and often starts in our schools, yet we continue to cut funding for school counselors, school social workers, and school psychologists" (Walker, 2013). Simply stated, not enough school-based mental health professionals are currently employed in U.S. schools. Yet, even if every school employed its own full-time school psychologist, counselor, and social worker, these professionals would still need to work hand-in-hand with educators to support students. Thus, because of limitations in available mental health professionals in the community and at school, serious efforts to improve school safety and foster students' mental health will involve collaboration between educators and school-based mental health professionals.

If armed—not with weapons as has been suggested by some legislators and others—but with the knowledge and skills to help support healthy, safe, and supportive school environments, educators, administrators, and school-based mental health professionals can work together to transform even the most challenging of educational environments (Chuck & Johnson, 2012). Solving complicated problems often involves getting buy-in from multiple parties and coordinated efforts from a range of stakeholders. Therefore, systematic efforts to improve students' mental health and make schools safer and more supportive for all students will need to involve all school personnel on some level. Essentially, creating safe schools and fostering students' mental health is *every* educator's concern.

Safe Schools and Student Mental Health: A–Z

Consistent with the title and focus of this book, educators can do a lot to help create safe schools and foster students' mental health. Through their roles as key members of school communities, they can support the aforementioned efforts, either directly through their own action or indirectly through supporting the efforts of their colleagues. Although not completely exhaustive, educators can support a range of services that aim to increase school safety and mental health. These include

(a) ensuring that the school is a safe place for all youth;
(b) making sure that effective behavior management practices are followed in every classroom;
(c) delivering social-emotional learning to all students;
(d) fostering student connections to peers, teachers, parents, caregivers, and other adults in the community;
(e) establishing school-wide positive behavior supports;
(f) incorporating principles of positive psychology into the school curriculum;
(g) focusing on improving the climate of the school to make it more responsive to student needs;
(h) ensuring that all the requisite social supports are provided to students;
(i) providing in-service to all staff so they have basic information about emotional and behavioral disorders;
(j) making sure that at-risk and vulnerable student populations get the additional support that they need;
(k) establishing school-family and community partnerships;
(l) implementing and enforcing anti-bullying policies and incorporating established bullying reducing programs if needed;
(m) implementing anti-violence curriculums and interventions as necessary;
(n) providing instruction or curricula that focus on having a healthy lifestyle (e.g., developing a vigorous exercise regimen; avoiding drugs, alcohol and tobacco; understanding nutrition and a healthy diet);
(o) establishing threat assessment teams to investigate potential acts of violence;
(p) putting systems in place that enable students to report potential threats and concerns;
(q) ensuring that all staff are trained in the basics of suicide prevention and intervention;
(r) developing and training school crisis teams;
(s) identifying students who need more intensive (Tier II and Tier III) interventions;
(t) providing small group interventions for at-risk students or those who have experienced a problem and need additional support (e.g., bereavement groups, anger management groups,

counseling for children who have failed a grade, social skills strategies for children who have been victimized by bullies, coping skills groups for students who have attempted suicide, etc.);

(u) providing school-based intensive individualized support, whenever possible, for those needing more comprehensive services;

(v) ensuring that effective referral sources are available for all children requiring more intensive services;

(w) collaborating with colleagues across school, home, and community settings to ensure accurate assessment and service delivery;

(x) respecting and celebrating cultural differences among students and their families;

(y) being cognizant of and attending to individual differences in students and families; and

(z) becoming involved. Yes, just becoming involved . . .

Practices, programs, policies, and strategies that focus on all the aforementioned topics are covered within this book. However, it is important to emphasize that schools do not need one program for social-emotional learning, another for violence prevention, and another for bullying prevention. Instead, programs and supports can be incorporated into an effective student support system under one umbrella consistent with a multi-tiered system of support (see Chapters 3, 4, 5, and 6). That is, in lieu of having separate silos for each concern, these can all be integrated into a unified and coherent system based on the individualized needs of each school.

The Structure of the Book

As previously discussed, educators are increasingly being engaged in efforts to help schools address students' mental health concerns and problems such as bullying, suicide, and school violence (Sulkowski et al., 2013; Yoon, Sulkowski, & Bauman, 2014). Thus, educators now are on the front line to address these critically important topics. However, like adjusting to any new and important role, supporting students' mental health and ensuring school safety may feel like a daunting task for many educators.

To make this task seem less formidable, this book covers issues and topics by providing relevant and easy-to-comprehend information. Ultimately, this book aims to help educators prevent, pre-empt, handle, and recover from significant problems that impact their schools. In addition, interviews from experts on a variety of the topics are imbedded in each chapter. Thus, this book draws on the work of leading experts in education, psychology, and related disciplines to craft a resource that is designed for educators to work effectively within existing school structures to make schools safer and to help students feel more supported.

The first section of this book (Chapters 1 and 2) focuses on creating safe schools and emotionally healthy learning environments. In Part I, the evolving role of educators is discussed as it pertains to school-based mental health as well as efforts to make schools safer and more secure. Part II (Chapters 3, 4, 5, and 6) discusses fostering student mental health using a multi-tiered model of supports, ways to incorporate social-emotional learning into every school, and the use of universal intervention (Tier I) practices (e.g., changing mindsets, encouraging grit, teaching mindfulness, decreasing anxiety, teaching emotional-self regulation skills, fostering resiliency, and creating resilient classrooms). It also focuses on implementing targeted (Tier II) and intensive (Tier III) interventions.

In Part III (Chapters 7, 8 and 9), ways to support nurturing learning environments are covered, such as improving school climate, providing requisite social support, fostering school connectedness and engagement, as well as integrating aspects of positive psychology into the schools. In particular, as previously discussed, this section describes how to support the whole student. Part IV (Chapters 10 and 11) discusses ways to improve student behavior throughout the entire school community by using school-wide, positive-behavior supports (SWPBS) and in the classroom through effective behavior management strategies. This section includes practical strategies for improving student behavior that can be incorporated by educators across different settings.

Part V (Chapters 12, 13 and 14) covers ways to identify and help vulnerable and victimized students. More specifically, this section discusses bullying prevention and intervention; helping students with emotional and behavioral disorders; and providing a wide variety of supports to at-risk youth. Part VI (Chapters 15 and 16) discusses ways to reduce school violence and prevent student suicide. An emphasis is placed on using evidence-based and field-tested strategies such as threat assessment (Cornell & Sheras, 2006) and following guidelines as recommended by the Substance Abuse and Mental Health Services Administration (2012), related to suicide prevention and intervention. Lastly, Part VII (Chapters 17 and 18) discusses preventing and responding to crises in the schools. In this section, developing school crisis response teams; implementing school crisis prevention, intervention, and postvention protocols, policies and procedures; and dealing with grief, bereavement, and trauma are covered.

This book is consistent with the *Framework for safe and successful schools* and, whenever possible, interventions are based on evidence-based practices that have been supported in the empirical literature. Consequently, this text expands upon the framework and it provides practical suggestions for educators, administrators, school-based mental health professionals, and all others who work in schools. The intention of our text is not to create additional burdens for educators and schools. Instead, our aim is to provide a needed resource to help infuse and integrate principles, practices, and programs to ensure student safety and promote mental health, and enable all readers, whether in pre-service education programs, in graduate school, or engaged in continuing education, to be on the cutting edge of research on all the included topics and to be able to apply this knowledge in their daily practice.

Conclusion

Currently, the roles of educators and student support personnel are evolving. As noted by Walker (2013), our U.S. schools have by default become the mental health system for our nation's children. Furthermore, according to recent trends, this evolution may prioritize efforts to create safe schools and foster students' mental health (Cowan et al., 2013; Kutash et al., 2006). In this vein, an effective model for safe and successful schools has now been endorsed by major professional educational and psychological organizations. In addition, the knowledge base on social emotional learning, mindfulness, anxiety reduction, resilient classrooms, school safety teams, responsive school climates, social support, positive psychology, school-wide positive behavior supports, student engagement, bullying prevention, cognitive behavioral therapy, trauma-sensitive schools, violence prevention, suicide prevention, threat assessment, crisis prevention and intervention, and related topics has increased exponentially during the past few decades. Thus, it has never been a more challenging and exciting time to be an educator.

Patrick Kennedy (2015), a former U.S. Congressman from Rhode Island who was a chief sponsor of the Mental Health Parity and Addiction Equity Act of 2008, described student mental health as a *force multiplier*. By this, Kennedy meant that students who possess high levels of mental health and emotional well-being are much more able to be successful in any endeavor or challenge that they face in life. When schools are safe and supportive and foster students' mental health, higher academic achievement and overall student success is inevitable. Thus, as expressed in this book, the factors that help students succeed are additive and interconnected. With this in mind, this book aims to provide you with state-of-the-art knowledge, evidence-based suggestions for prevention and intervention, and with the informed opinions of national and international experts. We intend for this to be the book that every educator needs to help create safe and supportive schools and to foster students' mental health. We invite you to read on.

References

Boli, J., Ramirez, F. O., & Meyer, J. W. (1985). Explaining the origins and expansion of mass education. *Comparative Education Review, 29,* 145–170.

Brock, S. E. (2015). Mental health matters. *NASP Communiqué, 43*(7), 1, 13–15.

Chuck, E., & Johnson, A. (2012). Armed guards, locked entryways, cameras: Schools seek security after Sandy Hook. *NBCNews.* Retrieved from: http://usnews.nbcnews.com/_news/2012/12/20/16042916-armed-guards-locked-entryways-cameras-schools-seek-security-after-sandy-hook?lite.

Cohen, J., McCabe, L., Michelli, N. M., & Pickeral, T. (2009). School climate: Research, policy, practice, and teacher education. *Teachers College Record, 111,* 180–213.

Cornell, D. G. (2015, February). *Secrets about school safety.* Paper presented at the annual convention of the National Association of School Psychologists. Orlando: FL.

Cornell, D., & Nekvasil, E. (2012). Violent thoughts and behaviors. In S. E. Brock & S. R. Jimerson (Eds.), *Best practices in school crisis prevention and intervention* (pp.485–502). Bethesda, MD: National Association of School Psychologists Press.

Cornell, D. G., & Sheras, P. L. (2006). *Guidelines for responding to student threats of violence.* Longmont, CO: Sopris West Educational Services.

Cowan, K. C., Vaillancourt, K., Rossen, E., & Pollitt, K. (2013). *A framework for safe and successful schools* [Brief]. Bethesda, MD: National Association of School Psychologists.

Cummings, J. R., Ponce, N. A., & Mays, V. M. (2010). Comparing racial/ethnic differences in mental health service use among high-need subpopulations across clinical and school-based settings. *Journal of Adolescent Health, 46,* 603–606.

Durlak, J. A., Weissberg, R. P., Dymnicki, A. B., Taylor, R. D., & Schellinger, K. B. (2011). The impact of enhancing students' social and emotional learning: A meta-analysis of school-based universal interventions. *Child Development, 82,* 405–432.

Dwyer, K., Osher, D., & Warger, C. (1998). *Early warning, timely response: A guide to safe schools.* Washington, DC: U.S. Department of Education.

Erbacher, T. A., Singer, J. B., & Poland, S. (2015). *Suicide in schools: A practitioner's guide to multi-level prevention, assessment, intervention and postvention.* New York: Routledge.

Espelage, D. L., Low, S., Polanin, J. R., & Brown, E.C. (2015). Clinical trial of Second Step© middle-school program: Impact on aggression and victimization. *Journal of Applied Developmental Psychology.* doi: 10.1016/j.appdev.2014.11.007

Farmer, E., Burns, B., Phillips, S., Angold, A., & Costello, E. (2003). Pathways into and through mental health services for children and adolescents. *Psychiatric Services, 54,* 60–66.

Flaherty, L. T., Weist, M. D., & Warner, B. S. (1996). School-based mental health services in the United States: History, current models and needs. *Community Mental Health Journal, 32,* 341–352.

Health Care Cost Institute (2012). *Children's health care spending report: 2007–2010.* Washington, DC; Author.

Horner, R. H., Sugai, G., & Anderson, C. M. (2010). Examining the evidence base for school-wide positive behavior support. *Focus on Exceptional Children, 42,* 1–14.

Horner, R. H., Sugai, G., Smolkowski, K., Eber, L., Nakasato, J., Todd, A. W., & Esperanza, J. (2009). A randomized, wait-list controlled effectiveness trial assessing school-wide positive behavior support in elementary schools. *Journal of Positive Behavior Interventions, 11,* 133–144. doi: 10.1177/1098300709332067

Hoyert, D. L., & Xu, J. Q. (2012, October 10). Deaths: Preliminary data for 2011. *National Vital Statistics Reports,* 61(6), 1–51. Retrieved from: www.cdc.gov/nchs/products/nvsr.htm.

Jeynes, W. H. (2007). *American educational history: School, society, and the common good.* Thousand Oaks, CA: Sage Publications.

Juszczak, L., Melinkovich, P., & Kaplan, D. (2003). Use of health and mental health services by adolescents across multiple delivery sites. *Journal of Adolescent Health*, 32(Supp. l6), 108–118. doi:–10.1016/S1054-139X(03)00073-9

Kalafat, J., & Lazarus, P. J. (2002) Suicide prevention in schools. In S. E. Brock, P. J. Lazarus, & S. R. Jimerson (Eds.), *Best practices in school crisis prevention and intervention* (pp. 211–223). Bethesda, MD: National Association of School Psychologists Press.

Kennedy, P. J. (2015, February). *My journey: Making mental health essential health.* Keynote address delivered at the annual convention of the National Association of School Psychologists. Orlando: FL.

Kluger, R. (2011). *Simple justice: The history of Brown v. Board of Education and Black America's struggle for equality.* New York, NY: Knopf Doubleday Publishing Group.

Kutash, K., Duchnowski, A. J., & Lynn, N. (2006). *School-based mental health: An empirical guide for decision-makers.* Research & Training Center for Children's Mental Health, Louis de la Parte Florida Mental Health Institute, University of Florida.

Merikangas, K. R., He, J., Burstein, M., Swanson, S. A., Avenevoli, S., Cui, L., . . . Swendsen, J. (2010). Lifetime prevalence of mental disorders in U.S. adolescents: Results from the National Comorbidity Survey Replication-Adolescent Supplement (NCS-A). *Journal of the American Academy of Child and Adolescent Psychiatry, 49,* 980–989. doi:10.1016/j.jaac.2010.05.017

Miller, D. (2011). *Child and adolescent suicidal behavior. School-based prevention, assessment, and intervention.* New York: Guilford Press.

Modzeleski, W., Feucht, T., Rand, M., Hall, J., Simon, T., Butler, L., et al. (2008). School-associated student homicides—United States, 1992–2006. *MMWR, 57,* 33–36.

National Research Council and Institute of Medicine. (2007). *Preventing mental, emotional, and behavioral disorders among young people: progress and possibilities.* Washington, DC: National Academic Press.

Neiman, S., & DeVoe, J. F. (2009). *Crime, violence, discipline, and safety in U.S. public schools: Findings from the School Survey on Crime and Safety: 2007–08 (NCES 2009-326).* Washington, DC: National Center for Education Statistics, Institute of Education Sciences, U.S. Department of Education.

Nekvasil, E. K., & Cornell, D. G. (2012). Student reports of peer threats of violence: Prevalence and outcomes. *Journal of School Violence, 11,* 357–375.

Perou, R., Bitsko, R. H., Blumberg, S. J., Pastor, R., Ghandour, R. M., Gfroerer, J. C. . . . Huang, L. N. (2013). Mental health surveillance among children – United States, 2005–2011. *MMWR, 62*(2), 1–35. Retrieved from: www.cdc.gov/mmwr/pdf/other/su6202.pdf

Poland, S., & Gorin, S. (2002). Preface. In S. E. Brock, P. J. Lazarus, & S. R. Jimerson (Eds.), *Best practices in school crisis prevention and intervention* (pp. xv–xviii). Bethesda, MD: National Association of School Psychologists Press.

Reinke, W. M., Stormont, M., Herman, K. C., Puri, R., & Goel, N. (2011). Supporting children's mental health in schools: Teacher perceptions of needs, roles, and barriers. *School Psychology Quarterly, 26,* 1–13.

Roberts, S., Zhang, J., & Truman, J. (2010). *Indicator of school crime and safety: 2010* (NCES 2011-002/NCJ 230812). Washington, DC: U.S. Department of Education, National Center for Education Statistics; U.S. Department of Justice, Office of Justice Programs, Bureau of Justice Statistics. Retrieved from: http://nces.ed.gov/pubs2011/2011002.pdf.

Rothbard, M. N. (1999). *Education: Free and compulsory.* Auburn, AB: Ludwig von Mises Institute.

Shaffer, D., & Craft, L. (1999). Methods of adolescent suicide prevention. *Journal of Clinical Psychiatry, 60,* (Suppl. 2), 70–74.

Siebold, S. (2013). *Arming teachers to protect students.* Washington Times. Retrieved from www.washingtontimes.com/news/2013/aug/26/siebold-arming-teachers-to-protect-students/.

Strichart, S. S., & Lazarus, P. J. (1986). Low-incidence assessment: Influences and issues. In P. J. Lazarus & S. S. Strichart (Eds.), *Psychoeducational evaluation of children and adolescents with low-incidence handicaps* (pp. 1–15). Orlando, FL: Grune & Stratton.

Substance Abuse and Mental Health Services Administration (2012). *Preventing suicide: A toolkit for high schools.* HHS Publication No. SMA-12-4669. Rockville, MD: Center for Mental Health Services, Substance Abuse and Mental Health Services Administration.

Sulkowski, M. L., Demaray, M. K., & Lazarus, P. J. (2012). Connecting students to schools to support their emotional well-being and academic success. *Communiqué, 40,* 1 & 20–22.

Sulkowski, M. L., & Joyce-Beaulieu, D. K. (2014). School-based service delivery for homeless students: Relevant laws and overcoming access barriers. *American Journal of Orthopsychiatry, 84,* 711–719. doi: 10.1037/ort0000033

Sulkowski, M. L., Joyce, D. J., & Storch, E. A. (2013). Treating childhood anxiety in schools: Service delivery in a response to intervention paradigm. *Journal of Child and Family Studies, 21,* 938–947. doi: 10.1007/s10826-011-9553-1

Sulkowski, M. L., & Michael, K. (2014). Meeting the mental health needs of homeless students in schools: A multi-tiered system of support framework. *Children and Youth Services Review, 44,* 145–151. doi: 10.1016/j.childyouth.2014.06.014

Sulkowski, M. L., Wingfield, R. J., Jones, D., & Coulter, W. A. (2011). Response to intervention and inter-disciplinary collaboration: Joining hands to support children and families. *Journal of Applied School Psychology, 27,* 1–16. doi: 10.1080/15377903.2011.565264

U.S. Department of Education. (1994). *National education goals.* Retrieved from: www.ed.gov/legislation/GOALS2000/TheAct/sec102.html.

U.S. Department of Education. (2001). *Twenty third annual report to Congress on the implementation of the Individuals with Disabilities Education Act.* Washington, DC: Author.

U.S. Department of Health and Human Services. (2000). *Report of the Surgeon General's conference on children's mental health: A national action agenda.* U.S. Department of Health and Human Services. Retrieved from: www.ncbi.nlm.nih.gov/books/NBK44233/.

Walker, T. (2013). Is mental health the next focus of the school safety debate? Retrieved from: http://neatoday.org/2013/12/13/is-mental-health-the-next-focus-of-the-school-safety-debate/.

Woolley, M. E., & Bowen, G. L. (2007). In the context of risk: Supportive adults and the school engagement of middle school students. *Family Relations, 56,* 92–104.

Yoon, J., Sulkowski, M. L., & Bauman, S. (2014). Teachers' responses to bullying incidents: Effects of teacher characteristics and contexts. *Journal of School Violence, 15,* 91–113. doi: 10.1080/15388220.2014.963592.

2 Safe and Supportive Schools

The public discourse around promoting safe and supportive schools has been heavily influenced by reactions to several highly publicized violent attacks that occurred in K-12 schools during the past couple of decades (Maguire, Weatherby, & Mathers, 2002; National Association of School Psychologists [NASP] & National Association of School Resource Officers [NASRO], 2014). Although every death that occurs in school is a tragedy and highly emotional reactions to incidents of school violence are to be expected, the public portrayal of schools as being dangerous is not warranted. In fact, major longitudinal studies of crime and safety in schools such as the Youth Risk Behavioral Surveillance System and Indicators of School Crime and Safety survey indicate that severe forms of school violence have been decreasing during the past two decades, while the use of school-based security and safety measures have been increasing (Jimerson, Hart, & Renshaw, 2012).

Unfortunately, however, during the same time, milder forms of school violence such as bullying have been increasing and becoming more prevalent in schools (see Chapter 12 for a review of school bullying). In addition, greater numbers of students report that they are carrying weapons in school, although it is difficult to assess the veracity of these anonymous self-reports on longitudinal studies (Dinkes, Kemp, Baum, & Snyder, 2009). Nevertheless, considering the former, efforts to promote school safety need to address incidents of school violence in their myriad of forms—not just severe incidents—and when doing so, these efforts also need to make students feel emotionally supported at school (NASP & NASRO, 2014). In support of this notion, a study of averted school attacks found that having a positive school climate and open and trusting relationships between students and educators were key factors in preventing school shootings, which often were averted by students who knew and reported the plans of a potential attacker (Daniels et al., 2010; Sulkowski, 2011). Thus, focusing on school climate is critically important to enhancing school safety efforts. In support of this perspective, Osher, Dwyer, Jimerson, and Brown (2012) advocate for a safe and effective school framework that aligns school safety, student support, and achievement across individual, classroom, school, and community levels. Specifically, they argue that despite often being viewed as independent from one another, student support, school safety, and students' performance at school are often interdependently related and interactive with each other. Therefore, comprehensive strategies to promote school safety are needed that enhance students' experiences at school, while bettering the overall school climate (Osher, Bear, Sprague, & Doyle, 2010).

As noted elsewhere in this text, research indicates that threats of violent attacks greatly outstrip actual attacks and schools generally are safe from violent attacks (Nekvasil & Cornell, 2012). In this regard, even though approximately 21 homicides occur in school settings per year, these deaths represent less than 1 percent of annual homicides among students between the ages of 5 and 18 in the U.S. (Modzeleski et al., 2008; Nekvasil & Cornell, 2012). Therefore, the likelihood of a life-compromising violent attack occurring in any particular school is exceedingly low (see Chapter 15 for information on threats of violence in schools).

In the wake of the tragic shooting that occurred at Sandy Hook Elementary in December of 2012, a cottage industry has sprung up to propose numerous strategies to mitigate school violence (Addington, 2009; Theriot & Orme, 2014). Some of these strategies appear to be promising, whereas others are unfeasible and capitalize on the public's fear. For example, some companies sell bulletproof backpacks, body shields, and mats that students can cloak themselves in to prevent being shot by an armed assailant (Stein & Cherkis, 2014). Meanwhile, others have proposed arming educators with firearms. Despite having the positive intention of protecting students, the likelihood of these approaches successfully being used to save lives during an armed attack is very low because school shootings are highly chaotic, usually over in a matter of seconds or minutes, and often end with the attacker completing suicide before first responders arrive (Vossekuil, Fein, Reddy, Borum, & Modzeleski, 2002). Moreover, without extensive training, it is extremely difficult to predict how anyone will react during a shooting and what will result from this response. For example, educators who carry weapons do not practice in a volatile crisis situation with moving target(s) and, as a result, there could be devastating repercussions for all who are involved. Also, when multiple individuals display weapons, it is problematic for the police and other first responders to differentiate attackers from defenders or armed bystanders.

In contrast to these questionable strategies to mitigate school violence, researchers, advocates, and policy makers have also proposed empirically grounded approaches in the wake of recent violent attacks at school. As a salient example, a position statement by an interdisciplinary group of expert researchers and mental health professionals was endorsed by more than 183 professional organizations and more than 200 prevention scholars and practitioners that represent over four million mental health professionals who specialize in school violence prevention and intervention. This position statement, available at the following link, advocates for using multifaceted and integrated prevention and intervention efforts to address school violence and promote school safety: http://curry.virginia.edu/articles/sandyhookshooting. More specifically, it calls for improved balance, communication, connectedness, and support for members of school communities to help prevent future school violence.

Figure 2.1 Five Elements of Healthy Working and Learning Environments

Table 2.1 Key Characteristics of Safe and Healthy Schools

Positive, Productive Relationships

- Social and emotional skills development of youth is supported using evidence-based programs as well as structured, natural opportunities for skill building.
- Collegial relationships among staff are supported and encouraged through systematic school planning.
- Professional development opportunities are provided for staff to support the development of the social and emotional competencies required to work with youth.
- Caring home and neighborhood adults are encouraged to volunteer in the classrooms and shared school spaces.
- School adults focus on student growth, rather than perceived ability.
- Specialized programs, practices, and policies are in place to support youth at high risk of social conflict or rejection,

Awareness and Respect for Diversity

- Students can see themselves in school materials. Curricula, classroom activities, and wall images represent the demographics of the school.
- School staff members reflect on their own potential biases and assumptions.
- Caring home and neighborhood adults for diverse groups are encouraged to both (a) volunteer at school, and (b) actively participate in school decision-making activities (e.g., parent advisory groups).
- Teachers reflect on the diverse backgrounds (i.e., culture, language, family history, religion) of their students and modify curricula to meet the needs of all students.
- School adults communicate high expectations for *all* students, regardless of background.
- School provides opportunities for staff and students to express their diverse backgrounds in creative and thoughtful ways.

Transparent and Unbiased Norms and Expectations

- School policies are applied to all students, regardless of gender, race, socioeconomic privilege, or perceived sexual orientation.
- Students and caring home and neighborhood adults are provided opportunities to participate in classroom and school-wide norm- and rule-setting activities.
- School rules and expectations are reiterated on a regular basis and are visible within classrooms and shared spaces.
- Professional development activities are provided for staff to support the development of positive classroom management practices.
- Schools provide restorative opportunities for students to correct harm caused by norm or rule breaking.

Individual Value and Shared Purpose

- School staff members share a sense of responsibility over school activities, milestones, and goals.
- Staff members are given opportunities to contribute to decisions related to future directions of school activities, including professional development planning.
- Students are encouraged to participate in governance councils and advisory committees.
- Students are encouraged to make shared contributions to the school and neighborhood communities through a variety of experiences, including service-learning projects.

Opportunities for Growth and Achievement

- Cooperative planning and professional development time for school staff is supported, encouraged, and expected.
- Curricula are rigorous and meaningful, emphasizing critical thinking, application of knowledge, and reflective learning.
- Academic and professional standards for students and staff, respectively, are high, but achievable.
- Achievements of staff and students are celebrated and widely highlighted.

Additionally, others have proposed similar models that aim to improve school safety through enhancing healthy working and learning environments in schools. One such model is discussed by O'Malley and Eklund (2012), which involves identifying and building on strengths of safe and healthy schools to mitigate violence. In this vein, fostering safe school climates involves establishing positive and productive relationships for all members of school communities, awareness of and respect for diversity, transparent and unbiased norms and expectations, individual value and shared purpose, and opportunities for growth and achievement. Figure 2.1 displays the five elements of healthy working and learning school environments and Table 2.1 provides further enumeration.

Efforts to Promote Safe and Supportive Schools

In general, extant efforts to promote safe and supportive schools involve ensuring the physical safety of the school environment, having effective safety procedures and policies in place, and promoting psychological safety among members of school communities (Cowan, Vaillancourt, Rossen, & Pollitt, 2013; Reeves, Kanan, & Plog, 2010). However, as adumbrated above, these efforts are complementary and it is unclear if the ultimate goal of promoting safe and supportive schools can be accomplished without at least mixing elements of the previously mentioned efforts. In other words, ensuring safe schools involves a hybrid approach—there is no single solution or approach. In thorough literature reviews, Dwyer, Osher, and Warger (1998); Sandoval, Brock, and Knifton (2013); and Strepling (1997) delineate key characteristics of safe and supportive schools. These characteristics are listed in Table 2.2.

Promoting physical safety

Common environmental design strategies can be employed to reduce threats of violence and promote safety in school settings. In addition, schools can employ school personnel that focus primarily on keeping schools safe and orderly. As salient efforts regarding the former, 68 percent

Table 2.2 Characteristics of Safe and Supportive Schools

- Focus on academic achievement and foster enthusiasm for learning.
- Involve families in meaningful ways.
- Develop links to the community.
- Emphasize positive relationships among students and staff. Teachers and students learn and use each other's names.
- Treat students with respect.
- Discuss safety issues openly.
- Create ways for students to share their concerns and help students feel safe expressing their feelings.
- Have in place a system for referring children who are suspected of being abused or neglected.
- Offer extended day programs for children.
- Promote good citizenship and character, and build a community of learners (using collaboration between students and teachers, school and home).
- Identify problems and assess progress toward solutions. Classroom meetings are held to discuss issues and problems.
- Support students in making the transition to adult life and the workplace.
- Develop and consistently enforce school-wide rules that are clear, broad-based, and fair.
- Ensure that classroom management includes firm, fair, and consistent rules and procedures.
- Use learning centers and the opportunity for cooperative group work.
- Make sure that leisure areas exist for discussions, downtime, and reading.
- Ensure that books, magazines, computers, tablets, and other resources are readily available.
- Display students' in-progress and completed work.
- Have students bring in plants and other objects that assist students in developing an identity of the classroom space as "ours."

Sources
From Dwyer, Osher, and Warger (1998); Sandoval, Brock, and Knifton (2013); and Strepling (1997).

of students (ages 12–18) report the presence of security guards or police officers in their schools, 70 percent report the presence of security cameras, and 11 percent report the use of metal detectors (Roberts, Zhang, & Truman, 2010). The concept of "target hardening" or the purposeful strengthening of the security of a building or setting to protect it in the event of an attack can help make a school more impervious to threats of violence (Addington, 2009). However, constructing and running schools like overly restrictive insular institutions is antithetical to the mission of schools as being open and nurturing educational institutions—environments in which diverse individuals and ideas can interact. Thus, with the aim of finding the right balance between being open and safe, Larson (2008) advocates for schools to employ a range of practical strategies that enhance school safety yet do not unduly interfere with the establishment and maintenance of a healthy school climate. Some of these include having administrators greet students when they arrive at school and at special events (e.g., ceremonies, dances), having educators present in hallways during times when a large number of students are transitioning, encouraging administrators to pop-in and periodically visit classrooms, having a clearly defined locker policy, enforcing a consistent and respectful dress code, and developing and implementing policies for parking automobiles on campus.

Other important strategies for increasing the physical safety of school campuses involve controlling campus access (Brown, 2006; Trump, 1998). In general, visitors should be required to report to a central office where they can check-in and be provided with an identifying nametag or identification badge (Brock, Sandoval, & Lewis, 2001). The person checking in individuals should be familiar with the student body and aware of school safety procedures. Additionally, all adults at school should be trained to greet and direct visitors to the main office where they can be checked to ensure that they have a legitimate reason for being at the school (Trump, 1998). Multiple entrance points in schools should be reduced by locking external doors to non-staff members; pedestrian and vehicular traffic should be routed through areas that can be supervised easily; and some schools may want to consider fencing their perimeters, especially if they are located in a neighborhood with high rates of violence (Larson, 2008). In this vein, schools located in high crime or violent communities will probably rely on different approaches to promote physical safety than will schools located in communities with low rates of violence.

Text Box 2.1 lists additional strategies that schools can employ to increase physical safety as well as some guidelines on how these strategies can be effectively employed.

Text Box 2.1 Strategies that Schools Can Employ to Increase Physical Safety

- Make school campuses safe and welcoming

- Ensure that school safety is on the educational agenda
- Ensure that the school handbook includes clear language about school safety

- Have a clearly defined locker policy

- Have positive posters and messages present
- Greet all students with a smile
- Have staff present in hallways during passing times
- Respect diversity of all students and families
- Have a school safety and healthy climate segment in meetings
- Behavioral expectations should be clearly delineated
- The handbooks should reflect state, county, and local statutes and ordinances
- Students and families should be informed that lockers are school property

(continued)

(continued)

	• Students should be advised that lockers could be searched at any time
	• Built-in locking mechanism should be used in which school staff know the combination or have access to a key
• Develop and enforce a school dress code	• Highly provocative and offensive clothing should be banned
	• Gang attire should be prohibited
	• Dress code expectations should be consistently enforced
• Review weapons and possession policies	• Attention is needed to determine the differences and boundaries between criminal offenses and disciplinary matters
	• Punishment should fit the nature of the offense
	• A 12-month suspension should be enforced for possession of a firearm in light of the Gun-Free School Zone Act of 1994
• Mandate crime reporting and tracking	• Crimes should be reported immediately
	• Data should be aggregated and regularly reviewed to identify potential trends
• Establish an emergency operations center	• Technology in the center should be current
	• A school communications network should be established
• Establish uniform visitor-screening procedures	• Name tags/badges should be required to be worn by school visitors
	• Picture ID cards should be required for staff and students
• Back up communications sources and channels	• Emergency emails and text messages should be considered
	• Internet and phone services should be regularly tested to ensure their functioning
• Remove obstacles to clear observation	• Unnecessary shrubs and other objects that block clear lines of sight should be removed
	• Impediments to navigating safely through the school should be removed
	• Parabolic/convex mirrors should be installed in hidden hallways/stairwells
	• Double-entry doors should be replaced with zig-zag designs
	• Bathrooms should be designed or modified to ensure better visibility by staff
• Have staff supervise students in high traffic areas and locker rooms	• Students should be discouraged from congregating in areas where they cannot be observed by staff
	• Staff should rotate supervision responsibilities
	• Coaches and/or other school personnel should be in the locker rooms when there are students present to ensure safety
• Have anonymous threat, bullying, cyberbullying, harassment, intimidation and potential suicide reporting boxes, lines, and websites	• Students should be reassured that they will not be punished for reporting threats
	• Students should be told that all reports will be appropriately addressed

	• Potential threats need to be acted upon immediately
	• Have a safety stop sign in the office—this sign should encourage staff to "drop everything" and immediately attend to the student who grabs the sign
• Quickly remove graffiti and fix broken windows/doors	• School environments that are clean, functional, and orderly tend to lower rates of violence and problematic behavior

Advances in security technologies such as video surveillance cameras, metal detectors and electromagnetic door locking systems, have given schools unprecedented opportunities to enhance their security. However, knowledge of the efficacy of these measures in reducing school violence is limited and research is needed on their potential to impact school climate (Brown, 2006). Currently, research on efforts to promote physical safety in schools is mixed and this may be because feeling safe, fearing being a victim of a crime, and worrying more generally may be different types of student experiences (Perumean-Chaney & Sutton, 2013). Research indicates that metal detectors tend to be associated with making students feel less safe and having locked doors and supervised hallways tend to increase students' worries that they could be victimized (Brown, 2006; McDevitt & Panniello, 2005). Further, research suggests that implementing visitor sign in, locker checks, hall passes, and dress codes largely do not impact students' perceptions of school safety (Perumean-Chaney & Sutton, 2013). Thus, considering how some security technologies and violence prevention strategies may exert a negative impact on students or have no significant effect, it is critically important to ensure that school campuses remain inclusive and welcoming, while these strategies are implemented. Ultimately, physical safety measures need to be individualized for the unique characteristics of school campuses; safety measures need to fit the school and community.

Michele Gay offers unique insights about school physical safety and discusses how educators can get involved in efforts to make schools safer and more emotionally supportive. Mrs. Gay is a former teacher and the Founder of Safe and Sound: A Sandy Hook Initiative, which aims to empower communities to improve the safety and security of schools through discussion, collaboration, planning and sharing of information, tools, and resources: www.safeandsoundschools.org/. Mrs. Gay also is the parent of Josephine (Joey) Grace, a seven-year-old child. Joey was one of twenty students and six staff members who died in the attack at Sandy Hook Elementary School.

Expert Interview 2.1 with Michele Gay

Co-founder of Safe and Sound: A Sandy Hook Initiative

PJL. Please tell us about Safe and Sound: A Sandy Hook Initiative. What is your mission?

MG. We are an all-volunteer, non-profit organization founded by parents who lost children on December 14, 2012 at Sandy Hook School. We are dedicated to empowering school communities to make their schools safer through collaboration, education, and practical problem solving.

We aim to provide the best tools and resources, expert opinion and discussion, and the frameworks for active participation and community collaboration in school safety. Our nationwide team of safety professionals and experts donates their experience, research, and content ideas to the mission. We offer materials and resources free of charge on our website, safeandsoundschools.org and fund the development of our materials on the website through donations, sponsorships, and public speaking.

PJL. What are some of the simple things that you believe schools can do to make our schools safer?

MG. School collaboration with local responders costs nothing but is invaluable to the safety of a school community. Creating a multidisciplinary safety team that includes these responders, as well as educators, mental health professionals, and parent and student representation is a powerful way to affect positive changes in school safety.

Access control is critical. The multidisciplinary safety team needs to think very seriously about who is granted access to the school building and campus before, during, and after school hours. Likewise, it is important to examine the building for possible entry points, such as doors, windows, and breakable glass (as was used to gain access to our school). Beyond that, it's important to look at how staff and students are equipped and trained to secure their locations within the building.

Developing *simple* response protocols and language are essential. And ensuring that these protocols are easily understood by all students, staff, and visitors is equally important. Police, fire, and medical responders can be of great help in developing and continually assessing these preparations.

Lastly, education, training, practice, and continual assessment of safety measures and practices create an active awareness and sense of safety in a school that translates into a confident, healthy learning community. Although our students and staff are unlikely to ever use the safety skills we teach in a school setting, they will surely carry them with confidence for the rest of their lives and into our communities.

PJL. You have been traveling around our country presenting to parents and educators, what are the major messages you wish to convey?

MG. We as school communities are not powerless against the threats to our schools' safety. We are a nation of innovators and problem solvers, and nothing is more important to us than our children. When we put our heads together and our minds to something, we can overcome the greatest challenges.

I am never more energized than when I spend time in a school community that "gets this." Seeing fire, police, medical, mental health, and education folks collaborating and reaching out to students, parents, and the community gives me great hope. There exists an amazing wealth of knowledge in prevention, response, and recovery just waiting to be shared.

PJL. How can educators and parents get more involved to make our schools safer?

Get out of your silo and get involved. As a modern society, we've learned to divvy up jobs and responsibilities in the interest of efficiency and specialization. It serves us well in most aspects of modern life but not so well when it comes to our children's safety. It is far too easy to assume that someone else is taking care of "this" or "that" because it is "their job." Parents focus on child rearing outside of school hours, shuttling kids to after-school activities, and surviving homework hours. Educators focus on curriculum and academic performance; police, fire, mental and medical professionals oversee safety and wellness. But how many things are we missing when we are not working together? Enough for 26 children and teachers to be murdered in a matter of minutes in one of the most peaceful communities in America.

As a Sandy Hook parent, I really didn't feel the need to ask if the classroom doors could be locked in an emergency, if the teachers had been trained with options for an intruder emergency, or even if the substitute teachers were trained and equipped to secure the classroom. Now I recognize that it is my responsibility, and that of every member of the school community to ask questions and actively participate in the safety of the school.

PJL. What legal, political, or public policy changes, if any, would you like to see to make schools and children safer? What have you found to be the biggest barriers to change as this relates to school safety and security?

MG. I often cite fire safety as the model for standard setting in other areas of school safety. We've not lost a life in a school fire in over 56 years. That is due to the collaboration of fire safety professionals, educators, and community leaders. This collaboration has led to multiple, redundant layers of fire safety in our schools (such as fire pulls, fire extinguishers, fire retardant construction materials and furnishings, lighted exit signs) as well as decades of fire safety education and training. The establishment of fire codes and regulations has mandated regular practice and inspection of schools for fire safety. It's time we began looking at securing our schools similarly.

The greatest barrier I see to change in school safety is fear—fear of change, fear of frightening children, fear of discovering difficult problems, and fear of unchartered territory. However, if you ask a frustrated administrator the same question, you are more likely to hear that expense is the issue. This indicates a view of school safety as an issue that can be "fixed" by hardware solutions, when in reality that is only a small part of creating a safe school. We've met with leaders in districts, with little to no budgets to address school safety, who have successfully tapped into the wealth of human resources within their community to educate and to train students and staff, creating a powerful culture of safety awareness and empowerment.

PJL. You have experienced dealing with profound grief. What have you and your family learned throughout this excruciating process?

MG. We each had unique relationships with our daughter, Joey, and we are, ourselves, unique individuals. Naturally, our grief and pain over losing her so tragically is an individual experience that each of us expresses very differently. One of the greatest challenges we discovered is learning to respect each other's grief. Individual, couple, and family therapy have helped us greatly with this challenge, but it takes constant effort to maintain mindfulness of each other's processes while tending to our own. I think that children's author Julia Cook described it best for our family. She says, "Grief is like a snowflake." In fact, that is the title of one of many books she gave my daughters. I've learned that every person experiences their grief journey differently.

The same lesson has served us well in our relationships within the group of 26 families that also lost a loved one on December 14. It is very important to recognize and respect the grief journeys of others. We share a terrible loss but choose individual paths to walk. Our family relies heavily on our faith and our service to others to carry on. We have realized that there will be no "moving on" or "getting over" the loss of Joey, but with our faith, it is possible to at least "carry on." We believe that Joey is very happy and safe now and that we will see her again one day. This faith and hope makes it possible to continue.

PJL. Please tell us your personal experience of letting go and how this might help others.

MG. For me, the burden of losing my precious daughter and having to carry on without her is enough to bear. I try very hard and very consciously each day to "let the rest go." To carry anger and judgment on top of it all is just too much for me to bear. Of course, it creeps back up on my shoulders regularly and it takes some effort to unload; but, it is work that has to be done. Keeping my daughter in the front of mind helps me with this. Despite the many challenges and frustrations

Joey had growing up autistic and apraxic she *never* gave up. Though she had every right to be angry, she chose to be happy and loving.

Surprisingly, most of the anger I deal with is not specifically directed toward the man who murdered my daughter and 25 other beautiful people. I believe it is my faith that allows me to release this particular burden. I know that I don't have to judge him. I trust that it's taken care of. He is not a part of my life or my daughter's. I understand that he was very sick and angry.

I did struggle early on with anger toward his family and the people that could have helped him. I still struggle with this from time to time. I also struggle with the fact that my daughter's safety was not protected at school. The way I deal with these struggles is through advocating for better safety preparation, mental health supports, education, and training in schools. Nothing is more important than protecting the safety of our children.

PJL. How has the community handled the tragedy in the aftermath—if there ever is an aftermath? What are the positives and negatives?

MG. Many in our community surrounded us with an immense bubble of love and protection. It was truly amazing. The outpouring of support from the across the country and around the world was like nothing I have ever seen. But each and every member of our community was hurt in some way, whether through the direct loss of a loved one, friend, or neighbor or through direct trauma. Beyond that, many were traumatized by the closeness of the tragedy itself.

I liken it to a band of the walking wounded. Everyone is suffering from injury of some sort, some certainly worse than others. At first, the most serious injuries take priority. After some time though, everyone has to attend to their own wounds. As people begin to get up and walk around amidst one another, they inadvertently bump into each other, reopening each other's wounds. Some become hurt by others and begin to protect themselves. When a person suffers any kind of physical injury, they become naturally protective of it. If you have ever broken a bone, you may have found yourself naturally shielding it from time to time so that others don't bump into it and cause you more pain. It is an unbelievable challenge for the community to walk around like this, learning to be mindful of so many wounds while being wounded themselves.

Adding to this challenge was the way others sought to divide us, whether intentionally or not. We were divided by charities into victim, survivor, teacher, and community member groups, and then further divided by politicians, religious groups, and local and state authorities. The initial feeling of connectedness and support that we experienced began to deteriorate.

Our family had a unique perspective and experience with this as we moved to Massachusetts a month after the tragedy. Having already taken new jobs in Massachusetts, we had to proceed with the move we had planned, only without Joey. It was unbelievably painful. Newtown was the place where she had lived all but the first two months of her life. We went back often for the support of our friends and church community, and the support of the other families that lost loved ones on December 14.

The combination of these trips back to Newtown and starting a new life in a town that was healthy and whole turned out to be extraordinary helpful to our family. We didn't have to give up the town and the friends and neighbors we loved (they were only 2 and a half hours away) and we didn't have to walk among all of the other wounded each day while trying to take care of our very hurt family. Our new community gave us a safe place to heal.

The support of other communities helped us as well. Community members from Columbine, Virginia Tech, and Nickel Mines have been very supportive of our family and the Newtown community. Their perspectives and experiences are helping many of us walk together again.

School Resource Officers

Commonly known as School Resource Officers (SROs), thousands of law enforcement officers have been deployed in schools across the U.S. since the 1960s (Finn & McDevit, 2005; K. Trump, personal communication, September 9, 2014). SROs are typically law enforcement officers from local or county law enforcement agencies assigned to schools in cooperative agreements with education officials. These officers are usually full-time, in-house school officers with police powers who are employed directly by the school district. Most SROs bring experience from other law enforcement positions, ranging from having worked basic patrol to units such as narcotics, gangs, juvenile units, and other specialized squads. According to Trump (2014), it is rare to see an officer come straight out of the police academy into an SRO position. Further, even with extensive law enforcement academy training and specialized police experience, effective SRO programs provide their officers with additional training specific to their jobs as SROs. Thus, these programs must integrate training in topics that are not necessarily central to policing. Some of these topics may focus on student and school-specific issues such as working with special education students, at-risk student populations, non-violent crisis de-escalation, teen suicide, lesson plans and classroom instruction, and school emergency planning (K. Trump, personal communication, September 9, 2014). Even though they often perform educational or related functions in schools, it is important to note that SROs differ from school security officers who are civilian district employees that perform security functions in schools yet are not sworn police officers.

The role of SROs is emerging and it will continue to do so in the foreseeable future. According to Girouard (2001), SROs perform a multifaceted role in that they can be expected to deliver specialized instruction or presentations (e.g., gang violence prevention); respond to threats of violence; counsel students who are in a state of crisis; enforce school rules and codes of conduct; collaborate with school administrators to ensure school safety; and serve as a liaison with law enforcement, schools, families, and the community. Thus, in addition to balancing security concerns and enforcing the law, SROs also must be able to function effectively in school environments, understand child development, and be familiar with education laws, policies, and practices.

School Resource Officers are central to President Barack Obama's plan for improving school safety in the aftermath of the shooting at Sandy Hook Elementary. This plan calls for creating federal incentives for schools to hire up to 1,000 or more SROs and counselors in schools across the U.S. (White House, 2013). Although SROs are encouraged to receive training in school and education-focused practices and policies such as crisis management and child development, no universal training requirements have been implemented to date and considerable variability exists in the practices of SROs across schools, districts, and states (Kim & Geronimo, 2010; Theriot & Orme, 2014).

Results from some preliminary studies suggest that security guards and SROs have a positive impact on students' safety perceptions (e.g., Brown, 2006; McDevitt & Panniello, 2005). However, others have actually identified more incidents of school crime and disruption when SROs are present in schools (Bachman, Randolph, & Brown, 2011; Nickerson & Martens, 2008; Mayer & Leone, 1999; Schreck, Miller & Gibson, 2003) and yet others have found that having security guards in schools is associated with increased fear of being victimized among students (Bachman et al., 2011; Theriot & Orme, 2014). Ultimately, much more research is needed on the impact of SROs and school security personnel on decreasing incidents of school violence, increasing student perceptions of safety and security, and improving school climate outcomes (Theriot & Orme, 2014). Moreover, increased research is needed on what standardized training components these individuals require to optimize their positive impact on students and other members of school communities (Kim & Geronimo, 2010).

Ken Trump, President of National School Safety and Security Services, provides important commentary about the role of SROs, their contribution to school safety, and current trends, both good and bad, to help make students safer in schools.

Expert Interview 2.2 with Ken Trump

President, National School Safety and Security Services

PJL. How do school resource officers contribute to the overall safety of a school? How would they fit in with a comprehensive school safety plan?

KT. Unfortunately, a lack of understanding of SRO programs by many representatives of academia, the media, elected officials, political special interest groups, and others have resulted in misinformation and misrepresentation of the programs as being reactionary and punitive when they are actually very proactive and preventative if professionally implemented by school and law enforcement officials. We find it somewhat ironic that those who vehemently oppose SROs working in schools do not question the presence of police and security measures elsewhere in society, such as at banks, malls, and other public places. It is a rather sad statement that some people would rather protect their money and their shopping conveniences better than our children and educators!

Most SROs (and other school safety personnel and school administrators) will tell you that SROs have prevented far more incidents from occurring than they have made actual arrests. SROs typically focus their functions on the "Triad Model" of serving as law enforcement officers, student counselors, and law-related educators. To fully understand the SRO role in school safety, SROs and school–law enforcement relationships must be viewed as the first-line of prevention, not as punitive or cuff'em-and-stuff'em programs focused on arresting students.

In three decades on the front lines of working in schools, I have seen some of the best SROs in the nation. These SROs certainly provide a visible law enforcement presence at school arrival and dismissal, in the cafeteria at lunchtime, and on patrol around campus. But they also can be found instructing a classroom on cyberbullying or date rape, helping a student who has been sexually abused at home, and serving as a coach for various school sports teams.

The key to successful SRO programs is simple: Relationships. Relationships lead to successful prevention and intervention whether that means helping the abused student or learning from a student tip about an individual who has a plot to shoot up the school. It's all about relationships.

PJL. How are officers assigned to SRO programs and what backgrounds must they have?

KT. Officers should be assigned to SRO programs because they have an interest in working with students and in schools, and because they want the job. SRO programs should not be a dumping ground where police chiefs send officers as a punishment or to get them away from other police units. Most SROs who have worked patrol and/or specialized police units (narcotics, homicide, gangs, vice, etc.) will readily acknowledge that being a SRO is the most demanding, but also the most rewarding, position they have ever held in the police department.

SRO selection should be a joint effort between school administrators and police department administrators. Police administrators may select a pool of potential SRO candidates based upon departmental job bidding procedures, union agreements, or other practices. But school administrators should have a say on who will be the SRO assigned to their buildings.

There also should be clear job descriptions for the SRO. Requirements for SRO training, identification of SRO supervision responsibilities, and SRO evaluation criteria should also be clearly defined. Again, these and other SRO program management issues should be jointly developed by the police agency and school district.

PJL. How might school resource officers not just stop homicides on campus, which are extremely rare, but reduce other types of violence on campus? Can you provide some success stories?

KT. Critics of SROs often point to incidences of high-profile school shootings where SROs were employed and shootings still occurred as reasons to downplay the value of SROs. However, there have been a number of cases where violent incidents occurred but thanks to the prompt intervention of an SRO already on scene, losses were minimized and attackers were quickly apprehended. In the past year alone, SROs were credited with quickly neutralizing an active student shooter at a Colorado high school, a knife-wielding student in a mass attack at a Pennsylvania high school, and an active shooter at an Oregon high school.

While the high-profile school shootings capture public and media attention, one of the hidden stories is how many plots of violent attacks at school are actually thwarted. Our research identified approximately 120 thwarted plots against schools between 2000 and 2010. Although this list is not comprehensive and many incidents likely went unreported, our study found many of the plots were stopped through the intervention of SROs.

But it is the day-to-day work of the SRO that really captures the success of good SRO programs. SROs have led chess clubs and tournaments and coached school sports teams. We even worked with an SRO who implemented a highly successful student reading program and behavior interventions using a canine in her school.

PJL. How might school resource officers reduce the influence of gang activity at school or around campus?

KT. SROs, like non-police district in-house campus security employees, can have a significant impact on preventing and intervening with gang-related activity at school. SROs serve as a link between the school, the police department, and the community. They can be the first to learn about gang activity that begins in the community and is likely to spill over into the school, and vice-versa.

SROs work with principals and other school staff to head-off gang-related assaults, fights, weapons-incidents, and related conflicts before they occur. By having good relationships with students, including those who are gang-affiliated, they can mediate conflicts between individuals associated with rival gangs before they escalate into violence in and around campus. SROs also provide a strong deterrent against non-students and gang-affiliated students who may otherwise muster up to fight outside at student arrival and at dismissal times.

PJL. Based on your knowledge of school safety, what are schools doing right and what are they doing wrong to ensure safe schools?

KT. Following high-profile incidents like the Sandy Hook shooting there is always a search to do something "new" in order to respond to the emotional security needs of parents, educators, and the broader society. Some of the buzz since the Newtown shootings, albeit from a relatively small percent of parents and schools, has been on ridiculous extremes like bulletproof backpacks for students, bulletproof white boards for classrooms, bulletproof blankets to protect against shooters and tornadoes, and teaching students and school staff to throw things at, and to attack, heavily armed gunmen. People are looking for the "Wow!" but not thinking about the "How!" in terms of the inability and unreasonableness of implementing these and other ideas.

We are seeing far too many school districts throw thousands of dollars into buying security equipment such as cameras based upon one-time grants or other budget allocations, only to have no budgets for maintenance and replacement in the months and years ahead. The result: Cameras that are not functioning, not being repaired and presenting a false sense of security, along with a potential liability risk to school districts.

Smart superintendents, principals, and school boards recognize that proactive security and preparedness efforts are not only the right thing to do, but also a strong tool for strengthening school–community trust and confidence in their leadership. School leaders must avoid knee-jerk reactions when the emotional tidal wave hits them by focusing on proven and reliable security and preparedness strategies. They must also ramp up their proactive communications on school safety and their crisis communications readiness.

Superintendents, principals, and school boards must invest as much, if not more, in their people and in dedicating time to safety and preparedness planning as they do in physical security enhancements. Too often we see well-intended school leaders who will be quick to drop some dollars for physical security equipment they can point to when talking with parents, but they are much more guarded in releasing time for training school staff, allocating resources for school mental health services, diversifying their lockdown or evacuation drills, and doing meaningful, detailed planning with their first responders.

Many of the security and preparedness measures schools really need are less flashy and fad-driven, and sometimes more discreet or even invisible. Employing Crime Prevention Through Environmental Design (CPTED) concepts in new school construction and renovations can make substantial improvements such as reconfiguring main entranceways to funnel visitors into the office while preventing people from walking directly into the building and enhancing hallway supervision with improved line-of-sight. Designs with safety in mind can also reducing bullying by putting restroom sinks in a common area on the outer portion of the bathrooms so adults can better supervise kids washing their hands after using the facilities.

We spend a good deal of our time in workshops not just focusing on active shooters, but also talking about day-to-day student supervision techniques that many school leaders mistakenly take for granted assuming that their teachers and support staff already know, yet they really have not been trained to do. We talk about the dangers of mishandling custody issues at elementary schools and how to de-escalate irate parents. We remind school leaders that while it is easy to point to more cameras or additional police at a school (neither of which on their own are bad things), it is equally important for school staff to build relationships with students, improve counseling and mental health support, conduct regular planning and cross-training with first responders, diversify lockdown and other emergency drills, and use proactive communication strategies with parents and the community.

The best school safety measures are often invisible, but they truly make schools safer.

PJL. Would hiring more school resource officers stop severe and rare forms of school violence. If not, what do you suggest?

KT. If a school district is hiring more SROs solely for the purpose of preventing school shootings, they are failing to understand the purpose and roles of SROs. The purpose for hiring an SRO should be to engage a professional with a unique disciplinary perspective who is there to support school administrators in building a comprehensive school safety strategy by implementing the Triad Model of law enforcement officer, student counselor, and law-related educator. Good SROs deal with everything from bullying and child abuse to educating students about the dangers of cyberspace to working on school emergency planning.

The key to effective SRO programs is an officer who builds relationships with students, as well as relationships with school administrators, staff, parents and the school community. It is all about relationships. So SRO programs must be viewed as prevention programs.

Of course, simply hiring more and more SROs is not the only solution, nor is it financially realistic. We also need more counselors, social workers, and school psychologists. We know from school shootings to bullying incidents that undiagnosed and/or untreated student mental health issues are often a common thread with violent and/or aggressive students. In general, we have far too few professionals on staff to meet these increasing mental health demands crossing the schoolhouse doors.

We must exercise caution, however, to avoid getting into the "We need more prevention" versus "We need more SROs and security" debate. It should not be an argument of more prevention OR more security. The argument should be more prevention AND better security.

We cannot successfully deliver prevention and education services in a school lacking reasonable security any more than we can have a prison-like environment without prevention and education services for children. The student who is violently attacked in the back hallway of the school is not going to benefit very much if he does not make it alive to the psychologist's office! Prevention and security must work hand-in-hand as part of a comprehensive approach to school safety.

PJL. There now is a movement to arm teachers or have designated teachers carry weapons on campus to protect their students? Is this a good idea or a bad idea?

KT. Firearms are standard tools of the trade for a law enforcement officer. Suggesting that trained, commissioned peace officers (SROs) work without firearms simply because they are in schools is ridiculous. To do so would lower the standard of equipment for a police officer and lower the officer's capacity to protect the lives of students, staff, and himself/herself. Doing so could also increase the liability potential for a school district and law enforcement agency.

Therefore, having SROs who are armed is an acceptable and expected best practice. Going beyond that and arming teachers and school support staff, however, is a high-risk and high-liability proposition, in my opinion. School districts considering arming teachers and school staff with guns would take on significant responsibility and potential liabilities that are beyond the expertise, knowledge-base, experience, and professional capabilities of most school boards and administrators.

It is also important to realize that the vast majority of teachers want to be armed, not with guns, but with the latest research on academic achievement, technology, and other tools to implement their educational objectives. In fact, teachers I talk with during my school security consulting and training projects consistently tell me that they have no desire to be armed. Unfortunately, the Sandy Hook Elementary School shootings resulted in the political hijacking of school safety by both the gun control and gun rights special interests, and this whole conversation on arming teachers has created a major distraction from sorely needed public policy programs and funding for meaningful comprehensive approaches to school safety and emergency preparedness.

The bottom line is that arming persons in pre-K-12 schools should be left to professional public safety officials: SROs who are sworn, commissioned career police officers.

PJL. What do educators need to know to work effectively with school resource officers to improve school safety?

KT. Educators and SROs have a lot they can learn from one another. It is a two-way street. Just as successful SRO programs require meaningful relationships between SROs and students, they also require meaningful relationships between the SRO and the school's administrators, teachers, and support staff.

Too often when SRO programs are not at maximum performance, it is due to a lack of understanding of roles and poor communication. SRO roles should be clear in their job descriptions, Memoranda of Understanding (MOU) agreements between the law enforcement agency and the school district, and in the minds of both the SRO and the building administrators. When roles are unclear and communication is poor, we see a lot of power struggles, personality conflicts, and finger pointing rather than teamwork, mutual respect, and meaningful collaboration resulting in safer schools.

Everyone in the school should know the role of the SRO. The SRO and principal should be clear on their respective roles and how to distinguish law enforcement versus school disciplinary matters. When those lines get blurry, as they do at times, even in the best of SRO programs,

SROs and principals must have mutual respect, trust and professionalism to communicate openly about their differences in opinions and protocols in order to work through sometimes difficult issues and incidents.

Understanding the role of the SRO goes beyond just the SRO and principal. The entire school staff, student body, and parents must also be educated about the role of the SRO. When everyone understands the role, boundaries, and benefits of the SRO program, those periodic obstacles that will naturally occur can be prevented and/or better managed when they arise.

Safety Policies and Procedures

Safe school plans and policies should be developed prospectively and continuously refined and updated. Anticipating threats to school safety and planning how to address these in advance can mitigate many of these threats (Cowan et al., 2013; Reeves et al., 2010). Moreover, only with adequate forethought and planning can a school respond effectively to chaotic and often highly distressing situations such as a violent attack. Although Chapter 15 covers threat assessment and Chapter 18 covers crisis management in greater depth, a brief review of general safety policies and procedures is discussed next. More specifically, content is provided on forming school safety teams, developing and implementing crisis plans, and collaborating with community agencies.

Safety Teams

All schools should develop safety teams that regularly meet to discuss safety policies and procedures. In general, these teams should be comprised of a school administrator, a school mental health professional, a school nurse, security personnel, teachers, and parents (NASP & NASRO, 2014). School safety teams aim to develop, foster, and maintain a safe and positive school climate by addressing issues such as threats of violence, emergency planning, campus security, bullying, gang violence, fighting, weapon carrying, sexual aggression, and vandalism. It is important for school safety teams to balance prevention, security, and crisis management practices—not just one or two of these foci. In addition, all members of school communities should know who is on the safety team and alternate team members are needed to help manage problems that could result from a team member being absent. Many school districts are now posting contact information for school safety team members on school websites, as well as resources related to ensuring student safety. As a salient example, the Cherry Creek School District in Greenwood Village, Colorado, lists the district's safety team members as well as safety policies and procedures on an easily accessible and clearly delineated webpage: www.cherrycreekschools.org/SafeSchools/Pages/default.aspx. Additionally, on this page, the district lists what to do during an emergency, how to report threats, safety and security resources, and messages from the Superintendent's Office about school safety. Figure 2.2 lists the Cherry Creek School District Comprehensive Safe Schools Plan.

Crisis Plans

Well-conceived and field-tested crisis plans can help to ensure rapid and effective responses to crises and acts of violence. Furthermore, having these plans in place and known by members of the school community can help individuals view crisis events as being more manageable and less emotionally traumatic (Reeves et al., 2010). According to Brock et al. (2009), crisis plans should include strategies for activating response protocols; contacting law enforcement officers, emergency responders, parents, and the media; de-escalating threats; identifying all crisis response personnel; communicating with staff; and communicating with parents and other stakeholders on an ongoing basis as a crisis unfolds and is addressed. Chapter 17 goes into greater depth on each of the aforementioned components that a crisis plan should address.

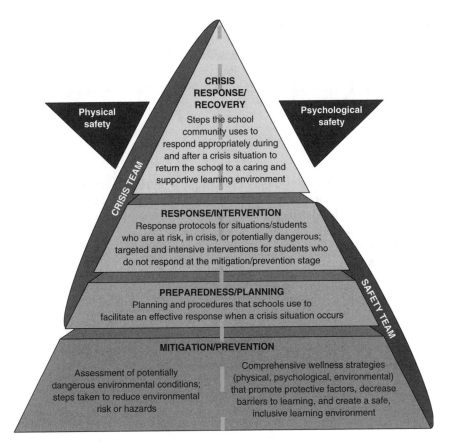

Figure 2.2 The Cherry Creek School District Comprehensive Safe Schools Plan

Collaborate with Agencies

In advance of a crisis event, it is important for schools to establish relationships with local agencies that can help with ensuring school safety and crisis response. If an event requires police intervention, school administrators will need to maintain regular contact with the police incident commander as well as liaison officers and public information officers to make sure that accurate and timely information is being collected and can then be disseminated to members of the school community (Reeves et al., 2010). Schools will also need to have positive and collaborative agreements set up in advance with emergency first responding agencies such as firefighters and paramedics who will need to know the layout of a school so they can nimbly navigate through its infrastructure. Lastly, a list of community providers should be developed and regularly updated so that members of the school can refer students and families to competent mental health professionals, social service agencies, and shelters.

Promoting Psychological Safety

Promoting safe and supportive schools involves ensuring the psychological safety of students in addition to protecting their physical safety. In general, schools that foster students' mental health and emotional well-being will also support their psychological safety and build resilience in them (Reeves et al., 2010). Therefore, efforts to promote psychological safety are highly overlapping with universal prevention and intervention approaches that aim to support the psychosocial functioning of all students. Moreover, they also infuse elements of positive psychology, aim to foster connectedness among members of school communities, involve effective behavior management, support highly at-risk and vulnerable students, and proactively prevent crises whenever possible. Therefore, as illustrated, promoting psychological safety espouses and integrates many of the concepts discussed in this text. Because of this, only brief descriptions of strategies to promote psychological safety are provided in this chapter, as subsequent chapters cover these strategies in greater depth.

Social-emotional Learning

Social-emotional learning (SEL), which is covered in Chapter 4, aims to create safe and emotionally supportive environments at school in which students can thrive academically and behaviorally. A wealth of research indicates that SEL is effective at improving positive or prosocial behavior among students, while decreasing negative behaviors (see Durlak, Weissberg, Dymnicki, Taylor, & Schellinger, 2011, for review). In addition, further highlighting the value of SEL, research indicates that it benefits students with and without behavioral problems, students of diverse ethnicities, and students who attend schools in rural, suburban, and urban settings; it can also be effectively implemented by educators—additional school personnel are not needed (Durlak et al., 2011).

Safe and Civil Schools

Safe and Civil Schools (SCS) is another framework that aspires to improve student behavior, discipline, and school safety. The SCS model aims to empower school staff with techniques to help all students behave responsibly and respectfully and some research suggests that the implementation of SCS results in reductions in disciplinary referrals, suspensions, expulsions, and tardiness. Conversely, SCS has been associated with improvements in student attendance and connectedness and perceptions of increased safety and climate (Ward & Gersten, 2013). Information on SCS and how to implement this framework in K-12 schools is available on the SCS website: www.safeandcivilschools.com/index.php.

School-wide Positive Behavioral Supports

School-wide positive behavioral supports (SWPBS), which is featured in Chapter 10, is an empirically supported framework that includes "proactive strategies for defining, teaching, and supporting appropriate student behavior to create positive school environments" (Office of Special Education Programs Technical Assistance Center on PBIS, 2010, para. 2). Support for students is delivered in multiple tiers in a SWPBS framework and all environments of the school are included in service-delivery efforts. In general, the SWPBS model centers on creating and maintaining universal or school-wide, targeted (classroom/group), and intensive (individualized) systems of support. Research support for SWPBS is extensive, as this framework is associated with reductions of problematic and aggressive student behavior as well as with increases in adaptive and prosocial behaviors (Horner et al., 2014).

Violence Prevention Programs

A study by McNeely and Falci (2004) found decreases in students' initiation of violence and increases in their cessation of violence when they receive adequate social support from educators. In addition, a study by Johnson, Burke, and Gielen (2011) found that student actions or how they treated each other and expectations for behavior (e.g., what types of behavior is tolerated, whether bullying is condoned) were the characteristics most responsible for the presence of school violence. Thus, primary prevention programs such as Second Step, that are designed to deter aggression and promote social competence of students, have potential to reduce school violence (Frey, Hirschstein, & Guzzo, 2000). The Second Step program includes classroom lessons to teach core social competencies and behavior management skills, teacher and staff training to encourage student generalization of skills and create consistent behavioral expectations throughout the school, follow-up support and preparation of on-site trainers to sustain ongoing program implementation, and a family component to encourage complementary school–home practices. Research supports the efficacy of Second Step in a range of school settings, and, more generally, meta-analytic studies provide support for the efficacy of multicomponent violence prevention programs (see Neace & Muñoz, 2012, for review). For example, a meta-analysis by Matjasko et al. (2012) found that violence prevention programs are moderately effective at reducing violence and aggressive behaviors in schools.

Bullying Prevention and Intervention

Chapter 12 covers current bullying prevention and intervention approaches. To promote psychological safety, many schools have implemented research-based multicomponent bullying prevention/intervention program such as the Olweus Bullying Prevention Program (Olweus & Limber, 2007), KiVA (Salmivalli, Kärnä, & Poskiparta, 2011), PeaceBuilders (Flannery et al., 2003), and Steps to Respect (Brown, Low, Smith, & Haggerty, 2011). In addition to reducing bullying and peer victimization more generally, bullying prevention/intervention programs aim to transform school environments to make them safer and more secure for all students. Although the previously mentioned bullying prevention/intervention programs have empirical support, they have not yet been tested with a range of different school-age populations and more research is needed on how these programs can be adapted to different K-12 school settings (Ttofi & Farrington, 2011).

Anti-bullying programs, such as those previously mentioned, have expanded dramatically in schools during the past two decades. In order to understand the impact of these efforts, Ttofi and Farrington (2011) conducted a meta-analytic review on the effectiveness of school-based anti-bullying intervention programs. Their analysis of 44 program evaluations that were published from 1983 to May 2009 showed that, overall, these programs are effective: on average, bullying decreased by 20–23 percent and victimization decreased by 17–20 percent. They found that the most important program elements that were associated with a decrease in bullying were parent training/meetings, improved playground supervision, disciplinary methods, classroom management, teacher training, classroom rules, a whole-school anti-bullying policy, school conferences, information for parents, and cooperative group work. In addition, the total number of elements and the duration and intensity of the program for teachers and children were significantly associated with a decrease in bullying. Also, one of their most significant findings was that programs needed to be intensive and long-lasting to have an impact on this disconcerting problem. This last point underscores an emphasis of this text: Efforts to promote school safety need to be field tested, empirically validated, and continually improved through ongoing evaluation.

Conclusion

Although rates of school violence appear to be declining at the aggregate level in the U.S., public perceptions of schools being unsafe or dangerous still abound. In addition to being driven by the heavy media coverage of recent tragedies such as the Sandy Hook shooting, this phenomenon may be also driven by increases in more common and less extreme incidents of school violence such as bullying and peer victimization. In response to problems with violence and aggressive behavior, many schools have increased their efforts to promote safe and supportive schools to prevent or mitigate these problems. In general, these efforts involve promoting the physical and psychological safety of schools. On one hand, some strategies to increase physical safety in school settings include increasing the use of security technologies, employing SROs, and re-thinking school safety plans, policies, and procedures. On the other hand, some strategies for increasing the psychological safety in schools involve implementing multicomponent prevention and intervention programs, supporting students' mental health more generally, and fostering safe and healthy learning environments. Ultimately, it is important for educators to view both physical and psychological strategies to promote safe and supportive schools—not as different approaches—but as mutually complementary.

References

Addington, L. A. (2009). Cops and cameras: Public school security as a policy response to Columbine. *American Behavioral Scientist, 52,* 1426–1446.

Bachman, R., Randolph, A., & Brown, B. L. (2011). Predicting perceptions of fear at school and going to and from school for African American and White students: The effects of school security measures. *Youth & Society, 43,* 705–726.

Brock, S. E., Sandoval, J., & Lewis, S. (2001). *Preparing for crises in the schools: A manual for building school crisis response teams.* Somerset, NJ: John Wiley & Sons Inc.

Brock, S. E., Nickerson, A. B., Reeves, M. A., Jimerson, S. R., Feinberg, T. & Lieberman, R. (2009). *School crisis prevention and intervention: The PREPaRE model.* Bethesda, MD: National Association of School Psychologists.

Brown, B. (2006). Understanding and assessing school police officers: A conceptual and methodological comment. *Journal of Criminal Justice, 34,* 591–604.

Brown, E. C., Low, S., Smith, B. H., & Haggerty, K. P. (2011). Outcomes from a school-randomized controlled trial of Steps to Respect: A bullying prevention program. *School Psychology Review, 40,* 423–433.

Cowan, K. C., Vaillancourt, K., Rossen, E., & Pollitt, K. (2013). *A framework for safe and successful schools [Brief].* Bethesda, MD: National Association of School Psychologists. Retrieved from: http://www.nasponline.org/Documents/Research%20and%20Policy/Advocacy%20Resources/Framework_for_Safe_and_Successful_School_Environments.pdf.

Daniels, J. A., Volungis, A., Pshenishny, E., Gandhi, P., Winkler, A., Cramer, D. P., & Bradley, M. C. (2010). A qualitative investigation of averted school shooting rampages. *The Counseling Psychologist, 38,* 69–95.

Dinkes, R., Kemp, J., Baum, K., & Snyder, T. (2009). *Indicators of school crime and safety: 2009 (NCES 2010-012).* Washington, DC: National Center for Education Statistics, Institute of Education Sciences, U.S. Department of Education.

Durlak, J. A., Weissberg, R. P., Dymnicki, A. B., Taylor, R. D., & Schellinger, K. B. (2011). The impact of enhancing students' social and emotional learning: A meta-analysis of school-based universal interventions. *Child Development, 82,* 405–432.

Dwyer, K., Osher, D., & Warger, C. (1998). *Early warning, timely response: A guide to safe schools.* Washington, DC: U.S. Department of Education.

Finn, P., & McDevitt, J. (2005). *National Assessment of School Resource Officer Programs. Final project report.* Document Number 209273. U.S. Department of Justice.

Flannery, D. J., Vazsonyi, A. T., Liau, A. K., Guo, S., Powell, K. E., Atha, H., Vesterdal, W., . . . Embry, D. (2003). Initial behavior outcomes for the PeaceBuilders Universal School-Based Violence Prevention Program. *Developmental Psychology, 39,* 292–308.

Frey, K. S., Hirschstein, M. K., & Guzzo, B. A. (2000). Second Step: Preventing aggression by promoting social competence. *Journal of Emotional and Behavioral Disorders, 8,* 102–112.

Girouard, C. (2001). *School resource officer training program.* U.S. Department of Justice, Office of Justice Programs, Office of Juvenile Justice and Delinquency Prevention.

Horner, R. H., Kincaid, D., Sugai, G., Lewis, T., Eber, L., Barrett, S., . . . Johnson, N. (2014). Scaling up school-wide positive behavioral interventions and supports: Experiences of seven states with documented success. *Journal of Positive Behavior Interventions,16,* 197–208.

Jimerson, S. R., Hart, S. R., & Renshaw, T. L. (2012). Conceptual foundations for understanding youth engaged in antisocial and aggressive behaviors. In S. R. Jimerson, A. Nickerson, M. J. Mayer & M. J. Furlong (Eds.), *Handbook of school violence and school safety: International research and practice, Second edition* (pp. 3–14). New York, NY: Routledge.

Johnson, S. L., Burke, J. G., & Gielen, A. C. (2011). Prioritizing the school environment in school violence prevention efforts. *Journal of School Health, 81,* 331–340.

Kim, C. Y., & Geronimo, I. (2010, January). Policing in schools: Developing a governance document for school resource officers in K-12 schools. *Education Digest, 75,* 28–35.

Larson, J. (2008). Best practices in school violence prevention. In A. Thomas & J. Grimes (Eds.), *Best practices in school psychology V.* (pp. 1291–1307). Bethesda: MD: National Association of School Psychologists.

McDevitt, J., & Panniello, J. (2005). *National assessment of school resource officer programs: Survey of students in three large new SRO programs.* National Institute of Justice (February 28, 2005), 1–3.

McNeely, C., & Falci, C. (2004). School connectedness and the transition into and out of health-risk behavior among adolescents: A comparison of social belonging and teacher support. *Journal of School Health, 74,* 284–292.

Maguire, B., Weatherby, G. A., & Mathers, R. A. (2002). Network news coverage of school shootings. *Social Science Journal, 39,* 465–470.

Matjasko, J. L., Vivolo-Kantor, A. M., Massetti, G. M., Holland, K. M., Holt, M. K., & Cruz, J. D. (2012). A systematic meta-review of evaluations of youth violence prevention programs: Common and divergent findings from 25 years of meta-analyses and systematic reviews. *Aggression and Violent Behavior, 17,* 540–552.

Mayer, M. J., & Leone, P. E. (1999). A structural analysis of school violence and disruption: Implications for creating safer schools. *Education and Treatment of Children, 22,* 333–356.

Modzeleski, W., Feucht, T., Rand M., Hall, J., Simon, T., Butler, L., . . . Hertz, M. (2008). School-associated student homicides – United States, 1992–2006. *Morbidity and Mortality Weekly Report, 57,* 33–36. Retrieved from: www.cdc.gov/mmwr/.

NASP and NASRO. (2014). *Best practice considerations for schools in active shooter and other armed assailant drills [Brief].* Bethesda, MD: National Association of School Psychologists.

Neace, W. P., & Muñoz, M. A. (2012). Pushing the boundaries of education: Evaluating the impact of Second Step®: a violence prevention curriculum with psychosocial and non-cognitive measures. *Child & Youth Services, 33,* 46–69.

Nickerson, A. B., & Martens, M. P. (2008). School violence: Associations with control, security/enforcement, educational/therapeutic approaches, and demographic factors. *School Psychology Review, 37,* 228–243.

Nekvasil, E., & Cornell, D. (2012). Student reports of peer threats of violence: Prevalence and outcomes. *Journal of School Violence, 11,* 357–375. doi: 10.1080/15388220.2012.706764

Office of Special Education Programs Technical Assistance Center (2010). *Implementation blueprint and self-assessment: Positive Behavioral Intervention and Support.* U.S. Department of Education, Office of Special Education Programs.

Olweus, D., & Limber, S. (2007). *Olweus Bullying Prevention Program: Teacher guide.* Center City, MN: Hazelden.

O'Malley, M., & Eklund, K. (2012). Promoting safe and healthy schools. In S. E. Brock & S. R. Jimerson (Eds.), *Best practices in school crisis prevention and intervention, Second edition* (pp. 151–176). Bethesda, MD: NASP.

Osher, D., Bear, G. G., Sprague, J. R., & Doyle, W. (2010). How can we improve school discipline? *Educational Researcher, 39,* 48–58.

Osher, D., Dwyer, K. P., Jimerson, S. R., & Brown, J. A. (2012). Developing safe, supportive, and effective schools: Facilitating student success to reduce violence. In S. R. Jimerson, A. B. Nickerson, M. J. Mayer, & M. J. Furlong (Eds.), *Handbook of school violence and school safety: International research and practice* (pp. 27–44). New York, NY: Routledge.

Perumean-Chaney, S. E., & Sutton, L. M. (2013). Students and perceived school safety: The impact of school security measures. *American Journal of Criminal Justice, 38,* 570–588.

Reeves, M. A., Kanan, L. M., & Plog, A. E. (2010). *Comprehensive planning for safe learning environments: A school professional's guide to integrating physical and psychological safety—Prevention through recovery.* New York, NY: Routledge

Roberts, S., Zhang, J., & Truman, J. (2010). *Indicators of school crime and safety: 2010 (NCES 2011-002/ NCJ 230812).* Washington, DC: National Center for Education Statistics, U.S. Department of Education, and Bureau of Justice Statistics, Office of Justice Programs, U.S. Department of Justice.

Salmivalli, C., Kärnä, A., & Poskiparta, E. (2011). Counteracting bullying in Finland: The KiVa program and its effects on different forms of being bullied. *International Journal of Behavioral Development, 35,* 405–411.

Sandoval, J., Brock, S. E., & Knifton, K. (2013). Acts of violence. In J. Sandoval (Ed.), *Crisis counseling, intervention, and prevention in the schools, Third edition* (pp. 212–228). New York, NY: Routledge.

Schreck, C. J., Miller, J. M., & Gibson, C. L. (2003). Trouble in the school yard: A study of the risk factors of victimization at school. *Crime & Delinquency, 49,* 460–484.

Stein, S., & Cherkis, J. (2014). *With school shootings routine, parents turn to bulletproof backpacks, child clothing.* Huffington Post. Retrieved on February 3, 2015 from www.huffingtonpost.com/2014/06/16/school-shootings_n_5497428.html.

Strepling, K. H. (1997). The low-aggression classroom: A teacher's view. In A.P. Goldstein & J. C. Conoly (Eds.), *School violence intervention: A practical handbook* (pp. 23–45). New York, NY: Guilford Press.

Sulkowski, M. L. (2011). An investigation of students' willingness to report threats of violence in campus communities. *Psychology of Violence, 1,* 53–65. doi: 10.1037/a0021592.

Theriot, M. T., & Orme, J. G. (2014). School resource officers and students' feelings of safety at school. *Youth Violence and Juvenile Justice, 14,* 130-146. doi: 1541204014564472.

Trump, K. (1998). *Practical school security: Basic guidelines for safe and secure schools.* Thousand Oaks, CA: Corwin Press.

Ttofi, M. M., & Farrington, D. P. (2011). The effectiveness of school based programs to reduce bullying: A systematic and meta-analytic review. *Journal of Experimental Criminology, 7,* 27–56. doi: 10.1007/s11292-010-9109-1

Vossekuil, B., Fein, R., Reddy, M., Borum, R., & Modzeleski, W. (2002). *The final report and findings of the Safe School Initiative: Implications for the prevention of school attacks in the United States.* Washington, DC: U.S. Secret Service, National Threat Assessment Center.

Ward, B., & Gersten, R. (2013). A randomized evaluation of the safe and civil schools model for positive behavioral interventions and supports at elementary schools in a large urban school district. *School Psychology Review, 42,* 317–333.

White House. (2013). *Now is the time: The President's plan to protect our children and our communities by reducing gun violence.* Retrieved on February 3, 2015 from: www.whitehouse.gov/sites/default/files/docs/wh_now_is_the_time_full.pdf.

Part II
Fostering Students' Mental Health

3   The Importance of Providing Mental Health Services in Schools

About 17 percent of children in the U.S. suffer from mental illness according to epidemiological studies (National Research Council & Institute of Medicine, 2009; Roberts, Attkisson, & Rosenblatt, 1998). Thus, about 340 youth will display clinically significant mental health problems in a school that contains 2,000 students. Furthermore, in addition to being prevalent, mental health problems also exert a markedly negative impact on students' functioning. A study by the World Health Organization indicates that mental health problems account for nearly half of all disabilities among individuals between the ages of 10 and 24 (Gore et al., 2011) and about 7.5 million U.S. children have been estimated to have an unmet mental health need (Kataoka, Zhang, & Wells, 2002).

The Scope of the Problem

This chapter addresses the scope of the problem of students' unmet mental health needs. This is followed by a discussion on the impact of adverse childhood experiences on mental health. The roles and functions of school-based mental health professionals are described and a case is made that school mental health services are a necessity—not a luxury—to help today's youth succeed in school and in life. A three-component approach to education with an emphasis on the critical importance of providing mental health and learning supports in schools is then provided. Finally, as an effective way to deliver mental health services in our schools, this chapter concludes with the presentation of a public health model that emphasizes prevention and focuses on the importance of making positive changes to the school environment rather than trying to change each child on an individual basis.

According to the New Freedom Commission on Mental Health (2003), approximately 5 percent to 9 percent of students meet eligibility criteria for "Emotional Disturbance,"[1] which is a special education classification that applies to students with serious emotional, behavioral, and mental health problems. In part, because of their emotional and behavioral problems, many of these youth will experience negative life outcomes such as not graduating from school and having a diminished quality of life. In support of this notion, and according to the Report of the Surgeon General's Conference on Children's Mental Health (Department of Health and Human Services [DHHS], 2000), 10 percent of U.S. children suffer from a mental disorder severe enough to limit daily functioning in their family, community, and school settings.

Even if they do not display mental health problems that result in a psychiatric diagnosis or special education classification, many other students suffer with mental health problems. Thirty percent of high school students in the U.S. felt so sad or hopeless that they stopped doing some usual activities almost every day for at least two consecutive weeks within the past year according to the Center for Disease Control and Prevention's bi-annual Youth Risk Surveillance Survey (CDC, 2014b). Additionally, and even more concerning, 17 percent of high school students reported that they had seriously considered suicide at some point during the 12 months prior to the survey's implementation. Stated differently, three out of ten youngsters felt so sad or hopeless during the past year that they were not able to lead fully productive lives, and one out of six students had seriously considered ending their own life. As a caveat, students with suicidal ideation typically feel sad and hopeless, so there is overlap between these two categories. Nonetheless, in a typical high school classroom with 30 students, during any given year, one would expect about nine students to feel sad or hopeless and about five to feel suicidal. These numbers alone highlight the mental health needs of youth in American schools.

In addition to displaying mental health problems that warrant acute care, millions of students fail to develop important social and emotional competencies that can protect their emotional well-being and are poorly bonded to supportive educational communities (Lazarus, 2012; Lazarus & Sulkowski, 2011). In this regard, research indicates that fewer than half of students (19 percent to 45 percent) develop competence in important social and emotional competencies such as empathetic responding, conflict resolution, and problem-solving skills prior to graduation (Klem & Connell, 2004). Moreover, less than a third (29 percent) of twelfth graders report that their school provides a caring and encouraging learning environment (Benson, 2006). The later problem may be even more dire than is reported, because the population sampled by Benson (2006) only included students who still remained in school (i.e., not school dropouts). In a sample of high school dropouts, only 41 percent of students reported that there was someone at school with whom they could discuss a personal problem and slightly more than half (56 percent) reported having a school staff member they could talk to about a school-related concern (Bridgeland, DiIulio, & Morison, 2006). This problem represents a significant barrier to graduating and subsequent success because a student's belief that nobody at school truly cares is the most frequently cited reason for dropping out (Kostering & Braziel, 2002). Clearly, more needs to be done to support at-risk students and ensure their long-term success in school and beyond.

The Impact of Adverse Childhood Experiences on Children's Mental Health

One of the most significant causes of mental health problems in youth is adverse childhood experiences (ACEs), which are highly stress-provoking experiences in childhood such as witnessing domestic violence, being physically abused, and experiencing neglect that can significantly disrupt physical and mental health (Blodgett, 2012; Rossen & Cowan, 2013). The National Survey of Children's Health (2011/2012) estimates that approximately 35 million children, from birth to 17 years of age, have experienced at least one ACE in their lifetime. The original ACE project by Felitti et al. (1998) brought to the forefront the impact of such experiences on individuals' well-being. Through a series of studies, Felitti et al. explored the long-term relationship between ACEs and a range of outcomes in adulthood and they highlighted the negative repercussions associated with ACEs that extend beyond childhood and into adulthood.

To date, the relationship between experiencing ACEs and the following outcomes have been investigated: physical health, emotional well-being, abuse, neglect, substance abuse in the home, having a relative with a mental illness or incarcerated, having a maternal figure treated violently, and parental separation or divorce (CDC, 2014a). As a whole, the initial ACE study revealed that almost two-thirds of the 17,000 participants sampled reported one or more ACEs and more than one in five reported three of more ACEs (CDC, 2014a). Moreover, the number of ACEs was positively correlated with a plethora of health risk factors and diseases and as the number of ACEs increased, the risk for the following health problems increased in a strong and graded fashion: smoking, alcoholism, drug use, obesity, physical inactivity, depression, suicide attempts, increased number of sexual partners and greater risk for sexually transmitted diseases, unintended pregnancies, heart and lung disease, cancer, skeletal difficulties, liver disease, and overall poor self-reported health (Felitti et al.,1998). Figure 3.1 highlights the negative impact of ACEs through the lifespan.

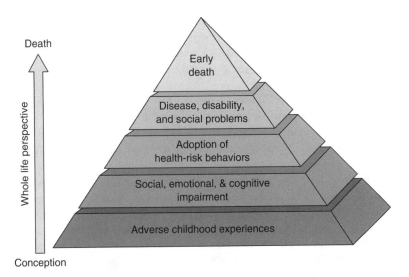

Figure 3.1 The Impact of Adverse Childhood Experiences

Since Felitti et al.'s seminal project, others have explored the effects of ACEs across other domains and within the context of childhood. For example, ACEs have been found to increase the risk for early initiation of illicit drug use by age 14, as well as the risk for suicide attempts in childhood, adolescence, and adulthood (Dube, Anda, Felitti, Chapman, Wiliamson, & Giles, 2001; Dube, Felitti, Dong, Chapman, Giles, & Anda, 2003). In a more recent study, Burke, Hellman, Scott, Weems, and Carrion (2011) found that over two-thirds of participants from birth to 20 years of age reported at least one or more ACEs.

The impact of ACEs is also evident at the neurobiological level. Stress can be defined as an individual's perception of how the body reacts to environmental stressors (McLaughlin & Christner, 2009). According to Danese and McEwen (2012), *allostasis* is our body's ability to detect environmental and physiological changes in order to activate certain response systems such as the endocrine, nervous, and immune systems. This activation in turn helps maintain stability in the face of such stressors. When a child is consistently exposed to stressors as a result of ACEs, also known as an allostatic overload, negative physiological and developmental changes often result (Danese & McEwen, 2012).

In a review of the literature, Danese and McEwen (2012) found that being exposed to repeated stress in childhood can lead to changes in the prefrontal cortex that correspond with inattentiveness, hyperactivity, impulsivity, and deficits in executive functioning. Moreover, over-activation of the stress-regulating HPA axis and higher levels of the stress hormone cortisol also have been found. Rossen and Cowan (2013) further note that overproduction of hormones such as cortisol and adrenaline can negatively affect development, memory, higher-order thinking skills, and learning more generally. Stress reactions can also be classified into four domains: Cognitive, emotional, behavioral, and physiological (McLaughlin & Christner, 2009). Thus, according to McLaughlin & Christner (2009), a child who has undergone a significant stressor such as an ACE may have a negative mindset (i.e., cognitive); appear anxious or irritable (i.e., emotional); react aggressively or regress to earlier behaviors such as bedwetting (i.e., behavioral); and may present with a host of physical symptoms such as headaches, stomach aches, and fatigue (i.e., physiological).

Students who have faced adversity may struggle with many of the skills needed for learning and achieving in school. They may have difficulty in (a) understanding the perspective of other people, (b) remaining attentive and focused during instruction, (c) engaging in effective problem-solving,

(d) communicating effectively, and (e) maintaining peer relationships (Cole et al., 2005). These students also may display deficits in executive functioning skills such as planning, setting goals, and emotional regulation. Moreover, children who have been exposed to ACEs may engage in aggressive behaviors, be defiant, withdraw socially, be highly reactive or on edge, and they may even become obsessed with perfectionism in their desire to maintain a sense of control over their lives (Cole et al., 2005).

Although the impact of early adversity in childhood is evident, the question remains how educators and school mental health professionals can work together to create learning environments that are responsive to such adversity? As described by Fitzgerald and Cohen (2012), schools provide ideal environments for addressing the negative effects of trauma and adversity. One proposed approach to creating trauma-sensitive schools is the Attachment, Self-Regulation, and Competency (ARC) model (Kinniburgh, Blaustein, Spinazzola, & van der Kolk, 2005). This model addresses issues and vulnerabilities stemming from childhood adversity by encouraging healthy social attachments, promoting self-regulation, and supporting competency across domains. The ARC model provides educators and school-based mental health professionals with principles to make trauma-informed decisions regarding the assessment and treatment of children who have faced adversity (Kinniburgh et al., 2005). The attachment component of this model focuses on the interactions between a child and his or her caregiver that have long-term implications for the child's identity formation and sense of self (Kinniburgh et al., 2005). The self-regulation component, in turn, addresses the lack of self-awareness and disconnect from emotional experiences that traumatized children often exhibit, and focuses on helping children identify, express, and adjust their emotions (Kinniburgh et al., 2005). Finally, the competency component of the ARC model supports children's cognitive, emotional, intrapersonal, and interpersonal competency development by helping them build such skills and connecting them with outside resources to support this endeavor (Kinniburgh et al., 2005). For more information on the ARC model visit www.traumacenter.org/research/ascot.php.

Additionally, the Flexible Framework model that was developed by Cole et al. (2005) as part of the Trauma and Learning Policy Initiative (TLPI) aims to help schools develop their own trauma-sensitive models. This framework emphasizes six main components: *leadership* by school and district-level administrators; *professional development* and training of staff; *access to resources and services* such as collaboration with mental health professionals; use of *academic and non-academic strategies* for traumatized students; changes to school *policies and procedures*; and *collaboration with families* to encourage their active engagement (Cole, Eisner, Gregory, & Ristuccia, 2013). For more information on the TLPI visit www.traumasensitive schools.org. Also from this site, the reader can download for free two texts, *Helping traumatized children learn: A report and policy agenda* and *Helping traumatized children learn: Creating and advocating for trauma-sensitive schools.*

Based upon the research related to the impact of ACEs on children's development, the governor of Massachusetts signed into law on September 13, 2014, provisions of An Act Relative to Safe and Supportive Schools as part of the legislature's omnibus Act Relative to the Reduction of School Violence and this is codified in Massachusetts General Laws as Chapter 69 Section 1p and is aligned with the TLPI flexible framework. The intention was to create a safe and supportive schools framework to improve educational outcomes for all students. The law includes a groundbreaking definition of safe and supportive schools as

> schools that foster a safe, positive, healthy, and inclusive whole-school learning environment that (i) enables students to develop positive relationships with adults and peers, regulate their emotions and behavior, achieve academic and non-academic success in school and maintain physical and psychological health and well being and (ii) integrates services and aligns

initiatives that promote students behavioral health, including social and emotional learning, bullying prevention, trauma sensitivity, dropout prevention, truancy reduction, children's mental health, foster care and homeless youth education, inclusion of students with disabilities, positive behavioral approaches that reduce suspensions and expulsions and other similar initiatives.
(http://traumasensitiveschools.org/get-involved/safe-and-supportive-schools/)

Consistent with the TLPI framework, Cole et al. (2005) provide several strategies for supporting the well-being of youngsters exposed to ACEs and trauma, and these are listed in Text Box 3.1.

Text Box 3.1 Supporting Children Exposed to Adverse Childhood Experiences

- Emphasize strengths but build a roadmap with students to work towards their areas of need
- Create predictable classrooms with routines
- Provide positive behavioral supports
- Help children learn how to identify and express their emotions
- Present information in a variety of modalities
- Review vocabulary and concepts before a lesson
- Use manipulatives and graphic organizers
- Provide plenty of concrete and abstract examples
- Determine if there is a need for a comprehensive evaluation (i.e., psychological, speech language, occupational, functional analysis of behavior)
- Foster caring, supportive relationships (e.g., praise for effort, create special jobs, assign a mentor)
- Involve children in extracurricular activities to build upon strengths and foster participation

Based on suggestions from Cole et al., 2005

Supporting Students' Mental Health and Emotional Well-Being

In response to this growing mental health crisis that has been illustrated above, President Bush's New Freedom Commission (2003) recommended that "all schools must be active partners in the mental health care of our children because of the important interplay between emotional health and school success" (p. 58). The Commission also stated that: "Federal, State, and local child-servicing agencies fully recognize and address the mental health needs of youth in the educational system" (p. 62). However, despite recognizing the importance of addressing students' mental health needs, a significant discrepancy exists between these needs and the provision of requisite services. For example, only 6–8 percent of U.S. children receive adequate mental health services in any setting (Kataoka, Zhang, & Wells, 2002) and less than 1 percent of students are identified and receive services for ED in schools (Becker et al., 2011).

Clearly, efforts are needed to support students' emotional well-being and mental health. Fortunately, schools may be an optimal environment to tackle this initiative. Research indicates that most (95 percent) youth spend at least 40 hours a week in school (Resnicow, Cross, & Wynder, 1993) and disparities in mental health service delivery are reduced in educational settings (Cummings, Ponce, & Mays, 2010). Further, research also indicates that rates for utilizing intervention programs in schools are higher than they are for clinics, due to reduced transportation obstacles and the familiarity of the school setting (Ginsburg, Becker, Newman-Kingery, & Nichols, 2008). Thus, in light of these findings, schools can be prime locations to reach youth who traditionally underuse mental health services.

Preventing Mental Health Problems

In addition to addressing students' mental health needs, schools also must work toward actively preventing mental health problems through supporting students' healthy development and emotional well-being. A report from the Institute of Medicine (2009) highlights the importance of promoting healthy self-esteem, social-emotional competence, and social inclusion to prevent and mitigate emotional, behavioral, and mental disorders in students. Although the importance of targeting these objectives may seem obvious to mental health professionals, this report represents an important shift in focus, as the Institute previously did not establish mental health promotion as an effective preventative intervention in 1994 (Durlak, Weissberg, Dymnicki, Schellinger, & Taylor, 2011).

In response to the Institute's concern to promote healthy self-esteem and social-emotional competence in youth, a corresponding shift in focus away from a medical model that primarily attends to the identification and treatment of youth with disabling conditions is needed. In this regard, incorporating a positive psychology approach into the schools can help. Positive psychology is the scientific study of what goes right in life and its basic premise is that the promotion of happiness and fulfillment should be a prime concern (Park & Peterson, 2008; Seligman & Csikszentmihalyi, 2000). Positive psychology seeks to complement the traditional clinical focus that is based on a medical or disease model, in which health and well-being are defined by an absence of a psychological disorder or psychosocial distress. In fact, researchers have found that the absence of mental illness does not invariably imply the presence of high levels of positive mental health and vice versa (Sin & Lyubomirsky, 2009). The aim of positive psychology is to help support human thriving and flourishing in *all* individuals, not just those who suffer with mental illness (Peterson & Park, 2003). Consequently, the ultimate goal of positive psychology in schools is congruent with the recommendations of the Institute of Medicine—to help *all* young people lead fulfilling lives. For further discussion regarding how educators can implement positive psychology into schools see Chapter 9.

The Roles of School-based Mental Health Professionals

In order to address the mental health crisis in U.S. schools, an adequate number of school-based mental health professionals must be employed. These individuals include school psychologists, school counselors, and school social workers, and, in some cases, school nurses and consulting child/adolescent psychiatrists. As emphasized by Cowen, Vaillancourt, Rossen, and Pollitt (2013) access to school mental health services needs to be available continuously and connected to the overall learning process. All school-based mental health professionals are trained in the organization and operation of schools, child development, family systems, consultation and collaboration with related professionals, assessment, school crisis response, and school-based mental health.

Although school-based mental health professionals may all deliver some overlapping services such as being willing and able to collaborate with allied professionals, provide short-term counseling, connect with families, and support social-emotional learning, each respective profession has its own core competencies and some individual professionals may have specialized skills within these professions (e.g., evaluating preschool children for autism, supporting children who have experienced a death of a parent or sibling, working with incarcerating youth). The current training requirements, roles, and core competencies of different school-based mental health professionals are discussed below.

School Psychologists

School psychologists have a minimum of an Educational Specialist (Ed.S.) degree, which requires at least 60 semester hours of coursework, a supervised practicum in the schools, and a 1,200 clock hour internship (or full school year) serving as an intern in school psychology. As a whole, school psychologists have extensive knowledge of learning processes; social, emotional, behavioral, and academic interventions; consultation and collaboration; typical and atypical development and behavior; special education; counseling, crisis prevention, and crisis intervention; psychological assessment; school systems; law; and ethical conduct in school and psychological settings. They specialize in analyzing complex student and school problems and in providing effective, evidence-based interventions. They work with parents and teachers to provide coordinated support to struggling learners and students experiencing emotional trauma, grief, and loss, as well as anxiety, depression, and other behavioral challenges. These professionals provide comprehensive psychological evaluations to students and they help develop individualized educational plans (IEPs) for students with disabilities (e.g., children with learning disabilities, autism, emotional and behavioral disorders), Section 504 accommodations, and response-to-intervention (RtI) service-delivery. School psychologists also respond to crises and have specialized training in suicide assessment, prevention, intervention, and postvention. Additionally, many are knowledgeable about conducting risk and threat assessments and they are capable of responding to many legal and ethical issues that impact students and schools (Cowen et al., 2013).

School Counselors

School counselors must have a minimum of a Master's degree in School Counseling to work in K-12 settings. They are frequently the first school-based mental health professionals to come into contact with students because they are involved with providing universal learning supports to the entire school population. Many school counselors are former teachers and have a solid foundation in curriculum development and instruction. They help students deal with their academic, personal, and career goals by designing, implementing, and evaluating a comprehensive school counseling program. They often are integral members of multidisciplinary teams that help develop IEPs for students with disabilities. They may facilitate individual and group counseling sessions for students experiencing difficulties (e.g., bereavement groups, social skills training, friendship groups, children in families undergoing divorce, victims of bullying, etc.). They work to promote safe learning environments and respond to student behaviors that impact the school climate, such as peer conflicts, student–teacher conflicts, and bullying. Working in tandem with teachers, parents, and community members, they help students with their transition from elementary school to middle school and from high school to college or into the workforce. Whereas school psychologists and school social workers often are assigned to multiple schools, school counselors typically are only assigned to one school. Additionally, middle schools and high schools often have more than one counselor, with one assigned to each grade level (Cowen et al., 2013).

School Social Workers

At the minimum, social workers must have a Master's degree in Social Work (MSW) to work in schools. Their preparation includes specialized training in systems theory, social justice, cultural diversity, consultation and collaboration, working with families and social service agencies, risk assessment and intervention, dropout prevention, and clinical interventions to support the mental health needs of students. They have special expertise in understanding community and family systems and linking students and their families with community support services, such as child protective services and domestic abuse shelters. These professionals work with high-risk families and vulnerable student populations and they often focus on providing supports to homeless and foster children, recent immigrants, migrant youth, students who have a high risk for truancy and dropping out of school, and students who are victims of abuse and neglect (Sulkowski & Michael, 2014). They help youth who may be transitioning from drug abuse treatment programs or the juvenile justice system to re-enter school, and students who are homebound for medical or behavioral reasons. Social workers work closely with all stakeholders to reduce barriers to learning that are created as a result of inadequate health care, neighborhood violence, and poverty (Cowen et al., 2013).

Addressing Shortages of School-based Mental Health Professionals

When these school-based mental health professionals are properly integrated into the schools, they complement each other and can offer more comprehensive and integrated services. Text Box 3.2 lists a range of the services provided by school-based mental health professionals. Ultimately though, not enough of these professionals are currently employed to ensure that all children in all schools get the services they need.

Text Box 3.2 Comprehensive Services Provided by School-based Mental Health Professionals

- Collecting, analyzing, and interpreting data to improve availability and effectiveness of mental health services
- Evaluating students for disability determination
- Designing and implementing interventions to meet the behavioral and mental health needs of students
- Promoting early intervention services
- Providing individual and group counseling
- Providing staff development related to positive discipline, behavior, and mental health (including mental health first aid)
- Providing risk and threat assessments
- Supporting teachers through consultation and collaboration
- Coordinating with community service providers and integrating intensive interventions into the schooling process

Cowen et al., 2013. Adapted with permission.

School mental health services are a necessity and not a luxury. Moreover, these services cannot be sporadic or disconnected from the learning process. In this vein, Cowen et al. (2013) state: "Just as children are not simply small adults, schools are not simply community clinics with blackboards" (p. 5.). Accessing school mental health services requires adequate staffing of school-based mental health professionals to ensure that services are of a high quality, appropriate to the school context, and effective. Every school and district must be supported to improve staffing ratios. Unfortunately, a lack of understanding of the need for mental health supports, a failure to fund the requisite services, and significant budget cuts have reduced access to school-based mental health professionals for many students.

In support of these findings, researchers examined the types of mental health problems in U.S. schools and the kinds of available provisions to address these concerns. Funding mechanisms and their impact on the delivery of services, the coordination of interventions, and potential barriers that might prevent schools from providing mental health support also have been examined. A study by Teich, Robinson, and Weist (2007) found that almost half of the schools surveyed reported having inadequate internal and community mental health resources and that these inadequacies served as a barrier to providing adequate support for young people's mental health and well-being.

In most districts, the ratio of school-based mental health professionals to students far exceeds the ratios established by their respective professional associations. For example, the recommended ratio of school psychologists to students is 1 to 500 to 700, when these professionals are providing comprehensive and integrated services, and should never exceed 1 to 1,000 (NASP, 2010). However, the actual national ratio is closer to 1 to 2,000 in most school settings in the U.S. Furthermore, many stakeholders including legislators and school board members are surprised to learn that the current ratio is so high and out of line with established recommended professional guidelines.

High ratios of school-based mental health professionals to students restrict the ability of these professionals to provide comprehensive, integrative, and preventative mental health services. These include important initiatives such as social-emotional learning, dropout prevention, school-wide positive behavioral supports, violence prevention, safety promotion, threat assessment, suicide prevention and intervention, etc. As a result of inadequate ratios, many districts may not include prevention and early intervention services that link mental health, school safety, and school climate (Cowen et al., 2013).

In order to improve access to mental health services for students, schools can establish effective partnerships with community mental health providers. However, even though they may provide excellent services, outside contract providers may be less familiar with schools and their culture, effective instruction practices, and the process of learning. In some charter schools or in some smaller districts, it is not uncommon to hire a community provider for just one function. For example, hiring a community-based psychologist to conduct psychological evaluations in lieu of hiring a school-based, school psychologist means that these community professionals are not there on an ongoing basis to provide consultation and collaboration; may not be familiar with the school's personnel and students; may not be available when a crisis occurs; are not providing primary prevention for the entire student body; and, most importantly, cannot offer the full range of necessary preventative services. In contrast, successful services that include school–community partnerships use a collaborative approach as an add-on to integrate these community supports into existing and comprehensive school initiatives to enhance services (e.g., providing after-school family therapy services to families of students who are struggling emotionally or behaviorally in school).

Moving From a Two- to a Three-Component Approach

In order to deal with the shortage of school-based mental health professionals, the National Center for Mental Health in Schools at UCLA and the National Association of School Psychologists developed a joint statement entitled *Enhancing the blueprint for school improvement in the ESEA reauthorization: Moving from a two to a three component approach* (see http://smhp.psych.ucla.edu/pdfdocs/enhancingtheblueprint.pdf).

This blueprint argues that through the Congressional re-authorization of the Elementary and Secondary Education Act (PL-89-10), schools must provide a coordinated approach to addressing barriers to learning and re-engaging disconnected students. The blueprint emphasizes that a failure to address these barriers will ensure that too many students struggle in school and that teachers will continue to divert essential instructional time to deal with problematic behaviors that interfere with classroom engagement. The document explains that the federal policy only addresses two components that are necessary for school reform. The first component includes the instructional factors that impact learning and the second component includes the governance and operations of schools. However, current research highlights a need for a third component, which is learning supports (Adelman & Taylor, 2006).

Learning supports in the blueprint are defined as "the resources, strategies and practices that provide physical, social, emotional and intellectual supports to enable all students to have an equal opportunity for success at school by directly addressing barriers to learning and teaching and by re-engaging disconnected students" (Adelman & Taylor, 2006, p.1). Most often, these supports are provided by school-based mental health professionals who collaborate with community-based providers and resources. Access to these learning supports has been found to transform schools in a positive way. More specifically, the provision of learning supports is associated with improvements in instruction, academic performance, behavior, school climate, family engagement, and data-based decision making (Cowen & Skalski, 2008). The authors of the blueprint argue that because learning supports are treated as secondary to school improvement efforts, the result is that learning supports often have no integrated or comprehensive focus. This makes them less effective and cost efficient.

It is becoming increasingly clear that learning supports must be given the same level of priority as instruction and management in schools. According to the authors of the blueprint (National Center for Mental Health in Schools at UCLA and the National Association of School Psychologists, n.d.), until the learning support resources and leadership are provided and the ensuing services become fully integrated into schools, only then can barriers to learning be removed. The authors emphasize that when this occurs, when the provision of comprehensive learning and mental health supports are provided for all students, school safety will be enhanced, the pipeline from schools to prisons will be mitigated, the achievement gap will be reduced, dropout rates will decline, and the promotion of well-being and responsible citizenship will be enhanced.

A Public Health Approach as a Way to Provide Essential Services

A public health approach for providing school-based mental health services can be used to support the mental health needs of students and address shortages of school-based mental health professionals. The Institute of Public Health (1988) defines public health as "what we as a society do collectively to assure the conditions in which people can be healthy" (p.1). The scientific core of public health is epidemiology, which identifies the risk factors, trends, and causes of health problems (Hemenway, 2004). Public health focuses directly on prevention, with the emphasis on eliminating problems before they get worse.

This is a transformative approach for the schools to undertake. In the past, the focus of school psychological services was on identifying children with *existing* problems for special education placement and services. When schools adopt a public health approach, the focus shifts. The goal then becomes to change the school environment and culture with the emphasis on *preventing* rather than *responding* to problems

As described by Hemenway (2004), the most notable public health advance of the nineteenth century was the "great sanitary awakening," which identified filth as both the cause of disease and a mode of transportation. As a result, sanitation changed the way society viewed health and people began to view the spread of illness as not resulting from poor moral conditions, but instead as due to unhealthy environments. Consequently, public health interventions began to emphasize the need to change the environment as well as individual's behavior. What followed was that early efforts to combat diseases such as tuberculosis succeeded primarily because they addressed poor sanitation in overcrowded urban neighborhoods rather than because of individual medical interventions. Moreover, this approach focused on how to change societal actions that could dramatically reduce disease. This meant that health could no longer be considered the sole responsibility of the individual.

Public health approaches have also been implemented in the past 40 years that focused on decreasing alcohol consumption and smoking, increasing physical exercise, and promoting "safe" sexual behavior to prevent sexually transmitted diseases and unwanted pregnancies (Miller, 2011). Moreover, life expectancy has increased from 47 years in 1900 to 78.7 in 2011 in the U.S. because of public health approaches to health that include vaccines to eliminate dreaded diseases such as polio, measles, mumps, diphtheria, rubella, tetanus, hepatitis B, chickenpox, and human papillomavirus (Organization of Economic Cooperation and Development, 2013. See http://gallery.mailchimp.com/de3259be81e52e95191ab7806/files/HAG2013.pdf).

One of the most successful applications of a public health approach to reducing death and injury involved the reduction of motor vehicle accidents over the past 60 years. In 1954, 38,000 people each year were killed in automobile accidents, and 1.5 million were injured. From the 1920s to the 1950s, automotive policy was dominated by the automobile industry. The federal policy at that time focused on instilling good habits in all drivers and punishing careless drivers. As described by Hemenway (2004), physicians who studied the automobile industry knew that the sources of death and injury—such as the steering column, windshield, dashboard, padded interiors, and passenger compartments—could easily be modified by technical improvements such as collapsible steering columns, padded interiors, shatterproof windshields, crush-resistant passenger compartments, and anchored seat belts.

Injury control experts realized that the best way to reduce collisions and injuries resulting from vehicle crashes, was by improving the vehicle, the equipment, and the highway rather than trying to change driver behavior. For example, it has been demonstrated that children not in restraint devices are 11 times more likely to die in a crash than those who are restrained. Thus, as a result of this knowledge, mandatory child safety seats became required in all vehicles (Kalbfleisch & Rivara, 1989). Other improvements, in addition to those that were previously listed, included airbags that cushion occupants in head-on collisions, gas tanks that do not rupture and explode, and cameras that help drivers see behind the car when they are backing up. Also better braking and a third brake light are ways vehicles have been improved to reduce collisions. In terms of highway safety, we now have better lighting, divided highways, limited-access roads, and improved signage.

Today's drivers are not any more careful than those in the 1950s, especially considering the current use of mobile devices while driving, the well-documented incidences of road rage, and the increase in traffic. Yet, the number of motor vehicle fatalities per mile driven in the U.S. has been reduced by 80 percent. As noted by Hemenway (2004), the key was reframing the policy from: "How can you change human nature?" to "What are the most cost effective ways to reduce injury?" A lesson learned was that it is "often easier to change the behavior of a few corporative executives at one point in time than that of two hundred million drivers on a daily basis" (Hemenway, 2004, p. 16.). Ultimately, this lesson has considerable applicability for educators and for the provision of school-based mental health services. That is, it is easier to change the school environment and the behavior of administrators and teachers, than to change the behavior of each child, every single day.

Conclusion

Because of the significant social, emotional, and behavioral problems experienced by today's students and the established linkage between mental health and school success, it is imperative for high-quality mental health services to be provided in schools. In addition, there must be adequate staffing of school-based mental health professionals to ensure that services are effective, comprehensive, and geared to the school and community. It is no longer sufficient to have only a reactive approach to the delivery of mental health services in schools, with the primary focus on providing services to referred children. Instead, it has become increasingly clear that a preventive approach is also necessary that emphasizes changing the school environment and delivering services to *all* children. As part of this proactive effort, helping students develop healthy self-esteem, establish meaningful relationships, and expand their social and emotional competencies must be part of this new equation.

Note

1 *Notice:* Some states use alternative terms to describe ED such as Seriously Emotionally Disturbed (SED), Emotionally Handicapped (EH), and Emotionally/Behaviorally Disordered (E/BD).

References

Adelman, H. S. & Taylor, L. (2006). *The implementation guide to student learning supports in the classroom and schoolwide: New directions for addressing barriers to learning.* Thousand Oaks, CA: Corwin Press.

Adolescent Health Measurement Initiative. (2011/12). National survey of children's health. [Data Query]. Retrieved from: www.childhealthdata.org/browse/survey?q=2257&r=1.

Becker, S. P., Paternite, C. E., Evans, S. W., Andrews, C., Christensen, O. A., Kraan, E. M., & Weist, M. D. (2011). Eligibility, assessment, and educational placement issues for students classified with emotional disturbance: Federal and state-level analyses. *School Mental Health, 3,* 24–34. doi: 10.1007/s12310-010-9045-2

Benson, P. L. (2006). *All kids are our kids: What communities must do to raise caring and responsible children and adolescents* (2nd ed.). San Francisco, CA: Jossey-Bass.

Blodgett, C. (2012). *Adopting ACEs screening and assessment in child serving systems.* Working Paper. WSU Area Health Education Center. Retrieved from: http://extension.wsu.edu/ahec/trauma/Documents/ACE%20Screening%20and%20Assessment%20in%20Child%20Serving%20Systems%207-12%20final.pdf.

Bridgeland, J. M., DiIulio, J. J., & Morison, K. B. (2006). *The silent epidemic. Perspectives of high school dropouts.* Washington, DC: Civic Enterprises and Peter D. Hart Research Associates for the Bill and Melinda Gates Foundation.

Burke, N. J., Hellman, J. L., Scott, B. G., Weems, C. F., & Carrion, V. G. (2011). The impact of adverse childhood experiences on an urban pediatric population. *Child Abuse & Neglect, 35,* 408–413.

Centers for Disease Control and Prevention (2013). *Mental health surveillance among children – United States, 2005–2011. 62*(Suppl 2). Washington, DC: U.S. Department of Health and Human Services, Centers for Disease Control and Prevention.

Centers for Disease Control and Prevention (2014a). *Adverse childhood experiences (ACE) study* Retrieved from: www.cdc.gov/violenceprevention/acestudy/findings.htmlChild and

Centers for Disease Control and Prevention (2014b). *Youth risk behavior surveillance – United States, 2013.* Retrieved from: www.cdc.gov/mmwr/pdf/ss/ss6304.pdf?utm_source=rss&utm_medium=rss&utm_campaign=youth-risk-behavior-surveillance-united-states-2013-pdf.

Cole, S. F., Eisner, A., Gregory, M., & Ristuccia, J. (2013). *Helping traumatized children learn: Creating and advocating for trauma-sensitive schools.* Boston, MA: Massachusetts Advocates for Children.

Cole, S. F., O'Brien, J. G., Gadd, M. G., Ristuccia, J., Wallace, D. L., & Gregory, M. (2005). *Helping traumatized children learn: Supportive school environments for children traumatized by family violence.* Boston, MA: Massachusetts Advocates for Children.

Cowen, K., & Skalski, A. K. (2008). *Ready to learn, empowered to teach: Excellence in education for the 21st century.* Bethesda, MD: National Association of School Psychologists. Retrieved from: http://www.nasponline.org/research-and-policy/ready-to-learn-empowered-to-teach.

Cowen, K. C., Vaillancourt, K., Rossen, E., & Pollitt, K. (2013). *A framework for safe and successful schools* [Brief]. Bethesda, MD: National Association of School Psychologists.

Cummings, J. R., Ponce, N. A., & Mays, V. M. (2010). Comparing racial/ethnic differences in mental health service use among high-need subpopulations across clinical and school-based settings. *Journal of Adolescent Health, 46,* 603–606. doi: 10.1016/j.jadohealth.2009.11.221

Danese, A., & McEwen, B. S. (2012). Adverse childhood experiences, allostasis, allostatic load, and age-related disease. *Physiology & Behavior, 106,* 29–39.

Doll, B., Cummings, J. A., & Chapla, B. A. (2014). Best practices in population-based mental health services. In P. L. Harrison & A. Thomas (Eds.), *Best practices in school psychology: System-level services* (pp. 149–163). Bethesda, MD: National Association of School Psychologists.

Dube, S. R., Anda, R. F., Felitti, V. J., Chapman, D. P., Williamson, D. F., & Giles, W. H. (2001). Childhood abuse, household dysfunction, and the risk of attempted suicide throughout the life span: Findings from the Adverse Childhood Experiences Study. *Journal of the American Medical Association, 286,* 3089–3096.

Dube, S. R., Felitti, V. J., Dong, M., Chapman, D. P., Giles, W. H., & Anda, R. F. (2003). Childhood abuse, neglect, and household dysfunction and the risk of illicit drug use: The adverse childhood experiences study. *Pediatrics, 111,* 564–572.

Durlak, J. A., Weissberg, R. P., Dymnicki, A. B., Schellinger, K. B., & Taylor, R. D. (2011). The impact of enhancing students' social and emotional learning: A meta-analysis of school-based universal interventions. *Child Development, 82,* 405–432. doi: 10.1111/j.1467-8624.2010.01564.x

Felitti, V. J., Anda, R. F., Nordenberg, D., Williamson, D. F., Spitz, A. M., Edwards, V., . . . Marks, J. S. (1998). The relationship of childhood abuse and household dysfunction to many of the leading causes of death in adults: The adverse childhood experiences (ACE) study. *American Journal of Preventive Medicine, 14,* 245–258.

Fitzgerald, M. M., & Cohen, J. A. (2012). Trauma-focused cognitive behavior therapy for school psychologists. *Journal of Applied School Psychology, 28,* 294–315.

Ginsburg, G. S., Becker, K. D., Newman-Kingery, J., & Nichols, T. (2008). Transporting CBT for childhood anxiety disorders into inner-city school-based mental health clinics. *Cognitive and Behavioral Practice, 15,* 148–158. doi: 10.1016/j.cbpra.2007.07.001

Gore, F., Bloem, P., Patton, G. C., Ferguson, B. J., Coffey, C., Sawyer, S. M. & Mathers, C. M. (2011). Global burden of disease in young people aged 10–24 years: A systematic analysis. *Lancet, 377,* 2093–2102.

Hemenway, D. (2004). *Private guns: Public health.* Ann Arbor: MI: University of Michigan Press.

Institute of Medicine. (2009). *Preventing mental, emotional, and behavioral disorders among young people: Progress and possibilities.* Washington, DC: National Academies Press.

Institute of Public Health (1988). *The future of public health.* Washington, DC: National Academy Press.

Kalbfleisch, J., & Rivara, F. (1989). Principles in injury control: Lessons to be learned from child safety seats. *Pediatric Emergency Care, 5,* 131–134.

Kataoka, S. H., Zhang, L., & Wells, K. B. (2002). Unmet need for mental health care among US children: Variation by ethnicity and insurance status. *American Journal of Psychiatry, 159,* 1548–1555.

Kinniburgh, K. J., Blaustein, M., Spinazzola, J., & van der Kolk, B. A. (2005). Attachment, self-regulation, and competency. *Psychiatric Annals, 35,* 424–430.

Klem, A. M., & Connell, J. P. (2004). Relationships matter: Linking teacher support to student engagement and achievement. *Journal of School Health, 74,* 262–273. doi: 10.1111/j.1746- 1561.2004.tb08283.x

Kostering, L. J., & Braziel, P. M. (2002). A look at high school programs as perceived by youth with learning disabilities. *Learning Disability Quarterly, 25,* 177–188.

Lazarus, P. J. (2012, February). *Advocating for the emotional well-being of our nation's youth.* Presidential keynote address presented at the annual convention of the National Association of School Psychologists. Philadelphia, PA.

Lazarus, P. J., & Sulkowski. M. L. (2011). The emotional well-being of our nation's youth and the promise of social-emotional learning. *Communiqué, 40* (2), 1, & 16–17.

McLaughlin, C. L. & Christner, R. W. (2009). Understanding stress: Helping students cope: Information for educators. Retrieved from: www.nasponline.org/educators/NASP_Stress_Article.pdf.

Miller, D. (2011). *Child and adolescent suicidal behavior: School-based prevention, assessment and intervention.* New York: Guilford Press.

National Association of School Psychologists. (2010). *Model for comprehensive and integrated school psychological services.* Bethesda, MD: Author. Retrieved from http://www.nasponline.org/assets/Documents/Standards%20and%20Certification/Standards/2_PracticeModel.pdf.

National Center for Mental Health in Schools at UCLA and the National Association of School Psychologists (nd). *Enhancing the Blueprint for School Improvement in the ESEA Reauthorization: Moving from a Two to a Three Component Approach.* Retrieved from http://smhp.psych.ucla.edu/pdfdocs/enhancingtheblueprint.pdf.

National Research Council and the Institute of Medicine. (2009). *Preventing mental, emotional, and behavioral disorders among young people: Progress and possibilities.* Washington, DC: The National Academies Press.

New Freedom Commission on Mental Health (2003). *Achieving the promise: Transforming mental health care in America. Final report for the President's New Freedom Commission on Mental Health (SMA Publication No. 03-3832).* Rockville, MD: Author.

Park, N., & Peterson, C. (2008). Positive psychology and character strengths: Application to strengths-based school counseling. *Professional School Counseling, 12,* 85–92.

Peterson, C., & Park, N. (2003). Positive psychology as the evenhanded positive psychologist views it. *Psychological Inquiry, 14,* 141–146.

Resnicow, K., Cross, D., & Wynder, E. (1993). The Know Your Body program: A review of evaluation studies. *Journal of Urban Health: Bulletin of the New York Academy of Medicine, 70,* 188–207.

Roberts, R. E., Attkisson, C. C., & Rosenblatt, A. (1998). Prevalence of psychopathology among children and adolescents. *American Journal of Psychiatry, 155,* 715–725.

Rossen, E. & Cowan, K. (2013). The role of schools in supporting traumatized students. *Principal's Research Review, 8*(6), 1–8.

Seligman, M. E., & Csikszentmihalyi, M. (2000). Positive psychology: An introduction. *American Psychologist, 55,* 5–14. doi: 10.1037/0003-066X.55.1.5

Sin, N. L., & Lyubomirsky, S. (2009). Enhancing well-being and alleviating depressive symptoms with positive psychology interventions: A practice-friendly meta- analysis. *Journal of Clinical Psychology, 65,* 467–487.

Sulkowski, M. L., & Michael, K. (2014). Meeting the mental health needs of homeless students in schools: A multi-tiered system of support framework. *Children and Youth Services Review, 44,* 145–151. doi: 10.1016/j.childyouth.2014.06.014

Teich, J., Robinson, G., & Weist, M. (2007). What kinds of services do public schools in the United States provide? *Advances in School Mental Health Promotion, 1,* 13–22. doi: http//dx.doi.org/10.1007/s10902-013-9476-1 Online publication.

U.S. Department of Health and Human Services. (2000). *Report of the Surgeon General's Conference on Children's Mental Health: A national action agenda.* Washington, DC: Author.

4 The Promise of Social-Emotional Learning

High-quality schools ensure that students master basic academic skills such as reading and math. If students fall behind in developing these skills, they are provided with academic supports that range from a little extra practice to inclusion in special education. Students who struggle academically are provided with these learning supports because educators believe that students' long-term success at school and in life is largely dependent on the successful development and application of academic skills. In fact, many educators consider teaching academic skills to be the main, if not, the key mission for schools.

However, emerging research indicates that academic skills do not develop in a vacuum. Moreover, the acquisition of these skills often is impacted by the social and emotional context in which they are taught (Elias et al., 1997). In other words, it is not enough to provide students with academic instruction only. Educators must also focus on the broader ecological context in which students learn. While learning to read, solve math problems, understand history, and apply science knowledge, students also must learn how to interact with others, form interpersonal relationships, establish and achieve goals, stay motivated, and manage setbacks and frustrations (Zins, Weissberg, Wang, & Walberg, 2004). These skills are not explicitly taught at school as part of the general curriculum, yet they are associated with the development and refinement of academic skills as well as other positive student outcomes (Dymnicki, Sambolt, & Kidron, 2013; Greenberg et al., 2003). Thus, instead of viewing students as containers to be filled with academic knowledge and seeing the development of academic skills and social and emotional skills as separate, it is important to view students as social participants in their learning and to understand that the relationship between academic and social-emotional skill development is inseparable (Lazarus & Sulkowski, 2011; Macklem, 2014).

As David Brooks (2007), the well-known journalist and *New York Times* columnist, writes:

> One thing is clear: It's crazy to have educational policies that, in effect, chop up children's brains into the rational cortex, which the government ministers to in schools, and the emotional limbic system, which the government ignores. In nature, there is no neat division. Emotional engagement is the essence of information processing and learning.

Brooks also notes, "Schools filled with students who can't control their impulses, who can't focus their attention, and who can't regulate their emotions will not succeed, no matter how many reforms are made by governors, superintendents or presidents" (A19). Thus, educators must incorporate a more holistic and integrated view of how children learn and succeed in school that includes both social and emotional influences.

From a practical standpoint, Lazarus and Sulkowski (2011) note that efforts to improve social-emotional skills should employ a two-pronged approach. The first prong involves teaching and modeling social-emotional skills across different settings. For example, a student who is sensitive to being disrespected and quick to react to a perceived social threat can be taught strategies to become less aggressive. This can be accomplished by changing the mindset of the student, by changing the way he or she interprets an event, as well as by changing the student's reaction to the situation. The second approach to improving social-emotional skills involves establishing a positive and supportive school environment to help students learn and apply these skills. This prong also involves incorporating an evidence-based, social-emotional learning (SEL) approach or program into the school's curriculum.

Defining Social-Emotional Learning

In 1994, the term "social-emotional learning" was coined by members of the Fetzer Institute, an organization that focuses on facilitating positive relationships among people because of a desire to increase health promotion and problem prevention efforts in schools (Macklem, 2014). In the years that followed, others fleshed out what SEL entailed, involved, and influenced in school settings. Then, in 1997, Elias defined SEL as the process of recognizing and managing emotions, establishing and maintaining positive interpersonal relationships, identifying and appreciating multiple perspectives, setting and pursuing positive goals, making responsible decisions, and effectively managing interpersonal conflicts. Thus, consistent with this definition, SEL involves developing and enhancing emotional regulation skills and adaptive behavior.

Years later, the Collaborative for Academic, Social, and Emotional Learning (CASEL, 2003, 2005), an organization that aims to advance the development of academic, social, and emotional competence for all students, redefined the goal of SEL as fostering the development of five key skills. These include self-awareness (knowing one's strengths and limitations), self-management (remaining in control of one's emotions while facing challenges), social awareness (understanding the emotional states of others and empathizing with them), relationship skills (being able to work with others and manage interpersonal conflicts), and responsible decision-making (making choices that ensure safety and ethical behavior) (CASEL, 2003, 2005). Thus, SEL is an umbrella term that applies to preventative efforts associated with enhancing students' learning and reducing emotional and behavioral problems (Desai, Karahalios, Persuad, & Reker, 2014; Hoffman, 2009). Text Box 4.1 provides specific examples that show how educators can incorporate these five key SEL competencies into the curriculum.

The aforementioned skills are invaluable for developing and maintaining positive and healthy relationships with a range of individuals including same-aged peers as well as with adults at school. Therefore, SEL also indirectly aims to foster healthier school climates by improving interpersonal relationships and social-emotional functioning for members of school communities (Elbertson, Brackett, & Weissberg, 2009). In this regard, it is a pervasive and transformative approach to improving school communities that stands alone, yet also meshes well with many of the tenets and goals of school-wide positive behavior support (SWPBS) programs and positive psychology approaches (Macklem, 2014; see Chapters 9 and 10 for a review of SWPBS and positive psychology approaches). These approaches to school-based service delivery overlap in salient ways that involve developing and applying positive behavioral expectations across the whole school, enhancing opportunities for cooperative learning, aiming to connect with students on an individualized and personal level, promoting prosocial behavior, and involving students in service-learning activities (Elbertson et al., 2009; Graczyk et al., 2000).

Need for Social-Emotional Learning

Why is it important for educators to teach social-emotional competencies within the school setting? Many students lack social-emotional skills and become disengaged from school while they progress from elementary to middle to high school (Blum & Libbey, 2004). In fact, results from a study by Klem and Connell (2004) indicate that 40–60 percent of students reported feeling

Text Box 4.1 Examples of How Educators Can Incorporate the Five Key SEL Competencies into the Curriculum

CASEL SEL skills	Self-Awareness	Self-Management	Social Awareness	Relationship Skills	Responsible Decision-Making
What these skills entail	Knowing one's strengths and limitations	Remaining in control of one's emotions while facing challenges	Understanding the emotional states of others and empathizing with them	Being able to work with others and manage interpersonal conflicts	Making choices that ensure safety and ethical behavior
Possible strategies for shaping these skills	• Have students journal on their strengths and limitations. • Have students describe strengths and weaknesses that exist in celebrities and relate this information back to themselves. • Have students attend to and write down their emotional reactions to events.	• Use diaphragmatic or deep breathing when distressed. • Use progressive muscle relaxation strategies. • Employ counting strategies until negative emotions dissipate. • Employ the "Stop, Look, Listen, and Think" technique. • Generate alternative explanations for events that cause anger or frustration.	• Have students view TV programs on mute and guess what the actors are thinking or feeling. • Have students look at pictures in magazines and guess what is happening socially and emotionally with the people. • Have students guess how the educator might have felt in response to positive and negative events/experiences.	• Have students list or describe how to "play nice" with other students. • Have students play/interact with another student and provide guidance on how to share and interact positively in live time. Role play with the students appropriate ways to interact with others. Seek information on why someone else would like interacting with students who acted in particular ways.	• Have students brainstorm their own set of rules that will maintain safety and ethical behavior and commit to following these rules. • Have students list unsafe and unethical behaviors that they have observed and describe ways to prevent or counteract these behaviors. • Have students describe how one of their moral heroes would handle challenging, immoral, or unsafe situations.

chronically disengaged from school by the time they reach high school. These students attended school less, did not participate as much as their peers during instruction, and rarely interacted with educators in a positive manner. Further, in a national sample of 148,189 students (grades 6–12), Benson (2006) found that only 29 percent of students indicated that their school provided a caring and encouraging or emotionally supportive learning environment and less than half (29–45 percent) of these students reported that they had developed social-emotional competencies such as empathy, problem-solving, and conflict resolution skills. Moreover, Benson (2006) also found that about 30 percent of high school students reported engaging in multiple high-risk behaviors (e.g., unprotected sex, substance use, aggressive behavior, suicide attempts) that negatively impacted their emotional well-being and academic success at school. Thus, improving social emotional competencies may be central to enhancing school engagement, learning, and positive long-term outcomes in students.

Applications of Social-Emotional Learning

Social-emotional learning has been applied to address a wide range of individual and systemic student problems. More specifically, SEL has been found to reduce internalizing (e.g., depression, anxiety, social withdrawal) and externalizing (e.g., conduct problems, oppositional behavior, hyperactivity) forms of psychopathology, deficits in empathy, perspective-taking limitations, and forms of maladaptive coping and problem-solving skills (Bird & Sultmann, 2010; Caldarella, Christensen, Kramer, & Kronmiller, 2009). Research also indicates that SEL is an effective approach for reducing substance use/abuse and incidents of school violence. In this regard, Wilson and Lipsey (2007) found that both universal and targeted SEL intervention approaches are effective for reducing violent behavior at school, and Tobler and Stratton (1997) found that SEL is effective for reducing the use of tobacco, marijuana, and alcohol among students. In addition to addressing emerging or extant problems, SEL also has been found to enhance positive student outcomes. In this regard, research indicates that the successful implementation of SEL is associated with student success in school and life in general (Zins & Elias, 2007). At the macro level, SEL helps mitigate risk factors while supporting resiliency and protective factors in youth (Guerra & Bradshaw, 2008).

Overall, the implementation of SEL has been associated with positive outcomes for students in schools. More specifically, this approach is associated with improvements in students' emotional well-being as well as in school performance, whereas a failure to achieve competence in these domains is associated with impairment in academic, social, and family functioning (Greenberg et al., 2003; Guerra & Bradshaw, 2008; Payton et al., 2008; Zins et al., 2004). As the best summary of this body of research to date, a meta-analysis by Durlak, Weissberg, Dymnicki, Taylor, and Schellinger (2011) evaluated 213 school-based SEL programs that included 270,034 K-12 students. Results of this investigation indicated that SEL programs were effective at all educational levels assessed (e.g., elementary, middle, high school) and across the different types of communities in which they were implemented (e.g., urban, suburban, rural). Moreover, as a testament to the important link between the development of social-emotional competence and academic achievement, students participating in SEL programs displayed an 11-percentile-point gain in academic achievement as well as improvements in social-emotional skills, attitudes about school, and school behavior compared to students in control schools that did not have SEL curricula in place. This truly is a remarkable finding. Even interventions that directly try to increase academic achievement by this magnitude often fail to do so.

Results of the Durlak et al. (2011) study suggest that SEL programs also help to buffer against the development of disruptive behavior and internalizing problems in students. This then suggests that SEL can facilitate positive outcomes among students as well as hedge against the development of emotional and behavioral problems. Lastly, results of the aforementioned study suggest that SEL is a transportable approach to improving school communities because it does not require employing additional school staff. In this vein, general education teachers and other school staff effectively implemented and conducted SEL, which suggests that SEL can be incorporated into routine educational practices by current members of school communities.

Well-designed SEL programs are grounded in solid theory, have empirical support, and involve the use of developmentally appropriate directions and instructional techniques. Essentially, these programs encourage students to learn, apply, and generalize the skills they acquire across multiple settings (CASEL, 2003). Furthermore, Macklem (2014) writes that the acronym "SAFE" can be used to inform educators about what makes for an effective and empirically supported SEL program. Using this acronym, "S" stands for "sequenced set of activities," "A" stands for "active

---

Text Box 4.2 Some Selected Social-Emotional Learning Programs that Have Empirical Support

Program	Grade level	Brief description	Developers
Caring School Community	Elementary Middle	A program that builds classroom and school-wide communities while developing students' social and emotional skills and competencies.	Developmental Studies Center (DSC)
I Can Problem Solve	Preschool Elementary Middle	A universal school-based program designed to enhance interpersonal cognitive processes and problem-solving skills.	Shure, 2001
Promoting Alternative Thinking Strategies	Preschool, Elementary, Middle	A program that helps students resolve conflicts, peacefully handle emotions, positively empathize, and make responsible decisions.	Channing Bete Company
Second Step	Preschool Elementary Middle	A program that helps reduce school violence and improve social-emotional skills in students.	Committee for Children
Incredible Years	Elementary Middle	A developmentally based, risk-factor reduction program that targets parents, teachers, and children.	Incredible Years, Inc.
Al's Pals/The Wingspan Approach	Preschool Elementary	A program that aims to develop children's social-emotional skills, problem-solving abilities, and healthy decision-making.	Wingspan, LLC.
Interpersonal Cognitive Problem Solving	Elementary	A curriculum that focuses on effective social skill development.	Shure & Spivak, 1988
Responsive Classroom	Elementary	A program that aims to facilitate the development of social, emotional, and academic skills.	Northeast Foundation for Children
Steps to Respect	Elementary Middle	A program that teaches children how to make friends; recognize feelings; and recognize, refuse, and report bullying.	Committee for Children
Lions Quest	Elementary Middle High	A program that promotes SEL, character education, bullying prevention, drug awareness, and service-learning.	Lions Clubs International Foundation

*See both the 2013 and 2015 *CASEL Guides* for a more complete list.

listening," "F" stands for "focus on developing personal and social skills," and the "E" stands for "explicit targeting of skills." Some examples of empirically supported SEL programs include the Caring School Community (Battistich, Schaps, & Wilson, 2004), the I Can Problem Solve (Boyle & Hassett-Walker, 2008; Shure, 2001), the Promoting Alternative Thinking Strategies (Bierman et al., 2010; Kusche & Greenberg, 1994) and the Social Decision-Making and Problem-Solving (Elias, 1991). Text Box 4.2 provides more information about these programs.

Barriers to Implementing SEL and Ways to Overcome These Barriers

Despite the obvious benefits associated with SEL, this approach to prevention and intervention is not widely implemented in schools across the U.S. This is likely because of various barriers to implementing SEL that exist in many school systems. Some of these barriers include the myopic focus of schools on academics to the neglect of educating the whole child, the concern with taking time from an already filled school day to focus on non-academic learning (especially with the accountability demands of high-stakes testing), the lack of knowledge about the positive impact of SEL on academic achievement and student behavior, the lack of legislation that supports SEL instruction, and the considerable amount of effort and time needed to implement SEL in schools with proper fidelity.

Currently, only the state of Illinois includes SEL as a required part of the general curriculum and variability exists regarding how SEL programs are implemented across this state. Moreover, surveys indicate that school-based mental health professionals are not well informed about SEL and its potential benefit for fostering positive student outcomes. This suggests that general education teachers, administrators, and school resource officers may be even less aware of its benefits (McKevitt, 2012). Thus, the dissemination of knowledge of SEL, how it can be applied to benefit students, not only emotionally, but also academically, and ways that this approach can be tailored to different grade levels needs to be shared with educators, administrators, school board members, and legislators.

To overcome these barriers, educators should be aware of the aforementioned research suggesting that SEL actually enhances academic achievement for students, perhaps to a degree that is even greater than some interventions that focus directly on increasing achievement. In addition, following the lead of Illinois, which implemented SEL in the general education curriculum in 2003 through the Children's Mental Health Act (Public Act 93-0495), educators can advocate for SEL to be integrated into official state learning standards (Gordon, Ji, Mulhall, Shaw, & Weissberg, 2011). Lastly, although research indicates that schools generally have the adequate infrastructure and personnel to implement SEL effectively (Durlak et al., 2011), it still is important for educators to receive training and professional development in SEL instruction on a regular basis. To help provide these trainings, administrators can reach out to school-based mental health professionals to conduct trainings and workshops on SEL (McKevitt, 2012).

Social-Emotional Learning Teams

Although SEL purports to influence and impact all members of school communities, specific individuals within these communities usually are more influential in the implementation of SEL and its maintenance. Therefore, SEL teams often are established to coordinate the efforts of these individuals and to help build capacity for systems-wide acceptance and inevitable change in schools. No specific formula exists for who should be included on these teams. However, to build capacity for change and implementation, it is important to include members of the school community that broker unique forms of expertise and power such as administrators, school-based mental health professionals, and respected educators who are invested in facilitating the positive social-emotional development of students. Thus, although a team-based approach to implementing SEL seems warranted—especially in preliminary or early stages of implementation—careful planning is still needed with regard to selecting team members to optimize the contributions of each team member and the team itself.

Inevitably, across schools, the people who comprise SEL implementation teams will vary in their training, experience, and involvement. Additionally, these individuals are charged with different tasks that range from trying to implement SEL to maintaining or expanding its scope. However, regardless of these differences, it is important for SEL team members and SEL programs more generally to respect and be contextualized within the context of the school community and culture (Small, Cooney, & O'Connor, 2009). Thus, members of SEL teams should ensure that the SEL programmatic efforts that they are trying to implement mesh well with social and cultural characteristics as well as with the current school-based efforts to support students (Macklem, 2014). For example, a middle school located in the south side of Chicago with an ongoing gang problem and a high incidence of violent deaths and injuries within the community would adopt a different approach or SEL program than a middle school located in an upper-class neighborhood in Palm Beach, Florida. Moreover, whenever possible, team members should aim to build on existing school and community strengths when implementing SEL programs and curricula.

Data Collection and Evaluation

Data collection and program evaluation are important for determining the efficacy of SEL in applied or non-research settings. To help in this regard, several instruments have been developed that can be used to evaluate the implementation of SEL curricula. Some of these include the Belief in SEL Teacher Scale (Brackett, Reyes, Rivers, & Elbertson, 2009), which measures students' perceptions of teachers' comfort and commitment to their emotional well-being, and the SEL Integration Scale (Collie, Shapka, & Perry, 2011), which helps members of school SEL teams to determine the degree to which SEL is integrated into the overall school environment.

Because of the large amount of variability across school environments, as well as marked differences in how SEL is implemented across schools, members of SEL teams have a formidable challenge when evaluating SEL program-related outcomes. At the most basic level, SEL programs will need to fit the ages and grade levels of the students for whom they were designed and validated. Although it is important to teach social and emotional competencies at all age levels, the way that these competencies are taught needs to reflect the developmental level and age of the students being instructed.

Implementing SEL

Several different approaches to helping students develop social and emotional competencies currently exist (CASEL, 2015). These include (1) infusing SEL in teaching practices; (2) infusing SEL into the academic curriculum; (3) creating organizational structures and policies that support students' social and emotional development; and (4) directly teaching SEL in free standing lessons (CASEL, 2015). Moreover, a combination of these approaches can be applied. At the middle or high school level, SEL can be implemented in the aforementioned ways, but it can also take place through character education, health promotion classes, or through targeted approaches that focus on violence prevention, substance use, dropout prevention, or anger management.

To date, several effective SEL programs have been developed and tested in a range of different school settings. CASEL (2013) has published the *2013 CASEL Guide to effective social and emotional learning programs: Preschool and elementary school edition* and the *2015 CASEL Guide: Effective social and emotional learning programs: Middle and high school edition.* These guides help educators select evidence-based programs, based on at least one carefully conducted evaluation. To be included in the guide, the programs must have been well-designed for classroom use and systematically promote SEL competence, as well as provide opportunities for practice and offer multiyear programming. In addition, they must espouse high-quality training and offer other implementation supports. In general, these programs employ a standard set of activities for educators to use with students, involve active listening, focus on augmenting personal and social skills, and explicitly foster the development of specific social and emotional skills. Programs and curricula have been created for students in specific grade levels. Thus, it is also vital to consider the backgrounds of students, their ages, and the whole school context when selecting and implementing SEL curricula.

Research has also found that SEL yields the best outcomes when the skills are embedded into the day-to-day curriculum and are connected with other school activities (Greenberg et al., 2003). In this regard, studies have also found that high-quality SEL program implementation is necessary for ensuring successful outcomes—just adopting a program will not guarantee positive student outcomes (Durlak et al., 2011). Initial training, as well as ongoing support such as coaching, consultation, and follow-up, enhances students' performance and the quality of teaching (CASEL, 2015). It is also is important to note that administrators can help ensure effective program implementation through setting high standards and allocating the necessary resources to program development, execution, and maintenance. Lastly, it is worth reiterating the important relationship between SEL and academic achievement by stating that research indicates that schools leaders who model SEL practices help create a school climate that enhances students' learning (Durlak, 2015).

Programming at the Elementary School Level

Research indicates that about half of kindergarten students have difficulty working in groups and about a fifth of these students have significant social skills problems (Whitted, 2011). Therefore, at the elementary level, SEL should focus on effectively managing interactions with peers and conforming to universal behavioral expectations. For example, these students will need to be able to interact successfully with others while they transfer from home to school and navigate through the school environment. To do this, young children will need to learn skills to self-regulate and demonstrate *effortful control*, which is the ability to resist impulses to engage in a behavior that may result in a short-term benefit but ultimately is problematic long-term, such as stealing food from another student. Essentially, effortful control is an important aspect of self-regulation and its absence is associated with impulsivity, poor attention control, and peer relationship problems (Mischel, 2014).

To help increase effortful control, Macklem (2014) reports that students will need to be taught skills related to self-awareness, self-management, and emotional expressiveness. Collectively, these skills operate in concert to help students build and maintain positive relationships. Although children often display some of these skills prior to attending school, educators who are equipped with SEL curricula are able to enhance students' knowledge about their emotional states and prosocial behaviors. Fundamentally, children need to learn that it is okay to experience a range of emotions, show these emotions and talk with others about them, and make positive behavioral choices in response to the emotions they are feeling.

Programming at the Middle School Level

Students in middle school usually have developed some skills to identify, express, and manage their emotions as well as to understand how other people feel. In addition, they display better abilities than young children to differentiate between more subtle emotions such as jealousy or shame. However, children at this age level still tend to deal with stress through behavioral rather than cognitive strategies (Kress & Elias, 2006). Therefore, SEL curricula that are used with middle school students should include specific behavioral strategies to help students manage their challenging behaviors and emotions. In this regard, SEL curricula at this level often involve teaching skills for making friends, dealing with negative social interactions (e.g., peer rejection, interpersonal conflicts), managing conversations with others, and anticipating how interactions with others might turn out (Macklem, 2014). Middle school students often are very sensitive to the influence of their peers and they place a high premium on what other students think about them. Therefore, SEL programs at the middle school level should emphasize the importance of facilitating social inclusion and school connectedness.

Programming at the High School Level

Implementation of SEL at the high school level is a challenge because fewer prevention and intervention programs exist for this age level. By the time students reach high school, they often are expected to have developed their social and emotional competencies to deal with a range of situations they encounter at school. However, a large percentage of students in high school display social-emotional problems (McNeely & Falci, 2004) and school disengagement reaches a high point at this age. In addition, many high school students often have given up on school and are in danger of dropping out. Consequently, it is important for high schools to provide these at-risk students with SEL competencies as well as social and emotional supports to re-connect them back to school.

As the high school curriculum becomes specialized into classes that focus on more narrow disciplines, it can be a challenge to fit SEL instruction into any particular class. In addition, it is not clear at this point what types of SEL lessons or curricula should be implemented at the high school level. However, more targeted interventions to help further refine students' social and emotional competencies such as specialized groups (e.g., circle of friends, a social skills group) or at the individual level to students who display identified problems may be warranted. Furthermore, some schools have implemented activities and practices that have helped with fostering social and emotional competencies in high school students, such as mindfulness-based stress reduction meditation to enhance emotional regulation (Burke, 2010).

In the following interview, Maurice Elias discusses successes, barriers, and common mistakes in implementing SEL into schools and how to ensure that SEL programs are implemented with integrity and fidelity.

Expert Interview 4.1 with Maurice J. Elias

Rutgers University

PJL. What are the particular successes that you have seen in specific school districts that have implemented Social Emotional Learning programs?

MJE. I have been involved in working with schools implementing SEL and related programs for almost 40 years so I have seen many successes. The greatest success came from the Developing Safe and Civil Schools (DSACS) project, funded for five years by the NJDOE. We worked with 250 schools to help them improve social-emotional and character development (SECD), as we call it in NJ, to accommodate the SEL and Character Education adherents. We worked with each school to assess and improve school culture and climate, systematically teach SEL skills and integrate them into academics, and identify sets of unifying core values. Even after the conclusion of the project, many schools have continued and a Network of Schools has developed in New Jersey to provide ongoing support for implementation across over 50 schools, with more joining in every month. There are also individual successes, schools that have implemented evidence-based SEL programs from the CASEL Safe and Sound Guide, as well as districts like urban Plainfield, New Jersey, which implemented SEL for 7 years and created a strong turnaround and New Brunswick, NJ, which just incorporated SEL into their K-8 student report cards.

PJL. We now know that Social Emotional Learning programs have positive academic, behavioral, and emotional consequences for children, yet most schools have not adopted SEL programs. What are some of the major barriers to implementation?

MJE. Much has been written about barriers to intervention and how to overcome them. The main barriers are a lack of staff familiarity with, understanding of, and training in SECD, especially at the administrator and policy levels; the tremendous proliferation of school mandates; the pervasive standardized test culture; and a tendency to think of problem areas in silos, rather than in integrative and developmental contexts. There must be a clear understanding that Social-Emotional and Character Development (SECD) is:

- A set of *skills and dispositions/essential life habits*
- that can be *built developmentally* if we do so with intentionality, focus, and continuity, in a positive, supportive, healthy school culture and climate, because
- *schools are the place* where most children can be reached systematically, and
- the same set of skills and habits ultimately *mediate academic, civic, and workplace success.*

In fact, true academic and life success integrates the intellectual, emotional, and social facets of learning. These are inextricably interconnected.

PJL. How can these barriers be overcome?

MJE. The list of obstacles contains the ways to overcome the barriers. SECD must be understood; training and opportunity must be available for Leadership Teams to form in schools, with a broad mandate around school culture and climate. These teams must have time to evolve into professional learning communities. Then, they need a three-year window in which to implement SECD plans. With my colleague, Jeff Kress, at Rutgers University, our research found that implementation is also aided by having an ongoing relationship with SECD experts. External expertise turns out to be an essential element of long-term sustainability (Kress & Elias, 2013). Finally, with colleagues at the College of St. Elizabeth in New Jersey (www.cse.edu) and Rutgers University, we are developing online credentialing programs in SEL Direct Instruction for teachers, counselors, school psychologists, social workers, and after-school program providers. In addition, we are providing School Focused SEL Leadership for principals, other administrators, and members of SEL, character, school culture and climate, and related leadership teams.

PJL. Districts are pressured to increase high-stakes test scores of students, yet schools are not measured on other outcomes, such as ensuring that schools are safer and more supportive to students' needs. How might we rectify this situation?

MJE. Schools should undertake systematic assessment of school culture and climate and SECD should be included on all student report cards. My colleagues and I have a guide that we developed in press to help schools do the latter. As for the former, there are excellent assessment resources, including the National School Climate Council (Jonathancohen@schoolclimate.org) and the Culture and Climate Assessment Lab at the College of St. Elizabeth (pheindel@cse.edu). The evidence is such that NOT to carry out systematic assessment in these areas can be considered educational malpractice.

PJL. What are some common mistakes that schools make when implementing SEL programs?

MJE. SEL programs require several other elements to be successful. First, they must be implemented with high degrees of fidelity. They require piloting and integration into the ecology of the school. Second, they require a minimum of two years to begin to register meaningful skill gains, so strong developmental continuity must be provided. Third, the skills taught in the programs must be linked to academics and other parts of the school routine. That is, they must become part of the language, fabric, and culture of the school. Finally, sustainability requires the existence of an implementation support system, including a Leadership Team to provide guidance and connection to others using the program that have more experience and can be called upon for consultative problem-solving. Some don't believe that programs are the best way to build SEL but even among those who do see programs as having a key purpose, the current understanding is that, at best, programs are necessary—but not sufficient—to produce generalizable skill gains in their recipients.

PJL. What do you think it takes to ensure that evidence-based SEL programs are implemented with integrity and fidelity in the classroom?

MJE. It is essential that the dosage of the program is adequate (at least 25–30 times over the course of the school year for at least 30 minutes per week), that there is systematic integration of the skills and values that are the focus of the programs into academic subject areas and all school routines (see Ray Pasi's book, *Higher Expectations*, 2001, published by Teachers College Press, for excellent examples of integration of SECD into academics for middle and high school), and that particular care is taken to ensure proper instructional accommodation for including special education students.

PJL. Can teachers implement these programs in their classrooms on their own or do they require assistance from a mental health personnel?

MJE. At Tier I, teachers do not require the assistance of mental health personnel to implement these programs. The pedagogy is constructivist, discovery-oriented, problem-based, and skills-focused and is well within the competence of a good teacher. What teachers do need, however, is support and assistance from others who have implemented the program they are using, or similar ones, to a greater degree. These individuals may be various student services and mental health personnel but it's the qualification of having prior implementation experience that is most important. It is useful to note that mental health personnel often have implementation experience with small groups, and this is not the same as regular classroom-based implementation.

At Tier II, teachers working with small groups generally would benefit from support in behavior management strategies, as the recipient populations in general may be a bit more difficult to deal with than the typical classroom group, where there is sometimes greater heterogeneity. Plus, the Tier II small group/individual context will be more congruent with the mental health personnel's experience, generally speaking.

PJL. What else would you like educators to know about selecting and implementing SEL programs in the schools?

MJE. Implementing SEL in schools can no longer be considered an option. It is a developmental right and ethical/moral imperative.

- Children need a supportive environment created by caring adults for them to succeed, and all children can succeed.
- Those working in the educational context, in any position, must act with respect, challenge, caring, safety, civility, support, inspiration, and encouragement of opportunity and resilience.
- We must go about this with No Alibis, No Excuses, and No Exceptions.

Ultimately, "We must prepare our children for the tests of life, not a life of tests" (Elias, 2001).

Conclusion

Awareness of the need to teach and support the whole student is growing. It is no longer reasonable or responsible for schools only to teach students academically to the neglect of teaching them social and emotional competencies. If a child is doing well academically, yet has few friends, cannot manage emotions, feels socially isolated, and has poor interpersonal skills, this student needs help to lead an emotionally rewarding life. Social-emotional learning is now a viable, evidence-based approach to supporting students' emotional well-being as well as increasing their academic achievement (Lazarus & Sulkowski, 2011). Consequently, it is important for educators working in states that may have limited SEL programs in place to advocate for its inclusion. The ultimate goal of SEL is to help students develop social and emotional competencies that help them develop healthy relationships, manage their emotional life, display positive and prosocial behaviors, and ultimately succeed in school and in life. What else could be a better student outcome?

References

Battistich, V., Schaps, E., & Wilson, N. (2004). Effects of an elementary school intervention on students' "connectedness" to school and social adjustment during middle school. *Journal of Primary Prevention, 24,* 243–262.

Benson, P. L. (2006). *All kids are our kids: What communities must do to raise caring and responsible children and adolescents (2nd ed.).* San Francisco: Jossey-Bass.

Bierman, K. L., Coie, J. D., Dodge, K. A., Greenberg, M. T., Lochman, J. E., McMahon, R. J., & Pinderhughes, E. (2010). The effects of a multiyear universal social-emotional learning program: The role of student and school characteristics. *Journal of Consulting and Clinical Psychology, 78,* 156–168.

Bird, K. A., & Sultmann, W. F. (2010). Social and emotional learning: Reporting a system approach to developing relationships, nurturing wellbeing and invigorating learning. *Educational and Child Psychology, 27,* 143–155.

Blum, R. W., & Libbey, H. P. (2004). School connectedness – Strengthening health and education outcomes for teenagers. *Journal of School Health, 74,* 231–235.

Boyle, D., & Hassett-Walker, C. (2008). Reducing overt and relational aggression among young children: The results from a two-year outcome evaluation. *Journal of School Violence, 7,* 27–42.

Brackett, M. A., Reyes, M. R., Rivers, S. E., & Elbertson, N. (2009). *Belief in SEL: Teacher scale.* New Haven, CT: Health, Emotion and Behavior Laboratory.

Brooks, D. (2007, March 1). A critique of pure reason. *New York Times.* Retrieved from: www.nytimes.com/2007/03/01/opinion/01brooks.html.

Burke, C. A. (2010). Mindfulness-based approaches with children and adolescents: A preliminary review of current research in an emergent field. *Journal of Child and Family Studies, 19,* 133–144.

Caldarella, P., Christensen, L., Kramer, T. J., & Kronmiller, K. (2009). Promoting social and emotional learning in second grade students: A study of the Strong Start curriculum. *Early Childhood Education Journal, 37,* 51–56.

CASEL. (2003). *Safe and sound: An educational leader's guide to evidence-based social and emotional learning (SEL) programs.* Chicago, IL: Author. Retrieved from: www.casel.org/pub/index.php.

CASEL. (2005). *Safe and sound: An educational leader's guide to evidence-based social and emotional learning programs—Illinois edition.* Chicago, IL: Author.

CASEL. (2013). *2013 CASEL Guide to Effective Social and Emotional Learning Programs: Preschool and Elementary School Edition.* Retrieved from: http://static.squarespace.com/static/513f79f9e4b05ce 7b70e9673/t/526a220de4b00a92c90436ba/1382687245993/2013-casel-guide.pdf .

CASEL. (2015). *2015 CASEL Guide: Effective Social and Emotional Learning Programs: Middle and High School Edition.* Retrieved from: www.casel.org/middle-and-high-school-edition-casel-guide?utm_source=Secondary+Guide+E-blast&utm_campaign=SEL+Handbook&utm_medium=email.

Collie, R. J., Shapka, J. D., & Perry, N. E. (2011). Predicting teacher commitment: The impact of school climate and social-emotional learning. *Psychology in the Schools, 48,* 1034–1048. doi: 10.1002/pits.20611

Desai, P., Karahalios, V., Persuad, S., & Reker, K. (2014). A social justice perspective on social-emotional learning. *Communiqué, 43,* 14–16.

Durlak, J. A. (2015). What everyone should know about implementation. In J. A. Durlak, C. E. Domitrovich, R. P. Weissberg, & T. P. Gullota (Eds.), *Handbook of social and emotional learning. Research and practice.* New York: Guilford.

Durlak, J. A., Weissberg, R. P., Dymnicki, A. B., Taylor, R. D., & Schellinger, K. B. (2011). The impact of enhancing students' social and emotional learning: A meta-analysis of school-based universal interventions. *Child Development, 82,* 405–432. doi: 10.1111/j.1467-8624.2010.01564.x

Dymnicki, A., Sambolt, M., & Kidron, Y. (2013). Improving college and career readiness by incorporating social and emotional learning. Washington, DC: College and Career Readiness and Success Center. Retrieved from: www.ccrscenter.org/products-resources/improving-college-and-career-readiness-incorporating-social-and-emotional.

Elbertson, N. A., Brackett, M. A., & Weissberg, R. P. (2009). School-based social and emotional learning (SEL) programming: Current perspectives. In A. Hargraves, A. Lieberman, M. Fullan, & D. Hopkins (Eds.), *Second international handbook of educational change* (pp. 1017–1032). Netherlands: Springer.

Elias, M. J. (1991). An action research approach to evaluating the impact of a social decision-making and problem-solving curriculum for preventing behavior and academic dysfunction in children. *Evaluation and Program Planning, 14,* 397–401.

Elias, M. J. (2001). Prepare children for the tests of life, not a life of tests. *Education Week, 2* (4), 40.

Elias, M. J., Zins, J. E., Weissberg, R. P., Frey, K. S., Greenberg, M. T., Haynes, N. M . . . Shriver, T. P. (1997). *Promoting social and emotional learning: Guidelines for educators.* Danvers, MA: ASCD.

Gordon, R., Ji, P., Mulhall, P., Shaw, B., & Weissberg, R. P. (2011). *Social and emotional learning for Illinois students: Policy, practice and progress—How Illinois SEL standards came to be and what the state has learned through putting them into practice.* Urbana, IL: Institute of Government and Public Affairs. Retrieved from http://casel.org/wp-content/uploads/IGPAIllinois-Report-SEL-chapter.pdf.

Graczyk, P. A., Weissberg, R. P., Payton, J. W., Elias, M. J., Greenberg, M. T., & Zins, J. E. (2000). Criteria for evaluating the quality of school-based social and emotional learning programs. In D. Goldman, R. Bar-On & J. D. A. Parker (Eds.), *The handbook of emotional intelligence: Theory, development, assessment, and application at home, school, and in the workplace* (pp. 391–410). San Franscisco, CA: Jossey-Bass.

Greenberg, M. T., Weissberg, R. P., O'Brien, M. U., Zins, J. E., Fredericks, L., Resnik, H., & Elias, M. J. (2003). Enhancing school-based prevention and youth development through coordinated social, emotional, and academic learning. *American Psychologist, 58,* 466–474. doi: 10.1037/0003-066X.58.6-7.466

Guerra, N. G., & Bradshaw, C. P. (2008). Linking the prevention of problem behaviors and positive youth development: Core competencies for positive youth development and risk prevention. *New Directions for Child and Adolescent Development, 122,* 1–17.

Hoffman, D. M. (2009). Reflecting on social emotional learning: A critical perspective on trends in the United States. *Review of Educational Research, 79,* 533–556.

Klem, A. M., & Connell, J. P. (2004). Relationships matter: Linking teacher support to student engagement and achievement. *Journal of School Health, 74,* 262–273. doi: 10.1111/j.1746-1561.2004.tb08283.x

Kress, J. S., & Elias, M. J. (2006). Building learning communities through social and emotional learning: Navigating the rough seas of implementation. *Professional School Counseling, 10,* 102–107.

Kress, J. S., & Elias, M. J. (2013). Consultation to support sustainability of Social and Emotional Learning initiatives in schools. *Consulting Psychology Journal: Practice and Research, 65* (2), 149–163.

Kusche, C. A., & Greenberg, M. T. (1994). *The PATHS (Promoting alternative thinking strategies) curriculum.* South Deerfield, MA: Channing-Bete.

Lazarus, P. J., & Sulkowski, M. L. (2011). The emotional well-being of our nation's youth and the promise of social-emotional learning. *Communiqué, 40,* 1 & 16–17.

Macklem, G. L. (2014). *Preventive mental health at school.* New York: Springer.

McKevitt, B. C. (2012). School psychologists' knowledge and use of evidence-based, social-emotional learning interventions. *Contemporary School Psychology, 16,* 33–45.

McNeely, C., & Falci, C. (2004). School connectedness and the transition into and out of health-risk behavior among adolescents: A comparison of social belonging and teacher support. *Journal of School Health, 74,* 284–292.

Mischel, W. (2014). *The marshmallow test: Mastering self control.* New York: Little, Brown & Company.

Pasi, R. (2001). *Higher expectations. Promoting social emotional learning and academic achievement in your school.* New York: Teachers College Press.

Payton, J., Weissberg, R. P., Durlak, J. A., Dymnicki, A. B., Taylor, R. D., Schellinger, K. B., & Pachan, M. (2008). *The positive impact of social and emotional learning for kindergarten to eighth-grade students: Findings from three scientific reviews.* Technical Report. Collaborative for Academic, Social, and Emotional Learning (NJ1).

Shure, M. B. (2001). *I can problem solve (ICPS): An interpersonal cognitive problem solving program, second edition.* Champaign, IL: Research Press.

Small, S. A., Cooney, S. M., & O'Connor, C. (2009). Evidence-informed program improvement: Using principles of effectiveness to enhance the quality and impact of family-based prevention programs. *Family Relations, 58,* 1–13.

Tobler, N. S. & Stratton, H. H. (1997). Effectiveness of school-based drug prevention programs: A meta-analysis of the research. *Journal of Primary Prevention, 18,* 71–128.

Wilson, S. J., & Lipsey, M. W. (2007). School-based interventions for aggressive and disruptive behavior: Update of a meta-analysis. *American Journal of Preventive Medicine, 33,* S130–S143.

Whitted, K. S. (2011). Understanding how social and emotional skill deficits contribute to school failure. *Preventing School Failure: Alternative Education for Children and Youth, 55,* 10–16. doi: 10.1080/10459880903286755

Zins, J. E., & Elias, M. J. (2007). Social and emotional learning: Promoting the development of all students. *Journal of Educational and Psychological Consultation, 17,* 233–255.

Zins, J. E., Weissberg, R. P., Wang, M. C., & Walberg, H. J. (2004). *Building academic success on social and emotional learning: What does the research say?* New York: Teachers College Press.

5   Universal Interventions to Support the Mental Health of All Students

One of the best ways to change the school environment is by developing a multi-tiered mental health continuum of care. This can be accomplished by providing mental health services to meet the needs of *all* students in the schools. Doll, Cummings, and Chapla (2014) refer to these services as population-based school mental health services. This approach is consistent with a prevention-focused public health model. The first tier represents the provision of universal screening and evidence-based curriculum and interventions for all students in the school. The second tier focuses on delivering selected or targeted interventions to high-risk students, which accounts for about 15–20 percent of the student body in a typical school. The third tier is geared toward the delivery of indicated and intensive services to those students requiring comprehensive supports. These services are often remedial and substantial and are designed to help students develop more effective behavioral, social, and emotional competencies. In a typical school, students receiving Tier III interventions may represent only about 1–5 percent of the school population (Doll et al., 2014).

Each school, depending on the characteristics of the community and student demographics, will have different needs. For example, inner-city schools, or schools in which most students receive free and reduced lunch, will usually have greater needs than schools in upper-middle-class neighborhoods. Schools in communities that are lower in socioeconomic status (SES) typically have more students who have endured more adverse childhood experiences (ACEs) and have fewer available community resources. Thus, students in these schools require greater support. See Figure 5.1.

To illustrate multi-tiered service delivery, all students could receive instruction on bullying and cyberbullying prevention and intervention at Tier I. At Tier II, students who are the perpetrators of bullying may require an intervention designed to teach them how to use their social influence or power more productively. Lastly, at Tier III, an array of interventions would be needed for students whose dysfunction is so severe that they require substantial services. For example, a student who was a chronic bullying victim and as a result often skipped school and became highly anxious, depressed, and suicidal would require individualized and intensive support such as counseling or therapy.

In the traditional school-based mental health delivery model, the major focus has been on the evaluation of students for special education placement and on the provision of support and remediation for those students who have met the criteria for emotional and behavioral disorders (EBD). However, in the population-based model, three additional goals are addressed (Doll et al., 2014). These include (1) promoting the psychological well-being of all students, (2) providing protective support to high-risk students, and (3) promoting caretaking environments for the more severely involved students to help them overcome challenges and risks (Doll & Cummings, 2008). As noted by Doll et al. (2014), population-based mental health services have a single purpose, which is "to foster the social, emotional, behavioral, and academic competence that students need to be successful in school and in life" (p. 150). This chapter will focus on how educators can deliver

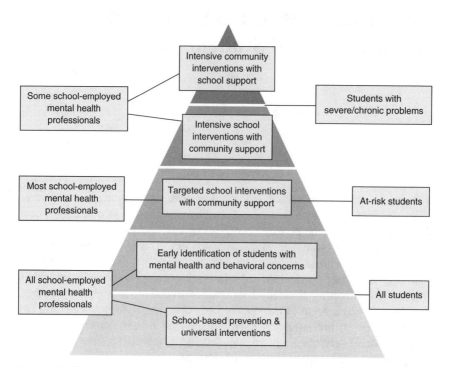

Figure 5.1 The Continuum of School Mental Health Services

Adapted from "Communication Planning and Message Development: Promoting School-Based Mental Health Services," by the National Association of School Psychologists, 2006, Communiqué, 35(1), p. 27. Copyright 2006 by the National Association of School Psychologists. Adapted with Permission

Tier I interventions in the classroom and the following Chapter 6 will focus on creating resilient classrooms and delivering Tier II and Tier III interventions.

Types of School-based Mental Health Interventions: Universal Interventions—Tier I

Given that 10 percent of U.S. children suffer from a mental disorder severe enough to limit their daily functioning in their family, community, and school setting, and that only 6–8 percent to 25 percent (CDC, 2013; Kataoka, Zhang, & Wells, 2002) of these youth receive therapeutic services outside of their school (Hoagwood & Johnson, 2003), the school itself has become the mental health provider for millions of students (Doll et al., 2014). Also, because there is a paucity of school-based mental health professionals to deliver all possible services to all students, educators must be the front-line allies for the provision of *basic* mental health support for students. This means that educators must focus on *universal* prevention and promote practices that are consistent with well-established principles and practices that support students' mental health and emotional well-being. As previously noted, the goal of universal prevention is the promotion of the psychological well-being of all students.

With this being the case, this chapter will highlight some basic universal (Tier I interventions) that can be delivered by teachers in their classroom. These classroom-based universal interventions will include strategies for (a) fostering growth mindsets, (b) encouraging grit, (c) teaching mindfulness, (d) decreasing anxiety (with an additional focus on reducing test anxiety), and (e) increasing emotional self-regulation. All these universal interventions may be considered subsets of social-emotional learning and are part of the paradigm of social-emotional intelligence. For example, mindfulness is a dimension of self-awareness, whereas grit is a dimension of motivation and persistence. By using these strategies and/or programs in their classes, educators will be able to foster the emotional well-being of their students.

Fostering Growth Mindsets

A *growth* mindset is the belief that our abilities and talents can be cultivated. In contrast, a *fixed* mindset is the belief that our abilities and talents are fixed and immutable (Dweck, 2006). According to Yeager and Dweck (2012), implicit theories are defined as the core assumptions about the malleability of personal qualities. They are called "implicit" because they are rarely made explicit and are called "theories" because they create a framework for judging the meaning of events in one's world and for making predictions.

Mindsets and Academic Achievement

Individuals can vary from having more of a fixed or entity theory of one's traits (e.g., intelligence, personality) to more of a malleable or incremental theory. For example, a student with a fixed theory sees intelligence as immutable to change and, consequently, could easily interpret academic setbacks as a sign that they lack intelligence or may be "dumb." Moreover, if they maintain this fixed and negative self-belief, they may not invest in efforts to improve their performance (Yeager & Dweck, 2012). In contrast, those with an incremental view of intelligence see intellectual ability as a skill set that can be developed over time. When students with a growth mindset encounter academic setbacks, they assume that with the right kind of instruction, studying, practice, and feedback that they can improve and succeed. Fortunately, research suggests that students' mindsets can be changed from a fixed mindset to a growth mindset and students become more resilient when this occurs (Blackwell, Trzesniewski, & Dweck, 2007).

Research also demonstrates that students can be taught to change their academically and socially relevant characteristics as well as to integrate these characteristics to change their lives for the better. In support of this notion, Yeager and Dweck (2012) explain that the fixed or entity theory is about measuring one's ability, and everything (difficult tasks, effort, setbacks) can measure ability. Basically, this theory is about threats and defenses in that individual's self-concepts are harmed when they do not measure up to their expectations. In contrast, an incremental or growth theory is about learning and developing, which allows for setbacks to be seen as an opportunity to foster growth. Yeager and Dweck (2012) further explain that the type of theory people adopt shapes their *goals, beliefs about effort, attributions*, and *learning strategies*. For example, students with fixed mindsets care more about looking smart or not appearing dumb; may set less challenging goals; may not give maximum effort as this would show that they lack ability or talents; and may consider giving up, cheating and/or becoming defensive when they encounter setbacks. Furthermore, students with fixed mindsets said they would look for someone who did worse than them when they encountered failure (Nussbaum & Dweck, 2008). In another study by Blackwell et al. (2007), students said they would probably resort to cheating if they failed a test. Moreover, in numerous studies, students with fixed mindsets have been found to eschew difficult or challenging tasks (e.g., Dweck, 2006). In contrast, students with growth mindsets may set high goals, understand that effort and perseverance are the keys to success, may attribute a setback to not studying or working hard enough, and may change their learning strategies such as asking for help, working with a tutor, using distributed practice, or getting more feedback (Dweck, 2006; Yeager & Dweck, 2012; Yeager, Trzesniewski, & Dweck, 2013).

The link between changing students' mindsets to increased academic performance is established by research. Good, Aronson, and Inzlicht (2003) examined whether students in middle school who received weekly mentoring e-mails for a year that explained the incremental theory would perform better on their statewide achievement test at the end of the year. The researchers found that students in the treatment group showed significantly higher verbal and math scores in comparison to the control group. What was most notable about these findings was that math test scores improved by more than one standard deviation among middle school girls compared to the control group that did not learn about the incremental theory of intelligence. In another study, Blackwell et al. (2007) designed two different interventions that were delivered to predominantly racial/ethnic minority seventh-grade students for eight sessions. Students were randomly assigned to learn either helpful study skills or the incremental theory along with study skills. Months after the conclusion of the intervention, the students who learned the incremental theory showed greater improvement in math grades relative to the control group by an estimated 0.30 higher grade point difference.

Mindsets and Personality

Similarly, Yeager, Trzesniewski, & Dweck (2013) implemented an intervention to promote adolescents' growth mindsets so that they could view their personalities as being more flexible. Implicit theories of personality involve the belief that personal characteristics can potentially change. As stated by Yeager, Trzesniewski, & Dweck (2013) this mindset is related to how adolescents respond to conflict and how they explain failures. In students transitioning into high school, for example, Yeager et al. (2014) found that fixed mindsets of personality were related to stress, poorer self-reported health, and lower grades in English, math, and science, as well as negative responses to social adversities. However, a brief growth mindset intervention that focused on how people can change given at the beginning of this transition reduced negative responses to social adversity, stress, and health concerns (Yeager et al., 2014). In another study, Yeager, Miu, Powers, & Dweck (2013) developed a workshop to promote growth mindsets that taught adolescent participants the idea that people can change their traits and roles in situations of victimization (e.g., bully, victim, winner, loser). The sessions included messages and activities related to how the brain changes through learning, how personalities can change, and how motivation involves more than personality. In contrast, participants in the control group received a coping skills workshop that taught skills for engaging in positive thinking and effective coping. Results indicated that participants who attended the growth mindset workshops experienced decreases in aggression, depression, conduct problems, and school absences (Yeager, Miu, et al., 2013).

Mindsets regarding personality have also been linked to the hostile attribution bias or the tendency to perceive negative actions from an individual as being intentional. For example, a hostile attribution bias occurs when a student accidently trips and spills juice on another student and the second student misperceives the spill as purposeful and responds with aggressive behavior. Yeager, Miu, et al. (2013) found that adolescents with fixed mindsets were more likely to exhibit this hostile attribution as well as engage more in aggressive reactions and desires. Yet, in the same study, a growth mindset intervention that discussed the malleability of personality was found to reduce such hostile attributions. Furthermore, this effect was durable at eight months post-intervention. Similarly, Yeager, Trzesniewski, Tirri, Nokelainen, and Dweck (2011) found that adolescents with fixed mindsets reported more desires of vengeance when recalling past conflicts with peers as well as when they responded to a hypothetical bullying scenario. A growth mindset intervention, however, had positive effects on reducing adolescents' desire for vengeance in the same study. These adolescents were less likely to view bullies as "bad people" and attributed their behaviors to other factors such as immaturity or a "bad home situation." These adolescents also reported feeling less ashamed regarding previously experienced victimization as well as less animosity towards bullies.

Process Praise and Inhibition

Another way of supporting growth mindsets is through praise and incentives. Research indicates that individuals that are praised for their work, effort, and use of strategies develop a growth mindset and as a result they believe that their ability is dependent upon their effort (Gunderson et al., 2013). Such "process praise" or praising effort as opposed to ability includes comments such as "I like the way you are working," "Nice job trying to put the books on the shelf," and "I like how you used your finger to follow along in the text." In contrast, praise that emphasizes an individual's ability leads to a fixed mindset. More specifically, person-specific praise, such as "You are fast" and "Good boy" links the positive feedback with innate and thus fixed traits. In particular, Gunderson et al. (2013) explored the relationship between parental praise in early childhood and the development of growth versus fixed mindsets in later childhood. Children who received process praise from parents between one and three years of age later developed a growth mindset. Essentially, these children believed that traits could be changed, sought situations that challenged them, attributed success and failures to effort rather than ability, and employed strategies to improve their performance.

Yeager and Dweck (2012) believe that sometimes the forces in a system are adequate to support learning (e.g., a quality curriculum, effective teachers, adequate resources), but students have mindsets that prevent them from fully taking advantage of these forces. Therefore, a precise intervention to change mindsets can help unlock learning opportunities and engagement, which can then lead to long-term effects on students' educational achievement (Yeager et al., 2014; Yeager & Walton, 2011). Text Box 5.1 displays additional suggestions to foster growth mindsets.

Text Box 5.1 Strategies to Foster Growth Mindsets

- Teach the incremental view of intelligence. One seventh-grade girl explains the concept this way: "Being smart is something you have to strive for. Most kids if they don't know an answer will not raise their hands. But I do. Because if I am wrong my mistake is corrected. Or I could say, 'I don't get this. Can you help me?' or 'How could this be solved?' Just by doing this I am increasing my intelligence." (Dweck, 2006, p.17).
- Give the message to all students that says: You are a capable person and I am interested in your development. When a student says, "I am not good at . . . ", tell the student, "Very few people are good at something the first time they make an attempt. We all have different learning curves and it may take you more time to catch on and be comfortable with the material. You may need more practice than others, but you will eventually learn. I have confidence in you."
- Use process praise. Remember to praise students for commitment and hard work, not for talent or intelligence. For example, say, "You truly worked hard to improve your score in science. You read the material over several times, outlined the chapters, highlighted the important points, developed flash cards and quizzed yourself. Your effort made a huge difference!"
- When students do not succeed, ask them to reflect on their experience. Ask, "What did you learn from your experience? How could you use this setback to help you learn and grow?"
- Help students stretch their skills by providing them challenges—both intrapersonal and interpersonal. For example, a third grade teacher could challenge all her students to earn a higher score on their next spelling test than they did on their last test, and if the majority of the students earn a higher score, she could give the entire class a reward. In this process, she could also incorporate peer tutoring. This would be particularly meaningful as students will get a reward if their fellow classmates improve their spelling skills. Or a physical education teacher could challenge her students to do just one more sit up or push up or run a faster 50 yard dash. In other areas, such as in music and tennis, the students can challenge their peers to move up a seat in the band or a rung on the tennis ladder, and in this way they can stretch their skills.
- When students have not been able to pass the requisite benchmarks or standards, consider giving students grades of "not yet."

Encouraging Grit

What makes people successful? What sets successful people apart? The answer to these age-old questions involves more than just talent and opportunity, or even brains and brawn (Duckworth & Gross, 2014). It also involves grit, which is defined as a personality trait that involves perseverance, commitment, and passion to achieve long-term goals (Duckworth, Peterson, Matthews, & Kelly, 2007). In this regard, an individual who has grit persists through challenges and setbacks, shows commitment, and continues to remain passionately involved with accomplishing a goal. Duckworth et al. (2007) equate grit to running a marathon whereby the individual continues along despite pain, boredom, fatigue, and other obstacles they experience along the path. Simply stated, when times get tough, those with grit keep going.

The impact of grit has been explored in a variety of contexts and it has been shown to be a predictor of success in academic, occupational, and social-emotional domains (Von Culin, Tsukayama, & Duckworth, 2014). Individuals with grit have been found to achieve higher levels of education, experience less job turnover, and show greater commitment to the success of their personal relationships (Duckworth et al., 2007; Eskreis-Winkler, Shulman, Beal, & Duckworth, 2014). Grit has also been associated with greater rates of high school completion and higher grade point averages among undergraduate students (Duckworth et al., 2007; Eskreis-Winkler et al., 2014).

Because grit involves determination, perseverance, and hard work, it is tied to deliberate practice. The concept of deliberate practice is based on the fundamental finding of a study by Ericsson, Krampe, and Tesch-Romer (1993) and this concept was later popularized by Colvin (2008). These scholars found that the way that an individual develops expertise in a skill has more to do with how he or she practices than with the number of practice repetitions. To understand this point, think of problems associated with extended practice of a faulty golf swing—the bad swing will become engrained and one's golf performance will not improve.

As discussed by Ericsson et al. (1993), individual differences even among elite athletes are closely related to the amount of deliberate practice. Many characteristics once believed to reflect innate talent actually have been shown to result from intense practice extended across at least a decade. Another important feature of deliberate practice lies in continually practicing a skill at more challenging levels with mastery as an end goal. For example, sticking with the golf analogy, deliberate practice in sports would be exemplified by Tiger Woods placing his ball in a sand trap 20 feet from the green and 70 feet from the hole, then lightly stepping on the ball, and practicing 100 wedge shots in order to improve his short game. Now applying this concept to an academic domain, in a spelling contest, deliberate practice would involve finding all the words a student cannot spell and spelling them correctly repeatedly until the words are mastered. In contrast to other forms of spelling bee preparation (e.g., playing word games, reading for pleasure, quizzing), deliberate practice is a solitary, effortful, and less enjoyable activity that aims to improve performance—it is an enterprise that requires grit. In studying National Spelling Bee winners, Duckworth, Kirby, Tsukayama, Berstein and Ericsson (2011) found that contestants who scored higher on grit were more likely to engage in deliberate practice and thus were more likely to advance to later rounds of the spelling bee.

Drawing from the positive relationship between grit, deliberate practice, and performance, what can be done within the classroom to promote grit in students? In general, fostering grit in students involves overcoming obstacles, experiencing failure, and feeling frustrated before reaching success. Moreover, as a roadmap to foster grit, Hoerr (2013) outlines a six-step process: (1) establish the environment, (2) determine the expectations, (3) teach the vocabulary, (4) create the frustration, (5) monitor progress, and (6) reflect and learn. As part of this process, teachers have to create a classroom environment that expects students to experience difficulties and frustration and consequently acknowledges hard work and effort on the road to success. This involves helping students set grit-related expectations for themselves. Hoerr (2013) suggests having students self-reflect on their perseverance and dedication to learning and practice. Students can also complete grit charts that show the number of times they have overcome a difficult task.

Facilitating this process involves incorporating a grit vocabulary (e.g., tenacity, perseverance, frustration) into everyday exchanges. For example, when providing feedback on a student's paper, a teacher may add "Good work, Carlos. Your paper shows perseverance and grit!" Teachers can help students work through difficulty, occasionally give students challenges to rise up to, and create appropriate levels of healthy frustration. For example, educators can have students work outside of their comfort zone, continually revise a project, or give them unclear directions that encourage innovative thinking (Hoerr, 2013). In order to help students persevere through these tasks, teachers can have students rate how hard they think the task will be before starting; encourage them to think about a time they thought they would not be successful but were; and have them reflect on their progress. However, as an important caveat, teachers must monitor students' frustration levels (e.g., thumbs up, thumbs down activity on how they are feeling) throughout this process and provide them with opportunities to reflect on what they have learned. To encourage such self-reflection, students can keep journals or logs to serve as a resource for future reference. In these entries, students can describe the tasks they completed, how they felt while doing so, and what they did to overcome difficulties.

Other ideas for promoting grit within schools include displaying posters that share messages of grit and showcasing students who have showed exceptional perseverance in academic and non-academic areas (Hoerr, 2013). Students can also be rewarded and acknowledged for the progress they make rather than just for achieving high grades. That is, teachers can praise a student who improves from a 50 percent to 65 percent on a spelling test, even though that student may be near the bottom of their class, as much as they would praise a student who continually earns 95 percent. Teachers can also lead discussions with students about what grit is and how famous individuals (e.g., athletes (Wilma Rudolph); presidents (Abraham Lincoln); scientists (Thomas Edison); aviation pioneers (the Wright brothers)) have shown relentless determination. As another strategy, Miller (2014) emphasizes the importance of providing ungraded feedback during formative evaluations. In this way, students can improve without the fear of earning a poor grade, and as a result, can view learning as a journey—a process of continual improvement.

Overall, the message conveyed to students by educators should be: We all learn by frustration and failure and only by hard work, effort, constructive feedback, and deliberate practice will we ever improve. Thus, to add a human element, teachers can model grit by sharing their own experiences of overcoming obstacles and succeeding in the face of challenges (Hoerr, 2013). Further, they can encourage their students to share their own similar experiences. These discussions help show children that everyone experiences challenges and that setbacks can be overcome with perseverance and determination. Another message that teachers can communicate is: It is okay to make mistakes, everyone does. A poignant example is shown in the film, *Monsieur Lazhar*, in which a teacher writes a poem on his last day in the classroom; he deliberately makes mistakes in the poem and proceeds to read it to his students. He then asks his students to correct his spelling and grammar, thereby communicating that everyone makes errors and this is part of learning and life.

Promoting Mindfulness

Kabat-Zinn (2003) defines mindfulness as "the awareness that emerges through paying attention on purpose, in the present moment, and non-judgmentally to the unfolding of experiences moment by moment" (p. 145). Simply put, mindfulness can be defined as being in the moment. It is the awareness that develops from attending to experiences as they occur (Hooker & Fodor, 2008). Being mindful involves becoming aware of one's internal and external experiences without labeling such experiences as "good" or "bad." As Hooker and Fodor (2008) note, mindfulness is simply being aware of the sights, smells, and sounds of our environment and the feelings, thoughts, and sensations these experiences elicit. Mindfulness essentially involves being in the now.

Two common mindfulness interventions include Mindfulness-Based Stress Reduction (MBSR) and Mindfulness-Based Cognitive Therapy (MBCT; Burke, 2010). The focus of MBSR and MBCT interventions is on teaching individuals how to engage in mindful meditation. Hooker and Fodor (2008) note that mindful meditation involves becoming aware and observant of the constantly changing stimuli that one experiences (both internally (i.e., in one's own mind) and externally (i.e., through one's afferent senses)). While traditional forms of meditation focus on achieving a relaxed state, the goal of mindfulness training is centered on becoming more aware and accepting of one's current state of being (Hooker & Fodor, 2008). In general, research suggests that MBST and MBCT are associated with positive outcomes in youth (Burke, 2010).

However, how can mindfulness be applied to school and classroom settings? To answer this question, Schonert-Reich et al. (2015) implemented a social-emotional learning curriculum called MindUp, that included mindfulness training components with school-age children. MindUp is a class-wide program that involves 12 weekly lessons that begin by teaching children mindfulness practices (e.g., breath-centered focus, actively listening to sounds without judgment). The lessons in the program then progress toward promoting executive functions (e.g., self-regulation), social-emotional learning (e.g., perspective taking), and positive emotions (e.g., optimism, gratitude, kindness). After implementing the MindUp program for four months in the regular classroom setting, performance on tasks of executive function, self-reported well-being, engagement in prosocial behaviors, and math performance all improved. For more information on the MindUp curriculum visit http://thehawnfoundation.org/mindup/.

Similarly, Metz et al. (2013) implemented another mindfulness-based program Learning to BREATHE (L2B) to explore its effects on emotional regulation, perceived stress, and reports of physical complaints among adolescents. Learning to BREATHE is a universal-level program that aims to teach adolescents mindfulness techniques and it provides opportunities for practice within the classroom setting (Broderick & Frank, 2014). The L2B program was developed around six thematic lessons: body awareness; understanding and working with thoughts; integrating awareness of thoughts, feelings, and sensations; reducing harmful self-judgments; and integrating mindful awareness into everyday life (Metz et al., 2013). Each lesson introduces one of these six themes, engages students through activities and discussions, and allows for opportunities for students to practice learned skills. Metz et al. (2013) found that among participants receiving the weekly L2B sessions, greater emotional self-regulation, fewer physical complaints (e.g., headaches, fatigue), and lower self-reported stress levels were observed. More information on the L2B program can be found at http://learning2breathe.org/.

In a recent study, Flook, Goldberg, Pinger, and Davidson (2015) developed and implemented a similar mindfulness-based curriculum (The Kindness Curriculum) with preschool children. The Kindness Curriculum is a program aimed at teaching young children prosocial skills (e.g., sharing, taking turns) through mindfulness techniques and kindness practices. The weekly Kindness Curriculum lessons were delivered for 12 weeks within the general education classrooms in 25–30-minute sessions. Flook et al. (2015) found that this program was linked to increased teacher-reported social competence, cognitive flexibility, and academic performance as well as fewer reports of selfish acts by preschool children (e.g., refusing to share with peers).

Types of Meditations

As explained by Renshaw (2012), the most foundational form of meditation is breathing meditation. However, many other forms exist such as body scan meditation, walking or movement meditation, compassion meditation, and Transcendental Meditation (Grossman, 2010; Harris, 2014;

Renshaw, 2012). During breathing meditation, individuals are asked to sit still, focus on their breath, and locate the sensation of breathing in their bodies. As noted by Renshaw, the "intent of this practice is to develop attentive awareness toward here-and-now bodily experiences using the breath as an anchor" (p. 410). As would be expected in practicing any type of new skill, this can be difficult at first. It is not unusual for individuals to let their minds wander or become distracted by thoughts of the past or future as well as by afferent stimuli and sensations. However, when this happens, individuals are encouraged to understand that this is a normal occurrence. Further, they are encouraged to maintain a non-judgmental attitude, and gently to redirect their attention back to their breath. Metaphorically speaking, if their attention wavers 1,000 times during a meditation session, all they have to do is re-focus 1,001 times. Text Box 5.2 provides a sample script for teaching students a breathing meditation.

Text Box 5.2 A Breathing Meditation

"Please make yourself comfortable. Sit in a straight position. Just close your eyes. Place your hands in your lap or on your knees. Now take a deep breath and let yourself relax. Focus your attention on your breath. Notice how the air feels as you breathe in and out. It might feel cool or it might feel warm, or it might even tingle, as the air flows in and out. Now focus on your chest and your stomach while breathing. Notice how your chest or stomach moves with each breath you take. Now just focus on your breath as you breathe in and out. Your only job is to sit and feel your breath. From time to time you might notice a sound in the room, or a feeling in your body, or you may notice that your mind is wandering. That is perfectly okay and normal, and can be expected. When this happens just let it pass, let it drift away, and refocus on your breath, breathing in and breathing out. Just sit and feel your breath."

(Now let students sit and meditate for the planned time period. This could last from two to 15 minutes based on the age of the students, the amount of experiences they have had with this practice, their level of receptivity and motivation, and the amount of time available.)

"As you come to the end of his meditation, just relax and feel the calm. This practice will help you relax and focus. It will also give you the energy to have a better day. Now if you want, just wiggle your toes, wiggle your nose, and wiggle your fingers. Now take three more breaths in and out. You may also want to put a smile on your face. Now when you are ready, open your eyes. Congratulate yourself for a job well done."

Partially adapted from Renshaw, 2012

Practical Suggestions for Teaching Mindfulness

Beyond these mindful curricula, Hooker and Fodor (2008) provide several practical suggestions for teaching children mindfulness. Such mindfulness lessons should first focus on helping children pay attention to concrete experiences in their environments. To promote awareness of objects, Hooker and Fodor (2008) suggest a drawing activity in which a child draws a picture of an object (e.g., a fruit, a brush, a shoe), spends time observing the actual object, and finally draws the object a second time and compares it to the original drawing. Other activities focus on promoting children's awareness of how they act upon their environment. One suggestion provided by Hooker and Fodor (2008) is to have children keep a daily journal for a week illustrating a daily routine (e.g., what do you do in the morning, after school). As the week progresses and the children become more aware of their environment, they may add more steps and details to their journal entries (e.g., waking up vs. rubbing eyes and pulling off warm blanket).

As stated above, mindfulness also involves an awareness of internal stimuli. To promote such mindfulness of the body, Hooker and Fodor (2008) suggest the Kabat-Zinn (1990) raisin activity.

As part of this activity, children are given three raisins or other small food items such as popcorn or chocolate. The children are instructed to bring their attention to the raisin and observe it carefully as they note its texture and smell and become aware of any thoughts or feelings these observations elicit. They are then told to bring the raisin toward their mouth, noting how their arm and hand moves. Finally, they begin chewing the raisin slowly and fully concentrating on its taste. This process is repeated for the remaining raisins as if each one were a novel experience. Another activity to promote mindfulness involves having children move about the classroom while focusing attention on their bodies. Hooker and Fodor (2008) suggest having children slowly walk around the classroom pretending, for example, that they are walking on eggshells or that they are secret agents on a mission. As the children slowly move about the classroom, they should focus on how their body is moving (e.g., muscles contracting, foot peeling off the ground, arms hanging, fast or slow pace).

Lastly, mindful breathing is an activity that can help children focus and be in the moment. Hooker and Fodor (2008) suggest starting by bringing attention to children's natural, rhythmic breathing. Mindful breathing exercises can be facilitated through counting (e.g., "one" as we inhale, "two" as we exhale) and by reminding children to stay focused on their breathing even when they begin to focus on other thoughts. Another activity that can be done with children is breathing buddies. As explained by Beach (2014), children can practice mindful breathing by lying on their backs and placing a stuffed animal on their stomach. As the children breathe in and breathe out they notice how their stuffed animal rises and falls. This activity can also be done by having children stand up and place their hands on their stomachs as they breathe in and out. These activities help children train and focus their mind, and can also help them calm and regulate their emotions.

Decreasing Anxiety

Twenge (2000) published a meta-analytic study of anxiety that assessed research conducted between the years 1952 and 1993 and the findings from this study are significant. More specifically, this investigation included 37 samples of elementary-age children and 13 samples of adolescents that were sampled over a 40-year time frame. Overall, results indicated that anxiety levels for U.S. youth have increased dramatically over the assessed time frame. In fact, in child samples, anxiety has increased almost a full standard deviation during a 40-year period. In line with these cross-comparisons, the average American child in the 1980s reported more anxiety than child psychiatric patients did in the 1950s. In a similar comparison, young adults also showed a significant and corresponding increase in anxiety.

Why are changes in anxiety levels important? Researchers have linked anxiety to a host of physical ailments including asthma, irritable bowel syndrome, inflammatory bowel disease, ulcers, and heart disease (Edelmann, 1992). Additionally, high levels of anxiety can impair mental performance and sometimes lead to drug and alcohol abuse (Smail et al., 1984). Severe anxiety is a predisposing factor to major depression and suicidal behavior (Bagby, Joffee, Parker, Kalemba, & Harkeness, 1995). Unfortunately, the prevalence of anxiety disorders is higher than that of virtually all mental disorders of childhood and adolescence (Costello et al., 1996) and is associated with negative long-term outcomes such as under-employment in adulthood and general unhappiness across the lifespan (Sulkowski, Joyce, & Storch, 2013; Twenge, 2000). Consequently, this increase in anxiety has profound effects on physical and mental health.

The increase in anxiety affects all those who work in schools. Presently, with an emphasis on high-stakes testing, school grades, and teacher compensation tied to student achievement, schools are raising the levels of anxiety in children and school personnel at a time when anxiety rates already are on the increase (Lazarus, 2012). Consequently, schools have highly anxious administrators, supervising highly anxious teachers, who are educating highly anxious students, who come home to highly anxious parents.

Twenge (2000) posited that the two most important variables that produced the rise in anxiety levels are high environmental threat and low degree of social connection. That is, the more threatened that children feel and the less they feel connected to other children, adults, and social institutions, the greater degree of anxiety they are likely to experience.

What can schools do to reverse this concerning trend? It appears that providing individual treatment to children with anxiety disorders will be insufficient to deal with this problem. First, there are not enough school-based mental health professionals to deal with this issue. Second, this increasing level of anxiety impacts all students—not just those with diagnosable mental disorders. The results of Twenge's study (2000) underscore the critical importance of establishing strong social attachments and bonds to others. Creative ways to help ensure that all students feel safe and connected to members of the school community will be discussed in Chapters 7 and 8. See Text Box 5.3 for strategies to decrease anxiety in youth.

Text Box 5.3 Some Strategies to Decrease Anxiety in Students

- Teach children what anxiety is: "An uncomfortable feeling people get when they worry about bad things happening to them or others in the future."
- Normalize anxiety: "We all feel anxiety sometimes. I feel anxious when I have to . . ," "I can understand why you'd feel anxious when you have to do that. I'd feel anxious too."
- Convey to students that anxiety will come and go over time.
- Convey to students that they can still do important things such as their schoolwork or play with friends, even if they feel anxious.
- Help ground highly anxious students and divert their attention away from the feared stimulus or situation: "Look here, look me in the eyes. You're going to be okay and I'm here to talk with you to help make things better."
- Reduce opportunities for students to avoid anxiety provoking, yet important, events and situations: "I can tell you're really anxious but you need to go to math class."
- Distract anxious students with humor.
- Pair reinforcers with anxiety provoking tasks. For example, a student could get extra computer time for reading aloud in class.
- Come up with a special handshake, catchphrase, or gesture to reinforce students who do not like overt teacher attention or being the center of attention.
- Ask anxious students about their feelings when other students are not around.
- Provide students with a visual prompt such as a stop sign so they can indicate visually when they are anxious or scared.
- Shelter students from scary movies, graphic images, and violent media.
- Do not lie to anxious youth by telling them that nothing bad will ever happen to them. Bad things happen to everyone. Instead, reinforce the message that they will be okay and that caring adults at school can help them.
- Teach students guided relaxation techniques that they can use when they take high-stakes tests.

Mitigating Test Anxiety

Test anxiety is a specific form of anxiety that attenuates students' performance on tests and other important academic tasks. Moreover, in this age of high-stakes testing, an era that is predicated on evaluating students based on their performance on standardized tests, overwhelming anxiety can be a crucial factor in determining if a student passes or fails a grade. Test anxiety is highly prevalent among school-age students. It has been estimated that approximately 20 percent of students in upper elementary school are hindered in demonstrating their ability because of test anxiety (Goonan, 2004). According to one study, between 34 percent and 41 percent of African-American third to sixth grade students are impacted by test anxiety (Turner, Beidel, Hughes, & Turner, 1993) and between 25 percent and 30 percent of American students suffer the effects of debilitating stress in evaluative situations (Hill & Wigfield, 1984). Moreover, Wigfield and Eccles (1989) report that as many as ten million students in elementary and secondary schools are performing below expectations on tests because of anxiety and deficiencies in their test-taking strategies.

According to Cizek and Burg (2006), test anxiety has two components. The first is *emotionality*. This is the physical component that is often observable and it has physiological manifestations such as pacing, pencil tapping, nervousness, sweating, fidgeting, and continually looking at the clock. The second is *worry*. This is the psychological or cognitive component of test anxiety. This is often evidenced in a student's preoccupation before and/or during testing with the concern of doing poorly or failing a test. Researchers have isolated the worry component as the primary factor that decreases test performance in students with high levels of test anxiety (Cizek & Burg, 2006).

Fortunately, interventions exist for reducing test anxiety (Erford & Moore-Thomas, 2004). Educators can have a positive impact on students' lives by teaching them more effective study preparation skills and by helping with reducing unwarranted anxiety that has a deleterious impact on their test performance. See Text Box 5.4, 5.5, and 5.6 on strategies to reduce test anxiety.

Text Box 5.4 Reducing Text Anxiety: Tips for Teachers

Teachers want their students to perform well on tests. Teachers spend much time and energy exposing students to academic concepts and providing opportunities for mastery. The importance of their efforts to prepare students for tests cannot be overemphasized. Here are a few suggestions:

- Establish a classroom environment in which testing is a natural part of the learning process. Communicate that testing is important and should be taken seriously. However, a classroom environment where learning is the goal rather than grades or test scores is less threatening.
- Avoid pop quizzes. Instead use frequent, brief, announced quizzes to accomplish the same goal but with less anxiety.
- Teach study skills throughout the year. Structure lessons so that previewing and reviewing material are integrated in the lesson. Previewing and reviewing help students develop metacognitive skills which have shown to increase motivation, memory and flexible knowledge.
- Build confidence through explicit instruction in test-taking strategies such as skimming over the entire test first, time management (answering easier questions first and skipping over and returning to harder questions later), how to read and follow directions, whether there is a penalty for guessing, etc.
- Give as much general information about the test as possible. Tell students about the time limits, if any; the length of the test; and the types of questions, such as multiple choice, true/false, fill in the blank, etc. Allow students to ask questions and clear up any misunderstandings beforehand. Unknown factors heighten anxiety.
- Balance curriculum coverage with time for reflecting and talking with students. Large volumes of new material can be overwhelming.
- Teach mastery of content. Repeated review and practice (overlearning) is an effective preventative strategy for reducing test anxiety.
- Avoid transmitting teacher anxieties about standardized testing due to school accountability systems. Emphasize to students that preparation is the key to doing their best. Don't communicate that the test is irrelevant or stupid.

- On testing day, make sure students have pencils, opportunities to use the restroom and drinking fountain, adequate space for working, good lighting, a comfortable room temperature, and freedom from distractions.
- Check that students with special instructional needs are accommodated.
- Most importantly, express confidence in students' abilities to do their best.

Suggestions from Cizek and Burg, 2006 and Lazarus and Lazarus, 2006.

Text Box 5.5 Decreasing Test Anxiety: Relaxation Script

Teachers can use this script when practicing with their students to help relieve students' anxiety about test taking. It is important to practice this relaxation script ahead of time so the activity becomes a habit with students. Practice in less stressful test-taking situations makes it easier to use when students have to take high-stakes tests. In presenting this relaxation script, it is important to speak slowly and in a relaxed and gentle voice. When three dots appear in the script, hesitate for about two to three seconds, then continue.

Relaxation Script

Sit comfortably in your chair. Close your eyes if you want. Let's breathe in and breathe out. Again, breathe in . . . breathe out. . . . Again, breathe in . . . breathe out. . . . Now, imagine that a warm and soft white cloud is covering your body. This gentle cloud makes you feel relaxed . . . breathe in . . . breathe out . . . and more relaxed, breathe in . . . breathe out . . . and even more relaxed . . . breathe in . . . breathe out. . . . Imagine this cloud covering your hair, your forehead, your eyes, your nose, your mouth, your neck, your shoulders, your chest, your arms, your fingers, and your stomach. You are feeling very relaxed . . . breathe in . . . breathe out. . . . This cloud of relaxation is now going down your upper legs, your lower legs, your ankles, your feet, and your toes. You can wiggle your toes if you want to. The more you wiggle your toes, the more relaxed you feel. Breathe in . . . breathe out. . . . Again, breathe in . . . breathe out . . . Let all your thoughts drift away into the sky. Let the cloud relax you. Breathe in . . . nice and slowly . . . breathe out . . . Notice how good your body feels . . . light and floating . . . calm and comfortable . . . relaxed . . . Silently, tell yourself that you are going to do your best today. That is the best you can do. When you open your eyes, you will feel calm and relaxed and ready to do your best. Breathe in . . . breathe out . . . now when you are ready, open your eyes. Notice how much more relaxed you feel.

Adapted from Lazarus and Lazarus (2006).

Text Box 5.6 Busting Test Jitters for Students

Before the test . . .

- Get a good night's rest and eat a balanced breakfast.
- Do the relaxation exercise.
  Don't say to yourself, I can't do this. This is hard. I'm not smart. I will fail. Instead, give yourself positive messages.

  o   I will do the best I can.
  o   I am capable of doing well.

(continued)

(continued)

- o   I know the material
- o   I can do it.
- o   I am prepared.

- Read or listen to the directions carefully.

  - o   Block out other thoughts.
  - o   Concentrate.

- If you get stuck—don't panic.

  - o   Take a deep breath and relax.
  - o   Give yourself a positive message.
  - o   Read or think about the question again to help you.

- After taking the test, reward yourself.

Increasing Emotional Self-Regulation

Emotional self-regulation is an individual's ability to recognize, understand, and integrate emotional information while managing his or her behavior (Zeman, Cassano, Perry-Parrish, & Stegall, 2006). A child who is capable of regulating his emotions, for example, might walk away from an upsetting situation and calm himself down by counting backwards from 20 to 1 or through taking deep breaths. In contrast, a child with poor emotional self-regulation may react to a similar situation with an angry outburst. In turn, children's ability to monitor and modify their emotional reactions is related to the ability to maintain positive relationships as well as to regulate their behavior (Supplee, Skuban, Trentacosta, Shaw, & Stoltz, 2011; Zeman et al., 2006). Children with effective emotional self-regulation skills are more likely to engage in positive behaviors and they are less likely to exhibit externalizing behaviors (e.g., outbursts, impulsivity), internalizing symptoms (e.g., depression, anxiety), and negative affect (Supplee et al., 2011; Zeman et al., 2006). They also perform better in school and earn higher grades. Parents rate children with good self-regulation as being better able to delay gratification and keep their impulses in check as well as being more socially competent, verbally fluent, rational, attentive, planful, and better able to deal with frustration and stress than their more impulsive peers (Shoda, Mischel, & Peake, 1990).

As a whole, emotional self-regulation is an integral skill for children to have in their social skills toolbox. In a series of famous experiments that have been called the marshmallow test, Walter Mischel (1974) posed a challenge to four-year-old children who were mostly children of faculty, graduate students, and employees at Stanford University. The experimenter told the preschool-aged participants that the experimenter had an errand to run, and if the child could wait until the experimenter came back, they could have two marshmallows instead of the one resting in front of them. If they could not wait until then, they could have only one marshmallow, but they could have it right away. As described by Goleman (1995), this is a challenge to try the soul of any four-year-old. This is the "eternal battle between impulse and restraint, id and ego, desire and self-control, and gratification and delay" (p. 81). In essence, this is a classic test of emotional self-regulation. Some of these four-year-old children were able to restrain their impulses. They talked to themselves, they turned their bodies around, they hid under the table, they covered their eyes, or they even tried going to sleep to do so. These emotionally self-regulated preschoolers were able to earn their two-marshmallow reward. But other preschoolers with less developed emotional regulation skills quickly grabbed the marshmallow, often immediately after the experimenter left the room (Mischel, 1974).

When these same students were followed up about 12 to 14 years later, preschoolers who resisted the temptation to immediately eat the marshmallow at age four, were found to be more personally effective, socially competent, and self-assertive in their adolescence. Further, they were better able to deal with the vicissitudes and challenges of life. They were viewed by their parents as being more trustworthy and dependable, and as having more self-reliance than their peers who, at age four, could not resist temptation. Moreover, the students were later evaluated as they were finishing high school, and it was found that the students who restrained their impulses had better grades and were more emotionally competent. They also had more staying power and could make effective plans and follow through on them (Mischel, Shoda, & Peake, 1988; Shoda et al., 1990). However, the most astonishing result from the aforementioned study was that the emotionally self-regulated students had significantly higher SAT scores than their more impulsive peers did. The top third of children who at age four resisted the longest in eating the marshmallow had an average quantitative score of 652 and an average verbal score of 610 on the SAT, whereas the bottom third of children who more quickly grabbed the marshmallow had average scores of 528 and 524 on the SAT respectively. This was a 210-point difference in total score on the SAT (Goleman, 1995).

In light of these findings, helping children develop their emotional self-regulation skills may have a positive impact on their well-being and success. Zeman et al. (2006) describes one way to accomplish this aim, which involves helping children become aware of their emotional states as well as the emotions of others. Using a feelings chart that matches facial expressions with different emotions can help children recognize their own emotions and express these with a feeling vocabulary (Bennett, 2007). Zeman et al. (2006) further suggest guiding children through decision-making when they encounter a negative situation. Through these teachable moments, educators and school-based mental health professionals can help children understand their feelings and find more positive ways to express their feelings (Joyce-Beaulieu & Sulkowski, 2015). For example, if a child is becoming upset because she wants a toy that a peer is playing with, a teacher can help the child decide how to best react to this situation (e.g., continue to become upset or play with a similar toy while they wait their turn). Davis and Levine (2013) further add that children can moderate negative emotions by learning how to reappraise the significance and outcome of a situation (e.g., How important is it to play with the toy? What else could you have done instead of becoming upset?). Finally, Zeman et al. (2006) suggest that brainstorming with children about different things they can do to help manage their emotions (e.g., taking deep breaths, slowly counting forwards or backwards, stepping away from a situation, going to a quiet area in the class, playing with a comforting toy) has utility. One approach that has been described to help students self-regulate their emotions is a form of mindfulness called the STOP technique that has been described by Renshaw, Bolognino, Fletcher, and Long (2015). See Text Box 5.7. Another approach is belly breathing and has been explained by Blue Cross Blue Shield of North Carolina. See Text Box 5.8.

Text Box 5.7 Increasing Emotional Regulation by the STOP Technique

STOP is an acronym that helps students regulate their emotions and to practice mindfulness when they encounter stressful situations. Tell students " 'S is for Stop!' When we realize we are in a stressful or difficult situation we can use this technique. The first thing we do is stop what we are doing. Remember, we are in charge of our feelings and actions. Our feelings are not in charge of us. Then after we stop, we move into T. 'T' stands for 'Take deep breaths.' We can take as many deep breaths as we need to help calm ourselves down. Next, 'O' is for observe what is happening

(continued)

(continued)

right now. Once we calm ourselves down, we can observe the small things in ourselves, such as, what we are feeling or thinking and what we want to do. And we can carefully observe others. Lastly, 'P' stands for 'Proceed positively.' Now that we are more calm and relaxed and have taken the time to notice how we are feeling and what is happening, we can make positive choices. We can now decide what we want to do and do it. Remember, we always want to do our best to be kind to ourselves and to others."

It is best to have students practice this technique when they are NOT is stressful situations. Then, when they encounter a difficult situation that requires this technique, they are more prepared to use it. This is consistent with the coaching philosophy of winning coaches: You play the way you practice.

Adapted from Renshaw, Bolognino, Fletcher, & Long (2015)

Text Box 5.8 Belly Breathing

1. Sit in a comfortable position and close your eyes if you want to.
2. Place your hands on your belly.
3. Inhale through your nose into your belly so your belly expands like a balloon
4. Slowly breathe out through your nose, using your stomach muscles to push your belly back in until all the air is pushed out.
5. Try to make your exhalation last as long as your inhalation.
6. Keep breathing in and out slowly for a few minutes.
7. As you go through the process, breathe in relaxation and breathe out stress. Let your body get more and more relaxed as you continue to belly breathe.

From Blue Cross Blue Shield of North Carolina

Beyond these suggestions, other approaches focus on developing children's emotional self-regulation through school-based interventions. One such approach is the Rochester Resilience Project, which aims to help elementary-aged children with emerging behavioral and social-emotional concerns develop emotional self-regulation (Wyman et al., 2010). As part of this program, Wyman et al. (2010) pair participants with adult mentors that help them practice essential emotional regulation skills in real-life situations. Such skills include monitoring emotions (e.g., establishing feeling check-ins); practicing self-control (e.g., teaching children to use a feeling thermometer to recognize the intensity of their emotions); and maintaining control and regaining equilibrium (e.g., using an imaginary umbrella to protect themselves from hurtful situations, taking a step back from an emotional situation). In a study exploring the effects of the Rochester Resilience Project, Wyman et al. (2010) found that this school-based intervention led to positive behavioral outcomes, including increased behavioral control, on-task behavior, effective social skills, and decreased disciplinary problems.

Further, Barnes, Vogel, Beck, Schoenfeld, and Owens (2008) employed a similar school-based intervention, specifically with children with emotional-behavioral disturbances who presented with sensory sensitivities. The Alert Program is an eight-week intervention that aims to teach children to recognize arousal states related to behavioral problems (e.g., loud sounds, touch, sudden movements) and to apply self-regulation strategies in response to these upsetting states. Barnes et al. (2008) noted improved behavior, self-regulation, and sensory processing in children receiving the Alert Program intervention.

It is also now known that children, even as young as age four, can be taught emotional self-regulation skills. As noted by Shoda et al. (1990), "preschoolers tended to wait longer when they were given effective strategies, or when they generated their own, for reducing the arousal while sustaining their goal-directed delay" (p. 979). This effectively means that all children can be taught the skills necessary for impulse delay and emotional self-regulation. Consequently, by teaching effective skills, engaging in conversation, providing classroom-based activities, and incorporating school-based interventions, children can be taught how to recognize, understand, and manage their emotions. For more techniques to help students self-regulate their emotions see Text Box 5.9.

Text Box 5.9 Techniques Teachers and Mental Health Professionals Can Use to Help Students Self-Regulate Their Emotions

- When a student makes a negative comment, consider this an opportunity to teach and talk about emotions.
- Label emotions that young children exhibit or help older children label their own emotions.
- Give students permission to feel their emotions. Indicate that emotions are neither good nor bad, but rather are normal and are experienced by everyone.
- Listen empathetically to students' description of their feelings. Make sure to give students time to experience and accept their feelings.
- If a student is having an emotional meltdown in a public place, move the student to a more private place where the student will not be on display. Do your best to set limits if the intensity of the emotion is too extreme. If a student is out of control (or is getting close to that point) use distraction rather than try to reason with the student.
- Offer to help the student with strategies for dealing with the intensity of the emotion or offer to set up an appointment with a school-based mental health professional.
- Teach the student strategies for calming down (e.g., belly breathing, the turtle technique, counting down, etc.).
- If problem-solving is warranted, help the student figure out how to prevent the problem from happening again or help the student explore alternative solutions.
- Help the student practice using calming or problem solving strategies when the student is feeling under control, not while in the midst of an emotional upheaval.
- Emphasize that everyone feels better when they are in control of their feelings rather than when their feelings are in control of them.
- Give homework that involves practicing the strategies taught or solving the problem(s).
- Give the student concrete cues or reminders to help the student use the strategies that he or she has practiced.
- Remind the student that you will be checking in to make sure that things are going okay and that the student is able to maintain emotional control.
- Reward the student with positive praise when they are able to handle a difficult situation by remaining in control of their feelings and actions.

Adapted from Macklem (2010, p.139)

Conclusion

In this chapter, we presented a number of universal interventions that can be provided by educators in the classroom and some of these require more study or training than others. However, providing universal mental health interventions does not always have to be particularly complicated, nor does it rely on intensive, multistep programs. Instead, it can be as simple as getting to know more about the personal lives of students and listening to their concerns. For example, a third grade teacher—Kyle Schwartz, in Denver, Colorado—sparked a movement after asking her students to share their struggles. She had been a teacher for three years and most of her students came from underprivileged backgrounds, with 92 percent qualifying for free and reduced lunch. She wanted to understand a bit more about their personal lives so she created a lesson plan, which she called, "I wish my teacher knew . . . " She asked her students to write down one thing they wanted to tell her but would not normally tell her in class. The responses she received were poignant and some were heartbreaking. The first note she received was from a student who said, "I don't have pencils at home to do homework." Another student spoke about missing her father. She wrote, "I wish my teacher knew how much I miss my dad because he got deported to Mexico when I was 3 years old and I haven't seen him in 6 years." Another wrote, "I wish my teacher knew sometimes my reading log is not signed because my mom is not around." Another girl wrote, "I wish my teacher knew I don't have a friend to play with me."

Since this activity, Ms. Schwartz has not only learned a lot more about her students, but she has seen a change in how they interact with each other. After the girl shared that she did not have anyone to play with at recess, the teacher arranged it so that the class would reach out, and the next day the girl was playing with a group of girls. Moreover, the teacher was able to ensure that her students received the necessary school supplies to succeed in class (retrieved from: www.dailymail.co.uk/news/article-3042711/I-wish-teacher-knew-don-t-pencils-home-homework-heartbreaking-letters-graders-wrote-teacher-eye-opening-lesson.html).

As a caveat, even if we use the most evidence-based strategies and programs to improve students' mental health, if we do not first reach out to students and listen with receptive ears, we will not hear of their struggles. Consequently, we must ask, listen, and care in order to understand the challenges that children are dealing with on a daily basis; only then will these mental health interventions have the power to improve children's lives.

References

Bagby, R. M., Joffe, R. T., Parker, J. D. A., Kalemba, V., & Harkeness, K. L. (1995). Major depression and the five-factor model of personality. *Journal of Personality Disorders, 9,* 224–234.

Barnes, K. J., Vogel, K. A., Beck, A. J., Schoenfeld, H. B., & Owen, S. V. (2008). Self-regulation strategies of children with emotional disturbance. *Physical & Occupational Therapy in Pediatrics, 28*(4), 369–387.

Beach, S. R. (2014). 8 ways to teach mindfulness to kids. Retrieved from: www.huffingtonpost.com/sarah-rudell-beach-/8-ways-to-teach-mindfulness-to- kids_b_5611721.html.

Bennett, B. (2007). Creating a school community for learning and healing. *The New Educator, 3*(4), 323–334.

Blackwell, L. S., Trzesniewski, K. H., & Dweck, C. S. (2007). Implicit theories of intelligence predict achievement across an adolescent transition: A longitudinal study and an intervention. *Child Development, 78*(1), 246–263.

Broderick, P. C., & Frank, J. L. (2014). Learning to BREATHE: An intervention to foster mindfulness in adolescence. *New Directions for Youth Development, 2014*(142), 31–44.

Burke, C. A. (2010). Mindfulness-based approaches with children and adolescents: A preliminary review of current research in an emergent field. *Journal of Child and Family Studies, 19*(2), 133–144.

Centers for Disease Control and Prevention (2013). *Mental health surveillance among children – United States, 2005–2011.* 62(Suppl 2). Washington, DC: U.S. Department of Health and Human Services, Centers for Disease Control and Prevention.

Cizek, G. J., & Burg, S. S. (2006). *Addressing test anxiety in a high-stakes environment.* Thousand Oaks, CA: Corwin Press.

Colvin, G. (2008) *Talent is overrated. What really separates world class performers from everybody else.* London: Penguin Books.

Costello, E. J. Angold, A., Burns, B. J. Stangl, D. K. Tweed, D. L. Erkanali, A., & Worthman, C. M. (1996). The Great Smoky Mountains Study of Youth. Goals, design, methods, and the prevalence of DSM-III-R disorders. *Archives of General Psychiatry, 53,* 1129–1136.

Davis, E. L., & Levine, L. J. (2013). Emotion regulation strategies that promote learning: Reappraisal enhances children's memory for educational information. *Child Development, 84*(1), 361–374.

Doll, B., & Cummings, J. A. (2008). Why population-based services are essential for school mental health, and how to make them happen in your school. In B. Doll & J. A. Cummings (Eds.), *Transforming school mental health services: Population-based approaches to promoting the competency and wellness of children* (pp. 1–22; A joint publication with the National Association of School Psychologists). Thousand Oaks, CA: Corwin Press.

Doll, B., Cummings, J. A., & Chapla, B. A. (2014). Best practices in population-based mental health services. In P. L. Harrison & A. Thomas (Eds.), *Best practices in school psychology: System-level services* (pp. 149–163). Bethesda, MD: National Association of School Psychologists.

Duckworth, A., & Gross, J. J. (2014). Self-control and grit related but separable determinants of success. *Current Directions in Psychological Science, 23,* 319–325.

Duckworth, A. L., Peterson, C., Matthews, M. D., & Kelly, D. R. (2007). Grit: Perseverance and passion for long-term goals. *Journal of Personality and Social Psychology, 92,* 1087–1101.

Duckworth, A. L., Kirby, T. A., Tsukayama, E., Berstein, H., & Ericsson, K. A. (2011). Deliberate practice spells success: Why grittier competitors triumph at the National Spelling Bee. *Social Psychological and Personality Science, 2,* 174–181.

Dweck, C. S. 2006. *Mindset.* New York: Random House.

Edelmann, R. J. (1992). *Anxiety theory, research and intervention in clinical and health psychology.* New York: Wiley.

Erford, B. T., & Moore-Thomas, C. (2004). Testing FAQ: How to answer questions parents frequently have about testing. In J. E. Wall & G. R. Walz (Eds.), *Measuring up: Assessment issues for teachers, counselors, and administrators* (pp. 535–555). Greensboro, NC: ERIC Clearinghouse on Counseling and Student Services.

Ericcson, K. A., Krampe, R. T., & Tesch-Romer, C. (1993). The role of deliberate practice in the acquisition of expert performance. *Psychological Review, 100,* 363–406.

Eskreis-Winkler, L., Shulman, E. P., Beal, S. A., & Duckworth, A. L. (2014). The grit effect: Predicting retention in the military, the workplace, school and marriage. *Frontiers in Psychology, 5,* 1–12.

Flook, L., Goldberg, S. B., Pinger, L., & Davidson, R. J. (2015). Promoting prosocial behavior and self-regulatory skills in preschool children through a mindfulness-based kindness curriculum. *Developmental Psychology, 51*(1), 44–51.

Goleman, D. (1995). *Emotional intelligence: Why it can matter more than IQ.* New York: Bantam Books.

Good, C., Aronson, J., & Inzlicht, M. (2003). Improving adolescents' standardized test performance: An intervention to reduce the effects of stereotype threat. *Journal of Applied Developmental Psychology, 24,* 645–662.

Goonen, B. (2004). Overcoming test anxiety: Giving students the ability to show what they know. In J. E. Wall, & G. R. Walz (Eds.), *Measuring up: Assessment issues for teachers, counselors, and administrators* (pp. 257–272). Greensboro, NC: ERIC Clearinghouse on Counseling and Student Services.

Grossman, P. (2010). Mindfulness for psychologists. Paying kind attention to the perceptible. *Mindfulness, 1,* 87–97.

Gunderson, E. A., Gripshover, S. J., Romero, C., Dweck, C. S., Goldin-Meadow, S., & Levine, S. C. (2013). Parent praise to 1-to 3-year-olds predicts children's motivational frameworks 5 years later. *Child Development, 84,* 1526–1541.

Harris, D. (2014). *10% Happier: How I tamed the voices in my head, reduced stress without losing my edge, and found self-help that actually works.* New York: Harper Collins.

Hill, K. T., & Wigfield, A. (1984). Test anxiety: A major educational problem and what can be done about it. *Elementary School Journal, 85,* 106–126.

Hoagwood, K., & Johnson, J. (2003). A public health framework: From evidence-based practices to evidence-based policies. *Journal of School Psychology, 41,* 3–21.

Hoerr, T. R. (2013). *Fostering grit: How do I prepare my students for the real world?* Danvers, MA: ASCD.

Hooker, K. E. & Fodor, I. E. (2008). Teaching mindfulness to children. *Gestalt Review, 12*(1), 75–91.

Joyce-Beaulieu, D. J., & Sulkowski, M. L. (2015). *Cognitive behavioral therapy in k-12 schools: A practitioner's workbook.* New York: Springer.

Kabat-Zinn, J. (1990). *Full catastrophe living: Using the wisdom of your body and mind to face stress, pain, and illness.* New York: Delacorte.

Kabat-Zinn, J. (2003). Mindfulness-based interventions in context: Past, present, and future. *Clinical Psychology: Science and Practice, 10,* 144–156.

Kataoka, S. H., Zhang, L., & Wells, K. B. (2002). Unmet need for mental health care among US children: Variation by ethnicity and insurance status. *American Journal of Psychiatry, 159,* 1548–1555.

Lazarus, P. J. (2012, February). *Advocating for the emotional well-being of our nation's youth.* Presidential keynote address presented at the annual convention of the National Association of School Psychologists. Philadelphia, PA.

Lazarus, P. J., & Lazarus, J. (2006, March). *Managing children's anxiety in a high-stakes environment.* Paper presented at the annual convention of the National Association of School Psychologists. Anaheim, CA

Macklem, G. L. (2010). *Practitioner's guide to emotion regulation in school-aged children.* New York: Springer

Metz, S. M., Frank, J. L., Riebel, D., Cantrell, T., Sanders, R. & Broderick, P. C. (2013). The effectiveness of the learning to BREATHE program on adolescent emotion regulation. *Research in Human Development, 10*(3), 252–272.

Miller, A. (2014). 5 steps to foster grit in the classroom. Retrieved from: www.edutopia.org/blog/foster-grit-in-classroom-andrew-miller.

Mischel, W. (1974). Processes in the delay of gratification. In L. Berkowitz (Ed.), *Advances in experimental social psychology.* (Vol. 7, pp. 249–292). San Diego, CA: Academic Press.

Mischel, W., Shoda, Y., & Peake, P. K. (1988). The nature of adolescent competencies predicted by preschool delay of gratification. *Journal of Personality and Social Psychology, 54,* 687–696.

Nussbaum, A. D. and Dweck, C. S. 2008. Defensiveness vs. remediation: Self-theories and modes of self-esteem maintenance. *Personality and Social Psychology Bulletin, 34,* 127–134.

Renshaw, T. L. (2012). Mindfulness-based practices for crisis prevention and intervention. In S. E. Brock & S. R. Jimerson (Eds.), *Handbook of school crisis prevention and intervention* (2nd ed., pp. 401–422). Bethesda, MD: National Association of School Psychologists.

Renshaw, T. L., Bolognino, S. J., Fletcher, S. P., & Long, A. C. J. (2015). Using mindfulness to improve well-being in schools. *NASP Communiqué, 43*(6), 4, 6, 8.

Schonert-Reichl, K. A., Oberle, E., Lawlor, M. S., Abbott, D., Thomson, K., Oberlander, T. F., & Diamond, A. (2015). Enhancing cognitive and social–emotional development through a simple-to-administer mindfulness-based school program for elementary school children: A randomized controlled trial. *Developmental Psychology, 51*(1), 52–66.

Shoda, Y., Mischel, W., & Peake, P. K. (1990). Predicting adolescent cognitive and self- regulatory competencies from preschool delay of gratification: Identifying diagnostic conditions. *Developmental Psychology, 26,* 978–986.

Smail, P., Stockwell, T., Canter, S., & Hodgson, R. (1984). Alcohol dependence and phobic anxiety states: I. A prevalence study. *British Journal of Psychiatry, 144,* 53–57.

Sulkowski, M. L., Joyce, D. J., & Storch, E. A. (2013). Treating childhood anxiety in schools: Service delivery in a response to intervention paradigm. *Journal of Child and Family Studies, 21,* 938–947. doi: 10.1007/s10826-011-9553-1

Supplee, L. H., Skuban, E. M., Trentacosta, C. J., Shaw, D. S., & Stoltz, E. (2011). Preschool boys' development of emotional self-regulation strategies in a sample at risk for behavior problems. *The Journal of Genetic Psychology, 172*(2), 95–120.

Turner, B. G., Beidel, D. C., Hughes, S., & Turner, M. W. (1993). Test anxiety in African American school children. *School Psychology Quarterly, 8,* 140–152.

Twenge, J. M. (2000). The age of anxiety? Birth cohort change in anxiety and neuroticism, 1952–1993. *Journal of Personality and Social Psychology, 79,* 1007–1021.

Von Culin, K. R., Tsukayama, E., & Duckworth, A. L. (2014). Unpacking grit: Motivational correlates of perseverance and passion for long-term goals. *The Journal of Positive Psychology, 9,* 306–312.

Wigfield, A., & Eccles, J. S. (1989). Test anxiety in elementary and secondary school students. *Educational Psychologist, 24,* 159–183.

Wyman, P. A., Cross, W., Brown, C. H., Yu, Q., Tu, X., & Eberly, S. (2010). Intervention to strengthen emotional self-regulation in children with emerging mental health problems: Proximal impact on school behavior. *Journal of Abnormal Child Psychology, 38*(5), 707–720.

Yeager, D. S., & Dweck, C. S. (2012). Mindsets that promote resilience: When students believe that personal characteristics can be developed. *Educational Psychologist, 47,* 302–314.

Yeager, D. S., & Walton, G. (2011). Social-psychological interventions in education: They're not magic. *Review of Educational Research, 81,* 267–301.

Yeager, D. S., Trzesniewski, K. H., & Dweck, C. S. (2013). An implicit theories of personality intervention reduces adolescent aggression in response to victimization and exclusion. *Child Development, 84,* 970–988.

Yeager, D. S., Miu, A. S., Powers, J., & Dweck, C. S. (2013). Implicit theories of personality and attributions of hostile intent: A meta-analysis, an experiment, and a longitudinal intervention. *Child Development, 84*(5), 1651–1667. doi:10.1111/cdev.12062

Yeager, D. S., Trzesniewski, K. H., Tirri, K., Nokelainen, P., & Dweck, C. S. (2011). Adolescents' implicit theories predict desire for vengeance after peer conflicts: Correlational and experimental evidence. *Developmental Psychology, 47,* 1090–1107.

Yeager, D. S., Johnson, R., Spitzer, B. J., Trzesniewski, K. H., Powers, J., & Dweck, C. S. (2014). The far-reaching effects of believing people can change: Implicit theories of personality shape stress, health, and achievement during adolescence. *Journal of personality and social psychology, 106,* 867–884.

Zeman, J., Cassano, M., Perry-Parrish, C., & Stegall, S. (2006). Emotion regulation in children and adolescents. *Journal of Developmental & Behavioral Pediatrics, 27*(2), 155–168.

6   Resilient Classrooms and Targeted and Intensive Interventions

Resilience has been defined as "good outcomes in spite of serious threats to adaptation or development" (Masten, 2001, p. 228). Basically, resilience is the ability to persist in the face of challenges and to bounce back from adversity. Based on decades of research on this topic, a movement has started that involves creating classrooms that foster student resilience. Resilient classrooms have been described as "places where all children can be successful emotionally, academically and socially" (Doll, Brehm, & Zucker, 2014, p. 7). This approach emphasizes that educators can deliberately create resilient classrooms by designing healthy environments for learning that enhance students' academic skills and foster their social-emotional well-being. Thus, this approach focuses on "changing classrooms, not kids" (Doll et al., 2014, p.7).

The focus of this chapter is to help educators create classroom conditions that promote resilience in *all* children and to ensure that students who are most at-risk to experience negative school and life outcomes get the additional support they need. The first half of the chapter focuses on what educators can do to create supportive classroom environments at the Tier I or universal service-delivery level, which involves promoting resilience in *all* students. As such, the beginning of this chapter can be considered a continuation of the notions in Chapter 5 that relate to providing universal interventions in schools. The second half of the chapter discusses how to deliver Tier II and Tier III mental health interventions that are designed to help *at-risk* students. As previously discussed in Chapter 5, the first tier represents interventions for all students in the school. The second tier focuses on delivering selected or targeted interventions to high-risk students. The third tier is geared toward the delivery of indicated and intensive services to those students requiring comprehensive supports.

Fostering Resilience

Reivich and Gillham (2010) note that three primary sets of circumstances require resilience: steering through the everyday stressors that most students confront such as academic pressures or social pressures, overcoming risk factors such as having a parent with mental illness, and recovering from adversity or trauma such as the loss of a parent or a natural disaster. Yeager and Dweck (2012) call "resilient" any behavioral, attributional, or emotional response to an academic or social challenge that is positive and beneficial for development (e.g., seeking new strategies, putting forth greater effort, solving conflicts peacefully). In addition, they describe any negative or not beneficial response to a challenge as being not resilient (e.g., helplessness, giving up, cheating, aggressive retaliation, p. 302). It is important to note that resilience is mediated by one's perspective or mindset. In this regard, Olson and Dweck (2008) report that resilience involves not only the presence of social, environmental, and academic hardships that determine an individual's response to adversity but also a person's interpretations of these events.

Risk and Protective Factors

Several *risk* factors exist that compromise healthy development. These factors include premature birth, maltreatment, parental illness or psychopathology, divorce, homelessness, incarceration of a parent, death of a family member, sexual abuse, and natural disasters (Filetti et al., 1998; Glantz & Johnson, 1999; Masten, Best, & Garmezy, 1990). However, several *protective* factors—qualities of the individual and the environment—also exist that buffer against risk factors and contribute to healthy development. In an extensive review, Matsen and Reed (2002) identify within-individual, within-family, and within-community protective factors. Within-individual protective factors include having an easy temperament in infancy and adaptability in childhood and adolescence; strong self-regulation skills; strong cognitive abilities and problem-solving skills; optimism and hope; positive self-perceptions and self-efficacy; a sense of faith and meaning; a good sense of humor; talents valued by the individual and others; and being seen as appealing to others. Fortunately, several of these protective factors can be cultivated. More specifically, factors such as self-efficacy, self-regulation, and optimism can be enhanced through skills-based training (Reivich & Gillham, 2010). In contrast, other protective factors such as having an easy temperament and a good sense of humor have been found to be difficult to influence through training.

In addition to within-individual factors, within-family factors have also been shown to impact resilience. These include a having a warm parenting style, having structured family interactions, and setting clear expectations (i.e., authoritative parenting). Additionally, having close relationships among family members and low discord between parents have been found to influence children's resilience. Other protective factors in the family include parental involvement in a child's education, socioeconomic advantage, and having parents with cognitive and personality strengths (e.g., optimism, self-regulation). Thus, children's resilience can benefit through family-level factors, even if they lack some within-person resiliency factors.

Walsh (2006) also identified other specific characteristics that resilient families share. These include finding meaning in adversity; being able to flexibility adapt to change; being open to emotional sharing; having connectedness and pulling together in times of crisis; maintaining clarity in regard to consistent and honest communication; engaging in collaborative problem solving; and finding and experiencing transcendence and spirituality, which involves having beliefs and values that offer meaning, purpose, and connections beyond personal lives and troubles (Pisano, 2014; Walsh, 2006). Again, similar to within-individual resiliency factors, some of these factors—such as parenting style—can be enhanced or taught, whereas others are less likely to be influenced through training (Reivich & Gillham, 2010).

As a third level of influence, within-community factors also impact resilience. For example, individuals who experience poverty (especially abject poverty) and live in neighborhoods that experience high levels of violence are more likely to experience mental health problems (Leventhal & Brooks Gunn, 2000; Margolin & Gordis, 2000). Youth who grow up in these high-risk environments are much more likely to end up in juvenile detention facilities, prison, and even die or be injured by violence than are youth who grow up in communities with more financial and social resources. To illustrate, Caputo (2014) found that nearly half of Chicago's 2,389 homicide victims—1,118—were under the age of 25. These statistics were collected from 2008 through 2012 and published by the *Chicago Reporter* in a series that was entitled: "Too Young to Die." Furthermore, of the young people who had been murdered, nearly 500 were 18 or younger and more than eight out of ten of those school-aged children were killed in the neighborhood where they lived, which tended to be racially segregated and poor. This report is available at http://chicagoreporter.com/homicides-chicago-down-number-children-killed-stays-same. For additional information, Jill Leovy's book, *Ghettoside* (2015), details the violence crisis that has impacted South Los Angeles, a crisis that, similar to the one in Chicago, places impoverished youth at an elevated risk of being injured or murdered.

In addition, a copious body of research now exists that highlights the impact not just of single risk experiences, but of cumulative risk (e.g., Dube et al., 2003; Dube et al., 2009; Felitti et al., 1998; Masten & Powell, 2003). In other words, regardless of the level of impact, risk and resiliency is determined by a preponderance of risk and protective factors as opposed to a single indicator. Moreover, a wide body of research supports a dose relationship between the number of adverse childhood experiences and adverse mental health and physical health outcomes that individuals experience. Moreover, in the most extreme of cases, a robust relationship exists between the number of adverse childhood experiences and early death (see Chapter 3 for further discussion).

One practical way to imagine the influence of protective factors and cumulative risk on a student's success is displayed in the following example. Imagine a group of children trying to trek 20 miles in the woods while carrying a backpack. Most of the children have their backpacks filled with all the requisite supplies such as food, water, sunscreen, a first aid kit, etc. and they have on the proper clothing and footwear (i.e., protective factors). Now imagine one child who starts out the trek without sufficient water, food, clothing, proper shoes and other supplies. Moreover, each adverse childhood experience (i.e., significant risk factor) the child has endured adds 20 additional pounds to his backpack. This child is at a distinct disadvantage compared to his peers. Not only does he lack the resources to complete the trek successfully, he also is carrying an additional burden along the journey. It is unlikely that he can keep up—or even walk—without the necessary resources, especially if he is carrying the weight of one, two, three or perhaps four adverse experiences. Simply stated, in order for this child to be successful, he needs to have his load lightened, acquire the necessary resources, and get the support of others to help carry his burden.

As noted by the Center on the Developing Child at Harvard University (2015), how individuals respond to stressful experiences varies dramatically, but extreme adversity always generates serious problems that require treatment. They report that "irrespective of constitutional strengths or the availability of supportive relationships that help build capacities to deal with a wide range of challenges or threats, extreme adversity can rarely be weathered without harm" (p. 6). Therefore, these youth will need significant interventions in order to succeed in school. They need educators, school-based mental health professionals, and others to help lighten the load and carry the burden. They need Tier II and Tier III interventions that will be discussed later in the chapter.

Fostering Resilience in Students

Decades of research in the behavioral and social sciences have produced evidence that children who do well despite serious hardships have at least one stable and committed relationship with a supportive parent, caregiver, or other adult (Center on the Developing Child at Harvard University, 2015). These relationships buffer children from developmental disruption and help them build capacities, such as adaptability, which enables them to respond to adversity and thrive. The combination of supportive relationships, adaptive skill building, and positive experiences help children develop resilience. In discussing implications for public policy and program direction, the Center on the Developing Child at Harvard University (2015) has emphasized that

> all prevention and intervention programs would benefit from focusing on combinations of the following factors: (1) facilitating supportive adult-child relationships; (2) building a sense of self-efficacy and perceived control; (3) providing opportunities to strengthen adaptive skills and self-regulatory capacities; and (4) mobilizing sources of faith, hope, and cultural traditions.
>
> (p. 10)

These four factors are discussed in the following to provide more specific direction for educators.

Supportive Adult–Child Relationships

Decades ago, Julius Segal (1988) coined the term "charismatic adult." He emphasized that children who overcome adversity and become resilient do so because of the presence in their lives of a charismatic adult. By this, Segal meant that a charismatic adult is a person from whom a child gathers strength (Brooks, 2012). When individuals who had difficult childhoods were asked to reflect on what helped them persevere and what factors contributed to their later success, the almost universal response was that there was at least one adult in their lives who steadfastly supported and believed in them (Brooks, 2012). This concept is well supported by the research literature. Despite the widespread belief that individual self-reliance, extraordinary grit, or some heroic strength of character can help children triumph over adverse childhood experiences or calamity, science now informs us that it is the reliable presence of at least one supportive relationship and multiple opportunities for developing effective coping skills that enable children to be successful in the midst of adversity (Center on the Developing Child at Harvard University, 2015).

Certainly, no educator can be a charismatic adult for every child. In fact, some of the most troubled students may need an entire student support team that is comprised of several caring adults to address their needs. Yet, as a general principle, it is exceedingly important to find ways to let children and adolescents know that they are special and appreciated. This is even truer for students who are angry, sullen, vulnerable, aggressive, and/or unpopular. Words and actions that communicate acceptance and encouragement can be uplifting, especially for students who are carrying too heavy of a burden on their own. Rather than only acknowledging high grades, educators can recognize a special talent, an act of kindness, a display of courage, a positive attribute, or an effort to improve academic skills or behavior. Some examples might include: "Nathaly, I loved your use of intense colors in your drawings. Your work is something special." "Sean, I liked how you made sure that everyone was included in the kickball game." "Tiffany, I noticed that when some of your friends said, 'let's not be friends with Rose anymore,' you told them that wasn't cool." "Yesenia, you have great posture. You look poised and ready to learn." "Annela, you improved on your spelling exam this week. You must have studied harder." "Silvana, I can tell that you are really paying attention by the questions you ask." Teachers can give encouragement out loud or deliver these words to the student in a personal note. Consistent with the adage that everybody's favorite sound is hearing their own name, educators should directly praise a student by using their name.

Self-Efficacy and Perceived Control

One way to build a *sense of self-efficacy* is by providing students with opportunities to contribute to others. The experience of making a positive difference in people's lives reinforces self-efficacy and self-respect. Robert Brooks (2015), a noted author and lecturer on resilience, reports that, when giving workshops, he asks his audience to reflect back on the most positive experience they had during their K-12 school years and the most frequent response he receives is having the opportunity to make a contribution. Some school examples Brooks (2002) provides involve engaging in charitable projects, contributing to a committee, beautifying the school, becoming buddies with a new student, and tutoring peers. Engaging in charitable projects could include raising money for children impacted by a disaster, helping out families in need, participating in a race or a walk for a worthy cause/organization, serving in a food kitchen, etc. As a powerful example of forming a committee to encourage participation, Brooks (2002) discusses how a social worker formed a committee of five children who were often absent from school. Their task was to research the question of what prompted students to be absent. Not only did the student committee prepare a written report of their findings but the students recommended that the school keep track of all the first graders who were often absent and to intervene early to help them. As a result, the attendance records of all the five students improved significantly as they all had a new reason to come to school.

When he was a principal, Brooks (2002) found that asking students to engage in school beautification by decorating school walls was a strong deterrent to vandalism. Even if students are willing to vandalize a wall in a school, they may hesitate to do so if the act would involve defacing a peer's artwork. Becoming buddies with new peers also is an effective way for youth to contribute to the school environment. As an example of how this can be done, Brooks (2002) describes how fifth grade students can be enlisted to become buddies with first grade students. They would spend time with the younger students by reading to them, helping them with their homework, or playing or coaching them in a sport. As a result, an atmosphere of cooperation permeated the school. Finally, engaging in peer tutoring is an excellent way to increase students' sense of competence and belonging. As reported by the Carnegie Council on Adolescent Leadership (Hornbeck, 1989), the Valued Youth Partnership Program was developed to reduce school dropout. The Carnegie report stated:

> A rise in tutors' self-esteem is the most notable effect of the program. . . . As a result, only 2 percent of all tutors have dropped out of school. This is remarkable, given that all of these students had been held back twice or more, and were reading at least two grade levels below their current grade placement.
>
> (p.47)

In addition, as a result of this program, the attendance of tutors soared, their grades improved, and their disciplinary problems became less severe.

One way to provide students a sense of perceived control is to have a teacher and students develop classroom rules and consequences together. This conjoint rule-making process gives students a sense of ownership. Moreover, students are more likely to remember and abide by rules that they have helped create. See Chapter 11 for information on effective behavior management strategies. Teachers also can give their class choices in order to increase students' perceived control. For example, when doing homework, if there are 20 math problems on the page the teacher could ask the students to select ten problems to complete. In a history class, six questions could be presented and students could work in small groups and select three to answer. Alternatively, students could be given a choice of what day of the week to take certain tests.

Adaptive Skills

One way to strengthen students' adaptive skills is by finding their "islands of competence." The term "islands of competence" was coined by Brooks (1999) to counteract the metaphor of seeing youth drowning in a sea of self-perceived inadequacy. To counteract this dismal image, he authored the term "island of competence" to instead portray an image of personal development and pride. Brooks noted that this image was not intended to illustrate mere wishful thinking; rather it was intended to stand as a "symbol of hope and respect, a reminder that all children have unique strengths and courage" (Brooks, 2002, p. 76).

The Case of Billy

To convey this concept, Brooks (2002) describes a young boy, Billy, who was referred to him for consultation and therapy. Brooks arranged to visit the boy at school, and when he arrived, he found an angry and depressed student hiding behind in the school bushes. Billy informed Brooks that he liked the bushes better than school. Rather than debating with the youth, Brooks asked him what he liked and was good at doing (i.e., what Billy perceived to be his island of competence). With alacrity, Billy responded that he liked to take care of his pet dog. With Billy's permission, Brooks mentioned this to the school principal and suggested that the school needed a pet monitor. As a result, the principal brought Billy into the office and told him that the school needed an able student to monitor all of the school's pets. The principal then inquired about Billy's interest in helping fulfill this important role. Billy beamed and happily accepted the job. However, Billy's new responsibilities required that he come to school early to check on the animals, a responsibility of which he happily complied. Later, after Billy settled into his role as the school's pet monitor, Billy's teacher was so impressed with the change in his behavior and attitude that she asked him to write a manual about how to take care of school pets. When Billy replied that he was not good at writing, the teacher offered to help and they worked together on the manual. Later that year, Billy gave a talk in every classroom about taking care of animals and his pet care manual was placed in the school library. Chapter 8 lists additional strategies for increasing feelings of school connectedness and engagement. See Chapter 5 for information on improving self-regulatory capacities.

Before moving on to the topic of cultural awareness and competence, in Expert Interview 6.1 with Sam Goldstein, Ph.D. he discusses suggestions for parents and teachers on how to foster resiliency in youth. This interview also covers why some young people are resilient when confronting adversity whereas others are not. Dr. Goldstein also discusses the research on characteristics of resilient children, the relationship between resilience and mental health and whether or not coping skills should be included in the school curriculum.

Expert Interview 6.1 with Sam Goldstein

Adjunct Assistant Professor, Department of Psychiatry, University of Utah

PJL. What are the most significant characteristics of resilient children?

SG. Resilient children possess certain qualities and/or ways of viewing themselves and the world that are not apparent in children who have not been successful in meeting challenges and pressures. Resilient children can translate this view or mindset into effective action. They are hopeful, possess high self-worth, and feel special and appreciated in the eyes of others. They have learned to set realistic goals and expectations for themselves. They have developed the ability to solve problems and make decisions effectively. Thus, they are able to view mistakes, hardships, and obstacles as challenges to confront rather than stressors to avoid. They are able to rely on productive coping strategies, and foster growth rather than defeat. They acknowledge and recognize their weaknesses and vulnerabilities but also appreciate their strengths and talents. They understand how to harness these strengths and talents to overcome their adversities. Their self-concept is filled with images of strength and competence. They possess effective interpersonal skills with peers and adults. They can seek out assistance and nurturance in a comfortable, appropriate manner from adults able to provide needed support. Finally, resilient children are able to define the aspects of their lives over which they have control and to focus their energy and attention on these rather than on factors over which they have little if any influence.

PJL. Is resilience something you either have or don't have, or can resilience be learned?

SG. The concept of resilience defines a process of education and parenting, essential to prepare children for success in all areas of their future lives. The phenomenon of resilience is biopsychosocial. That is, some individuals are genetically endowed and have parents that foster resilience, such as Anne Frank. They simply are more optimistic even in the face of challenging adversities. However, biology is not destiny. Through day in and day out interactions, parents and educators are able to strengthen children's abilities to be resilient and to meet life's challenges with thought-fulness, confidence, purpose, and empathy. Every interaction with a child provides an educational opportunity to help the child weave a strong and resilient personal fabric. Though in the class-room the outcome of specific activities is important, even more vital are the lessons learned from the process of dealing with each issue, assignment, or problem. The knowledge gained provides the nutrients from which the seeds of resiliency develop and flourish.

PJL. What seems to make some young people resilient in the face of difficult circumstance whereas others are not?

SG. Though some children are temperamentally more optimistic and stress hardy, numerous scientific studies have demonstrated that the day in and day out interactions children have with the adults in their lives foster a resilient mindset and enhance their ability to cope with stress, adversity, and problems more effectively.

PJL. What is the relationship between resilience and mental health?

SG. Given the complexity of our species and the culture we have created, the relationship between resilience and mental health is complex and multi-directional. The mental health, developmen-tal, behavioral challenges children face do not have single or simple etiologies or solutions. All appear to arise from a complex interaction of biological, environmental, and cognitive influences. Further, all of these influences to some extent are idiosyncratic to the individual. Resilience explains in part why some children cope better with challenges and adversities and demonstrate better mental health despite these phenomena. As such, resilience can be best viewed as a protec-tive factor in the face of mental health challenges.

PJL. What suggestions might you have for parents who are trying to rear resilient children?

SG. Though children come into this world with their own unique temperaments, parents are able to strongly influence whether a child will develop the characteristics and mindset associated with resilience or whether they will be burdened with low self-worth, self-doubt, and a diminished sense of hope. Developing a resilient mindset in today's society is not a luxury but an essential compo-nent for a successful future. Parents hope for happiness, success in school, and satisfaction in their children's lives. They would like their children to develop solid friendships and transition happily and healthily into adult life. To reach these goals, children must develop the inner strength to deal competently and successfully day after day with the challenges and demands they encounter. This capacity to cope and feel competent we call resilience. Parents begin this process by appreciating ten critical guideposts, obstacles, and strategies to foster resilience in their children. The guideposts are:

1. Listening effectively and actively.
2. Practicing empathy in all interactions.
3. Accepting children for who they are and helping them to set realistic expectations and goals.
4. Loving children in ways that help them feel special and appreciated.
5. Helping children experience success by identifying and reinforcing their islands of competence.
6. Helping children recognize that mistakes are experiences from which to learn.
7. Teaching children to solve problems and make decisions.
8. Disciplining in ways that promote self-discipline and self-worth.
9. Helping children develop the skills to modify and change the adverse, repetitive interactions they often have (negative scripts).
10. Helping children develop responsibility, compassion, and a social conscience by providing them with opportunities to make contributions.

PJL. How can educators help foster resilience in children and adolescents?

SG. Teachers can and do have a powerful role in children's ability to cope with adversity and enhance resiliency. First and foremost, they must avail themselves of the science and general knowledge available concerning resilience. Second, they must be provided with opportunities to learn to apply these behaviors and qualities in their daily interactions with students.

Teachers can help all students feel special and appreciated, creating traditions and special times in the classroom. In doing so, this conveys to students that they are important. Teachers should also not miss significant occasions in the classroom, including birthdays. Teachers should be demonstrative with positive attention and work to build up as opposed to chip away at children. Feedback about errors is important but feedback and support for success is even more important. Teachers must also help children feel accepted for who they are. The best way to help children change self-defeating behaviors is to create an atmosphere in which children feel safe, secure, and willing to take risks. It is therefore critical that teachers make adjustments in classroom assignments and expectations based upon children's capabilities.

Teachers must also nurture students' islands of competence by enjoying and celebrating their accomplishments and emphasizing students' input in creating success. Teachers should also take the time to help children develop strengths and appreciate and acknowledge the unique strengths of each student. Teachers must also help children learn to cope with mistakes by serving as a model for dealing with mistakes and setbacks, emphasizing that mistakes are not only accepted but expected, and are necessary for growth. Finally, teachers should avoid providing contingent reinforcement only for success and instead should reward effort and serve as a model of responsibility, caring for all students.

PJL. Should teaching resilience be something that is included in a school's curriculum?

SG. In many ways, resilience is synonymous with good coping. Good coping or stress hardiness should absolutely be included as part of the social, emotional curriculum provided to students in all grades.

Cultural Awareness and Competence

Culture includes the shared ideas, symbols, values, and beliefs among members of a group. It can encompass any of the following categories: race, ethnicity, language, socioeconomic status, disability, sexual orientation, gender identity, and religious/spiritual identity (Banks & McGee Banks, 2004). According to Jones (2014), culture is the lens through which people view the world. Consequently, culture affects everything people do, think, and feel in any given day.

The U.S. is becoming a more culturally diverse society, especially as this relates to the racial and ethnic composition of the nation. According to the 2010 census, minorities account for 37 percent of the total population (U.S. Census Bureau, 2010). In 2010, Hispanic/ Latino(a), African American, Asian, and Native American/American Indian individuals accounted for 22 percent, 14 percent, 4 percent, and 1 percent of the school-age population (5–17 years of age) respectively. In addition, children with two or more races made up 3 percent of the population, and for the first time in 2011, racial and ethnic minorities constituted more than half of all children born in the United States (U.S. Census Bureau, 2012). Therefore, in light of these demographic estimates, it is critically important for educators to display cultural competence, which has been described as "the ability to work effectively with people from a variety of cultural, ethnic, economic, and religious backgrounds often different from themselves" (Miranda, 2014, p. 13).

Self-Awareness

To help all students, educators must develop cultural competence. The tripartite model for developing cultural competence is often recommended and consists of three dimensions: *self-awareness, knowledge*, and *skills* (Miranda, 2014). First, in order to understand another culture, educators must understand their own culture and how it impacts their worldview. For Caucasians this stage requires individuals to examine their own values, beliefs, assumptions and personal biases in regard to ethnic minorities. Ultimately, this process requires openness and a capacity for self-reflection.

According to Miranda (2014), there are at least five steps in developing cultural self-awareness. First, one needs to acknowledge one's personal biases and prejudices. Second, a person must be aware that there are cultural standards, beliefs, and attitudes that differ from one's own. The third step is respecting and valuing cultural diversity. The fourth step is a willingness to move past one's comfort level and reach out to engage more fully with different cultural groups. And the final step in the self-awareness process is developing a comfort level in novel situations with different minority populations.

Knowledge

Learning about the worldview, traditions, customs, beliefs, and values of different cultures is essential. In the following are a few ways to do this. An educator can read biographies, fiction, and nonfiction and see movies, plays, and television shows to learn about different cultures. An individual can gain valuable knowledge through an immersion experience or by participating in the daily life of another culture. An educator can engage in deep conversations with a cultural mediator who is a person from a different cultural group. Often, people are generally willing to share their experiences if they believe that the individual inquiring about their culture is genuinely interested (Miranda, 2014). Most importantly, an educator can just ask students about their beliefs, attitudes, and experiences and show a sense of curiosity, appreciation, and respect. This is not only an excellent way to learn about different cultures but it also helps connect with students from diverse communities.

Application

Applying knowledge in a culturally sensitive way and communicating through a cultural lens helps students feel appreciated and also fosters resilience. One way for educators to show they appreciate the diverse cultural experiences of their students is to engage in supportive educational activities in the classroom. For example, educators can have students bring in food (if allowed) that is indigenous to their culture. Students can give presentations that inform their classmates of their heritage. This might include discussing language, culture, religion, traditions, celebrations, dance, art, literature, and music of their culture. Discussions can center on both similarities and differences of various cultures. Teachers and students can research, discuss, and/or give reports on the unique contributions of different cultural and ethnic groups, and guest speakers from the community can present to the class.

The works of individuals who are diverse in terms of culture, ethnicity, language, religion, gender, and sexual orientation can be highlighted and the unique contributions of people with disabilities can be discussed. In addition, educators can actively work to reduce stereotype threats in the classroom. The term stereotype threat refers to being at risk of confirming, as self-characteristic, a negative stereotype about one's group (Steele & Aronson, 1995). For example, if a girl is told or socialized to believe that boys are better at math, she will be more likely to score lower on a math test—not because of her ability level—but because of being influenced by a stereotype threat. Therefore, educators can focus on how women have been critical leaders in science, technology, engineering, and math (STEM) fields to help reduce the surreptitious and negative effects of stereotype threat. Of course, many other stereotype threats exist and this is just a single example of what educators can do to help reduce barriers to learning and optimal performance in the classroom. The importance of mobilizing sources of faith and hope will be discussed in Chapter 18. In addition to the previously discussed strategies, Text Box 6.1 lists additional ways that teachers can foster resilience.

Text Box 6.1 Some Strategies to Foster Resilience in Students

- Be that one stable supportive adult in a child's life. Be that educator from whom a child can gather strength.
- Help children find positive meaning in a negative event by asking them to reflect on what they learned through the setback, what they can work on to do better in the future, and to recognize what went well, even if the overall outcome was not what they wanted.
- Make sure that students get enough physical exercise. Physical activity can alter brain structure and function, while also reducing the expression of pro-inflammatory genes.
- Focus on each student's islands of competence and find at least one positive thing to say about each child regardless of their abilities. This lets each student know that they are special in some way. For example, for students who have difficulties with academics, teachers can say, "I love your smile." "You truly put a lot of effort into this work. People that work hard are successful in life." "I appreciate your kindness." "You are curious, which is a great trait to have." "You certainly know how to make your classmates laugh." "You are so good at making friends." "I like the way you don't give up." "I noticed that your work has improved in math, and each day you will get just a little bit better at it."
- Tell students that you are going to give them a challenge that requires that everyone work together to solve a problem or complete a task. Celebrate each group's accomplishments. For the group that finished last, applaud their persistence. Tell them that they worked longer, and they never gave up. Make sure that if there is a long race in school, such as the one mile run, mandate that all the students that finish early stand at the finish line and cheer those still running.
- Have students in upper grades tutor students in lower grades. This enables older students to know that they can help another student learn which increases their sense of self- efficacy and helps the younger student feel that they have a buddy who will support them.
- Help support a growth mindset. When students say, "This is too hard or I can't do this" the teacher can respond with "It is too hard now, and you can't do this yet. But you can learn every day, and eventually you will be able to accomplish this task."
- Give out praise or accolades for most improved or for good effort.
- Read stories about individuals who, despite all odds, became successful. Ask students to research famous people who overcame great obstacles in their lives such as Helen Keller, Louis "Louie" Zamperini, and Oprah Winfrey.
- Discuss writers who were rejected for their manuscripts but never gave up. For example, Margaret Mitchell received 38 rejections from publishers before finding one to publish her novel, *Gone With The Wind*. It sold 30 million copies. After 23 rejections, Frank Herbert finally landed a publisher, and *Dune* became the best science fiction novel of all time. Stephen King once wrote, "The nail in my wall would no longer support the weight of the rejection slips impaled upon it. I replaced the nail with a spike and just kept on writing," http://www.litrejections.com/best-sellers-initially-rejected/.
- Encourage students and families to develop shared activities that create a sense of meaning and to set goals for engaging in these activities on a regular basis.
- Encourage students to write diaries, logs, or journals or create art work, songs, or plays following a group hardship. For example, in the aftermath of a tornado that partially demolished their school, students in Kissimmee, FL, created a play about the event, and months later the school chorus performed a medley of songs at the annual convention of the National Association of School Psychologists.
- Create support groups for students who have had setbacks such as a divorce or death in the family or have suffered significant losses due to a natural disaster.

Resilient Classrooms and Classroom Supports

Three lines of research have guided efforts to design resilient classrooms (Doll et al., 2014). The first focused on results from longitudinal research on how children develop competencies in the midst of adversity (Doll & Lyon, 1998; Masten, 2001). Essentially, these studies involved tracking children across time to determine what within-child, within-family and within-community characteristics predict life success (e.g., educational attainment, employment, financial independence, and social adjustment). It is interesting to note that the best predictors of success in children have been found to be within-family and within-community factors—not within child characteristics (Doll et al., 2014; Werner, 2013).

The second line of research on how to design resilient classrooms focused on evaluating programs that aim to support students that have been impacted by poverty. Students in these programs often are from communities that have been impacted by violence, have limited access to health care, and experience high rates of family stress and discord. Consistent with this line of research, several programs have established efficacy such as the School Development Program (Comer, Haynes, Joyner, & Ben-Avie, 1996), the Primary Mental Health Project (Cowen et al., 1996) and Success for All (Slavin & Madden, 2001). Although these programs are all slightly different in their aims and the populations with whom they have been applied, they all focus on strengthening personal relationships among members of the community, family, and school.

The third line of research with the same goals that were established above examined the education of children with disabilities. This line of research included data that are germane to one out of every 11 children attending public schools in the U.S. (U.S. Department of Education, 2010). Much of this research examined how children with disabilities learn and socialize in regular education classrooms. Doll et al. (2014) focused on regular education classrooms because students with disabilities typically spend 80 percent of the school day in this environment (U. S. Department of Education, 1999). In general, research in special education settings has demonstrated that students with disabilities capacity to learn can be improved when classmates support, help, and befriend them; when they are provided with instruction that focuses on their own personal strengths; when they are taught to apply the academic content in meaningful ways; and when they are assigned to teachers who have been described as caring and nurturing (Johnson, Johnson, & Anderson, 1983; Pullin, 2008; Reschly & Christenson, 2006). Moreover, the social integration of students with disabilities improves when the social environment supports frequent peer interaction with non-disabled classmates (NRC/IOM, 2004). From their review of the literature in each of these three lines of research, Doll et al. (2014) identified six characteristics of classrooms that enable children to be successful academically, socially, and emotionally. These are listed in Table 6.1.

Table 6.1 Six Characteristics of Resilient Classrooms

1. Students perceive themselves as competent and effective learners.
2. Students develop academic self-determinism; that is, they set and work hard toward self-selected learning goals.
3. Students behave according to expectations set by the school and only require a minimal amount of adult supervision.
4. There are nurturing and supportive relationships between teachers and students.
5. Students have emotionally fulfilling and ongoing relationships with their classmates.
6. Families are aware of and strengthen the learning that happens in school.

Source: Doll et al. (2014, pp. 8–9).

Note
Basically, there are two links that connect students to their classroom communities. The first link emphasizes the self-agency of the students, which includes autonomy, self-regulation, and self-efficacy (characteristics 1–3). The second link emphasizes caring and connected relationships among members of school communities (characteristics 4–6)

In Expert Interview 6.2, Beth Doll, Ph.D. discusses how to identify and prioritize a school's mental health needs, how to create and manage a nurturing school environment, and how to provide population-based mental health services that support all children. She also discusses how schools can strengthen protective factors in their students, what teachers can do to promote positive peer relationships, and how to help ignored and rejected students.

Expert Interview 6.2 with Beth Doll

University of Nebraska-Lincoln

PJL. What are some strategies that you have found to be most successful in identifying and prioritizing a school's mental health needs?

BD. Two aspects of my strategies are important: (1) The most successful strategies are simple, so that the assessment of mental health needs doesn't overpower interventions to promote mental health; and (2) their foundation is in reliable data that provide the school with useful answers to 10 or 12 carefully targeted questions. It is important, too, that the targeted questions are framed around the solid tradition of developmental research. Stretching back more than 60 years, developmental risk research has identified the positive supports that are highly predictive of psychological wellness (Werner, 2013) and developmental epidemiological research has described the unexpected prevalence of childhood disturbances and mental disorders (Centers for Disease Control, 2013). Consequently, operational definitions of mental health need to describe the presence of psychosocial competence as well as the absence of disorder.

With these as my organizing principles, I have found that the students are an untapped resource for planning and decision-making. I build my profile of a school's mental health needs around their answers to a few strategically planned questions about their satisfaction with their relationships with adults and peers; the adequacy of the relationship between their families and the school; and their experiences with anxiety, mood, conduct problems, and self-regulation. These are the factors that predicted children's success despite the odds in longitudinal studies of developmental risk and resilience. These surveys are almost effortless to collect in this era of computer administered survey tools. Students have told me that surveys like these should be anonymous, but I am torn between two options. Anonymous student surveys make it impossible to follow up with specific students who indicate high needs for support; however, identifiable student surveys will discourage some students from responding frankly and so the results are somewhat less accurate.

Student surveys are not the only relevant data sources for planning. Teachers or other staff can also contribute to a profile but their information is second-hand (based on observations of and experiences with students) and they are describing what they believe students are experiencing; and while students are often absent, school staff are typically in the room when plans are made for mental health services so it is less urgent that staff perceptions be captured in data. There may also be school records that inform mental health profiles – such as attendance records, playground discipline notes, or office referral records. Still, if these are not reliably kept, it may be more time-consuming to collate and enter these records into databases than to simply computer-administer a survey.

The central challenge in prioritizing mental health needs is balancing the urgency of competing needs for services with the high prevalence of some needs within a school. I typically draft these out on a two-dimensional matrix, and I prioritize mental health services in the very urgent/very prevalent quadrant. That said, some options for mental health supports are very low in cost and have very high impact, and such low cost/high benefit services will also become part of my planning.

PJL. What suggestions do you have for engaging parents in the process of supporting students' mental health?

BD. Parents are among the busiest people in our communities and when there are too many demands on their time, they prioritize—they do some things and not others. So that families put our mental health initiatives at the top of their "to do" lists, we need to pay attention to families' top priority: their kids. My most effective communications with families have been student mediated moments. If the students write a family newsletter, and the students' pictures and work are prominent, families read the newsletter. When students in a bereavement group invited their families to school, and the students planned their demonstrations for the family night, 80 percent of the parents attended. And when the parents attended, they participated. One more detail: my family work has been most effective when at least half of my communications with parents are celebrating their kids' accomplishments rather than focusing on their deficits.

PJL. How can educators create and manage a nurturing school environment?

Schools and educators need to start from a clear definition of what constitutes a "nurturing school environment." The National Research Council/Institute of Medicine (2004) nicely summarized this research and makes the clear case that two factors are important to the environment: the availability of warm and caring relationships among adults and students in the school; and supports for the students' emerging autonomy including their self-regulation and sense of self-efficacy. Caring teachers are not enough. As one middle school teacher explained, when we let students skip their homework because they don't have electricity at home to light their studies, we are unintentionally telling them that we don't expect any more of you. Caring has to be combined with high expectations and a commitment to helping students succeed. Other recent research has demonstrated that the absence of negativity is more critical than the presence of positive supports (Ang, 2005). Thus, above all else, we should do no harm.

In the past, our default was to assume that the social context operating in a school was positive unless there was evidence to the contrary. However, recent examinations have demonstrated that students do not necessarily speak up unless they are asked (Doll et al., 2014). As one example, when my daughter was a high school sophomore, a teacher/basketball coach was dismissed after he was found to have engaged in serial sexual relationships with several students in the school. I asked a car full of the students, "Did you know that this was happening?" Their immediate and cynical response was "Of course." "Everybody knew." "It was obvious." But it hadn't been obvious to the school administration.

Creating nurturing environments in a school has to be a shared endeavor. Teachers, students, and their families are co-responsible for making the school that they want to be part of. However, teachers and administrators must take the lead in engaging the full school in the task. This task begins by paying attention to the learning environment of a school. Next, check in with the students and ask them their experiences in the school, and what students or adults could do to make the school even better. I have used two alternative strategies for these check-ins: I have convened brief (35 minutes) and topically focused classroom meetings in which students identify classroom practices that are important to them and need to be continued, and pitfalls with a suggestion for fixing them. The *Resilient Classrooms* book (Doll et al., 2014) talks about ways to use classroom data to focus these meetings and build them into plans for change; the Child Development Project (1996) has structured instructions for classroom meetings in *Ways We Want Our Class to Be*. Alternatively, I have sometimes worked with a smaller student leadership group of 3–6 students who co-direct a plan for examining the classroom environment and making suggestions for change. In some cases, it is possible to identify microchanges that are simple modifications in routines and practices (often suggested by students) that make important improvements to the classroom environment. Examples include creating a fair and mutually agreed-upon routine for the class to choose soccer teams, embedding a strategy that guides students through management of homework and classroom assignments, or changing the seat arrangements so that no one is sitting too close to the pencil sharpener. There is no risk in such minor modifications and, if student data or feedback shows that the environment improves, there may not be a need to implement more ambitious interventions.

PJL. How might schools strengthen protective factors in their students? Are there any well-known evidence-based programs that might help?

BD. Fortunately, we know a lot about which protective factors matter; the developmental risk and resilience research is one of the few areas of psychology with multiple studies, conducted across various continents and in different decades, but showing highly consistent results replicated across independent research groups (Werner, 2013). Students are successful despite the odds when they have positive friendships with peers, an internal locus of control, expect that they can succeed, value learning and believe that it is worth their while, are engaged in their communities, have a close bond with at least one parent or caretaker, are well nurtured by parents or another caretaker who steps in when parents are unable, have positive adults in their lives whom they respect and emulate, and attend effective schools. Schools that work to make these factors broadly available to their students are contributing to their success. A good strategy is to start with the protective factors that are most under the control of the school, and then gradually build in additional supports. I emphasize the use of data (student surveys, school records, work products) because data allow the school to figure out which protective factors are already strong (and not waste valuable time and attention on strengthening factors that are already strong) and attend to those protective factors that are inconsistent or weak. In some cases, minor modifications to school routines and practices can prompt important changes in the students' experiences of support. However, when these minor modifications are not sufficient, there are now many alternative manualized interventions that schools can adopt. Several manualized programs are described in the Chapter 8 of the *Resilient Classrooms* book (Doll, et al., 2014); examples include Second Step (Frey, Hirschstein, Guzzo, 2000), Promoting Alternative Thinking Strategies (Greenberg, Kusche, & Mihalic, 1998), Linking the Interests of Families and Teachers (Eddy, Reid, & Fetrow, 2000), Positive Action Program (Flay & Allred, 2003), and Coping Power (Lochman, Wells, & Lenhart, 2008).

PJL. What might teachers do to ensure that their individual classroom supports positive peer relationships?

There are four key classroom supports that help peers develop healthy and supportive relationships:

1. Provide students with many different opportunities to have fun doing things together with classmates—both classmates who are friends and classmates who are not yet friends. Sometimes allow the students to choose and other times assign partners. The "things" that they do can be work, peer tutoring, classroom chores, or other activities; it does not necessarily need to be playing together. Time spent having fun together is the currency of friendships and these opportunities create possibilities for more and different friendships in the class.

2. In classroom meetings, small discussions, or integrated into the curriculum, lead the class through decisions about the peer social norms that they expect in their classroom. Then once a decision is reached, write it down and post it somewhere prominent in the classroom. In the absence of prompts from adults, groups of students can drift into ways of treating each other that are thoughtless or self-absorbed. Small prompts and reminders are ways to shift the expectations in the class.

3. Assistance in repairing peer conflicts is sometimes more important than preventing the conflicts altogether. Developmentalists will tell us that peer conflicts are opportunities

for reduction of egocentrism, and that peers are "agents of mutual socialization." That is, peers help each other socialize. Thus, preventing conflicts altogether removes some of these opportunities for students to practice compromise, negotiation, and mediation. Alternatively, efforts that coach students through compromise and negotiation are providing essential life skills that students will need far into the future.

4. Many elementary classes are trapped into repeated and unrepaired conflicts—how to choose teams for soccer, how to react to minor teasing or taunts, what to do if a new student wants to join the group. These are prime opportunities to practice compromise, negotiation, and problem solving; leading the full class through decisions about solutions provides a valuable model for what students can do themselves, the next time they encounter a tough conflict.

It is always important to remember that mentally healthy adults are able to solve problems, make decisions, and regulate their own behavior so that they reach their goals. Classrooms promote students' wellness when they prompt students to be slightly more independent and self-determined than they were the year before.

PJL. Oftentimes, there are students that are either ignored or rejected by their classmates. How might teachers help ensure these youth are better accepted by their peers?

This has to be a two-pronged attack: it is important to build the peer acceptance within the full classroom group, but it is also important to strengthen the social competence of students who are isolated in the group. During classroom meetings with the peer group, I raise the topic of children's exclusion using a fictional story about children of similar age and situation. For example, with late elementary grades, I might show some clips from the video, "Stand By Me." Then I lead the class to problem solve: "Whose job is it to fix this—the kid, the class, or the adults? What could the kid do to fix this? What could the teacher do? What could the other kids in class do? And then, the pivotal question: How do we want our class to be, and what are we going to do to make that happen?"

Still, many neglected and rejected students are likely to be struggling with important deficiencies in social competencies. And so they may need help thinking through social situations (social cognition and social problem solving); they might have social anxieties; difficulties with social behaviors; struggle with empathy; or may need accommodations like game clinics on the playground that teach a small group new games to play. I sometimes use a friendship group to help isolated children set goals and plan strategies to make friends. (A brief curriculum for the group is in the appendices of the *Resilient Playgrounds* book; Doll & Brehm, 2010). It is sometimes useful to be on the playground or in the lunchroom when students are gathering together, and to surreptitiously coach or prompt isolated students to use their social strategies. (*"Remember, you planned to ask Rodrigo if you could join today's soccer game."*)

PJL. You have written about shifting from a conventional approach for providing psychological services that focuses only on individual problems to population-based services that support all students. Can you explain what you mean and why you see this as the best approach to take to support student mental health?

BD. My working definition of population-based mental health services has three key elements: (1) Identify and prioritize the mental health needs in a school—and use that data to develop a coherent plan for moving forward. (2) Use the entire school as an instrument to support students' psychological wellness and to prevent/remediate disturbances. Whole school contributions to mental health might include playground policies and the recess paraprofessional; classroom teachers; before and after school programs; or workgroups of kids. (3) Deliver a blend of school-wide, class-wide, small-group and individual services to meet the most pressing mental health needs and the most students.

I am not so naïve as to think that we can altogether stop focusing on individual services. However, it is clear that our schools and communities do not have sufficient mental health resources (people, money, time) to tackle the frequency and the urgency of children's mental health needs one child at a time. So, inherently, individually focused services translate directly into a large number of children with needs that are entirely unmet. That is unacceptable to me. For the same reason, I'm very committed to gathering needs assessment data to identify and to profile the mental health needs in a school. Traditionally, policy makers and mental health leadership have justified the constraints on mental health resources by arguing that other children did not have an urgent need for services. Once research emerged documenting the gap between the need for and availability of services, this rationale was clearly unsupported. And so I am committed to data-informed, population-based services.

PJL. What are the most important things you want educators to know about providing effective mental health services for all children?

BD. First, it is as much about promoting wellness as it is "fixing" or preventing disturbances. And support for the psychological resilience of children has been integral to child rearing practices since the beginning of civilization. Second, both nature and nurture contribute to children's psychological wellness and their psychosocial disturbances.

Targeted Interventions: Tier II

As previously discussed in Chapter 5, at the universal level of mental health service delivery or Tier I, schools can implement school-wide mental health supports such as changing mindsets, mitigating anxiety, teaching mindfulness, encouraging grit, and helping students modulate their emotions. Also at the Tier I level, educators can foster resilience, and create resilient and supportive classrooms. These supports are designed to benefit all students and they are not targeted toward any particular groups of students. Overall, the purpose of Tier I mental health supports is to bolster the emotional well-being of all students and prevent the development of mental health problems.

A key concept within a multi-tiered system of support (MTSS) mental health model is that the intensity of intervention should be matched to the severity of the concern with the focus and intensity increasing as the student moves from one tier to the next higher one. Unfortunately, many students do not adequately respond to Tier I, or universal interventions, and continue to display or develop mental health problems. These students need more targeted interventions or Tier II mental health supports (Sulkowski & Michael, 2014). Although no single model exists for delivering Tier II services within a mental health delivery system, compared to previous decades, schools across the U.S. are providing more of these services to meet the unique needs of the students they serve (Kutash, Duchnowski, & Lynn, 2006). Within a MTSS mental health model, Tier II services aim to both address emerging mental health problems as well as curtail their further development. Furthermore, the delivery of Tier II mental health services should match the unique needs of the student population as well as the availability of school resources (Vaillancourt, Cowan, & Skalski, 2013).

As perhaps the most common Tier II intervention for students with behavioral or mental health problems, group-based interventions (e.g., counseling, therapy) often are delivered by a school psychologist, social worker, or counselor to students who display extant or emerging risk factors (e.g., anxiety, depression, grief, anger problems, social skills deficits, few peer relationships; Sulkowski, Joyce, & Storch, 2012). These interventions generally are delivered to a small percentage of the school population (usually 10–15 percent) and they require consent from caregivers because they are not part of general education programming. Thus, it is important for members of student support teams to identify and select students who may benefit from group-based interventions and then structure intervention groups in a manner that ensures that all group members can succeed. Therefore, educators need to be able to screen in the "right" students to ensure that they benefit from a treatment while also screening out students that either do not need to participate in the group or could be highly disruptive to the progress of other group members. For example, it would be counter-therapeutic to include a student who displays highly disruptive oppositional or defiant behavior in a group of students who are learning social skills. This student would display negative social skills that encumber the progress of other members.

Different strategies exist for identifying students who can benefit from group-based interventions. In schools that implement universal screeners for emotional and behavioral problems, school-based mental health professionals could identify students with elevated scores on these measures and assess them more intensely to determine the nature of these problems. For example, a school psychologist could assess students scoring in the elevated range on a behavioral screener and then follow-up with an omnibus behavior rating scale such as the Behavior Assessment System for Children, Third Edition (BASC-3; Reynolds & Kamphaus, 2015). The BASC-3 is a commonly used measure that allows for a more in-depth understanding of students' emotional, behavioral, and mental health problems.

Teacher Referrals

Although not as reliable as identifying students through universal or whole-school screening, teacher referrals are a common approach to identifying students with behavior and mental health problems (Eklund et al., 2009; Eklund & Dowdy, 2014). Furthermore, other schools track students based on office discipline referrals or other strategies to identify students with disruptive behavior. However, these approaches are subject to teacher and administrator bias and they tend to under-identify large numbers of students such as those with internalizing behavior problems (e.g., anxiety, depression; Eklund & Dowdy, 2014; Sulkowski et al., 2012). In addition, waiting for teacher reports of disciplinary problems to emerge can result in missing early opportunities to identify students with significant behavioral, emotional, and mental health problems (Severson, Walker, Hope-Doolittle, Kratochwill, & Grasham, 2007). Therefore, it is important for school-based mental health professionals and educators to work together to help identify students who display less conspicuous forms of psychopathology such as anxiety as well as emerging behavioral problems. Even if schools do not use universal screeners, then it is still recommended that schools use the aforementioned strategies to identify students with troubling behaviors. That is, it is better to identify a proportion of the students who require supports, than none at all. Chapter 13 discusses signs of emotional and behavioral problems in students.

Several studies support the efficacy of group-based interventions for various forms of emotional, behavioral, and mental health problems. For example, research supports the use of group-based cognitive-behavioral therapy (CBT) for treating childhood anxiety, depression, mild social skills problems, and anger and aggression problems (Clarke, Rohde, Lewinsohn, Hops, & Seeley, 1999; DeRosier, 2004; Lochman & Wells, 2004; Masia-Warner, Fisher, Shrout, Rathor, & Klein, 2007). Cognitive-behavioral therapy aims to reduce maladaptive thoughts and behaviors as well as teach more effective ways of thinking, acting, and managing emotions (Joyce-Beaulieu & Sulkowski, 2015). In addition to addressing specific forms of psychopathology, group-based intervention groups also help support students who experience more general adjustment issues such as making and keeping friends, getting along with others, and displaying appropriate behavior across different contexts. Further, these interventions can help students who display risk factors that make them more susceptible to developing mental health problems. For example, preliminary research supports the potential for group-based interventions to improve peer acceptance and the inclusion of vulnerable students such as students with physical disabilities (Frederickson & Turner, 2003).

Newly developed, evidence-based computerized intervention programs also display utility for helping at-risk students who could benefit from Tier II services. As a salient example of one such program, the Camp Cope-A-Lot (CCAL; Khanna & Kendall, 2008), a computerized therapy program, has been specifically designed to address childhood anxiety and related concerns such as social skill problems. Camp Cope-A-Lot includes six computer-assisted anxiety-reductive therapy sessions that can be followed with six therapist-directed exposure therapy sessions and is designed for use with children and youth. Although more research is needed on CCAL, results from one study on the efficacy, feasibility, and likeability of CCAL (Khanna & Kendall, 2010) found that 81 percent of youth who received CCAL had greater reductions in their anxiety compared to youth in a control condition at post-treatment. Considering these positive findings and the potential for computerized intervention programs to reach greater numbers of students, these types of interventions may become a key way that schools can provide students with Tier II mental health supports (Sulkowski et al., 2012).

Intensive Interventions: Tier III

Students who do not respond effectively to Tier I or Tier II mental health supports and interventions need increasingly intense support in the form of Tier III mental health interventions. Tier III mental health services can involve providing individualized therapy or counseling to students with mental health problems such as individualized CBT (Sulkowski et al., 2012). Currently, compared to other forms of psychotherapy, CBT has the strongest empirical support and the greatest current potential to help students in school settings who are in need of Tier III mental health support (Joyce-Beaulieu & Sulkowski, 2015). Students in need of Tier III services can be identified by their lack of response to previously tried interventions or if they have already displayed marked emotional, behavioral, or mental health problems such as a diagnosable psychiatric disorder, an Emotional Disturbance (ED) special education classification, or a manifested serious adjustment problem, such as bereaving the loss of an important caregiver (Wright & Sulkowski, 2013). Thus, students who likely would benefit from Tier III mental health supports already are experiencing considerable psychosocial distress and functional impairments in their academic, social, and family functioning. These students may experience episodes of significant distress, negative mood, or self-loathing; refuse to attend school; be fearful or afraid when they are there; display frequent and severe behavior problems; have difficulty making and keeping friends; and frequently receive disciplinary write-ups, suspensions, and expulsions.

Empirical support for CBT is extensive (Kendall 2011), even for use in school settings by appropriately trained mental health professionals. More specifically, research supports the use of CBT to help students with Attention-Deficit/Hyperactivity Disorder, Post-Traumatic Stress Disorder, Obsessive-Compulsive Disorder (OCD), Depression, and a range of anxiety disorders (Albano & Kendall, 2002; Creed, Reisweber, & Beck, 2011; Kendall, 2011; Masia-Warner et al., 2007; Mychailyszyn et al., 2011; Salloum, Sulkowski, Sirrine, & Storch, 2009). In addition, CBT has been successfully adapted across a broad array of school settings to help diverse student populations (Mychailyszyn, Méndez, & Kendall, 2010; Neil & Christensen, 2009). Further, research by Ginsburg, Becker, Kingery, and Nichols (2008) found that CBT was effective for helping highly at-risk populations of students in inner-city schools when it was delivered in school-based mental health clinics.

Unfortunately, however, not all school-based mental health professionals are well-prepared to deliver intensive or Tier III mental health supports such as CBT (Wright & Sulkowski, 2013). These individuals need to be trained adequately to deliver these interventions, often through seeking additional training and supervised practice (Mychailyszyn et al., 2010). In schools that do not have individuals who are trained in delivering intensive Tier III mental health interventions, community-based practitioners can be located and engaged through making appropriate referrals or developing partnerships. To locate these individuals, databases maintained by the

American Psychological Association (APA), the International Obsessive-Compulsive Disorder Foundation (IOCDF), the Anxiety and Depression Association of America (ADAA), and other professional psychological associations can be consulted. Lastly, in the absence of providing CBT or intensive interventions directly in school, it behooves members of school communities to reach out to community practitioners and collaborate to ensure that treatment gains generalize across settings (Sulkowski, Wingfield, Jones, & Coulter, 2011).

As a second promising individualized intervention that can support students who display intensive mental health needs, the use of solution-focused therapy (SFT) is increasing among school-based mental health professionals (Murphy, 2008). Solution-focused therapy is a relatively short-term intervention for various mental health problems that was developed for helping individuals in a few sessions. This therapeutic approach views people as experts in their own experience and it focuses on tapping into people's unique specific strengths and competencies that they can use to enhance the quality of their lives. Moreover, according to the SFT model, clients hold the key to their own solutions and success (Corcoran & Stephenson, 2000). Thus, with SFT, a therapist aims to assist clients to discover and tap into their past successes, employ adaptive resources, and utilize their strengths to create solutions to the problems they are facing.

Research support for SFT is far less robust than it is for CBT. Some studies suggest that SFT is an effective intervention for reducing mental health problems in students at school (Birdsall & Miller, 2002; Corcoran & Stephenson, 2000; Newsome, 2005; Young & Holdorf, 2003). However, the research support for SFT has been criticized for being built on studies that employ non-rigorous designs. For example, some researchers report that most SFT studies are limited in their use of standardized outcome measures, adequate baselines, control groups, or other experimental procedures (e.g., Franklin, Biever, Moore, Clemons, & Scamardo, 2001). Moreover, others contend that even when control groups are employed, study results may not generalize because of problems related to having small sample sizes, loose participation criteria, and poorly standardized intervention procedures (e.g., Coady, Stalker, & Levene, 2000). Thus, considerable more research is needed on the use of SFT, particularly in school settings as a Tier III intervention for students experiencing significant mental health problems.

Non-Responders to Intensive Interventions

Despite receiving intensive or Tier III interventions, some students still will not respond adequately to treatment and therefore may require alternative education placement or special education services. As a point of clarification, alternative education placement does not require the student to be classified with a disability; whereas a student must be classified with a disability to receive special education services. As seen in Figure 5.1 in the previous chapter, these are students with severe/chronic problems who require intensive community interventions with school support or intensive school interventions with community support. Often, these students suffer from extreme forms of psychopathology such as having psychotic symptoms and/or are classified as being Emotionally Disturbed (ED). In addition, these students also have frequently been impacted by multiple adverse life events and they may live in highly unstable homes or communities. For example, a student who attempted suicide and is highly emotionally disorganized or psychotic may require hospitalization and receive educational services in the hospital. After being stabilized, that same student may return to a self-contained classroom or school for students with severe ED. See Chapter 13 for information on psychopathology and special education classification and Chapter 14 for information on supporting highly at-risk and vulnerable student populations.

A group of students that have been found to be highly resistant to a traditional school-based behavioral or mental health approach is students who display psychotic symptoms (e.g., delusions, hallucinations, illusions). Although experiencing episodes of psychosis is not uncommon among students, severe and chronic childhood psychosis and schizophrenia is rare (see Chapter 13 for more information on childhood psychopathology). Therefore, most interventions for children with psychotic symptoms should focus on acute symptom remission and mental health stabilization. Inevitably, this will involve consulting with a psychiatrist who will likely treat the student with some form of antipsychotic medication, which shows efficacy in reducing psychotic symptoms. These students (depending on the level of stabilization) may also require small special education classes, family intervention, and a wide range of supports from school-based or community-based mental health professionals

To facilitate effective psychiatric consultation, Sulkowski, Jordan, and Nguyen (2009) discuss ways to overcome barriers that exist across school and medical settings. These include directly reaching out to physicians and describing how they can help facilitate positive mental health outcomes in students, working with district-level personnel to ensure that open communication is not hobbled by district policy or information-sharing laws, finding ways to compensate physicians for the time they invest in consultative services, clearly delineating the nature of services that will be provided to various students across settings, working out effective plans to assess and manage medication management plans, and proactively working out ways that school and medical providers can best support each other's efforts to help students. Because childhood psychosis is highly disturbing and potentially suggestive of the manifestation of greater psychosocial problems, this form of psychopathology often flummoxes educators and school-based mental health professionals. However, through consulting with medical professionals who are more familiar with low-incidence cases of psychopathology, educators and school-based mental health professionals can do a lot to support these students—students who often are treatment non-responders who need intensive services (De Maio, Graham, Vaughan, Haber, & Madonick, 2015).

Another group of students that have been found to be highly resistant to a traditional school-based behavioral or mental health approach includes students who display conduct problems. These students often are identified because of the highly aggressive, disruptive, manipulative, and antisocial behaviors they display at school and in other settings. Often these students get into trouble and display disregard for the rights and well-being of others. Thus, because of their antisocial and disruptive behavior and the negative impact it has on the school environment, it is critically important for members of school communities to intervene on the behalf of these students.

To address students with serious conduct problems or highly disruptive behaviors, some school districts have alternative schools or alternative school programs that are housed in schools. These schools usually have a smaller ratio of students to staff and they may have staff members with specific training in behavior modification and classroom management. See Chapter 11 for information on effective behavior management strategies. In addition, they may have more on-site, school-based mental health professionals. Unfortunately, however, despite these benefits, alternative schools still often are criticized for being overcrowded and understaffed. In fact, one study found that 33 percent of U.S. school districts reported being unable to enroll new students in alternative schools and programs because of staffing or space limitations (Carver & Lewis, 2010). In addition, another study found that students with conduct problems were disproportionately likely to drop out of school and that these students also generally did not respond to contemporary school-based interventions to help improve their behavior problems (Bierman at al., 2013). Therefore, room for great improvement exists with regard to helping students with conduct problems be successful in school and life.

One promising approach regarding the former is the delivery of multi-systemic therapy (MST). This form of therapy is a highly intensive, family-focused, and community-based treatment approach that usually is used for youth who display a history of conduct problems and violent behavior. The Family Services Research Center (FSRC) of the Department of Psychiatry and Behavioral Sciences at the Medical University of South Carolina is credited with developing MST and it includes some specific components. These include effective coordination between members of the school, community mental health and social service, juvenile justice, and family settings as well as the effective monitoring of the youth receiving treatment. In general, the over-all goals of MST are to reduce aggressive and violent behavior as well as to improve the youth's ability to make good decisions when choosing his/her peer group and to allow family members to be better able to monitor the youth's behavior. Research support for MST is favorable, as the treatment has been associated with reductions in violent behavior, substance abuse, and delin-quency, especially if the MST emphasizes developing healthy peer relationships and addresses risks and protective factors at school (van der Stouwe, Asscher, Stams, Deković, & van der Laan, 2014). For more information on MST, MUSC provides an overview of the treatment approach and its components: http://academicdepartments.musc.edu/psychiatry/research/fsrc/mst.pdf.

Conclusion

Within the past few decades there has been an accumulation of research on risk factors that compro-mise healthy development and protective factors that buffer against negative experiences and foster resilience. In order to promote resilience, all prevention and intervention programs should focus on "(1) facilitating supportive adult-child relationships; (2) building a sense of self-efficacy and per-ceived control; (3) providing opportunities to strengthen adaptive skills and self-regulatory capacities; and (4) mobilizing sources of faith, hope, and cultural traditions" (Center on the Developing Child at Harvard University, 2015, p. 10). Consistent with this recommendation and with an understand-ing of the factors that support resilience, a movement has recently emerged to take this knowledge beyond the three ecosystems of the individual, family, and community and extend it to creating classrooms and schools that promote healthy youth development (Doll et al., 2014). However, this goal can only be successfully achieved if creating nurturing school environments becomes a shared enterprise. Administrators, teachers, school-based mental health professionals, families, and stu-dents all need to be part of this process and take the information provided in this chapter and put it to work in classrooms and schools.

In addition to creating resilient classrooms at the Tier I level, there will always be students at higher risk for social-emotional and behavioral problems that require Tier II and III level interven-tions in order to succeed in school. In this regard, it is important for educators and school-based mental health professionals to work together to identify those students most at-risk and get them the help they need. Typically, students first receive Tier II interventions and if sufficient progress has not been made, then they receive additional supports at the Tier III level. Currently, CBT and SFT are seen as the best mental health interventions for high-risk students, with CBT having more empirical support. Moreover, there will be students who require even more intensive, ongoing interventions, which typically include special education or alternative education services. A group of students who may not respond to Tier III interventions are students who display psychotic symptoms. These youth will require intensive supports, small special education classes with a wide-range of assistance from mental health professionals, family interventions, and ongoing con-sultation with a psychiatrist who will most likely treat these youth with antipsychotic medications which shows efficacy in reducing psychotic symptoms. Another group of non-responders are often those youth with serious conduct problems or highly disruptive behaviors, for whom alter-native education programs or special education services are warranted. For students with a history of conduct problems and violent behavior, MST has shown promising results.

References

Albano, A. M., & Kendall, P. C. (2002). Cognitive behavioural therapy for children and adolescents with anxiety disorders: Clinical research advances. *International Review of Psychiatry, 14*, 129–134.

Ang, R. P. (2005). Development and validation of the teacher–student relationship inventory using explora-tory and confirmatory factor analysis. *Journal of Experimental Education, 74*, 55–73.

Banks, J. A., & McGee Banks, C. A. (Eds.). (2004). *Multicultural education: Issues and perspectives* (5th ed.). Hoboken, NJ: Wiley.

Bierman, K. L., Coie, J., Dodge, K., Greenberg, M., Lochman, J., McMohan, R., & Pinderhughes, E. (2013). School outcomes of aggressive-disruptive children: Prediction from Kindergarten risk factors and impact of the Fast-Track Prevention Program. *Aggressive Behavior, 39,* 114–130.

Birdsall, B., & Miller, L. (2002). Brief counseling in the schools: A solution-focused approach for school counselors. *Counseling and Human Development, 35,* 1–9.

Brooks, R. B. (1999). Fostering resilience in exceptional children. The search for islands of competence. In V. Schwean & D. Saklofske (Eds.), *Handbook of psychological characteristics of exceptional children* (pp. 563–586). New York: Academic/Plenun Publishers.

Brooks, R. B. (2002). Creating nurturing classroom environments: Fostering hope and resilience as an antidote to violence. In S. E. Brock, P. J. Lazarus, & S. R. Jimerson. (Eds.), *Best practices in school crisis prevention and intervention* (pp. 67–93). Bethesda, MD: National Association of School Psychologists.

Brooks, R. B. (2012). Stories about charismatic adults: Relationships that change lives. Retrieved from http://www.drrobertbrooks.com/monthly_articles/1212

Brooks, R. B. (2015). Resilience: The common underlying factor. Retrieved from http://www.drrobert brooks.com/monthly_articles/resilience-common-underlying-factor

Caputo (2014, April). Homicides in Chicago down, number of children killed stays the same. *Chicago Reporter.* Retrieved from http://chicagoreporter.com/homicides-chicago-down-number-children-killed-stays-same/

Carver, P. R., & Lewis, L. (2010). *Alternative schools and programs for public school students at risk of educational failure: 2007–08 (NCES 2010–026).* U.S. Department of Education, National Center for Education Statistics. Washington, DC: Government Printing Office.

Clarke, G. N., Rohde, P., Lewinsohn, P. M., Hops, H., & Seeley, J. R. (1999). Cognitive-behavioral treatment of adolescent depression: Efficacy of acute group treatment and booster sessions. *Journal of the American Academy of Child and Adolescent Psychiatry, 38,* 272–279.

Coady, N., Stalker, C., & Levene, J. (2000). A closer examination of the empirical support for claims about the effectiveness of solution-focused brief therapy: Stalker et al. respond to Gingerich. *Families in Society, 81,* 223–230.

Center on the Developing Child at Harvard University. (2015). *Supportive relationships and active skill-building strengthen the foundations of resilience: Working paper 13.* www.developingchild.harvard.edu.

Centers for Disease Control and Prevention (2013). *Mental health surveillance among children – United States, 2005–2011.* 62 (Suppl 2). U. S. Department of Health and Human Services, Centers for Disease Control and Prevention, Washington, DC.

Child Development Project (1996). Ways we want our class to be: Class meetings that build commitment to kindness and learning. Ideas from the Child Development Project. Oakland, CA. Developmental Studies Center.

Comer, J. P., Haynes, N. M., Joyner, E. T., & Ben-Avie, M. (1996). *Rallying the whole village: The Comer process for reforming education.* New York: Teachers College Press.

Corcoran, J., & Stephenson, M. (2000). The effectiveness of solution-focused therapy with child behavior problems: A preliminary report. *Families in Society, 81,* 468–474.

Cowen, E. L., Hightower, A. D., Pedro-Carroll, J. L., Work, W. C., Wyman, P. A., & Haffey, W. G. (1996). *School-based prevention for children at risk: The primary mental health project.* Washington, DC: American Psychological Association.

Creed, T. A., Reisweber, J., & Beck, A. T. (2011). *Cognitive therapy for adolescents in school settings.* New York, NY: Guilford Press.

De Maio, M., Graham, P., Vaughan, D., Haber, L., & Madonick, S. (2015). Review of international early psychosis programmes and a model to overcome unique challenges to the treatment of early psychosis in the United States. *Early Intervention in Psychiatry, 9,* 1–11.

DeRosier, M. E. (2004). Building relationships and combating bullying: Effectiveness of a school-based social skills group intervention. *Journal of Clinical Child and Adolescent Psychology, 33,* 196–201.

Doll, B., & Brehm, K. (2010). *Resilient playgrounds.* New York: Routledge.

Doll, B., Brehm, K., & Zucker, S. (2014). *Resilient classrooms: Creating healthy environments for learning, 2nd Edition.* New York: Guilford Publications.

Doll, B., & Lyon, M. (1998). Risk and resilience: Implications for the practice of school psychology. *School Psychology Review, 27,* 348–363.

Dube, S. R., Fairweather, D., Pearson, W.S., Felitti, V.J., Anda, R.F., & Croft, J.B. (2009). Cumulative childhood stress and autoimmune disease. *Psychological Medicine, 71,* 243–250.

Dube, S. R., Felitti, V. J., Dong, M., Chapman, D. P., Giles, W. H., & Anda, R. F. (2003). Childhood abuse, neglect, and household dysfunction and the risk of illicit drug use: The adverse childhood experiences study. *Pediatrics, 111,* 564–572.

Eddy, J. M., Reid, J. B., & Fetrow, R. A. (2000). An elementary school-based prevention program targeting modifiable antecedents of youth delinquency and violence: Linking the Interests of Families and Teachers (LIFT). *Journal of Emotional & Behavioral Disorders, 8,* 165–176.

Eklund, K., & Dowdy, E. (2014). Screening for behavioral and emotional risk versus traditional school identification methods. *School Mental Health, 6,* 40–49. doi: 10.1007/s12310-013-9109-1

Eklund, K., Renshaw, T. L., Dowdy, E., Jimerson, S. R., Hart, S. R., Jones, C. N., & Earhart, J. (2009). Early identification of behavioral and emotional problems in youth: Universal screening versus teacher-referral identification. *California School Psychologist, 14,* 89–95. doi: 10.1007/BF03340954

Felitti, V. J., Anda, R. F., Nordenberg, D., Williamson, D. F., Spitz, A. M., Edwards, V., & Marks, J. S. (1998). The relationship of childhood abuse and household dysfunction to many of the leading causes of death in adults: The adverse childhood experiences (ACE) study. *American Journal of Preventive Medicine, 14,* 245–258

Flay, B. R., & Allred, C. G. (2003). Long-term effects of the Positive Action® program. *American Journal of Health Behavior, 27,* S6-S21. doi:10.5993/AJHB.27.1.s1.2

Franklin, C., Biever, J., Moore, K., Clemons, D., & Scamardo, M. (2001). The effectiveness of solution-focused therapy with children in a school setting. *Research on Social Work Practice, 11,* 411–434.

Frederickson, N., & Turner, J. (2003). Utilizing the classroom peer group to address children's social needs an evaluation of the Circle of Friends intervention approach. *Journal of Special Education, 36,* 234–245.

Frey, K. S., Hirschstein, M. K., & Guzzo, B. A. (2000). Second step: Preventing aggression by promoting social competence. *Journal of Emotional and Behavioral Disorders, 8,* 102–112. doi:10.1177/106342660000800206

Ginsburg, G. S., Becker, K. D., Kingery, J. N., & Nichols, T. (2008). Transporting CBT for childhood anxiety disorders into inner-city school-based mental health clinics. *Cognitive and Behavioral Practice, 15,* 148–158.

Glantz, M. D., & Johnson, J. L. (Eds.) (1999). *Resilience and development: Positive life adaptations.* Dordrecht, Netherlands: Kluwer Academic Publishers.

Greenberg, M. T., Kusche, C., & Mihalic, S. F. (1998). *Blueprints for violence prevention: Promoting alternative thinking strategies.* Boulder: University of Colorado, Institute of Behavioral Science, Center for the Study and Prevention of Violence.

Hornbeck, D. W. (1989). *Turning points. Preparing American youth for the 21st century.* New York: Carnegie Council on Adolescent Development.

Johnson, D. W., Johnson, R. T., & Anderson, D. (1983). Social interdependence and classroom climate. *Journal of Psychology. 114,* 135–142.

Jones, J. (2014). *Best practices in providing culturally responsive interventions.* In P. L. Harrison & A. Thomas (Eds.), *Best practices in school psychology: Foundations* (pp. 49–60). Bethesda, MD. National Association of School Psychologists.

Joyce-Beaulieu, D. J., & Sulkowski, M. L. (2015). *Cognitive behavioral therapy in k-12 schools: A practitioner's workbook.* New York: Springer.

Kendall, P. C. (2011). *Child and adolescent therapy: Cognitive-behavioral procedures.* New York: Guilford Press.

Khanna, M. S., & Kendall, P. C. (2008). Computer-assisted CBT for child anxiety: The coping cat CD-ROM. *Cognitive and Behavioral Practice, 15,* 159–165. doi:10.1016/j.cbpra.2008.02.002

Khanna, M. S., & Kendall, P. C. (2010). Computer-assisted cognitive behavioral therapy for child anxiety: Results of a randomized clinical trial. *Journal of Consulting and Clinical Psychology, 78,* 737–745. doi:10.1037/a0019739

Kutash, K., Duchnowski, A. J., & Lynn, N, (2006). *School-based mental health: An empirical guide for decision-makers.* Tampa, FL: University of South Florida, The Louis de la Parte

Florida Mental Health Institute, Department of Child & Family Studies, Research and Training Center for Children's Mental Health.

Leovy, J. (2015). *Ghettoside. A true story of murder in America.* New York: Random House.

Leventhal, T., & Brooks-Gunn, J. (2000). The neighborhoods they live in: The effects of neighborhood residence on child and adolescent outcomes. *Psychological Bulletin, 126,* 309–337.

Lochman, J. E., & Wells, K. C. (2004). The coping power program for preadolescent aggressive boys and their parents: Outcome effects at the 1-year follow-up. *Journal of Consulting and Clinical Psychology, 72,* 571–578.

Lochman, J. E., Wells, K. C., & Lenhart, L. A. (2008). *Coping power: Child group facilitator's guide.* New York: Oxford University Press.

Margolin, G., & Gordis, E. B. (2000). The effects of family and community violence on children. *Annual Review of Psychology, 51,* 445–479.

Masia-Warner, C., Fisher, P. H., Shrout, P. E., Rathor, S., & Klein, R. G. (2007). Treating adolescents with social anxiety disorder in school: An attention control trial. *Journal of Child Psychology and Psychiatry, 48,* 676–686. doi:10.1111/j.1469-7610.2007.01737.x

Masten, A. S. (2001). Ordinary magic: Resilience processes in development. *American Psychologist, 56,* 227–238.

Masten, A. S., Best, K. M., & Garmezy, N. (1990). Resilience and development: Contributions from the study of children who overcome adversity. *Development and Psychopathology, 2,* 425–444.

Masten, A. S., & Powell, J. L. (2003). A resilience framework for research, policy, and practice. In S. L. Luthar (Ed.), *Resilience and vulnerability: Adaptation in the context of childhood adversities* (pp. 1–25). New York: Cambridge University Press.

Masten, A. S., & Reed, M. G. J. (2002). Resilience in development. In C. R. Snyder & S. J. Lopez (Eds.), *Handbook of positive psychology* (pp. 74–88). New York: Oxford University Press.

Miranda, A. H. (2014). Best practices in increasing cross-cultural competency. In P. L. Harrison & A. Thomas (Eds.), *Best practices in school psychology: Foundations* (pp. 9–19). Bethesda, MD. National Association of School Psychologists.

Murphy, J. J. (2008). *Solution-focused counseling in schools.* Alexandria, VA: American Counseling Association.

Mychailyszyn, M. P., Beidas, R. S., Benjamin, C. L., Edmunds, J. M., Podell, J. L., . . . Kendall, P. C. (2011). Assessing and treating child anxiety in schools. *Psychology in the Schools, 48,* 223–232. doi:10.1002/pits.20548.

Mychailyszyn, M. P., Mendez, J. L., & Kendall, P. C. (2010). School functioning in youth with and without anxiety disorders: Comparisons by diagnosis and comorbidity. *School Psychology Review, 39,* 106–121. doi:10.1002/pits.20548.

National Research Council and Institute of Medicine. (2004). *Engaging schools: Fostering high school students' motivation to learn.* Committee on Increasing High School Students' Engagement and Motivation to Learn; Board of Children, Youth, and Families; Division of Behavioral and Social Sciences and Education. Washington, DC: National Academies Press.

Neil, A. L., & Christensen, H. (2009). Efficacy and effectiveness of school-based prevention and early intervention programs for anxiety. *Clinical Psychology Review, 29,* 208–215.

Newsome, W. (2005). The impact of solution-focused brief therapy with at-risk junior high school students. *Children & Schools, 27,* 83–90.

Olson, K., & Dweck, C.S. (2008). A blueprint for social cognitive development. *Perspectives on Psychological Science, 3,* 193–202.

Pisano, M.C. (2014). Best practices in services to children in military families. In P. Harrison & A. Thomas (Eds.), *Best practices in school psychology: Foundations* (pp. 181–190). Bethesda, MD: NASP.

Pullin, D. C. (2008). Individualizing assessment and opportunity to learn: lessons from the education of students with disabilities. In P. A. Moss, D. C. Pullin, J. P. Gee, E. H. Haertel, & L. J. Young (Eds.), *Assessment, equity and opportunity to learn* (pp. 333–351). New York: Cambridge University Press.

Reivich, K., & Gillham, J. (2010). Building resilience in youth: The Penn Resiliency Program. *NASP Communiqué, 38,* 6.

Reschly, A. L., & Christenson, S. L. (2006). Prediction of dropout among students with mild disabilities: A case for the inclusion of student engagement variables. *Remedial and Special Education, 27,* 276–292.

Reynolds, C. R., & Kamphaus, R. W. (2015). Behavior Assessment System for Children, Third Edition. Pearson Education.

Salloum, A., Sulkowski, M. L., Sirrine, E., & Storch, E. A. (2009). Overcoming barriers to using empirically supported therapies to treat childhood anxiety disorders in social work practice. *Child and Adolescent Social Work Journal, 26,* 259–273. doi: 10.1007/s10560-009-0173-1

Segal, J. (1988). Teachers have enormous power in affecting a child's self-esteem. *The Brown University Child Behavior and Development Newsletter, 4,* 1–3.

Severson, H. H., Walker, H. M., Hope-Doolittle, J., Kratochwill, T. R., & Gresham, F. M. (2007). Proactive, early screening to detect behaviorally at-risk students: Issues, approaches, emerging innovations, and professional practices. *Journal of School Psychology, 45,* 193–223.

Slavin, R. E., & Madden, N. A. (2001). *Success for all: Research and reform in elementary education.* Mahwah, NJ: Erlbaum.

Steele, C. M., & Aronson, J. (1995). Stereotype threat and the intellectual test performance of African Americans. *Journal of Personality and Social Psychology, 69,* 797–811.

Sulkowski, M. L., Jordan, C., & Nguyen, M. L. (2009). Current practices and future directions in psychopharmacological training and collaboration in school psychology. *Canadian Journal of School Psychology, 24,* 237–244. doi: 10.1177/0829573509338616

Sulkowski, M. L., Joyce, D. K., & Storch, E. A. (2012). Treating childhood anxiety in schools: Service delivery in a response to intervention paradigm. *Journal of Child and Family Studies, 21,* 938–947. doi:10.1007/s10826-011-9553-1

Sulkowski, M. L., & Michael, K. (2014). Meeting the mental health needs of homeless students in schools: A multi-tiered system of support framework. *Children and Youth Services Review, 44,* 145–151. doi: 10.1016/j.childyouth.2014.06.014

Sulkowski, M. L., Wingfield, R. J., Jones, D., & Coulter, W. A. (2011). Response to intervention and interdisciplinary collaboration: Joining hands to support children's healthy development. *Journal of Applied School Psychology, 27,* 118–133. doi: 10.1080/15377903.2011.565264

U.S. Census Bureau. (2010). *National resident population estimates by race, Hispanic origin, and age: 2000 and 2009.* Washington, DC. Author. Retrieved from http://www.census.gov/compendia/statab/2012tables/12s0010.pdf

U.S. Census Bureau. (2012). *Most children younger than 1 are minorities.* Washington, DC. Author. Retrieved from http://www.census.gov/newsroom/releases/archives/population/cb12-90.html

U.S. Department of Education. (1999). *Twenty-first annual report to Congress on the implementation of the Individuals with Disabilities Act.* Washington, DC: Author.

U.S. Department of Education, Office of Special Education and Rehabilitative Services. (2010). *Twenty-ninth annual report to Congress on the implementation of the Individuals with Disabilities Education Act, 2007, Vol. 1.* Washington, DC: Author.

Vaillancourt, K., Cowan, K. C., & Skalski, A. K. (2013). *Advocating for comprehensive and coordinated school mental health services.* In J. D. Desrochers and G. Houck (Eds.), Depression in children and adolescents: Guidelines for school practice. Bethesda, MD: NASP.

van der Stouwe, T., Asscher, J. J., Stams, G. J. J., Deković, M., & van der Laan, P. H. (2014). The effectiveness of Multisystemic Therapy (MST): A meta-analysis. *Clinical Psychology Review, 34,* 468–481.

Walsh, F. (2006). *Strengthening family resilience* (2nd ed.). New York. Guilford Press.

Werner, E. E. (2013). What can we learn about resilience from large-scale longitudinal studies? In S. Goldstein & R. B. Brooks (Eds.), *Handbook of resilience in children* (pp. 87–104). New York, NY: Springer.

Wright, S., & Sulkowski, M. L. (2013). Treating childhood anxiety: How school psychologists can help. *Communiqué, 41,* 1 & 12.

Yeager, D. S., & Dweck, C. S. (2012). Mindsets that promote resilience: When students believe that personal characteristics can be developed. *Educational Psychologist, 47,* 302–314.

Young, S., & Holdorf, G. (2003). Using solution-focused brief therapy in individual referrals for bullying. *Educational Psychology in Practice, 19,* 271–282.

Part III
Supporting Nurturing Learning Environments

7 School Climate and Social Supports

Dostoyevsky's classic novel, *Anna Karenina*, begins with the famous words: "All happy families are alike; each unhappy family is unhappy in its own way." Similarly, all safe and supportive schools share similar characteristics; however, schools that fail in this regard do so in many different ways. According to the latest research, safe and supportive schools have a healthy school climate, which involves providing students with rich instruction, ample opportunities to interact with others, and the security they need to feel safe at schools, as well as social support from key peers, educators, caregivers, and other members of school communities (Cowan, Vaillancourt, Rossen, & Pollitt, 2013; Dwyer, Osher, & Warger, 1998; O'Malley & Eklund, 2012).

This chapter reviews the interrelated concepts of school climate and social support. More specifically, the quantity and quality of social supports help determine the climate of the school which influences school safety and students' academic achievement and emotional well-being. Additionally, an emphasis is placed on the importance of providing social supports and creating a positive school climate in order to enhance educational opportunities for children from low-income neighborhoods and inner city schools. Lastly, this chapter concludes with a section on enhancing social support and school climate for lesbian, gay, bisexual, transgender, and questioning students (LGBTQ), a population of students that traditionally has been neglected and subjected to hostile environments, and helping families headed by LGBT caregivers feel respected and welcome in schools.

Enhancing School Climate

Cohen, McCabe, Michelli, and Pickeral (2009) define "school climate" as "the quality and character of school life that is based on patterns of people's experiences of school life and reflects norms, goals, values, interpersonal relationships, teaching and learning practices, and organizational structures" (p. 182). Further, these authors describe a positive school climate as an environment in which people are engaged and respected. Thus, a positive school climate is one that fosters student development and learning in a way that is necessary for productive, contributive, and satisfying life in a democratic society. Moreover, a positive school climate allows for the existence of norms, values, and expectations that support people feeling socially, emotionally, and physically safe. In this environment "students, families, and educators work together to develop, live, and contribute to a shared school vision; and educators model and nurture an attitude that emphasizes the benefits of, and satisfaction from, learning" (p. 182). Cohen et al. (2009) also emphasize that school climate is more than an individual experience; it is a group phenomenon that reflects the character and quality of a school.

The Influence of School Climate

School climate has a critical and powerful influence on academic, social, and behavioral outcomes (Cohen et al., 2009). School climate also is a highly important factor that influences students' perceptions, attitudes, and behaviors (Ferrans & Selman, 2014). Overall, students who have positive perceptions of their school climate exhibit greater attachment to their school and have stronger academic values and feelings of academic competence (Blum, McNeely, & Rinehart, 2002; Roeser & Eccles, 1998; Roeser, Eccles, & Sameroff, 2000).

Research illustrates that responsive school climates are correlated with safe, caring, participatory, and effective risk-prevention and health-promotion efforts (Catalano, Haggerty, Oesterie, Fleming, & Hawkins, 2004). In addition, students who have positive views of their school's climate tend to feel more socially bonded and are less likely to experience emotional distress or attempt suicide (Catalano et al., 2004; Loukas & Robinson, 2004; McNeely, Nonnemaker, & Blum, 2002; Roeser, Eccles, & Sameroff, 2000). In contrast, the presence of a negative school climate is associated with elevated aggressive behavior among students (e.g., Aspy et al., 2004; Bond, Carlin, Thomas, Rubin, & Patton, 2001); substance abuse and weapon carrying behaviors (Coker & Borders, 2001; Kuperminc, Leadbeater, Emmons, & Blatt, 1997; Loukas & Robinson, 2004); and misconduct and delinquency (Battishtich & Horn, 1997; Gottfredson, Gottfredson, Payne, & Gottfredson, 2005).

The Phenomenology of School Climate

Types of School Climate

The pioneering work of Diana Baumrind (1966) provides a framework to understand the construct of school climate. As a developmental researcher, she noted that parenting practices (also called parenting styles) are the patterns of discipline and affection that parents display with their children. Baumrind (1966) described these practices as falling along two distinct dimensions: control and responsiveness. Control is considered the manner and strictness with which parents impose limits and discipline their children. On the other hand, responsiveness is concerned with acceptance, caring, and affection. Thus, control describes the behavioral aspects of parenting, whereas responsiveness describes the emotional aspects of this process. Lastly, Baumrind described four parenting practices: uninvolved, permissive, authoritarian, and authoritative practices that involve different degrees of responsiveness and control.

Baumrind's (1966; 1991) parenting styles have been applied to describe school environments or climate. To date, four different types of school climate have been described and researched: negligent, permissive, authoritarian, and authoritative (e.g., Chaux, 2012; Ferrans & Selman, 2014; Hughes, 2002). Out of these styles, the authoritative style has been associated with the most favorable outcomes for students. Negligent environments tend to be low in nurturing teacher–student relationships and have poor structure and order, whereas permissive environments are described as having nurturing teacher–student relationships yet they do not have clear and consistent rules for safety in place. In authoritarian environments, teachers do not establish supportive relationships and instead focus on maintaining strict order, whereas in authoritative environments teachers create caring relationships with students while simultaneously establishing order with clear and consistently enforced rules (Ferrans & Selman, 2014).

Recent studies have explored four school-level indicators reflective of students' perceptions of school climate: safety, order, care, and empowerment. As might be expected, schools that are perceived as being safe, orderly, caring, and empowering by students have the most desirable student-related outcomes (Ferrans & Selman, 2014). Schools with the aforementioned characteristics fit the definition of an authoritative school environment and are effective at helping students fulfill their personal needs for safety, order, connection, support, and power (Chaux, 2012; Ferrans & Selman, 2014).

School Climate and Safety

In the Safe Schools Initiative, a study conducted by the U.S. Secret Service, 37 cases of school shootings were analyzed with the goal of identifying a profile of school shooters in an effort to create safer schools (Fein et al., 2002). Although the results of the study failed to identify a typical profile for school shooters, it did reveal that at least one person knew about the attacker's plan yet did not report the threat to an adult in the majority of shootings. As noted by Lazarus (2001), a number of reasons these concerns went unreported have been identified. These included the person(s) who knew about the shooter's plan (a) did not take the threat seriously; (b) did not want to get the potential shooter in trouble; (c) felt obligated to maintain the code of silence that often separates students from faculty and staff; (d) feared being perceived as a snitch; (e) feared being ostracized or harmed by friends or peers; (f) feared being retaliated against by the student who threatened violence; (g) believed that they would not be taken seriously, that nothing would be done, or that school authorities would be ineffective in their response; or, most disturbing of all, (h) they wanted to be part of the plot, sought revenge on fellow classmates and/or faculty, and wanted to create chaos in the school. These concerns were in some way related to students' trust in adults, their feeling of safety and protection by authorities, their sense of being part of a caring community, and their sense of having power to make a difference. Collectively, these concerns are all integral components of school climate.

The finding that at least one student had prior knowledge of an impending attack in the majority of researched school shootings is especially poignant because it implies that many of these attacks could have been prevented if this knowledge was shared with a responsible adult. Consequently, this finding encouraged Pollack, Modzeleski, and Rooney (2008) to interview 15 individuals who had prior knowledge of a school shooting threat to determine what factors influenced their decision about whether or not to report their knowledge of the threat. Of the 15 individuals interviewed, six attended schools in which the shooting was prevented and nine attended schools where the threat was carried out. The interviews revealed that the students' perceptions of school climate predicted their willingness to report threats of violence to adults. Essentially, students who reported threats endorsed having a positive relationship with at least one adult in their school and they claimed that the relationship greatly influenced their decision to report. Additionally, students who reported threatening students also stated that they trusted that school officials would handle the situation appropriately. However, in contrast, those who did not trust school officials to respond effectively to a potential threat expressed reluctance to report the threat. Thus, as a promising approach to reducing risk for serious incidents of violence, schools can work to promote a positive, nurturing, and authoritative school climate. Chapter 15 goes in depth regarding threat reporting and violence prevention.

Similar patterns of behavior have been noted in studies that have investigated less severe forms of school violence such as bullying. More specifically, teacher disciplinary practices and the way they treat students have been found to influence students' decision to either take action against bullies or be passive bystanders (Ferrans & Selman, 2014; Ferrans, Selman, & Feigenberg, 2012). Additionally, Ferrans and Selman (2014) found that students report that they chose not to intervene when witnessing bullying because they did not believe it was their business and they did not believe that their teachers would respond appropriately if they were notified. These attitudes were reportedly shaped by the treatment students received from their teachers and the perceived norms set by the climate of the school. Students were less likely to take action and confide in an adult if they perceived that their teachers were uncaring or hostile, or if their school had a history of using inconsistent or punitive discipline. Students attributed the cultural norms of the school to the way teachers handled similar situations in the past, implying that students modeled their teachers' behavior. That is, if teachers did not intervene when they witnessed bullying, then it was unlikely that students would do so on their own accord.

Further supporting the important dynamic between teachers' and students' behavior, a recent study by Yoon, Sulkowski, and Bauman (2014) found that teachers who perceived that a school climate was hostile were less likely to intervene during incidents of student bullying. Chapter 12 discusses bullying prevention and intervention.

In addition to aggressive behavior directed at others, research also indicates that peers often know in advance when a student is planning suicide. Although some suicides may occur without warning, about 80 percent of individuals that attempt or complete a suicide provide some warning or indication to another person before they do so (Ainsworth, 2000). Unfortunately, similar to the "code of silence" that exists against reporting threats of violence in unfavorable school climates, the majority of individuals with information on a peer's suicidal ideation do not report it to an adult (Syvertsen, Flanagan, & Stout, 2009). In a study by Pisano et al. (2012), researchers examined predictors of help-seeking behavior among adolescents from 12 high schools in rural/underserviced communities who seriously considered suicide in the past year. Students in this study who reported having suicidal ideations or knew of a peer who had suicidal ideation were interviewed to determine their help-seeking behaviors. In the aforementioned study, only 23 percent of students with suicidal thoughts told an adult about their own suicidal ideation.

As suggested by Pisano et al. (2012), positive attitudes about help-seeking from adults at school, perceptions that adults would respond to suicide concerns, willingness to overcome peer secrecy requests, and greater coping support and engagement with the school were associated with students' increased disclosure of suicidal ideation and help-seeking behavior. In addition, students identified perceived support from teachers and the school as a major factor influencing their decision to disclose information on their own or another student's suicidal ideation. Students that did disclose information were also more likely to report help-seeking behavior as a norm set by their school environment and were more likely to rate the adults in their school as available, approachable, and responsive to the needs of the students. Students were also more likely to confide information to an adult if they felt a sense of school connectedness. Chapter 16 discusses suicide assessment, prevention, and intervention.

A pattern can be seen in these findings related to students not sharing information on school violence or a threat because they do not feel personally responsible to get involved due to the prevailing norms of the school and because they are concerned that adults will not take an appropriate action. Regarding the former, students may feel that they are not part of a supportive community, fear experiencing negative repercussions associated with reporting (e.g., being targeted by the potential perpetrator), or underestimate the seriousness of the threat. These findings are consistent with the principles of the bystander effect, which is characterized as a social phenomenon in which being part of a large group creates a diffusion of responsibility within the individuals of the group (Darley & Latane, 1970). As a result, the likelihood of the individuals taking action to intervene when they witness situations in which their help may be needed is diminished. The bystander effect operates when individuals in a group are faced with a diffusion of responsibility and they take cues from other members of the group to determine whether the situation requires their assistance and to decide what course of action to take (Latane & Darley, 1968). This phenomenon may have been occurring in the study by Ferrans and Selman (2014) in that students chose not to intervene when their peers were being bullied. If students perceive that the adults in their school will not take proper action even if they are made aware of the instances of bullying, it may normalize the behavior and shape their perception that violence is acceptable. Similarly, this phenomenon appears to have also been observed in the aforementioned study by Pisano et al. (2012) in which students attributed the cultural norms of the school to the environment shaped by the attitudes and treatment they received from adults in the school.

Darley and Latane's (1968; 1970) seminal research also highlights the impact of school climate in that they found that bystanders consider their own safety before proceeding to take action. This was also evident in the studies by Ferrans and Selman (2014), Pisano et al. (2012), and Pollack et al. (2008) as students reportedly were more reluctant to get involved and take action if they feared repercussions for themselves, whether these repercussions were social or safety-oriented. It is therefore unsurprising that school climates that included trusting and positive attitudes toward adults in the school were reportedly major factors in influencing students' decisions to report threats and acts of school violence (which includes suicide) to adults. These patterns emphasize the importance of identifying and understanding the factors that contribute to the formation of a school climate that promotes positive and trusting relationships and forges connections between the students and the adults in school.

Studies have indicated that students are more likely to trust their teachers if they perceive them to be fair, supportive, caring, and respectful. Research indicates that students judge their teachers' fairness by the way they implement school rules and policies with a norm of equity (Hallinan, 2008). Students are also more likely to perceive that their teachers are caring if they listen to them, encourage their efforts, and treat them as individuals by respecting their respective cultures. Pollack et al. (2008) state that simple gestures such as regularly greeting students, talking to them, and addressing them by name can help students feel connected and part of the school. Dobransky and Frymier (2004) suggest that teacher–student relationships can be strengthened if communication occurs at the individual and coordinate level as opposed to the hierarchical teacher–student level. This point is supported by studies that underscore the value of treating students more like equals in the learning process through appreciating their voice and opinions, which, in turn, allows them to feel more like a part of the school community (McNeely, Nonnemaker, & Blum, 2002; Solomon, Watson, Battistich, Schaps, & Delucchi, 1996). Essentially, consistent with an authoritative school climate, educators should strive to build relationships with students that place less emphasis on the imbalance in authority, and focus more on encouraging autonomy and independence through support and care.

In summary, an authoritative school climate is one in which in which fair and consistent disciplinary rules and practices are applied, order is maintained, and perceived support, care and respect from teachers and school administrators enable students to feel a sense of belonging, dignity, and school community. In this positive school climate, students feel safe and trust adults to make the best decisions. Consequently, students feel personal responsibility for members of their school community and are empowered to take action when they become aware of a threatening situation.

Enhancing Social Support

Social support has been defined as the overall "perception one has of being cared for, valued, and included by others within a network of caregivers, teachers, peers, and community members" (Saylor & Leach, 2009, p. 71). Thus, descriptions of social support refer to the interpersonal, psychosocial, and material resources available to individuals that enhance their functioning or buffer against adverse outcomes (Cohen, 2004; Demaray & Malecki, 2003). These resources vary across settings, however. For example, students receive social support from their peers, educators, and other school personnel in schools as well as from caregivers, relatives, friends, and other individuals in home and community settings (Sulkowski, Demaray, & Lazarus, 2012).

Different types of social support have been established in the literature. These include *emotional*, *instrumental*, *informational*, and *appraisal* supports. Emotional support involves having emotional attachments and feeling cared for by others, whereas instrumental support involves being the recipient of time and various supportive resources (e.g., materials and homework assistance; Tardy, 1985). Informational support often involves receiving helpful advice such as information from a peer about an upcoming social event. Lastly, appraisal support generally involves receiving evaluative feedback such as feedback from a teacher on an assignment. Although different individuals can provide different amounts of social support, each form can be provided by various individuals in a student's social network (Malecki & Demaray, 2003).

The Influence of Social Support

To help ensure positive academic and social-emotional outcomes, it is important for students to receive social support from their educators, peers, and caregivers. Research indicates that students who feel supported by their teachers and peers tend to feel better connected to the school environment, display strong academic initiative, and have higher rates of school engagement (Garcia-Reid, Reid, & Peterson, 2005; Wang & Eccles, 2012). Moreover, students who feel supported by caregivers, peers, and educators have been found to display higher rates of school attendance, receive higher grades, and spend more hours studying than students who feel unsupported or experience only one or two of these sources of social support (Rosenfeld, Richman, & Bowen, 2000).

In addition to having a positive impact on students' academic achievement, social support also has been found to have a positive influence on students' social-emotional functioning. More specifically, experiencing teacher, caregiver, and peer social support is positively related to a healthier self-concept, higher self-esteem, and improved social competence (Chu, Saucier, & Hafner, 2010; Demaray, Malecki, Davidson, Hodgson, & Rebus, 2005; Malecki & Demaray, 2003; Nettles, Mucherah, & Jones, 2000). Yet, on the other hand, a perceived lack of social support from peers and caregivers has been associated with social-emotional problems such as the development of anxiety, depression, and other psychological problems (Demaray et al., 2005; Rueger, Malecki, & Demaray, 2010).

Developmental Considerations

The influence of social support appears to vary as it is delivered by different individuals at different ages. In early childhood, social support from primary caregivers tends to be most valued, as students in elementary school tend to select their caregivers over their friends when asked with whom they would like to spend the majority of their time (Nickerson & Nagle, 2005). However, students in middle school often report that they prefer to spend time with their peers or friends over their caregivers, yet they still value caregivers as important sources of support (Malecki & Demaray, 2003; Nickerson & Nagle, 2005). Finally, many students report that their friends are more supportive than their caregivers are when they transition into late adolescence (Bokhorst, Sumter, & Westenberg, 2009). Thus, in general, as students advance through their K-12 education, they tend to rely more on their peers and less on their caregivers for social support.

The impact of teacher support also may vary across student ages. Research by Malecki and Demaray (2002) suggests that perceived teacher support decreases as students' grade level increases. Similarly, a study by Bokhorst et al. (2009) indicates that younger students (ages 9–12) perceive that they receive more social support from their teachers than older students do (ages 13–18). Moreover, in the same study, older students reported that their peers and caregivers were stronger sources of social support than their teachers were. Declines in perceived teacher support across time likely are associated with transitions from having a single or few teachers in elementary school to having many teachers and a rotating class schedule in secondary school (Bokhorst et al., 2009). Additionally, similar to parental influences, as peer influences increase into adolescence, teacher influence also likely diminishes and, subsequently, the impact of teacher social support also may attenuate (DeWit, Karioja, Rye, & Shain, 2011).

Results from the aforementioned studies should be interpreted with caution. Although students report reductions in teacher social support as they transition through grades, and report that they receive less social support from teachers when compared to their peers or caregivers, this does not devalue the support they receive from educators. As previously noted, teacher social support is associated with better academic and social-emotional outcomes for students (Chu et al., 2010; Demaray et al., 2005; Garcia-Reid et al., 2005; Malecki & Demaray, 2003; Nettles et al., 2000; Rosenfeld et al., 2000; Wang & Eccles, 2012). Therefore, as suggested by Grapin, Sulkowski, and

Lazarus (2015), educators can increase their efforts to make a positive impact on students, particularly in secondary school when their perceived social support tends to diminish. Specifically, they can redouble efforts to implement emotionally supportive tutoring, small-group work, opportunities to participate and share during instruction, cooperative learning experiences, and ways to connect with educators and other school community members. Table 7.1 lists general strategies that educators can employ to provide students with social support.

Gender

Research indicates that girls perceive that they receive higher levels of social support from a variety of sources (e.g., peers, teachers) when compared to their male counterparts (Bokhorst et al., 2009; Rueger, Malecki, & Demaray, 2008; Rueger Malecki, & Demaray, 2010). Further, perceived levels of social support may impact male and female students' social and emotional functioning differently. For example, the perceived lack of global support (i.e., combined social support from parents, teachers, and peers) is a significant predictor of internalizing symptoms (e.g., depression, anxiety) in male students, yet the same lack of global support is more closely related to externalizing symptoms (e.g., hyperactivity, oppositional/defiant behavior) in girls (Rueger et al., 2008). However, although between-gender differences may exist with regard to the impact of social support, social support is fundamental to engendering positive social-emotional outcomes for both sexes, especially during adolescence when students place a high premium on their social relationships.

Culture

Culture can influence the way individuals perceive their relationships with friends, family members, and educators as well as how they access social support (Goebert, 2009). For example, in individualistic cultures (i.e., cultures that emphasize anonymity, independence,

Table 7.1 General Strategies that Educators Can Employ to Provide Students with Social Support

- Greet all students by their name.
- Ask students how they are feeling each day.
- Provide praise to students liberally.
- Encourage peer buddies and peer mediation programs.
- Support a range of extracurricular clubs, programs, and activities at various skill or ability levels.
- Check-in with students who are struggling academically or socially-emotionally each day.
- Allow all students opportunities to respond and/or participate during instruction.
- Have an open door policy in place in case students need to request additional support.
- Give students the benefit of doubt when they report experiencing adversity and describe how it is negatively impacting their performance at school.
- Convey worries or concerns about at-risk students to school-based mental health professionals such as school psychologists, counselors, and social workers.
- Encourage collaborative learning.
- Consult with community agencies and providers to help provide wraparound support.
- Engage big brother/sister programs in the community to support students who lack social support at home.
- Actively welcome caregivers into school and the classroom.
- Invite positive community members and stakeholders to the school.
- Involve all students in whole-class and collaborative instructional activities.
- Organize classrooms in a way that facilitates positive peer interaction.
- Advocate for the provision of Tier II and III services to support highly at-risk, vulnerable, and impacted students.
- Develop interventions that engage culturally, linguistically, generally disenfranchised students.
- Encourage students to identify and develop their strengths.

and self-efficacy), relationships are believed to be freely chosen and individuals often are encouraged to express their concerns and needs to significant others. However, in collectivist cultures (i.e., cultures that stress interdependence, responsibility to the family and community and group efficacy), relationships tend to be more group-oriented and individuals often view their interpersonal relationships as obligations to a greater community or extended family system. In light of these differences, individuals in collectivist cultures may be more reluctant to seek support when under duress because of a concern about potentially upsetting others in their social network (Goebert, 2009).

When trying to increase social support for students who are racial and ethnic minorities, educators should consider unique stressors that these individuals may have experienced such as discrimination, alienation, and acculturative stress (Grapin et al., 2015). Fortunately, social support can be an effective buffer against the deleterious effects of these experiences. For example, when compared to European American students, peer social support appears to be more strongly associated with school identification and school engagement among African American students (Wang & Eccles, 2012). This finding seems to suggest that having strong peer relations is an important protective factor for African American students. Moreover, Garcia-Reid et al. (2005) found that social supports provided to Latino students by their parents, teachers, and friends were positively associated with school engagement.

Socioeconomic Status

Social support and its influence on important outcomes may be influenced by students' socioeconomic status (SES). In support of this notion, a study by Malecki and Demaray (2006) found that the relationship between SES and academic performance is moderated by perceived support from caregivers and classmates. In this regard, students' perceived social support from caregivers and classmates predicted the grade point averages for low-SES students. That is, those students who had the most social support earned, on average, higher grades. However, in addition to research on students from low SES backgrounds, research is needed to clarify the influence of social support on student outcomes for individuals from a range of SES backgrounds.

Social Support and School Climate: Overlapping Constructs

It is easy to envision how efforts to increase social support can improve school climate and how improving school climate can cause students to feel more supported socially. For example, a school implementing a social-emotional learning (SEL) program that improves the overall health of the school climate likely will also cause students to feel more socially supported because they will be exposed to more positive social interactions with their peers and educators. Similarly, efforts to improve social support for students such as implementing peer- and teacher-relationship building interventions (e.g., circle of friends) also will likely improve the school climate. Therefore, efforts to improve school climate and provide students with social support are complementary.

In the following interview Kevin Dwyer discusses the role of school climate and social support in helping students in inner city schools and in high poverty areas.

Expert Interview 7.1 with Kevin Dwyer

School Psychological Consultant

PJL. You have been working and providing services to inner city schools and schools in high poverty areas. What have you learned about how to make these schools more supportive and caring and how to create positive learning climates for students?

KD. Four specific things come to mind. First, help schools better value their children, families, and staff. Second, give schools the resources they need to maximize *conditions for learning* so that every child can become academically and socially competent. Third, do all that is necessary to ensure partnerships between teachers and principals that foster academic excellence and social-emotional competence in all students. Fourth, develop a school climate that personifies mutual caring and connectedness among all members, with an emphasis on teaching and rewarding positive behaviors.

PJL. What do educators who work in inner-city schools need to know that may differ from what educators who work with students in middle-class environments need to know?

KD. Teachers who work in inner-city schools need to be master teachers who consistently focus on high standards and expectations, believe in their students, and successfully support and use each child's strengths to reach mastery. Teachers in these settings must be knowledge seekers and problem solvers and also be able to team with peers and parents effectively. These strengths also are important to possess when working in middle-class settings; however, the stressors of poverty, including students feeling valueless or being negatively impacted by community violence, can be best addressed by skilled teachers who can create a caring and respectful school climate and who know how to work well with others to maximize their strengths as well as set high academic, social, and behavioral expectations.

PJL. Some schools across the nation have been called "drop out factories," which have failed children from poor neighborhoods and especially children of color. What can educators and all stakeholders do to turn this situation around?

KD. In regard to graduation, in 2001, Robert Balfanz (2014) of John Hopkins University coined the term "drop-out factories" which describes schools where less than 60 percent of the freshman class remained enrolled four years later. These schools are typically big high schools that teach only poor kids of color. They are concentrated in 15 states. Many are in major cities, but others are in smaller, decaying industrial cities or in the south. Presently, the number of high schools labeled drop-out factories have decreased from more than 2000 to less than 700. However, with regard to urban school systems, the progress that has occurred more generally in education has not been evenly shared and there are even some unfortunate regressions. Many urban schools are now becoming more and more segregated by both income and race. Unfortunately, many parts of the south are almost all segregated as are many urban districts. We continue to poorly educate poor children, and this is a national disgrace.

But this does not need to be the case. Recently, Diplomas Now, a partnership of three national nonprofits that works with 30,000 students in 40 of the toughest middle schools and high schools in big cities, focused on students in transition—those struggling sixth and ninth graders. They identified these students based on their attendance, behavior, and course performance, and found that it was possible to identify by the middle of ninth grade just about all the students that would eventually drop out. They reorganized the entire school with teams of teachers who shared a common group of students. The schools then added more time for math and English and provided coaching for teachers and principals. Administrators and faculty welcomed students to school, helped with homework, and called them when they didn't show up. The initial findings were impressive (Balfanz, 2014). In the 2012–2013 school year, there was a 52 percent reduction in students failing math and a 69 percent reduction in students failing English. Also there was a 70 percent reduction in suspensions and a 41 percent reduction in chronically absent students. Unfortunately, many secondary schools that educate poor students of color are not specifically designed for them, and will need to be redesigned to make a significant difference. Basically, these students need a great deal more academic and social support to stay in school.

PJL. Based on your involvement, what practices have been most successful in creating safe and supportive schools and in fostering student mental health?

KD. What has impressed me while working to create successful schools in low-income districts are *universal preventive practices*. These practices need to be part of the system's strategic plan and aligned with the school's annual yearly progress (AYP). Additionally, proper buy-in, training, and ongoing fidelity monitoring is needed to implement these practices effectively. I think the early prevention and intensive intervention paradigm has greatly helped schools become safer and has reduced the reactive response of punishment and police action on the part of schools. For example, training all staff in de-escalation practices has reduced office referrals and class disruptions in many schools. School Resource Officers with this training are less punitive and threatening than police.

Schools have begun to recognize that helping students become more adept problem solvers, promoting practices consistent with research on fostering student mental health, and developing evidence-based prevention practices make schools safer. Due to the increased number of stressors imposed by poverty, low-income schools often need to implement a range of intensive interventions in addition to universal supports. When doing so, schools that utilize their trained staff or partner with mental health community services have better outcomes as measured by outcome data such as fewer behavioral referrals of students receiving interventions and better attendance. Schools that adroitly coordinate these services and include agency staff in their planning efforts and trainings to ensure that all parties speak the same language are more successful at fostering student mental health.

One of the best things I have seen is when School Support Teams (SST) spend effective time on frequently monitoring their intervention plans for students referred and where the principal is part of the SST.

PJL. More specifically, what have successful schools done to address school violence and gang violence that seems to work best?

KD. Violence is best addressed before it happens. As a possible trigger for school violence, addressing bullying is valuable and restorative justice helps. I do not think we are very successful in addressing gang violence. What we might be looking at with gangs is preventing recruitment.

PJL. What practices and strategies have you found to work best to engage parents?

KD. All parents want their children to learn and graduate. One thing that has started to help engage students from urban or disadvantaged backgrounds is for schools to hire a family engagement paraprofessional and train this person to communicate with families. These specialists should have or develop connections with supportive institutions in the community. Another strategy that has helped to engage parents and educators involves having teachers contact parents with positive news about their child. Hosting special student events that encourage teachers to meet, greet, and connect with parents is helpful.

Regarding engaging parents for students from low-SES backgrounds or poverty, parent engagement requires a far greater understanding of what families in poverty are coping with on a day-to-day basis. We know that families value education, want to connect with members of school communities, and want to know about their child's learning. But many barriers to "engagement" exist, especially among families impacted by poverty. For example, parents have complex work schedules and few have employment schedules that allow for school visits without loss of pay or even job loss.

PJL. What other suggestions do you have for superintendents, principals, educators, and school staff?

KD. Put the conditions for learning into the school's vision statement and strategic plan. Review all policies, procedures, and practices to ensure that they conform to best practices in education. Be transparent in addressing problems and keep stakeholders informed about results. Remind all stakeholders that change takes continued commitment, resources, and time. Progress is incremental. Principals must be supported as instructional leaders. They need to be cheerleaders for a positive school climate and actively monitor student progress. Educators and staff are best involved when they are well trained in quality preventive and early intervention service-delivery efforts that create a positive school climate.

The next section of this chapter discusses an integrated approach to enhancing school climate and providing social support for lesbian, gay, bisexual, transgender and questioning (LGBTQ) students who often do not feel accepted and are often subjected to a hostile school environment. A considerable amount of research indicates that these students are at-risk for being victimized at school and having their needs neglected by educators.

Enhancing Climate and Social Support for LGBTQ Students

Safe and supportive environments are essential to the learning and overall well-being of all students. Yet, hostile school climates are a reality that many lesbian, gay, bisexual, transgender and questioning (LGBTQ) youth face. LGBTQ students may experience their school climate as hostile when they hear peers or teachers make negative remarks about students' sexual orientation and gender expression. In addition, they may experience the climate this way when teachers, staff, and students fail to support them when they are bullied or harassed; when they feel invisible in the curriculum; when they are excluded from participating in extracurricular activities or establishing clubs; or when they feel there is no one in the school to talk to regarding their personal issues or safety concerns. Thus, in the absence of receiving social support, they may have negative perspectives of the school climate.

Feeling Unsafe and Disconnected

In general, LGBTQ youth are more likely to report feeling unsafe and socially disconnected at school. Research consistently confirms that LGBTQ students experience fear, harassment, discrimination, social isolation, and physical violence on a daily basis because they do not conform to the prevailing heterosexual norms of U.S. high schools (see Adelman & Woods, 2006). Further, according to research by Kosciw, Greytak, Palmer, and Boesen (2014), such hostile school climates can have adverse effects on LGBTQ students' well-being and result in negative outcomes such as absenteeism, poor academic performance, low self-esteem, and depression. In addition, research cited by the Gay–Straight Alliance (n.d.) notes that youth harassed on the basis of their sexual orientation are also more than twice as likely to seriously consider suicide and they also are more likely to smoke, drink or use drugs and become victims of violence; and they are three times more likely to carry a weapon for safety (for more information visit http://www.gsanetwork.org/about-us). Thus, considering these findings, it is imperative for educators and school-based mental health professionals to consider the unique needs of LGBTQ students.

However, it is also important to emphasize that identifying as LGBTQ does not automatically put a student at risk (Fisher, 2014). However, identifying as an LGBTQ student within hostile, heterosexist, and homophobic environments increases the risk for a range of negative experiences (Fisher & Kennedy, 2012). Instead, recent research by Russell, Toomey, Ryan, and Diaz (2014) suggests that LGBTQ students who come out as lesbian, gay, or bisexual at school have higher self-esteem and lower levels of depression as young adults when compared to lesbian, gay, and bisexual students who do not disclose their sexual orientation or gender identity at school. Furthermore, in the same study, students were more likely to perceive their school climate as accepting if they came out at school. Consequently, consistent with research on effective strategies for supporting all students, efforts to improve school climates can mitigate risks that uniquely impact LGBTQ students (Fisher, 2014; Kosciw et al., 2014).

Creating Policy

Developing and enforcing a comprehensive and inclusive policy that protects students on the basis of actual or perceived sexual orientation or gender identify is the single most important action that a school or school district can take to create a safe and supportive environment for LGBTQ students (Fisher & Kennedy, 2012; Kosciw et al., 2014). In this regard and as noted by Fisher (2014), this policy sets the stage for all other efforts to improve the school culture for these students. Additionally, implementing a policy that protects all students regardless of their actual or perceived sexual orientation or gender identity can improve social support through making schools more inclusive.

After a comprehensive policy has been developed, it is critical that all educators and other school staff know the policy, recognize behaviors that violate the policy, and understand how they are expected to respond whenever they witness LGBTQ harassment, intimidation, bullying, or social exclusion (Fisher, 2014). Further, consistent with this policy, it is imperative to include language related to zero tolerance of harassment, discrimination, and violence, as well as the use of derogatory or hate speech directed toward LGBTQ students. As emphasized by Weiler (2003), these policies should apply to all students and school personnel and they should be enforced by faculty and staff for all incidents, including minor ones such as name calling and ambiguous teasing.

Training School Personnel

In a research review, Whitman (2013) concluded that school personnel have not been adequately trained in LGBTQ issues in education preparation programs, and recommends that teachers, administrators and school-based mental health professionals need to receive more in-service education with a focus on *knowledge*, *awareness*, and *skill development*. In the area of knowledge, at minimum, school personnel need a better understanding of sexual and gender identity development, the appropriate language and terminology related to LGBTQ individuals, an appreciation of the experiences that these students encounter, and the extant research findings that highlight the negative academic and mental health outcomes for LGBTQ students. To increase awareness, school personnel should be encouraged to explore their own attitudes, stereotypes, assumptions, and prejudices as these relate to LGBTQ individuals. Moreover, they should explore this awareness in a way that facilitates open discussion of ways in which their preconceived notions may cause harm to others. Also, consistent with Whitman's (2013) recommendations, educators will need to hone specific skills to provide assistance to LGBTQ students such as responding appropriately and consistently to bullying and harassment, integrating LGBTQ topics into the curriculum, and being a visible support person. Further, school-based mental health professionals may need to develop more affirming counseling skills.

Intervening

Consistent with the aim of increasing social support, it is critical for all faculty and staff to be provided with the knowledge, skills, and dispositions needed to intervene effectively whenever harassment, intimidation, or bullying occur as well as engage LGBTQ students at school in a positive manner. In addition, students will need these same skills. Espelage and Rao (2013) further emphasize that schools need to create expectations for bystander behavior and teach bystanders how to respond whenever they witness bullying. In many instances, bystanders may wish to intervene but may not have the knowledge, skills, courage, or implicit permission to do so. This may especially be the case in a non-supportive or hostile school climate in which bystanders are afraid of negative repercussions from the perpetrator(s) or their peers if they intervene. Consequently, changing the norms and expectations regarding student behavior may be necessary to reduce the harassment of LGBTQ students.

Wernick, Kulick, and Inglehart (2013) explored three factors: hearing homophobic language, seeing teachers intervene, and seeing other students intervene to understand factors that influence students' intention to intervene in LGBTQ bullying situations. They found that students were more likely to intervene when students witnessed teachers or other students intervene, the latter being the most significant determinant. However, hearing homophobic language did not impact students' likelihood to intervene. Drawing from these results, Wernick et al. (2013) emphasized teaching intervention strategies to peers as well as fostering student leadership in multi-level, anti-bullying programs. More specifically, they emphasized eliminating homophobic language from schools, increasing students' willingness to intervene to disrupt bullying incidents, having educators stop bullying when it occurs, and adopting evidence-based bullying prevention/intervention programs. For example, if students hear peers use degrading language against individuals they perceive to be LGBTQ, then they can be taught that it is okay to say: "We don't use language like that in our school. It's not cool."

Changing the Environment

To create positive environments and better support LGBTQ students at school, Weiler (2003) suggests addressing misconceptions about LGBTQ youth, displaying pro-LGBTQ posters, using gender neutral language, and providing students with LGBTQ resources as well as literature authored by individuals who are LGBT. To help accomplish many of these aims, the Gay, Lesbian, and Straight Education Network (GLSEN) provides a toolkit for infusing the curriculum with lessons addressing various issues. *The Ready, Set, Respect! Toolkit* provides elementary level teachers with developmentally appropriate lessons that help address issues that focus on inclusion, diversity, and disrespectful behaviors. The toolkit can be downloaded via the GLSEN website at http://glsen.org/readysetrespect.

Another approach for creating safe and supportive learning environments for LGBTQ students involves Safe Space or Safe Zone Programs. Safe Space Programs are workshops and procedures that aim to provide educators, administrators, and other stakeholders with resources and skills-training for working with sexual minority youth and curbing anti-LGBTQ school climates (Ratts et al., 2013). Moreover, Safe Space Programs help improve social support by helping faculty and staff become and identify themselves as LGBTQ allies (Ratts et al., 2013). Such LGBTQ allies can promote their support for students by displaying symbolic stickers or place cards (e.g., rainbow triangles) that help promote safe environments and signal to students that they are available to provide support. GLSEN provides resources for creating safe spaces for LGBTQ youth that can be retrieved at http://glsen.org/safespace.

Two programs that aim to further the knowledge and skills of school-based professionals for creating supportive learning environments for LGBTQ youth are the Massachusetts Safe Schools Program and the Reduction of Stigma in Schools (RSIS) program. The Massachusetts Safe Schools Program was established to provide a variety of services to help schools support and engage LGBTQ youth. Specifically, this program aims to help schools develop policies against the harassment of LGBTQ youth; to provide school staff with crisis and suicide intervention training; to establish school-based support groups; and to provide counseling services to families of LGBTQ youth (Szalacha, 2003). The RSIS program focuses on providing educators, administrators, and support staff with school-based, professional development that is delivered by other trained educators (Payne & Smith, 2011). Through RSIS, stakeholders learn about the risks of stigmatizing LGBTQ youth, how to provide education and tools for creating more positive learning environments, and how to become allies to LGBTQ youth by providing opportunities for dialogue and understanding (Payne & Smith, 2011).

Efforts to create a safe and supportive environment for LGBTQ youth should also include peer social support groups. The research literature indicates that Gay–Straight Alliances (GSAs) can help promote a sense of safety and support for LGBTQ students at the middle and high school level. In a recent study, Quasha, McCabe, and Ortiz (2014) found that participation in GSAs is associated with higher academic achievement and perceived social support, lower dropout rates and absenteeism, and fewer reports of hearing derogatory remarks and of feeling unsafe for LGBTQ youth. Further, Quasha et al. (2014) also explored the school climates in two middle schools with and without such alliances. Results of their investigation indicate that the middle school with a GSA reported fewer incidents of physical and verbal bullying and greater support from the staff to maintain safe environments. The Gay Straight Alliance Network is a national leadership organization for youth that provides resources for establishing and supporting such peer support groups (for more information visit http://www.gsanetwork.org/).

Cowan and Klotz (2012) provide several additional strategies for fostering support and creating safe environments for LGBTQ students. One such strategy is to promote positive dialogue among all stakeholders in school communities. Cowan and Klotz emphasize the use of positive and respectful language such as using the terms "respect" and "acceptance" rather than "tolerance." Further, they advocate for disseminating fact sheets to identify harassment and bullying and leading classroom discussions about all aspects of diversity. Lastly, Cowan and Klotz emphasize that it is imperative to identify and spread key messages regarding respect and acceptance and point out the harm derogatory language can cause to positive school climates, even if it is unintentional.

In the following interview Troy Loker discusses how to help establish a more supportive school climate for LGBTQ students, frequent misconceptions about LGBTQ youth, how educators should respond to bullying and harassment, and the advantages of establishing Gay–Straight Alliances in schools.

Expert Interview 7.2 with Troy Loker

Honolulu District, Hawaii Department of Education

PJL. We know that lesbian, gay, bisexual, transgender, and questioning (LGBTQ) students are frequently the target of bullying and intimidation. What would you like educators to know about this problem?

TL. Educators should know that LGBTQ students are victimized at significantly higher rates than their heterosexual peers (Button, O'Connell, & Gealt, 2012). These heightened rates of victimization are associated with many negative educational and mental health outcomes for LGBTQ students, such as truancy, low grade point averages (GPAs), low self-esteem, depression, substance use, and suicidal thoughts and behaviors (e.g., Button et al., 2012; D'Augelli, 2002; Espelage, Aragon, Birkett, & Koenig, 2008; Goodenow, Szalacha, & Westheimer, 2006, Kosciw et al., 2014; Pearson, Muller, & Wilkinson, 2007). LGBTQ youth also experience substantial indirect hostility at school, which involves frequently hearing their peers say homophobic remarks or using the word "gay" in a negative way (Kosciw et al., 2014). While those comments are not necessarily direct harassment, they are still distressing to LGBTQ students and they negatively impact school climate.

PJL. GLSEN's 2013 National School Climate Survey found that 74 percent of LGBTQ students experienced verbal harassment in the past year because of their sexual orientation and 55 percent because of their gender expression. What can educators do to help reduce this problem?

TL. It is critical that educators respond every time they witness LGBTQ harassment. In the eyes of an LGBTQ student, there likely is no better way to demonstrate a lack of support than to ignore a homophobic or transphobic remark or attack. It is the inaction from educators that helps explain why a majority of victimized LGBTQ students do not tell staff about being harassed or assaulted. Consistently responding to incidents of anti-LGBTQ language and behavior not only helps interrupt the specific incident at hand, but it demonstrates to the victim, the perpetrator, and the bystanders that students will not get away with such behavior.

Beyond responding to specific incidents of harassment, educators can reduce anti-LGBTQ behaviors by taking a proactive approach with students. In a study by a lead researcher in the area of risk and protective factors for LGBTQ youth, within a nationally representative sample, Stephen T. Russell and his colleagues (Russell, Seif, & Truong, 2001) found that the best predictor of school-related outcomes for LGBTQ students was the student–teacher relationship, even more so than other social, peer, family, or demographic variables. When these students get along with their teachers, feel that they are treated fairly, and feel like their teachers care about their well-being, they are significantly more likely to experience lower levels of peer difficulties and improved academic engagement.

The number of supportive educators also makes a difference. National School Climate Survey data tell us that when LGBTQ students are able to identify more than ten supportive educators at school they are much more likely to feel safe at school (Kosciw et al., 2014). Beyond the improved sense of safety, they are also more likely to feel connected to their school community, earn better grades, and have greater post-secondary aspirations than when LGBTQ students are unable to identify any supportive educators at school.

PJL How can educators proactively demonstrate that they are supportive of LGBTQ students and facilitate the development of positive student–teacher relationships?

TL. Many simple educator actions can communicate respect and acceptance of diversity that will lead LGBT students to view them as supportive. In fact, educators have the power to set a welcoming and supportive tone for their class or school from the very beginning of the year. It can be as easy as placing a Safe Space or LGBT-inclusive diversity poster on the wall of the educator's classroom or office. Educators can also establish classroom or school expectations for behavior that include treating everyone with respect. To help define that expectation to students, educators can describe behaviors that will not be tolerated, such as name calling and harassment based on race, ethnicity, religion, gender, sexual orientation, gender identity and expression, disability, and any other cultural or personal characteristic. When educators articulate statements that are purposefully inclusive and when they enumerate specific diversity characteristics, they provide clear communication about the scope of their support. Another way to help communicate interest in students' well-being and to open the door for self-disclosure is for teachers to collect "get to know you" papers at the beginning of the year. Including a question about what students prefer to be called can be particularly important for transgender students, as it provides an opportunity for them to clarify their preferred name and preferred gender pronouns.

PJL. How should educators respond to anti-LGBTQ language and behavior?

TL. The steps for interrupting anti-LGBT behaviors should look similar to best practices for addressing other problematic behaviors. If an educator observes a homophobic comment, a transphobic comment, a racist comment, or any other type of offensive verbal attack, it is best to firmly interrupt the incident with a statement such as: "Those words are unacceptable at our school." Educators should then name the behavior and briefly explain how the behavior is unacceptable. For instance, a teacher could say "Calling someone a faggot is both derogatory and harassment. That offensive and aggressive language goes against our school's expectation for you to be respectful towards others."

There are then three important follow-up steps to reduce the likelihood of future anti-LGBTQ behaviors and to reduce any harm caused by the incident. First, try to turn this negative event into an opportunity for a teachable moment. Discussing respectful behavior, providing education about biased behaviors, and helping to build empathy are all examples of educator efforts that could be provided in the moment or at a slightly later time depending on the situation. This education could occur privately with the perpetrator or more publicly with a larger group. Either way, education is key to making a positive difference in individual behavior and school climate.

The second follow-up component is to check in with the targeted student. By seeing how the student is doing, it will communicate your interest in the student's well-being and provide an opportunity to assess whether or not more support is needed. Students react differently, so it is important not to assume how the student is feeling or what the student needs. It is also important to learn if the incident is part of a larger pattern of repeated bullying behaviors.

Finally, the perpetrator must be held accountable in a way that is consistent with other types of behavioral infractions. Similar to the way educators would be communicating a lack of support if they ignored an instance of anti-LGBTQ behavior, educators would also show themselves as biased if they provided less than appropriate disciplinary consequences for an anti-LGBTQ behavior.

PJL. There has been a great change in awareness by the general public about problems gay and lesbian youth face due to their sexual orientation. Has this change led to a safer school climate for LGBTQ youth?

TL. Since 2001, GLSEN has conducted a National School Climate Survey every two years. Their national data show some significant improvements in school safety over time, though there is still much room for improvement. For instance, in 2001 about four out of five LGBTQ students heard homophobic remarks frequently or often at school. By 2013 that ratio went down to three out of five. Frequency of direct verbal harassment has shown the greatest rate of improvement. In 2007, almost half (45 percent) of LGBTQ students reported being verbally harassed frequently or often, and in 2013, this number dropped to just over a quarter (27 percent) of LGBTQ students. The frequency of physical harassment and physical assault has been decreasing as well, but to a lesser degree than verbal harassment (Kosciw et al., 2014).

It is difficult to pinpoint the exact causes of the improvements. The change in general public awareness undoubtedly has made a difference, but there have also been tangible changes in the supports for LGBTQ students at school. More students than ever before are reporting that their schools have established anti-bullying/harassment policies and Gay–Straight Alliances, that their teachers include positive representations of LGBT people or events during instruction, and that students have access to textbooks that include LGBT-related content. Perhaps most importantly, the number of staff members that LGBTQ students view as supportive has been increasing (Kosciw et al., 2014).

PJL. What are the most frequent misconceptions about LGBTQ youth?

TL. Some people believe that LGBTQ individuals hardly even exist within their school or community as well as believe that society somehow has an influence on the development of an individual's sexual orientation or gender identity. This line of thinking is rooted in the idea that having a sexual orientation or gender identity that is anything other than heterosexual male or heterosexual female is in some way unnatural, a personal choice, or pathological. These are clear misconceptions.

It has been more than four decades since the American Psychological Association (APA) declared that homosexuality was not a mental disorder, and the fifth edition of the *Diagnostic and statistical manual (DSM-V)* no longer lists being transgender as a disorder. Many experts view that gender identity and sexual orientation are determined based on a mixture of biological and environmental factors, not by a single gene or a single environmental variable (APA, 2008). This means that individuals do not have a personal choice in determining same- or opposite-gender attractions. The use of conversion or reparative therapy to change a person's sexual orientation has also been declared unethical by the APA. Attempts to change sexual orientation through such therapy have been found to not be safe or effective (APA, 2008).

LGBTQ individuals also live in every community. Census data shows that same-sex couples live in over 99 percent of all counties in the United States. Recent research from the Williams Institute of the UCLA School of Law indicates that 3.5 percent of the U.S. adult population identify as lesbian, gay, or bisexual, and 0.3 percent, or 700,000 adults, identify as transgender. This research also found that 11 percent of the adult population report some degree of same-sex attraction (Gates, 2011). It is important for educators to know that a significant proportion of LGBT individuals first self-identify as LGBT during their adolescence. While there is considerable individual variability in identity development, many LGB youth become aware of their same-sex attractions as early as ten years old and self-identify as LGB at age 15 (e.g., D'Augelli, 2002).

Simply stated, LGBTQ identity development most often occurs prior to adulthood, and variations in sexual orientation and gender identity are naturally occurring aspects of human diversity.

PJL. On the GLSEN website there are listed lesson plans that educators can access to build safe, inclusive, and affirming classrooms for all students? Can you tell us some more about this?

TL. Many of GLSEN's anti-bullying lessons were originally designed for No Name Calling Week, a bullying-prevention initiative celebrated every January in schools across the country. Broken down by elementary, middle, and high school levels, these lesson plans also can be used throughout the year and not just during a school-wide, No-Name-Calling Week initiative.

To further promote inclusive and affirming classrooms, GLSEN also has elementary level, literature-based lesson plans that include LGBT-themed literature, secondary level history lesson plans that include audio-recorded interviews from American LGBT historical figures, and additional lesson plans that address LGBT-inclusive family diversity as well as gender role diversity. For more information, visit http://glsen.org/educate/resources/lesson-plans.

PJL. The Safe Space Kit is GLSEN's Guide to Being an Ally to LGBT Students. The guide provides concrete strategies that will help support LGBT students, educate about LGBT bias, and advocate for changes in your school. The kit guides educators through making an assessment of your school's climate, policies and practices and also outlines strategies to advocate for change, including posting a Safe Space Sticker or Safe Space Poster in your classroom or office. What have you found to be the most effective strategies to advocate for change at the school and/or district level?

TL. Essentially, positive change occurs by increasing the number of active LGBTQ allies, which is the goal of the Safe Space Kit. Being an ally to LGBTQ students involves gaining cultural competence around LGBTQ youth issues, reflecting on personal and systems-level biases, and making a commitment to improve outcomes for all students, regardless of their sexual orientation, gender identity, or gender expression.

To help move schools and districts forward in providing safer school environments, it is important to build allies at all levels. That is, you need to have allies who are teachers, student services personnel, parents, community members, school building administrators, and district level supervisors and administrators. Using the strategies and resources in the Safe Space Kit helps to build allies across all these levels.

PJL. How might a concerned educator go about founding a Gay–Straight Alliance (GSA) club at school? What are the advantages of having such a club in schools? Also, how can barriers to forming a GSA club be reduced?

TL. Similar to other non-academic clubs in school, a GSA is a student-initiated and student-run club that operates under the guidance of a faculty advisor. Proactively demonstrating your inclusive support for all students, regardless of their sexual orientation, gender identity, or gender expression, is a great way to show to students that you would serve as a positive role model and potential GSA advisor. Communicating your interest and encouragement of their efforts can provide the sense of student empowerment needed to launch and sustain a GSA.

GSAs can provide a safe space for students to be themselves, can add visibility to LGBTQ students' needs, and can become actively engaged in promoting anti-bullying and school improvement efforts. Research consistently shows that schools with GSAs have a variety of better outcomes for LGBTQ students, including an improved sense of safety, reductions in school-based homophobic language, higher GPAs, lower dropout rates, and even lower rates of suicide attempts (e.g., Goodenow et al., 2006; Kosciw et al., 2014; Walls, Kane, & Wisneski, 2010).

Administrators are the best advocates or worst barriers for GSAs. Unfortunately, administrators still often discourage or block students and educators from establishing or sustaining a GSA. When this happens, it is important to first share data and stories about the hostile environments LGBTQ students experience and the positive impact associated with GSAs. Unfortunately, that is not always enough to change an administrator's decision. Instead of advocating for doing what is right for student safety and well-being, pointing out the legal issues may be more effective. A concerned educator could share that the 1984 Equal Access Act requires public secondary schools to provide equal access for all extracurricular clubs. More specifically, U.S. Department of Education Secretary Arne Duncan issued a policy letter in 2011 articulating that the protections in this law apply to GSAs just as they apply to religious, political, or other student-initiated groups. If a GSA still is blocked or treated unfairly compared to other extracurricular clubs, a call to the American Civil Liberties Union (ACLU) often helps expedite decisions to become compliant with this law.

PJL. What else would you like school administrators, educators, and parents to know about how to help LGBTQ students?

TL. We must be willing to openly engage in dialogue about the needs of LGBTQ youth. LGBTQ students are present in every school, yet the well-being of these students is far too often never discussed. If we can advocate amongst our peers for systemic school improvement efforts, we can equip educators with the knowledge and skills to enhance school safety for all students, regardless of their sexual orientation, gender identity, or gender expression.

Also, we can include information about LGBTQ youth in undergraduate curricula as I have found that future educators are more enlightened about the needs to these youth and want to be as supportive as possible.

Establishing an Inclusive School Climate for Families Headed by LGBT Caregivers

All students display the best academic and social-emotional outcomes when they receive social support from a range of different individuals and when their families feel accepted. Unfortunately, however, schools are typically structured to accommodate traditional families that include a father, and/or mother, and children, which means that they often tacitly embrace a heteronormative perspective on the constellation of the families they serve (Herek, 2007). This is evident in the expectations educators hold on what is considered a family structure, specifically the expectation that students come from one- or two-parent heterosexual households (Fox, 2007). Yet, between one-fifth and one-third of gay men and lesbians currently are rearing children (U.S. Census Bureau, 2010). Lofquist (2011) reports there are an estimated 594,000 same-sex couple households in the United States, 115,000 of which report having biological, step, or adopted children. Moreover, these numbers do not include data on children whose caregivers are lesbian, gay, bisexual, or transgender (LGBT) and not necessarily in a same-sex relationship. Consequently, it has been estimated that seven million students are being raised by parents who are LGBT (Kosciw et al., 2014). As Ryan and Martin (2000) explain, the significant prevalence of children from households with LGBT caregivers has led educators and related professionals to consider the needs of these children and their families. However, despite this growing phenomenon, there are major gaps in professionals' knowledge about LGBT issues and families (Ryan & Martin, 2000), which highlights a need for increased attention toward addressing the needs of these students and families.

Families headed by LGBT caregivers vary across social and economic factors, relationship statuses (e.g., single, partnered, married, divorced), and how they were formed (e.g., biological, adopted, or fostered; Lamme & Lamme, 2002). Therefore, a great deal of diversity exists among family constellations. However, when compared to heterosexual families, research indicates that LGBT parents and their children suffer from the stigmatization and challenges of an unsupportive community and heteronormative school system across a range of contexts, even though children from these families usually experience normal developmental outcomes (Allen, 2013). In spite of this stigma, these students usually do as well in school and life as their peers from families that are comprised of a father and a mother.

Heteronormative perspectives on child rearing and education often are propagated in schools, even without an explicit intention to do so. In this regard, Fox (2007) explains that heteronormative perspectives are frequently communicated in schools through classroom books, letters sent home, posters in the hallways, conversations staff members have with students, and any curricular materials that imply that mother–father caregiver relationships are the only normal family structure. In the realm of children's literacy, for example, Emfinger (2007) reviewed print literature regarding LGBT topics and found that these resources are exceedingly limited, and when books about LGBT caregivers do make it to press, most focus on explaining parental sexuality and family structure rather than focusing on the everyday activities of these households. To address this paucity of information, Emfinger recommends that libraries stock books and multimedia resources that include diversity in family make-up because all children need to see their own experiences reflected and validated at home and at school.

In an investigation, Averett and Hedge (2012) surveyed the attitude, comfort, preparation, and disposition of early childhood educators and school social workers with regard to families headed by gay and lesbian caregivers. Although these education professionals reported positive attitudes and dispositions toward these families as well as a willingness to take action by including LGBT friendly literature or symbols in their workspaces, few felt comfortable interacting with LGBT caregivers (Averett & Hedge, 2012). In a related study by Martino and Cumming-Potvin (2011), some teachers reported a willingness to include LGBT themes into their curriculum; however, they felt hesitation to actually do so because of "parental surveillance." That is, they personally espoused inclusionary attitudes and willingness yet their concerns about the negative repercussions that could ensue on the part of parents and the community if they incorporated LGBT content into their lessons outweighed their own attitudes.

Many LGBT parents identify heteronormativity as a primary factor that creates an unwelcoming atmosphere for their children in schools. Fox (2007) explains that parents feel unwelcome when they receive letters addressed to mothers and fathers, when their families are considered non-traditional, and when the term "gay families" is used as an umbrella term to suggest that all members of the family share the same sexuality. Similarly, Mercier and Harold (2003) interviewed lesbian parents about their relationships with their children's schools. These parents expressed their apprehension to share their sexual orientation with educators at the school where their children attended, as many were wary of the possibility that a negative reaction could occur from their children's peers. Yet, parents in this same study shared that parent involvement was significantly more prevalent in schools that advocated for respectful and inclusive attitudes toward all families. In light of these findings, and consistent with a family-centric approach to fostering school connection and engagement, Herbstrith (2014) recommends that schools plan events and activities around the theme of diversity to help students, teachers, and all other stakeholders understand and support an array of different family structures, whatever these structures may be.

Connecting with families headed by LGBT caregivers involves creating a welcoming school environment (e.g., displaying LGBT-friendly and safe icons, using enrollment forms that leave a space for information about families as opposed to assuming their constellation), addressing home–school communications to "Dear Families" rather than "Dear Mom and Dad," raising awareness of the issues that children from families headed by LGBT caregivers face, using inclusive language, stocking books and multimedia resources in the library about LGBT individuals and their families, and taking a proactive stance in teaching educators how to be more supportive and comfortable with family diversity. Further, the aforementioned efforts to connect better with all families should be taught in teacher training programs, graduate school courses, and through in-service education (Lamme & Lamme, 2002).

Conclusion

This chapter emphasized the critical importance of establishing an authoritative school climate that is deemed to be supportive and caring; where students and faculty feel connected and bonds of trust have been developed; and where clear and fair rules have been created and are administered equitably. A school with a positive climate is also a safer school because students are more likely to tell an adult if there is a threat of violence as well as to intervene to help prevent peer suicide and bullying incidents. Essentially, schools with a healthy school climate and ample social supports are schools where all students feel respected, regardless of their socio-economic status, sexual orientation, race, ethnicity, gender, disability, or religion; and everyone is treated with dignity.

References

Adelman, M., & Woods, K. (2006). Identification without intervention: Transforming anti-LGBTQ school climate. *Journal of Poverty, 10*(2), 5–26.

Ainsworth, P. (2000). *Understanding depression.* Mississippi: University Press of Mississippi.

Allen, D. W. (2013). High school graduation rates among children of same-sex households. *Review of Economics of the Household, 11,* 635–658.

American Psychological Association (2008). *Answers to your questions: For a better understanding of sexual orientation and homosexuality.* Washington, DC: Author. [Retrieved from www.apa.org/topics/sorientation.pdf.]

Aspy, C. B., Oman, R. F., Vesely, S. K., McLeroy, K., Rodine, S., & Marshall, L. (2004). Adolescent violence: The protective effects of youth assets. *Journal of Counseling and Development, 82,* 268–276.

Averett, P. E., & Hegde, A. (2012). School social work and early childhood student's attitudes toward gay and lesbian families. *Teaching in Higher Education, 17,* 537–549.

Balfanz, R. (2014, June 7). Stop holding us back. *New York Times.*

Battishtich, V., & Horn, A. (1997). The relationship between students' sense of their school as a community and their involvement in problem behaviors. *American Journal of Public Health, 87,* 1997–2001.

Baumrind, D. (1966). Effects of authoritative parental control on child behavior. *Child Development, 37,* 887–907.

Baumrind, D. (1991). *Effective parenting during the early adolescent transition.* In P. A. Cowan, & E. M. Hetherington, Family Transitions (Vol. 2, pp. 111–163). Hillsdale, NJ: Erlbaum.

Blum, R. W., McNeely, C., & Rinehart, P. M. (2002). *Improving the odds: The untapped power of schools to improve the health of teens.* Center for Adolescent Health and Development. Minneapolis: University of Minnesota.

Bokhorst, C., Sumter, S., & Westenberg, M. (2009). Social support from parents, friends, classmates, and teachers in children and adolescents aged 9 to 18 years: Who is perceived as most supportive. *Social Development, 19,* 417–426. doi: 10.1111/j.1467- 9507.2009.00540.x

Bond, L., Carlin, J. B., Thomas, L., Rubin, K., & Patton, G. (2001). Does bullying cause emotional problems? A prospective study of young teenagers. *British Medical Journal, 323,* 480–482.

Button, D., M. O'Connell, D.J., & Gealt, R. (2012). Sexual minority youth victimization and social support: The intersection of sexuality, gender, race, and victimization. *Journal of Homosexuality, 59,* 18–43.

Catalano, R. F., Haggerty, K. P., Oesterie, S., Fleming, C. B., & Hawkins, J. D. (2004). The importance of bonding to schools for healthy development: Findings from the social development research group. *Journal of School Health, 74,* 252–262.

Chaux, E. (2012). *Educación, convivencia y agresión escolar.* Bogotá, Colombia: Ediciones Uniandes.

Chu, P. S., Saucier, D. A., & Hafner, E. (2010). Meta-analysis of the relationships between social support and well-being in children and adolescents. *Journal of Social and Clinical Psychology, 29,* 624–645.

Cohen, S. (2004). Social relationships and health. *American Psychologist, 59,* 676–684. doi:10.1037/0003-066X.59.8.676

Cohen, J., McCabe, L., Michelli, N. M., & Pickeral, T. (2009). School climate: Research, policy, practice, and teacher education. *Teachers College Record, 111,* 180–213.

Coker, J. K., & Borders, L. D. (2001). An analysis of environmental and social factors impacting adolescent problem drinking. *Journal of Counseling and Development, 79,* 200–208.

Cowan, K. C., & Klotz, M. B. (2012). Tips for building commitment to create safe, supportive schools for LGBTQ students. *Communiqué, 40*(8), 10–12.

Cowan, K. C., Vaillancourt, K., Rossen, E., & Pollitt, K. (2013). *A framework for safe and successful schools [Brief].* Bethesda, MD: National Association of School Psychologists. Retrieved from www.nasponline.org/resources/framework-safe-and-successful-schools.aspx.

D'Augelli, A. R. (2002). Mental health problems among lesbian, gay, and bisexual youths ages 14 to 21.*Clinical Child Psychology and Psychiatry, 7,* 1359–1045.

Darley, J. M., & Latane, B. (1970). *The unresponsive bystander: Why doesn't he help?* New York: Appleton Century Crofts.

Demaray, M. K., & Malecki, C. K. (2003). Importance ratings of socially supportive behaviors by children and adolescents. *School Psychology Review, 32,* 108–131.

Demaray, M. K., Malecki, C. K., Davidson, L. M., Hodgson, K. K., & Rebus, P. J. (2005). The relationship between social support and student adjustment: A longitudinal analysis. *Psychology in the Schools, 42,* 691–706. doi: 10.1002/pits.20120

DeWit, D., Karioja, K., Rye, B., & Shain, M. (2011). Perceptions of declining classmate and teacher support following the transition to high school: Potential correlates of increasing student mental health difficulties. *Psychology in the Schools, 48,* 556–572. doi: 10.1002/pits.20576

Dobransky, N. D., & Frymier, A. B. (2004). Developing teacher–student relationships through out of class communication. *Communication Quarterly, 52,* 211–223.

Dwyer, K., Osher, D., & Warger, C. (1998). *Early warning, timely response: A guide to safe schools.* Washington, DC: U.S. Department of Education.

Emfinger, K. (2007). Rethinking welcoming literacy environments for LGBT families. *Childhood Education, 84,* 24–28.

Espelage, D. L., Aragon, S. R., Birkett, M., & Koenig, B. W. (2008). Homophobic teasing, psychological outcomes, and sexual orientation among high school students: What influence do parents and schools have? *School Psychology Review, 37,* 202–216.

Espelage, D. L., & Rao, M. A. (2013). Safe schools: Prevention and intervention for bullying and harassment. In E. S. Fisher & K. Komosa-Hawkins (Eds.), *Creating safe and supportive learning environments:*

A guide for working with lesbian, gay, bisexual, transgender, and questioning youth and families (pp. 140–155). New York: Routledge.

Fein, R. A., Vossekuil, B., Pollack, W. S., Borum, R., Modzeleski, W., & Reddy, M. (2002). *Threat assessment in schools: A guide to managing threatening situations and to creating safe school climates.* Washington, DC: United States Secret Service and United States Department of Education.

Ferrans, S. D., & Selman, R. L. (2014). How students' perceptions of the school climate influence their choice to upstand, bystand or join perpetrators of bullying. *Harvard Educational Review, 84,* 162–187.

Ferrans, S., Selman, R. L., & Feigenberg, L. (2012). Rules of the culture and personal needs: Witnesses' decision-making process to deal with situations of bullying in middle school. *Harvard Educational Review, 82,* 445–470.

Fisher, E. S. (2014). Best practices in supporting students who are lesbian, gay, bisexual, transgender, and questioning. In P. Harrison & A. Thomas (Eds.), *Best practices in school psychology: Foundations* (pp. 191–203). Bethesda, MD: National Association of School Psychologists.

Fisher, E. S., & Kennedy, K. S. (2012). *Responsive school practices to support lesbian, gay, bisexual, transgender, and questioning students and families.* New York: Routledge.

Fox, R. K. (2007). One of the hidden diversities in schools: Families with parents who are lesbian or gay. *Childhood Education, 83,* 277–281.

Garcia-Reid, P., Reid, R. J., & Peterson, N. A. (2005). School engagement among Latino youth in an urban middle school context: Valuing the role of social support. *Education and Urban Society, 37,* 257–275. doi:10.1177/0013124505275534

Gates, G. J. (2011, April). *How many people are lesbian, gay, bisexual, and transgender?* Williams Institute, UCLA School of Law. Retrieved from http://williamsinstitute.law.ucla.edu/wp-content/uploads/Gates-How-Many-People-LGBT-Apr-2011.pdf.

Gay-Straight Alliance Network (n.d.). Frequently asked questions about GSA network. Retrieved from https://gsanetwork.org/about-us/faq.

Goebert, D. (2009). Social support, mental health, minorities, and acculturative stress. In S. Loue & M. Sajatovic (Eds.), *Determinants of minority mental health and wellness* (pp. 125–148). New York: Springer. doi: 10.1007/978-0-387-75659-2_7

Goodenow, C., Szalacha, L., & Westheimer, K. (2006) School support groups, other school factors, and the safety of sexual minority adolescents. *Psychology in the Schools, 43,* 573–589.

Gottfredson, G. D., Gottfredson, D. C., Payne, A., & Gottfredson, N. C. (2005). School climate predictors of school disorder: Results from a national study of delinquency prevention in schools. *Journal of Research in Crime and Delinquency, 42,* 412–444.

Grapin, S., Sulkowski, M. L., & Lazarus, P. J. (2015). A multilevel framework for increasing social support in schools. *Contemporary School Psychology, 20,* 93–106. doi: 10.1007/s40688-015-0051-0

Hallinan, M. T. (2008). Teacher influences on students' attachment to school. *Sociology of Education, 81,* 271–283.

Herbstrith, J. C. (2014). Best practices in working with LGBT parents and their families. In P. Harrison & A. Thomas (Eds.), *Best practices in school psychology: Foundations* (pp. 205–215). Bethesda, MD: National Association of School Psychologists.

Herek, G. M. (2007). Confronting sexual stigma and prejudice: Theory and practice. *Journal of Social Issues, 63,* 905–925.

Hughes, J. N. (2002). Authoritative teaching: Tipping the balance in favor of school versus peer effects. *Journal of Psychology, 40,* 485–492.

Kosciw, J. G., Greytak, E. A., Palmer, N. A., & Boesen, M. J. (2014). *The 2013 National School Climate Survey: The experiences of lesbian, gay, bisexual and transgender youth in our nation's schools.* New York: GLSEN.

Kuperminc, G. P., Leadbeater, B. J., Emmons, C., & Blatt, S. J. (1997). Perceived school climate and difficulties in the social adjustment of middle school students. *Applied Developmental Science, 1,* 76.

Lamme, L. L., & Lamme, L. A. (2002). Welcoming children from gay families into our schools. *Educational Leadership, 59,* 65–69.

Latane, B., & Darley, J. M. (1968). Group inhibition of bystander intervention in emergencies. *Journal of Personality and Social Psychology, 10,* 215–221.

Lazarus, P. J. (2001, May). Breaking the code of silence: What schools can do about it. *Communiqué, 29*(7), 28–29.

Lofquist, D. (2011). Same-sex couple households: American community survey briefs. *US Census Bureau.*

Loukas, A., & Robinson, S. (2004). Examining the moderating role of perceived school climate in early adolescent adjustment. *Journal of Research on Adolescence, 14,* 209–233.

McNeely, C. A., Nonnemaker, J. M., & Blum, R. W. (2002). Promoting school connectedness: Evidence from the national longitudinal study of adolescent health. *Journal of School Health, 72,* 136–146.

Malecki, C. K., & Demaray, M. K. (2002). Measuring perceived social support: Development of the child and adolescent social support scale (CASSS). *Psychology in the Schools, 39,* 1–18. doi: 10.1002/pits.10004

Malecki, C.K., & Demaray, M. K. (2003). What type of support do they need? Investigating student adjustment as related to emotional, informational, appraisal, and instrumental support. *School Psychology Quarterly, 18,* 231–252. doi: 10.1521/scpq.18.3.231.22576

Malecki, C. K., & Demaray, M. K. (2006). Social support as a buffer in the relationship between socioeconomic status and academic performance. *School Psychology Quarterly, 21,* 375–395. doi: 10.1037/h0084129

Martino, W. & Cumming-Potvin W. (2011). Investigating teachers' approaches to addressing same-sex parenting and non-normative sexuality in the elementary school classroom. *Curriculum Inquiry, 41,* 480–501.

Mercier, L., & Harold, R. (2003). At the interface: Lesbian-parent families and their children's schools. *Children & Schools, 25,* 35–47.

Nettles, S., Mucherah, W., & Jones, S. (2000). Understanding resilience: The role of social resources. *Journal of Education for Students Placed at Risk, 5,* 47–60. doi:10.1207/s15327671espr0501&2_4

Nickerson, A. B., & Nagle, R. J. (2005). Parent and peer attachment in late childhood and early adolescence. *Journal of Early Adolescence, 25,* 223–249. doi: 10.1177/0272431604274174

O'Malley, M., & Eklund, K. (2012). Promoting safe and healthy schools. In S. E. Brock & S. R. Jimerson (Eds.), *Best practices in school crisis prevention and intervention, Second edition* (pp. 151–176). Bethesda, MD: NASP.

Payne, E. C., & Smith, M. (2011). The reduction of stigma in schools: A new professional development model for empowering educators to support LGBTQ students. *Journal of LGBT Youth, 8,* 174–200.

Pearson, M., Muller, C., & Wilkinson, L. (2007). Adolescent same-sex attraction and academic outcomes: The role of school attachment and engagement. *Social Problems, 54,* 523–542.

Pisano, A. R., Schmeelk-Cone, K., Gunzler, D., Petrova, M., Goldston, D. B. . . . Tu, X. (2012). Associations between suicidal high school students' help-seeking and their attitudes and perceptions of social environment. *Journal of Youth and Adolescence, 41,* 1312–1324.

Pollack, W. S., Modzeleski, W., & Rooney, G. (2008). *Prior knowledge of potential school-based violence: Information students learn may prevent a targeted attack.* Washington, DC: United States Secret Service and United States Department of Education.

Quasha, S., McCabe, P. C., & Ortiz, S. O. (2014). A program review of a middle school gay- straight alliance club. *School Psychology Forum, 8,* 91–102.

Ratts, M. J., Kaloper, M., McReady, C., Tighe, L., Butler, S. K., Dempsey, K., & McCullough, J. (2013). Safe space programs in K-12 schools: Creating a visible presence of LGBTQ allies. *Journal of LGBT Issues in Counseling, 7,* 387–404.

Roeser, R. W., & Eccles, J. S. (1998). Adolescents' perceptions of middle school: Relation to longitudinal changes in academic and psychological adjustment. *Journal of Research on Adolescence, 8,* 123–158.

Roeser, R. W., Eccles, J. S., & Sameroff, A. J. (2000). School as a context of early adolescents' academic and social-emotional development: A summary of research findings. *Elementary School Journal, 100,* 443–471.

Rosenfeld, L. B., Richman, J. M., & Bowen, G. L. (2000). Social support networks and school outcomes: The centrality of the teacher. *Child Adolescent Social Work Journal, 17,* 205– 226. doi: 10.1023/A:1007535930286

Rueger, S., Malecki, C., & Demaray, M. (2008). Gender differences in the relationship between perceived social support and student adjustment during early adolescence. *School Psychology Quarterly, 23,* 496–514. doi: 10.1037/1045-3830.23.4.496

Rueger, S., Malecki, C., & Demaray, M. (2010). Relationship between multiple sources of perceived social support and psychological and academic adjustment in early adolescence: Comparisons across gender. *Journal of Youth and Adolescence, 39,* 47–61. doi: 10.1007/s10964-008-9368-6

Russell, S. T., Seif, H., & Truong, N. L. (2001). School outcomes of sexual minority youth in the United States: Evidence from a national study. *Journal of Adolescence, 24,* 111–127.

Russell, S. T., Toomey, R. B., Ryan, C., & Diaz, R. M. (2014). Being out at school: The implications for school victimization and young adult adjustment. *American Journal of Orthopsychiatry, 84,* 635–643.

Ryan, D., & Martin, A. (2000). Lesbian, gay, bisexual, and transgender parents in the school systems. *School Psychology Review, 29,* 207–216.

Saylor, C. F., & Leach, J. B., (2009). Perceived bullying and social support in students accessing special education inclusion programming. *Journal of Developmental and Physical Disabilities, 21,* 69–80. doi: 10.1007/s10882-008-9126-4

Solomon, D., Watson, M., Battistich, V., Schaps, E., & Delucchi, K. (1996). Creating classrooms that students experience as communities. *American Journal of Community Psychology, 24,* 719–748.

Sulkowski, M. L., Demaray, M. K., & Lazarus, P. J. (2012). A little help from my friends: Social support in schools and links to students' emotional well-being. *Communiqué, 41,* 1 & 6–8.

Syvertsen, A. K., Flanagan, C. A., & Stout, M. D. (2009). Code of silence: Students' perceptions of school climate and willingness to intervene in a peer's dangerous plan. *Journal of Educational Psychology, 101,* 219–232.

Szalacha, L. A. (2003). Safer sexual diversity climates: Lessons learned from an evaluation of Massachusetts safe schools program for gay and lesbian students. *American Journal of Education, 110,* 58–88.

Tardy, C. H. (1985). Social support measurement. *American Journal of Community Psychology, 13,* 187–202. doi: 10.1007/BF00905728

U.S. Census Bureau. (2010). *Census Bureau releases estimates of same-sex married couples.* Washington, DC: Author. Retrieved from www.census.gov/newsroom/releases/archives/2010_census/cb11-cn181.html

Walls, N. E., Kane, S. B., & Wisneski, H. (2010). Gay-straight alliances and school experiences of sexual minority youth. *Youth & Society, 41,* 307–332.

Wang, M., & Eccles, J. (2012). Social support matters: Longitudinal effects of social support on three dimensions of school engagement from middle to high school. *Child Development, 83,* 877–895. doi: 10.1111/j.1467-8624.2012.01745.

Weiler, E. M. (2003). Making school safe for sexual minority students. *Principal Leadership, 4,* 10–13.

Wernick, L. J., Kulick, A., & Inglehart, M. H. (2013). Factors predicting student intervention when witnessing anti-LGBTQ harassment: The influence of peers, teachers, and climate. *Children and Youth Services Review, 35,* 296–301.

Whitman, J. S. (2013). Training school professionals to work with lesbian, gay, bisexual, transgender, and questioning students and parents. In E. S. Fisher & K. Komosa-Hawkins (Eds.), *Creating safe and supportive learning environments: A guide for working with lesbian, gay, bisexual, transgender, and questioning youth and families.* (pp. 123–139). New York: Routledge.

Yoon, J., Sulkowski, M. L., & Bauman, S. (2014). Teachers' responses to bullying incidents: Effects of teacher characteristics and contexts. *Journal of School Violence, 15,* 91–113. doi: 10.1080/1538 8220.2014.963592

8 School Connectedness and Engagement

Human beings are social creatures that require safe, secure, and supportive relationships to thrive. In support of this notion, having positive relationships with caregivers, peers, and others is associated with mental health, physical health, and overall emotional well-being (Bond et al., 2007; Lee, Dean, & Jung, 2008; Yoon, Lee, & Goh, 2008). Furthermore, the belongingness hypothesis (i.e., humans have an emotional need to be an accepted member of a group) and Maslow's hierarchy of needs (i.e., basic needs must be met before individuals will strongly desire secondary or higher-level needs) suggest that feelings of belonging and social connectedness are fundamental human needs (Baumeister & Leary, 1995; Maslow, 1943). Thus, as a social species, humans naturally interact with each other to bond and create meaningful relationships.

This chapter further highlights how important it is for students to feel socially connected and engaged. In addition, certain populations of children have unique challenges and may need extra support from educators. One such population is children in military families who move on average three times more often than children in civilian life (Collins, 2009), with the majority of these children being educated in public schools (Pisano, 2014). A second population includes youth from socially and economically marginalized families that often have low social capital and are not adequately supported by social institutions. To help illustrate concepts presented, this chapter concludes with a section on unique issues impacting students from these two groups. Additionally, ways that educators can help these youth to feel better connected to their school and peer group are discussed.

Social Connection vs. Disconnection

Despite spending as much as 80 percent of their time around other people such as caregivers, classmates, siblings, and friends, children may be particularly vulnerable to feeling socially disconnected and lonely (Asher & Paquette, 2003). In this regard, research indicates that as many as 80 percent of youth and 40 percent of adults report feeling lonely "at least some time," with levels of loneliness gradually diminishing through middle adulthood (Berguno, Leroux, McAinsh, & Shaikh, 2004). Thus, from these findings, it appears that loneliness is more clearly related to perceptions of social isolation than to objective social isolation (i.e., how disconnected a person is from other people). On one hand, individuals can live relatively solitary lives and not feel lonely; however, on the other, some people can have what appear to be rich social lives and still feel lonely and socially disconnected.

According to Hawkley and Cacioppo (2010), loneliness is defined as "a distressing feeling that accompanies the perception that one's social needs are not being met by the quantity or especially the quality of one's social relationships" (p. 218). Therefore, children who have limited peer relationships and do not have supportive caregivers in their lives may be uniquely vulnerable to feeling socially disconnected, disengaged, and lonely. Findings from an early study on child loneliness indicate that about 10 percent of elementary school-aged children report feeling lonely either "always" or "most of the time" (Asher, Hymel, & Renshaw, 1984). In addition to experiencing negative emotions, these students are at risk for having difficulties at school as they often are rejected by their peers, perceived negatively by teachers, and generally feel misunderstood by others (Asher & Paquette, 2003; Woodhouse, Dykas, & Cassidy, 2012). Moreover, a growing body of research indicates that feeling lonely or socially disconnected is associated with a range of negative outcomes such as having physical health problems (e.g., cardiovascular disease, obesity, substance abuse, compromised immunity), mental health problems (e.g., anxiety, depression, heightened stress levels), and increased risk for suicide as well as experiencing impaired cognitive performance and cognitive decline, school dropout, and reduced executive functioning (see Hawkley and Cacioppo, 2010, for review). Even more concerning, chronic and intense loneliness or social disconnection has been found to be more deleterious to one's health across the lifespan than being obese. Also highly concerning, loneliness has been found to attenuate emotional well-being to a degree that is similar to the effects of living in poverty (Hawkley & Cacioppo, 2013). Lastly, social disconnection was found to be associated with premature death in a relatively recent study (e.g., Luo, Hawkley, Waite, & Cacioppo, 2012). Thus, although this may sound hyperbolic, according to research, a lack of social engagement and connection can literally kill people.

Social Connectedness

In direct contrast to loneliness or social isolation, social connectedness involves feeling bonded and connected with others. Lee and Robins (1995) report that social connectedness involves being "able to feel comfortable and confident within a larger social context than family or friends" (p. 232). Additionally, this definition also involves having the ability to identify with individuals who are perceived to be different from oneself. Thus, feeling socially connected involves experiencing a bond with nurturing individuals that provide social support while also fostering an understanding of one's own identity.

School Connectedness

School connectedness can be subsumed under a broader category of social connectedness; however, it pertains more directly to how connected students feel to the overall school social environment. With this in mind, school connectedness involves a range of subjective assessments about how comfortable students feel in the physical environment of the school campus as well as in the presence of their peers, educators, administrators, and other school personnel. Similar to the subjective experience of feeling socially disconnected more generally, school connectedness is more clearly related to perceptions of being bonded with others at school than it is to how many people with whom a student regularly affiliates.

Consistent with the aforementioned definition, a variety of terms are used to describe the construct of school connectedness. These include school belonging, school attachment, school bonding, school connection, and school engagement (Johnson, 2009; Libbey, 2004). However, the construct of school connectedness essentially involves the belief by students that "individuals in the school care about their learning as well as about them as individuals" (Wingspread Declaration on School Connections, 2004, p. 233). Furthermore, even more broad definitions of school connectedness can also involve non-immediate members of school communities such as caregivers and community members because of the influence that these individuals can have on students' perceptions of the school environment (Rowe, Stewart, & Patterson, 2007).

Impact of School Connectedness on Achievement

Preliminary research on school connectedness has established that having a sense of school membership or belonging is critical for increasing school retention and reducing dropout

(Wehlage, Rutter, Smith, Lesko, & Fernandez, 1989). Subsequent research has established a link between school connectedness and a range of positive student or educational outcomes including students' academic motivation, self-esteem, self-regulation skills, attitudes toward school, academic achievement, and quality of peer relationships (Anderman & Freeman, 2004; Hagborg, 1994; Osterman, 2000). In a study that involved examining the impact of school connectedness on the academic performance of economically disadvantaged sixth grade students, results indicated that perceptions of school connectedness declined thorough the year (Niehaus, Moritz-Rudasill, & Rakes, 2012). However, students who reported less significant declines in school connectedness had higher levels of academic achievement at the end of the year than students did who reported greater declines in connectedness. In particular, compared to girls, boys were found to be at greater risk for experiencing negative outcomes (e.g., lower school support, lower GPAs, more discipline referrals) associated with declines in school connectedness across the school year.

Impact of School Connectedness on Mental Health

School connectedness also has been found to predict students' mental health and emotional well-being. One study by Resnick et al. (1997) found that students' perceptions of school connectedness were negatively correlated with emotional distress, suicidality, violence, and substance use. Moreover, school connectedness was found to predict about 13 percent to 18 percent of the variance in emotional distress in different age groups in this study. In another study, high levels of connectedness were found to predict optimism, lower levels of depression, reduced behavior problems at school, and improved overall academic performance (Anderman, 2003). Further, the strength of the link between individual connectedness and depression was found to be significantly reduced in schools with higher levels of school connectedness, which suggests that having high levels of social bonding at school can improve students' mental health. However, in the same study, when students reported having high levels of school connectedness, these ratings were negatively associated with social rejection. Overall, this suggests that when the general level of school connectedness is high (i.e., when most students feel socially bonded), the students who do not feel socially connected might feel particularly rejected. In other words, they might feel like they are being left out when other students are being included. Therefore, it is important for all students to feel connected and engaged at school—not just the students who are naturally included.

One study on the impact of school connectedness on students' mental health found that perceptions of school connectedness overlapped highly with mental health problems, particularly depression, across time. Specifically, a study by Shochet, Dadds, Ham, and Montague (2006) found that students' ratings of their belongingness at school explained between 26 percent to 46 percent of the variance in their general mental health functioning and between 38 percent and 55 percent of their depression symptoms across the course of one year. Further, even after controlling for prior mental health symptoms, school connectedness was found to predict depressive symptoms one year later for boys and girls, anxiety symptoms for girls, and general mental health functioning for boys. Thus, results of this study highlight school connectedness's important role on the development and maintenance of mental health functioning and mental health problems in students.

Impact of School Connectedness on Other Important Outcomes

A considerable body of research indicates that school connectedness influences a range of other important outcomes for students such as their engagement in risk-taking behaviors, delinquency and violent behavior, and social relationships. In this regard, Catalano, Oesterle, Fleming, and Hawkins (2004) found that feeling socially bonded at school in fifth and sixth grade was associated with the delayed initiation of alcohol and other drug use and reduced drug abuse in later life as well as reduced delinquency and crime, lower rates of involvement in gang activity and violence, and delayed sexual activity. Similarly, school connectedness was found to impact students' involvement in health-risk and deviant behavior such as use of alcohol, marijuana, cigarettes as well as violent behavior in an earlier study by Dornbusch, Erickson, Laird, and Wong (2001). The authors of this study speculated that students who did not feel socially bonded to the school environment were more likely to associate with delinquent peers who also felt disengaged from school.

In a seminal study, Hagborg (1994) found that eighth grade students who reported having lower levels of school connectedness were more likely to be receiving counseling for having problems at school, as well as to be experiencing low self-esteem, family problems, and inter-personal difficulties when compared to students with higher levels of school connectedness. Providing further support for the important role of school connectedness on student outcomes, Maddox and Prinz (2003) conclude that school connectedness can help prevent against the devel-opment of substance use, delinquency, antisocial behaviors, and high-risk behaviors in students such as having unprotected sex. These authors suggest that feeling bonded to the school com-munity mediates the effects of weak or impaired parental attachment on students' psychosocial development. Thus, even if students experience adversity in their home or community, educators can help these students stay socially engaged engaged at school and subsequently help support their success at school and beyond.

School Engagement

Similar to school connectedness, school engagement is another term that is commonly used to describe relationships at school (Libby, 2004). Although definitional differences exist regarding this construct, these definitions usually involve the following: having a desire to attend school and to engage in instruction, regularly completing assignments, having positive affect toward school or liking school, having social connections at school, identifying with the school or having school spirit, and following school rules and meeting behavioral expectations. Therefore, consistent with this broad definition, school connectedness is an aspect of overall school engagement.

As one might expect, the different components of school engagement are interrelated. Thus, students who like and feel socially bonded at school will also likely be engaged in instruction, identify with the school, and meet behavioral expectations. Conversely, however, students who dislike and do not feel socially connected at school are more likely to disengage during instruc-tion, not identify with the school, and display behavior problems (Finn & Rock, 1997). Therefore, it is important to ensure that students feel safe and emotionally supported at school as well as excited and proactive about their own learning and development.

Guthrie and Wigfield (2000) argue that school engagement mediates the relationship between academic instruction and achievement. In light of this, they argue that students must be engaged behaviorally, cognitively, and emotionally to optimize learning and growth. Behavioral engage-ment involves participating in enriching academic, social, and extracurricular activities and it has been found to improve students' academic performance and protect students from dropping out (Fredricks, Blumenfeld, & Paris, 2004). Cognitive engagement involves being supported in one's efforts to comprehend complex ideas and master cognitive skills and it has been found to predict students' interest in school and desire to achieve (Greene, Miller, Crowson, Duke, & Akey, 2004). Lastly, emotional engagement relates to the relationships that students have with educators, peers, and the school environment more generally. The influence of being emotionally engaged at school on students' educational performance is best understood through the range of risk factors that social-emotional learning (SEL) reduces and the resiliency factors it supports that predict students' success at school and beyond. See Chapter 4 for a review of SEL and its positive effects on students' engagement and learning, and see Chapter 6 for a discussion on the importance of creating classrooms that foster resilience.

In the most comprehensive investigation to date, Wang and Eccles (2012) researched the impact of behavioral, cognitive, and emotional engagement on students' developmental trajectories from seventh grade to eleventh grade. They employed a multidimensional approach to investigate how engagement impacts students' participation at school, sense of school belonging, and self-regulated learning. In this study, the average growth trajectories of school participation, sense of belonging to school, and self-regulated learning were found to decrease from seventh through eleventh grades and the rates of decline varied across these three types of engagement. In this regard, students' sense of emotional engagement did not significantly predict students' academic achievement independent from their behavioral or cognitive engagement. Thus, even if students feel connected or emotionally bonded at school, it is still important for them to have opportunities to participate in learning opportunities and intellectually engage with instruction.

Strategies for Increasing School Connectedness and Engagement

Results from the aforementioned study by Wang and Eccles (2012) indicate that school engagement tends to decline as students transition into high school. Similarly, students' sense of school connectedness tends to decline as they advance through primary and secondary education (Marks, 2000; Ryan & Patrick, 2001). In fact, research indicates that about half (40–60 percent) of students feel disconnected and chronically disengaged from school by the time they reach high school (Furrer & Skinner, 2003; Klem & Connell, 2004). Thus, it is unfortunate that a substantial percentage of students feel both disconnected and disengaged from school when they are still in their formative years of education. Furthermore, a concerning number of students are at risk for dropping out when they are legally allowed to do so because they are less interested in what school has to offer and they no longer feel bonded to others at school. In support of this notion, research indicates that about 28 percent of U.S. students do not graduate from high school each year and many of these students do not graduate because they feel disengaged from school (Editorial Projects in Education Research Center, 2011; Fredricks et al., 2004).

However, to combat this problem, educators can reach out to at-risk students, family members of these students, and to community members directly. Similar to the adage that it takes a village to raise a child, it takes a community to educate a student. Students need support from a range of dedicated individuals and they must be provided with multiple levels of influence and support (Rowe et al., 2007). Consequently, one of the best ways to support at-risk or vulnerable students is to increase their connections with adults in the school. Chapter 15 discusses strategies to help highly vulnerable student populations.

Facilitating Community-Level Connections and Engagement

The types of community agencies, organizations, and people that influence student success vary considerably across communities. In large metropolitan communities, a wide array of resources may be present. However, in rural and impoverished inner-city communities, resources may be limited and stretched thin. Therefore, educators in these communities need to be proactive and identify individuals, groups, and agencies that can provide needed services. More specifically, in order to identify important community-level connections that can help students feel bonded and engaged at school, educators should tap into existing knowledge of these connections from people who have been working and living in the community for an extended period of time. Although considerable variability exists in their roles and titles, these individuals may be experienced teachers, administrators, other school staff, and trusted community members.

It is useful for educators to map out the various resources in their community that they can utilize to help students—especially highly at-risk students—to feel more connected and engaged at school. Some of these resources include big brother/sister organizations, community-based mental health service agencies, Boy Scouts and Girl Scouts, Boys and Girls Clubs, medical and dental clinics that accept Medicaid or sliding scale payment, social service agencies, national and local nonprofit agencies, shelters, tutoring/academic support centers, and churches, synagogues, mosques, and other religious organizations. Often, setting up healthy school–community partnerships enables students to feel more connected to their environment (Eagle, Dowd-Eagle, & Sheridan, 2008).

In Expert Interview 8.1 Donna Poland, Ph.D., discusses ways that administrators, teachers, and others can increase student engagement. Furthermore, Dr. Poland discusses ways that educators can engage important community members and organizations to increase school connectedness and engagement. Lastly, she describes ways that educators can overcome problems associated with accomplishing the former aims.

Expert Interview 8.1 with Donna Poland

Nova Southeastern University, Former Middle School Director

PJL. As a principal who has worked in middle schools and high schools in both the public and private sectors, what practices have you used to help increase student engagement? What seems to work best?

DP. During the past 34 years, I have had the privilege of being a teacher and an administrator for students in every grade level from the time they enter kindergarten through high school graduation. Elementary children want to join with their parents in fun and rewarding activities that provide opportunities to contribute to their school community. At this age, parents and school staff play a crucial role in modeling "giving back" and "making a difference" in the young child's most immediate world—the classroom and school. Demonstrations of school engagement in elementary school include student generated positive messages and thematic artwork in the hallways, student government and safety patrol positions, and making care packages for our military or the less fortunate. By the time students reach middle school, they are ready to generate their own ideas with adult guidance. They are concerned about the needs of others and making the school a safe place. They are starting to self-advocate for clubs and activities that will enrich their school experience. As they enter high school, they begin to use their self-advocacy skills to partner with school faculty and parents in meaningful ways of giving back and making a difference. Examples of high school engagement would be participating in committees such as school safety and food services; volunteering to be student ambassadors for new students; serving as an officer for various clubs; and developing community service projects. Whether the child is in a private or a public school setting, the developmental needs for engagement are the same; however, the resources available may be different. It's critical to provide many varied opportunities for students to play an important role in the school community.

PJL. How do you make sure that schools have an inclusive environment where fostering student connections are a high priority? What have you found to work best?

DP. It is vital that every student, no matter the size of the school, feels a sense of belonging. One of the first challenges for every school administrator is to make large schools feel small. My largest public high school had 4,000 students, while my private high school had 750. The techniques for ensuring an inclusive environment may be more challenging depending on the size, but the same strategies apply to small and large schools. Some of the effective strategies I've used have been creating schools within a school, establishing grade-level houses, dividing students into teacher teams, and assigning counselors according to the alphabet rather than by grade level. By using this last approach, counselors can attend to their students and their families as they move from grade to grade.

After an effective structure and schedule has been established to help ensure that all students feel included, the next goal is to design activities that promote connections between adults and students. Establishing an advisory period that meets at least once per week, and assigning a cadre of students to a teacher, who will partner with the same group throughout their school experience, will help build close relationships. During the advisory period the students focus on activities such as character lessons, school safety discussions, and community service initiatives. One of the great resources I have used to base advisory activities on is *40 Developmental Assets for Adolescents (ages 12–18)* from the Search Institute; available at www.search-institute.org/content/40-developmental-assets-adolescents-ages-12-18.

This program focuses on 40 assets (both internal and external) and provides guidance on how to take action. Categories of external assets include support, empowerment, boundaries and expectations, and constructive use of time. Internal assets categories include commitment to learning, positive values, social competencies, and positive identity.

PJL. What effective strategies or practices have you used to enhance school/community/family partnerships?

DP. I have discovered that parents need as much support in making school connections as our students do. We have to reach out to parents to include them in school life and to ensure that they feel confident in the work we do with their children. When they understand that we need them to help their children grow and thrive, then they begin to feel comfortable in their own role as a partner. To that end, it is important to provide innovative ways (beyond the Open House experience) for parents and students to enjoy a partnership with the school. Guest speakers on specific topics such as "Navigating the Teen Years," "Cyber-safety," "Building Resiliency in Children," and "Growing up in a Global Society" are examples of parent and student training that always seem to be appreciated. Additionally, creating events that are student driven and that include faculty and entire families is a good way to make schools feel like a welcoming environment. Cooking contests that include family competition, cook-outs, beach or park cleanups, Bingo Night, school carnivals that parents help sponsor, and Junior Achievement or Career Day are some examples of ways to create family engagement.

PJL. What problems have you encountered related to increasing school engagement, fostering student connections and enhancing school/community/family partnerships and how have you addressed or solved these?

DP. It's been my experience over the years in both private and public schools that parents have very complicated work schedules, child care issues, etc. They have to work hard to arrange time to come to school in the evening or during the day. When their children are involved in an activity or benefit from their attendance, they will move mountains to be at the event. I have had student groups perform before meetings, provided "get out of tardy sweep" passes to the children whose parents attend, orchestrated student-led meetings and trainings, and provided food, childcare, and open gyms for families. The trick is to figure out what draws your particular parent population to the school and what are the obstacles they have to overcome in order to attend. Another strategy that works well in today's technological age is to videotape training sessions and share materials with absent parents via e-mail or on the school's website. Also, consider building a Parent Advisory Committee that is comprised of a representative group of parents who can bring ideas and concerns to the table for athletes, performing arts students, academically focused students, and that represent the cultural, racial, and economic make-up of your school. This group of parents can be your ambassadors for getting other parents involved in school functions.

PJL. Have you found that there are ways that principals should respond to the aforementioned concerns that differ between the public and private schools? Also, how might the approaches be adapted depending on the racial, ethnic, and socioeconomic makeup of the community?

DP. As stated earlier, my experience has been that there really is not much of a difference between the needs of parents and students in public and private schools when creating a sense of belonging, safety, and security. The inclusive activities and adult/student/parent connections are equally as effective. The level of challenge in getting parent participation has varied depending on the community that the school serves. Many public schools that serve high socioeconomic families are very similar to private schools. I've been an administrator in both settings. I've also been an administrator in Title II schools and in a magnet school. While the income levels, family dynamics, and cultural experiences differ, I've been able to get very high parent involvement when the programming for their children and the involvement opportunities cater to their interests and needs. The key to getting any parent population engaged in the school community is to find out "who" they are and "what" their needs are. This can be done through surveys, town hall meetings, blogs, and parent advisory committees.

PJL. What specific advice do you have for principals and educational staff who are trying to increase student engagement and connections and forge effective linkages to families and the community?

DP. The best advice I can give is that all principals and educational staff need to create an embracing environment for parents and students that will make them feel joyful when they enter. I remember when I first became an administrator that my former principal said, "Parents will come to school carrying an emotional mindset from their own experiences in school. If it was a bad experience, they will feel anxious. If it was a good experience, they will easily become your partner." Our first challenge is to build trust within the school community. This can only be done if you have taken the time to listen and respond to parents' needs. Our second challenge is to create meaningful opportunities for students to "make a difference" in their school community. The most telling evidence is when students don't want to go home as soon as school ends because they are needed and feel valued as a member of the school community. This occurs when they are on athletic teams, in the school play, participating in a club activity, or working with their classmates and teachers on a service project. Creating a sense of belonging for every student and parent will ensure that school plays an unforgettable and important role in their lives.

Addressing the Needs of Vulnerable and At-Risk Students

Highly at-risk and vulnerable students may need to receive wraparound services to help them remain connected to school. Wraparound service-delivery involves coordinating key stakeholders that help support youth across a range of settings (Eber, Sugai, Smith, & Scott, 2002). Students who may be in need of wraparound service-delivery include youth with histories of having serious conduct problems, violent behavior and sexual perpetration, volatile episodes of emotional dysregulation, live in highly unstable or unsafe settings, and have been subjected to high levels of trauma and abuse. School-based mental health professionals who are often part of wraparound service-delivery include social workers, counselors, school psychologists, teachers, and administrators. Community-based individuals who often assist in this regard include members of social service agencies, mental health clinics, juvenile justice and law enforcement, private practitioners, and medical/clinical centers. Additionally, including parents and important caregivers is essential to ensure the success of wraparound service-delivery to help highly at-risk students stay engaged and be successful in school (Eagle et al., 2008).

Facilitating Family-Level Connections and Engagement

Family influences robustly impact how well children do in school. Children who have supportive and engaged caregivers are far more likely to be successful in school, whereas children from abusive, neglectful, and highly unstable environments are at a distinct disadvantage (Sulkowski & Michael, 2014; Williams & Sanchez, 2011). Moreover, a combination of a welcoming school environment and high rates of parental involvement has been associated with fostering school engagement and positive academic outcomes for students (Moreno, Lewis-Menchaca, & Rodriguez, 2011). Therefore, because of the important influence that parents and caregivers have on students, educators and other school-based professionals must implement a family-centered approach to understanding the immediate family factors that influence students' academic and social-emotional functioning.

According to Sheridan, Taylor, and Woods (2008), rather than viewing a student's behavior in isolation, utilizing a family-centric approach involves implementing proactive practices whereby school-based professionals facilitate positive family interactions with a student. The ultimate goal of employing a family-centric approach to facilitate family-level connections and engagement involves fostering positive working relationships between key caregivers and invested members of the school community to support family strengths that ultimately have a positive impact on children while also addressing and mitigating family problems that may negatively impact a student.

Research clearly indicates that efforts to encourage parent/family engagement in students' education result in positive outcomes for students, families, and educators (Christenson, 1995; Hickman, Greenwood, & Miller, 1995; Sheridan et al., 2008). Essentially, through being involved with students' education, caregivers can be crucial allies that support the efforts of educators. Dunst (2000) describes three key factors that help educators and school-based mental health professionals ensure that students feel socially connected at school. These include: (1) ensuring that efforts to engage family members and caregivers are proactive and positive in nature; (2) orienting interactions with family members toward the benefit of the student; and (3) focusing on supporting family/caregiver strengths and mutual partnerships as opposed to pathologizing caregivers and families. Thus, the onus is then on school-based professionals to reach out to family members, to prioritize the importance of addressing the needs of their child, and to ensure that family members feel that they are respected and supported. Following guidelines that are delineated by Roberts and Magrab (1991), Text Box 8.1 lists additional principles for utilizing a family-centric approach to engage family members and caregivers.

Text Box 8.1 Principles for Utilizing a Family-centric Approach to Engage Family Members

- Establish clear, honest, and respectful communication with family members to build trust and facilitate positive partnerships.
- Use a strength-based approach when interacting with families in which positive family factors are highlighted.

(continued)

(continued)

- Use shared decision-making processes to empower caregivers to give voice to what they think will benefit their students academically, socially, and emotionally.
- Pay attention and be sensitive to cultural and linguistic factors that influence relationships between families and schools.
- Treat each meeting or form of communication with family members as a unique event—do not use a "cookie cutter" approach.
- Coordinate the provision of concrete services and necessities (e.g., food, shelter, clothing) if the family lacks these resources.
- Reach out to extended family members who may not be legal guardians yet still have a strong influence over a student.
- Establish regular open houses and meeting times in which family members and school staff can interact, discuss ways to support students, and enrich their collaborative relationships.
- Reinforce family members for their positive efforts to support students and acknowledge barriers that negatively impact a student's learning or problems that have a deleterious effect on the family.

Facilitating School-Level Connections and Engagement

Universal or whole-school efforts to facilitate school-level connections and engagement involve providing services to all students. Although there is not yet a codified way to deliver these particular services, Rowe et al. (2007) discuss ways to promote school connection and engagement through their review of targeted efforts to improve school organization and environment; teaching, learning, and curriculum; and key partnership development.

School Organization and Environment

School organization and environment involves the interaction between policy, organization, procedures, and emotional and physical settings that influence students. These factors have been called the "hidden curriculum" and they have a robust influence on relationships between educators, students, and caregivers (Lister-Sharp, Chapman, Stewart-Brown, & Sowden, 1999). They also are influenced by norms and values that become incorporated into codes of discipline and conduct, organizational procedures, and the actual attitudes that members of school communities adopt (Smith & Sandhu, 2004). Therefore, it is important for schools to adopt policies, practices, and procedures that help students stay engaged and feel connected to members of the school community. Additionally, educators need to help with maintaining the social and physical environment at school so that it is appealing and welcoming.

Research indicates that schools that value and support positive interpersonal relationships have a strong sense of community, practice social justice and inclusion for all students, and empower students to have a voice in determining school policies that foster higher degrees of engagement and connectedness (Konu, Lintonen, & Rimpelä, 2002; Rowe et al., 2007; Smith & Sandhu, 2004). Because of the importance of having the aforementioned practices in place, educators can support the development, implementation, and maintenance of specific organizations that reach out to and include students of diverse backgrounds and experiences. In this regard, educators ought to support student-run organizations (e.g., student council), extra-curricular clubs and activities, intramural sport and athletic clubs, tutoring and mentoring opportunities, leisure and social activities, and culturally enriching and inclusive clubs and organizations (Rowe et al., 2007). Furthermore, Markham and Aveyard (2003) advocate for including students and student-run organizations in the decision-making procedures at school as relationships between students and educators tend to improve by doing so. Ultimately, the relationships that students and educators build are integral to fostering and solidifying social connectedness and engagement (Voisin et al., 2005).

Addressing the Physical Environment

Efforts to improve the physical environment at school often are limited by financial and logistical issues. Overcrowded, poorly maintained, and underfunded schools will struggle to maintain current obligations and not be able to change their physical environment drastically. However, even schools that have been neglected for years can make slight modifications to their buildings and grounds to help improve students' feelings of connectedness to these environments. Safe, clean, pleasant, and welcoming school environments are associated with improvements in prosocial behavior at school as well as with higher degrees of school connectedness (Johnson, 2009; Konu et al., 2002; Smith & Sandhu, 2004). Therefore, educators can help to enhance the overall physical environment of the school to improve connectedness through maintaining adequate supervision to prevent vandalism, coordinating regular clean-ups of school grounds, displaying students' artwork on campus, and working with local nonprofit organizations that can help beautify the campus through planting trees and flowers as well as providing students with opportunities to become involved with agricultural activities such as growing vegetables, fruits and herbs; developing a butterfly sanctuary; and raising animals. Chapter 2 provides additional information on improving physical and emotional environments in schools.

Teaching, Learning, and Curriculum

The delivery of engaging teaching, effective learning strategies, and an enriching curriculum is important for helping students stay on task during instruction as well as connected to the school community. For students to stay engaged and actively participate in class, they will need ample opportunities to interact regularly with others. This concept highlights the need for providing them with multiple opportunities to respond and participate with peers (Hulac, Terrell, Vining, & Bernstein, 2011). In general, teaching and learning activities that have been found to engage students' learning and keep them feeling connected include facilitating rich class discussions, working collaboratively in small groups, providing cooperative learning activities, and engaging in shared tasks and peer mentoring (Korinek, Walther-Thomas, McLaughlin, & Williams, 1999; Rowe et al., 2007; Smith & Sandhu, 2004).

The success of the aforementioned teaching and learning strategies highlights the strong social need that students have and how important it is for them to feel socially connected to others while they engage in instruction. Similarly, the core tenants of social-emotional learning (SEL) also aim to foster student engagement and connectedness (see Chapter 4 for more information on SEL). Thus, efforts to help students stay academically and emotionally connected to school and the curriculum should be thought of as two sides of the same coin. Furthermore, it also is important for students to apply what they learn to their everyday lives. Students often are too present-minded and shortsighted to understand how learning abstract concepts in school will enhance their overall reasoning and critical thinking abilities. However, if educators can effectively break down abstract concepts through using real-world examples and embed learning, some students who otherwise would disengage might be able to understand and appreciate these concepts. This notion of deriving meaning from direct experience is called "experiential learning" and it has been found to help facilitate school connectedness and engagement (Rowe et al., 2007; Teranishi, 2007).

Developing Key Partnerships

Maintaining school connectedness and engagement among students requires dedicated educators and other members of school communities to prioritize these efforts on a regular basis. Unfortunately, however, educators often feel stretched thin because of expectations that their students will meet benchmarks on statewide standardized achievement tests. These educators often feel overburdened and wonder how they will find time to prioritize initiatives that focus on fostering school connectedness and engagement.

To address this concern, it is important to emphasize that increasing academic achievement and bolstering school connectedness and engagement are complementary and can be addressed concomitantly. From the bottom up, concerned teachers can team up and support each other with their efforts to help all students feel socially connected and stay engaged at school. From the top down, district leaders and administrators can provide more flexibility to educators at the school-building level to implement programs such as SEL and effective curricula that foster engaging teaching and the implementation of effective learning strategies, while also providing opportunities to allow for rich social interactions that enhance learning. Text Box 8.2 lists specific ways that various members of school communities can help facilitate school connectedness and engagement.

Text Box 8.2 Ways that Members of School Communities Can Help Facilitate School Connectedness and Engagement

- Focus on barriers to success in school in lieu of student problems or deficits.
- Avoid stigmatizing language, labeling students, and being culturally insensitive.
- Become educated about the struggles of highly at-risk and vulnerable student populations and actively work to make these students feel comfortable at school.
- Support and respect LGBT students through displaying safe-space stickers and posters that are available through the Gay, Lesbian & Straight Education Network (GLSEN).
- Take action when bullying or peer victimization occurs. This involves addressing the bully, the victim, and student bystanders.
- Display student work products and pictures around the classroom and school.
- Provide highly mobile students (e.g., homeless students, foster care youth) with a safe space or locker to store their personal possessions.
- Have classroom pets, plants, and lounging areas accessible to students.
- Have regular check-in meetings with students to understand how they are doing in and outside of school; this provides them with an opportunity to open up and it helps to solidify teacher–student relationships.
- Allow students to participate in creating and buying into school and classroom rules
- Establish "new student" groups, mentoring programs/initiatives, and friendship groups.
- Provide students with healthy snacks and drinks.
- Allow students to explore their own creative pursuits and celebrate students' creative efforts.
- Integrate art, music, movement, and non-traditional activities into instruction and regular school practices.
- Connect lessons and instructional activities to students' interests, hobbies, and personally meaningful topics.
- Provide a range of extracurricular learning opportunities, experiences, and opportunities for students to socialize.

Facilitating Peer-to-Peer Connections and Mitigating Peer Conflict

Research on the effects of peer connections has expanded during the past few decades. More than 40 years ago, two salient researchers made significant contributions in this regard

(Garbarino & deLara, 2002). One of these individuals, Ronald Rohner (1975), was an anthropologist who studied 118 cultures around the world in an effort to understand how rejection influenced the lives of children and adolescents. He found that different cultures express rejection in a variety of ways. However, in every culture, youth who were socially rejected also were maladjusted. From this research, Rohner concluded that rejection is a form of emotional cancer, a form of psychological malignancy. Another prominent researcher, Stanley Coopersmith (1974), studied young people in the U.S. to understand how and why they experienced acceptance and how it impacted them (Coopersmith & Feldman, 1974). His conclusion parallels the findings of Rohner. That is, children need acceptance to feel good about themselves and they will do almost anything to get it. As a poignant example, this can even include engaging in painful initiation rituals such as being "jumped into" a gang or committing crimes to be accepted by peers.

Through knowing the former, it becomes increasingly clear that educators need to ensure that every child feels accepted in his or her classroom and at school. Research indicates that students' friendships are created or strengthened when they engage in fun or challenging activities together. In support of this idea, Doll, Brehm, and Zucker (2014) provide suggestions that are applicable for fostering social connections on the playground. For example, educators can teach students to play non-competitive games that have no clear winners or losers. Further, teachers can hold game clinics that involve teaching a new game during recess to a small group of isolated students. Then, once the game is underway, anyone can join in and participate, thus making the experience inclusive of all students yet establishing the isolated students as early participants in the game. Furthermore, Doll et al. (2014) also suggest that teachers can add developmentally appealing games to the playground and pay special attention to games that can be played by students with limited athletic ability or can be played in dyads, as well as in small or large groups.

It is important for educators to ensure that students feel socially connected during unstructured times in the school day when they interact with and engage their peers. Some of these times include during lunch, recess, "bell work," and study hall. In particular, during lunchtime, educators can make it mandatory for all children to sit in groups and interact with each other. Moreover, they can require all children to participate with each other during activities and ensure that no student is excluded. Over time, this can become part of the classroom culture. The mantra can be: *In our class, no one sits alone* and students can be commended during weekly classroom meetings for including others as well as for engaging in acts of kindness.

During classroom activities, Doll et al. (2014) suggest that educators find multiple tasks for students to do together and for them to occasionally mix them up to work with unexpected partners. This can be for instructional tasks, classroom privileges, or chores. It may be helpful for children who lack friends to give out rewards (e.g., stickers, line leader assignments, homework passes) that are based on the input from the teacher. In this way, these students may be perceived more positively as they develop competence with completing helpful tasks in the classroom and interacting with their peers. Additionally, educators can incorporate the jigsaw method as part of their instructional strategies, which is an instructional strategy that hinges on students' contributions to a group or a team.

In addition to fostering positive interpersonal relations, educators spend a good deal of instructional time trying to prevent peer conflicts. Conflicts in human relationships are inevitable; however, the frequency and intensity of conflicts can be reduced. With that said, a proactive approach to prevention is warranted. In this regard, Doll et al. (2014, p. 103) offer a myriad of strategies for reducing conflicts on the playground so that students can learn how to manage conflicts more successfully and have more fun together.

Some of these strategies include: (1) conduct a recess workshop in which students tour the playground together. During this time, they are educated about the rules, routines, proper use of equipment, and actions that supervisors may take when there are problems; (2) write down easy to follow rules about playground games (e.g., soccer, kickball, basketball) that students often argue about; (3) invite local athletes to school to discuss good sportsmanship; (4) ensure that playground games are situated so that they do not interfere with each other; (5) add more supervisors to the playground and have them circulate as necessary to help students resolve conflicts; (6) attempt to solve predictable arguments in advance with classroom meetings and by practicing good problem-solving skills. Or after a major conflict has occurred, have students discuss ways that the situation could have been better resolved; (7) hold a recess school for any student who has to sit out recess more than three times in a month. During this time, the student should over-practice the right way to play games or interact with classmates on the playground; (8) if it has been found that older children have been intimidating or bullying younger children on the playground, then reschedule recess so that both groups are not on the field at the same time.

Social Justice and Fostering School Connectedness and Engagement

Social justice involves treating all students fairly, with respect, and empowering them with the same opportunities, protections, and rights that all other students have (Shriberg et al., 2008). Unfortunately, however, students from marginalized populations and groups do not have the same rights, opportunities, and protections that students from the majority group have. These groups may include students from low-income families, racial and ethnic minority groups, children of migrant workers, and linguistically diverse or English language learners (Raffaele & Knoff, 1999). Moreover, students from marginalized families that have had negative experiences at school or with members of school communities are likely to be even more disengaged from school because of erosions in trust and perceptions of not fitting in based on past experiences (Harris, 2011). The cultural values and expectations that currently are espoused in many U.S. schools reflect White middle-class values, which can cause culturally and linguistically diverse students to feel alienated and misunderstood (Hong, 2011). Additionally, marginalized youth might feel like they must discard their own values and beliefs if they want to fit in and feel socially connected at school.

Anti-immigrant sentiment. Currently, a new wave of anti-immigrant sentiment is impacting children and families who have recently immigrated to the U.S. In support of this notion, almost half (42 percent) of Americans identify immigration as a "very big problem" that impacts the country (Pew Research Center, 2006). Furthermore, xenophobia has risen considerably in the U.S. since the 1990s and hate crimes have become more prevalent against immigrants (McDevitt, Shively, & Subramanian, 2011; Potok, 2008). Perhaps even more concerning is that legislative acts such as the Illegal Immigration Reform of 1996 and the Enhanced Border Security and Visa Entry Reform Act of 2002 have contributed to a hostile dynamic between U.S.-born individuals and immigrants and have eroded school and family connections in immigrant communities (Androff, Ayon, Becerra, & Gurrola, 2011; Massey, Durand, & Malone, 2003). Additionally, English language only policies that exist in many U.S. states serve to alienate linguistically diverse students and families, which further reduces family–school connections (Bartolomé, 2008). Essentially, acts that purport to limit or exclude immigration drastically reduce the provision of social services to undocumented immigrants or send them back to their country of origin, discriminate against English language learners, and require educational institutions to report foreign students to the U.S. Immigration and Naturalization Service disenfranchise an important and growing group of students and place these students at risk for negative academic and social outcomes (Massey et al., 2003; Sulkowski, Bauman, Wright, Nixon, & Davis, 2014).

Fortunately, research indicates that culturally and linguistically diverse students who feel socially connected in their neighborhood and have positive relationships with educators tend to be resilient and to succeed academically (Brown, 2008; Maurizi, Ceballo, Epstein-Ngo, & Cortina, 2013). In addition, many marginalized populations have and maintain a strong sense of collectivism, which can enhance resilience in these student populations (McPherson, Alves, Burns, & Diaz, 2014). Therefore, concerned educators can capitalize on strong community bonds to increase student and family connections and collaborations.

Youth in Military Families

Approximately 1.98 million children and adolescents had one or both parents in the military in 2009 according to the U.S. Department of Defense (2010). These included 1.25 million youth who had parents in active duty and 728,000 who had parents in the reserves. Because of deployments, more than two million youth have experienced the absence of one or both of their parents at some point during their development.

Compared to previous decades, the smaller and professionalized composition of the contemporary U.S. military influences the educational needs of children in military families (Fletcher, 2013). Having a smaller military concentrates more responsibilities, hardships, and stressors on fewer families and it increases the likelihood that children will experience their caregivers going through multiple and long-term deployment cycles during different phases in their lives (Meagher, 2007). As noted by Tanielian and Jaycox (2008), these deployments can place a heavy emotional burden on families. Family members experience concerns about the safety of their loved ones who serve in various branches of the military. Ultimately, these concerns may be highly distressing to children who depend on family members for love, guidance, and support. As evidence of this notion, research indicates that children in military families have significantly higher rates of anxiety and behavior problems when compared to children from nonmilitary families (Chandra et al., 2010). Moreover, these effects are even exaggerated in families that have been impacted by long-term and multiple deployments. Thus, many children from military families struggle to adjust to the absence of an important caregiver and worry about the safety of their caregiver.

One factor that influences distress experienced by children in military families is the amount and type of media coverage a conflict or war garners. For example, the extensive media coverage during the Iraq war was associated with elevated worries in children about their parent's safety and possible death (Huebner & Mancini, 2005). Moreover, research indicates that children who had a parent deployed between 2006 and 2007 (or around the time of the U.S. troop surge) had an 11 percent higher rate of visits to clinics due to behavioral or mental health issues compared to children whose parents were not deployed (Gorman, Eide, & Hisle-Gorman, 2010).

In addition to children in active duty (or full-time) military families, Pisano (2014) points out that children whose parents are members of the National Guard and Reserve also are impacted by their parent's service. Because these youth do not typically live on military bases, they may not have easy access to supportive organizations such as Army Community Services and Military One Source. Pisano (2014) further notes that families on active duty live in communities with other families in similar circumstances, which enables them to connect easily with other active duty families that are dealing with the same problems and thereby receive support from their neighbors. Moreover, families in these communities can relate to the deployment experiences of each other, and understand the emotional hardship that this entails. However, families of the National Guard and Reserve do not have such connections and often feel isolated because their neighbors and friends may not understand their experiences (Segal & Segal, 2003).

In addition to discussing the aforementioned risks, it is important to stress that children from military families show the same type of behavioral and mental health outcomes that their peers do from nonmilitary families during peacetime. Additionally, being connected to the military can imbue feelings of pride, civic responsibility, duty, purpose, and patriotism. Thus, children in military families may feel increased respect for a parent who is making an important sacrifice to serve their country (Pisano, 2014). Essentially, it is not military service that negatively impacts children—it is the stress of war, active deployment, injuries (both physical and psychological) and death that takes a toll on children and families.

Unique Challenges Experienced by Youth in Military Families

As previously noted, one of the biggest challenges children from military families face is being separated from their parents because of deployment. Even more burdensome, when a single parent is deployed, children will need to be placed with another caregiver or friend and they will have to adjust to a new lifestyle, community, peers, or school. As one would suspect, this can be particularly challenging and disorienting for children.

Collins (2009) reports that students in active-duty military families have extremely high mobility rates. They move about every two to three years on average and they can often experience six to nine relocations during their K-12 school years (U.S. Department of Defense, 2009). These youth may also have to adjust to changes in the school curriculum and teaching methods, which can impact their academic achievement and progress. In addition, they may have to deal with understanding and interpreting different school regulations and policies, taking different high-stakes exams that vary state by state, and adjusting to new school cultures. Regarding their social lives, these youth frequently have to make new friends, find a new peer group, and adjust to a new home, neighborhood, and school. At the same time, if they had a positive experience in their last location, then they will experience loss—loss of their friends, peer group, school, community and all the other related connections (e.g., clubs, sports teams, activities, scouts, places of worship, etc.). Or if they had a special connection to an important adult (e.g., a mentor, a football coach, a pastor, etc.) or held a position in their school or community (e.g., a captain of the soccer team, member of the cheerleaders, secretary of the computer club, etc.), they will experience feelings of loss when they have to relocate. Furthermore, as emphasized by Pisano (2014), in those circumstances where children from military families have special education needs or require other accommodations, they may have difficulty getting needed services because of differences in regulations, resource availability, and evaluations that are required to receive extra support and services.

Youth in military families often need to adjust to deployments as well as the return of their parent. In some cases, they may need to deal with both physical and mental injuries suffered by their parents and with changes in the parental relationship. It is estimated that up to 30 percent of military personnel returning from the wars in Iraq and Afghanistan have incurred a mild to moderate traumatic brain injury (TBI) during deployment (Glasser, 2006), while up to 26 percent of service members develop symptoms of posttraumatic stress (PTSD) or a major depressive disorder (MDD; Tanielian & Jaycox, 2008). It is also common for service members with a TBI to also have PTSD, particularly if a blast-related injury occurred that resulted in loss of consciousness (Kennedy et al., 2007). It has been estimated that roughly one half of service members seek treatment for either TBI or mental health concerns and the increase in suicides of returning service members is a national concern.

The suicide rate of soldiers jumped 80 percent from 2004 to 2008, and while this rate leveled off in 2010 and 2011, it soared 18 percent in 2012 according to a story in *Time* magazine aptly titled "The war on Suicide? More U.S. soldiers have killed themselves than have died in the Afghan war. Why can't the army win the war on suicide?" (Gibbs & Thompson, 2012.) The authors of this report explain that combat trauma alone cannot account for the aforementioned trend. Nearly a third of the suicides from 2005 to 2010 were among troops who had never deployed and 43 percent had deployed only once. Only 8.5 percent had deployed three or four times. Moreover, nearly 95 percent of suicide cases were male and the majority of these individuals were married. As might be expected, all war-related injuries and losses—both physical and psychological—impact the overall stability of families of military personnel as they struggle to manage and treat the injuries and their effects, which in many cases can overwhelm their ability to cope with adversity (Tanielian, Jaycox, Adamson, & Metscher, 2008).

Helping Youth in Military Families

Forging connections with children in military families is paramount to helping students from these families and this can be achieved by developing a relationship between the child, his or her family, and the school. In a longitudinal study, the best predictor of how well a youth will cope with the deployment of a parent was found to be the health and well-being of the nondeployed parent (Flake, Davis, Johnson, & Middleton, 2009). Moreover, according to the U.S. Army (2012), the mental state of the nondeployed parent is considered a stronger influence on the child than having a caregiver go through multiple deployments or experience threats of injury or death. Consequently, it is important for school personnel to develop a relationship with the parents and to help support them during all phases of deployment. These include pre-deployment, deployment, rest and relaxation (also called sustainment), reunion, and reintegration (see Pisano, 2014, for an extended discussion on the impact of the five major stages of deployment and its impact on children and families). It also is important for educators to make sure that parents or caregivers are given the opportunity to share any concerns regarding how their child is coping at home and to let them know that they should feel free to speak with the child's teacher or a school-based mental health professional at any time (Rahill, 2013).

Although most children and families experience some type of decline in well-being during the absence of a parent, most children and families do find ways to adjust. Thus, educators should be sensitive to the wide variability in how military families respond to their experiences. Furthermore, each child will have different needs, even within the same family. For example, Rahill (2013), a school psychology graduate educator whose husband was deployed for one year in Afghanistan, noted that one of her sons wanted to talk in school with his friends and teachers about the deployment of his father, whereas her other son did not want to feel different from his peers so he told no one at school about his father's deployment.

Collins (2009), a school superintendent, provides these suggestions in order to establish bonds between the school and children and families and to enable every child to feel a sense of stability. It is important to emphasize that these ideas are not entirely specific to children from military families and many of these ideas can be modified and used with any new student entering the school. For example, ideas similar to these were shared with school districts in the aftermath of Hurricane Katrina when students from Mississippi and Louisiana were relocated to school systems all across the country. These strategies are listed below:

1. Develop a Welcome Packet for Military Children

Include information about the mission of the school district, graduation requirements, curriculum requirements, attendance requirements, dress code requirements, immunizations, and school calendar, as well as school-specific information about clubs and organizations, a map of the school, and bell schedule. Also include information about resources for military families, including special workshops, orientations, and transition activities. (See a sample Checklist for Transferring Students on the Military Child Education Coalition website at www.militarychild.org.)

2. Establish a Buddy Program for Military Children at Each School

A buddy is another student in the school that can be paired with a recently arrived military student. This individual can serve as a key source of information about the school, its programs, extracurricular activities, sports, expectations, and traditions and can be someone to sit with at lunch and at athletic events. The Junior Student to Student and the Student to Student transition programs developed by the Military Child Education Coalition are effective models (www.militarychild.org).

3. Encourage Parents and Guardians to Be Active in the School

Their presence in the school may provide a sense of comfort to ease their child's transition. Encourage their involvement in the PTA, on committees, and on school and district planning teams. In addition, parents may be able to share some insights into how the school can make their child feel more connected and engaged. Publicize volunteer opportunities in school newspapers and on the school and district websites.

4. Promote Student Participation in Extracurricular Activities

Extracurricular activities are an excellent way for students to meet classmates and quickly feel a part of the school, so help them explore all the options. Military students may come to the school after the deadline for signing up for activities, auditioning for drama productions, or trying out for sports—encourage teachers and coaches to find a place for them anyway.

5. Encourage Parents, Guardians, and Students to Become Involved with National Organizations

Involvement in national organizations such as Boy Scouts, Girl Scouts, and 4H will help families connect to the community. Association with national organizations also will pave the way for continued connections when the families move to a different community, where the organization can provide a sense of continuity.

Another way that teachers can connect with children in military families is to help them keep a journal that they can share with their deployed parent (Pisano, 2014). In doing so, the teacher could prompt the student with questions to stimulate their writings or they could help them write e-mails or letters. But the most important thing an educator can do is to be there for the child, listen with empathy, and provide support and reassurance.

In the following interview Katie Eklund, Ph.D., who has worked directly with many military families, discusses the challenges that youth in military families face, especially when their parents are deployed. She offers strategies on how to help children deal with deployments and strategies that educators can use in the classroom. In addition, she offers suggestions on how to help youth deal with the death of a parent and provides a description of internet and web resources available.

Expert Interview 8.2 with Katie Eklund

University of Missouri

PJL. What are some unique educational and psychological challenges that children in military families face?

KE. Since September of 2001, well over two million U.S. troops have been deployed for tours of duty and approximately two million school-aged children have parents who are active duty military. Military-connected youth are at an increased risk of behavioral and academic concerns due to normal developmental stressors as well as stressors induced by military life. This includes traumatic events, such as parent separation, deployment, and/or parent death, frequent moves and relocation, and injuries to an active duty parent. Due to the job requirements, military families move more frequently than civilians, and service members are often separated from their families for months at a time due to training and/or deployment duties. Supportive schools and staff can help shield students from many of these negative outcomes and can help promote positive academic, social, emotional, and health-related outcomes.

PJL. How might educators and school-based mental health professional help mitigate these challenges and support these youth using a school-wide approach?

KE. School-based mental health professionals, such as school psychologists, social workers, and counselors are essential to providing behavioral and emotional supports to military connected youth. For example, school psychologists are trained to design, implement, and evaluate school-wide policies and practices that can address the unique needs of military children. These include broad *universal prevention* strategies that promote resiliency enhancing skills intended to sustain families through challenges. All educators are called on to create a culture of caring at school, where each person is treated with respect and kindness. Social emotional learning skills can be taught in each classroom so that children develop effective coping and problem-solving skills to address any concern they might face. Educators are encouraged to ask children and families about military connections as well as work to understand the unique experiences of military connected youth. Schools or classrooms can develop a "wall of heroes" where military connected students can place pictures of their parent or write a message describing why their mom or dad is their hero.

PJL. What classroom-based strategies have you found to be most useful?

KE. Educators are encouraged to develop *targeted strategies* that help families experiencing multiple deployments, combat-related injuries, posttraumatic stress disorder, or a parent's death. During parent deployment, for example, children can be encouraged to keep a journal describing their activities at home and school while mom or dad is away, including pictures or drawings that may highlight favorite activities or memories. Technological advances have also made it possible for students to create short videos or messages that can be easily attached to an e-mail and sent overseas. Students can also be encouraged to talk openly about their experiences during deployment, understanding that routines and responsibilities at home have changed. By setting aside even 30–45 minutes a week to help a child stay connected to a deployed parent, educators are building an important family–school connection that will go a long way in not only demonstrating the value and worth of each service member, but in honoring the unique experiences of military youth.

PJL. How might the process of deployment and multiple deployments impact children in military families?

KE. Having a parent or family member who is deployed can place a number of new demands on a child. Not only can the actual time the parent is away place a significant burden on the family system, but also each stage of the deployment cycle (i.e., pre-deployment, deployment, sustainment, reunion, reintegration) presents new challenges that every family member will have to learn how to successfully navigate. This can include the ever-changing dates of when mom or dad may be deployed (including only a few hours notice for those in Special Forces) as well as the post-deployment period, when service members come home from war and must be reintegrated into families whose internal rhythms have changed. Many times children have taken on new roles and experienced multiple developmental changes during the long months a parent has been away. Additional patience and understanding are needed to traverse a service member's reintegration into the family.

The mental health and capacity of parents or caretakers also relates strongly to how well children adapt to the stress of deployment. Mental health issues in a parent often impede the parent's ability to respond to a child's needs in an adaptive fashion. Family-centered interventions are needed to help support a child within the context of their family, as well as provide additional resources to help mom or dad facing their own mental health needs, and/or parenting needs within the family.

It is important to note that families respond to deployments differently; many are distressed but can sustain health and wellness, while others experience a great deal of difficulty when faced with these significant stressors. This range of responses calls for school personnel to employ a wide range of strategies that support health and wellness, screen for behavioral and emotional risk, and engage students and families who struggle most.

PJL There are a number of different educational resources available to help educators and school-based mental health professionals provide effective services to these students and their families. What have you found to be the most helpful?

KE. A number of programs, websites, and agencies have surfaced over the last 20 years, increasing the availability of services provided to military children and their families. The Military Child Education Coalition (MCEC; www.militarychild.org) is a nonprofit organization dedicated to ensuring quality educational opportunities for all military children. MCEC provides professional development training and publishes resources for educators and agencies working with military connected youth, in addition to offering materials and services for military children and families. Military OneSource (militaryonesource.mil) also provides a number of helpful resources to military connected youth and their families, including tips on deployment, parenting, relationships, grief, and childhood services.

One constant of military life is experiencing multiple relocations to new installations, also known as a Permanent Change of Station (PCS). The PCS has an especially profound impact on children with disabilities and their families as they experience gaining and losing special education service providers, as well as new laws and regulations guiding special education practices upon entering into new districts and states. As school mental health providers are often involved in special education decisions, including eligibility and placement considerations as well as the development of IEP goals and objectives, practitioners must be prepared to support military youth with special needs. A number of support services are available to help ease this transition. These include the Exceptional Family Member Program (EFMP), benefits through the Extended Health Care Option (EHCO), and TRICARE benefits specifically targeting military youth with special needs.

PJL. How might school administrators, teachers, and school-based mental health professionals best respond when it has been confirmed that a parent, caregiver, brother, or sister of a student has died as a result of military deployment? What practices and supports have you found to be the most helpful and what should all educators know about how to help students and families cope and grieve? Also what specific resources would you recommend for schools to use to help students and faculty following these tragic deaths?

KE: It can be traumatic for a child to lose their parent or family member, especially when a service member does not return home. Educators can best be supportive of students in a number of important ways. First, be clear when communicating with children. Do not lie or tell half-truths about the event. It is important to use the word "death" when talking about someone who has passed away. Referring to death using phrases such as "going to sleep" may only serve to incite fear of bedtime for many children.

Second, many children will need to talk about the event more than once. Educators should encourage students to ask questions and stay open to the discussion as needed over time. Allow the child to guide the conversation and direct what information or support he or she may need.

And finally, don't assume all children grieve in the same way. As grief can affect how children express their feelings, relate to others, and behave, be aware that there is no one way for a child to understand or cope with a traumatic event. Teachers and school personnel can be an important source of support, and should establish an open line of communication between home and school. It is helpful for children to have multiple sources of support. A number of resources are available that address traumatic grief in military children (www.nctsnet.org) and can provide resources for teachers and parents faced with the difficult task of helping children cope with loss, death, and grief (www.nasponline.org).

PJL. Please provide some resources that educators can consult to help children from military families.

KE. Stephanie Rahill (2013) has listed these links which educators will find helpful.

- Military OneSource (www.militaryonesource.com) contains information for caregivers about parenting, children's mental health, behavioral and emotional functioning, and information about common concerns for families such as homework completion, tutoring, participation in activities, and more.
- Military Child Education Coalition (www.militarychild.org) provides information and resources to parents and school personnel about transitions, impact of deployments, school change, and other common stressors for children.
- Military Kids Toolkit (www.militaryfamily.org) contains information provided by military children ages 6 to 11 years old about the best and hardest parts of living a military life.
- Military Homefront (www.militaryhomefront.dod.mil) is the official Department of Defense website for the military community and family policy.
- MyMilitaryLife is a new app that can be downloaded by family members. This app, created by the National Military Family Association, provides personalized to-do lists and access to resources to use to accomplish goals and tasks.
- Operation Military Kids (http://www.operationmilitarykids.org/public/home.aspx) provides information about programs and support options for children in the communities in which they live.
- The Educator's Guide to the Military Child During Deployment (www2.ed.gov/about/offices/list/os/homefront/homefront.pdf) provides school personnel with interventions that can be used in the classroom for children experiencing the deployment of a parent.

In addition, the Coalition to Support Grieving Students (https://grievingstudents.org/) was developed that has state-of-the-art information related to helping children deal with grief and bereavement. Educators can find videos, PowerPoint presentations, pdf files, and other related resources. This is especially important as I have found that teachers want information of this topic, yet have not been well prepared to handle such painful issues as the death of a parent, caregiver, sibling or friend.

Facilitating School Connectedness for Marginalized Students

It is important for educators to prioritize fostering positive interactions and relationships with students and families that may feel disconnected and disengaged from the school community. While discussing ways to increase school connectedness for marginalized youth, McPherson et al. (2014) report that "a critical step for schools to take is to encourage familial collaboration and participation in order to promote positive experiences for students and families in hopes of breaking the cycle of perpetual dissatisfaction with schools" (p. 14). Ultimately, this involves creating an open and welcoming environment for all students and families.

To help establish connections, schools can have regular meetings that are open to everyone and host diverse members of the community who can discuss critical issues that are impacting youth in the community. Further, to lessen the burden on families, schools can provide inexpensive meals such as spaghetti dinners or partner up with local restaurants to provide catering services. For these meetings, schools can also provide volunteer babysitting services for children while their parents are participating. In addition, educators can set up a special parent/caregiver room in the school in which these individuals can interact with other members of the school community such as teachers and administrators. To promote engagement among students and caregivers from marginalized populations, educators can promote volunteer opportunities for interested individuals to help improve and beautify the school campus. One of the best ways to do this is for educators to directly ask parents to become involved and then tell them how needed their services are. For example, educators can coordinate opportunities to plant trees, clean up litter, and re-paint parts of the school. These opportunities help students and members of the community feel invested in efforts to support the school community. Moreover, as another way to engage members of marginalized populations, schools can create parental advisory boards that allow for caregivers to voice their opinions on how best to support students, impact school organization and governance, and capitalize on community strengths (Halgunseth, 2009; Jeltova & Fish, 2005; McPherson et al., 2014). This might also involve connecting with community leaders and powerbrokers such as local ministers, community advocates, civil rights attorneys and representatives, and others. In addition, community elders might need to be engaged to allow certain members of marginalized populations to feel comfortable expressing themselves and participating more fully in efforts to support and educate their children.

Collectively, the aforementioned efforts aim to bridge gaps that may exist between school culture and the culture of families and community members. The success of these efforts then depends on how convenient educators can make it for students and their family members to participate and feel included in the day-in and day-out functioning of schools (Halgunseth, 2009). Simply increasing interactions between educators and members of marginalized populations is a starting place; however, efforts to understand and celebrate the unique culture, social history, and shared experiences among these individuals goes much further for fostering trust and meaningful community–school relationships that span across generations (Good, Masewicz, & Vogel, 2010; McPherson et al., 2014). Essentially, through accepting and reaching out to all students and families independent of their individual differences, educators can make impressive strides toward increasing student connectedness and engagement.

Conclusion

Having positive relationships with caregivers, peers, and others is associated with emotional well-being, mental health, physical health, and overall positive life outcomes. To facilitate success in school, it is critically important for students to feel socially connected to members of the school community and engaged in instruction. In this regard, a number of studies have found a link between school connectedness and a range of positive student or educational outcomes including students' academic motivation, self-esteem, self-regulation, attitudes toward school, academic achievement, and quality of peer relationships. Fortunately, a range of strategies exist to help increase students' sense of connectedness and engagement at the community, family, school, and classroom levels. Additionally, through enacting change in the organization and environment of schools, utilizing teaching strategies that help foster a sense of connection and mutual responsibility, ensuring that curricula are culturally relevant to all populations represented in the community, and by reaching out to key stakeholders, educators can reconnect and engage students who may feel alienated or marginalized at school. Lastly, to increase connectedness and engagement for all students, educators should reach out to students from military families and historically marginalized populations and focus on increasing social justice at school. Like threads in a spider web, each individualized effort to connect with a student results in an increasingly sophisticated and strong web of interconnections that enables each student to thrive.

References

Anderman, L. H. (2003). Academic and social perceptions as predictors of change in middle school students' sense of school belonging. *Journal of Experimental Education, 72,* 5–22.

Anderman, L. H., & Freeman, T. M. (2004). Students' sense of belonging in school. *Advances in Motivation and Achievement, 13,* 27–63.

Androff, D. K., Ayon, C., Becerra, D., & Gurrola, M. (2011). US immigration policy and immigrant children's well-being: The impact of policy shifts. *Journal of Sociology and Social Welfare, 38,* 77–98.

Asher, S. R., Hymel, S., & Renshaw, P. D. (1984). Loneliness in children. *Child Development, 55,* 1456–1464.

Asher, S. R., & Paquette, J. A. (2003). Loneliness and peer relations in childhood. *Current Directions in Psychological Science, 12,* 75–78.

Bartolomé, L. I. (2008). Focus on policy: Understanding policy for equity in teaching and learning: A critical-historical lens. *Language Arts, 85,* 376–381.

Baumeister, R. F., & Leary, M. R. (1995). The need to belong: Desire for interpersonal attachments as a fundamental human motivation. *Psychological Bulletin, 117,* 497–529.

Berguno, G., Leroux, P., McAinsh, K., & Shaikh, S. (2004). Children's experience of loneliness at school and its relation to bullying and the quality of teacher interventions. *Qualitative Report, 9,* 483–499.

Bond, L., Butler, H., Thomas, L., Carlin, J., Glover, S., Bowes, G., & Patton, G. (2007). Social and school connectedness in early secondary school as predictors of late teenage substance use, mental health, and academic outcomes. *Journal of Adolescent Health, 40,* 357–359.

Brown, D. L. (2008). African American resiliency: Examining racial socialization and social support as protective factors. *Journal of Black Psychology, 34,* 32–48. doi:10.1177/0095798407310538.

Catalano, R. F., Oesterle, S., Fleming, C. B., & Hawkins, J. D. (2004). The importance of bonding to school for healthy development: Findings from the Social Development Research Group. *Journal of School Health, 74,* 252–261.

Chandra, A., Larea-Cinisomo, S., Jaycox, L., Tanielan Bing Han, T., Burns, R., & Ruder, T. (2010). Children on the home front: The experiences of children from military families. *Journal of the American Academy of Pediatrics, 125,* 16–25.

Christenson, S. L. (1995). Families and schools: What is the role of the school psychologist? *School Psychology Quarterly, 10,* 118–132.

Collins, R. (2009). *Five things school leaders can do to build connections.* Alexandria, VA. American Association of School Administrators. Retrieved from www.aasa.org/content.aspx?id=8996.

Coopersmith, S., & Feldman, R. (1974). *The formative years: Principles of early childhood education.* San Francisco: Albion.

Doll, B., Brehm, K., & Zucker, S. (2014). *Resilient classrooms: Creating healthy environments for learning, 2nd Edition.* New York: Guilford Publications.

Dornbusch, S. M., Erickson, K. G., Laird, J., & Wong, C. A. (2001). The relation of family and school attachment to adolescent deviance in diverse groups and communities. *Journal of Adolescent Research, 16,* 396–422.

Dunst, C. J. (2000). Revisiting "rethinking early intervention." *Topics in Early Childhood Special Education, 20,* 95–104. doi: 10.1177/027112140002000205

Eagle, J. W., Dowd-Eagle, S. E., & Sheridan, S. M. (2008). Best practices in school–community partnerships. In A. Thomas & J. Grimes (Eds.), *Best practices in school psychology V* (pp. 953–967). Bethesda, MD: National Association of School Psychologists.

Eber, L., Sugai, G., Smith, C. R., & Scott, T. M. (2002). Wraparound and positive behavioral interventions and supports in the schools. *Journal of Emotional and Behavioral Disorders, 10,* 171–180.

Editorial Projects in Education Research Center. (2011). *National graduation brief 2011.* Bethesda, MD: Editorial Projects in Education.

Finn, J. D., & Rock, D. A. (1997). Academic success among students at risk for school failure. *Journal of Applied Psychology, 82,* 221–234.

Flake, E., Davis, B., Johnson, P., & Middleton, L. (2009). The psychosocial effects of deployment on military children. *Journal of Developmental and Behavioral Pediatrics, 30,* 271–278.

Fletcher, K. L. (2013) Helping children with the psychological effects of a parent's deployment: Integrating today's needs with lessons learned from the Vietnam War. *Smith College Studies in Social Work, 83,* 78–96.

Fredricks, J. A., Blumenfeld, P. C., & Paris, A. H. (2004). School engagement: Potential of the concept, state of the evidence. *Review of Educational Research, 74,* 59–109.

Furrer, C., & Skinner, E. (2003). Sense of relatedness as a factor in children's academic engagement and performance. *Journal of Educational Psychology, 95,* 148–162.

Garbarino, J., & deLara, E. (2002). *And words can hurt forever: How to protect adolescents from bullying, harassment and emotional violence.* London: The Free Press.

Gibbs, N., & Thompson M. (2012, July 23). The war on Suicide? More U.S. soldiers have killed themselves than have died in the Afghan war. Why can't the army win the war on suicide? *Time,* Retrieved from http://content.time.com/time/subscriber/article/0,33009,2119337-2,00.html.

Glasser, R. J. (2006). *Wounded: Vietnam/Iraq.* New York: George Braziller.

Good, M. E., Masewicz, S., & Vogel, L. (2010). Latino English language learners: Bridging achievement and cultural gaps between schools and families. *Journal of Latinos and Education, 9,* 321–339. doi:10.1080/15348431 .2010.491048

Gorman, G., Eide, M. & Hisle-Gorman, E. (2010). Wartime military deployment and increased mental and behavioral health complaints. *Pediatrics, 126,* 1058.

Greene, B. A., Miller, R. B., Crowson, H. M., Duke, B. L., & Akey, K. L. (2004). Predicting high school students' cognitive engagement and achievement: Contributions of classroom perceptions and motivation. *Contemporary Educational Psychology, 29,* 462–482.

Guthrie, J. T., & Wigfield, A. (2000). Engagement and motivation in reading. In M. L. Kamil, P. B. Mosenthal, P. D. Pearson, & R. Barr (Eds.), *Handbook of reading research* (pp. 403–422). Mahwah, NJ: Lawrence Errlbaum.

Halgunseth, L. (2009). *Family engagement, diverse families, and early childhood programs: An integrated review of the literature.* Washington, DC: The National Association for the Education of Young Children.

Hagborg, W. J. (1994). An exploration of school membership among middle-and high-school students. *Journal of Psychoeducational Assessment, 12,* 312–323.

Harris, L. (2011). Secondary teachers' conceptions of student engagement: Engagement in learning or in schooling?. *Teaching and Teacher Education, 27,* 376–386.

Hawkley, L. C., & Cacioppo, J. T. (2010). Loneliness matters: A theoretical and empirical review of consequences and mechanisms. *Annals of Behavioral Medicine, 40,* 218–227.

Hawkley, L. C., & Cacioppo, J. T. (2013). Loneliness and health. In M. C. Gellman & J. R. Turner (Eds.), *Encyclopedia of behavioral medicine* (pp. 1172–1176). New York: Springer.

Hickman, C. W., Greenwood, G., & Miller, M. D. (1995). High school parent involvement: Relationships with achievement, grade level, SES, and gender. *Journal of Research & Development in Education. 28,* 125–134.

Hong, S. (2011). *A cord of three strands: A new approach to parent engagement in schools.* Cambridge, MA: Harvard Education Press.

Hulac, D., Terrell, J., Vining, O., & Bernstein, J. (2011). *Behavioral interventions in schools: A response-to-intervention guidebook.* New York: Routledge

Huebner, A. J. & Mancini, J. A. (2005). *Adjustment among adolescents in military families when a parent is deployed. A final report submitted to the Military Family Research Institute and the Department of Defense Quality of Life Office.* Falls Church, VA: Department of Human Development, Virginia Tech.

Jeltova, I., & Fish, M. C. (2005). Creating school environments responsive to gay, lesbian, bisexual, and transgender families: Traditional and systemic approaches for consultation. *Journal of Educational and Psychological Consultation, 16,* 17–33. doi:10.1207/ s1532768xjepc161&2_2

Johnson, S. L. (2009). Improving the school environment to reduce school violence: A review of the literature. *Journal of School Health, 79,* 451–465.

Kennedy, J. E., Jaffee, M. S., Leskin, G. A., Stokes, J. W., Leal, F. O. & Fitzpatrick, P. J. (2007). Post-traumatic stress disorder-like symptoms and mild traumatic brain injury. *Journal of Rehabilitative Research and Development, 44,* 895–920.

Klem, A. M., & Connell, J. P. (2004). Relationships matter: Linking teacher support to student engagement and achievement. *Journal of School Health, 74,* 262–273.

Konu, A. I., Lintonen, T. P., & Rimpelä, M. K. (2002). Factors associated with schoolchildren's general subjective well-being. *Health Education Research, 17,* 155–165.

Korinek, L., Walther-Thomas, C., McLaughlin, V. L., & Williams, B. T. (1999). Creating classroom communities and networks for student support. *Intervention in School and Clinic, 35,* 3–8.

Lee, R. M., Dean, B. L., & Jung, K. R. (2008). Social connectedness, extraversion, and subjective well-being: Testing a mediation model. *Personality and Individual Differences, 45,* 414–419.

Lee, R. M., & Robbins, S. B. (1995). Measuring belongingness: The Social Connectedness and the Social Assurance scales. *Journal of Counseling Psychology, 42,* 232–241.

Libbey, H. P. (2004). Measuring student relationships to school: Attachment, bonding, connectedness, and engagement. *Journal of School Health, 74,* 274–283.

Lister-Sharp, D., Chapman, S., Stewart-Brown, S., & Sowden, A. (1999). Health promoting schools and health promotion in schools: Two systematic reviews. *Health Technology Assessment, 3,* 1–22.

Luo, Y., Hawkley, L. C., Waite, L. J., & Cacioppo, J. T. (2012). Loneliness, health, and mortality in old age: A national longitudinal study. *Social Science and Medicine, 74,* 907–914.

McDevitt, J., Shively, M., & Subramanian, R. (2011). *Research briefing: Understanding trends in hate crimes against immigrants and Hispanic-Americans.* NCJ 234632, Washington, DC: ABT Associates.

McPherson, C., Alves, A., Burns, M., & Diaz, Y. (2014). A social justice perspective on: Family–school–community collaboration. *Communiqué, 43*(3), 12–14.

Maddox, S. J., & Prinz, R. J. (2003). School bonding in children and adolescents: Conceptualization, assessment, and associated variables. *Clinical Child and Family Psychology Review, 6,* 31–49.

Marks, H. M. (2000). Student engagement in instructional activity: Patterns in the elementary, middle, and high school years. *American Educational Research Journal, 37,* 153–184.

Markham, W. A., & Aveyard, P. (2003). A new theory of health promoting schools based on human functioning, school organization and pedagogic practice. *Social Science & Medicine, 56,* 1209–1220.

Maslow, A. H. (1943). A theory of human motivation. *Psychological Review, 50,* 370–396.

Massey, D. S., Durand, J., & Malone, N. J. (2003). *Beyond smoke and mirrors: Mexican immigration in an era of economic integration.* New York, NY: Russell Sage Foundation.

Maurizi, L. K., Ceballo, R., Epstein-Ngo, Q., & Cortina, K. S. (2013). Does neighborhood belonging matter? Examining school and neighborhood belonging as protective factors for Latino adolescents. *American Journal of Orthopsychiatry, 83,* 323–334. doi:10.1111/ ajop.12017

Meagher, I. (2007). *The war list: OEF/OIF statistics.* Retrieved from www.ptsdcombat.com/documents/ ptsdcombat_war-list_oef-oif-statistics.pdf.

Moreno, R. P., Lewis-Menchaca, K., & Rodriguez, J. (2011). *Parental involvement: A critical view through a multicultural lens.* Albany, NY: SUNY Press.

Niehaus, K., Moritz-Rudasill, K. M., & Rakes, C. R. (2012). A longitudinal study of school connectedness and academic outcomes across sixth grade. *Journal of School Psychology, 50,* 443–460.

Osterman, K. (2000). Students' need for belonging in the school community. *Review of Educational Research, 70,* 323–367.

Pew Research Center (2006). *No consensus on immigration problem or proposed fixes: America's immigration quandary.* Retrieved on November, 16, 2014 from www. people-press.org/files/legacy-pdf/274.pdf.

Pisano, M. C. (2014). Best practices in services to children in military families. In P. L. Harrison & A. Thomas (Eds.), *Best practices in school psychology: Foundations* (pp. 181–190). Bethesda, MD. National Association of School Psychologists.

Potok, M. (2008). *Anti-Latino hate crimes rise for fourth year in a row.* Retrieved November, 11, 2014 from www.splcenter.org/blog/2008/10/29/anti-Latino-hate-crimes-rise-forfourth-year/.

Raffaele, L. M., & Knoff, H. M. (1999). Improving home-school collaboration with disadvantaged families: Organizational principles, perspectives, and approaches. *School Psychology Review, 28,* 448–466.

Rahill, S. (2013). Supporting children facing the deployment of a parent. *Communique, 41*(8), 4.

Resnick, M. D., Bearman, P. S., Blum, R. W., Bauman, K. E., Harris, K. M., Jones, J., . . . & Udry, J. R. (1997). Protecting adolescents from harm: Findings from the National Longitudinal Study on Adolescent Health. *JAMA, 278,* 823–832.

Roberts, R. N., & Magrab, P. R. (1991). Psychologists' role in a family-centered approach to practice, training, and research with young children. *American Psychologist, 46,* 144–148.

Rohner, R. (1975). *They love me, they love me not: A worldwide study of the effects of parental acceptance and rejection.* New Haven: CT: HRAF Press.

Rowe, F., Stewart, D., & Patterson, C. (2007). Promoting school connectedness through whole school approaches. *Health Education, 107,* 524–542.

Ryan, A. M., & Patrick, H. (2001). The classroom social environment and changes in adolescents' motivation and engagement during middle school. *American Educational Research Journal, 38,* 437–460.

Segal, M. W., & Segal, D. R. (2003). Implications for military families of changes in the Armed Forces of the United States. In G. Caforio, (Ed.), *Handbook of the sociology of the military* (pp. 225–233). New York: Kluwer Academic/Plenum.

Sheridan, S. M., Taylor, A. M., & Woods, K. E. (2008). Best practices in working with families: Instilling a family-centered approach. In A. Thomas & J. Grimes (Eds.), *Best practices in school psychology V* (pp. 995–1008). Bethesda, MD: National Association of School Psychologists.

Shochet, I. M., Dadds, M. R., Ham, D., & Montague, R. (2006). School connectedness is an underemphasized parameter in adolescent mental health: Results of a community prediction study. *Journal of Clinical Child and Adolescent Psychology, 35,* 170–179.

Shriberg, D., Bonner, M., Sarr, B. J., Walker, A. M., Hyland, M., & Chester, C. (2008). Social justice through a school psychology lens: Definition and applications. *School Psychology Review, 37,* 453–468.

Smith, D. C., & Sandhu, D. S. (2004). Toward a positive perspective on violence prevention in schools: Building connections. *Journal of Counseling & Development, 82,* 287–293.

Sulkowski, M. L., Bauman, S., Wright, S., Nixon, C., & Davis, S. (2014). Peer victimization in youth from immigrant and non-immigrant U.S. families. *School Psychology International, 35,* 649–669. doi: 10.1177/0143034314554968.

Sulkowski, M. L., & Michael, K. (2014). Meeting the mental health needs of homeless students in schools: A multi-tiered system of support framework. *Children and Youth Services Review, 44,* 145–151. doi: 10.1016/j.childyouth.2014.06.014

Tanielan, T., & Jaycox (2008). Summary. In T. Tanielian & L. J. Jaycox (Eds.), *Invisible wounds of war: Psychological and cognitive injuries, their consequences, and services to assist recovery* (pp. xix–xxxiii). Santa Monica, CA: RAND.

Tanielian, T., Jaycox, L. H., Adamson, D. M., & Metscher, K. N. (2008). Introduction. In T. Tanielian & L. J. Jaycox (Eds.), *Invisible wounds of war: Psychological and cognitive injuries, their consequences, and services to assist recovery* (pp. 3–18). Santa Monica, CA: RAND

Teranishi, C. S. (2007). Impact of experiential learning on Latino college students' identity, relationships, and connectedness to community. *Journal of Hispanic Higher Education, 6,* 52–72.

U. S. Army (2012). Army 2020: *Generating health and discipline in the force: Ahead of the strategic reset.* Washington, DC: U.S. Department of Defense.

U.S. Department of Defense (2009). *DODEA partnership.* Washington, DC. Author.

U.S. Department of Defense. (2010). *Report on the impact of deployment of members of the armed forces on their dependent children.* Washington, DC: Author

Voisin, D. R., Salazar, L. F., Crosby, R., Diclemente, R. J., Yarber, W. L., & Staples-Horne, M. (2005). Teacher connectedness and health-related outcomes among detained adolescents. *Journal of Adolescent Health, 37,* 17–23.

Wang, M. T., & Eccles, J. S. (2012). Social support matters: Longitudinal effects of social support on three dimensions of school engagement from middle to high school. *Child Development, 83,* 877–895.

Wehlage, G. G., Rutter, R. A., Smith, G. A., Lesko, N., & Fernandez, R. R. (1989). *Reducing the risk.* New York, NY: Falmer.

Williams, T. T., & Sánchez, B. (2011). Identifying and decreasing barriers to parent involvement for inner-city parents. *Youth & Society, 45,* 54–74.

Wingspread Declaration on School Connections. (2004). Wingspread declaration on school connections. *Journal of School Health, 74,* 233–234.

Woodhouse, S. S., Dykas, M. J., & Cassidy, J. (2012). Loneliness and peer relations in adolescence. *Social Development, 21,* 273–293.

Yoon, E., Lee, R. M., & Goh, M. (2008). Acculturation, social connectedness, and subjective well-being. *Cultural Diversity and Ethnic Minority Psychology, 14,* 246–255.

9   Positive Psychology

Positive psychology is both a theoretical and applied psychological movement that strives to understand the factors that help people function and flourish at optimal levels. Thus, it is a psychological approach that helps individuals build quality lives by focusing on positive subjective experiences, positive character, and positive institutions (Suldo, 2013). Moreover, positive psychology is about using scientifically informed perspectives related to what makes life worth living and it focuses on aspects of the human condition that lead to happiness, fulfillment, and flourishing (Linley, Joseph, Harrington, & Wood, 2006). As such, positive psychology has practical and powerful implications for the fields of psychology and education (Chafouleas & Bray, 2004).

The Three Pillars of Positive Psychology

Just as every structure is only as strong as its base, positive psychology also needs a sturdy theoretical foundation. In this regard, positive psychology is grounded in research and interventions that have been found to improve psychological well-being. As the scaffolding that holds up positive psychology, Suldo (2013) states that the following three pillars undergird this psychological perspective: (1) *positive subjective experiences*, (2) *positive character*, and (3) *positive institutions*.

The first pillar, *positive subjective experiences* are comprised of well-being, contentment, and satisfaction (in the past); flow and happiness (in the present); and hope and optimism (for the future). Positive subjective experiences do not exist as solitary moments in time. In fact, each of these past, present, and future experiences is relative and unique to each individual's perception of his or her own reality (Seligman, 2003; Seligman & Csikszentmihalyi, 2000).

The second pillar, *positive character,* refers to the positive traits that an individual is capable of possessing and expressing. Peterson and Seligman (2004) investigated positive traits that they found in the writings of moral philosophers, ancient spiritual leaders, and educators, as universal virtues that existed across time periods and cultures. They noted that there are six core values that constitute the broadest virtues. They then defined character strengths as the "psychological processes or mechanisms that define these virtues" (p. 13). Specifically, they identified 24 character strengths and these have been subsumed under six main virtues or core values (Values in Action-Inventory of Strengths, 2015). The first core value, categorized as *wisdom and knowledge*, includes traits such as creativity, curiosity, judgment, love of learning, and perspective. The second core value categorized as *courage*, includes bravery, perseverance, honesty, and zest. The third is termed *humanity* and it includes the attributes of kindness, love, and social intelligence. The fourth is *justice* and it includes fairness, leadership, and teamwork. The fifth is *temperance* and it includes forgiveness, humility, prudence, and self-regulation. Lastly, the sixth core value is categorized as *transcendence* and it includes appreciation of beauty and excellence, gratitude, hope, humor, and spirituality. Individuals interested in determining their own character strengths may take the VIA Inventory of Strengths at http://www.viacharacter.org/www/The-Survey.

Finally, the third pillar of positive psychology is called *positive institutions*. This pillar describes the concept of optimal living experiences at the universal level. This pillar brings together the first two pillars and it incorporates them into the larger context of life as well as the overall community in which individuals live. These communal institutions exist within families, places of work, society, culture, and especially within schools. In order to fit properly within the framework of positive psychology, positive institutions such as schools must nurture and support the individuals they serve, and therefore, one of the goals of positive psychology is to help institutions thrive (Molony, Hilbold, & Smith, 2014). Further, positive institutions must help to foster healthy living, harmony, and sustainability (Linley et al., 2006). Ultimately, this concept emphasizes that the overall well-being and quality of life can be enhanced at the systems-level for the benefit of those who are part of the system. In summary, each of the three pillars of positive psychology—positive subjective experiences, positive character, and positive institutions—all function independently and in unison to contribute to the well-being of individuals.

Positive Psychology and Traditional Psychology

The formal application of psychology is fairly new in comparison to other approaches to enhancing well-being. In fact, it probably was not until the mid-twentieth century, following the trauma of World War II, that psychology became more commonly known. The goal of psychology at such a tumultuous time was to gain a deeper understanding of psychological problems and to learn how to remedy them (Seligman, 2007). Thus, "traditional psychology" became a discipline that uses a "disease model" of human functioning (i.e., looking at abnormal functioning and psychopathology) and it is devoted to healing mental illness (Suldo, 2013). To this day, most members of society are familiar with the traditional clinical psychological approach that has utility for identifying and addressing maladies such as suffering, selfishness, dysfunctional family systems, and ineffective institutions (Gable & Haidt, 2005). However, positive psychology researchers have suggested that an overemphasis on the disease model and the treatment of mental disorders has detracted from the other missions of psychology such as making lives

---

Text Box 9.1 The Major Differences between Traditional Psychology and Positive Psychology

Traditional Psychology		*Positive Psychology*
Disease Model		*Health* Model (Suldo, 2013)
Repair *worst* things in life		Build the *best* things in life (Suldo, 2013)
Overcome deficiencies		Develop competencies
Focus on *psychopathology* (e.g., anxiety, depression, antisocial behavior)		Focus on *subjective well-being* (e.g., joy, satisfaction, gratitude, flow, optimism, hope; Suldo, 2013)
Avoid pain		Seek pleasure
Oriented towards human and institutional *deficits*	*VS.*	Oriented towards human and institutional *strengths*
Reactive (healing already existing illnesses)		*Preventive* (encouraging practices that enhance flourishing and prevent mental and emotional illness)
Relief from suffering by *treating illness* (Seligman & Pawelski, 2003)		Address suffering by *maximizing human potential* (Terjesen, Jacofsky, Froh, & DiGiuseppe, 2004)
Study *human suffering* (Gable & Haidt, 2005)		Study *human flourishing* (Gable & Haidt, 2005; Seligman, 2011)

more fulfilling, developing prevention programs, and nurturing excellence. In addition, there is also benefit to studying individuals who flourish (Fredrickson, 2009; Seligman, 2011). In short, clinical psychology focuses on ameliorating mental distress and positive psychology focuses on helping individuals lead a more enriched life. Consequently, both approaches complement each other and provide a more balanced approach to advancing the human condition. Text Box 9.1 outlines the differences between traditional and positive psychology.

Subjective Well-Being

Subjective well-being is a core concept in positive psychology and is comprised of three related yet separate constructs: life satisfaction, positive affect, and negative affect (Diener, 2000). Subjective well-being involves holistic and global assessments that encompass all facets of a person's life (Diener, 1984). More specifically, life satisfaction relates to an individual's evaluation of his or her life. This evaluation can occur cognitively (i.e., in one's mind) or affectively (i.e., in one's feelings). On the one hand, cognitive well-being involves the evaluation of global life satisfaction (e.g., How satisfied am I with my life as a whole?) as well as the evaluation of more specific life domains (e.g., How satisfied am I with my work, family, and career?). On the other hand, affective well-being involves the moods and feelings an individual experiences. Positive affect involves pleasant feelings such as happiness and pride, while negative or unpleasant affect involves such feelings as guilt and envy.

In a seminal article, Diener (1984) noted that well-being is inherently subjective because it involves judgments made by the individual based on his or her unique experiences. For example, a struggling student may report being satisfied with her recent academic performance after receiving a "C" on a spelling quiz. However, an above-average student with the same grade may be disappointed.

It is important to enhance subjective well-being in youth as it has been linked to healthy psychosocial functioning. For example, increased subjective well-being has been linked to goal setting, participation in peer groups, formation of close interpersonal relationships, and gratitude (Bird & Markle, 2012). Moreover, subjective well-being involves the presence of positive factors as well as the absence of negative factors. In a dual factor model, mental health is viewed in terms of indicators of wellness (specifically, subjective well-being) as well as traditional indicators of psychopathology, namely internalizing and externalizing distress. Preliminary research based on the dual factor model has indicated that the presence of average to high subjective well-being and the absence of psychopathology has been associated with optimal academic success (Suldo, Thalji, & Ferron, 2011) .

The Benefits of Using Positive Psychology in Schools

Based on increasing subjective well-being and fostering both individual and institutional strengths, positive psychology is closely aligned with other topics addressed in this text, such as social-emotional learning, resilience, student engagement and connectedness, mindfulness, growth mindsets, social supports, school climate, and school-wide positive behavior support. As such, many of the practices that support the aforementioned topics relate to the use of positive psychology in schools. However, the central focus of positive psychology in schools has been on how to help children become happier and more fulfilled by using a strength-based orientation.

The Relationship between Positive Psychology and Education

How then is positive psychology related to education? Chafoules and Bray (2004) state that the major goal of education has been to master academic, social, or behavioral content. However, adherents to a positive psychology approach view that the goal of education is to raise children who are "happy, healthy, and morally good" (Park & Peterson, 2008, p. 85). Martin Seligman, a pioneering positive psychologist, identified a reciprocal relationship between positive emotions, exploration or discovery, and mastery (Seligman, 2011). He concluded that positive emotions lead to exploration, which leads to mastery and feeling positive emotions. Thus, there is a reciprocal loop in which increasing positive emotions in students improve their academic engagement and academic performance. Overall, Seligman (2011) advises that positive psychology provides a more balanced, positive perspective on education that focuses on helping children to develop positive characters and lead healthy and fulfilling lives. In turn, this approach has the added benefit of facilitating the mastery of academic content.

The application of positive psychology to student outcomes is an emerging and promising area for research that has many potential benefits (Huebner & Hills, 2011; Molony et al., 2014; Suldo et al., 2015). In a relevant review, Miller and Nickerson (2007) discuss six areas of positive psychology that appeal to student development: gratitude, forgiveness, flow, mindfulness, hope, and optimism. Research on gratitude indicates that it is a powerful emotion related to a high level of well-being; it creates a feeling of being valued and affirmed and it promotes an appreciation of social supports (McCullough & Emmons, 2003). In addition, research indicates that grateful adolescents earn higher GPAs, enjoy more social connections, experience higher life satisfaction, and are less anxious and depressed than students who are less grateful (Froh, Emmons, Card, Bono, & Wilson, 2011). Forgiveness decreases anger and fosters positive development in youth, especially among individuals with aggressive or depressive behaviors. Flow makes life more vibrant and exciting and it can be promoted by working with teachers, parents, and students to identify engaging activities and appropriate levels of challenge (Csikszentmihalyi, 1997). As a related concept, mindfulness helps children become more self-aware, calm, and focused, and it can be explicitly taught. For example, by using a mindfulness program, children have been found to benefit on tasks of executive function, self-reported well-being, engagement in prosocial behaviors, and math achievement (Schonert-Reich et al., 2015). Finally, fostering hope and optimism can help decrease students' depressive thinking and negativity. Hope has been positively related to self-worth, life satisfaction, academic achievement, social competence, and athletic success (Marques Lopez, & Pais-Ribero, 2011). Optimism is related to physical and psychological health outcomes, and optimists are seen as active problem solvers (Seligman, 2002). In addition, research indicates that increasing optimism can reduce symptoms of anxiety, depression, hopelessness, and behavior problems in youth (Seligman et al., 2009).

Positive Peer Cultures and Families

Positive psychology also may be related to other beneficial outcomes among students. One of these areas involves positive peer cultures. Positive peer cultures were developed as a preventative approach to negative peer influences (Steinebach, Steinebach, & Brendtro, 2013). Such positive peer groups involve the use of group dialogue and problem-solving skills. Ultimately, positive peer cultures focus on fostering concern and respect among peers. Moreover, Steinebach et al. (2013) explain that creating positive peer cultures to enhance youth development is a well-researched, evidence-based practice. Further, this practice epitomizes the focus of positive psychology, which aims to enhance students' strengths rather than remediate their weaknesses.

Positive psychology research has also been examined within the context of engaging family members. Sheridan, Warnes, Cowan, Schemm, and Clarke (2004) espouse a family-centered positive psychology approach for working with students and families that focuses on strength building rather than on remediating problems or deficiencies. This approach to positive psychology contends that child outcomes will be enhanced if family members help identify child needs, establish social support and partnerships, promote family strengths and resources, and foster new skill development, rather than simply receiving services from professionals. Results of their case study investigation of a special needs child indicate that a family-centered, positive psychology approach can be both acceptable and effective in reducing negative behaviors in both the school and community (Sheridan et al., 2004). An emphasis on this approach has implications for educators and school-based mental health professionals, who when consulting with parents can (a) form working collaborative relationships, (b) focus on family identified rather than professionally determined needs, (c) help them identify both their child's and family's strengths and resources, and (d) use these strengths and resources to enhance the child's and family's skills and competencies.

Subjective Well-being and Positive Correlates

As described in the preceding section, subjective well-being is concerned with an individual's evaluation of his or her life as well as both positive and negative affect. *Life satisfaction* is one area that has been explored, as it relates to increasing subjective well-being. Park (2004) explains that life satisfaction has been linked to positive correlates such as self-control, self-esteem, motivation, extraversion, and resiliency. Adolescents who report high levels of life satisfaction report higher satisfaction across school, interpersonal, and intrapersonal variables (Proctor, Linley, & Maltby, 2010).

Similarly, subjective well-being has been investigated in relation to other positive correlates. For example, positive affect, has also been linked to greater involvement in positive leisure activities (Palen & Coatsworth, 2007). Character strengths (i.e., morally valued personality traits like courage, kindness, and wisdom) have been shown to predict subjective well-being (Gillham et al., 2011). Other factors such as hope, self-esteem, and optimism have also influenced the subjective well-being of students, especially of ethnically diverse youth (Morgan, Vera, Gonzalez, Vacek, & Coyle, 2011). Basically, students who possess these character strengths or attributes are happier and more fulfilled.

Also, meta-analytic research of positive psychology interventions has linked increased subjective and psychological well-being to decreased symptoms of depression (e.g., Boiler, Haverman, Westerhof, Riper, Smit, & Bohlmeijer, 2013; Sin & Lyubomirsky, 2009).[1] In turn, increasing well-being in children can lead to increased learning, academic motivation and self-efficacy, and life satisfaction (Pajares, 2009; Seligman, Ernst, Gillham, Reivich, & Linkins, 2009).

The dual factor model of mental health which considers both subjective well-being and psychopathology has been studied in youth. For example, Schaffer-Hudkins, Suldo, Loker, and March (2010) investigated the relative influence of subjective well-being and psychopathology on 10–16-year-olds' perceptions of overall physical health. Although psychopathology was predictive of physical health, subjective well-being (including life satisfaction), negative affect, and positive affect were found to be more predictive in this study. The researchers contend that adolescents' positive emotions and moods as well as their satisfaction with life, could be more important than having symptoms of anxiety or depression for predicting their physical health. Overall, perceived good health was strongly linked to life satisfaction and feeling strong, excited, and proud. Students who said they felt anxious, depressed, sad, and lonely also reported being less physically healthy. Based on these finding, the authors conclude that a comprehensive model of mental health must integrate both positive and negative indicators. Likewise, subjective well-being has been found to be a better predictor of future academic achievement in middle school students than psychopathology is (Suldo et al., 2011). Results from the aforementioned studies suggest that subjective well-being is integral to students' mental health and academic functioning.

The effects of stressors on the subjective well-being in adolescents have also been investigated. Several coping strategies (e.g., using humor, planning, venting, and active coping) have been found to assuage stressors (e.g., death of a loved one, financial difficulties) and the use of these coping strategies has been found to be associated with increased positive affect among ethnically diverse students from urban communities (Vera et al., 2012). In particular, using active coping strategies such as direct problem solving has been related to positive affect and subjective well-being in adolescents (Coyle & Vera, 2013). In summary, increasing life satisfaction, increasing positive affect and decreasing negative affect is essential in helping children and adolescents achieve a good quality of life and not just correct pathology or illnesses (Park, 2004).

Strengths, Adaptive Abilities, and Positive Correlates

As previously discussed, positive psychology aims to help students by building competencies rather than correcting flaws or weaknesses (Seligman, 2002). Positive psychology can increase students' hopes about the future, levels of optimism, their ability to live mindfully, experience gratitude and forgiveness, and become engaged in meaningful activities (Miller & Nickerson, 2007). Moreover, extant research highlights the many benefits of positive psychology and its related concepts. For example, researchers reported that grade point averages (GPAs) were better predicted by the character strengths of perseverance, honesty, fairness, gratitude, hope, and perspective than by IQ (Park & Peterson, 2009). This finding underscores the benefits of helping children develop character strengths at an early age. Positive psychology's focus on fostering strengths and adaptive abilities has been linked with healthy self-esteem, vitality, positive affect, and lower perceived stress (Wood, Linley, Maltby, Kashdan, & Hurling, 2011). Moreover, fostering such strengths can lead to fulfillment, academic achievement, and decreased psychopathology in youth (Park & Peterson, 2008). Further, in a study by Park and Peterson (2009), youth who possessed the character strengths of honesty, prudence, and love demonstrated fewer externalizing behaviors (aggression), whereas youth who possessed the character strengths of zest, hope, and leadership demonstrated fewer internalizing problems (anxiety and depression). As such, positive psychology, its various components (e.g., flow, gratitude, mindfulness, optimism), and its focus on strengths and virtues can benefit students' overall well-being, mental health, learning, and functioning in and beyond the classroom.

Promoting Positive Psychology

How Administrators Can Promote Positive Psychology

Positive psychology has practical applications in school settings beyond its theoretical underpinnings. In particular, positive psychology provides a preventative rather than reactive model of prevention/intervention that schools can employ. However, in order for these prevention and intervention efforts to be implemented effectively, the support of school leaders is needed. In this vein, it is important for school administrators to be on board with efforts to implement positive psychology approaches. Fortunately, there are ways that administrators can help with incorporating positive psychology in school settings. Some of these ways are described below.

Promote Positive Psychology and Ensure Supports

School administrators can provide support for the effective implementation of positive psychology into the curriculum by openly expressing their endorsement of activities and/or programs (Suldo et al., 2015). In addition, they can (a) ensure that teachers have the requisite training, support, consultation, materials and resources to infuse positive psychology into the daily curriculum; (b) allocate time throughout the day or week for these activities; (c) help establish the school's expectation regarding building character strengths; (d) offer community and parent meetings to highlight how the school will support building positive character strengths in children and how the school will serve as a positive institution; (e) support positive psychology clubs on campus; and (f) provide ways that students can highlight their character strengths. Thus, as established leaders, school administrators can use their influence to promote positive psychology for the benefit of the students they serve (Brannon, 2008).

Encourage Consultation and Collaboration

Administrators can encourage consultation between teachers and school-based mental health professionals to apply positive psychology principles with proper integrity and fidelity. For example, they can help teachers identify their own personal character strengths and in turn apply positive psychology principles in the classroom (Akin-Little, Little, & Delligatti, 2004). In addition, they can support data-based approaches to program and intervention implementation such as conjoint behavioral consultation, which is a family-centered positive psychology approach that involves collaboration among educators, caregivers, and school-based mental health professionals. This consultation model can be used to help implement positive psychology practices into the school and to improve overall student functioning (Sheridan, Eagle, Cowan, & Mickelson, 2001). Administrators can also help put a team together composed of educators, school-based mental health professionals, parents, and students who can work collaboratively to infuse positive psychology into schools.

How School-based Mental Health Professionals Can Promote Positive Psychology

School-based mental health professionals can champion aspects of positive psychology that help students establish positive emotions, gratitude, goal fulfillment, optimism, character strengths, flow, hope, kindness, and positive relationships (Molony et.al., 2014; Shoshani & Steinmetz, 2013). Mental health professionals can be the primary role models in demonstrating how to incorporate positive practices into various school-wide contexts, even if specific interventions are delivered by educators. School-based mental health professionals can also work closely with teachers in order to provide instruction and guidance on how to implement positive psychology practices at the classroom level. If requested by teachers, and if time permits, they can work with students in the classroom to teach and model skills such as self-control, social awareness, group participation, social decision-making, and problem-solving and encourage the students to practice these in different situations.

How Educators Can Promote Positive Psychology

As the professionals who spend the most time each day with students, teachers have a unique opportunity to implement elements of positive psychology in school settings. Further, with this aim in mind, a recent study by Suldo (2013) established a set of strategies for educators to integrate the ideas of positive psychology within schools. It is worth noting that these strategies were developed from direct feedback from students. These strategies are listed in Table 9.1.

One way that all professionals can increase the application of positive psychology in schools involves inspiring feelings of gratitude among students (Suldo et al., 2015). Gratitude can be modeled by all school personnel as they outwardly display thankful interactions. More directly, as suggested by Suldo (2013), school personnel can implement a school-wide intervention whereby all students are instructed to list five things they are grateful for before they leave school at the end of each day. Teachers can also encourage students to keep a gratitude journal to notice and appreciate feelings of gratitude on a daily basis. Students can also share in class (in either small groups or as a whole class) their personal examples of feelings of gratitude.

Table 9.1 What Students Say about How Teachers Can Use the Principles of Positive Psychology

- Take actions to help students improve their moods (create positive emotional environment by being in a cheerful and upbeat mood in the presence of the students).
- Respect students (e.g., respond to students who make a mistake privately rather than bringing attention to it in the presence of the entire class).
- Express an interest in students' wellness and well-being.
- Identify unique strengths of each and every student then regularly acknowledge these.
- Share personal experiences with students.
- Take an interest in students' academic progress.
- Offer additional academic assistance such as tutoring sessions during lunch or after school (allowing students to ask questions in a more intimate and casual atmosphere).
- Use varied teaching strategies (fun and interactive lessons such as review games instead of traditional "take-home" study guides).
- Give students rewards (e.g., extra computer time, homework passes).
- Help students improve their grades.
- Respect individual learning preferences.
- Explicitly state permission to ask questions.
- Respond to questions in a positive manner.
- Check for understanding (re-teach the material until all students demonstrate full comprehension).

Another significant gratitude intervention is a gratitude visit. This intervention involves expressing one's gratitude to another person. Prior to the gratitude visit, students write a letter of appreciation and then hand deliver it to someone who has been especially helpful and kind. As noted by Seligman (2002), both the writers and the recipients of the letters report that this experience is overwhelmingly meaningful. Another suggestion for cultivating gratitude is provided by Molony et al. (2014). More specifically, a school psychologist who wanted to foster gratitude distributed Post-it notes in a variety of colors, sizes and shapes for students to surprise others with messages of gratitude. They reported that the recipients who used the Post-it notes experienced positive feelings and subsequently left surprise notes for others as a result—thus passing it forward. Engaging in activities such as these can radically change a school's climate and create a culture of caring. Additionally, as demonstrated in a study by Froh, Yurkewicz, and Kashdan, (2009), gratitude practice among children has a significant relationship with increasing positive affect, life satisfaction, optimism, social support, and prosocial behavior.

Another approach to implementing positive psychology involves the simple practice of performing acts of kindness. Results from a study by Layous, Nelson, Oberle, Schonert-Reichl, and Lyubomirsky (2012) support this notion. In this investigation, randomly assigned students (ages 9 to 11) were divided into one of two groups. Every week one group was instructed to perform three acts of kindness, whereas the other group was instructed to visit three places; anywhere they wished. Examples of kind acts included "gave my mom a hug when she was stressed by her job," "gave someone some of my lunch," and "vacuumed the floor." The results of the study demonstrated that students in both conditions improved in subjective well-being but students who performed kind acts significantly improved in their ratings of peer acceptance (or sociometric popularity). Layous et al. (2012) note that doing acts of kindness for others benefits the givers, earning them both popularity and improved well-being. Thus, prosocial behavior can influence peer acceptance and the relationship between these variables is largely bidirectional. That is, children who feel accepted are more likely to do good things for others, and in turn, children who do acts of kindness gain the acceptance of their peers. Moreover, increasing peer acceptance among youth is important, as it is associated with a variety of crucial social and academic outcomes, including a reduced likelihood of being bullied.

If positive psychology practices, such as expressing gratitude or performing acts of kindness, are implemented at the universal or school-wide level, the overall well-being of all students is likely to increase, while levels of depression and anxiety are likely to decrease concomitantly (Suldo, 2013). Moreover, engaging in such activities can both directly and indirectly mitigate risk factors for psychopathology (e.g., rumination, loneliness, being bullied); and therefore, decrease the prevalence of mental disorders across the lifespan (Layous & Lyubomirsky, 2014). Text Box 9.2 lists two examples of exercises that educators can use to implement positive psychology. Furthermore, Table 9.2 profiles three well known and researched positive psychology programs.

Text Box 9.2 Examples of Exercises in the Positive Psychology Curriculum

Three Good Things. Students are instructed to write down three positive things that happened each day for a week. These can be relatively small or large in importance (I answered a really hard question on my math exam. This amazing guy asked me to go to a party with him!) After the positive event that they list, students should be encouraged to write a reflection related to one of these questions: Why did this good thing happen? What does this mean to you? How can you increase the likelihood that it will happen more in the future?

Using Signature Strengths in a New Way. Researchers believe that students can get more satisfaction out of life if they learn to identify which of the character strengths they possess in abundance. Then, they use these strengths as much as possible with friends, family, in hobbies, and in school. Students take the VIA Signature Strengths test for children, which can be found at VIA Inventory of Strengths at www.viacharacter.org/www/The-Survey. In addition, the website authentic-happiness. com has several lessons in the curriculum that focus on helping youth identify character strengths in themselves and others and using the strengths in new ways and/or applying these strengths to overcome challenges.

Table 9.2 The Positive Psychology Program (PPP; Selgiman et al., 2009)

PPP

- Designed by Martin Seligman and his colleagues at the University of Pennsylvania, the PPP curriculum emphasizes the positive psychology prevention approach to well-being and resilience by helping students develop an increased capacity for positive emotions, identify and use their strengths, engage in activities that are meaningful to them, and develop close relationships.
- The PPP consists of 20–25 lessons for teaching positive psychology through discussions, in-class activities, homework assignments, and journal activities. These lessons can be embedded in the high school curriculum and classroom teachers can serve as service providers.
- Examples of lesson topics include: introductory lesson: the three paths to happiness, expressing gratitude, optimism lessons, identifying strengths, and examining meaning. Research has shown that interventions that use this promotion model reduce depression and increase life satisfaction (Kranzler, Hoffman, Parks, & Gillham, 2014).

Strong Kids and Strong Teens:

- Designed by the late Kenneth Merrell and his colleagues at the Oregon Resiliency Project at the University of Oregon. The focus of Strong Kids and Strong Teens is on promoting resilience and coping by teaching social and emotional skills. It can be used at the universal level or for children deemed to be at risk.
- There are different program curriculums: Pre-K, K-2, Grades 3-5, Grades 6-8, and Grades 9-12. The series was designed to be easy to use, brief, and to target skills that are known to build competence to thwart internalizing problems such as anxiety and depression. Lessons highlight concepts in emotional identification and management; behavioral activation; managing stress and relaxation

---

(continued)

Table 9.2 (continued)

strategies; identifying cognitive errors and reframing techniques; and social problem solving and goal setting. Students are seen as active participant in role playing activities and they engage in real-world applications. Prevents and treats internalizing problems (i.e., depression and anxiety) by teaching students how to modify irrational thoughts, manage stress through relaxation techniques, and learn problem-solving and goal-setting skills (Merrell & Gueldner, 2010).
- According to Tran, Gueldner and Smith (2014), the Strong Kids curriculum can be implemented with a high degree of fidelity, teaches basic social and emotional concepts that are essential to promote wellness and resilience, and it can help protect youth that have internalizing problems.

The Penn Optimism Program (POP; Seligman, Reivich, Jaycox, & Gillham, 1995; Shatté, Gillham, & Reivich, 2000) and now known as the *Penn Resiliency Program* (Gillham & Revitch, 2004)

- These programs employ a 12-week group-intervention design that aims to prevent depression and increase optimism.
- These programs teach students how to challenge irrational beliefs by devising worst-case, best-case, and most-likely scenarios in order to create numerous solutions to scenarios and problems.
- They also teach "assertiveness and negotiation, countering procrastination, decision-making skills, and combining these skills with more optimistic thinking in a comprehensive problem-solving model" (Shatté et al., 2000).

Note
Research suggests that the aforementioned programs are effective for promoting hope and optimism, and reducing depressive symptoms in youth (Miller, Nickerson, & Jimerson, 2014; Sin & Lyubomirsky, 2009).

In the following interview, Terry Molony discusses how to incorporate the practice and principles of positive psychology into the field of education.

Expert Interview 9.1 with Terry Molony

Philadelphia College of Osteopathic Medicine and Cherry Hill (NJ) Public Schools

PJL. As a former National Association of School Psychologists (NASP) School Psychologist of the Year and the Chair of the NASP Interest Group on Positive Psychology you have been celebrated for your work in the area of positive psychology. What do you see as the most significant contributions that this new area of practice and research can make to the field of education?

TM. Positive psychology can teach skills of self-awareness and resiliency to students. Helping students become more self-aware and identify their character strengths or virtues and teaching them how to use these in their everyday lives can enhance their well-being. Teaching students how to develop "positivity portfolios" related to different emotions can teach them that they have some power over changing their emotions. If students engage with their portfolio and elicit the positive feelings that they initially felt and described, then they can learn to change their feelings and thinking. Self-awareness and self-monitoring can be extremely empowering and can help students learn at an early age about their own accountability for their emotions and actions.

PJL. How might we use the insights and the research in this area to make schools physically and psychologically safer?

TM. If positive psychology were practiced in a school, a climate of caring would be established system-wide because everyone would be practicing gratitude, and students' and teachers' strengths would be acknowledged, respected, and celebrated on a regular basis. Students and teachers would become aware of the beneficial impact of using their character strengths on themselves and others. This practice would lead to a welcoming school climate and an appreciation of diversity—not simply tolerance. The knowledge that everyone is using different character strengths at a different time or in a different way would lead to enormous amounts of productivity.

Students and teachers who concentrate on flow (i.e., a highly focused and creative state) would be engaged in meaningful and relevant learning activities that would deepen the understanding and conceptualization of academic goals. It seems logical that this would increase intrinsic motivation for students, which, besides resulting in greater learning, would also result in greater independence and a stronger internal locus of control. Teachers and other school staff would experience more powerful feelings of self-efficacy and affirmation, thus leading to greater job satisfaction and less job burnout.

PJL. What are some things that teachers can do to incorporate principles and practices of positive psychology in the schools?

TM. Teachers can be role models for positive psychology. They can demonstrate how optimistic attributions can lead to more creative problem-solving and increased positive emotions. They can teach children about the flow experience, so that children can deepen and enrich their learning, which would likely lead to greater academic achievement. Teachers can create classrooms of gratitude and caring that would probably result in fewer behavioral disruptions. In some lower-level elementary classrooms I have observed, teachers have students sit on the floor and go around the room and say something kind to another student once a week in an exercise for character education. While the intentions of this activity are positive, this seems somewhat contrived and the compliments might be forced. In contrast, a classroom engaged in positive psychology would have ongoing spontaneous expressions of appreciation and gratitude throughout the whole day.

Teachers would reap the most benefits from positive psychology if they practice it in their daily lives before incorporating these principles in the classrooms. Once they experience its positive effects, it would be easy to find ways to infuse it throughout the curriculum. In math, expressions of gratitude or kindness could be used as the content for teaching skills about counting, measuring, or graphing. Identifying the benefits of using character strengths could be topics for essays. Describing the strengths or lack of strengths the characters in books display can be topics for written assignments or discussion. One creative teacher had her students develop PowerPoint presentations for positive emotions.

PJL. With all the demands now being placed on educators, will using positive psychology create more time demands on already stressed teachers?

TM. Because the tenets of positive psychology are so easy to understand and use, incorporating them into the school day would not take additional time or effort. Also, as mentioned earlier, if a teacher practices positive psychology in his or her everyday life, it would become second nature to incorporate examples or activities throughout the day. In addition, a teacher who uses positive psychology daily in schools would probably enhance his or her life; this would lead to satisfaction in all aspects of life and work, which would make it even more meaningful to use in classrooms.

PJL. In your practice as a school psychologist, will you please share some things you have done to help foster student mental health using positive psychology?

TM. My elementary school practice has been greatly enhanced by Fifth Grade Positive Psychology groups that I have facilitated. This is an easy and flexible way to incorporate positive psychology into one's practice. Our club is open to any fifth graders who are interested in learning about positive psychology and the meetings occur during the lunch hour. Membership is flexible and students can attend as often or as infrequently as they like. We focus on the themes of positive psychology, including gratitude, positive emotions, optimistic vs. pessimistic attribution style, flow, character strengths, etc. We have developed different activities based on research articles, books, and book chapters by experts in the field. The gratitude activities include things like writing gratitude notes and leaving surprise Post-it notes for family members, teachers, or friends to who they wish to thank. We have made positivity portfolios, in which we talk about the calming impact of positive emotions when we are under stress. We borrow some concepts and terminology from Cognitive Behavior Therapy when we teach about the optimistic and pessimistic attribution styles and how we can change our ways of thinking when these get in the way of accomplishing our goals. When we talk about flow, we help the students become aware of their level of engagement, and what learning activities lead to greater engagement. As a follow-up, we teach students advocacy skills to discuss their learning needs with their teachers. A major topic that we cover is character strengths or Seligman and Peterson's virtues in action. The students identify the signature strengths they think are their strongest and they pay attention to when they use them and they also decide if they would like to develop other strengths.

I have also incorporated positive psychology in my practice in parent meetings as well as during in-services for teachers and other school personnel. At parent meetings, I always discuss positivity portfolios and how families can use them. Many parents have later told me that they made positivity portfolios with their children one weekend and that it was a wonderful family bonding experience. It was also something that the children used throughout the school year when they were stressed over tests.

Incorporating positive psychology might take a little extra work, but that extra time and effort has increased my joy and satisfaction as a school psychologist exponentially!

Conclusion

The theoretical principles and practical applications of positive psychology have significant and far-reaching benefits for school communities. Although students gain valuable knowledge and skills as they progress through their educational years, the emphasis of schooling often is on the mastery of academic content to the exclusion of other life-enhancing skills. Considering that parents generally state that they want their children to lead happy and fulfilling lives (as well as to have positive relations with others) it is discouraging that instruction in this regard is not provided at school (Diener & Lucas, 2004). However, as the impact of positive psychology practices become better known, it is hoped that this will change in the near future.

Furthermore, because mental illness accounts for about half of all disabilities in children and young adults aged 10–24 years old (Gore et al., 2011), it is apparent that millions of students can benefit from what positive psychology espouses. Namely, they should be provided with the opportunity to flourish and reach their full potential. In addition to academic skills, students need to learn how to live their lives with a greater sense of gratitude, kindness, optimism, mental stability, joy, and overall fulfillment. Ultimately, by not only teaching the principles of positive psychology, but by genuinely incorporating these into every aspect of the school system, students can be taught the most important skill of all—learning how to build and maintain an emotionally rewarding and fulfilling life.

Note

1 A meta-analysis is a type of statistical analysis that aims to compare and contrast results from different studies to identify patterns among study results. Through using this approach, sources of disagreement among results can be understood and contextualized. In addition, use of meta-analytic techniques can elucidate other interesting relationships or patterns that can be established within the context of multiple studies.

References

Akin-Little, K., Little, S. G., & Delligatti, N. (2004). A preventative model of school consultation: Incorporating perspectives from positive psychology. *Psychology in the Schools, 41*, 155–162.

Bird, J. M., & Markle, R. S. (2012). Subjective well-being in school environments: Promoting positive youth development through evidence-based assessment and intervention. *American Journal of Orthopsychiatry, 82*, 61–66. doi:10.1111/j.1939- 0025.2011.01127.x

Bolier, L., Haverman, M., Westerhof, G. J., Riper, H., Smit, F., & Bohlmeijer, E. (2013). Positive psychology interventions: A meta-analysis of randomized controlled studies. *BMC Public Health, 13,* 119. doi:10.1186/1471-2458-13-119

Brannon, D. (2008). Character education: It's a joint responsibility: Instilling positive character traits in children requires teachers, parents, and administrators to work together. *Kappa Delta Pi Record, 44,* 62–65.

Chafouleas, S. M., & Bray, M. A. (2004). Introducing positive psychology: Finding a place within school psychology. *Psychology in the Schools, 41*, 1–5.

Coyle, L. D., & Vera, E. M. (2013). Uncontrollable stress, coping, and subjective well-being in urban adolescents. *Journal of Youth Studies, 16*, 391–403.

Csikszentmihalyi, M. (1997). *Finding flow: the psychology of engagement in everyday life.* New York: Basic Books.

Diener, E. (1984). Subjective well-being. *Psychological Bulletin, 95,* 542–575. doi: 10.1037/0033-2909.95.3.542

Diener, E. (2000). Subjective well-being: The science of happiness and a proposal for a national index. *American Psychologist, 55*, 34–43.

Diener, M. L., & Lucas, R.E. (2004). Adults desires for children's emotions across 48 countries. *Journal of Cross Cultural Psychology, 35,* 525–547.

Fredrickson, B. (2009). *Positivity: Groundbreaking research reveals how to enhance the hidden strengths of positive emotions, overcome negativity and thrive.* New York: Crown.

Froh, J. J., Emmons, R. A., Card, N. A., Bono, G., & Wilson, J. A. (2011). Gratitude and the reduced costs of materialism in adolescents. *Journal of Happiness Studies, 12,* 289, 302.

Froh, J., Yurkewicz, C., & Kashdan, T. (2009). Gratitude and subjective well-being in early adolescence: Examining mechanisms and gender differences. *Journal of Adolescence, 32*, 633–650.

Gable, S. L., & Haidt, J. (2005). What (and why) is positive psychology? *Review of General Psychology, 9*, 103–110. doi:10.1037/1089-2680.9.2.103

Gillham, J., Adams-Deutsch, Z., Werner, J., Reivich, K., Coulter-Heindl, V., Linkins, M., . . . & Seligman, M. E. (2011). Character strengths predict subjective well-being during adolescence. *The Journal of Positive Psychology, 6*, 31–44.

Gillham, J., & Reivich, K. (2004). Cultivating optimism in childhood and adolescence. *Annals of the American Academy of Political and Social Science, 591,* 146–163. http://dx.doi.org/10.1177/0002716203260095

Gore, F., Bloem, P., Patton, G. C., Ferguson, B. J., Coffey, C., Sawyer, S. M., & Mathers, C. M. (2011). Global burden of disease in young people aged 10–24 years: A systematic analysis. *Lancet, 377*, 2093–2102.

Huebner, E. S., & Hills, K. J. (2011). Does the positive psychology movement have legs for children in schools? *The Journal of Positive Psychology, 6*, 88–94.

Kranzler, A., Hoffman, L. J., Parks, A. C., & Gillham, J. E. (2014). Innovative models of dissemination for school-based interventions that promote youth resilience and well-being. In M. J. Furlong, R. Gilman, & E. S. Huebner (Eds.), *Handbook of positive psychology in schools,* 2nd ed. (pp. 381–397). New York: Routledge.

Layous, K., & Lyubomirsky, S. (2014). Benefits, mechanisms, and new directions for teaching gratitude to children. *School Psychology Review, 43,* 153–159.

Layous, K., Nelson, S. K., Oberle, E., Schonert-Reichl, K. A., & Lyubomirsky, S. (2012). Kindness counts: Promoting prosocial behavior in preadolescents boosts peer acceptance and well-being, *Plos One, 7*, e51380.

Linley, P. A., Joseph, S., Harrington, S., & Wood, A. M. (2006). Positive psychology: Past, present, and (possible) future. *The Journal of Positive Psychology, 1*, 3–16. doi:http://dx.doi.org.ezproxy.fiu.edu/10.1080/17439760500372796

McCullough, M., Emmons, R. (2003). Counting blessings versus burdens: An experimental investigation of gratitude and subjective well-being in daily life. *Journal of Personality and Social Psychology, 84,* 377–389.

Marques, S., Lopez, S., & Pais-Ribero, J. (2011). Building hope for the future. A program to foster strengths in middle school students. *Journal of Happiness Studies. 12,* 139–152.

Merrell, K. W., & Gueldner, B.A. (2010). *Social and emotional learning in the classroom: Promoting mental health and academic success.* New York: Guilford.

Miller, D. N., & Nickerson, A. B. (2007). Changing the past, present, and future: Potential applications of positive psychology in school-based psychotherapy with children and youth. *Journal of Applied School Psychology, 24,* 147–162.

Miller, D. N., Nickerson, A. B. & Jimerson, S. R. (2014). Positive psychological interventions in U.S. schools: A public health approach to internalizing and externalizing problems. In M. J. Furlong, R. Gilman, & E. S. Huebner (Eds.), *Handbook of positive psychology in schools* 2nd ed. (pp. 478–494). New York: Routledge.

Molony, T. M., Hilbold, M., & Smith, N. D. (2014). Best practices in applying positive psychology in schools. In P. L. Harrison, & A. Thomas (Eds.), *Best practices in school psychology: Student-level services* (pp. 199–212). Bethesda, MD: NASP.

Morgan, M. L., Vera, E. M., Gonzales, R. R., Conner, W., Vacek, K. B., & Coyle, L. D. (2011). Subjective well-being in urban adolescents: Interpersonal, individual, and community influences. *Youth & Society, 43,* 609–634.

Palen, L. A., & Coatsworth, J. D. (2007). Activity-based identity experiences and their relations to problem behavior and psychological well-being in adolescence. *Journal of Adolescence, 30,* 721–737.

Park, N. (2004). The role of subjective well-being in positive youth development. *The Annals of the American Academy of Political and Social Science, 591,* 25–39.

Park, N., & Peterson, C. (2008). Positive psychology and character strengths: Application to strengths-based school counseling. *Professional School Counseling, 12,* 85–92.

Park, N., & Peterson, C. (2009). Strengths of character in schools. In R. Gilman, E. S. Huebner, & M. J. Furlong (Eds.), *Handbook of positive psychology in schools.* (pp. 65–76). New York: Routledge.

Pajares, F. (2009). Toward a positive psychology of academic motivation. The role of self- efficacy beliefs. In R. Gilman, E. S. Huebner, & M. J. Furlong (Eds.), *Handbook of positive psychology in schools* (pp. 149–160). New York: Routledge.

Peterson, C. & Seligman, M. (2004). *Character strengths and virtues. A handbook and classification.* Washington, DC: American Psychological Association.

Proctor, C., Linley, P. A., & Maltby, B. (2010). Very happy youths: Benefits of very high life satisfaction among adolescents. *Social Indicators Research, 98,* 519–532.

Schonert-Reichl, K. A., Oberle, E., Lawlor, M. S., Abbott, D., Thomson, K., Oberlander, T. F., & Diamond, A. (2015). Enhancing cognitive and social–emotional development through a simple-to-administer mindfulness-based school program for elementary school children: A randomized controlled trial. *Developmental Psychology, 51(1),* 52–66.

Seligman, M. (2007). Frequently asked questions. *Positive Psychology Center.* Retrieved March 7, 2014, from http://www.positivepsychology.org/faqs.htm.

Seligman, M. E. (2002). Positive psychology, positive prevention, and positive therapy. *Handbook of Positive Psychology, 2,* 3–12.

Seligman, M. E., & Csikszentmihalyi, M. (2000). Positive psychology: An introduction. *American Psychologist, 55,* 5–14. doi: 10.1037/0003-066X.55.1.5

Seligman, M. E., Ernst, R. M., Gillham, J., Reivich, K., & Linkins, M. (2009). Positive education: Positive psychology and classroom interventions. *Oxford Review of Education, 35,* 293–311.

Seligman, M. E. P. (2003). Positive psychology: Fundamental assumptions. *The Psychologist, 16,* 126–127.

Seligman, M. E. P. (2011). *Flourish: A visionary new understanding of happiness and well-being.* New York: Free Press.

Seligman, M. E. P., & Pawelski, J. O. (2003). Positive psychology: FAQs. *Psychological Inquiry, 14,* 159–163.

Seligman, M. E. P., Reivich, K., Jaycox, L., & Gillham, J. (1995). *The optimistic child.* New York: Houghton Mifflin.

Shaffer-Hudkins, E., Suldo, S., Loker, T., & March, A. (2010). How adolescents' mental health predicts their physical health: Unique contributions of indicators of subjective well-being and psychopathology. *Applied Research in Quality of Life, 5,* 203–217.

Shatte, A. J. Gillham, J. E. & Revitch, K. (2000). Promoting hope in children and adolescents. In J. E. Gillham (Ed.), *The science of optimism and hope* (pp. 215–234). Philadelphia, PA: Templeton Foundation Press.

Sheridan, S. M., Eagle, J. W., Cowan, R. J., & Mickelson, W. (2001). The effects of conjoint behavioral consultation results of a 4-year investigation. *Journal of School Psychology, 39,* 361–385.

Sheridan, S. M., Warnes, E. D., Cowan, R. J., Schemm, A. V., & Clarke, B. L. (2004). Family-centered positive psychology: Focusing on strengths to build student success. *Psychology in the Schools, 41,* 7–17.

Shoshani, A., & Steinmetz, S. (2013). Positive psychology at school: A school-based intervention to promote adolescents' mental health and well-being. *Journal of Happiness Studies, 15,* 1289–1311. doi: 10.1007/s10902-013-9476-1.

Sin, N. L., & Lyubomirsky, S. (2009). Enhancing well-being and alleviating depressive symptoms with positive psychology interventions: A practice-friendly meta- analysis. *Journal of Clinical Psychology, 65,* 467–487.

Steinebach, C., Steinebach, U., & Brendtro, L. K. (2013). Positive youth psychology: Lessons from positive peer culture. *Reclaiming Children & Youth, 21,* 15–21.

Suldo, S (2013, October 30). *Positive people & positive practices: Insights from the field of positive psychology.* Presentation at the FASP Annual Conference, Orlando, FL. Powerpoint presentation retrieved from flash-drive obtained at FASP Conference.

Suldo, S., Hearon, B. V., Dickinson, S., Esposito, E., Wesley, K. L., Lynn, C., & Hin Lam, G. Y. (2015). Adapting positive psychology interventions for use with elementary school children. *NASP Communiqué, 43*(8).

Suldo, S., Thalji, A., & Ferron, J. (2011). Longitudinal academic outcomes predicted by early adolescents' subjective well-being, psychopathology, and mental health status yielded from a dual factor model. *Journal of Positive Psychology, 6,* 17–30.

Terjesen, M. D., Jacofsky, M., Froh, J., & DiGiuseppe, R. (2004). Integrating positive psychology into schools: Implications for practice. *Psychology in the Schools, 41,* 163–172. doi:http://dx.doi.org/10.1002/pits.10148

Tran, O. K., Gueldner, B. A., & Smith, D. (2014). Building resilience in schools through social and emotional learning. In M. J. Furlong, R. Gilman, & E. S. Huebner (Eds.), *Handbook of positive psychology in schools, second ed.* (pp. 298–312). New York: Routledge.

Veenhoven, R. (2005). Is life getting better? How long and happily do people live in modern society? *European Psychologist, 10,* 330–343.

Vera, E. M., Vacek, K., Coyle, L., Gomez, K., Jorgenson, K., Luginbuhl, P., . . . Steele, J. C. (2012). Subjective well-being in urban, ethnically diverse adolescents: The role of stress and coping. *Youth & Society, 44,* 331–347.

VIA (2015). VIA classification of character strengths and virtues. Retrieved from www.viacharacter.org/www/Character-Strengths/VIA-Classification#nav.

Wood, A. M., Linley, P. A., Maltby, J., Kashdan, T. B., & Hurling, R. (2011). Using personal and psychological strengths leads to increases in well-being over time: A longitudinal study and the development of the strengths use questionnaire. *Personality and Individual Differences, 50,* 15–19.

Part IV

Improving Student Behavior

10 School-wide Positive Behavior Supports

School-wide positive behavior support (SWPBS) is a proactive, systematic, and inherently positive approach to engendering meaningful behavioral and educational change in school settings (Simonsen & Sugai, 2009). Essentially, SWPBS is a system of behavioral strategies and supports that are implemented to improve the outcomes of all members of the school community as well as to improve the overall climate in schools.[1] Therefore, SWPBS is broad in its scope and it is applicable to all K-12 educational settings (Sugai & Horner, 2006). As an increasingly important and popular movement to improve students' behavior, SWPBS and how it can be applied by educators in school settings are discussed in this chapter. In addition, empirical support for SWPBS is discussed and service delivery is covered within a multi-tiered framework. Although this chapter is not an exhaustive review on the use of positive behavior support intervention strategies in school settings, it provides a foundation on which subsequent knowledge and experience with this topic can be built.

Language related to SWPBS was first introduced into educational law following the passage of the Individuals with Disabilities Education Act (IDEA) in 1997 and it centered on using behavioral strategies to meet the needs of students with significant problems and disabilities (Carr et al., 2002). Since then, a marked expansion in interest and the application of SWPBS has been experienced in the U.S. as language related to SWPBS has been incorporated into the No Child Left Behind Act of 2001 and has been appropriated by state education agencies (SEAs) in their policies for how educational services should be delivered by local educational agencies (LEAs). As a result, most educators are now familiar with various overlapping SWPBS plans that exist in the schools in their state. However, it is important to note that variability exists in how these plans actually are implemented and how they benefit students.

Core Elements of School-wide Positive Behavior Support

The use of data to identify relevant outcomes and to make informed decisions about intervention planning is central to the philosophy undergirding SWPBS as an evidence-based practice. In this regard, Simonsen and Sugai (2009) identify four critical elements of SWPBS that include *outcomes, data, practices*, and *systems*. The term *outcomes* in SWPBS relates to observable and measurable goals that are contextualized to fit school, district, community, state, and federal characteristics. Further, outcomes or outcome data must be collected within a reasonable timeframe to ensure the utility of the data for making informed decisions. Data then are collected within a SWPBS framework to determine the present level of performance being displayed by a student, group of students, or students generally. Thus, *data* are used to prioritize a need for intervention; to select objective outcomes to aspire toward that are observable, measurable, and specific; and to evaluate measurable progress toward the achievement of established goals. Data are thus integral to the successful implementation of SWPBS because they are used to guide the selection of specific intervention strategies, monitor their progress, and evaluate outcomes.

The critical element of *practices* involves all of the tasks and duties that are conducted by SWPBS team members. These include employing a function-based perspective when evaluating student behavior, generating acceptability of behavioral approaches to behavior modification in schools, training appropriate staff and support personnel, collecting accurate and useful data on student behavior, using data to make programming-related decisions, and checking the integrity of data. Essentially, within a SWPBS framework, *practices* relate to the actual task of implementing service delivery. Finally, *systems* within this framework relate to the way that SWPBS is embedded and integrated within schools and communities. Implementing SWPBS is not as simple as taking a model and applying it "out-of-the-box." Instead, the main components of SWPBS must be tailored to specific educational environments and school communities.

Applying Core Elements of School-wide Positive Behavior Support

It is important to note that data used in most SWPBS programs usually are gleaned from extant data collection processes at school. These data are sometimes called "naturally occurring school data" and, among other data sources, they may include office discipline referrals, in-school suspensions, and incidents of out-of-school suspensions (Joyce-Beaulieu & Sulkowski, 2015). Thus, schools implementing elements of SWPBS should capitalize on data that schools already are collecting as part of their standard operating evaluation procedures and should be consistent with extant laws that govern educational practices in public K-12 schools. However, as suggested by Simonsen and Sugai (2009), these data can be aggregated and presented more clearly in tables, graphs, and images to increase their impact as well as comprehension among members of SWPBS teams and beyond.

Research suggests that a wide array of school personnel can become involved with supporting SWPBS practices (Crone, Hawken, & Bergstrom, 2007). However, the formation and maintenance of a school-level SWPBS team is a key practice to the success of SWPBS efforts. In support of this notion, one study found that creating a SWPBS team was the most successful way to ensure effective behavior assessment and change in schools (Goh & Bambara, 2012). Therefore, each school should have its own SWPBS team and common members on this team include the school principal, at least one school-based mental health professional such as a school psychologist who is trained in systems-wide service delivery methods, and educators from different grade levels and disciplines (Sugai & Horner, 2002; Sugai & Horner, 2006). To ensure the success of SWPBS efforts, teams must have clearly defined roles for each team member, follow specific plans of implementation and action, and meet regularly to review data. Additionally, SWPBS members must regularly hone their skills and knowledge through professional development and meeting with colleagues about innovations and ways that they can improve their own practices (Simonsen & Sugai, 2009).

School-wide positive behavior support practices should be grounded in research, preventative in nature, consistent with desired outcomes (e.g., improving school climate, reducing student misbehavior), and well matched with local norms and cultural practices. In other words, SWPBS practices must fit within existing systems. Often these practices involve the implementation of school-wide contingency management programs such as token economies that encourage students, classes, and even educators to be reinforced for regularly displaying positive behaviors and interventions that aim to increase prosocial interactions and facilitate the development of social skills (Sugai & Horner, 2002).

Regarding the later point, savvy administrators also are using SWPBS strategies to encourage desirable behavior among educators. This might involve incentivizing teachers as well as students for reductions in office discipline referrals and other behavioral infractions. Although some members of the school community may initially feel uncomfortable with being included in SWPBS initiatives, research indicates that implementing SWPBS across the board for all members of educational communities is associated with improvements in school organizational health (Bradshaw, Koth, Bevans, Ialongo, & Leaf, 2008).

Multi-tiered School-wide Positive Behavior Support

Intervention strategies and supports under a SWPBS framework often are organized into a three-tiered prevention service delivery framework that is conceptually similar to other service delivery frameworks for providing services at schools such as response-to-intervention or Multi-tiered Systems of Support (MTSS; Bohanon & Wu, 2011; Sugai, & Horner, 2009). The provision of services within this framework allows for various intervention approaches and data management strategies to be delivered on a continuum to students that display different needs (Office of Special Education Programs Center on PBIS, 2004). The tiers included in SWPBS usually are organized into *primary* (universal), *secondary* (selective), and *tertiary* (indicated) levels of service delivery. Figure 10.1 displays a three-tiered model of SWPBS.

Primary Tier Interventions

Primary tier intervention services under a SWPBS framework are available to all students across all different school environments, including in and outside of classrooms. These intervention services are preventative in nature and they often include setting and teaching positively stated behavioral expectations, rules, norms, and procedures that all members of the school community are expected to follow. In addition, the development and implementation of a school-wide reinforcement system is a critical component of primary tier interventions within a SWPBS framework (Sugai & Horner, 2002; Sugai & Horner, 2009).

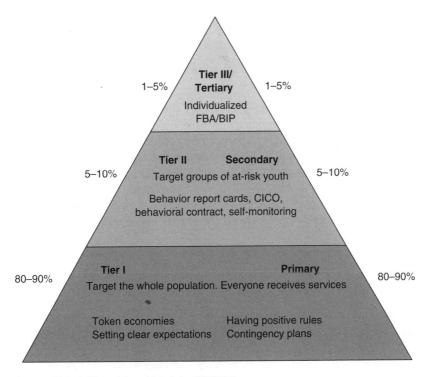

Figure 10.1 A Three-Tiered Model of SWPBS

Schools implementing primary tier interventions within a SWPBS framework generally emphasize that all members of school communities follow certain codes of conduct and that these codes become adopted and enforced. These codes of conduct, which usually are few in number so they will be easy to learn, are explicitly taught to all students and staff members. To help with this process as well as the successful adoption of specific rules, visual prompts such as posters are displayed in various locations around the school such as in classrooms, hallways, the main office, and lunchrooms to reinforce behavioral expectations. Behavioral expectations and rules should be worded positively and descriptively so that students will know how to behave in specific contexts (e.g., "walk on the right side of the hall," "return your lunch tray to the counter after eating"). Furthermore, school-wide expectations should encourage prosocial behavior among students and ensure the safety of the school environment (e.g., be respectful of others, be safe, be an active learner; Simonsen & Sugai, 2009).

Providing regular, consistent, and positive reinforcement for meeting behavioral expectations is essential for the successful implementation of SWPBS. This often is accomplished through implementing a token economy for all students that encourages these individuals to earn a range of primary (e.g., food, drinks), secondary (i.e., token; e.g., bingo chips, student bucks), and social reinforcers (e.g., praise, recognition). At the primary tier of SWPBS, token economies should allow for specific individuals, whole classrooms, grades, and the entire student body to receive reinforcers (Sugai & Horner, 2002).

In addition to positive reinforcement, it also is crucial for misbehavior and rule violations to be met with pre-determined and consistent consequences. A one-size-fits-all approach to delivering consequences is contraindicated. Instead, Simonsen and Sugai (2009) recommend for SWPBS programs to be constructed in a way that allows for consequences to be delivered on a continuum that begins with less intrusive and mildly adverse consequences for minor infractions (e.g., ignoring/ extinction, differential reinforcement) followed by more adverse consequences for moderate infractions (e.g., response cost, time out), and even more adverse consequences for serious incidents of misbehavior (e.g., detention, suspension). Thus, while implementing SWPBS, punishment should fit the nature of the infraction. However, from a philosophical perspective as well as in its direct application in schools, SWPBS aims to prevent behavioral infractions proactively.

Secondary Tier Interventions

According to Crone, Hawken, and Horner (2004), secondary tier intervention services under an SWPBS framework focus on increasing instructional structure, the intensity of instruction, the frequency and intensity of reinforcement, or a combination of these aims. Thus, secondary tier interventions are designed to assist students who did not adequately respond to primary tier interventions and need additional behavioral supports. However, students who are provided with secondary tier interventions should still have access to school-wide or primary interventions and reinforcers. Additionally, prior to receiving secondary tier interventions, students should be evaluated by a SWPBS team to ensure the goodness of fit between the student and the intervention approach.

Simonsen and Sugai (2009) report that secondary tier interventions are characterized as having:

> (a) regular and frequent daily behavior assessments (self or other), (b) direct alignment with school-wide behavioral expectations, (c) regular and frequent daily positive reinforcement for displays of appropriate behavioral expectations, (d) group-based contingencies that involve positive reinforcers for whole classrooms on the basis of individual student/group performance, (e) behavioral reporting to and positive reinforcement opportunities by parents, and (f) routine progress review and intervention adjustments on the basis of student responsiveness.

(p. 137)

Essentially, schools have a lot of leeway in how they provide secondary tier interventions. However, they often adopt one or more specific approaches to address the needs of students who can benefit from these interventions, such as daily behavior report cards, self-monitoring interventions, behavioral contracts, and check-in/check-out to provide students with extra behavioral supports (Hulac, Terrell, Vining, & Bernstein, 2011). Table 10.1 provides a brief summary of each of the aforementioned secondary tier interventions as well as information on their implementation.

Tertiary Tier Interventions

Tertiary tier interventions involve developing individualized interventions for students who have not successfully responded to primary or secondary interventions. Thus, these interventions should be tailored to specific students because of the needs they display. To assess these needs, it is often important to conduct a functional behavior assessment (FBA; also referred to as a functional assessment of behavior), which is a systematic assessment practice that aims to determine the functions of specific behaviors or what is driving and maintaining these behaviors. Essentially, the FBA process aims to elucidate antecedents (As) that happen before problematic behaviors (Bs) and consequences (Cs) that occur afterward that may reinforce the problematic behaviors (Simonsen & Sugai, 2009; Sugai & Horner, 2002). Crone, Hawken, and Horner (2015) describe the FBA process as being integral to any and all successful SWPBS programs. Moreover, they emphasize the importance of establishing positive working relationships between educators and school-based mental health professionals and behavior analysts to ensure the integrity of this

Table 10.1 Secondary Tier Interventions

	What does the intervention involve?	*Problems the intervention might be used for*	*Who might be involved?*
Daily behavior report cards	Developing and applying customized behavior rating forms that help with evaluating specific student behaviors on a regular basis.	• Aggressive behavior • Work completion • Compliance • Use of adaptive behavior	• Teacher • Behavior specialist • Administrator • Guidance counselor • Parent
Self-monitoring interventions	Involves the student paying attention to his or her own behavior and then comparing it to a specific standard or achievable goal.	• Impulsive behaviors • Affective dysregulation • Inattention • Hyperactivity	• Teacher • Behavior specialist • Classroom aid
Behavioral contracts	Delineates the expectations of student and teacher (and sometimes parents) for carrying out a specific plan or course of action.	• Externalizing behavior problems • Low rates of compliance	• Teacher • Administrator • Behavior specialist • Parents
Check-in/ check-out	Students are presented with daily/ weekly goals and then receive frequent feedback on meeting the goals throughout the day or week.	• Poor attendance • Frequently late • Low social connection • Frequently losing work	• Teachers • Guidance counselors • Administrators

process. Thus, even if not directly involved with the development of a FBA, it is important for educators to be behaviorally minded.

The overall goal of an FBA is to establish the functions maintaining a problematic behavior, which can then provide insight into ways that the problematic behavior can be replaced or modified. Therefore, data collected during the FBA process should help inform the development of a behavior intervention plan (BIP) or a behavior improvement plan. As implied by the name, a BIP aims to modify problematic student behavior in a positive way. More specifically, these plans often involve (a) modifying antecedent conditions that contribute to problematic behavior, (b) teaching replacement behaviors that meet the same function as the problematic behavior yet are less disruptive to instruction, (c) changing the provision of reinforcement or the amount of reinforcement a student is receiving, (d) building in successive approximations to allow a student to make progress toward achieving a behavioral goal, and (e) using extinction to reduce the occurrence of the problematic behavior (Simonsen & Sugai, 2009). Text Box 10.1 lists examples of each of the strategies that often are included in a BIP.

Text Box 10.1 Behavior Intervention Plan Strategies and Examples

Behavior intervention plan strategies	*Examples*
• Modifying antecedent conditions that contribute to problematic behavior.	• A teacher moves a student who is frequently distracted during class away from the window.
• Teaching replacement behaviors that meet the same function as the problematic behavior yet are less disruptive to instruction.	• A teacher teaches an impulsive student to raise her hand in lieu of calling out to obtain attention.
• Changing the provision of reinforcement or the amount of reinforcement a student is receiving.	• An administrator decides to increase the number of tokens that are provided to students for displaying positive classroom behaviors.
• Building in successive approximations to allow a student to make progress toward achieving a behavioral goal.	• A classroom aid helps a student learn how to get ready for lunch by reinforcing him for every step of the process or behavioral sequence.
• Using extinction to reduce the occurrence of the problematic behavior.	• A teacher stops calling on students who do not raise their hands quietly.

To the greatest degree possible, the FBA and BIP process should be seamless. In other words, after the completion of an FBA, which should identify target behaviors for intervention, the creation of a BIP to address these target behaviors should naturally follow. Therefore, individuals who provide tertiary tier assessment and intervention services will need a strong background in behavior modification and applied behavior analysis (ABA), which usually results from graduate training and supervised experience. Clearly, only a small minority of school personnel such as school psychologists and behavior specialists will have this training and the related skill set. Therefore, it will be important for educators to contact these individuals to help address the needs of students who may benefit from tertiary tier intervention services. For a more extensive discussion about implementing the FBA and BIP process, the reader is referred to the *Miami-Dade*

Functional Assessment of Behavior Manual: Linking Interventions to Assessment for Students with Challenging Behaviors. Basic Workshop available at http://ebdprogram.dadeschools.net/pdfs/FAB_manual.pdf. Furthermore, accompanying forms to use to assess challenging behaviors in students are available at http://ese.dadeschools.net/forms.asp#fab.

Implementation of SWPBS

Over the past decade, the implementation of SWPBS has increased markedly in K-12 schools across the U.S. and beyond. Over 6,000 schools that are spread out across 40 states have adopted SWPBS and many more schools have infused elements of SWPBS in their regular practices (Simonsen & Sugai, 2009). In general, the process of adopting SWPBS and applying it in school systems does not happen overnight. Instead, it usually takes a few years to implement fully all tiers of the model and all aspects of the prevention/intervention approach.

To implement SWPBS successfully, this is what is required: A commitment is needed from about 80 percent of school personnel, an administrator will need to be actively involved in the process, district-level support must be provided, a school-based team needs to be developed and meet regularly, and an efficient data management system needs to be designed and implemented. In addition, Simonsen and Sugai (2009) recommend for school-based teams to receive about six days of training that should be spread out across the year in the first couple of years of implementation. In these trainings, team members should identify clear behavioral outcomes that would enhance the school environment, establish what data will be collected and regularly monitored, determine what interventions and services will be provided across tiers, and coordinate how the team will engage the rest of the school community to ensure adequate program buy-in and successful implementation.

In subsequent years, members of the SWPBS team will need to engage continually with the rest of the school community as well as maintain the SWPBS program in place. Further, they will need to receive periodic training to help with this process. In this regard, Simonsen and Sugai (2009) recommend that they receive at least three days of training across the second year that the school is implementing SWPBS. In subsequent years, SWPBS teams will also need to receive periodic trainings, especially if new members are added to the team. Additionally, it is important for schools that are implementing SWPBS to schedule professional development opportunities on a regular basis for all members of the school community to learn about SWPBS and effective ways to improve student behavior. To help with the implementation of SWPBS, educators can consult the Office of Special Education Programs (OSEP) Center on Positive Behavioral Intervention Supports (PBIS) for helpful guides and resources: www.pbis.org.

SWPBS in Application

The implementation of SWPBS-related practices should be done flexibly. All school climates are different and it is important to consider the impact of unique cultural and community-related factors that influence student and educator behaviors in schools (Fallon, O'Keeffe, & Sugai, 2012). Therefore, educators will need to adapt extant SWPBS protocols and interventions to the schools in which they work. Fortunately, even though marked differences exist in students' native language, cultural context, and familiarity with the ways in which schools work, certain universal behaviors can signal mismatches between students and their environment. In this vein, a study by Lassen, Steele, and Sailor (2006) found the application of SWPBS in urban school communities over the course of three years to result in significant reductions in office discipline referrals and suspensions as well as increases in standardized math and reading achievement scores. Thus, SWPBS displays promise in improving student behavior and academic achievement in challenging and disadvantaged school communities.

The application of SWPBS requires careful assessment across a range of school environments and settings. To help with this process, the School-wide Evaluation Tool (SET; Sugai, Lewis-Palmer, Todd, & Horner, 2001) has been developed. The SET includes 28 items that are organized into seven subscales that represent the seven key features of school-wide PBS:

- School-wide behavioral expectations are defined.
- These expectations are taught to all children in the school.
- Rewards are provided for following the expectations.
- A consistently implemented continuum of consequences for problem behavior is put in place.
- Problem behavior patterns are monitored and the information is used for ongoing decision-making;
- An administrator actively supports and is involved in the effort.
- The school district provides support to the school in the form of functional policies, staff training opportunities, and data collection options.

Educators can learn how to administer and score the SET to help with evaluating the implementation of SWPBS as well as to assess the school climate in a more systematic manner. While administering the SET, the assessor must interview administrators, teachers, staff members, and students; review permanent products and documents at school (e.g., school handbooks, training curricula); and determine what existing data systems the school is using. In addition, this assessment process involves randomly sampling students and others to assess their knowledge of SWPBS practices such as whether they can recite specific school rules or behavioral expectations. Research on the SET supports its reliability and validity for use in schools when it is implemented with fidelity, especially in elementary school settings (Horner et al., 2004; Vincent, Spaulding, & Tobin, 2009). The SET can be downloaded for review on OSEP Center on PBIS's resource page: www.pbis.org/resource/222/school-wide-evaluation-tool-set-v-2-1.

Empirical Support for SWPBS

An impressive amount of research has been conducted on the various components and aspects of SWPBS. A review of research by Horner, Sugai, and Anderson (2010) found that over 46 studies have been published that review an aspect of SWPBS during the last 20 years. Although considerable variability exists across these studies and their foci, research on SWPBS generally aims to establish the efficacy of interventions at the different levels of service delivery: primary, secondary, and tertiary.

Research on the efficacy of primary tier SWPBS intervention approaches indicates that these interventions significantly reduce problematic student behavior and increase school cohesion and climate (Bradshaw et al., 2008; Horner et al., 2009, 2010; Kilian, Fish, & Maniago, 2006; Knoff, 2012; Safran & Oswald, 2003). In a salient study on this topic by Bradshaw, Mitchell, and Leaf (2010) that included 37 elementary schools and utilized a randomized controlled trial and five-year longitudinal study design, results indicated that office discipline referrals associated with problem behavior and the proportion of students receiving out-of-school suspensions were significantly reduced when schools were able to implement SWPBS with high fidelity.

Research also supports the efficacy of secondary tier SWPBS interventions. More specifically, Horner et al. (2010) report that the efficacy of a range of secondary tier SWPBS interventions has been supported by research, especially check-in/check-out (CICO), which involves presenting students with daily/weekly goals that they then receive frequent feedback on while they work toward achieving them. According to Horner et al. (2010), "the research support for CICO is strong and comes largely from single-case research documenting functional relations between the implementation of CICO and a reduction in problem behavior" (p. 9). Lastly, tertiary tier

SWPBS interventions also are empirically supported. In general, a wealth of studies has established that the FBA process is an effective way to determine the functions of students' behavior (Crone et al., 2015; Kazdin, 2001; Miltenberger, 2011). Similarly, following the FBA process, the development and implementation of a BIP that is matched to the nature of the behavioral concern is associated with reductions in problematic behaviors and increases in desirable ones (Crone & Horner, 2012; Fallon et al., 2012).

In the following interview, Rob Horner discusses the importance of designing effective learning environments, effective strategies for enhancing academic and social behaviors of students, the most important goals of behavior management, and some lessons learned in implementing SWPBS in schools.

Expert Interview 10.1 with Rob Horner

University of Oregon

PJL. It has been noted in the SWPBS literature that "children will learn best in schools with effective behavior systems." The shift is from looking for tactics to "control" student behavior to building school-wide systems that define, teach, monitor, and acknowledge appropriate social behavior. Can you elaborate on this idea?

RHH. Behavior support is about the design of effective environments. Effective environments, especially effective learning environments, share four features. They are socially *predictable* in that students are very clear about what behaviors are expected. The expectations are *consistent* across people, places, and time. The interactions that students have with adults and peers are much more likely to be *positive* than corrective or negative. And the environment is perceived by students as being both physically and emotionally *safe*. Creating these features requires big shifts in the traditional vision of discipline in schools. The first shift is to focus on features of the *context* (setting) as much as on the students. The second shift is to invest in *prevention* of problems rather than only responding to problems. It is this emphasis on prevention that leads to defining and teaching expectations proactively. The third shift emphasizes the use of *acknowledgements* (or rewards) not just as a behavior change strategy, but as a learning mechanism for improving the precision and fluency of positive behavior. The fourth major shift is on the *collection and use of data* not just for accountability but for continuous improvement. We have learned that effective environments have highly efficient ways to document (a) if they are doing the practices they claim to do, and (b) if those practices are benefiting students. These data are used at least every 3–4 months to adjust efforts in the school to improve the effectiveness of the setting.

PJL. What are the most effective strategies for improving classroom and school environments? How do effective school-wide behavior support systems make a significant difference in improving school climates? What can we learn from current research on school-wide behavior support programs?

RHH: Educators have a wealth of research defining effective strategies for enhancing both academic and social behavior in schools. The real shift in recent years has been on tailoring these strategies to make them extremely efficient, and then combining effective, efficient strategies with systematic implementation procedures (cf. Fixsen et al., 2005).

Three lessons learned to date include:

1. *Effective academic procedures need to be delivered with effective social supports to achieve the academic gains targeted throughout the country.* Good academic practices delivered in behaviorally chaotic contexts are much less likely to be effective.

2. *Effective behavior support requires a "whole-school" focus.* The days when we viewed behavior support as only something done with individual students or in isolated classrooms is over. We need to define practices that are consistent throughout the school to make the system accessible to all students.

3. *A central feature of schools that wish to deliver equitable education is the development of behavior support that is delivered with multiple tiers of intensity.* This is true for reading, math, and writing too, but is especially important for social behavior. Too often schools build a single (if solid) strategy for supporting students, and that strategy works with 70–80 percent of the students; the remaining students are allowed to fail. Effective educational settings will have Tier I evidence-based strategies for academic and behavior support systems that are proactive and efficient. But they will also have screening procedures to identify students at risk for failure early, and elevated intervention practices (Tier II, Tier III) that can be accessed early when children are at risk. These higher intensity supports should alter otherwise negative academic or social trajectories.

PJL. What are the most important goals of classroom management, especially as they relate to discipline?

RHH: Create classrooms that are effective learning environments. Start by defining the behaviors you wish to see from students. Then define the features of instructional settings that would be likely to teach, support, and improve those behaviors. Then define the most common behavioral errors (acting out behaviors) that challenge the setting, and ensure that the reinforcers that naturally maintain these undesirable behaviors are extremely unlikely to be accessed in the classroom. Finally always build in a practical process for regularly assessing (a) Are we doing what we claim to do? and (b) Are these procedures benefiting students?

There is very compelling research indicating that classrooms that are effective have a small number of key features. Students are taught expected behaviors in the first ten days of school. Students are taught classroom routines to make it clear when, why, and how to be successful in the classroom. Students are given cooperative strategies so the benefits of one student benefit all. Students become invested in the academic and social success of their peers, not in their personal success at the expense of their peers. In addition, issues around organization of space, systems of communication, and functional strategies for acknowledging positive behavior are well documented. Roy Mayer, Brandi Simonson, Terry Scott and many others have guided us well in defining the features of an effective classroom management system.

An often under-emphasized feature of classroom management is effective instruction. Teaching well is among the most powerful behavior support strategies available to schools. Explicit instruction that challenges the students to apply their creativity and competence is effective. Every student, not just those easy to teach, should be able to define (a) the goals of instruction, (b) the concepts/strategies being taught, (c) examples of what the "it" looks like, and (d) examples of what it is not. Teaching well engages students, gives them clarity about how to succeed, and through their success, encourages the acquisition of specific and generalized competence.

Poor teaching is demanding, ambiguous, and only rewarding for those privileged students who are easy to teach. Poor teaching is among the most effective ways of developing problem behavior in the classroom.

PJL. What do you find are the most common mistakes that educators make in managing their classroom and how can their mistakes be corrected?

RHH: In general we are very impressed with teachers. They are tremendously committed, hard working, and skilled. The mistakes we see in classrooms are more the direct result of poor preparation in university programs, unclear expectations by the school and/or district, and insufficient administrative support.

1. Teachers who build one lesson plan and expect it to work with all students will teach to the "able" and struggle with those who are academically challenged. Teach with clarity to minimize the number of students that need more help. Identify those who are struggling early, and use differentiated instructional systems to maximize the success of all students.
2. Establish behavioral expectations and classroom routines during the first ten days of school. Invest in prevention more than on procedures that involve waiting for students to struggle and then focusing on remediation.
3. When you intervene, use practices that are tailored to the academic or social mistakes students make. Use functional assessment information to guide the selection of effective and efficient strategies. Do not simply adopt a packaged program as the one option for all problems or all struggling students, regardless of their need.

PJL. It has also been noted that now the "challenge is becoming less one of identifying strategies and procedures that work than in defining the process of implementing these practices in all 110,000 schools across the nation." What are the major barriers to implementation and what approaches have you found that work best in getting educators to buy into establishing school-wide positive behavior supports in their schools?

RHH: Effective practices combined with effective implementation results in valued outcomes. Effective practices implemented poorly do not generate outcomes. We have under-valued the technology of "implementation." Dean Fixsen and Karen Blase are helping the field discover an alternative that focuses on (a) how to select practices that are effective, (b) how to build the teams that will enhance fidelity and sustainability, (c) how to build the "drivers" related to effective selection of personnel, training of personnel, coaching of personnel, performance feedback data systems, and administrative supports, and (d) how to use data systems to assess both the fidelity of implementation and the impact on student outcomes.

A major barrier at this time is the belief that training alone is sufficient to implement a new practice. Training without coaching, selection, performance feedback, administrative support, and functional data systems is seldom sufficient.

We also load most of the obligation for implementation on teachers. We need better ways to document role and capacity of district, regional and state agencies to support effective implementation. Sustained and scaled implementation of evidence-based practices will not occur without the active support of school districts and state agencies. While students will always be the "unit of impact" in education, and schools will soon become the "unit of analysis," we have yet to appreciate that school districts are the "unit of implementation." Without much more attention to the role of school districts as active contributors to the implementation process (not just monitors of competence) we will continue to struggle with large-scale implementation.

School-wide Positive Behavior Intervention Support (PBIS) is now being used in 21,000 schools across the U.S. Our modest success in scaling up PBIS is directly related to efforts to follow the guidance of Fixsen and Blase when they encourage attention to teams, drivers, administrative supports, and functional data systems.

PJL. If a school wanted to implement school-wide positive behavior supports, what resources do you recommend to help get them started?

RHH: There is a wealth of resources on the www.pbis.org website. There also are state PBIS coordinators in 44 states, and any school wishing to adopt PBIS should (a) look for their coordinator (listed on the pbis.org website) and (b) advocate at their district/region for a coordinated plan of adoption.

Teams may also find three "blueprints" useful for planning PBIS implementation, or for developing grant applications to fund PBIS implementation: (a) PBIS Implementation Blueprint, (b) PBIS Evaluation Blueprint, and (c) PBIS Professional Development Blueprint. Each of these is available from the www.pbis.org website.

PJL. Can you describe a school system that is doing an exemplary job implementing school-wide positive behavior supports? What does this school system do differently that sets them apart?

RHH: Many school systems are doing PBIS well. We have over 15,000 schools that actively measured the fidelity of their PBIS implementation in 2013–2014, and the majority of these schools are reaching fidelity criteria within 28–30 months. We recently acknowledged the work done in Wisconsin as a state that (a) invested in a strong and diverse state leadership team, (b) built training, coaching, and evaluation supports at the state, regional, and district levels, (c) actively supported districts in their assistance to adopting schools, (d) consistently measured both fidelity and student outcomes, and (e) used their data to adjust personnel, technology, and training foci. We need more Wisconsins.

PJL. What type of training and consultation are available for schools that want to implement school-wide positive behavior supports?

RHH: The U.S. Department of Education's Office of Special Education Programs (OSEP) funds a national Technical Assistance Center on PBIS that I co-direct with George Sugai and Tim Lewis. Part of our task is to work with states and districts that wish to build the capacity to implement PBIS. Our focus is always to build capacity as locally as possible, and the result is that today most states have strong systems of effective training and implementation support. Missouri is a good example of a state that invested well in building local capacity, and now has a state team that can support any school in the state. Michigan is also a state where extensive effort has been made to extend both academic and behavior supports throughout the intermediate districts in the state. Any family, teacher or school administrator wishing to adopt PBIS should start with their district leadership, determine state PBIS coordinators by reviewing the state map available at www.pbis.org and, if those resources are ineffective, then contact us at the national technical assistance center.

Conclusion

The past few decades have witnessed a significant increase in the implementation of SWPBS programs and supports in K-12 schools across the U.S. These programs aim to improve student behavior and the school climate as a whole through the application of positive and effective behavioral strategies. Prevention and intervention services are delivered across multiple tiers that include *primary* (universal), *secondary* (selective), and *tertiary* (indicated) tiers. In general, all students receive primary tier supports, whereas students receiving secondary and tertiary tiered services should display a need for these services that has not been met with the provision of universal or primary tiered behavioral supports.

Research on the efficacy of SWPBS has grown considerably and it continues to grow. Currently, several large and well-designed studies support the efficacy of SWPBS as a whole and many other studies support the effectiveness of specific interventions that are commonly subsumed within an SWPBS framework. Because of its robust empirical support, utility for all members of school communities, and flexibility to be implemented across a range of K-12 school settings, SWPBS displays considerable promise for improving student outcomes and transforming school communities. In addition, as an integral part of effective SWPBS programs, FBAs allow for collaboration among educators, school-based mental health professionals, and behavior analysts to understand

and improve student behavior. Furthermore, everyone wins—students, educators, administrators, caregivers—through these conjoint efforts.

Note

1 *Notice:* Different authors and resources use different terms to describe SWPBS. Some of these include Positive Behavior Support (PBS), Positive Behavioral Intervention Support (PBIS), and School-wide Positive Behavioral Intervention Support (SWPBIS). Although slight differences may exist among these different models, they all are highly overlapping. In some instances PBIS may refer to the individual classroom, whereas SWPBS refers to the entire school. Therefore, SWPBS as a general term (i.e., not a specific model) is used for convenience in this text.

References

Bohanon, H., & Wu, M. J. (2011). Can prevention programs work together? An example of school-based mental health with prevention initiatives. *Advances in School Mental Health Promotion, 4,* 35–46.

Bradshaw, C. P., Koth, C. W., Bevans, K. B., Ialongo, N., & Leaf, P. J. (2008). The impact of School-Wide Positive Behavioral Interventions and Supports (PBIS) on the organizational health of elementary schools. *School Psychology Quarterly, 23,* 462–473.

Bradshaw, C. P., Mitchell, M. M., & Leaf, P. J. (2010). Examining the effects of school-wide positive behavioral interventions and supports on student outcomes: Results from a randomized controlled effectiveness trial in elementary schools. *Journal of Positive Behavior Interventions, 12,* 133–148.

Carr, E. G., Dunlap, G., Horner, R. H., Koegel, R. L., Turnbull, A. P., Sailor, W., . . . & Fox, L. (2002). Positive behavior support evolution of an applied science. *Journal of Positive Behavior Interventions, 4,* 4–16.

Crone, D. A., Hawken, L. S., & Bergstrom, M. K. (2007). A demonstration of training, implementing, and using functional behavioral assessment in 10 elementary and middle school settings. *Journal of Positive Behavior Interventions, 9,* 15–29.

Crone, D. A., Hawken, L. S., & Horner, R. H. (2010). *Responding to problem behavior in schools: The behavior education program.* New York: Guilford Press.

Crone, D. A., Hawken, L. S., & Horner, R. H. (2015). *Building positive behavior support systems in schools: Functional behavioral assessment, second edition.* New York: Guilford.

Crone, D. A., & Horner, R. H. (2012). *Building positive behavior support systems in schools: Functional behavioral assessment.* New York: Guilford Press.

Fallon, L. M., O'Keeffe, B. V., & Sugai, G. (2012). Consideration of culture and context in School-wide Positive Behavior Support: A review of current literature. *Journal of Positive Behavior Interventions, 14,* 209–219. doi: 1098300712442242.

Fixsen, D. L., Naoom, S. F., Blase, K. A., Friedman, R. M., & Wallace, F. (2005). Implementation research: A synthesis of the literature. Tampa, FL: University of South Florida, Louis de la Parte Florida Mental Health Institute, The National Implementation Research Network (FMHI Publication #231).

Goh, A. E., & Bambara, L. M. (2012). Individualized positive behavior support in school settings: A meta-analysis. *Remedial and Special Education, 33,* 271–286.

Horner, R. H., Sugai, G., & Anderson, C. M. (2010). Examining the evidence base for school-wide positive behavior support. *Focus on Exceptional Children, 42,* 1–14.

Horner, R. H., Sugai, G., Smolkowski, K., Eber, L., Nakasato, J., Todd, A. W., & Esperanza, J. (2009). A randomized, wait-list controlled effectiveness trial assessing school-wide positive behavior support in elementary schools. *Journal of Positive Behavior Interventions, 11,* 133–144. doi: 10.1177/1098300709332067

Horner, R. H., Todd, A. W., Lewis-Palmer, T., Irvin, L. K., Sugai, G., & Boland, J. B. (2004). The School-Wide Evaluation Tool (SET): A research instrument for assessing school-wide positive behavior support. *Journal of Positive Behavior Interventions, 6,* 3–12.

Hulac, D., Terrell, J., Vining, O., & Bernstein, J. (2011). *Behavioral interventions in schools: A Response-to-intervention guidebook.* New York: Routledge.

Joyce-Beaulieu, D., & Sulkowski, M. L. (2015). *Cognitive-behavioral therapy in K-12 schools: A practitioner's workbook.* New York: Springer.

Kazdin, A. E. (2001). *Behavior modification in applied settings.* Long Grove, IL: Waveland Press.

Kilian, J. M., Fish, M. C., & Maniago, E. B. (2006). Making schools safe: A system-wide school intervention to increase student prosocial behavior and enhance school climate. *Journal of Applied School Psychology, 23,* 1–30.

Knoff, H. M. (2012). *School discipline, classroom management, and student self-management: A positive behavioral support implementation guide.* Thousand Oaks, CA: Corwin Press.

Lassen, S. R., Steele, M. M., & Sailor, W. (2006). The relationship of school-wide positive behavior support to academic achievement in an urban middle school. *Psychology in the Schools, 43,* 701–712.

Miltenberger, R. (2011). *Behavior modification: Principles and procedures.* Belmont, CA: Cengage Learning.

Office of Special Education Programs Center on Positive Behavioral Interventions and Supports. (2004). *School-wide positive behavior support implementers' blueprint and self assessment.* Eugene, OR: University of Oregon.

Safran, S. P., & Oswald, K. (2003). Positive behavior supports: Can schools reshape disciplinary practices? *Exceptional Children, 69,* 361–373.

Simonsen, B., & Sugai, G. (2009). School-wide positive behavior support: A systems-level application of behavioral principles. In A. Akin-Little, S. G., Little, M. Bray, & T. J. Kehle (Eds.), *Behavioral interventions in schools: Evidence-based positive strategies* (pp. 125–140). Washington, DC, U.S.: American Psychological Association.

Sugai, G., & Horner, R. H. (2002). The evolution of discipline practices: School-wide positive behavior supports. *Child & Family Behavior Therapy, 24,* 23–50.

Sugai, G., & Horner, R. H. (2006). A promising approach for expanding and sustaining school-wide positive behavior support. *School Psychology Review, 35,* 245–259.

Sugai, G., & Horner, R. H. (2009). Responsiveness-to-intervention and school-wide positive behavior supports: Integration of multi-tiered system approaches. *Exceptionality, 17,* 223–237.

Sugai, G., Lewis-Palmer, T., Todd, A., & Horner, R. H. (2001). *The School-Wide Evaluation Tool (SET).* Eugene, OR: University of Oregon.

Vincent, C., Spaulding, S., & Tobin, T. J. (2009). A reexamination of the psychometric properties of the school-wide evaluation tool (SET). *Journal of Positive Behavior Interventions, 12,* 161–179. doi: 10.1177/1098300709332345

11 Effective Behavior Management Strategies

In light of legislation such as No Child Left Behind (NCLB) and Race to the Top, educators are under considerable pressure to ensure that students are making adequate yearly progress (AYP). In addition, educators also must meet the complex needs of an increasingly diverse student population that includes students with substantial learning and behavioral challenges (Wehby & Lane, 2009). Although many students display adequate school readiness skills that help facilitate their success at school, many others do not. Subsequently, these students must be taught what is expected of them and how to be successful in school. Students who lack school readiness skills may struggle with following expectations, routines, and prompts that other students seem naturally to know and understand (Greene, Ablon, & Goring, 2003). Further, students can become disruptive, non-compliant, and even aggressive when they are asked to perform behaviors that they do not possess or know how to display (Greene & Ablon, 2005). Ultimately, without proper instruction and intervention, students who lack the skills they need to be successful in school will be more challenging to teach and their disruptive behavior can overwhelm even the most patient of educators (Walker, Irvin, Noell, & Singer, 1992).

This chapter discusses effective behavior management strategies that any educator can implement to help improve student behavior. A particular emphasis is placed on using positive and non-punitive behavior modification approaches as well as using antecedent manipulations or behavior modification strategies that involve manipulating the environment to prevent the likelihood of an undesirable behavior. In addition, efforts to increase student engagement are covered and ways to increase positive behaviors while reducing undesirable ones are discussed. In general, this chapter outlines a wealth of effective behavior strategies that can be implemented in a range of school settings.

Why Effective Behavior Management Is Important

Disruptive classroom behavior has been identified as one of the biggest reasons why educators choose to leave the profession. The National Education Association (NEA) reports that 20 percent of new teachers leave the classroom within the first three years of teaching and this percentage is close to 50 percent in schools that are located in urban and high poverty communities (NEA, 2002). Thus, despite having positive and admirable intentions, many teachers burn out from having to deal with students' problematic behaviors. Often, educators who leave the field report that they felt ill-prepared to deal with student misbehavior and that their coursework in college did not adequately prepare them to manage challenging student behavior (Gonzalez, Brown, & Slate, 2008). However, effective behavior management strategies can be learned and applied at any point in one's career (Knoster, 2008).

In addition to reducing misbehavior, the positive effects of having effective behavior management strategies in place can carry over to impact an entire school community. Thus, when teachers manage behavior effectively students become more academically successful because of increased instructional time and they feel safer and more supported at school (Dwyer, Osher, & Hoffman, 2000). The relationship between stable, orderly, safe, and emotionally supportive learning environments and positive student outcomes is clearly established. Further, research indicates that the majority of incidents of bullying or peer victimization occur in unstructured and chaotic environments (Craig, Pepler, & Atlas, 2000; Durlak, Weissberg, Dymnicki, Taylor, & Schellinger, 2011; Kern & Clemens, 2007). Therefore, educators with strong behavior management skills also support the emotional well-being of students, especially students who may be vulnerable to being victimized by peer aggression (Sulkowski, Bauman, Wright, Nixon, & Davis, 2014).

Effective Behavior Management Strategies

All good teachers share one thing in common. This commonality is that they employ effective behavior management strategies. By doing so, these educators are both able to increase instructional time, opportunities to engage, and feelings of being safe and secure at school. In addition, they are able to reduce discipline problems, disruptions to learning, and negative interactions in the classroom (Dwyer et al., 2000). Thus, effective behavior management really is about prevention—prevention of behaviors that negatively impact learning and instruction.

A wealth of research indicates that educators can employ three proactive strategies to prevent behavior problems at school. These strategies generally involve maximizing structure and clarifying expectations, actively engaging students during instruction, and acknowledging appropriate behavior (Hulac, Terrell, Vining, & Bernstein, 2011; Simonsen, Fairbanks, Briesch, Myers, & Sugai, 2008; Wehby & Lane, 2009). It is worth noting that these strategies are sometimes dismissed as being too time consuming, especially among educators that frequently are functioning in "crisis mode" or have to respond regularly to student misbehavior (Hulac et al., 2011). However, this concern is misguided because the use of preventative strategies actually aims to save time in the long run by reducing behavior that derails instruction and leads to a loss of instructional time (Wehby & Lane, 2009). Thus, as implied by the adage that "an ounce of prevention is worth a pound of cure," time allocated toward implementing proactive strategies to mitigate behavior problems at school before they occur is, ultimately, a worthy investment (Emmer, Sabornie, Evertson, & Weinstein, 2013).

Maximizing Structure and Clarifying Expectations

A seminal, yet still relevant, study on the use of behavior management strategies with students illustrates that setting clear classroom rules and behavioral expectations can have a massive impact on students' behavior. Specifically, Madsen, Becker, and Thomas (1968) found that setting clear expectations and explaining rules reduces problematic student behavior by 50 percent. Thus, clearly and explicitly explaining behavioral rules and expectations can be both instructional and largely influence students' future behavior. Moreover, these effects can even be enhanced by something as simple as having students recite expectations to show that they have learned what is expected of them (Hulac et al., 2011).

In addition to having clear behavioral expectations in place, posting classroom rules is associated with reductions in problematic student behavior as well as with increases in academic engagement and work completion (Simonsen et al., 2008). However, the mere act of establishing rules obviously will not have an impact if they are not skillfully implemented, carried out, and reinforced. Therefore, it is important for educators to select and implement rules that will facilitate instruction as well as directly benefit students. In other words, rules must be good for both educators and students and not lead to unfruitful power struggles that take away from instructional time. In this regard, Hulac et al. (2011) lists qualities associated with "good rules" that include promoting safety, allowing for instruction to be optimized for all students, minimizing disruptions, maximizing students' time on task, appearing to be fair for all students, and are mutually agreed upon by both educators and students. Regarding the last point, it may be beneficial for an educator to work with his or her class at the beginning of the school year to develop classroom rules. When doing so, students should feel free to contribute their own suggestions for various rules that can be modified by others and potentially voted on. Essentially, all ideas should be entertained, yet not adopted. It is interesting to note that by allowing students to create their own rules, the rules that they end up agreeing on are often very similar to the ones that adults develop; however, when students feel that they have contributed to creating the rules, they will be more likely to follow them (Rademacher, Callahan, & Pederson-Seelye, 1998).

Rules should also be positively stated to tell students what is expected of them. Moreover, they should be clearly and unambiguously presented, written in a way that makes it easy to observe if followed or violated, and easily enforceable (Miltenberger, 2011; Rademacher et al., 1998). Negatively stated rules (e.g., "don't talk out of turn") do not tell a student what he or she should be doing (only what they should not be doing), which is far less instructive than the former. As a general principle, it is beneficial to tell students what they can do to be successful at school. In addition, trying to implement non-enforceable rules can undermine an educator's credibility and his or her ability to enforce other behavioral expectations. In this vein, it is easy to think of problems associated with making unrealistic threats that will not be taken seriously by students: "You will all get detention if you do not quiet down right now." Thus, rules should be written in a way that help enforce appropriate and mutually agreed on behavioral expectations that increase instructional time and underscore an educator's role as a classroom leader (Rademacher et al., 1998).

Seating and Classroom Arrangements

Depending on the setting and context, designing seating and classroom arrangements to modify students' problematic behavior can be challenging, but when done correctly it can be highly effective. In classrooms with ample space and possibilities for various seating arrangements, educators have leeway in how they physically structure the classroom environment. However, this will not be the case in classrooms with limited space or with constraints on how desks, instructional materials, and other resources can be arranged.

Research on the setting and arrangement of the classroom indicates that it is important for teachers to consider what types of behaviors students should display prior to arranging the classroom (Wannarka & Ruhl, 2008). More specifically, teachers wishing to facilitate collaboration and mutual problem-solving among groups of students should consider clustering their desks or work stations together. Conversely, teachers who desire students to interact less and complete more independent work should consider arranging students' desks and workstations in rows. However, depending on the range of instructional tasks and the degrees of collaboration that may be involved, dynamic educators likely will not stick to either one of these extremes. Rather, they can arrange and re-arrange the room to fit the nature of instructional tasks that will vary throughout the instructional period or day.

Proximity Control

Proximity control relates to the way that an educator uses his or her physical presence to influence students' behavior. Although this behavior management strategy may seem overly simplistic, a study by Shores et al. (1993) found that proximity control is one of the most effective strategies for managing student misbehavior. In general, when teachers are closer (or more proximal) to students, their disruptive behavior decreases and they are more likely to comply with requests or behavioral expectations (Lampi, Fenty, & Beaunae, 2005).

Because of its simplicity, proximity control is one of the easiest behavior management techniques to employ, yet research indicates that this technique is underutilized (Gunter, Shores, Jack, Rasmussen, & Flowers, 1995). As a strategy, proximity control can be employed in a number of different ways. For example, it is common for educators to seat students who are frequently disruptive or off-task near their own desk or workspace, yet other educators regularly patrol the classroom and use proximity control with all students in a systematic manner. In the moment, an educator can employ proximity control by moving toward a student or group of students who are misbehaving. In this case, the student(s) usually will stop misbehaving once he or she observes that an educator is aware of their behavior and is moving toward them.

Early research suggests that proximity control is most effective when an educator is within 3 feet of a student (Etscheidt, Stainback, & Stainback, 1984). This likely is because the student is aware of the educator's presence and the possibility that he or she could deliver an immediate punishment or a consequence. Overall, proximity control has appeal because it is easy to implement, is often effective at modifying behavior, and is able to be used with a particular student or with groups of students. Text Box 11.1 lists specific strategies for effectively using proximity control.

Text Box 11.1 Strategies for Effectively Using Proximity Control

- Stand within three feet of the student(s) you want to influence.
- Randomly move throughout the classroom when students may not be expecting you to move.
- Display low emotion or reactivity in proximity to students.
- Keep interactions with students brief.
- Ensure that interactions are not overly verbose.
- Prompt the student to look or pay attention to you if he or she is distracted.
- Regularly cycle through the classroom to be close to all students at some point during instruction.
- Place highly disruptive students near where the educator usually delivers instruction.
- Ensure that all students in the class can be seen and easily reached at all times.
- Recruit other school personnel (e.g., teacher's aides) to help with proximity control.
- Create and do not break the emotional tension associated with proximity control until the student gets back on task or complies with a request.
- Use a business-like tone of voice (i.e., not weak or overly emotional) when speaking with students in proximity.
- Maintain strong yet non-threatening eye contact with students in proximity.

Actively Engaging Students

High Rate of Opportunities to Respond

Effective instruction enables students to interact regularly with the educator and each other. Expecting students to sit back, be still, and be compliant for long periods of time is not realistic and this expectation likely will lead to misbehavior. Instead, it is critically important for educators to help all students to feel engaged in instruction by allowing them ample opportunities to answer questions, state their thoughts, engage in rich dialogue, raise their hands, and write in front of their peers. This may be especially true for students who regularly disrupt instruction. Research by Wehby, Symons, Canale, and Go (1998) found that highly disruptive and aggressive students receive less than half as many opportunities to respond during instruction when compared to their peers who generally are not disruptive. Similar results were found in a study by Carr, Taylor, and Robinson (1991), who found that students who were classified as having problematic classroom behaviors received the fewest opportunities to participate during class. Research also indicates that increasing students' opportunities to respond during instruction reduces incidents of misbehavior classroom-wide, even for students that often disrupt instruction (see Sutherland and Wehby, 2001, for review). This phenomenon likely results from having students actively engaged, responding, and complying with instructional demands. Thus, providing students with opportunities to respond or behave in class can take away opportunities to misbehave (Wehby & Lane, 2009).

Some experts recommend that students should have at least two to three opportunities to respond, interact, practice, or engage per minute of instruction, which can seem like a daunting task to accomplish (e.g., Hulac et al., 2011; Sutherland, Adler, & Gunter, 2003). However, these opportunities can be relatively brief and non-intrusive, such as raising one's hand in response to a question (e.g., "How many think 'B' is the correct answer?") or personally recording an answer (e.g., "Write down the number that you think is most accurate"). From a developmental perspective, educators should expect students, especially young students, to have difficulty sitting still and being passive during instruction. Students need to engage actively with their teachers and peers; they need to learn through doing and through being social. Therefore, it is important for educators to provide students with ample opportunities to interact and respond. If they fail to do this, the students will probably respond anyway; however, instead of doing so in a prosocial way that facilitates learning, it is likely that they will disrupt the classroom environment and instruction. Text Box 11.2 lists strategies for increasing opportunities to respond.

Text Box 11.2 Strategies for Increasing Opportunities to Respond

- Provide students with 2–3 opportunities per minute to respond during instruction.
- During instruction, provide students with multiple and shorter tasks to complete.
- Use combinations of oral, written, gestured, and non-verbal opportunities to respond.
- Mix easy questions with more challenging ones and make sure that less able students are given the opportunity to respond.
- Ensure that students get answers right at least half the time if a correct answer exists.
- Couple meaningful feedback with opportunities to respond.
- Provide students with sufficient time (at least a few seconds) to respond before moving on.
- Praise correct or prosocial responses.
- Correct but do not criticize inaccurate responses.
- Self-evaluate how frequently you provide students with opportunities to respond and the types of responses that occur.

High Probability Requests

High probability requests are requests with which students likely will comply. As one might expect, not all requests are alike and students are more likely to comply with some requests rather than others. For example, getting a student to comply with the request to "please hand me a Kleenex" is far more likely to result in compliance when compared to a request to stay after class to complete extra math problems.

Educators can use high probability requests to increase students' compliance with requests across different contexts. This process has been called "behavioral momentum" and it essentially involves first establishing a compliant environment in which high probability requests (i.e., requests that students likely will comply with) are given, which then increases the likelihood that a student will comply with low probability or less preferred requests (Mace & Belfiore, 1990).

Overall, the process of pairing a sequence of high probability requests with low probability requests has been found to be an effective strategy for improving student behavior in general, while reducing misbehavior (Ardoin, Martens, & Wolfe, 1999; Wehby & Lane, 2009). As an example of this strategy, an educator could pair a request to be the "classroom helper" (a high probability request) with a low probability request such as completing all class work until it is time to hand out materials.

Choice Making

Choice making involves decreasing the aversive nature of a request or expectation through incorporating student preferences or preferred activities into the request. Therefore, as an example, an educator using choice making might allow a student to stand up near his desk during instruction instead of sitting in a chair if he is more engaged and compliant during instruction. Choice making essentially involves decreasing the aversive nature of tasks while increasing the likelihood that a student will comply with the task through what has been termed the Premack Principle, which generally states that high probable behaviors will reinforce the occurrence of less probable behaviors (Miltenberger, 2011). This principle has also frequently been called Grandma's rule, which is illustrated by the example, "You have to finish your vegetables (low probability) before you can eat any ice cream (high probability)."

Choice making enables students to exert greater control over their lives by giving them greater control over being reinforced (Shogren, Faggella-Luby, Bae, & Wehmeyer, 2004). Additionally, this intervention approach has appeal as a preventive or early intervention because it does not require problematic or disruptive behaviors to occur prior to its implementation. Lastly, in addition to being effective at reducing problematic behaviors, choice-making interventions can be effective at increasing task engagement and compliance for a range of students with academic and behavioral problems (Dunlap et al., 1994; Jolivette, Wehby, Canale, & Massey, 2001). Although more research still is needed to establish the efficacy of choice making across a range of different conditions, Shogren et al. (2004) found that providing participants with choice options resulted in clinically significant reductions in their display of problematic behaviors in a meta-analysis of single-subject studies ($N = 13$) that included 30 participants in total. Thus, choice making interventions appear to be effective and easy to implement (Wehby & Lane, 2009).

Effective Strategies for Acknowledging Appropriate Behavior

Providing Positive Reinforcement

Positive reinforcement increases the likelihood that a behavior will occur in the future (Miltenberger, 2011). By using positive reinforcement, an educator can set up conditions in which either a desirable behavior (e.g., raising a hand to respond to a question) or an undesirable behavior (e.g., calling out in class) can be increased by acknowledging and responding to the behavior. In the first example, the positive reinforcement is intended, whereas in the second example, it is unintended. Therefore, a teacher may think that she is punishing a student for acting out by scolding him in class. However, if the action of doing so actually increases the likelihood that the student will act out again, the teacher's action actually is positively reinforcing the student's acting out behavior (due to inadvertently providing attention). Conversely, a principal may think that she is positively reinforcing a student for walking away from a fight, yet if the student does not want to be publicly recognized by his peers for doing so, the principal's behavior may be counterproductive and could actually decrease the likelihood that the student will walk away from the next fight.

Many different tangible objects, activities, and social behaviors serve as positive reinforcers. Their influence will vary across different students, while they also are impacted by contextual factors (Miltenberger, 2011). In this regard, food will be much more reinforcing for someone who has not eaten for a while and it will be maximally reinforcing for someone who is starving. Therefore, when using positive reinforcement in educational settings, it is important to remember that, like any menu, some options will be more appealing than others for specific individuals. Some people love spicy *pad thai*; others prefer meat and potatoes. Moreover, it is important to provide an array of options or activities as students get satiated and require a variety of reinforcers. Students may prefer having extra time for outdoor recess on a brisk fall day, whereas they may prefer extra classroom computer time on a cold dreary afternoon. Listening to music in the music center, receiving a homework pass, getting a token or sticker, painting in the art center, or serving as the line leader will have varying degrees of reinforcement power depending on the characteristics of the student and contextual factors.

Social reinforcers such as praise are potent for most students and are easy to deliver (Hulac et al., 2011). In general, research on the impact of praise on improving student behavior has been favorable in that educators who display high rates of praise for positive student behaviors experience higher rates of student on-task behavior and lower rates of disruption in their classrooms (Matheson & Shriver, 2005). In light of these results, and because students who display problematic behavior in schools often receive low rates of praise (Sprick, Knight, Reinke, & McKale, 2006), "students prone to behavioral problems need praise more often than other students" (Hulac et al., 2011, p. 66). Text Box 11.3 provides recommendations on how educators can deliver effective praise.

Text Box 11.3 How Educators Can Deliver Effective Praise

Although most students respond well to praise and recognition, it is important to remember that praise may cause some students to feel uncomfortable and even to shut down in some cases (Hulac et al., 2011). Often praise is ineffectual for two reasons: (1) because it will cause students to be perceived negatively by peers (e.g., teacher's pet), and (2) because students will not trust the sincerity of the praise, perhaps because of the difficulties they may have with trusting adults or people at school. Therefore, to overcome these caveats and ensure that praise is effective, Hulac et al. (2011) recommend that educators provide praise that has the following characteristics:

- Descriptive in nature
- Delivered in proximity to students
- Inclusive of the student's name
- Genuine and sincere
- Specific—it should tell the student what he or she has done well

---

Group Reinforcement

Positive reinforcement strategies can be expanded beyond reinforcing particular students to focus on whole classes and beyond (see Chapter 10 for information on Positive Behavior Support (PBS)). However, it is important for educators to be aware of evidence-based group reinforcement strategies for improving classroom behavior. These strategies generally involve positively reinforcing whole classrooms of students for the collective success of a class in achieving desired outcomes and goals. Thus, the focus of these strategies is for a group of students to learn and to display a common set of behaviors that reduce distractions while encouraging learning for all students (Simonsen et al., 2008). Further, when implementing group reinforcement, educators should carefully ensure that students will not be punished for failing to meet group goals or be rewarded in the absence of making a worthy contribution.

The most salient and heavily researched group reinforcement behavioral intervention is the Good Behavior Game (GBG; Barrish, Saunders, & Wolf, 1969; Tingstrom, Sterling-Turner, & Wilczynski, 2006). The GBG is a group-reinforcement, positive behavior support intervention that involves rewarding students and ultimately whole classes for displaying appropriate on-task behaviors during instructional times. To implement the GBG, a class is divided into two teams and a point is given to a team for any inappropriate behavior that is displayed by one of its participants. Each day, the team with the fewest number of points at the conclusion of the game wins a group reward. However, if both teams keep their points below a preset level, then both teams share in the reward. Initial research on the GBG that was conducted shortly after its development supports its efficacy (Barrish et al., 1969). However, since the debut of this group-based behavior management strategy, many other studies have supported its efficacy. Thus, the GBG has been established as an effective intervention (for review, see Tingstrom et al., 2006).

Positive Practice

While using positive practice, the educator has the student perform the correct or appropriate behavior consistent with school rules or behavioral expectations. For example, a teacher who sees a student run down the hallway can ask the student to return to the beginning of the hallway and practice walking. After a dozen times, the student will get the idea and it will be less likely that the student will run in the school building the next day (Kazdin, 2001). When using positive practice, it is most important for students to be able to learn from their mistakes and display the appropriate behavior or expectation.

Effective Strategies for Responding to Inappropriate Behavior

Despite the near perfect use of proactive behavior management strategies, it is inevitable that some students still will misbehave and disrupt instruction. Therefore, educators also will need effective strategies to respond to student misbehavior. These strategies might involve changing reinforcers that maintain the problematic behaviors or using other reductive techniques that likely will improve student behavior and not result in unintended negative consequences (e.g., causing students to shut down). Thus, the next section of this chapter covers some effective strategies for responding to inappropriate or challenging behavior in school settings.

Strategies to reduce inappropriate or problematic behaviors are often called reductive strategies. These strategies can involve delivering punishment (i.e., presenting a stimulus that reduces the likelihood that a particular behavior will occur in the future (Miltenberger, 2011)). However, delivering punishment in school settings is a controversial topic because of its questioned efficacy as well as the possibility that punishment can have unintended side effects (e.g., causing students to give up or shut down). Therefore, prior to administering a punisher, Alberto and Troutman (2006) recommend asking the following questions: (a) Have reinforcement-based procedures been considered first? (b) Does the student have access to a pool of reinforcers from which to deduct payment? (c) Are there clear rules for appropriate behavior and are penalties for a violation of these rules clear? (d) Has the magnitude of the penalty relative to the infraction been considered? (e) Is there a way for the student to earn back lost reinforcers? (f) Is there adequate reinforcement available to the student? Thus, if these conditions have not been met, it may be inappropriate to use the following strategies. Moreover, considering the following conditions, punishment should only be used to modify behavior in students on rare occasions.

Differential Reinforcement

Various forms of differential reinforcement exist that basically involve decreasing a problem behavior (i.e., extinguishing it) while trying to increase a more desirable behavior or increase the periods of time in which the problem behavior does not occur. To illustrate the application of differential reinforcement, consider a child who frequently calls out during instruction. If the student occasionally raises her hand yet all too frequently calls out without doing so, a teacher can only reinforce (i.e., acknowledge the student) when she raises her hand while ignoring her calling out behavior in the absence of hand raising. Alternatively, the teacher could choose only to call on the student if she has been quiet or displayed an absence of the problem behavior for a certain amount of time (e.g., a couple of minutes) or if the student is quiet in the moment that a specific question or prompt has been posed.

A wealth of research indicates that differential reinforcement is effective for reducing problem behaviors while increasing desired ones (see Petscher, Rey, and Bailey (2009) for a review). However, it often is a challenge for educators to identify accurately when behaviors are functioning as reinforcers, or when they are serving a different function. Therefore, it can be helpful for educators to collaborate with school-based behavior experts such as school psychologists, special educators, or behavior specialists who can help with identifying the functions of problematic behaviors as well as possible ways to change these behaviors.

Extinction and Planned Ignoring

Extinction is defined as "a procedure in which the reinforcer is no longer delivered for a previously reinforced response that results in the decrease in the probability or likelihood of a response" (Kazdin, 2001, p. 454). Thus, although extinction aims to reduce problematic behavior by stopping the reinforcement of it, it does not inform the student of better ways to behave or even about specific behavioral expectations. Moreover, during extinction, students often escalate their behavior—the behavior that was previously being reinforced—in an effort to once again receive the reinforcer; this escalation process has been termed an "extinction burst." Therefore, educators should anticipate an increase in problematic behaviors once they stop reinforcing them. For example, in the absence of being called on, a student may begin to wave her hand vigorously and then begin calling out to get a teacher's attention. However, as previously discussed, extinction can be used as part of the differential reinforcement process, which can reduce the likelihood of an extinction burst because the student is being reinforced for engaging in a different behavior or for not engaging in the problematic behavior.

In school settings, planned ignoring is a common form of extinction. Planned ignoring involves actively avoiding engaging in undesirable interactions with students. This concept should not be confused with acquiescing or avoiding conflict, because planned ignoring actually is a goal-oriented strategy for behavior modification as opposed to being a conflict-avoidant approach. This is because planned ignoring involves actively planning what the target behavior, behavioral goal, or pre-specified criterion for reinforcement is for a particular student. This is based on the understanding that all behaviors that are inconsistent with achieving or approximating the pre-selected behavior will be ignored as long as they are not dangerous (i.e., will cause significant harm to the student or others).

Therefore, assuming that a reinforcement-for-a-desirable-behavior approach is in place, if the goal for the day is to increase a student's in-seat behavior, he or she should be reinforced for all successful approximations with achieving this desired outcome, even if he or she is displaying other problematic or undesirable behaviors (e.g., complaining, talking out of turn, etc.). It is important to note that planned ignoring should only be used to extinguish behaviors that can be ignored without compromising the safety of the student or the classroom environment. For example, physically aggressive behaviors such as hitting, kicking, and grabbing other students should not be ignored and must be responded to immediately.

Response Cost and Time Out

Response cost essentially involves reducing a problematic behavior by eliminating or reducing a reinforcer when the behavior occurs. Thus, students lose something they like, desire, or value when they engage in some sort of undesirable behavior. Response cost often is used in conjunction with a token economy system that involves providing students with tokens that represent currency that can be used to purchase desired objects or outcomes. Thus, when used in conjunction with response cost, a student would lose tokens for engaging in undesired behavior. Overall, response cost is associated with few negative outcomes as long as students can earn reinforcers back for correcting their behavior and, when used with token economies, this combined intervention approach has strong efficacy for modifying students' behavior (Little, Akin-Little, & Cook, 2009).

In contrast to response cost or losing something for displaying an undesirable behavior, time out involves removing a student from an environment or situation that is reinforcing for a specific period of time or preventing a student from receiving reinforcement for a specific period of time without removing the student from the setting. Thus, in time out, the student is prevented from receiving all forms of reinforcement in the environment, whereas in response cost, the student is prevented from receiving a specific reinforcer. Although time out is a commonly used intervention approach by educators and many teachers report that it is an effective behavior modification strategy, research indicates that implementing time out effectively is crucial for its success (Noell & Witt, 1999). As a caveat, time out is only effective for the student who wants to be with

---

Text Box 11.4 Effective Strategies for Implementing Time Out

- Time out area

  o The time-out area should be easily accessible, and in such a location that the child can be easily monitored while in time-out.

  o For example, a chair in the corner of a classroom is one such spot. Placing a kitchen timer on the table is a good way to keep the child informed of how much time he has left to serve.

- Amount of time spent in time out

  o Time out should not exceed one minute per year of age. Generally, it is considered more effective to have short periods of time out, 5 to 10 minutes, rather than to have long periods, such as half an hour to an hour.

  o Aim for compliance with a behavioral expectation and then reinforce a child for complying.

- Procedures for time out

  o When a child is told to go into time out, an educator should only say: "you are in time out for . . ." and then state the particular infraction. There should be no further discussion or bargaining.

  o Use a timer with a ringer. Set the timer for the length of the time out and tell the child he must stay in time out until he hears a ring.

  o While in time out, the child should not be permitted to talk, and the educator should not communicate with the student in any way.

  o The students also should not make noises in any way, such as mumbling or grumbling.

  o While in time out, students should not be allowed to play with any toys, objects, or manipulatives.

  o Any violation of time out should result in automatic resetting of the timer for another time out period.

others in the classroom. Children who prefer to be alone and do not want attention from others may prefer to be removed from the classroom, and, in this way, time out negatively reinforces their behavior, which means that it allows them to escape from an aversive situation/stimulus (Walker, Shea, & Bauer, 2004). Text box 11.4 lists effective strategies for implementing time out.

Overcorrection and Restitution

Overcorrection generally involves penalizing an undesirable behavior by requiring an individual to perform some other type of behavior to make up for the undesirable one (Kazdin, 2001). Thus, for writing on his desk with a marker, a student may be required to stay after class to clean up his desk as well as all the other desks in the room (Little et al., 2009). Restitution, the process of restoring something that has been lost or stolen, is similar to overcorrection and it has been found to be effective for reducing a range of problematic behaviors, especially for vandalism (Alberto & Troutman, 2006; Little et al., 2009). Technically, these behavior modifications are considered punishers because they reduce the likelihood that an individual will engage in the problematic behavior again. However, unlike other forms of punishment, overcorrection and restitution have social value and allow for teaching prosocial behaviors.

Using Technology for Behavior Management

ClassDojo is a recently developed program and app that has been created to help teachers effectively manage student behavior. A free account and app is available for teachers, students, and parents by going to www.classdojo.com. ClassDojo helps teachers encourage students in the classroom by rewarding students with points when they engage in positive behaviors, such as working hard, turning in homework, staying on task, being persistent, engaging in teamwork, participating in class, demonstrating insight, helping others, and any other behavior the teacher decides is noteworthy. When using this program, each student is given an avatar by their teacher and when the student displays a positive behavior, they are given credit by their teacher and their avatar receives one point. Teachers can also take away points for negative behaviors, such as not turning in homework, being late, getting out of seat, or interrupting; however, they are not required to use this form of response cost. All of the students' avatars, along with the points received, can be displayed on a screen or a smart board to show individual and class-wide behavioral performance. Consequently, this program provides students with immediate feedback about their behavior and they can also see how their behavior compares to their classmates. Moreover, this program is customizable. For example, when a student engages in a negative behavior, the teacher can be choose to record it; however, the ClassDojo display setting can be customized so that it is up to the teacher to decide if negative behavior is displayed for other students to see. By not displaying negative behavior on the screen the teacher can promote positive class norms while not visibly reinforcing negative actions.

Teachers using ClassDojo can either use a computer, a tablet, or a smart phone to reinforce students with points and ClassDojo works on any iOS/Android device or web browser. In addition, ClassDojo helps teachers communicate with parents and administrators and keeps them in the loop with free instant messaging and reports. According to the ClassDojo website, support is available 24/7 and the website also has a number of videos to help teachers get started.

Presently, due to the newness of the program, there are no empirically validated research studies supporting the efficacy of ClassDojo; however, the authors' school psychology graduate interns report, based on their consultation with teachers, that it is a worthwhile tool for managing K-12 student behavior and communicating with parents. Most importantly, it is data driven, and data can be collected and monitored on each individual student and on an entire class. The interested reader can go to the website and take short tutorials that will help them set up ClassDojo for their classes.

Managing Highly Disruptive and Explosive Behavior

Educators often report that they struggle to manage highly disruptive or explosive behavior in school settings. Although this behavior can sometimes be ignored or extinguished in safe and tightly controlled clinical settings, it is not reasonable to ignore it in school settings where other students or members of the school community are negatively affected. For example, a student who is in the middle of an emotional meltdown can derail instruction, damage school materials, and even scare or hurt other students and school staff. In these cases, it is not reasonable for educators to ignore these behaviors while the classroom is cleared and the class waits for the explosive student to calm down due to exhaustion or in the absence of reinforcement. Instead, a different approach is needed to help the student regain emotional control as well as allow instruction to continue unabated.

Adults often operate under the "little adult" hypothesis when understanding children's behavior and placing expectations on them. Consistent with this hypothesis, adults expect children to have the same strengths, abilities, and skills that adults have and to be able to utilize these qualities when under duress, when solving a problem, or when trying to get a need met. This is a faulty expectation, however, as children often need to be taught how to be successful when facing new challenges and how to problem solve in ways to get their needs met.

Thus, new approaches to addressing and managing challenging student behavior are now focusing less on stopping bad behavior and instead on teaching youth how to display positive behavior to be successful in their environment. Essentially, these approaches aim to teach students how to do well and get their needs met so they do not have to engage in problematic behavior to fulfill similar needs. For example, instead of shouting out to get a teacher's attention, teaching a student to quietly raise his or her hand is a simple adjustment that allows the student to obtain teacher attention that also does not disrupt the classroom environment. Although it may not be intuitive, this increasing positive focus on student behavior may be even more relevant for students who display highly disruptive or explosive behavior.

To help students who display explosive or highly disruptive behavior, Greene (2009) espouses a *Collaborative & Proactive Solutions* (CPS) model. This model includes three sequential steps: changing the lens, identifying language skills and unsolved problems, and solving problems. The step of changing the lens is grounded in the philosophy that students will do well if they can. In other words, most problematic behaviors displayed by students result from not knowing how to behave better or lacking the skills to do so as opposed to being willfully difficult. Thus, instead of viewing students as manipulative, coercive, unmotivated, and attention seeking, this model encourages educators to view these students as lacking the necessary skills to meet their needs more effectively.

Greene (2009) identifies many student-related behavioral problems as resulting from deficits in language skills and problem-solving abilities. Therefore, the second step of the CPS model involves assessing skills and abilities that need to be enhanced. Often, highly disruptive and explosive students struggle to meet tacit behavioral expectations that most students naturally identify and meet. When this is the case, these students will need to be taught specifically how to identify rules and expectations so that they can modify their behavior accordingly. Then, after these students learn how to identify the requisite behavioral expectations, the language skills and problem-solving abilities of these students can be shaped to enable them to meet expected behavioral norms.

The final step of the CPS model involves helping students solve problems that contribute to undesirable behavior. To do this, Greene (2009) espouses three specific plans. The first plan, Plan A, involves solving the problem unilaterally. Thus, Plan A involves having a student solve a problem on their own and it should be used only when a student has previously displayed the capacity to solve the same or a similar problem. The second plan, Plan B, involves solving the problem collaboratively and proactively with a caring adult. This plan is the crux of the problem-solving component of the CPS model. Plan B involves providing the student with empathy to understand the student's problem and open him or her up to efforts to address the problem. Essentially, this step aims to ready the student to engage in a problem-solving dialogue. Lastly, Plan C involves setting an unsolved problem aside for the time being (not to give in to problematic behavior, but because the particular behavior is outside of the current focus of behavior modification/change). Regarding Plan C, it is important for educators not to try to change too many behaviors at the same time. It is also necessary to ensure that students display fundamental language skills and the requisite problem-solving abilities prior to tackling behavioral challenges. Text Box 11.5 provides additional information on the application of the CPS model.

Text Box 11.5 Applying the CPS Model to Practice

- Changing the Lens: *Students naturally do well if they can—we need to help them do well!*

  - Questions to ask yourself:
    - Who is this student?
    - How am I misunderstanding this student?
    - How can he/she do well?
    - What is getting in the way of this student doing well?
    - How can I help this student do well?

- Identifying language skills and unsolved problems: *Many students come to school with deficits that need to be ameliorated through teaching and education*

  - Some lagging areas on which to focus:
    - Managing transitions
    - Placing things in sequential order
    - Persevering on tasks
    - Understanding behavioral expectations and tacit rules
    - Paying attention to time
    - Delaying gratification
    - Understanding consequences of one's behavior
    - Understanding a range of solutions to a problem
    - Managing one's emotions or emotional reactions
    - Understanding the perspective of others
    - Initiating and maintaining prosocial interactions
    - Expressing concerns, thoughts, wants, and needs in words
    - Comprehending what is said or verbal language more generally
    - Understanding the middle ground, shades of gray, or nuances
    - Adjusting to changes to plans or expectations
    - Understanding the impact of situational factors
    - Obtaining attention in a prosocial and adaptive manner
    - Respecting the rights of others
    - Having and expressing empathy for others

- Solving problems (Plan B): *Many students do not directly learn problem-solving skills outside of school—they need to be taught them directly and work with educators to apply them*

(continued)

(continued)

Three Steps of Plan B: The CPS Model as Illustrated Through a Hypothetical Dialogue:

Step 1 (Empathy):

Teacher: Steve, I've noticed that you get really upset at the beginning of math instruction. I also heard you yell at Molly when you were doing math problems. What's up?

Student: I really hate math! It sucks.

Teacher: I hear that. A lot of students hate math, yet it can be useful to know. What makes it so bad for you?

Student: It is really hard. It makes me feel stupid.

Teacher: Well, I know that you are smart and math takes a while to learn. Would you be willing to chat with me to better understand the problem that you're having with math?

Student: I guess so.

Step 2 (Define the problem):

Teacher: Okay, right now we're doing fractions and I noticed that you're not contributing much in class lately and your math homework is incomplete. Is this a hard unit?

Student: Yes. I hate fractions. They make no sense.

Teacher: Does the math work make you feel upset and not want to not be in class.

Student: Yes. When doing math, sometimes I feel dumb and angry.

Step 3 (An invitation to problem-solve together):

Teacher: I get it. Fractions can be confusing. Sometimes it takes a while to learn them. Though you may feel dumb about math, it is really that you need more instruction and practice, then you will get it. Would you be willing to tell me more so that I can make sure that math is not so bad?

Student: Okay. Yes. I'm worried that I will bomb the next test. I don't know this stuff. I'm trying but it is hard.

Teacher: I am glad you are trying. How does it sound if I postpone the next test? Other students are also struggling with fractions, so I can delay the test until all students get a better handle on the topic. Also, maybe I can do a better job of teaching fractions. I can discuss this with Mrs. Rivera. She really is good at teaching math. Also, I won't call on you to answer questions about fractions in class until you have this down. We can meet after class and I will help you get it.

Student: That sounds good.

Teacher: Cool. Thank you for chatting with me about this. Is there anything else I can do to help?

Student: I dunno. . .

Teacher: Are you sure?

Student: Well. . . . Sitting near Molly kind of is annoying. She's always messing with me. She laughed at my last math grade. If she was a guy I would have hit her.

Teacher: I am glad you maintained self-control and I can see how her laughing at your grade could get you so angry. Would it help if I moved you to the other side of the room?

Student: Yeah, I think so.

Teacher: No problem. Consider it done!

Student: Thank you.

In Expert Interview 11.1, Ross W. Greene discusses how to deal with explosive children and explains that both children with challenging behaviors and their caregivers tend to respond well to interventions that are non-punitive, non-adversarial, collaborative, proactive, skill-building, and relationship-enhancing and that lagging skills are the most frequent source of challenging behaviors.

Expert Interview 11.1 with Ross W. Greene

Founding Director, Lives in the Balance

PJL. You have written extensively about the explosive child. What have you learned about children who have severe temper tantrums and/or become explosive or violent?

RWG. I've learned that these students and their caregivers are frequently misunderstood. These children are often viewed as attention-seeking, manipulative, coercive, unmotivated, and limit-testing . . . and their caregivers are frequently viewed as passive, permissive, inconsistent, and non-contingent disciplinarians. I've learned that these children are lacking crucial cognitive skills, especially in the global realms of flexibility/adaptability, frustration tolerance, and problem-solving. I've learned that these youth and their caregivers need help in ways that incentive programs and adversarial, punitive interventions—such as discipline referrals, detentions, suspensions, and corporal punishment—do not provide. And I've learned that both the children and their caregivers tend to respond quite well to interventions that are non-punitive, non-adversarial, collaborative, proactive, skill-building, and relationship-enhancing. I've learned these things from thousands of parents and teachers and staff in many dozens of inpatient psychiatry units, residential facilities, and juvenile detention settings.

PJL. How should a teacher de-escalate a student who appears to be heading toward an emotional explosion? What are the most effective strategies?

RWG. De-escalation is a crisis *management* strategy. While it's good for teachers to know how to defuse and de-escalate, it's even more important for them to know how to proactively identify and solve the problems that are causing the behaviors that would necessitate de-escalation so that de-escalation strategies aren't necessary in the first place. Those problems are actually highly predictable. So the focal point of intervention should be on what the teacher does before the explosion—crisis *prevention*—rather than on what the teacher does once a student is predictably heading in that direction.

PJL. If a student is in the midst of an emotional explosion and is throwing chairs, knocking over material in the classroom, etc., what should a teacher do? How might the teacher protect the safety of the child and the other students in the classroom?

RWG. Sometimes it's necessary to clear the classroom of the other students as a means of keeping the other students safe and de-escalating the student who's exploding. Sometimes the student who's upset can be calmed without clearing the classroom. But, once again, we don't want de-escalation to be our primary long-term strategy. Better to proactively identify and solve the highly predictable problems that are causing the student to become upset in the first place; that should set the stage for the classroom teacher to be relying far less often on de-escalation strategies.

PJL. How might teachers figure out what precipitated this behavior and help prevent it in the future?

RWG. I've created an instrument called the *Assessment of Lagging Skills and Unsolved Problems (ALSUP)* to help teachers and other school staff proactively identify a student's lagging skills and the specific expectations a student is having difficulty meeting (these are called unsolved problems) in association with those lagging skills. When lagging skills and unsolved problems are identified proactively, a student's challenging behaviors become highly predictable and the stage is set for solving those problems (and teaching those skills) proactively. When, as is too often the case, our primary assessment focal point is *behavior* (rather than lagging skills and unsolved problems), we miss all of the important information about lagging skills and unsolved problems that makes challenging episodes predictable.

PJL. What seems to work best with this type of child, carrots or sticks, or a combination of both?

RWG. I'm not a big fan of carrots *or* sticks. I'm not allergic to carrots and sticks, I just find that they aren't especially effective at solving the problems that are precipitating challenging behaviors or teaching students the skills they're lacking. Indeed, I actually find that punishment—and the failure to achieve an anticipated reward—often *precipitate* or *fuel* challenging episodes. I find that once caregivers move into problem-solving mode—rather than finding bigger sticks and sweeter carrots—they often discover that they don't need all those carrots and sticks anymore.

PJL. When children become explosive should they be suspended? Should we maintain a zero tolerance policy regarding this type of behavior? What is wrong with using overly punitive responses to problematic student behavior?

RWG. The data are in on zero tolerance policies, and they didn't work . . . in fact, they made things worse. But that shouldn't really be surprising . . . suspensions, detentions, discipline referrals, and paddlings don't solve the problems that are precipitating challenging episodes and don't teach students the skills they're lacking. There are highly effective, non-punitive, non-adversarial ways to help students understand that we don't approve of the behaviors they exhibit when expectations are placed upon them that they lack the skills to meet. There are highly effective, non-punitive, non-adversarial ways to reduce those behaviors. Ineffective interventions don't keep the other students safe. Ineffective interventions don't convince the other students (and their parents) that we're taking the challenging behavior seriously. Only *effective* interventions accomplish those missions.

PJL. Do children that become explosive often require special education services?

RWG. Some behaviorally challenging students have difficulties—in realms such as language processing and communication skills, sensory/motor skills, and academic skill areas such as reading and math—that may require special education services. And there are behaviorally challenging students whose behavior is so extreme or who have been so over-corrected, over-directed, and over-punished for such a long time that they need an "environment transplant"—a separate program—to address their needs. But solving the problems that are precipitating challenging episodes and teaching the majority of lagging skills on the *Assessment of Lagging Skills and Unsolved Problems* do not require special education services. What's mostly required is a classroom teacher who's been trained to solve problems collaboratively and proactively and school leaders who made sure that they and the classroom teachers received that training.

PJL. What types of interventions and accommodations can be provided to help these youth?

RWG. I've spent most of my professional career developing and refining a model that is now called *Collaborative & Proactive Solutions*, as described in my books *The explosive child* and *Lost at school*. The model helps adults understand the true factors—lagging skills—that are contributing to the difficulties of behaviorally challenging students; use the ALSUP to proactively identify lagging skills and unsolved problems; and engage students in solving those problems collaboratively and proactively. The website of my nonprofit, *Lives in the balance* (www.lives inthebalance.org), is loaded with free resources to help educators and parents learn about and implement the model. Some students may also need medical intervention to address issues such as hyperactivity, impulsiveness, inattention, and emotion regulation . . . but nowhere near the number who are receiving such intervention.

PJL. What would you like teachers, administrators, and support personnel to know about working with children who engage in explosive behavior?

RWG. I'd like them to know about the various lagging skills that can make it difficult for these students to respond adaptively to various expectations; that these children deserve our compassion and understanding every bit as much as children with other forms of developmental delays; that it's far more productive to focus on the problems that are giving rise to challenging behaviors than on the behaviors themselves; that it's crucial to get these children talking to us so we can understand what's really making it difficult for them to meet our expectations; that it's far more productive to work collaboratively with children to solve problems than to impose our will; and that most of the work can be done proactively rather than in the heat of the moment. If teachers, administrators, and support personnel knew about all those things, we'd be helping behaviorally challenging students far better than we often do now. Information on helping behaviorally challenged children can be accessed at www.livesinthebalance.org/

Conclusion

It is critical for educators to use effective behavior management strategies to maintain control of the classroom, to teach socially sanctioned norms of behavior, and to avoid burning out. Moreover, effective behavior management is associated with increases in instructional time and improvements in the overall school climate, which is crucial for student success and well-being. Ideally, educators will be able to avert the majority of problematic student behaviors by employing preventative strategies that involve maximizing structure and clarifying expectations, actively engaging students during instruction, and acknowledging appropriate behavior. However, even the most highly trained and diligent educator must deal with incidents of student misbehavior. Therefore, it is important for educators to know effective strategies to respond to inappropriate behaviors that occur at school. Some of these strategies include the use of differential reinforcement, extinction and planned ignoring, response cost and time out, and overcorrection and restitution. These reductive strategies for addressing misbehavior ought to be employed following or along with preventive strategies such as acknowledging appropriate behavior, delivering engaging instruction, clearly establishing behavioral expectations, and providing adequate structure to the educational environment. Lastly, for behavior problems that are too disruptive to address using the aforementioned strategies, innovative approaches such as the CPS model are worth utilizing.

References

Alberto, P., & Troutman, A. C. (2006). *Applied behavior analysis for teachers.* New York: Pearson.

Ardoin, S. P., Martens, B. K., & Wolfe, L. A. (1999). Using high-probability instruction sequences with fading to increase student compliance during transitions. *Journal of Applied Behavior Analysis, 32,* 339–351.

Barrish, H. H., Saunders, M., & Wolf, M. M. (1969). Good behavior game: Effects of individual contingencies for group consequences on disruptive behavior in a classroom. *Journal of Applied Behavior Analysis, 2,* 119–124.

Carr, E. G., Taylor, J. C., & Robinson, S. (1991). The effects of severe behavior problems in children on the teaching behavior of adults. *Journal of Applied Behavior Analysis, 24,* 523–535.

Craig, W. M., Pepler, D., & Atlas, R. (2000). Observations of bullying in the playground and in the classroom. *School Psychology International, 21,* 22–36.

Dunlap, G., DePerczel, M., Clarke, S., Wilson, D., Wright, S., White, R., & Gomez, A. (1994). Choice making to promote adaptive behavior for students with emotional and behavioral challenges. *Journal of Applied Behavior Analysis, 27,* 505–518.

Durlak, J. A., Weissberg, R. P., Dymnicki, A. B., Taylor, R. D., & Schellinger, K. B. (2011). The impact of enhancing students' social and emotional learning: A meta-analysis of school-based universal interventions. *Child Development, 82,* 405–432.

Dwyer, K. P., Osher, D., & Hoffman, C. C. (2000). Creating responsive schools: Contextualizing early warning, timely responses. *Exceptional Children, 66,* 347–365.

Etscheidt, S., Stainback, S., & Stainback, W. (1984). The effectiveness of teacher proximity as an initial technique of helping pupils control their behavior. *The Pointer, 28,* 33–35.

Emmer, E., Sabornie, E., Evertson, C. M., & Weinstein, C. S. (2013). *Handbook of classroom management: Research, practice, and contemporary issues.* New York: Routledge.

Gonzalez, L. E., Brown, M. S., & Slate, J. R. (2008). Teachers who left the teaching profession: A qualitative understanding. *Qualitative Report, 13,* 1–11.

Greene, R. W. (2009). *Lost at school: Why our kids with behavioral challenges are falling through the cracks and how we can help them.* New York: Simon and Schuster.

Greene, R. W., & Ablon, J. S. (2005). *Treating explosive kids: The collaborative problem-solving approach.* New York: Guilford Press.

Greene, R. W., Ablon, J. S., & Goring, J. C. (2003). A transactional model of oppositional behavior: Underpinnings of the Collaborative Problem Solving approach. *Journal of Psychosomatic Research, 55,* 67–75.

Gunter, P. L., Shores, R. E., Jack, S. L., Rasmussen, S., & Flowers, J. (1995). On the move: Using teacher/student proximity to improve student's behavior. *Teaching Exceptional Children, 28,* 12–14.

Hulac, D., Terrell, J., Vining, O., & Bernstein, J. (2011). *Behavioral interventions in schools: A response-to-intervention guidebook.* New York: Routledge.

Jolivette, K., Wehby, J. H., Canale, J., & Massey, N. G. (2001). Effects of choice-making opportunities on the behavior of students with emotional and behavioral disorders. *Behavioral Disorders, 26,* 131–145.

Kazdin, A. E. (2001). *Behavior modification in applied settings.* Long Grove, IL: Waveland Press.

Kern, L., & Clemens, N. H. (2007). Antecedent strategies to promote appropriate classroom behavior. *Psychology in the Schools, 44,* 65–75.

Knoster, T. (2008). *The teacher's pocket guide for effective classroom management.* Baltimore, MD: Paul H. Brookes Publishing Company.

Lampi, A. R., Fenty, N. S., & Beaunae, C. (2005). Making the three Ps easier: Praise, proximity, and precorrection. *Beyond Behavior, 15,* 8–12.

Little, S. G., Akin-Little, A., & Cook, C. R. (2009). Classroom applications of reductive procedures: A positive approach. In A. Akin-Little, S. G. Little, M. A. Bray, & T. J. Kehle (Eds.), *Behavioral interventions in schools* (pp. 177–188). Washington, DC: American Psychological Association.

Mace, F. C., & Belfiore, P. (1990). Behavioral momentum in the treatment of escape-motivated stereotypy. *Journal of Applied Behavior Analysis, 23,* 507–514.

Madsen Jr, C. H., Becker, W. C., & Thomas, D. R. (1968). Rules, praise, and ignoring: Elements of elementary classroom control. *Journal of Applied Behavior Analysis, 1,* 139–150.

Matheson, A. S., & Shriver, M. D. (2005). Training teachers to give effective commands: Effects on student compliance and academic behaviors. *School Psychology Review, 34,* 202–219.

Miltenberger, R. (2011). *Behavior modification: Principles and procedures.* Belmont, CA: Cengage Learning.

National Education Association. (2002). *Attracting and keeping quality teachers.* Retrieved from www.nea.org/teachershortage/index.html

Noell, G. H., & Witt, J. C. (1999). When does consultation lead to intervention implementation? Critical issues for research and practice. *Journal of Special Education, 33,* 29–35.

Petscher, E. S., Rey, C., & Bailey, J. S. (2009). A review of empirical support for differential reinforcement of alternative behavior. *Research in Developmental Disabilities, 30,* 409–425.

Rademacher, J. A., Callahan, K., & Pederson-Seelye, V. A. (1998). How do your classroom rules measure up? Guidelines for developing an effective rule management routine. *Intervention in School and Clinic, 33,* 284–289.

Shogren, K. A., Faggella-Luby, M. N., Bae, S. J., & Wehmeyer, M. L. (2004). The effect of choice-making as an intervention for problem behavior: A meta-analysis. *Journal of Positive Behavior Interventions, 6,* 228–237.

Shores, R. E., Jack, S. L., Gunter, P. L., Ellis, D. N., DeBriere, T. J., & Wehby, J. H. (1993). Classroom interactions of children with behavior disorders. *Journal of Emotional and Behavioral Disorders, 1,* 27–39.

Simonsen, B., Fairbanks, S., Briesch, A., Myers, D., & Sugai, G. (2008). Evidence-based practices in classroom management: Considerations for research to practice. *Education and Treatment of Children, 31,* 351–380.

Sprick, R., Knight, J., Reinke, W., & McKale, T. (2006). *Coaching classroom management: A toolkit for administrators and coaches.* Eugene, OR: Pacific Northwest Publishing.

Sulkowski, M. L., Bauman, S., Wright, S., Nixon, C., & Davis, S. (2014). Peer victimization in youth from immigrant and non-immigrant U.S. families. *School Psychology International, 35,* 649–669. doi: 10.1177/0143034314554968

Sutherland, K. S., Adler, N., & Gunter, P. L. (2003). The effect of varying rates of opportunities to respond to academic requests on the classroom behavior of students with EBD. *Journal of Emotional and Behavioral Disorders, 11,* 239–248.

Sutherland, K. S., & Wehby, J. H. (2001). The effects of self-evaluation on teaching behaviors behaviors in classrooms for students with emotional and behavioral disorders. *Journal of Special Education, 35,* 161–171.

Tingstrom, D. H., Sterling-Turner, H. E., & Wilczynski, S. M. (2006). The good behavior game: 1969–2002. *Behavior Modification, 30,* 225–253.

Walker, H. M., Irvin, L. K., Noell, J., & Singer, G. H. (1992). A construct score approach to the assessment of social competence: Rationale, technological considerations, and anticipated outcomes. *Behavior Modification, 16,* 448–474.

Walker, J., & Shea, T. M., & Bauer, A. M. (2004). *Behavior management: A practical approach for educators (8th edn).* Upper Saddle River, NJ: Pearson.

Wannarka, R., & Ruhl, K. (2008). Seating arrangements that promote positive academic and behavioural outcomes: A review of empirical research. *Support for Learning, 23,* 89–93.

Wehby, J. H., Symons, F. M., Canale, J., & Go, F. (1998). Teaching practices in classrooms for students with emotional and behavioral disorders: Discrepancies between recommendations and observations. *Behavioral Disorders, 24,* 52–57.

Wehby, J. H., & Lane, K. L. (2009). Proactive instructional strategies for classroom management. In A. Akin-Little, S. G. Little, M. A. Bray, & T. J. Kehle (Eds.), *Behavioral interventions in schools* (pp. 141–156). Washington, DC: American Psychological Association.

Part V

Identifying and Helping Vulnerable, Victimized, and At-Risk Youth

12   Bullying Prevention and Intervention

Use of the word "bullying" is commonplace in the news, media, and in general conversation. People talk about being bullied in the workplace, during meetings, while making business deals, and in virtually any situation in which people live and work. However, as implied, the term bullying often is over-generalized and misapplied. Furthermore, in addition to definitional misunderstandings, a lot of confusion exists about how bullying impacts victims. On one end of the spectrum, some people dismiss bullying with a "boys will be boys" type of attitude, which seems to suggest that bullying is permissible because aggressive behavior is natural. On the other end, others describe being bullied as being the singular reason why a tiny, yet still concerning, number of students engage in violent attacks at schools. As will be discussed in this chapter, both of these extreme positions are misguided. This chapter aims to reduce confusion regarding bullying, especially as it occurs in schools, and provides educators with the information they need to help reduce bullying at school. With these aims in mind, effective interventions and prevention programs are discussed.

Bullying Definition

The term "bullying" generally is used to describe unwanted, intentional, aggressive behavior that involves a real or perceived power imbalance between the bully and the victim (Olweus, 1993). The power difference between bullies and victims can take many forms. For example, a bully may be physically stronger, display more adroit interpersonal skills, have a higher social status, be more tech savvy, or have other qualities that give them an edge or allow them to dominate a victim.

Bullying can be subdivided into various forms that include physical aggression (e.g., hitting, kicking, shoving), verbal aggression (e.g., name calling, teasing, threatening), and relational aggression (e.g., social exclusion, spreading rumors). Although many people believe that boys are more likely to engage in physical forms of bullying and girls are more likely to engage in relational forms, research indicates that boys and girls both engage in relational aggression to similar degrees, yet boys are more likely to engage in physical aggression (Card, Stucky, Sawalani, & Little, 2008). Lastly, with the exception of physical aggression, these forms of aggressive behavior can also be perpetrated in cyberspace (i.e., cyberbullying) and via the use of cyber technology (e.g., computers, smart phones, video games).

Prevalence of Bullying, Harassment, and Peer Victimization

Research indicates that bullying is the most prevalent form of aggressive or violent behavior that occurs in schools (Ross, 2002). Even though specific prevalence estimates vary considerably across studies, large epidemiological studies generally find that 10–28 percent of students report being bullied by their peers and that about half of students will be bullied at some point during their educational career (Nansel, Overpeck, Pilla, Ruan, Simons-Morton, & Scheidt, 2001; Roberts, Zhang, Truman, & Snyder, 2012). In addition, research indicates that about 10–25 percent of youth report having been cyberbullied within the past year (Kowalski & Limber, 2013; Võllink, Bolman, Dehue, & Jacobs, 2013). These findings, coupled with the belief that aggressive behavior is part of the human condition, have led some individuals to conclude that all schools (if not all classrooms) are affected by bullying to some degree.

The prevalence and nature of bullying and cyberbullying vary by a range of school characteristics and developmental considerations of students. Research suggests that bullying behaviors are extant even in preschoolers and that bullying gradually becomes more prevalent in middle childhood and adolescence (Hanish, Kochenderfer-Ladd, Fabes, Martin, & Denning, 2004). Moreover, bullying tends to peak in middle school and then it declines as children advance through high school (Swearer, Wang, Maag, Siebecker, & Frerichs, 2012). As students mature into adolescence, the bullying behaviors they perpetrate tend to become more complex and representative of the intimate relationships they are forming. In this regard, bullying may be expressed in the form of sexual harassment, sexual violence, dating violence, and hurtful relationship manipulation (Espelage & Holt, 2007). Thus, because of variability in the prevalence and nature of bullying behaviors within and across school settings, it is important for school districts to collect their own data on the prevalence and nature of bullying that occurs in local school communities.

Cyberbullying

Research indicates that 95 percent of teens (ages 12–17) regularly use the internet and 77 percent own a cell phone (Lenhart, 2012), which indicates that millions of youth potentially could be victimized by cyberbullying. Although cyberbullying is similar to bullying that occurs in physical settings and most youth are bullied and victimized across these settings, some unique characteristics of cyberspace influence the way that aggression is transmitted in this realm (Dempsey, Sulkowski, Nichols, & Storch, 2009). For example, victims of bullying in cyberspace may struggle to identify their victimizers because of a degree of anonymity that cyberspace can provide. In addition, cyberspace offers a potentially unlimited audience for bullying, especially in social networks where victims can be targeted at any time. Moreover, bullies often do not see how their behavior impacts victims first hand, which can lead to cruel behavior that perpetrators might not engage in in-person. This phenomenon has been called the "online disinhibition effect" and it has been observed empirically. For example, Patchin and Hinduja (2006) found that 37 percent of teens surveyed reported that they had said things to another person via electronic communication that they would not say in a face-to-face interaction. Text Box 12.1 lists various ways that students can be bullied in cyberspace.

Text Box 12.1 Various Ways that Students can be Bullied in Cyberspace

- *Flaming:* Online "fights" using electronic messages with angry and vulgar language, may include insults or threats.
- *Harassment:* Repeatedly sending offensive, rude, and insulting messages.
- *Denigration:* "Dissing" someone online. Sending or posting gossip or rumors about a person to damage his or her reputation or friendships.
- *Impersonation:* Pretending to be someone else and sending or posting material to get that person in trouble or danger or to damage that person's reputation or friendships.
- *Sexting:* Sending partially nude, nude or demeaning photographs through cyberspace.

- *Cyberbullying by proxy:* Convincing others to send flame or hate mail to the victim, and then when the victim responds, forwarding responses to an authority figure who then punishes the victim.
- *Polling:* Establishing virtual polling places online to enable fellow students to vote on undesirable characteristics, such as which student is the fattest, ugliest, sluttiest, geekiest, etc.
- *Using bash boards:* Posting online racist remarks or gossip to online forums.
- *Taking stealth pictures:* Taking embarrassing photos or videos of someone and posting these online.

Sources: Myers, McCaw & Hemphill, 2011; Willard, 2007

Negative Consequences

Bullying and cyberbullying[1] have been associated with a range of negative outcomes in all students who are affected. Victims of bullying tend to be less engaged in school, have higher rates of absences, and often experience declines in their grades (Cornell, Gregory, Huang, & Fan, 2013; Juvonen, Wang, & Espinoza, 2011). Moreover, lower rates of school graduation, student participation in school activities, and performance on standardized tests are reported in schools that have been found to have high rates of bullying (Espelage, & De La Rue, 2012; Mehta, Cornell, Fan, & Gregory, 2013). In addition to academic problems, victimized youth also are at risk for experiencing negative psychosocial outcomes. Research indicates that these youth experience higher rates of depression, anxiety, social adjustment, and physical health problems (Dempsey et al., 2009; Espelage, Low, & De La Rue, 2012; Gini & Pozzoli, 2009; Ttofi, Farrington, Lösel, & Loeber, 2011). They also tend to have low self-esteem and to be at risk for suicidal behaviors (Bauman, Toomey, & Walker, 2013; Card et al., 2008; Klomek et al., 2013). See Text Box 12.2 for information on the link between being bullied and suicide. Lastly, the negative psychosocial correlates associated with being bullied appear to have an enduring impact on some individuals. In this vein, a recent study found that students who were bullied in childhood were substantially more likely to develop an anxiety disorder (e.g., agoraphobia, generalized anxiety, and panic disorder) and to have an elevated risk for suicide in adulthood when compared to non-victimized individuals (Copeland, Wolke, Angold, & Costello, 2013).

Text Box 12.2 The Link between Bullying and Suicide

A lot of attention has focused on high profile suicides of youth who had histories of being bullied. In many cases, these youth were horrendously bullied and many opportunities were missed by others to help stop them from being victimized. However, considering that about a quarter of students report that they have been victimized by peer aggression and that about seven out of 100,000 students will die by suicide each year (Bridge, Goldstein, & Brent, 2006), the relationship between being victimized by peer aggression and suicide usually is impacted by other factors such as having a history of mental illness (e.g., depression, anxiety), limited social support, low degrees of social connectedness, feelings of hopelessness, problems with substance abuse, and difficulties coping with distress. Therefore, the relationship between bullying and suicide is best thought of as an indirect one that increases the risk of suicidal behavior (e.g., suicidal thoughts, suicidal gestures, suicide attempts, suicide completion) in victims who may already be vulnerable (Bauman et al., 2013; Klomek et al., 2013).

Bullies also experience negative academic and psychosocial outcomes related to their problematic behavior. Bullies display an elevated risk for delinquency, truancy, poor school adjustment, and social problems (Bender & Lösel, 2011; Farrington & Ttofi, 2011). In adulthood, they are at risk for social maladjustment, criminal behavior, antisocial personality disorder, and incarceration (Copeland et al., 2013; Ttofi et al., 2011). Further establishing the concerning relationship between bullying behavior in childhood and later criminal behavior, one early study found that 60 percent of high school bullies had been convicted of a crime by the age of 24 (Olweus, 1993) and a more recent study found that the likelihood of being charged with a criminal offense over a decade after engaging in bullying was significantly higher among bullies than it was among individuals who reported having not previously engaged in bullying behavior (Ttofi et al., 2011).

It has been argued that bully-victims or youth who are both bullied and bully others display the most dismal outcomes of youth on the bully–victim continuum (Swearer et al., 2012). In general, bully-victims often are afflicted by a range of psychosocial adjustment problems such as depression, anxiety, suicidality, low self-esteem, hyperactivity, aggression, and delinquency (Menesini, Modena, & Tani, 2009). These youth have been described as being impulsive and as having difficulties regulating negative emotions. They may misjudge social cues and social situations, experience peer relational problems as a result thereof, and react aggressively toward others when they feel threatened, upset, or confused as they try to gain peer acceptance (Salmivalli & Nieminen, 2002). Perhaps the most vulnerable group of youth affected by bullying, bully-victims have been found to be at risk for significant, negative long-term outcomes. Specifically, they have been found to be at risk for depression, panic disorder, agoraphobia (females only), and suicidality (males only) in adulthood (Copeland et al., 2013). However, despite these findings, these youth have been traditionally understudied and research on the bully-victim phenomenon is still emerging.

Vulnerable Groups of Students

Certain groups of students are frequently targeted by bullies. These students tend to stand out from their peers in some observable, noticeable, or discernible way and they may not conform to prevailing norms that govern students' behavior. In addition, they may display unique vulnerabilities because of social biases against them, the influence of overt or tacit prejudices, social and economic marginalization and disenfranchisement, and even outward hostility directed toward members of their group. Thus, being victimized may be a common experience for certain vulnerable groups of students.

Lesbian, Gay, Bisexual, Transgender, and Questioning Students

Ninety percent of U.S. lesbian, gay, bisexual, transgender, and questioning (LGBTQ) students report that they have heard their peers use the word "gay" as a derogatory term (Kosciw, Greytak, & Diaz, 2009). However, what is even more alarming is that over 85 percent of these youth report having been verbally harassed because of their sexual orientation and 44 percent of LGBTQ youth report being physically aggressed for the same reason (Kosciw et al., 2009).

The content of bullying messages frequently is homophobic in nature and it is often independent of the victim's sexual orientation. In other words, regardless of whether a student identifies with being gay, straight, or otherwise, it is likely that he or she will be harassed by peers for "being gay," which can be personally distressing. In this regard, research suggests that being bullied because of one's real or perceived sexual orientation may be among the most distressing ways in which youth can be harassed, especially for male students. Compared to male students who were bullied for a range of other reasons, Swearer, Turner, Givens, and Pollack (2008) found that boys who were bullied by being called "gay" displayed higher levels of psychological distress and more negative attitudes about school overall.

Although peer victimization does not completely explain all the vulnerabilities in LGBTQ students, it is a major contributor to overall psychosocial distress in these youth (Robinson

& Espelage, 2012). In general, LGBTQ students report greater levels of depression, anxiety, substance abuse, and suicidal behaviors as well as higher rates of compromised academic performance when compared to their peers who identify as heterosexual (Espelage, Aragon, Birkett, & Koenig, 2008). Similar to the general long-term risks associated with being victimized, LGBTQ individuals who were bullied in their childhood have been found to display long-term psychosocial adjustment problems into adulthood. Specifically, these individuals have been found to be at a pronounced risk for experiencing adult mental health problems (e.g., depression, anxiety, suicidality), abusing drugs and alcohol, and contracting life-disruptive sexually transmitted diseases such as human immunodeficiency virus (HIV).

On a more positive note, emerging research suggest that acceptance and support for LGBTQ students may be increasing, which, in turn, might reduce the vulnerability of these youth to bullying. According to a recent study (Russell, Toomey, Ryan, and Diaz, 2014) LGBT students who reported "being out" (i.e., openly disclosing their lesbian, gay, bisexual, or transgender sexual orientation) at high school had better psychosocial adjustment in young adulthood. Similarly, a study by Ryan, Legate, and Weinstein (2015) found that experiencing negative reactions related to coming out was associated with higher rates of depression and lower self-esteem. However, feeling like one's autonomy is respected and supported by others during the coming out process mediated the relationship between experiencing negative reactions and feeling greater degrees of depression and lower self-esteem. In light of these findings, schools can work to establish a supportive and inclusive climate where it is safe for students to come out and communicate their sexual identity to others. Moreover, educators can help to ensure that LGBTQ students feel accepted and respected during this process as way to offset distress and negative self-perceptions.

Racial, Ethnic Minority, and Immigrant Students

Bullying of racial and ethnic minority students is an exceedingly complicated phenomenon. These youth may be bullied by members of a cultural majority group, members from other minority groups, or by members of their own group. Institutional racism, prejudice, and xenophobia can all contribute to the victimization of racial minority youth, especially in relatively homogenous communities that are intolerant of outsiders or others. Moreover, as racial minority youth adjust to and adapt to cultural elements of the majority culture in which they live, they may be at risk for being criticized or even ostracized by members of their own racial or cultural group who resent their efforts to assimilate (Mendez, Bauman, & Guillory, 2012). This phenomenon, the concept of cultural marginalization, may be particularly poignant because these students may feel isolated or excluded by members of the majority group and their own group.

Results from an early study on the topic suggest that one in five minority students often experience race-related bullying at school (Charach, Pepler, & Ziegler, 1995). Further, subsequent studies suggest that minority adolescents still experience similar rates of bullying and discrimination from both their same-race and cross-race peers (e.g., Russell, Sinclair, Poteat, & Koenig, 2012). Regarding gender differences associated with being bullied, a study by Klomek, Marrocco, Kleinman, Schonfeld, and Gould (2008) found that male students are more likely than female students to be belittled or physically harmed by their peers because of their race or ethnicity. Thus, minority males may be particularly likely to be bullied or victimized by peer aggression.

Although research on how minority youth experience bullying is still emerging, several studies have investigated this phenomenon among African American youth. Research suggests that African American youth (32 percent) are more likely to be victimized by physical aggression than White (21 percent) and Latino (19 percent) youth are (Turner, Finkelhor, Hamby, Shattuck,

& Ormrod, 2011). Lastly, research suggests that being bullied because of one's race or ethnicity is associated with a range of negative psychosocial outcomes. A recent study by Mendez, Bauman, Sulkowski, Nixon, and Davis (2014) found that students who were victimized because of their race were 1.4 times more likely than students bullied for other reasons to report a severe emotional impact from the experience. More specifically, other studies suggest that being bullied because of one's race is associated with higher rates of depression, problems with peer relations, social exclusion and rejection, loneliness, substance abuse, truancy, and academic failure (Cooke, Williams, Guerra, Kim, & Sadek, 2010; Fitzpatrick, Dulin, & Piko, 2010; Nansel et al., 2001; Russell et al., 2012).

Research on bullying of immigrant youth still is emerging, especially within the U.S. context. Some studies have found that immigrant youth are more likely to be bullied than their non-immigrant peers (e.g., Graham & Juvonen, 2002; von Grünigen, Perren, Nägele, & Alsaker, 2010), whereas other studies have found either the opposite or no relationship between immigrant status and the likelihood of being bullied (e.g., Hanish & Guerra, 2000; Strohmeier, Spiel, & Gradinger, 2008). These mixed findings may be due to the influence of contextual variables, as immigrant youth are more likely to be bullied or aggressed in societies with low cultural diversity that harbor anti-immigrant sentiments (Jasinskaja-Lahti, Liebkind, & Perhoniemi, 2006; Juvonen, Nishina, & Graham, 2006). In a recent study conducted in the U.S., Sulkowski, Bauman, Wright, Nixon, and Davis (2014) found that youth from immigrant families are more likely than their non-immigrant peers to report being victimized by physical aggression and to be victimized because of their race, religion, and family income.

Students with Disabilities

Although disabilities are heterogeneous and range considerably in their severity and level of impairment, children with disabilities are more likely to be victimized by peer aggression in general. In this regard, research indicates that students with disabilities are twice as likely to be victims of peer aggression when compared to their peers without disabilities (Rose, Espelage, Aragon, & Elliott, 2011). Furthermore, students with severe disabilities that negatively impact their social functioning may be even more likely to be victimized (Rose, 2010). More specially, students with autism and related disorders that are characterized by poor communication and ineffective social skills display an elevated risk of being victimized (Rose, Monda-Amaya, & Espelage, 2011).

Even students with less severe disorders such as learning disabilities (LD) also display an elevated risk for being victimized. In a meta-analysis of 152 studies, 80 percent of children with an LD diagnosis were socially "rejected" by their peers and these students were also found to be markedly less likely to be selected as "friends" by their peers (Baumeister, Storch, & Geffken, 2008). Overall, research suggests that students with both conspicuous and inconspicuous disabilities tend to be bullied more often than their non-disabled peers (Carter & Spencer, 2006). Moreover, in response to being bullied, these youth tend to report higher levels of depression and loneliness, and to be perceived as being less socially popular than their non-disabled counterparts (Rose, Forber-Pratt, Espelage, & Aragon, 2013).

Bullying Prevention and Intervention in Schools

Legal Considerations and Student Rights

As of April 2015, all U.S. states and the District of Columbia have laws that require schools to address bullying. Furthermore, results of court cases such as *Davis v. Monroe County Board of Education* (1994) suggest that schools are required to protect students from sexual harassment.

Civil rights laws such as Title IV and Title VI of the Civil Rights Act of 1964, Section 504 of the Rehabilitation Act of 1973, Titles II and III of the Americans with Disabilities Act, and the Individuals with Disabilities Education Improvement Act (IDEIA) all require schools to protect youth from discrimination and harassment, especially if they are from a protected class (e.g., a class that is defined by race, disability, or religion). Although sexual orientation is not a protected class under current federal legislation, some state laws do offer protections to LGBTQ youth. However, the proposed Student Non-Discrimination Act of 2015, which would have extended protections against harassment to youth based on their actual (or perceived) sexual orientation and identity, failed to pass. This means that LGBTQ individuals are not currently considered a protected class at the federal level. Text Box 12.3 lists steps that members of school communities should take to comply with extant laws and protect students from bullying.

Text Box 12.3 What Educators can do to Comply with Laws to Combat Bullying

- Investigations by schools of possible harassment must be conducted expediently, thoroughly, and consistently.
- Schools should make known to students and parents specific procedures for reporting bullying and harassment, as well as who to contact if cases are not handled expediently.
- Schools should advise students and parents of alternative reporting mechanisms (e.g., police) in cases of violence or other criminal activity.
- Schools should assess whether bullying experiences constitute a potential civil rights violation.
- Schools should be aware that there is consistent evidence that Zero Tolerance policies, originally applied to cases of school violence and weapon possession on campuses, but sometimes extended to bullying and harassment, are not effective.
- Knowledge of legal, procedural, and policy issues is central for schools in the effort to prevent bullying.
- Most legislation focuses on reporting, investigating, and intervening when bullying has occurred, but prevention efforts should be a key focus for school-based anti-bullying and harassment efforts.

Note
These recommendations are adapted from the American Educational Research Association (2013).

Bullying Prevention Programs

Schools have two main options they can select to prevent and address bullying. One option involves adopting and implementing a multicomponent bullying prevention/intervention program such as the Olweus Bullying Prevention Program (Olweus & Limber, 2007), KiVA (Salmivalli, Kärnä, & Poskiparta, 2011), PeaceBuilders (Flannery et al., 2003), Steps to Respect (Brown, Low, Smith, & Haggerty, 2011), and many others. The previously mentioned programs all have empirical support; however, none of them have been shown to be universally effective across internationally and racially/ethnically diverse school settings. Therefore, it is extremely important for educators to select programs that address bullying based on their empirical support as well as in their ability to adapt to local school characteristics. Good places to start in this regard are the National Registry of Evidence-Based Programs and Practices (www.nrepp.samhsa.gov/), the Model Programs Guide (www.ojjdp.gov/mpg/), and the Blueprints for Healthy Youth Development (www.colorado.edu/cspvblueprints/).

It is important to underscore that even if a school adopts a well-matched, evidence-based bullying prevention/intervention program, the utility of this program and any promising results likely will be significantly compromised if it is not implemented with adequate integrity and fidelity. That is, if the program is not implemented according to the same protocol on which it was developed and empirically tested, it is unlikely that the program will be as effective when it is implemented in an altered form. However, even greater caution is warranted if schools plan to implement a bullying prevention/intervention program that is not vetted by the previous resources. Unfortunately, some multicomponent bullying prevention/intervention programs that are both readily and commercially available for schools to purchase have no empirical support, theoretical grounding, or even practical appeal. Even worse, some of these programs have been criticized for being insensitive, if not deleterious, to the social and educational needs of LGBTQ students and are inconsistent with research-based position papers and statements produced by organizations such as the American Psychological Association (APA) and the National Association of School Psychologists (NASP). As a final word of caution, it is important to note that controversial, if not counterintuitive bullying prevention/intervention programs, can easily be confused with evidence-based programs with proven utility in web browser searches.

The second way that schools can prevent or reduce bullying involves adopting individual approaches to mitigating bullying. In this regard, research indicates that bystander interventions are the most effective (Pozzoli, Ang, & Gini, 2012). Most importantly, when bystanders act as defenders of victims (or potential victims of bullying), incidents of bullying tend to attenuate along with the negative effects of this phenomenon (Polanin, Espelage, & Pigott, 2012). Therefore, considerably more research is needed on ways in which youth and others can be taught to be more effective defenders of victims of peer aggression (Hanish et al., 2013). Text Box 12.4 lists specific strategies that students can employ to address bullying incidents and prevent themselves from becoming victims. Expert Interview 12.1 with Susan Swearer, an internationally recognized expert on bullying and bullying prevention, discusses additional ways that schools and educators can prevent and reduce bullying.

Text Box 12.4   Some Strategies Students Can Use to Deal with Bullying

- Seek assistance from an adult, friend or classmate when a potentially threatening situation occurs.
- Be assertive (not aggressive) when possible.
- Use humor to de-escalate a potential threatening situation.
- Avoid unsafe places or walk away before a potential bullying encounter occurs.
- Agree with or own a belittling comment to defuse it.
- Walk in the school with friends or a small group of like-minded peers.
- Use positive self-statements to maintain positive self-esteem during an incident.
- Avoid getting emotionally upset when bullying occurs as this only encourages bullying.

Source: Bonds & Stoker (2000).

The most effective strategy to deal with cyberbullying

- Stop. Don't do anything. Take time to calm down.
- Block. Block the cyberbully or limit all communication to those on your buddy list.
- Tell. Inform a trusted adult.

Source: www.stopcyberbullying.org

In the following interview, Dr. Susan Swearer discusses how prevalent bullying is in today's schools, what seems to work in preventing bullying and frequent mistakes made by educators in coping with this problem. She further highlights practical strategies that educators and administrators can use to make schools more supportive and discusses the role that parents have in helping their children cope with bullying.

Expert Interview 12.1 with Susan M. Swearer

University of Nebraska – Lincoln

PJL. How prevalent is bullying in today's schools? Has it actually increased in the last few decades or are we just now becoming more aware of the problem? If it has increased, why do you think this is the case?

SMS. Involvement in bullying varies dramatically across studies. When we distill the research, we can state that close to half of youth will be involved in bullying as a perpetrator, a victim (or both—bully-victim), or as bystanders at some point during their school years. The level or the duration of involvement depends on multiple factors such as peer group influences, family influences, mental health functioning, and school climate. Bullying is a complex social relationship problem that is influenced by multiple factors. Certainly, we are becoming more aware of the problem and the media has shed important light on the issue as well. When I started studying bullying in 1998, there was very little cyber or electronic bullying, primarily because there wasn't such ubiquitous access to cell phones, computers, and electronic gaming systems. So, the ability to bully 24 hours-per-day, seven days per week has obviously increased. It's no longer just a face-to-face phenomenon that typically occurred on the playground. Bullying occurs across the lifespan and includes verbal, physical, relational, and/or electronic forms.

PJL. What is the school's responsibility to prevent or stop bullying?

SMS. Adults in schools have the mandate to provide a free, appropriate, and safe educational environment for all children. Schools are 100 percent responsible to create a healthy and positive educational environment and adults and students are 100 percent responsible to treat each other in kind, respectful, and caring ways.

PJL. What is commonly done but does not seem to work in bullying prevention? And what are frequent mistakes that educators make regarding developing or implementing bullying prevention programs?

SMS. Unfortunately, one thing that is all too common is that teachers and administrators ignore bullying or downplay the seriousness of bullying. That obviously doesn't work. The number one mistake that educators make regarding implementing bullying prevention programs is not implementing them with high treatment integrity and fidelity. One educator told me that they purchased one of the widely used bullying prevention and intervention programs and it was sitting on a shelf in his office. Getting 100 percent of staff and students to buy-in to bullying prevention and intervention programming is important. Another mistake that educators frequently make is using a program that doesn't have evidence to support its' effectiveness. We always recommend that schools use a bullying prevention program that is theoretically based and that has outcome data to support its effectiveness. We also urge educators to collect data on their bullying prevention and intervention efforts. If we don't collect data in our schools, we have no idea if our efforts are working or not.

PJL. What seems to work best in bullying prevention?

SMS. Bullying prevention and intervention strategies that target the entire school (all adults, students, and parents) combined with small group approaches for at-risk youth, combined with individual intervention for involved youth. Basically, a coordinated set of prevention and intervention approaches will work best in bullying prevention.

PJL. How can adults spot subtle forms of bullying?

SMS. Adults need first to be aware of their students or their children's social relationships. Who are they friends with? Do they have conflicts with certain people? What are the cliques like in the school? In the classroom? Once adults have a good sense of children's relationships, then they're in a better place to spot the more subtle forms of bullying—social exclusion, rumor spreading, manipulation, etc. It's also important that adults help foster trusting relationships with youth, so that children and adolescents will be more likely to report the bullying that they experience or witness.

PJL. What are the most important things that administrators can do to help prevent bullying and mitigate it when it occurs?

SMS. The most important thing that administrators can do to help prevent bullying is to model healthy, respectful behavior. The second most important thing to do is to invest fully in creating a healthy, positive school climate. When the consistent message is, "We treat everyone with kindness and respect" is communicated and modeled, bullying prevention has a real chance. However, when bullying does occur, the best thing administrators can do is to focus on intervention first and to help the students who are bullying learn more prosocial and adaptive ways of interacting with others. As Ben Franklin said, "An ounce of prevention is worth a pound of cure!"

PJL. What are the most important actions that teachers can take to prevent bullying?

SMS. The first step that teachers can take to prevent bullying is to treat all colleagues and their students with kindness and respect. Everyone is responsible for creating a culture of caring in our schools and communities. Teachers need to address social-emotional learning in their classrooms and recognize that students with high social and emotional skills are also those students who are academically engaged and less likely to be involved in bullying.

PJL. What are the best approaches that teachers can take when they see a student bullying another child?

SMS. When a teacher sees a student bullying another child, they can simply and firmly state, "We don't do that here," or "We treat others kindly. That didn't look so kind." Letting students know that teachers are watching and that they're concerned is a basic step in bullying prevention. If the student persists in bullying others, the teacher should meet with that student alone and talk with him or her about the behaviors that they witnessed. If the bullying behaviors persist, then involving the school psychologist or school counselor and/or adult caregivers is an important next step. The goal is to help the student who is perpetrating the bullying behaviors to stop bullying and to learn and demonstrate healthier social interaction skills. That will help everyone and will create a caring and respectful environment.

PJL. Are there particular children that seem to be most at risk for being bullied and how can we identify and help them?

SMS. This really varies by schools and communities and is influenced by larger societal norms and values. So, any perceived difference where someone stands out puts them at risk for being bullied. Adults in schools need to be aware of students who might be isolated or who are seen as "different." In some schools, differences whether due to gender identity, socioeconomic status, popularity, sexual orientation, clothing, body composition, family background, religious orientation, and a host of other factors might place particular children at risk for being bullied. The adults in the school are responsible for being aware of these children and protecting them. Adults can help them by making sure they're connected in school and in after-school activities where they can develop and hone their talents.

PJL. What should be the role of the parents in helping their child if the child is a bully, a target or even a bystander?

SMS: Parents and adult caregivers should first and foremost model healthy social relationships and make sure that they are not involved in bullying themselves. Second, adults need to create a healthy home environment where their children will feel comfortable talking with them about social relationships, bullying, friendships, and other issues that all children face at some point. There are some great parent handouts at www.stopbullying.gov that address what to do if their child is bullying others, is being bullied, or is witnessing bullying. The best advice for parents is to listen non-judgmentally and then to ask, "How can I help you with this situation?"

PJL. What were the most important things you want educators to know about bullying?

SMS. I want educators to know that bullying is not an "epidemic" and that we have many, many great schools and communities where bullying really doesn't happen. I also want educators to know that they have a profound responsibility to create safe school environments where everyone can learn and thrive. Together, we have the power to create kinder and braver homes, schools, and communities.

How Educators Can Address School Bullying

Efforts of educators to prevent and address school bullying ought to focus on facilitating safe and supportive learning environments for all students instead of only propagating an anti-bullying agenda. Because aggressive behavior is highly prevalent and it is impossible to eradicate it completely from social settings, educators can help inoculate students and other members of school communities against the negative effects of bullying through protecting the physical safety of students, making sure that they feel emotionally bonded with other students and adults at school, and fostering a school climate that encourages prosocial behaviors (Craig, Pepler, & Atlas, 2000).

To protect the physical safety of students, educators should be present in loosely structured social settings or in places in which bullying is more likely to occur, such as in hallways, playgrounds, free periods, study halls, and the cafeteria. In addition, educators should work toward increasing openness between students and adults at school so that students feel comfortable to report incidents of bullying or problems more generally. See Text Box 12.5 for strategies to help improve educator–student relationships. Similarly, and consistent with an effort to improve school climate more generally, educators can implement programs such as positive peer reporting in addition to having an anonymous bullying incident report box. Positive peer reporting is a research-based intervention that involves reinforcing students for engaging in positive social interactions with others (e.g., helping a student pick up dropped materials, inviting other students to participate in an activity, sharing supplies with a peer, speaking up to protect a student against verbal abuse). This intervention can be implemented school-wide or classroom-wide and it provides students an opportunity to "report" prosocial behaviors to educators who then reinforce the students who display these desirable behaviors (Moroz & Jones, 2002).

Text Box 12.5 Strategies for Improving Educator–Student Relationships

- Know every student's name and three key things about them.
- Greet students by name every day while they arrive at school or at the classroom.
- Schedule periodic "check-in" times with students to hear about what is happening in their lives in and outside of school.
- Find a way for each student to participate in class each and every day.
- Provide at least three statements of encouragement or recognition of something positive for every correction or critical statement.
- Find and connect students with members of the school or local community with whom they can identify.
- Schedule in periods that involve active collaboration and allow for students to be complimented for displaying prosocial behavior.
- Model good emotional regulation skills.
- Model empathy and concern for others.
- Regularly go over behavioral expectations and revisit established classroom rules.
- Become aware of and validate students' strengths, particularly when dealing with vulnerable students.

To help establish a school climate that encourages prosocial behaviors and discourages peer aggression, educators should actively express that bullying, teasing, and harassment will not be tolerated and that specific consequences will occur for these behaviors. Consequences must be consistent with extant school policies; however, to engage students and help establish a classroom climate that does not condone bullying, educators can work with students to identify specific consequences for specific problematic behaviors. For example, a teacher could stimulate a class activity at the beginning of the year that involves trouble-shooting consequences and remediation strategies for bullying incidents, which involves input from all students in the classroom. Text Box 12.6 lists comprehensive strategies that teachers and administrators can employ to prevent and address bullying incidents, Text Box 12.7 discusses myths regarding bullying that are essential for educators to understand and Text Box 12.8 provides an example of a teacher addressing a bullying incident.

Text Box 12.6 Strategies for Prevention and Intervention

- Provide workshops or materials to increase awareness and knowledge of bullying and dispel myths among all school personnel, parents and community stakeholders. See Text Box 12.7.
- Provide workshops to students on safe new media use. Discuss the dangers associated with the inappropriate use of cyberspace. Explain the concept of cyberbullying and its forms and emphasize that it is the responsibility of all students to prevent it from occurring.
- Survey all students using an anonymous questionnaire to determine the bullying problem in each school. Include questions related to: What types of bullying occur on campus? Where does bullying take place? How safe do students feel from bullying and harassment? How many students are involved?
- Develop a bullying coordinating committee consisting of a school administrator, a school psychologist or counselor, teachers, parents, and students.
- Develop an effective anti-bullying school policy and establish clear and enforceable rules and sanctions. In doing so, make sure that school policies are consistent with board of education rules and state statutes. School rules should be posted and discussed with all students so that they have a clear understanding of expectations.

- Consider having students sign a pledge that can include: (a) We will not bully other students. (b) We will help others who are being bullied by speaking out and by getting adult help. (c) We will use extra effort to include all students in activities at our school.
- Provide comprehensive training to all teachers and school staff about bullying prevention and intervention.
- Use survey results to make necessary changes to the school environment to create a safer and more supportive school climate. This may include extra monitoring and supervision.
- Develop a number of different ways that students can report bullying to adults. Investigate every report, provide follow up and take administrative actions as necessary.
- Increase adult supervision in areas found to be problematic on the survey. Bullying often occurs in school hallways, cafeterias, playgrounds, locker rooms and restrooms.
- Intervene consistently when bullying occurs—never ignore it. Empower teachers with effective strategies to confront bullying on the spot.
- Hold separate follow-up meetings with perpetrators and targets. Provide support and protection to a victimized student. Conflict resolution or peer mediation strategies are not appropriate in this process because the target is being abused by the perpetrator and there is an unequal balance of power. During this process, the teacher can help the vulnerable child learn to assert himself more effectively. Also, the educator can teach the perpetrator how to get his or her needs met in alternative ways. If possible, involve parents in the process.
- Have class meetings where students can discuss peer relations as well as any problems with bullying.
- Teach all students how to be "upstanders" and encourage them to take action to stop bullying when it occurs.
- Help foster nurturing relationships and friendship patterns within the school and classroom. This is especially important as the number and quality of friends protect children from being victimized. That is, youngsters who have a number of friends, especially those who are strong or popular, are less likely to become targets (Pelligrini & Long, 2004).
- Consider adopting a structured bully prevention program. Effective programs focus on knowledge, attitude change, and skill development taught through modeling, role play and practice.
- Continue these efforts over time. Patience is required as it may take up to three years to change the culture of the school and make a difference.

These aforementioned strategies are based on best practices recommended by the U.S. Department of Health and Human Services through their website, Stop Bullying Now; the seminal principles of Dan Olweus (1993) and his Bullying Prevention Program; and critical components of such anti-bullying programs such as Bully Proofing Your School, Bully Busters, Steps to Respect, and PATHS (Providing Alternative THinking Strategies).

Source: Adapted from Lazarus & Pfohl (2011).

Text Box 12.7 Myths about Children Who Bully

- Children who bully are loners.
- Children who bully have low self-esteem.
- Being bullied toughens up a student and prepares him to be a man.
- Most students will learn how to combat being bullied on their own.
- We don't have bullying in our schools.
- A student must be stronger and bigger to be a bully.

Source: Garrity, Jens, Porter, Sager, & Short-Camilli, (2000) and Lazarus, P. J. (2011)

(continued)

(continued)

Facts about Children Who Bully

- Children who bully have an easier time making friends than do victims.
- Children who bully have average to high average self-esteem and feel it is their right to intimidate other students.
- Being bullied creates scars. Rather than toughening up a student, it makes the victim feel more vulnerable and anxious and less able to perform academically and socially. As a result, bullied students feel less connected to the school and often less prepared for life.
- Most chronic victims will need help from school staff to avoid being victimized. If handling bullying was so easy, they probably would not have been victimized in the first place.
- All schools have bullying; however, for various reasons students are reluctant to report it to school staff. Also, some schools have less bullying than others.
- A student can be more socially sophisticated, more technologically savvy, and/or more popular to be a bully. In cyberspace, the disinhibition effect enables students (who may actually be weaker and smaller) to bully others who would not do so in person.

Text Box 12.8   An Example of a Teacher Responding to a Bullying Incident

Eastman Middle School surveyed their study body to find out about their perceptions of campus safety and bullying in their school. One of the findings was that physical bullying often occurred when students changed classes and unbeknownst to staff many of these incidents occurred when some of the eighth grade boys had targeted sixth grade boys. As a result of this data, the school staggered class schedules so that each grade transitioned at a different time and teachers were now required to stand outside their classroom to monitor students. Consequently, Mrs. Givens, a sixth grade math teacher, is standing in the hallway during a class transition. She observes Juan, a large sixth grade boy, as he walks down the hall. Juan is yelling at Manuel, a much smaller boy, "Get out my way" as he walks by him and intentionally bangs him with an elbow. Manuel does not appear hurt but looks upset. She calls both boys over. She reminds Juan about the no bullying policy. She tells him that according to the school's policy she will write up the details of the incident and that he will be contacted later by the school administrator. Manuel states that although Juan has been unfriendly he has never pushed him before. Mrs. Given knows that according to the school's anti-bullying policy, if this is Juan's first incident, the administrator will have a serious talk with him. However, if this is Juan's second incident, then further action will be taken, which includes informing Juan's parents as well as an after school detention(s). Mrs. Givens firmly states to the boys, "We do not tolerate bullying in our school. We pride ourselves on being a caring community. Juan you know the rules will be enforced. Go on to class."

How Educators Can Address Cyberbullying

Because incidents of cyberbullying usually occur outside of the watchful eyes of educators, members of school communities often feel powerless to address this phenomenon. However, even if educators are not part of (or even aware of) the social networks in cyberspace that allow cyberbullying to occur, they can educate students about taking precautions to help protect themselves from being bullied in cyberspace. Text Box 12.9 lists specific ways that students can make themselves less vulnerable to being a victim of cyberbullying. To help teach these strategies, educators can schedule brief meetings to inculcate them in their students' minds, while also encouraging students to voice things that they can do to help protect themselves from cyberbullying.

Text Box 12.9 Strategies to Prevent Being Victimized by Cyberbullying

- Never accept friend/network requests from unfamiliar people.
- Employ the "mom" principle: Do not post or share photographs or movies that you would not be willing to share with your mother, father, or other important caregiver.
- Employ the "forever" principle: Assume that everything in cyberspace will be there forever.
- Employ the "no privacy" principle: Assume that everyone can get access to the information about you in cyberspace.
- Employ the "ex" principle: Would you be okay with your ex-boyfriends/girlfriends having access to content that you are planning to share.
- Block threatening or questionable people from seeing your profile and personal information.
- Do not post provocative, scandalous, or inflammatory remarks in cyberspace.
- Do not reply or retaliate to incidents of cyberbullying.
- Regularly change passwords to sites/applications and immediately delete profiles that have been hacked.
- Avoid sites, networks, and applications that have poor security, readily provide access to personal information, or encourage interactions among strangers.
- Ensure that you can approve information before it is posted or shared socially.
- Limit involvement in social networking to a few familiar sites.
- Avoid joining sites that do not have adequate privacy settings.
- Never, never, never engage in sexting!

Students regularly sign up for and quit social networking sites as they wax and wane in popularity. Often as adults and educators become aware of the sites that are in vogue and start paying attention to these sites, students migrate to other less well-known sites. For example, as the average age of Facebook users has increased into 2013, many adolescents are leaving the site or using alternative sites to communicate with their same-aged peers (Olsen, 2013). Instead, students now commonly use a range of other social networking sites that often have lower privacy controls, allow for more risky interactions among members, and have little monitoring or oversight. Table 12.1 lists social networking sites that students commonly use, as well as risks associated with these sites.

Table 12.1 Social Networking Sites that Students Commonly Use as Well as Risks Associated with These Sites

Site	Description	Risks
Snapchat	A photo messaging application that allows users to take and share brief videos with each other that are supposed to be erased shortly after sharing.	<ul><li>Shared content often is pornographic.</li><li>Users can take screen shots to preserve images</li><li>A data breech occurred in late 2013 compromising user accounts and identities.</li></ul>
Ask.fm	A social networking site that allows users to ask others questions, with the option of anonymity.	<ul><li>Questions often are offensive or aggressive (e.g., why are you a loser?).</li><li>Associated with several cyberbullying cases that resulted in suicide.</li></ul>
Pheed	A social networking application that allows individuals to stream what they are doing as well as share media.	<ul><li>Includes a young demographic of users (ages 14–25).</li><li>Allows multiple streams of information sharing that can be used to bully others.</li></ul>

(continued)

Table 12.1 (continued)

Site	Description	Risks
Twitter	A social networking site that allows users to send and read "tweets," which are text messages limited to 140 characters.	• Users can post inflammatory tweets and responses to other tweets. • Bullies can quickly reach a large audience using the site.
Vine	An application that individuals can use to post short videos of themselves or others.	• The application can be used to post harmful videos of others without their knowledge. • The application often is used to tease or harass
Creepy	An application that aggregates data from social networking sites to locate people's location and places they regularly frequent.	• Allows for the accessing of sensitive personal information (e.g., pictures, geotag data). • Provides information on people's behavioral patterns and potential location.
Instagram	A media sharing and social networking site that allows users to connect through a variety of social networking sites.	• Few privacy controls over who can view posted material. • Can result in the disclosure of geotag information.
Kik Messenger	An instant messenger service designed for use on smartphones and other media devices.	• Difficult for parents/caregivers to monitor. • Often used to post inappropriate content, pictures, and secretive messages.

Conclusion

Bullying and cyberbullying have garnered a lot of attention among members of the general public during the past few decades. In general, being victimized by bullying is associated with negative outcomes, especially among youth who are already at risk for mental health problems and psychosocial difficulties. Although no surefire strategy exists for preventing or addressing all incidents of bullying, educators can implement a range of strategies to address this phenomenon. Research-based prevention and intervention packages exist, such as the Olweus Bullying Prevention Program (Olweus & Limber, 2007), KiVA (Salmivalli et al., 2011), PeaceBuilders (Flannery et al., 2003), and Steps to Respect Program (Brown et al., 2011) that can be implemented school- or even district-wide. However, at the individual and classroom level, educators also can take steps to mitigate bullying by promoting safe and supportive learning communities. More specifically, educators can make efforts to help ensure that all students feel safe and socially bonded to others at school. Lastly, cyberbullying represents a new challenge for educators and others who aim to facilitate the well-being of students. Currently, more research is needed on effective strategies to stop cyberbullying. However, educators can help youth to protect themselves in cyberspace and reduce risks associated with cyber-communication.

Author's Note

In this book, we use the terms bully, victim, and bystander as these descriptions are more commonplace in the scientific literature. However, these terms label an individual with a pejorative trait. In other words, these terms label "who you are," rather than "this is what you are doing." Often, these distinctions present false dichotomies and may not best represent reality. Individuals may engage in bullying at one time and be the target at another time. In presenting workshops on this topic, we prefer to use the terms perpetrator, target, and witness or "upstander." These terms represent behaviors. The term perpetrator focuses on a particular incident. The term bully, because it is a trait or label, leaves the individual less open to change. Individuals who are targets of a bullying attack may not consider themselves victims. Labeling the person a victim implies that the person is in a helpless position, where he or she can do little about the situation. The term target is more respectful. Moreover, a bystander is a passive person. A person who is a witness has more of an obligation to intervene. An "upstander" is a new term in the literature that requires a person who sees bullying to take an active part to stop it.

Note

1 *Notice:* Because of similarities between bullying in physical settings and cyberspace and how these forms of aggressive behavior impact youth, these terms will be subsumed under the term "bullying" in the remainder of the chapter.

References

American Educational Research Association. (2013). *Prevention of bullying in schools, colleges, and universities: Research report and recommendations.* Washington, DC: American Educational Research Association.

Bauman, S., Toomey, R. B., & Walker, J. L. (2013). Associations among bullying, cyberbullying, and suicide in high school students. *Journal of Adolescence, 36,* 341–350. doi: 10.1016/j.adolescence.2012.12.001

Baumeister, A. L., Storch, E. A., & Geffken, G. R. (2008). Peer victimization in children with learning disabilities. *Child and Adolescent Social Work Journal, 25*(1), 11–23.

Bender, D., & Lösel, F. (2011). Bullying at school as a predictor of delinquency, violence and other anti-social behaviour in adulthood. *Criminal Behaviour and Mental Health, 21*(2), 99–106.

Bonds, M., & Stoker, S. (2000). *Bully proofing your school: A comprehensive approach for middle schools.* Longmont, CO: Sopris West.

Bridge, J. A., Goldstein, T. R., & Brent, D. A. (2006). Adolescent suicide and suicidal behavior *Journal of Child Psychology and Psychiatry, 47,* 372–394. doi: 10.1111/j.1469-7610.2006.01615.x

Brown, E. C., Low, S., Smith, B. H., & Haggerty, K. P. (2011). Outcomes from a school-randomized controlled trial of steps to respect: A bullying prevention program. *School Psychology Review, 40,* 423–433.

Card, N. A., Stucky, B. D., Sawalani, G. M., & Little, T. D. (2008). Direct and indirect aggression during childhood and adolescence: A meta-analytic review of gender differences, intercorrelations, and relations to maladjustment. *Child Development, 79,* 1185–1229. doi: 10.1111/j.1467-8624.2008.01184.x

Carter, B. B., & Spencer, V. G. (2006). The fear factor: Bullying and students with disabilities. *International Journal of Special Education, 21*(1), 11–23.

Charach, A., Pepler, D., & Ziegler, S. (1995). Bullying at school: A Canadian perspective. *Education Canada, 35,* 12–18.

Cook, C. R., Williams, K. R., Guerra, N. G., Kim, T. E., & Sadek, S. (2010). Predictors of bullying and victimization in childhood and adolescence: A meta-analytic investigation. *School Psychology Quarterly, 25,* 65–83.

Copeland, W. E., Wolke, D., Angold, A., & Costello, E. J. (2013). Adult psychiatric outcomes of bullying and being bullied by peers in childhood and adolescence psychiatric outcomes of bullying and being bullied. *JAMA Psychiatry, 70,* 419–426.

Cornell, D., Gregory, A., Huang, F., & Fan, X. (2013). Perceived prevalence of teasing and bullying predicts high school dropout rates. *Journal of Educational Psychology, 105,* 138–149.

Davis v. Monroe County Board of Education (M.D. GA August 29, 1994), 74 F.3d 1186 (11th Cir.), 91 F.3d 1418 (11th Cir. 1944).

Dempsey, A. G., Sulkowski, M. L., Nichols, R., & Storch, E. A. (2009). Differences between peer victimization in cyber and physical settings and associated psychosocial adjustment in early adolescence. *Psychology in the Schools, 46,* 962–972. doi: 10.1002/pits.20437

Craig, W. M., Pepler, D., & Atlas, R. (2000). Observations of bullying in the playground and in the classroom. *School Psychology International, 21,* 22–36.

Espelage, D. L., Aragon, S. R., Birkett, M., & Koenig, B. W. (2008). Homophobic teasing, psychological outcomes, and sexual orientation among high school students: What influences do parents and schools have? *School Psychology Review, 37,* 202–216.

Espelage, D. L., & De La Rue, L. (2012). School bullying: Its nature and ecology. *International Journal of Adolescent Medicine and Health, 1,* 3–10. doi: 10.1515/ijamh.2012.002

Espelage, D. L., & Holt, M. K. (2007). Dating violence & sexual harassment across the bully-victim continuum among middle and high school students. *Journal of Youth and Adolescence, 36,* 799–811.

Espelage, D. L., Low, S., & De La Rue, L. (2012). Relations between peer victimization subtypes, family violence, and psychological outcomes during adolescence. *Psychology of Violence, 2,* 313–324. doi:10.1037/a0027386

Farrington, D. P., & Ttofi, M. M. (2011). Bullying as a predictor of offending, violence and later life outcomes. *Criminal Behaviour and Mental Health, 21,* 90–98.

Fitzpatrick, K., Dulin, A., & Piko, B. (2010). Bullying and depressive symptomatology among low-income African American youth. *Journal of Youth and Adolescence, 39,* 634–645.

Flannery, D. J., Vazsonyi, A.T., Liau, A.K., Guo, S., Powell, K.E., Atha, H., Vesterdal, W., & Embry, D. (2003). Initial behavior outcomes for the PeaceBuilders Universal School-Based Violence Prevention Program. *Developmental Psychology, 39,* 292–308.

Gini, G., & Pozzoli, T. (2009). Association between bullying and psychosomatic problems: A meta-analysis. *Pediatrics, 123,* 1059–1065.

Garrity, C., Jens, K., Porter, W., Sager, N., & Short-Camilli, C. (2000). *Bully-proofing your schools: A comprehensive approach for elementary schools* (2nd edn). Longmont, CO: Sopris West.

Graham, S., & Juvonen, J. (2002). Ethnicity, peer harassment, and adjustment in middle school: An exploratory study. *Journal of Early Adolescence, 22,* 173–199. doi:10.1177/0272431602022002003

Hanish, L. D., Bradshaw, C., Espelage, D. L., Rodkin, P. C., Swearer, S., & Hone, A. (2013). Looking toward the future of bullying research: Recommendations for research and funding priorities. *Journal of School Violence, 12,* 283–295. doi: 10.1080/15388220.2013.788449

Hanish, L. D., & Guerra, N. G. (2000). The roles of ethnicity and school context in predicting children's victimization by peers. *American Journal of Community Psychology, 28,* 201–223. doi: 10.1023/A:1005187201519

Hanish, L. D., Kochenderfer-Ladd, B., Fabes, R. A., Martin, C. L., & Denning, D. (2004). Bullying among young children: The influence of peers and teachers. In D. Espelage & S. Swearer (Eds.), *Bullying in American schools: A social ecological perspective on prevention and intervention* (pp. 141–160). Mahwah, NJ: Erlbaum Publishers.

Jasinskaja-Lahti, I., Liebkind, K., & Perhoniemi, R. (2006). Perceived discrimination and well-being: A victim study of different immigrant groups. *Journal of Community and Applied Social Psychology, 16,* 267–284. doi:10.1002/casp.865

Juvonen, J., Nishina, A., & Graham, S. (2006). Ethnic diversity and perceptions of safety in urban middle schools. *Psychological Science, 17,* 393–400. doi:10.1111/j.14679280.2006.01718.x

Juvonen, J., Wang, Y., & Espinoza, G. (2011). Bullying experiences and compromised academic performance across middle school grades. *Journal of Early Adolescence, 31,* 152–173.

Klomek, A. B., Kleinman, M., Altschuler, E., Marrocco, F., Amakawa, L., & Gould, M. S. (2013). Suicidal adolescents' experiences with bullying perpetration and victimization during high school as risk factors for later depression and suicidality. *Journal of Adolescent Health, 53,* 37–42.

Klomek, A. B., Marrocco, F., Kleinman, M., Schonfeld, I. S., & Gould, M. S. (2008). Peer victimization, depression, and suicidiality in adolescents. *Suicide and Life-Threatening Behavior, 38,* 166–180.

Kosciw, J. G., Greytak, E. A., & Diaz, E. M. (2009). Who, what, when, where, and why: Demographic and ecological factors contributing to hostile school climate for lesbian, gay, bisexual, and transgender youth. *Journal of Youth and Adolescence, 38,* 976–988.

Kowalski, R. M., & Limber, S. P. (2013). Psychological, physical, and academic correlates of cyberbullying and traditional bullying. *Journal of Adolescent Health, 53,* S13–S20.

Lazarus, P. (2011, July). *Breaking the cycle of bullying and creating a school climate where everyone belongs.* A workshop presented at the annual conference of the Hawaii Association of School Psychologists. Honolulu, HI.

Lazarus, P. J. & Pfohl, W. (2011). Bullying. In A. Canter, L. Z. Paige, & S. Shaw (Eds.), *Helping children at home and school III* (pp. S4H8-1-4). Bethesda, MD. National Association of School Psychologists Press.

Lenhart, A. (2012). *Teens, smartphones & texting: Texting volume is up while the frequency of voice calling is down. About one in four teens say they own smartphones.* Washington, D.C.: Pew Research Center's Internet & American Life Project.

Mehta, S., Cornell, D., Fan, X., & Gregory, A. (2013). Bullying climate and school engagement in ninth-grade students. *Journal of School Health, 83,* 45–52. doi: 10.1111/j.1746-1561.2012.00746.x

Mendez, J. J., Bauman, S., & Guillory, R. M. (2012). Bullying of Mexican immigrant students by Mexican American students: An examination of intracultural bullying. *Hispanic Journal of Behavioral Sciences, 34,* 279–304.

Mendez, J. J., Bauman, S., Sulkowski, M. L., Nixon, C., & Davis, S. (2014). Racially-focused peer victimization: Prevalence, psychosocial impacts, and the influence of coping strategies. *Psychology of Violence, 6,* 103–111. doi: 10.1037/a0038161.

Menesini, E., Modena, M., & Tani, F. (2009). Bullying and victimization in adolescence: Concurrent and stable roles and psychological health symptoms. *Journal of Genetic Psychology, 170,* 115–134.

Moroz, K. B., & Jones, K. M. (2002). The effects of positive peer reporting on children's social involvement. *School Psychology Review, 31,* 235–245.

Myers, J. J., McCaw, D. S., & Hemphill, L.S. (2011). *Responding to cyberbullying: An action tool for school leaders.* Thousand Oaks, CA: Corwin

Nansel, T. R., Overpeck, M., Pilla, R. S., Ruan, W. J., Simons-Morton, B., & Scheidt, P. (2001). Bullying behaviors among US youth: Prevalence and association with psychosocial adjustment. *JAMA, 285,* 2094–2100. doi: 10.1001/jama.285.16.2094

Olsen, P. (2013). Here's where teens are going instead of Facebook. *Forbes.* Retrieved on January 6, 2014 from www.forbes.com/sites/parmyolson/2013/11/12/heres-where-teens-are-going-instead-of-facebook/

Olweus, D. (1993). *Bullying at school: What we know and what we can do.* Oxford, UK: Blackwell Publishers.

Olweus, D., & Limber, S. (2007). *Olweus Bullying Prevention Program: Teacher guide.* Center City, MN: Hazelden.

Patchin, J. W., & Hinduja, S. (2006). Bullies move beyond the schoolyard a preliminary look at cyberbullying. *Youth Violence and Juvenile Justice, 4,* 148–169.

Pelligrini, A. D., & Long, J. D. (2004). Part of the solution and part of the problem: The role of peers in bullying, dominance, and victimization during the transition from primary school to secondary school. In D. L. Espelage & S. M. Swearer (Eds.), *Bullying in American schools: A social-ecological perspective on prevention and intervention* (pp. 107–117). Mahwah, NJ: Lawrence Erlbaum.

Polanin, J. R., Espelage, D. L., & Pigott, T. D. (2012). A meta-analysis of school-based bullying prevention programs' effects on bystander intervention behavior. *School Psychology Review, 41*(1), 47–65.

Pozzoli, T., Ang, R. P., & Gini, G. (2012). Bystanders' reactions to bullying: A cross-cultural analysis of personal correlates among Italian and Singaporean students. *Social Development, 21*(4), 686–703.

Roberts, S., Zhang, J., Truman, J., & Snyder, T. (2012). *Indicators of school crime and safety: 2011* (NCES 2012-002/NCJ 236021). Washington, DC: National Center for Education Statistics, U.S. Department of Education, and Bureau of Justice Statistics, Office of Justice Programs, U.S. Department of Justice.

Robinson, J. P., & Espelage, D. L. (2012). Bullying explains only part of LGBTQ–heterosexual risk disparities implications for policy and practice. *Educational Researcher, 41,* 309–319.

Rose, C. A. (2010). Bullying among students with disabilities: Impact and implications. In D. L. Espelage & S. M. Swearer (Eds.), *Bullying in North American schools: A socio-ecological perspective on prevention and intervention* (2nd edn) (pp. 34–44). Mahwah, NJ: Lawrence Erlbaum.

Rose, C. A., Espelage, D. L., Aragon, S. R., & Elliott, J. (2011). Bullying and victimization among students in special education and general education curricula. *Exceptionality Education International, 21,* 2–14.

Rose, C. A., Forber-Pratt, A. J., Espelage, D. L., & Aragon, S. R. (2013). The influence of psychosocial factors on bullying involvement of students with disabilities. *Theory Into Practice, 52,* 272–279.

Rose, C. A., Monda-Amaya, L. E., & Espelage, D. L. (2011). Bullying perpetration and victimization in special education: A review of the literature. *Remedial and Special Education, 32,* 114–130. doi:10.1177/0741932510361247

Ross, D. M. (2002). Bullying. In J. Sandoval (Ed.), *Handbook of crisis counseling, intervention, and prevention in the schools* (2nd edn) (pp. 105–135). Mahwah, NJ: Lawrence Erlbaum.

Russell, S. T., Sinclair, K. O., Poteat, V. P., & Koenig, B. W. (2012). Adolescent health and harassment based on discriminatory bias. *American Journal of Public Health, 102,* 493–495.

Russell, S. T., Toomey, R. B., Ryan, C., & Diaz, R. M. (2014). Being out at school: The implications for school victimization and young adult adjustment. *American Journal of Orthopsychiatry, 84,* 635–643.

Ryan, W. S., Legate, N., & Weinstein, N. (2015). Coming out as lesbian, gay, or bisexual: The lasting impact of initial disclosure experiences. *Self and Identity, 14,* 549–569.

Salmivalli, C., Kärnä, A., & Poskiparta, E. (2011). Counteracting bullying in Finland: The KiVa program and its effects on different forms of being bullied. *International Journal of Behavioral Development, 35,* 405–411.

Salmivalli, C., & Nieminen, E. (2002). Proactive and reactive aggression among school bullies, victims, and bully-victims. *Aggressive Behavior, 28,* 30–44.

Strohmeier, D., Spiel, C., & Gradinger, P. (2008). Social relationships in multicultural schools: Bullying and victimization. *European Journal of Developmental Psychology, 5,* 262–285. doi:10.1080/17405620701556664

Sulkowski, M. L., Bauman, S., Wright, S., Nixon, C., & Davis, S. (2014). Peer victimization in youth from immigrant and non-immigrant U.S. families. *School Psychology International, 35,* 649–669. doi: 10.1177/0143034314554968

Swearer, S. M., Turner, R. K., Givens, J. E., & Pollack, W. S. (2008). "You're so gay!": Do different forms of bullying matter for adolescent males? *School Psychology Review, 37,* 160–173.

Swearer, S. M., Wang, C., Maag, J. W., Siebecker, A. B., & Frerichs, L. J. (2012). Understanding the bullying dynamic among students in special and general education. *Journal of School Psychology, 50,* 503–520.

Ttofi, M. M., Farrington, D. P., Lösel, F., & Loeber, R. (2011). Do the victims of school bullies tend to become depressed later in life? A systematic review and meta-analysis of longitudinal studies. *Journal of Aggression, Conflict and Peace Research, 3,* 63–73.

Turner, H. A., Finkelhor, D., Hamby, S. L., Shattuck, A., & Ormrod, R. K. (2011). Specifying type and location of peer victimization in a national sample of children and youth. *Journal of Youth and Adolescence, 40,* 1052–1067.

Völlink, T., Bolman, C. A., Dehue, F., & Jacobs, N. C. (2013). Coping with cyberbullying: Differences between victims, bully-victims and children not involved in bullying. *Journal of Community and Applied Social Psychology, 23,* 7–24.

von Grünigen, R., Perren, S., Nägele, C., & Alsaker, F. D. (2010). Immigrant children's peer acceptance and victimization in kindergarten: The role of local language competence. *British Journal of Developmental Psychology, 28,* 679–697. doi:10.1348/026151009X470582

Willard, N. (2007). *Cyberbullying and cyberthreats: Responding to the challenge of online social aggression, threats and distress.* Champaign, IL: Research Press.

13 Childhood Emotional and Behavioral Disorders

Emotional and behavioral disorders (EBD) encompass a broad category of disorders that affect students and school communities. These disorders may be described using general terms (e.g. anxiety, depression, disruptive behavior) or they may be narrowly defined in diagnostic terms in the *Diagnostic and statistical manual of psychiatric disorders, 5th Edition* (DSM-V; American Psychiatric Association (APA, 2013)). However, it is worth noting that general definitions as well as a specific EBD diagnosis is contextual in that observed behaviors depend on many individual and environmental factors. For example, a child displaying disruptive behaviors during reading instruction (e.g., talking out of turn, hitting other students) may display these behaviors for a range of reasons. On one hand, the child may lack appropriate social skills to ask for help. On the other, the child might be negatively influenced by his or her peers, have not had appropriate instruction, be experiencing a mental health problem, or be impacted by any number of other factors. Whatever the case, the great majority of educators—not just special educators—will have students with EBDs in their classes and will be expected to help address the academic and social-emotional needs of these youth.

This chapter provides information on students with EBDs so that educators will be more aware of the unique needs and characteristics of these students. Although educators are not direct mental health providers, they are on the front lines of efforts to help students with emotional, behavioral, and social problems succeed in school. Therefore, although this chapter is highly informational, the provided information is crucial for educators to know to help support students as well as the efforts of school-based mental health professionals. In addition, information on student emotional and behavioral disorders can help with having a greater capacity to champion coordinated efforts to support the needs of all students while reducing prejudice against a vulnerable student population.

There is a wide body of research that underscores that the education of youth with disabilities has not been as effective as that of their non-disabled peers (e.g., President's Commission on Excellence in Special Education, 2002; Reschly & Christenson, 2006). For example, students with disabilities drop out of school twice as often as their classmates, they enter into higher education at half the rate, and they are much less likely to be gainfully employed post-graduation. Moreover, this is even more of a problem for children with EBDs than it is for students in other disability categories (Kern, 2015). Currently, students with EBDs have low rates of graduation (approximately 50 percent), high rates of arrest, poor academic achievement, and unfavorable post-school outcomes (Van Acker, 2004; Wagner, Kutash, Duchnowski, Epsten, & Sumi, 2005). And to further illustrate this point, one study found that only 20 percent of students classified as having EBD who exited the schools during the 2006–2007 academic year graduated with a diploma (Smith, Katsiyannis, & Ryan, 2011). Moreover, according to Kern (2015), research indicates that "this group of students fares worse than other disability group along almost any dimension we consider" (p. 24).

A number of issues contribute to difficulties with providing effective services for students with EBDs (Kern, 2015). Some of these are listed in the following. First, many educators believe that their job is to teach students academics and not remedy emotional and behavioral problems. Second, many teachers are not sufficiently trained to respond to students' behavior challenges. In support of this notion, almost half of college and university training programs in elementary education offer no courses on effective behavior or classroom management (State, Kern, Starosta, & Divatia Mukherjee, 2011). Third, many educators blame parents when a child lacks behavioral control. Blaming parents for behavioral problems in students is understandable, yet it can easily provide an excuse not to muster the effort or find the resources to help these vulnerable students. Fourth, students with problem behaviors often disrupt the classroom environment and as a result impede both their own academic performance and that of their fellow classmates (Ling, Hawkins, & Weber, 2011). Collectively, these issues have led to schools to rid themselves of students with emotional and behavioral challenges, resulting in exclusion of students with EBDs to increasingly restrictive placements. Moreover, due to the complex behavioral challenges presented by students with EBDs, evidence from research has noted that when these youth are placed in self-contained classes, only approximately 30 percent of class time is devoted to instruction (Wehby, 2003). Lastly, the complex societal issues often associated with the label "emotional disturbance," such as stigma, poverty, race/ethnicity, family concerns (e.g., parental mental health), and having limited access to mental health services further contribute to the problem of students with EBDs receiving the services they need.

In general, students with EBDs often are criticized, blamed, and even ostracized because of their emotional and behavioral problems, many of which they have little control over. Regardless of the problematic behaviors that they display, these students already have significant vulnerabilities that place them at risk for having negative interpersonal interactions with important caregivers, educators, and peers that can degrade important relationships. Therefore, even though it can be a challenging, it is important for educators to provide students with emotional and behavioral problems the empathy and support they need to remain interpersonally connected to adults at school and to feel emotionally supported. Further, along with their efforts to make all students feel safe and supported at school, educators can also help reduce the negative stigma associated with being labeled with an EBD. Unfortunately, this stigma negatively brands students as being problem students and may exacerbate the development of a coercive dynamic between teachers and students with EBDs.

Adverse Childhood Experiences that Impact Students

The first step to supporting students with emotional problems is to understand what these children experience and how their symptoms and problems may act as barriers to learning and success. Only with this understanding can educators calibrate their efforts to help these students, as there is no effective "one-size-fits-all" approach to supporting students. For example, it is often standard practice to punish children for misbehavior that they do not know how to control. In some instances, this may be analogous to punishing a child for having a medical problem and disrupting school functioning. Oftentimes, a child who acts out or responds with defiance is in fact displaying a normal reaction to toxic stress resulting from chronic negative experiences such as traumatic abuse.

For example, Blodgett (2012) found that more than 20 percent of children in ten targeted schools in Spokane, Washington, had undergone two or more Adverse Childhood Experiences (ACE), which are inherently disruptive experiences in childhood that produce significant and potentially damaging levels of stress and associated physical changes (e.g., having been homeless, witnessing domestic violence, or having a caregiver who is incarcerated or using drugs). Compared with children who had no known stressors, these children were two to four times more likely to have problems with school attendance, behavior, academics, and health; and as the number of ACEs increased, so did these problems. For more information on ACEs, review Chapter 3, which discusses providing mental health services in schools.

As a result of reading about the research regarding ACEs, and the effects of stress and trauma on children, Ryan Powers, the school principal at Mary E. Baker Elementary School in Brockton, MA, began organizing his staff so that they could begin to understand how stress and trauma impact children's learning. He noted that when one of the presenters from the district attorney's office overlaid the map of the Brockton School District with maps of gun violence and drug offenses, there was an "aha moment" when the staff realized what their students were witnessing and asked what they could do (Bornstein, 2013). They realized that some students had experienced a disproportionate number of ACEs that were impacting their functioning. As a result, the school started creating choices for children who felt overwhelmed or felt as if their emotions were getting the best of them. Blodgett noted that when children violate rules or expectations, they are often met with punishment or by having to reason with an adult about their behavior. Yet, when children who have been impacted by toxic stress react to change, loss, or threat, they will often violate rules because they feel profoundly out of control. This can be interpreted as a survival reaction and it may actually be intended to help children control the situation. As a result of this understanding, youngsters were given options that did not involve punishment or having to engage in a conversation or a confrontation with an adult if they felt emotionally distraught. Instead, they could go for a walk, put on headphones, listen to classical music, take a break, or sit on a beanbag chair. The approach moved from reflexive discipline and toward responses that helped children calm themselves and build emotional resilience. Educators also made an effort to start paying attention to how they spoke to children. They began each day by greeting each child by name or with a handshake or a touch on the shoulder. They also made the first session of the morning about building a sense of community. As a result of these changes, according to Bornstein (2013), office referrals decreased by 75 percent from the initial baseline estimate.

As a caveat, not all children who have a high number of ACEs have an emotional or mental health disorder, yet as the number of these events that a child is exposed to increases, so does the risk for developing one of these disorders (Feletti et al., 1998). Consequently, research also indicates that children with psychiatric disorders and mental health problems are at increased risk to experience ACEs such as abuse (Mandell, Walrath, Manteuffel, Sgro, & Pinto-Martin, 2005). Thus, the risk factors can go in both directions and educators should keep in mind that both ACEs and mental health problems negatively impact children's learning and behavior.

Emotional and Mental Health Disorders that Impact Students

Although a comprehensive review of EBDs and how these disorders impact students is beyond the scope of this chapter, a foundation for understanding various EBDs and related problems that negatively impact students is provided. Various disorders and problems are discussed as they relate to each other on established dimensions or diagnostic categories. In addition, the latter part of the chapter discusses ways that educators can help students with EBDs.

Internalizing and Externalizing Disorders

Emotional and behavioral disorders often are described as being internalizing (e.g., involving mood or anxiety problems that negatively impact the student) or externalizing in their nature (e.g., involving behavioral problems that disrupt academic and social environments; Saklofske, Joyce, Sulkowski, & Climie, 2013). By their very nature, externalizing disorders or the behavioral problems associated with these disorders are easy to notice in school communities (Sulkowski, Joyce, & Storch, 2013). These disorders include Conduct Disorder (CD), Oppositional Defiant Disorder (ODD), Intermittent Explosive Disorder (IED), and Attention-Deficit/Hyperactivity Disorder (AD/HD). Table 13.1 lists the main symptoms of externalizing disorders, prevalence rates, gender differences, and functional consequences associated with each disorder.

Table 13.1 Externalizing Behavior Disorders

Disorder	Prevalence	Core Symptoms	Gender Differences	Functional Consequences
Conduct Disorder	4%	Aggression to people and animals; destruction of property; deceitfulness, lying, or stealing; serious violations of rules.	Males are more likely to engage in fighting, vandalism, stealing, and have discipline problems at school; females are more likely to exhibit lying, substance abuse, truancy, running away, and prostitution.	High rates of school suspension and or expulsion; legal difficulties; risk-taking behavior; substance abuse; incarceration.
Oppositional Defiant Disorder	3%	Angry/irritable mood; argumentative/defiant behavior; vindictiveness.	More common in males than in females (1.4:1).	Affected individuals experience frequent conflicts with caregivers, teachers, peers, and partners; social problems often result in impairments in emotional, social, academic, and occupational functioning.
Intermittent Explosive Disorder	3%	Recurrent behavioral outbursts representing a failure to control aggressive impulses; the magnitude of aggressiveness is grossly out of proportion to the provocation or precipitating stressors; outbursts are not premeditated.	More common in males than in females (2.3:1).	Commonly experience a loss of relationships; occupational and financial instability; legal problems.
Attention Deficit/ Hyperactivity Disorder	5%	Inattention; hyperactivity; impulsivity.	More common in males than in females (2:1).	Reduced school performance and academic success; peer rejection; interpersonal conflict; substance abuse; unemployment.

As previously mentioned, students with externalizing disorders are easy to notice and difficult to ignore at school. These are the students who most commonly disrupt instruction and frustrate other members of school communities. Too frequently, they are labeled as the "bad apples." However, when engaged at school, these students can be highly successful and make positive contributions to the classroom environment (Wilson, 2004). Thus, it is important for educators to catch students with behavioral problems being good and acknowledge them for doing so with praise before they have a chance to display problematic behaviors (McCurdy, Mannella, & Eldridge, 2003). In addition, some youth with certain EBDs such as AD/HD may benefit from a psychiatric consultation from an outside child and adolescent psychiatrist. Text Box 13.1 lists information on the controversy of treating children with AD/HD with psychiatric medication.

Text Box 13.1 Controversies Associated with Psychiatric Treatment for AD/HD

According to the American Academy of Pediatrics (AAP), treatment recommendations for children with AD/HD should vary by age:

- For children who are 4–5 years old, evidence-based parent- and/or teacher-administered behavior therapy should be used as a first-line treatment and a commonly used stimulant medication such as methylphenidate should be used if behavior interventions are deemed ineffective and the child is still at least experiencing moderate functional impairments.
- For children who are 6–18 years old, a US Food and Drug Administration–approved medication for AD/HD and/or evidence-based parent and/or teacher-administered behavior therapy should be used as a first-line treatment for AD/HD (preferably both).

Prior to beginning treatment with young children, it is important for a medical professional to weigh the risks of starting medication at an early age against the harm of delaying treatment as well as the importance of taking the school environment and placement into consideration as part of any treatment plan.

This information was adopted from the American Academy of Pediatrics: www.cdc.gov/ncbddd/adhd/guidelines.html

---

In contrast to youth with externalizing disorders, youth who are afflicted by internalizing disorders are less easily noticed in schools (Sulkowski et al., 2013). These youth often suffer from depression or anxiety and they may try to hide their symptoms and attempt to remain unnoticed in school settings (Wright & Sulkowski, 2013). Internalizing disorders include Major Depressive Disorder (MDD), Persistent Depressive Disorder (Dysthymia), Generalized Anxiety Disorder (GAD), Social Anxiety Disorder, Specific Phobia, Separation Anxiety Disorder, Panic Disorder, and Selective Mutism. Table 13.2 lists the main symptoms of internalizing disorders, gender differences, and functional consequences associated with each disorder. Because of the often covert nature of their symptoms, youth with internalizing symptoms often are described as "flying under the radar" and they may not be identified and provided with supportive services, which is unfortunate because these disorders also are associated with negative long-term outcomes such as under-employment in adulthood, substance abuse, and general unhappiness across the lifespan (Sulkowski et al., 2013). To help identify these youth, Text Box 13.2 provides signs that a student may be affected by an internalizing disorder.

Table 13.2 Internalizing Behavior Disorders

Disorder	Prevalence	Core Symptoms	Gender Differences	Functional Consequences
Major Depressive Disorder	7%	Depressed mood; diminished interest or enjoyment in daily activities; insomnia or hypersomnia; psychomotor agitation or retardation; feelings of guilt or worthlessness; difficulty concentrating and making decisions; recurrent thoughts about death.	Females are more likely to be affected (2:1); females with depression also display a higher rate of suicide attempts, but not completion.	Impairment is highly variable ranging from an inability to engage in self-care to mild functional impairment,
Dysthymia	1%	Depressed mood for most of the day for more days than not; poor appetite/overeating; insomnia or hypersomnia; low energy or fatigue; Low self-esteem; poor concentration and difficulty making decisions; feelings of hopelessness.	Not well established but likely more prevalent in females.	Effects are similar to Major Depressive Disorder.
Generalized Anxiety Disorder	1%	Excessive anxiety and worry (apprehensive expectation) that occurs more days than not; the individual has difficulty controlling worry.	Females are more likely to be affected (2:1).	Excessive worrying negatively impacts individuals' capacity to do tasks quickly and efficiently; many missed days at school/work.
Social Anxiety Disorder	7%	Marked fear or anxiety about one or more social situations in which a person is exposed to possible scrutiny by others; fear of negative evaluation.	Females report a greater number of social fears as well as comorbidities; males are more likely to have fears of dating, abuse substances, and to display externalizing behavior problems.	Elevated risk of school dropout; Under-employment; poor self-reported quality of life; relationships problems; substance abuse
Specific Phobia	5–16%	Marked fear about a specific object or situation (e.g., heights, certain animals, blood, etc.).	Females are more likely to be affected (2:1).	Increased risk of academic, social, and family functioning impairments; avoidance of situations and settings related to the phobia.
Separation Anxiety Disorder	4%	Developmentally inappropriate and excessive fear or anxiety related to separating from an attachment figure (e.g., parent, caregiver)	Females are more likely to be affected (2:1).	Associated with high levels of social, occupational, and physical disabilities; school avoidance and dropout; occupational impairments; dependence on caregivers.
Panic Disorder	3%	Recurrent and unexpected panic attacks involving a quick and intense fear and/or discomfort.	Females are more likely to be affected (2:1).	High levels of social, occupational, and physical disabilities; frequent medical visits; frequent absence from school and work.
Selective Mutism	1%	Consistent failure to speak in specific social situations in which there is an expectation for speaking, despite speaking in other situations; impairment interferes with functioning because of social communication deficits.	Not clearly established.	Social impairment; social isolation; academic delays and under-achievement; peer victimization; school refusal; dropout.

Text Box 13.2 Signs that a Student May be Affected by an Internalizing Disorder

- Signs that a child may be depressed

  - irritable mood and edginess
  - increase in tantrums and oppositional behavior
  - crying spells and difficulty articulating sadness
  - social withdrawal
  - sudden reluctance to play games/engage in play
  - declines in academic performance
  - low motivation
  - confusion and difficulty making decisions
  - trouble focusing and paying attention
  - low desire to participate in class or in extra-curricular activities
  - thoughts about death and dying
  - excessive guilt and shame.

- Signs that a child may be anxious

  - physiological arousal (e.g. tachycardia, sweating, trembling)
  - avoidance of people or social situations
  - racing and rapid thoughts
  - excessive worry about oneself or caregivers
  - avoidance of eye contact
  - difficulty staying engaged and focused
  - somatic symptoms (e.g. stomachaches, headaches)
  - reluctance to engage or work with peers
  - unexplained poor performance on tests or other stressful evaluations
  - excessive absences and/or tardiness.

Importantly, some disorders display elements of both externalizing and internalizing problems. For example, Disruptive Mood Dysregulation Disorder, which was added to the latest version of the DSM (DSM-5; 2013), describes students who are impacted by feelings of depression as well as irritability and acting out behaviors. In general, these youth are described as being moody, frustrated, and prone to temper outbursts.

Similarly, childhood depression can present as irritability, agitation, and moodiness as opposed to pervasive sadness, social withdrawal, and anhedonia (i.e., an inability to experience pleasure from activities usually found enjoyable). Therefore, it is critically important for educators to avoid assuming that a student's disruptive behaviors are purposively malicious, as they could also be a manifestation of depression or another emotional disorder (Salloum, Sulkowski, Sirrine, & Storch, 2009).

Co-morbidity

Although psychiatric disorders are grouped in categories because of their related features, many children have co-morbid (i.e., co-occurring or "occurring together") disorders that have different features. For example, according to a review by Axelson and Birmaher (2001), 25–50 percent of youth with depression also have an anxiety disorder and 10–15 percent of children with an anxiety disorder also have depression. This example illustrates how psychiatric disorder co-morbidity estimates vary depending on the primary or most problematic disorder that a child has and this is because different pathogeneses contribute to psychopathology. For example, a child with Social Anxiety Disorder may avoid social situations with other children because of fear associated with being judged or perceived negatively. Subsequently, the child may have few friends or avoid fun social activities such as birthday parties, sleepovers, or joining clubs, team sports, or extracurricular activities, which can then contribute to feelings of social isolation, loneliness, and depression. Conversely, a child with depression may be highly anxious around other people because of highly self-critical and judgmental thoughts that often occur with the disorder (e.g., "Nobody likes me," "I'm a loser," "I don't belong").

In general, the more co-morbid disorders that a child displays, the more likely it is that his or her psychosocial functioning will be highly impaired. Unless specific pre-determined diagnostic rule-outs exist (e.g., a child cannot be diagnosed with ODD if he or she has been diagnosed with CD), co-morbid disorders are most likely to occur from a similar diagnostic category. Thus, in this regard, it is common for youth with an externalizing disorder such as ODD to also have AD/DH or a child with GAD to have MDD (APA, 2013). Moreover, it is not uncommon for youth to have disorders that are very different in their diagnostic criteria and for multiple co-morbidities to occur across different clusters of diagnoses. For example, in a seminal investigation, Angold, Costello, and Erklani (1999) found that children with AD/HD were 10.7 times more likely to have CD and 5.5 times more likely to have MDD.

As a final note on this topic, the presence of co-morbid disorders does not necessarily mean that separate interventions will be needed to treat the symptoms of each co-morbid condition. For example, if a child's depression is related to social impairment associated with having a severe anxiety disorder, successfully treating the child's anxiety could result in reductions in depression as the child may start engaging in more enjoyable social activities (Pence, Sulkowski, Jordan, & Storch, 2010). However, if the depression seems mostly unrelated to anxiety or symptoms of another psychiatric disorder, directly treating depression through an evidence-based treatment such as cognitive-behavioral therapy (CBT) or with a serotonin reuptake inhibitor (SRI) may be warranted.

Bipolar Disorder

Bipolar Disorder, also known as manic-depression in previous versions of the DSM, involves experiencing unusual and severe shifts in mood, energy, and activity levels. The disorder is marked by episodes of mania (i.e., significantly elevated mood, energy, and activity) as well as periods of depression that often follow episodes of mania. When affected, children with Bipolar Disorder may struggle with completing routine tasks and behaving appropriately at school. Moreover, emotional volatility associated with this disorder can put a significant strain on relationships.

Diagnosing Bipolar Disorders in children is controversial. During the last decade, the number of children receiving the diagnosis of Bipolar Disorder has grown significantly (Moreno, Laje, Blanco, Jiang, Schmidt, & Olfson, 2007). Research suggests that Bipolar Disorder symptoms often first present in the late teens or early adult years and more than half of cases occur before age 25 (Kessler, Berglund, Demler, Jin, Merikangas, & Walters, 2005).

It is critically important to note that the majority of children who present with symptoms resembling Bipolar Disorder likely do not have the disorder and that psychiatric medication should only be used after safer and more benign psychological and behavioral interventions have been exhausted. Symptoms of the disorder overlap highly with externalizing behavior problems and the medications that are used to treat Bipolar Disorder often have significant side effects (Pataki & Carlson, 2013). Moreover, some scholars question the validity of the diagnosis of Bipolar Disorder in children, largely because of serious ethical violations among leading pediatric bipolar researchers (Kaplan, 2011). Text Box 13.3 lists additional information on this controversy.

Text Box 13.3 Controversy regarding Pediatric Bipolar Disorder

In a 2008 Congressional Investigation several researchers at Massachusetts General Hospital who have been forceful in their efforts to encourage children to be diagnosed with Bipolar Disorder were found to have violated federal and university regulations by secretly receiving large sums of money from the pharmaceutical companies that produced the medications that they prescribed. These researchers have since been sanctioned for violating conflict of interest policies of Massachusetts General Hospital and Harvard Medical School and the credibility of their work has been questioned by other mental health experts (Kaplan 2011).

Autism Spectrum Disorder

An Autism Spectrum Disorder (ASD) diagnosis reflects the full range of autistic symptoms that youth may display that are emotional and behavioral in nature. Previously, ASD was broken up into discrete diagnostic categories: Autism, Asperger's Disorder, and Pervasive Developmental Disability. However, because of significant overlap in symptoms across these disorders as well as problems with differentiating youth across and between diagnostic categories, the former discrete categories have been included on a broader ASD diagnostic spectrum (APA, 2013). In general, ASD is characterized by deficits or marked delays in verbal and non-verbal communication, social interaction (e.g., social reciprocity, developing and maintaining relationships), rigidities and restricted patterns of behavior, and by the presence of stereotypic and repetitive behaviors. In addition to displaying impairments in social communication and interaction across multiple settings and often having restricted, repetitive, patterns of behavior, interests, or activities, youth with ASD also often display limitations in their cognitive functioning (i.e., intelligence) and language impairments (e.g., poor language comprehension, expressive language difficulties, slow or delayed language production).

Although prevalence rates vary across studies, most estimates suggest that about 1 percent of youth display symptoms consistent with an ASD diagnosis (APA, 2013). Yet, more recent studies indicate that the prevalence rates have increased from 1.16 percent to 2 percent from 2007 to 2012 among U.S. children ages 6–17 (Blumberg et al., 2013). Thus, consistent with these estimates, it is likely that more children with ASD will be served by schools within the near future.

Depending on the constellation and severity of their symptoms, the educational performance of youth with ASD is highly variable and they require a range of educational and behavioral supports. In this regard, higher functioning youth with ASD may only require social skills training, whereas youth with ASDs that need "very substantial support" will need a range of academic and social-emotional supports to help them be successful at school. In all cases, it is important for educators and especially preschool educators to refer these youth to student support teams for a complete assessment of their strengths, weaknesses, and needs and then determine the best educational placement for these youth. This is extremely important, as research indicates that early identification and intervention for students with ASD is associated with better long-term outcomes.

As a final note, considerable confusion and controversy exists regarding the etiology or origin of ASD. Text Box 13.4 lists controversies associated with putative causes of ASD, such as vaccines. Essentially, as a heterogenic condition, current research clearly indicates that there is no single factor that predicts the development or cause of ASD. However, in the largest-ever study of its kind, research by Sandin et al. (2014) suggests that the risk of autism is influenced equally by genetic and environmental factors. In scientific terms, environmental factors include a broad range of influences. In autism, these can be as varied as parental age, birth complications, maternal nutrition at conception and exposure to pollution and toxins during early brain development. This does not mean that half of autism cases are caused by genetic and half by environmental factors. In other words, the development of autism is not an either/or scenario. Instead, a complex interaction of genetics and environmental factors, working together, seem to underlie the development of ASD.

Text Box 13.4 Controversy over Vaccines and Autism

Great confusion exists regarding the cause of ASD. For example, no credible evidence exists suggesting that vaccine exposure increases risk for developing ASD symptoms at any stage of child development (Flaherty, 2011). The original research that was published suggesting a link between environmental factors such as measles, mumps, and the rubella vaccination and the development of ASD symptoms has been proven to be fraudulent and the journals that published this research have since retracted and discounted the papers (Godlee, Smith, & Marcovitch, 2011). Moreover, in January 2010, a five-member tribunal of the British General Medical Council found three dozen charges, including four counts of dishonesty and 12 counts involving the abuse of developmentally challenged children, of misconduct committed by Andrew Wakefield, who was the lead author on since-retracted papers linking ASD with vaccine exposure. And as of 2010, Wakefield has been removed from the Medical Register, which effectively prevents him from practicing medicine or engaging in medical research in the United Kingdom.

Obsessive-Compulsive and Related Disorders

Obsessive-Compulsive Disorder (OCD) formally was categorized as an anxiety disorder in the previous version of the DSM. Now, however, OCD is classified as an Obsessive-Compulsive and Related Disorder (OCRD) and it is listed with a range of disorders that share similar features. These disorders include OCD, Body Dysmorphic Disorder (BDD), Hoarding Disorder, Trichotillomania (Hair-Pulling Disorder), and Excoriation (Skin-Picking) Disorder. Table 13.3 lists the main symptoms of OCRDs, prevalence rates, gender differences, and functional consequences associated with each disorder.

Obsessive-Compulsive and Related Disorders can be grouped according to whether they are compulsive (i.e., reduce anxiety or distress) or impulsive (i.e., increase stimulation, produce a desirable feeling) in their nature. For example, a child with obsessive thoughts about being contaminated by germs will experience anxiety when he comes into contact with an object that is perceived to be contaminated. Then, to reduce his anxiety associated with feeling contaminated or dirty, the child may wash excessively to neutralize his anxiety and temporarily mitigate his obsessive thoughts about contamination. In contrast to compulsive or anxiety-reductive behaviors, impulsive hair-pulling behaviors associated with Trichotillomania can occur when a child is bored or during episodes of low stimulation. Importantly, problematic behaviors associated with some OCRDs may appear as both compulsive and impulsive depending on the context. For example, skin-picking behaviors associated with Excoriation Disorder may occur impulsively. This is similar to hair-pulling behaviors that occur during periods of low stimulation or compulsively to reduce distress, as some children report that the behavior reduces distress.

Tic Disorders

Tic disorders are characterized by sudden and non-rhythmic motor movements or vocalizations (tics) that usually present in childhood. Three major tic disorder classifications are listed in the DSM: Tourette Disorder (TD), Persistent (Chronic) Motor or Vocal Tic Disorder (PM/VTD),

Table 13.3 Obsessive-Compulsive and Related Disorders

Disorder	Prevalence	Core Symptoms	Gender Differences	Functional Consequences
Obsessive-Compulsive Disorder	2%	Presence of obsessions (i.e., recurrent and persistent thoughts, urges, or images that cause distress), and/or compulsions (i.e., repetitive behaviors or mental acts that an individual feels driven to perform).	Males are more likely to be affected in childhood; in adulthood, females are slightly more likely to be affected.	Impaired quality of life; high levels of social, academic, occupational, and family functioning.
Body Dysmorphic Disorder	2%	Preoccupation with one or more perceived deficits or flaws in one's physical appearance that are not observable or appear slight to others; at some point, the individual has performed repetitive behaviors or mental acts in response to appearance concerns.	Rates are roughly equivalent.	Impaired psychosocial functioning; avoidance of social situations; low quality of life; school dropout; seeking of unnecessary surgery.
Hoarding Disorder	2%	Persistent difficulty discarding or parting with possessions, regardless of their actual value; this difficulty results in the accumulation of possessions and causes functional impairment.	Slightly more common among males.	Quality of life is impaired; health risks; impairment in relationships; risk for fire and accidents
Trichotillomania	1%	Recurrent hair pulling that results in hair loss.	Females are significantly more likely to be affected (10:1).	Loss of hair; avoidance of activities and settings where hair loss can be noticed.
Excoriation Disorder	1%	Recurrent skin picking that results in lesions.	Females are more likely to be affected (3:1).	Excessive time is allocated to picking (greater than an hour per day); noticeable lesions.

and Provisional Tic Disorder (PTD). Tourette Disorder is characterized by the presence of multiple motor and one or more vocal tics that can occur at any point during the illness, whereas PM/VTD involves having either single or multiple motor or vocal tics—but not both. Provisional tic disorder is characterized by the presence of short-lived motor or vocal tics.

Research indicates that provisional or transient tics are common in children, as almost a quarter (24 percent) of youth display tics at some point during childhood (Snider et al., 2002). However, relatively few children (3 percent) by comparison meet diagnostic criteria for Tourette Disorder or Persistent Motor or Vocal Tic Disorder (Khalifa & von Knorring, 2003). Tic disorders are associated with a range of functional impairments and children often have difficulty controlling their tics, especially under stress or when excited (Conelea et al., 2011).

Tics also negatively impact school adjustment, as children with tics often struggle to develop and maintain positive peer and teacher relations and to achieve academically (Carter et al., 2000; Sulkowski, McGuire, & Tesoro, 2015). One study found that 25 percent of students with tic disorders had difficulties writing in class, 22 percent struggled with completing homework, 22 percent had trouble concentrating on schoolwork, 19 percent had problems with being prepared for class, and 18 percent were teased by peers (Storch et al., 2007). Further, children with tics have been found to have high rates of learning disabilities and to experience significant academic problems in general (Burd, Freeman, Klug, & Kerbeshian, 2005).

Trauma and Stress-Related Disorders

These disorders include Posttraumatic Stress Disorder (PTSD), Acute Stress Disorder, Reactive Attachment Disorder, Disinhibited Social Engagement Disorder, and Adjustment Disorder. Twelve-month prevalence rates for these disorders are as follows: PTSD (4 percent), Acute Stress Disorder (6–50 percent depending on the traumatic stressor), Reactive Attachment Disorder (less than 1 percent), Disinhibited Social Engagement Disorder (less than 1 percent), and Adjustment Disorder (5 percent to 20 percent; APA, 2013). In general, symptoms of trauma and stress-related disorders develop in response to experiencing a significant threat to one's safety/well-being (e.g., being involved in an auto accident, experiencing a natural disaster, being abused by a caregiver) or to the safety or well-being of someone else who is important to the child (e.g., experiencing a parent being injured badly in an accident).

The impact of traumatic stress on youth is highly variable and specific to particular individuals. The majority of youth exposed to traumatic or highly stressful events will naturally recover within a few weeks or months post-exposure without intervention. However, when significant distress related to the event lasts for more than one month, it is important to consider a preliminary diagnosis of PTSD or changing an Acute Stress Disorder diagnosis to PTSD. In school, students who have been impacted by a traumatic event or who are suffering from a Trauma and Stressor-Related Disorder may become easily triggered, be highly reactive to minor provocations, shut down easily, and engage in self-compromising behaviors (e.g., refuse to do work, engage in physical altercations, neglect future-oriented goals and plans). It is important for educators to notice changes in students' demeanor or behavior that may be related to exposure to a traumatic event. Further, beyond just noticing these changes, educators also can provide these students with the support they need, which may involve recognizing their distress, validating their emotional experience, allowing them adequate time and a safe space to experience difficult emotions, speaking with them in a calm voice, and conveying to them that adults at school are concerned about their well-being.

At first, educators may feel uncomfortable discussing a trauma with a student and believe that they do not know exactly what to say or they may be concerned that they may make the situation worse by talking about the trauma. Yet, ignoring the trauma may inadvertently convey that the educator is indifferent to the student's feelings or that he or she thinks the event is unimportant. Thus, by acknowledging their experience, traumatized students will understand that their distress has been recognized and affirmed and that the educator cares. In addition, it is important for educators to reduce additional stressors that may trigger strong and potentially overwhelming memories in youth who have been exposed to trauma. Text Box 13.5 lists signs that a student may be affected by trauma.

Text Box 13.5 Signs that a Student may be Affected by Trauma

- Having frequent memories of the event, or in young children, engaging in play in which some or all of the trauma is repeated over and over.
- Having upsetting and frightening dreams.
- Acting or feeling like the experience is happening again.
- Developing repeated physical or emotional symptoms when reminded of the event.
- Worrying about dying at an early age.
- Losing interest in activities.
- Having physical symptoms such as headaches and stomachaches.
- Showing more sudden and extreme emotional reactions.
- Having problems falling or staying asleep.
- Showing irritability or angry outbursts.
- Having problems concentrating.
- Acting younger than their age (for example, clingy or whiny behavior, thumbsucking).
- Showing increased alertness to the environment.
- Repeating behavior that reminds them of the trauma.

Note: These signs were adapted from Facts for Families—PTSD by *the American Academy of Child and Adolescent Psychiatry* (2011)

Childhood Psychosis

Symptoms of psychosis include delusions (i.e., fixed beliefs that are impervious to change in light of conflicting evidence), hallucinations (i.e., perception-like experiences that occur without an external stimulus), disorganized speech, grossly disorganized or abnormal behavior (e.g., catatonic behavior, mutism, stupor), and negative symptoms (i.e., diminished emotional expression and avolition or a decrease in self-motivated functional behaviors (APA, 2013)). Delusions and auditory hallucinations are more common than visual hallucinations in children experiencing psychosis (David et al., 2011).

Childhood psychosis is rare and considerable care is needed to avoid confusing these symptoms with other issues such as obsessive thinking or developmentally normal magical thinking. Therefore, if an educator suspects that a student is experiencing psychosis, it is important to refer this student to a competent school-based mental health professional who can evaluate him/her or refer the student to a community-based practitioner with expertise in low-incidence psychiatric problems for an evaluation.

In general, the earlier that psychosis presents, the more impairing it will likely be across the lifespan (Kumra & Schultz, 2008). Therefore, children who display psychotic symptoms will likely experience considerable and long-term disruption in their academic, occupational, social, and family functioning. In light of this, these youth will likely need considerable emotional and behavioral supports at school and they will likely be prescribed an antipsychotic medication (e.g., Abilify©, Seroquel©, Geodon©, Risperdal©). Antipsychotic medications have been found to be effective at reducing symptoms of psychosis (e.g., delusions, hallucinations) and at improving a patient's overall functioning. However, they are associated with a lot of side effects such as anticholinergic effects (e.g., dry mouth, gastrointestinal symptoms, tachycardia), extrapyramidal effects (e.g., akinesia (inability to initiate movement) and akathisia (inability to sit still or remain motionless)), and decreased metabolism, which can result in weight gain. In addition, because of these side effects and because antipsychotic medications reduce dopamine levels in the brain, which is the neurotransmitter that is most closely associated with pleasure, getting individuals to stay on antipsychotic medications can be a challenge. Essentially, they stop taking these medications when they feel better and because they want to feel more pleasure or zest. Therefore, it is important for educators to consult with school nurses to ensure that a student is regularly taking his or her medication as well as to report immediately any of the aforementioned side effects.

Childhood Emotional and Behavioral Disorders at School

Psychiatric, medical, and mental health disorders that are identified and diagnosed by psychologists, psychiatrists, psychiatric nurses, and other clinical or community-based mental health professionals may or may not overlap with classification criteria or procedures that are employed in schools to support students with EBDs. Therefore, even if a child has been diagnosed with a psychiatric disorder by a mental health professional, the child's diagnosis does not require that the student be evaluated for similar concerns at school nor does it automatically enable the student to receive supports such as early intervention services, accommodations, or special education services.

Schools have a range of options that they can use to support students with EBDs or suspected EBDs. However, uniformity in understanding these options across school systems currently is lacking. Thus, students with EBDs receive different services under different laws across states, districts, and schools. For example, depending on established practices and decisions made by a student support team,[1] a child with a psychiatric diagnosis may receive special education services under the Individuals with Disabilities and Educational Improvement Act (IDEIA), accommodations under Section 504 of the Americans with Disabilities Act (ADA), or interventions under a multi-tiered system of support (MTSS)/response-to-intervention (RtI) framework, which is an intervention service delivery model that purports to address and mitigate problems in students before they become severe and warrant special education intervention. Alternatively, the same child may not be evaluated or receive any services if it is determined that his or her disorder is not impacting his or her educational performance, which is the total involvement of the student in the educational environment. Thus, educational performance includes such things as a student's social interaction, emotional development, communication, behavior and participation in classroom activities, as well as his or her academic achievement.

Relevant IDEIA classification categories. Several different IDEIA classification categories can be invoked to provide students with EBDs with special education services and supports. Thirteen disability classification categories are included in IDEIA and the names of these categories vary in their adoption across states. For example, the category of Emotional Disturbance (ED) that is utilized by many states is called Emotional/Behavioral Disabilities (E/BD) in the Florida Statutes and State Board of Education Rules (Florida Department of Education, 2013, p. 270). Therefore, it is important for educators to obtain copies of IDEIA provisions and state statutes for their particular state, which are usually freely available through state departments of education.

Even though 13 different classification categories are included in IDEIA, only three of these categories are regularly used to classify students with EBDs. These include ED, Other Health Impairment (OHI), and Autism. Across states, the following criteria often are considered for an ED classification:

A condition exhibiting one or more of the following characteristics over a long period of time and to a marked degree that adversely affects a child's educational performance: (A) an inability to learn that cannot be explained by intellectual, sensory, or health factors. (B) an inability to build or maintain satisfactory interpersonal relationship with peers and teachers. (C) inappropriate types of behavior or feelings under normal circumstances. (D) a general pervasive mood of unhappiness or depression. (E) a tendency to develop physical symptoms or fears associated with personal or school problems

(OSERS; 2006, p. 46756)

The term includes schizophrenia, and does not apply to children who are socially maladjusted, unless it is determined that they have an emotional disturbance. Although not required by IDEIA, some state statutes require a physician to document a student's EBD for him or her to be classified or eligible to receive special education services.

Notice how IDEIA ED classification criteria do not encompass any specific symptoms or features of EBDs. Instead, they focus on the impacts of EBDs. Therefore, even though ED often is used to classify students with externalizing pathology (e.g., conduct problems, oppositional and defiant behavior), students with a range of internalizing, externalizing, or other psychiatric disorders also can be classified with ED.

The category of OHI is intended for "acute or chronic health conditions" that impact students' educational performance (OSERS 2006, p. 46540). The following definition has generally been adopted across states to describe OHIs, although these criteria are not exhaustive (p. 46550):

Other health impairment means having limited strength, vitality, or alertness, including a heightened alertness to environmental stimuli, that results in limited alertness with respect to the educational environment, that—(i) Is due to chronic or acute health problems such as asthma, attention deficit disorder or attention deficit hyperactivity disorder, diabetes, epilepsy, a heart condition, hemophilia, lead poisoning, leukemia, nephritis, rheumatic fever, sickle cell anemia, and Tourette syndrome; and (ii) Adversely affects a child's educational performance.

(OSERS 2006, p. 46757)

Although the OHI definition is broad and it encompasses a range of health/mental health-related problems that impact students, this classification is most commonly invoked to classify students with AD/HD and to allow them to receive special education services (Wodrich & Spencer, 2007). In this regard, some school-based educational professionals view OHI as being synonymous with AD/HD; however, this view seems to be more of an artifact of previously established practices than a valid practice that is consistent with OHI definitions. In support of this notion, youth with a range of internalizing and externalizing psychopathology can be classified with having an OHI and provided with supportive services in addition to students with AD/HD symptoms and medical problems (Sulkowski et al., 2013).

The third category used to classify students with EBDs is Autism. As previously discussed, it is important to identify children with ASD as early as possible as these children are eligible for special education as soon as identified. Moreover, the sooner these children are identified and receive services the better the outcome. Under IDEIA autism is defined as:

A developmental disability significantly affecting verbal and nonverbal communication and social interaction, generally evident before age three, that adversely affects a child's educational performance. Other characteristics often associated with autism are engagement in repetitive activities and stereotyped movements, resistance to environmental change or change in daily routines, and unusual responses to sensory experiences. Autism does not apply if a child's educational performance is adversely affected primarily because the child has an emotional disturbance.

(OSERS, 2006)

Independent of the IDEIA criteria under which students with EBDs are classified, it is important to emphasize that being classified does not necessitate any particular educational placement or any specific accommodations. For example, a student with AD/HD, depending on the severity of the disorder, may not need any accommodations, may require accommodations under Section 504 of ADA, or, if the disorder is particularly severe, may require special education placement under IDEIA. One student with AD/HD may present as hyperactive, whereas another will not. Moreover, a student may have a co-morbid disorder such as ODD, MDD or a specific learning disability (SLD) that requires additional services and supports. Some students with AD/HD may have significant problems with organization and planning and their disorder may significantly compromise their peer relationships. As a result, they may require help with organizing and planning their work as well as social skills training; whereas others with AD/HD may have more intact organization and planning skills and adequate social skills. Some students with a high intelligence quotient (IQ) and AD/HD may be able to use their superior intellectual ability to compensate and succeed in the classroom, whereas those with lower cognitive skills may require more supports and curriculum modifications.

The main point is that each student is unique and accommodations, supports, and the potential special educational placements need to depend on the child's needs and not on his or her diagnosis or classification. In addition, being classified under IDEIA does not require for students to be placed in a self-contained classroom; and in fact, educators should make concerted efforts to provide students with supportive services in the least restrictive environment whenever possible. In this regard, most students with EBDs should be allowed access to the general education setting for portions of the day and the opportunity to interact with diverse groups of peers.

Conclusion

Almost 20 percent of students in the U.S. suffer from mental illness and a significant percentage (5–9 percent) meet criteria for serious emotional disturbance. However, less than 1 percent are classified as EBD and receive services in the schools (Becker et al., 2011). If unaddressed, these youth are at risk for experiencing impairments in their daily functioning in family, community, and school settings. In addition, they are at an elevated risk for developing academic problems and negative long-term outcomes. Thus, it is important that students with severe EBDs, such as youth with childhood psychosis, receive a full range of supportive services that may involve school-based mental health professionals as well as professionals in the community (e.g., psychiatrists, clinical psychologists, social workers, physicians, applied behavioral analysts, etc.).

Childhood EBDs encompass a wide range of internalizing and externalizing forms of psychopathology. Additionally, many groups of psychiatric disorders, specific diagnoses, and clusters of symptoms are subsumed under the EBD framework. Unfortunately, however, perfect overlap does not exist between understanding and classification of psychopathology across medical, psychological, and educational fields. Therefore, educators will need to be aware of psychiatric disorders and symptoms that present in childhood. Further, they will need to understand how these disorders are classified under IDEIA, when it is appropriate to refer a student for a psychoeducational evaluation, and the resources available both within the school and the community to help students with EBDs. Most importantly, as public education has moved toward an inclusionary model for special education services, regular teachers may need more knowledge than is typically taught as part of their undergraduate or graduate training on how best to provide the necessary supports and accommodations to help youth with EBDs succeed in school. It is no longer just the special educator's responsibility to help these students.

Note

1 "Student support team" is a generic term to describe a group of allied professionals and educators who collaborate to evaluate and provide students with disabilities and problems with supportive services. Depending on the district or state, student support teams also may be called individualized educational plan (IEP) teams, response-to-intervention (RtI) teams, pupil appraisal teams, or other terms.

References

American Academy of Child and Adolescent Psychiatry. (2011). Facts for families—posttraumatic stress disorder. Retrieved at http://www.aacap.org/App_Themes/AACAP/docs/facts_for_families/70_post traumatic_stress_disorder_ptsd.pdf

American Psychiatric Association. (2013). *Diagnostic and statistical manual of mental disorders (5th edn).* Washington, DC: Author.

Angold, A., Costello, E.J., & Erklani, A. (1999). Comorbidity. *Journal of Child Psychology and Psychiatry, 40,* 57–87. doi: 10.1111/1469-7610.00424

Axelson, D. A., & Birmaher, B. (2001). Relation between anxiety and depressive disorders in childhood and adolescence. *Depression and Anxiety, 14,* 67–78. doi: 10.1002/da.1048

Becker, S. P., Paternite, C. E., Evans, S. W., Andrews, C., Christensen, O. A., Kraan, E. M., & Weist, M. D. (2011). Eligibility, assessment, and educational placement issues for students classified with emotional disturbance: Federal and state-level analyses. *School Mental Health, 3,* 24–34. doi: 10.1007/s12310-010-9045-2

Blodgett, C. (2012). Adopting ACEs screening and assessment in child serving systems. Unpublished manuscript. Retrieved from http://extension.wsu.edu/ahec/trauma/Documents/ACE%20Screening%20 and%20Assessment%20in%20Child%20Serving%20Systems%207-12%20final.pdf

Blumberg, S. J., Bramlett, M. D., Kogan, M. D., Schieve, L. A., & Jones, J. R. (2013, March 13). Changes in prevalence of parent-reported autism spectrum disorder in school-aged U.S. children: 2007 to 2011-2012. *National Health Statistics Reports, 65,* 1–11. Retrieved from www.cdc.gov/nchs/data/nhsr/nhsr065.pdf

Bornstein, D. (2013, November 13). Schools that separate the child from the trauma. *New York Times.* Retrieved from http://opinionator.blogs.nytimes.com/2013/11/13/separating-the-child-from-the-trauma/

Burd, L., Freeman, R. D., Klug, M. G., & Kerbeshian, J. (2005). Tourette Syndrome and learning disabilities. *BMC Pediatrics, 5,* 34. doi:10.1186/1471-2431-5-34

Carter, A. S., O`Donnell, D. A., Schultz, R. T., Scahill, L., Leckman, J. F., & Pauls, D. L. (2000). Social and emotional adjustment in children affected with Gilles de la Tourette`s syndrome: Associations with ADHD and family functioning. *Journal of Child Psychology and Psychiatry, 41,* 215–223. doi: 10.1111/1469-7610.00602

Conelea, C. A., Woods, D. W., Zinner, S. H., Budman, C., Murphy, T., Scahill, L. D., . . . Walkup, J. (2011). Exploring the impact of chronic tic disorders on youth: Results from the Tourette Syndrome Impact Survey. *Child Psychiatry and Human Development, 42,* 219–242. doi: 10.1007/s10578-010-0211-4

David, C. N., Greenstein, D., Clasen, L., Gochman, P., Miller, R., Tossell, J. W., . . . & Rapoport, J. L. (2011). Childhood onset schizophrenia: High rate of visual hallucinations. *Journal of the American Academy of Child & Adolescent Psychiatry, 50,* 681–686.

Flaherty, D. K. (2011). The vaccine-autism connection: A public health crisis caused by unethical medical practices and fraudulent science. *Annals of Pharmacotherapy, 45,* 1302–1304.

Feletti, V. J., Anda, R. F., Nordenberg, D., Williamson, D. F., Spitz, A. M., Edwards, V., . . . & Marks, J. S. (1998). Relationship of childhood abuse and household dysfunction to the many leading causes of death in adults. *American Journal of Preventive Medicine, 14,* 245–258. doi: 10.1016/S0749-3797(98)00017-8

Florida Department of Education, Bureau of Exceptional Education and Student Services. (2013). *A resource manual for the development and evaluation of exceptional student education programs: Volume 1-B, Florida statutes and state board of education rules.* Tallahassee, FL: Author.

Godlee, F., Smith, J., & Marcovitch, H. (2011). Wakefield's article linking MMR vaccine and autism was fraudulent. *BMJ, 342.* c7452. doi: 10.1136/bmj.c7452

Individuals with Disabilities Education Improvement Act of 2004. 20 U.S.C. § 1400 et seq.

Kaplan, S. L. (2011). *Your child does not have bipolar disorder: How bad science and good public relations created the diagnosis.* Santa Barbara, CA: Praeger.

Kern, L. (2015). Addressing the needs of students with social, emotional, and behavioral problems: Reflections and visions. *Remedial and Special Education 36,* 24–27.

Kessler, R. C., Berglund, P., Demler, O., Jin, R., Merikangas, K. R., & Walters, E. E. (2005). Lifetime prevalence and age-of-onset distributions of DSM-IV disorders in the National Comorbidity Survey Replication. *Archives of General Psychiatry, 62,* 593–602.

Khalifa, N., & von Knorring, A. L. (2003). Prevalence of tic disorders and Tourette syndrome in a Swedish school population. *Developmental Medicine and Child Neurology, 45,* 315–319.

Kumra, S., & Schulz, S. C. (2008). Editorial: Research progress in early-onset schizophrenia. *Schizophrenia Bulletin, 34,* 15–17.

Ling, S., Hawkins, R. O., & Weber, D. (2011). Effects of a classwide group contingency designed to improve the behavior of an at-risk student. *Journal of Behavioral Education, 20,* 103–116.

Mandell, D. S., Walrath, C. M., Manteuffel, B., Sgro, G., & Pinto-Martin, J. A. (2005). The prevalence and correlates of abuse among children with autism served in comprehensive community-based mental health settings. *Child Abuse and Neglect, 29,* 1359–1372. doi: 10.1016/j.chiabu.2005.06.006

McCurdy, B. L., Mannella, M. C., & Eldridge, N. (2003). Positive behavior support in urban schools: Can we prevent the escalation of antisocial behavior? *Journal of Positive Behavior Interventions, 5,* 158–170.

Moreno, C., Laje, G., Blanco, C., Jiang, H., Schmidt, A. B., & Olfson, M. (2007). National trends in the outpatient diagnosis and treatment of bipolar disorder in youth. *Archives of General Psychiatry, 64,* 1032–1039.

Office of Special Education and Rehabilitative Services, Department of Education (2006). Federal register: Part II Department of Education, 34 CFR Parts 300 and 301, Assistance to states for the education of children with disabilities and preschool grants for children with disabilities; Final rule. Author.

Pataki, C., & Carlson, G. A. (2013). The comorbidity of ADHD and bipolar disorder: Any less confusion? *Current Psychiatry Reports, 15,* 1–7.

Pence, S. L., Jr., Sulkowski, M. L., Jordan, C., & Storch, E. A. (2010). When exposures go wrong: Trouble-shooting guidelines for managing difficult scenarios that arise in exposure-based treatment for obsessive-compulsive disorder. *American Journal of Psychotherapy, 64,* 39–53.

President's Commission on Excellence in Special Education. (2002). *A new era: Revitalizing special education for children and their families.* Washington, DC: U.S. Department of Education.

Reschly, A. L., & Christenson, S. L. (2006). Prediction of dropout among students with mild disabilities: A case for the inclusion of student engagement variables. *Remedial and Special Education, 27,* 276–292.

Saklofske, D. H., Joyce, D. J., Sulkowski, M. L., & Climie, E. (2013). Models of personality assessment for children and adolescents. In C. R. Reynolds (Ed.), *The Oxford handbook of child psychological assessment* (pp. 348–365). New York: Oxford University Press. doi: 10.1093/oxfordhb/9780199796304.013.0015

Salloum, A., Sulkowski, M. L., Sirrine, E., & Storch, E. A. (2009). Overcoming barriers to using empirically supported therapies to treat childhood anxiety disorders in social work practice. *Child and Adolescent Social Work Journal, 26,* 259–273. doi: 10.1007/s10560-009-0173-1

Sandin S., Lichtenstein, P., Kuja-Halkola, R., Larsson, H., Hultman, C. M. & Reichenberg, A. (2014). The familial risk of autism. *Journal of the American Medical Association, 311,* 1770–1777. doi: 10.1001/jama.2014.4144

Section 504 of the Rehabilitation Act of 1973. 29 U.S.C. § 794.

Smith, C. R., Katsiyannis, A., & Ryan, J. B. (2011). Challenges of serving students with emotional and behavioral disorders: Legal and policy considerations. *Behavioral Disorders, 36,* 185–194.

Snider, L. A., Seligman, L. D., Ketchen, B. R., Levitt, S. J., Bates, L. R., Garvey, M. A., & Swedo, S. E. (2002). Tics and problem behaviors in schoolchildren: Prevalence, characterization, and associations. *Pediatrics, 110,* 331–336.

State, T. M., Kern, L., Starosta, K. M., & Mukherjee, A. (2011). Elementary pre-service teacher preparation in the area of social, emotional, and behavioral problems. *School Mental Health, 3,* 13–23. doi:10.1007/s12310-010-9044-3

Storch, E. A., Merlo, L. J., Lack, C., Milsom, V. A., Geffken, G. R., Goodman, W. K., & Murphy, T. K. (2007). Quality of life in youth with Tourette's syndrome and chronic tic disorder. *Journal of Clinical Child and Adolescent Psychology, 36,* 217–227. doi: 10.1080/15374410701279545

Sulkowski, M. L., Joyce, D. J., & Storch, E. A. (2013). Treating childhood anxiety in schools: Service delivery in a response to intervention paradigm. *Journal of Child and Family Studies, 21,* 938–947. doi: 10.1007/s10826-011-9553-1

Sulkowski, M. L., McGuire, J. F., & Tesoro, A. (in press). Treating tics and Tourette's Disorder in school settings. *Canadian Journal of School Psychology.*

U.S. Department of Education. (2013). *Part B data & notes.* Retrieved from www.ideadata.org/PartBData. asp

VanAcker, R. (2004). Current status of public education and likely future directions for students with emotional and behavioral disorders. In L. M. Bullock & R. A. Gable (Eds.), *Quality personnel preparation in emotional/behavioral disorders: Current perspectives and future directions* (79–93). Denton, TX: Institute for Behavioral and Learning Differences.

Wagner, M., Kutash, K., Duchnowski, A. J., Epstein, M. H., & Sumi, W. C. (2005). The children and youth we serve: A national picture of the characteristics of students with emotional disturbances receiving special education. *Journal of Emotional and Behavior Disorders, 13,* 79–96. doi:10.1177 /1063426605013002020

Wehby, J. H. (2003*). Promoting academic success as an incompatible behavior.* Paper presented at the Council for Children with Behavioral Disorders International Forum, Las Vegas, NV.

Wilson, D. (2004). The interface of school climate and school connectedness and relationships with aggression and victimization. *Journal of School Health*, *74*, 293–299.

Wodrich, D. L., & Spencer, M. L. (2007). The other health impairment category and health-based classroom accommodations: School psychologists' perceptions and practices. *Journal of Applied School Psychology, 24,* 109–125.

Wright, S., & Sulkowski, M. L. (2013). Treating childhood anxiety: How school psychologists can help. *Communiqué, 41,* 1, 12.

14 Highly Vulnerable Student Populations

Specific groups of students are vulnerable to experiencing significant academic and social-emotional problems that negatively impact their quality of life and long-term functioning. However, these youth differ in the ways that they are vulnerable and how these vulnerabilities impact them. Some youth are subjected to highly adverse settings that lack critical environmental and developmental supports (e.g., safety, security, supportive caregivers, stable conditions for learning, adequate living conditions). These students include homeless students, students who are in foster care settings, and students who are in juvenile and criminal justice systems. In general, these students often lack support from important family members and caregivers, are highly transient, frequently change schools, experience extreme disruption in their lives, and often display marked academic and social-emotional problems.

This chapter discusses the plight of these students as well as ways that educators can help them. Other vulnerable populations have been discussed in previous chapters (e.g., students with mental health problems, LGBT students, etc.); however, homeless students, students who are in foster care settings, and students who are in juvenile and criminal justice systems share a unique vulnerability that places them at a distinct risk. Essentially, they have all experienced environmental instability and likely have had their academic, family, and community stability challenged. Although highly vulnerable and at-risk students face formidable challenges, educators can do a lot to help stabilize these students and help protect them from experiencing negative academic and life outcomes.

Highly Vulnerable Students

Highly vulnerable students such as students who are homeless, in foster care, and who have been in juvenile justice settings are some of the most misunderstood students that attend schools (Jozefowicz-Simbeni & Israel, 2006; Pecora, 2012; Skowyra & Cocozza, 2007). Often, these students are incorrectly labeled as deviant, disruptive, or even deleterious to the school environment and the education of their peers. However, these students are highly variable and it is unfairly pejorative to make any assumptions about any particular student who may fall into one or more of the aforementioned categories of risk. In addition, despite displaying unique vulnerabilities, many of these students also display considerable strengths and resiliency factors that enable them to succeed in school and life in spite of the formidable challenges and barriers they face (Kidd & Shahar, 2008; Milburn et al., 2009).

Homeless Students

Research indicates that the number of homeless students enrolled in U.S. public schools is at an all-time high (Aviles de Bradley, 2011; Miller, 2011; Sulkowski & Michael, 2014). Rates of homeless students have increased 72 percent since the beginning of the 2008 economic recession and 10 percent from the 2011–2012 school year, which places the number of U.S. homeless students at over a million (National Association for the Education of Homeless Children and Youth [NAEHCY], 2014). Moreover, whether or not they are identified as homeless, approximately two million students may live on the streets on any given night (Edidin, Ganiam, Hunter, & Karnik, 2012; Miller, 2011). Thus, student homelessness is a prevalent and growing problem and most educators will encounter homeless students in the schools in which they work (Sulkowski & Joyce-Beaulieu, 2014; Sulkowski & Michael, 2014).

Research indicates that approximately 87 percent of homeless school-age youth are enrolled in school, yet only 77 percent of these students regularly attend school and more than 50 percent of homeless children miss more than two weeks of school per year. Moreover, 40 percent of these students attend two or more different schools each year (National Center on Family Homelessness (NCFH), 2009; U.S. Department of Education, 2004). Homeless students are highly at risk for experiencing poor academic outcomes, largely because of attendance problems, instability in where they attend school, and other related barriers to learning. Thus, the road to graduation is challenging for homeless students, as evidenced by statistics indicating that only about 25 percent of these students graduate from high school (NCFH; 2009). Furthermore, at some point during their K-12 educational career, 45 percent of homeless students will repeat at least one grade, 25 percent will fail a class, and 42 percent will be in jeopardy of failing a class at any given time (Buckner, Bassuk, & Weinreb, 2001). Regarding their proficiency with academic skills, homeless students on average are 16 percent less proficient in math and reading than their non-homeless peers are (NCFH, 2009). Therefore, homeless students are one of the most at-risk populations of youth to experience marked academic problems.

Although homeless students generally value their education and desire to succeed in school (Rafferty, 1995), formidable barriers to their educational success exist. As many as 86 percent of homeless students might meet diagnostic criteria for a psychiatric disorder (Ginzler, Garrett, Baer, & Peterson, 2007), 70 to 90 percent report using illicit drugs (Edidin et al., 2012; Nyamathi et al., 2010), and one study found that 84 percent of homeless youth screened positive for childhood physical and/or sexual abuse (Keeshin & Campbell, 2011). Many of these students are desperate or face dire circumstances that make them more likely to engage in extremely risky and self-compromising behaviors. In this regard, research indicates that a concerning number of homeless youth engage in "survival sex" or the practice of trading sexual favors for getting basic needs met (e.g., food, shelter; Walls & Bell, 2011) and some studies suggest that up to 63 percent of homeless youth have some form of a sexually-transmitted disease or infection (Busen & Engebretson, 2008; Rice, Milburn, & Rotheram-Borus, 2007).

Largely because of the extreme stressors they face and the difficulties that they experience coping with various adversities, it is not surprising that a large percentage of homeless students are psychologically maladjusted. In fact, research suggests that 50 percent of homeless students regularly experience suicidal thoughts (Yoder, Hoyt, & Whitbeck, 1998) and 20–40 percent of homeless students will attempt suicide at some point prior to adulthood (Greene & Ringwalt, 1996; Molnar, Shade, Kral, Booth, & Watters, 1998). When considering these statistics, keep in mind that only about 3 percent of non-homeless youth attempt suicide (King et al., 2001). Moreover, actual mortality rates among homeless students —often related to suicide and drug overdose—are estimated to be between eleven and forty times higher than they are for their non-homeless peers (Edidin et al., 2012).

Helping Homeless Students

Educators and other members of school communities can help provide a strong foundation at school for homeless students to succeed. In fact, for some homeless students such as unaccompanied youth[1] who do not have a consistent adult caregiver taking care of them, adults at school may be the only adults that they regularly interact with and trust (Jozefowicz-Simbeni & Israel, 2006; Julianelle, 2008). Therefore, it is important for educators to make homeless students feel welcome, safe, and secure at school. To do this, educators can work with other members of the school and local community to ensure that the physical, social, emotional, and academic needs of homeless students are being supported both in and outside of school by reaching out directly to them and to the individuals in their lives who help support them such as relatives, step and surrogate parents, neighbors, social workers, group home directors, mentors, and others.

It is important to emphasize that educators may not know much about homeless students and that these youth usually do not identify with the label of "homeless" because of shame, embarrassment, lack of understanding of the term (e.g., we have a home—we live in Trailhead's Campground) or because of concerns that Child Protection Service (CPS) workers may try to remove them from their current living situation and force them to live in an undesirable setting, such as with an abusive biological parent (Aviles de Bradley, 2011; Kidd, Miner, Walker, & Davidson, 2007; Miller, 2011). Therefore, it is critically important for educators to carefully broach discussions with homeless students or students whom they think might be homeless. Specifically, they should be sensitive to the stress that these students often experience, and the difficulties they may face with activities that usually are not problematic for students living in stable settings such as turning in assignments on time. They should openly express that they are not trying to cause them any more stress and rather are there to help them feel safe and supported at school. In addition, it is important for educators to recognize and compliment the strengths that homeless students display. Research indicates that many homeless students display high amounts of independence, resourcefulness, self-esteem, and they may be taking care of other individuals such as younger siblings (Cleverly & Kidd, 2010; Milburn et al., 2009). Therefore, it is important to recognize the considerable amount of resiliency and adaptive behaviors displayed by these youth and address the needs of homeless students on a case-by-case basis.

Youth do not automatically come into school and announce that they are homeless. This is often due to shame, embarrassment, and fear of rejection by peers and teachers. However, these youth need to be identified because they have specific rights mandated by law and can access additional supportive school and community services. Table 14.1 lists some common signs of student homelessness. However, there is no cut-off number of signs that need to be present to predict homelessness and certainly many homeless youth will not display all or even a majority of these characteristics. Nonetheless, educators may wish to consult this table in addition to other information sources provided by colleagues or community members before broaching this topic with students or their families.

The McKinney–Vento Act (McK-VA; 42 U.S.C. §11431 et seq.), which was re-authorized under No Child Left Behind (NCLB; P.L. 107–110, 2001), was enacted to prevent homeless students from being barred enrollment in schools or forced to transfer to schools when their place of residence or shelter changed (Sulkowski & Joyce-Beaulieu, 2014). In other words, the McK-VA guarantees the rights of homeless students to a "free and appropriate public education," even if they cannot furnish documents that usually are required to enroll in school such as a birth certificate or a social security card (Sulkowski & Michael, 2014). In addition, the act requires every local education agency (LEA) to employ a homeless liaison who is charged with the task of actively identifying all homeless youth who reside within the LEA in which they work as well as facilitating the enrollment of these youth, the coordination of needed services and supports (e.g., stable housing in the community, health and dental care, the provision of basic necessities), and appropriate educational services. Therefore, to support the physical and other needs of homeless students, it is important for educators to contact the homeless liaison who is working in their respective LEA and consult with this individual to ensure that a homeless student in their school is provided with important resources and referrals to requisite agencies (Sulkowski & Joyce-Beaulieu, 2014). Text Box 14.1 lists the major provisions in the McK-VA and what these provisions mean for educators who work with homeless students.

Table 14.1 Common Signs of Student Homelessness

- Lack Of Continuity in Education
  - Attendance at many different schools
  - Lack of records needed for enrollment
  - Gaps in skill development

- Poor Health/Nutrition
  - Lack of immunizations and/or immunization records
  - Unmet medical or dental needs
  - Chronic hunger
  - Hoarding, inappropriately saving, or stealing food
  - Excessive fatigue (falling asleep in class)

- Transportation and Attendance Problems
  - Erratic attendance or tardiness
  - Inability to contact parents
  - Numerous absences
  - Avoidance of field trips and activities that involve engaging parents

- Poor Hygiene
  - Lack of basic health supplies
  - Lack of shower facility or resources to stay clean

- Not Ready for Class
  - Lack of basic school supplies
  - Concern for the safety of belongings/possessions
  - Incomplete or missing homework

- Social or Behavioral Cues
  - Difficulty trusting people
  - Avoidance of events that include parents at school
  - High emotional reactivity
  - Associating with other homeless students
  - Avoidance of talking about parents or caregivers
  - Difficulty with sharing family experiences
  - Shame about one's background, home, or living situation

- Reactions by Parent, Guardian, or Child
  - Anger or embarrassment when asked about current address
  - Mention staying with grandparents, other relatives, friends, or in a motel
  - Making comments such as:
    - "I don't remember my last school"
    - "We've been moving around a lot"
    - "Our address is new—I can't remember it" (may hide lack of a permanent address)
    - "We're going through a bad time right now"

Note
These warning signs were adapted from resources provided by the Arizona, Illinois, and Pennsylvania Departments of Education. They are available at the following link: www.azed.gov/wp-content/uploads/PDF/CommonSignsofHomelessness. pdf.

Text Box 14.1 The McKinney-Vento Act and what this Act Means For Educators

The McK-VA is a federal law that guarantees the immediate enrollment and stability of school place-ment for homeless students. The McK-VA allows for the provision of federal funding to states for the purpose of supporting the homeless students they serve.

(continued)

(continued)

Defining Homeless

Under McK-VA, homeless students are defined as: "individuals who lack a fixed, regular, and adequate nighttime residence." Furthermore, examples of children who would fall under this definition are provided in the act:

- children and youth sharing housing due to loss of housing, economic hardship or a similar reason
- children and youth living in motels, hotels, trailer parks, or camp grounds due to lack of alternative accommodations
- children and youth living in emergency or transitional shelters
- children and youth abandoned in hospitals
- children and youth awaiting foster care placement
- children and youth whose primary night-time residence is not ordinarily used as a regular sleeping accommodation (e.g. park benches, etc.)
- children and youth living in cars, parks, public spaces, abandoned buildings, substandard housing, bus or train stations
- migratory children and youth living in any of the above situations.

Enrollment and Transportation Issues

The McK-VA requires LEAs to enroll homeless youth immediately, even if they lack documents that usually are required for enrollment such as immunization records or proof of residence. Further, if it is in the student's best interest, the act ensures that homeless students receive transportation to and from their school of origin.

School District Responsibilities

LEAs must designate a homeless liaison that is charged with the task of ensuring that homeless students are identified and provided with adequate educational services. The liaison must reach out to homeless students at school and in the community to increase their access to school services. School districts are also required to track their homeless students and report that data annually to the state educational agency (SEA).

A list of resources to assist educators with helping homeless students as well as the names and contact information for homeless liaisons in each LEA is included on the webpage for the Department of Education (DOE) in each state. For example, the Arizona DOE's webpage includes a compendium of resources for educators under a page entitled "McKinney-Vento Homeless Education" (www.azed.gov/populations-projects/home/homeless/), as well as a link to a regularly updated spreadsheet that lists all of the homeless liaisons within the state by their respective placement. Further, state DOE webpages also often include valuable resources for homeless liaisons and educators more generally to identify homeless students; facilitate their enrollment; provide them with needed transportation to and from school; identify and collaborate with community resources; help provide homeless students with behavioral health, mental health, and medical care services; and seek funding to help homeless students (Sulkowski & Joyce-Beaulieu, 2014). Lastly, under the McK-VA, each state is required to have a designated coordinator for homeless education who is responsible for helping to schedule and conduct trainings, workshops, and in-services for LEAs and school personnel on meeting the needs of homeless students in the state (Sulkowski & Michael, 2014).

Foster Care Youth

Youth are placed in out-of-home care settings such as in foster care because of maltreatment and when parents cannot effectively manage the youth's serious health, emotional, and behavioral problems. On any given day in the U.S., over 650,000 children and adolescents are placed in out-of-home care and approximately 400,000 are placed out of their homes in licensed foster family homes and in non-family group homes and residential treatment settings (U.S. Department of Health and Human Services (DHHS), 2012). These youth live in a variety of placements such as in foster family homes, supervised independent living shelters, and in other institutional settings and the need for foster placements exceeds the availability of homes by about 30 percent (DHHS, 2012).

Instability in their living placements is high among youth in foster care settings and rates of turnover also are concerning. Almost half (44 percent) of youth in foster care report that they have lived in more than three placement settings and 38 percent reside in group homes, shelter care, or other institutions. An identical percentage of youth in foster care (38 percent), report having a long-term goal of "emancipation" or aging out of long-term foster care when they turn 18 years old, have established an adequate place to live, and are making progress leading to independence (e.g., enrolling in educational programs, maintaining employment). Regarding this goal, sadly only about 10 percent of youth in foster care leave the system by emancipation. Overall, the stability of the living placement has been found to be an influential determinate of outcomes for youth in foster care. For example, a study by Rubin, O'Reilly, Luan, and Localio (2007) found that unstable living conditions were associated with the manifestation of behavioral problems in youth in foster care and that youth living in stable conditions was a robust predictor of well-being among these youth.

Despite the small percentage of youth that leave the foster care system by emancipation, most of these youth graduate from high school (74 percent) and plan to attend college (70 percent; McMillen, Auslander, Elze, White, & Thompson, 2002; Pecora, 2012). However, few of these youth (3–11%) graduate with a bachelor's degree, when compared to 28 percent of 25–34-year-old individuals in the general population who graduate with this degree (Pecora et al., 2006). Thus, despite having strong ambitions, many of these youth are not able to achieve their educational goals. Similar to homeless students, youth in foster care settings also commonly experience considerable academic problems in K-12 schools. Research indicates that about one- third to one half of youth in foster care are retained at least once during their schooling experience (Advocates for Children of New York, 2000; Courtney, Terao, & Bost, 2004; Pecora et al., 2006). Furthermore, children in foster care often are placed in special education, are referred for disciplinary problems, drop out of school, and lag behind their peers in reading, writing, and math achievement (Quest, Fullerton, Geenen, & Powers, 2012; Scherr, 2008; Zima et al., 2000).

In addition to experiencing academic problems, youth in foster care are also highly at risk for experiencing other adverse life events. For example, research indicates that approximately 50–66 percent of these youth experience at least one traumatic event in their lifetime, such as abuse, neglect, exposure to domestic violence, or being victimized in a violent attack among other events (Copeland, Keeler, Angold, & Costello, 2007; Finkelhor, Turner, Ormrod, & Hamby, 2009). Research by Berlin, Vinnerljung, and Hjern (2011) indicates that poor academic achievement among youth in foster care settings is a significant risk factor for developing social-emotional problems. For example, they found that a majority of boys (60 percent) and 42 percent of girls in long-term foster care had low grades in primary school (compared to 22 percent and 11 percent respectively in the general population). Furthermore, they found that youth in foster care were much more likely than their peer counterparts to attempt suicide, engage in serious criminal activity, and become dependent on public welfare before age 25.

Supporters of foster care note that although 70–80 percent of children in out-of-home care have been abused, neglected, or mistreated in some way in their home of origin, further mistreatment in another setting usually is averted in the majority of foster care cases (Chamberlain, Price, Leve, Laurent, Landsverk, & Reid, 2008; Lawrence, Carlson, & Egeland, 2006). However, even if subsequent mistreatment is prevented, considering that the majority of these youth have been mistreated at some point, it is not surprising that youth in foster care also display high rates of psychiatric and mental health problems. In this regard, research indicates that as many as 63 percent of youth in foster care meet diagnostic criteria for a psychiatric disorder, with the highest rates for Oppositional Defiant Disorder (29 percent), Conduct Disorder (21 percent), Major Depressive Disorder (19 percent), and Attention-Deficit/Hyperactivity Disorder (15 percent; White, Havalchak, Jackson, O'Brien, & Pecora, 2007). Moreover, behavioral and mental health problems have been associated with placement breakdowns for youth in foster care (Oosterman, Schuengel, Wim Slot, Bullens, & Doreleijers, 2007), which highlights the importance of addressing these problems to improve the stability of living placements for youth in this situation.

Helping Youth in Foster Care

Establishing and maintaining healthy connections and attachments to important adults such as primary caregivers is essential to feeling secure and supported. Thus, because of the strained relationships that youth in foster care have had with their parents or caregivers that resulted in their removal, these students may feel psychologically vulnerable and have difficulty with trusting and forming new relationships with caregivers and adults such as teachers, case workers, and school-based mental health professionals (Britner & Kraimer-Rickaby, 2005; Leslie et al., 2005). In addition, youth in foster care, especially if they have been abused or have had to change their residence often or attend new schools, may experience negative emotions such as anger, confusion, ambivalence, and disinterest when others might expect them to feel positive emotions such as happiness and gratitude from being helped, supported, or engaged at school or elsewhere (Scherr, 2008). Furthermore, these youth may withdraw, isolate themselves socially, repeatedly test rules and boundaries, appear overly passive and/or dependent, or engage in paradoxical or even self-compromising behaviors such as starting fights with new caregivers and adults who are trying to help them (McKellar, 2007).

However, despite these challenges, concerned educators are well positioned to help youth in foster settings, even if they do not have a lot of experience working with this population. A study by Ahrens, DuBois, Richardson, Fan, & Lozano (2008) found that youth in foster care that were mentored by or connected to important adults were more likely to have favorable overall health outcomes and were less likely to report having experienced serious health, behavioral health, and mental health problems such as transmitting a sexually transmitted infection, getting into a physical altercation that resulted in injury, or experiencing suicidal ideation. Moreover, in the same study, students who reported having meaningful connections with adults also were more likely to experience positive academic outcomes such as enrolling in college classes when compared to their peers without these connections.

Consequently, educators can redouble their efforts to forge meaningful connections with youth in foster care and they can do this by establishing enduring and stable relationships with these students. Youth in foster care may experience significant variability in their daily moods, social behavior, and academic performance that is related to the instability that they face in their lives (Scherr, 2008). Consequently, educators should not be surprised and can expect that these students will act inconsistently. Thus, according to McKellar and Cowan (2011), it is important for educators to be patient and consistent with their efforts to develop trusting relationships with students in foster care, as these students may be primed to expect that educators and other adults will abandon them or neglect their needs. In addition, the previous authors recommend

Table 14.2 Recommendations for Educators to Help Support Students in Foster Care

- Orient the new student to the classroom: When the child is first enrolled in the school, the teacher should help the child to understand how the classroom is organized and the academic and behavioral expectations for all students.
- Determine academic needs: Use task and error analyses to assess the child's knowledge and skills relevant to the curriculum. If the school has a tutoring program, consider whether the foster child might benefit by serving as a tutor or receiving tutoring.
- Reinforce strong social skills: Many foster children have good interpersonal skills and are eager for approval and affection. Interventions that capitalize on such characteristics, such as cooperative learning and positive reinforcement, should be implemented.
- Teach executive skills: Goal setting, problem-solving, and organization are important skills for all students and these are ones that children in foster care can carry with them if they do change schools. Start with small but meaningful goals that can be accomplished in a few weeks.
- Establish relationships with foster parents: School personnel should establish and maintain a good relationship with the foster parents to facilitate the foster parent's involvement in the child's education. They need to feel welcome in the school and should be kept fully informed, because any intervention involving home–school contingencies requires full cooperation of the foster parents. Teachers need to monitor the completion of assignments and work with the foster parents to make sure that homework is completed.
- Consider the appropriate involvement of biological parents: The extent, timing, and type of involvement of the biological parents in the child's education should be discussed by the school team, the foster parents, and the child's case manager.
- Limits to accessing information: The foster child's rights to confidentiality and privacy may result in less background information available to the school team than what is typically available for planning assessment and intervention services. However, the teacher should ask the foster parents about the child's special needs, problems, or interests.
- Seek health information: The school nurse should be asked to assess the child's health needs and to attempt to obtain immunization records from the child's previous school.
- Use strategies that are effective with abused children: Special attention should be given to the child management approaches used with foster children who have experienced abuse and/or neglect.

Source: Reproduced from: NASP *Communiqué*, Vol. 36, #4 December 2007; Foster Care for Children: Information for Teachers, By Nancy McKellar, Ph.D., Wichita State University.

that educators combat stigmatization associated with being involved with the foster care system. They need to be sensitive to various difficulties that these students have with completing certain assignments that may be emotionally overwhelming, such as constructing a family tree. Table 14.2 lists additional recommendations for educators to help support students in foster care.

In Expert Interview 14.1, Shamika Patton, a child case worker and school psychologist, discusses her experiences working with abused and neglected youth who often end up in the foster care system. In addition she discusses how educators should respond to help this highly vulnerable student population.

Expert Interview 14.1 with Shamika Patton

Seminole Tribe of Florida

PJL. You have been a case worker and supervisor working with abused and neglected children and those in foster care for the Florida Department of Children and Families, and now work overseeing programs for the Seminole Tribe of Florida. Have you seen this problem of abuse and neglect increasing over the past few decades? If so, why do you think that is the case?

SP. Yes. I just recently reviewed statistical data and according to an article written by the Sun-Sentinel, investigators working for the Broward Sheriff's Office removed more than 1,525 children from their families during the 12 months ending June 30, 2013, compared with 1,129 in the same period the prior year (2012). In recent years, the number of child deaths in Broward County at the hands of a parent/caregiver has increased dramatically. This unfortunate increase has led to the Department of Children and Families being more careful during abuse investigations and being more guarded about allowing children to remain in the home with a parent while receiving services to preserve the placement with the family.

I strongly feel that issues that contribute to the mental health instability of parents have increased over the past years. I have seen recent cases in the child welfare system of parental mental instability or psychopathology related to cruel and unusual/bizarre punishment of children (e.g., children being hog-tied in closets without being fed, children being burned with an iron/cigarettes, an infant hospitalized with 22 fractures, or death threats from parents).

Also, there has been an increase in sexual abuse cases due to some parents being unaware/ uninterested in knowing risks associated with allowing children to be too independent or being careless with who's caring for their children. Most children are sexually abused by someone they know. Some parents are allowing their children to stay over at a friend or family member's house and are not aware of signs that they are being abused by their male cousin, stepfather, or friend of the family. Also, some of the children who are sexually abused "act-out" or sexually perpetrate against their siblings or other children in the foster home or neighborhood,which causes more abuse/trauma.

In addition, the effects of the weakened economy have indirectly contributed to an increase in the cases of abuse or neglect. Due to the inability of finding employment, some individuals turn to drugs, alcohol, and/or prostitution which limit their ability to care appropriately for their children. Another issue that has arisen over the years is the number of infants being substance exposed to various illegal drugs in utero, which has in some cases caused a delay in the child's development. It is a very unpleasant sight to see the traumatic effects of a newborn infant suffering from withdrawal of cocaine, or methamphetamine in the hospital.

Further, the increase in domestic violence cases is very concerning over the past couple of years. Some parents are staying in relationships despite ongoing domestic violence because their partner is their only source of support. Individuals in these relationships experience depression, low self-esteem, and neglect. All of these stressors have a direct effect on the safety and well-being of children.

PJL. If a teacher sees a child in her class that has marks or injuries on his or her body that may indicate physical abuse, what should the teacher do? Should the teacher talk to the child about this or should he/she refer the child to the school psychologist, school counselor, school social worker, or principal?

SP. If a teacher sees a mark or even suspects abuse or neglect he/she is mandated by law to call the state's abuse hotline. Once the teacher reports the abuse to the hotline, that information is confidential and only given to the investigator. The investigator may contact the individual who makes the report for follow-up information if needed.

I would not recommend that the teacher talk to the child about the abuse unless the child is initiating the conversation. If any detailed information is reported to the teacher, the teacher may be subject to testifying in court at a later date as a factual witness. Also, probing the child or talking in detail about the abuse might cause more emotional trauma to the child. The teacher should allow the investigator to speak to the child and ask questions, so the investigation is not compromised. If the child is emotionally distraught, the child should be referred to the school psychologist, school counselor, or social worker for immediate brief counseling.

PJL. What would be the best way to talk to a child about any type of abuse?

SP. I would not recommend the teacher probe or question the child about suspected abuse. The investigator assigned to the child's case will conduct their investigation. However, if the child initiates conversation, the teacher should take a supportive approach to the conversation. The educator should accept what the child says and not question any story inconsistencies, if any. Do not ask leading questions, request details, or encourage the child to disclose details of the abuse/ neglect. Make no promises or guarantees beyond your control, but ensure your support. Inform the child that there is someone that will talk to them to help protect them.

PJL. What are the obligations of all educators if they suspect that a child has been abused or neglected?

SP. Although every person has a responsibility to report suspected abuse or neglect, some occupations are legally required to do so. All school teachers, school officials, or school personnel are obligated to report any suspicion of abuse, abandonment, and/or neglect. In many states, a professionally mandatory reporter of child abuse/neglect is legally required to provide his or her name to the Abuse Hotline Counselor when reporting. A professionally mandatory reporter's name is entered into the record of the report, but is held confidential. Failure to report child abuse is a third degree felony offense.

PJL. What are the best practices for school staff to follow who have to deal with suspected child abuse or neglect?

SP. Staff should contact the abuse hotline first; staff should notify a principal or assistant principal/school social worker/counselor of any suspicion. Staff should not call or confront a parent or even disclose any suspicion to the other parent. Any type of confrontation can sometimes lead to a parent fleeing with the child or further abuse to the child.

PJL. What are the most important things you want educators to know about child abuse and neglect?

SP. I believe it is very important for educators to be aware of the physical/emotional/mental trauma that a victim of abuse/neglect has endured. If it is known that a child is in foster care or out of the home with a relative, it is very important to be sensitive to the child's recent lifestyle change. Allow the child to adapt academically to their traumatic event. The following symptoms will directly affect their school functioning: sleep problems, anxiety and aggression, problems with attention and hyperactivity, and preoccupation with details of traumatic events. Therefore, be supportive, understanding, and nurturing.

In conclusion, I believe that we as professionals must be willing to put into action the community services necessary to break the cycles of abuse from generation to generation. I have seen teenagers in foster care having children at an early age who ultimately, sooner than later, enter the foster care system. We must see the sense of urgency to be more preventive instead of being reactive. We must get out and into the communities and provide the love and support many families need. As a case manager, the genuine love and support that I showed children and families on my caseload encouraged them to do better in their lives and community and to never walk through the child welfare system again.

Youth in Juvenile Justice Settings

About 1.6 million youth under the age of 18 are arrested in the U.S. each year (Puzzanchera & Kang, 2013). These youth include juvenile delinquents (i.e., minors who have committed offenses that would be classified as crimes if they were legally recognized as adults) and "status offenders," or youth who have committed offenses that only apply to children such as running away from home or school truancy. Although most cases involving arrested juveniles do not go to trial and instead result in probation without confinement or incarceration, approximately 70,000 U.S. youth under the age of 20 are in residential settings within the juvenile justice system including in detention centers, shelters, boot camps, and group homes (Sickmund, Sladky, Kang, & Puzzanchera, 2011). A large asymmetry exists between males and females in juvenile justice and criminal justice settings. For example, some estimates suggest that males outnumber females in these settings by seven to one. In addition, minority youth are over-represented in these settings, with African American youth making up 41percent of juveniles in residential placements (Sickmund et al., 2011).

The academic achievement and related outcomes of youth who engage in criminal or delinquent behaviors have received considerable empirical attention over the greater part of the last century (Glueck & Glueck, 1950; Katsiyannis, Ryan, Zhang, & Spann, 2008). Overall, results of this body of research indicate that these youth tend to underperform by a considerable margin when compared to their non-delinquent peers. In particular, youth in juvenile justice settings have been found to display pervasive deficits in core and foundational academic skill areas such as in reading and math. For example, in a study of 271 youth with juvenile delinquent histories, the great majority of these youth (95–98 percent) were reading below grade level (Beebe & Mueller, 1993) and in a more recent study, almost half (44 percent) of youth with juvenile delinquent histories were found to be reading at the elementary level (Zamora, 2005). In the aforementioned study by Zamora (2005), a similar yet slightly larger percentage (48 percent) of youth displayed elementary-level mathematics skills. In general, as a group, youth in juvenile justice settings tend to display serious academic skill deficits and problems. Additionally, they have been found to be maladjusted in other functional domains.

Although youth in juvenile justice settings often are thought of as being malicious and even predatory, many of these youth are afflicted by serious mental health problems. Research indicates that about 60–65 percent of these youth have a diagnosable psychiatric or mental health disorder and 20 percent of them display serious or extremely elevated forms of psychopathology (Skowyra & Cocozza, 2007; Teplin, Abram, McClland, Dulcan, & Mericle, 2002). Moreover, having substance abuse problems, being exposed to violent behavior, and having early sexual activity are all common in youth in juvenile justice settings (see Braverman and Murray (2011) for review). Lastly, similar to other highly mobile and highly at-risk students, a concerning percentage of these youth engage in suicidal behavior. For example, research suggests that youth in juvenile justice settings may be about 11 times more likely to attempt suicide compared to their peers who have not been impacted by the juvenile justice system (Thompson, Kingree, & Ho, 2006). In addition, a study by Thompson, Ho, and Kingree (2007) found that while controlling for demographic variables and a range of risk factors, being identified as a "juvenile delinquent" was associated with an increased risk for suicidal behavior at both one- and seven-year follow-ups.

Helping Students in Juvenile Justice Settings

Transitioning from the juvenile justice system to school is a formidable challenge for many students. They often must overcome academic coursework and credit deficits, changes in their school or grade cohort, problems associated with starting classes late, instructional deficits and inadequate access to the curriculum, and challenges with re-establishing (or even with establishing) their identity as students (Osher, Amos, & Gonsoulin, 2012; Quinn, Osher, Poirier, Rutherford, & Leone, 2005). They also tend to miss many days of school because of lingering legal issues and complications associated with the sometimes slow-moving juvenile justice system (Balfanz, Spiridakis, Neild, & Legters, 2003). In addition, youth impacted by the juvenile system may encounter negative attitudes and biases toward them and they may be inappropriately placed in restrictive school settings, such as in alternative schools that may focus more heavily on controlling disruptive student behavior than on providing enriching and appropriately-matched instruction (Osher, Sidana, & Kelly, 2008). Essentially, they must then overcome a combination of both personal and systemic challenges to be successful in school post-reintegration. It is not surprising then that many students who have been impacted by the juvenile system struggle to extricate themselves from the negative influences of these settings, especially if they feel like they have been inappropriately victimized and do not feel hopeful about their future. Unfortunately, this then puts many of these youth on a path toward re-offending and facing increasingly more serious punishments. This problematic trajectory has been called the "school-to-prison pipeline" and it is described as a phenomenon that leads to the criminalization of delinquent student behavior and the gradual transfer of students from educational to penal settings. Text Box 14.2 describes the school-to-prison pipeline and how it impacts highly vulnerable students.

Text Box 14.2 The School-to-Prison Pipeline and Vulnerable Students

The pervasive problem in the U.S. in which disadvantaged students are removed from school and placed in the juvenile justice system and eventually the criminal justice system has been called the "school-to-prison pipeline." This phrase regularly is used by organizations such as the American Civil Liberties Union (ACLU) and the Justice Policy Center that champions social justice and educational reform initiatives. Essentially, the "school-to-prison pipeline" described the upshot of a range of public, social, and political institutions being neglectful or derelict in providing disadvantaged and highly vulnerable youth with the academic, behavioral, and emotional supports they need to be successful in school and beyond. Thus, instead of being supported, these youth are placed in unstable, overly harsh, and violent settings such as juvenile and criminal justice settings that further exploit their risk factors and contribute to the creation of a vicious circle of violent offending and increasingly more restrictive forms of punishment for these individuals.

Supporting the academic success of students in juvenile justice settings is extremely important for helping these youth succeed in life as well as for reducing a major social and financial burden on society. The majority of individuals in prison in the U.S. have not completed high school and many of these individuals were incarcerated before they dropped out (Balfanz et al., 2003). Although some of these individuals complete General Educational Development (GED) degrees, which indicates that they have achieved basic proficiency in science, mathematics, social studies, reading, and writing, these youth still struggle vocationally and economically when compared to their peers who graduate with high school diplomas (Osher et al., 2012). More specifically, they tend to achieve lower rates of employment and they earn far less across the lifespan. Therefore, preventing dropout and ensuring that students impacted by the juvenile system have the opportunity to graduate from high school is important for the well-being of these youth as well as for helping them be better adjusted to society.

Educators can help youth from juvenile system settings in several ways. First, they can help to provide students with intensive transitional services to help them reintegrate into school settings, especially if they display academic skills deficits or a history of poor school attendance. Some of these services might involve peer or teacher mentorship, flexible academic tutoring, and mental health counseling. Considerable care is needed to assess and understand the academic profiles of youth who have encountered the juvenile justice system, as they likely will display both instructional and academic skills deficits from receiving fragmented instruction and learning opportunities. Second, it is important for educators to avoid applying overly punitive forms of school discipline such as Zero Tolerance policies, as these policies are ineffective and contribute to the school-to-prison pipeline (American Psychological Association Zero Tolerance Task Force, 2008). Sometimes students who transition from juvenile justice settings are treated as if they have two strikes against them, even if they have no previous history of having discipline problems at the specific school or district they are entering (Osher et al., 2008). Moreover, research indicates that Zero Tolerance policies for school discipline have no meaningful impact on reducing problematic behaviors at school and instead create additional problems for at-risk or vulnerable students, such as criminalizing minor behavior infractions and overly discriminating against students from minority backgrounds (American Psychological Association Zero Tolerance Task Force, 2008). See Chapter 15 on threat assessment and reducing school violence, and for more information on the impact of Zero Tolerance policies.

Restorative Justice

In lieu of implementing overly punitive forms of school discipline that may unfairly punish particular groups of highly vulnerable students, schools can implement restorative justice programs that aim to reduce antisocial behaviors at school and find fitting solutions for delinquent behavior. Restorative justice programs utilize extant school and community resources to deal with problematic student behaviors without resorting to the juvenile justice system. In addition, they also focus on maintaining a safe and supportive school environment for all students, including those who have been accused of engaging in delinquent behavior (Karp & Breslin, 2001).

Essentially, restorative justice is based on a philosophy of reparation, which involves holding students directly accountable for their actions and requiring them to undo harm/damages they have done to others. Within the restorative justice model, student misbehavior is viewed as a violation of a relationship, either between the offender and the victim or between the offender and the school community (Drewerey, 2004). Consequently, restorative justice focuses heavily on relationship building (Payne & Welch, 2015). Therefore, in order to repair the harm caused, the offending student and those individuals whose trust was violated must reconcile to mend the relationship. This practice also involves all relevant stakeholders (e.g., victims, parents, educators) in a decision-making process that clearly articulates how reparations will be met. Thus, as an example of restorative justice, a child who starts a fight with another student and as a result destroys personal property might be required to apologize to the victim and his/her family as well as to others who have been impacted by his actions and pay for any damages or costs incurred. Furthermore, this student might also be required to engage in prosocial behaviors of some kind, such as cleaning up trash outside the school building or volunteering for a local non-profit organization to undo his harmful actions. Thus, it is not enough for the aggressor to simply say they are sorry, for appropriate restitution, they need to do something to make the situation better and/or help the victim feel better.

Unfortunately, rather than using restorative justice practices, many schools, especially those in neighborhoods with predominately African American populations, frequently use punitive discipline practices to control student behavior (Skiba, Michael, Nardo, & Peterson, 2002). Moreover, some schools now even involve police officers in efforts to address minor incidents of student misbehavior and school violations, a trend that can produce harsher consequences for offending students who are found responsible or guilty (Berger, 2002). Ultimately, this practice results in even more students being placed into the juvenile justice system. A recent study conducted by Payne and Welch (2015), using a national random sample, found that schools with a greater percentage of Black students are less likely to use such restorative justice practices (e.g., student conferences, peer mediation, restitution, and community services), practices that enhance community building. Unfortunately, this is occurring despite the evidence that a restorative justice approach can help create a positive school climate, build a sense of community, and improve student outcomes (Riestenberg, 2012). As noted by Payne and Welch (2015), "the racially disparate use of restorative justice . . . is troubling" (p. 555), especially because a proportionally higher number of racial minority students end up in juvenile justice settings. That is, schools that need restorative justice programs the most are the least likely to use them.

Although more research on restorative justice is needed across a range of different educational settings, preliminary studies indicate that such programs effectively reduce recidivism rates among juvenile delinquents and promote positive relationships among students, teachers, and other members of school communities (McKlusky et al., 2008). In addition, restorative justice practices are generally preferred by students and school community members over the traditional sanctions of detentions, suspensions, and expulsions (Drewery, 2004; Fields, 2003). Thus, restorative justice is a promising approach to addressing delinquent behavior in schools that warrants further empirical investigation and consideration. For further information, Text Box 14.3 lists the six core aspects of restorative justice as described by Amstutz and Mullet (2005).

Text Box 14.3 Six Core Aspects of Restorative Justice

Restorative justice is a research-based educational practice that is used to reduce suspensions, expulsions, and disciplinary referrals in K-12 schools. Restorative justice practices are variable and they can take a variety of forms that are centered on the following principles:

- focus on relationships first and rules and disciplinary practices second
- give voice to the person harmed and the person who caused the harm
- engage in collaborative problem-solving
- enhance personal responsibility
- empower change and growth
- include strategic plans for restoration/reparation.

Amstutz and Mullet (2005)

Cross-cutting Strategies for Helping Highly Vulnerable Students

At the most fundamental level, students who are homeless, in foster care settings, and who have been in juvenile justice settings need to feel a sense of safety and stability before they are fully ready to maximize their potential. From a hierarchy of needs perspective in which basic needs (e.g., food, shelter, etc.) need to be achieved before higher level needs can be prioritized (e.g., self-actualization), these youth must be free of chronic physical and emotional harm, feel supported by caregivers at home and school, and be able to foster meaningful connections with others (Kenrick, Griskevicius, Neuberg, & Schaller, 2010).

Because it is important for all students to feel supported to optimize their learning, Chapters 7 and 8 list specific ways that educators can provide students with social and emotional supports that also apply to highly vulnerable youth. In addition, it is important for educators to address specific issues that often complicate the delivery of educational services and supports to homeless students, students in foster care, and students from juvenile justice settings. For example, youth from all of these populations experience delays and disruptions in receiving educational records when they transfer schools and move across educational settings (Julianelle, 2008; Osher et al., 2012; Pecora, 2012; Sulkowski & Joyce-Beaulieu, 2014). Therefore, educators may need to come up with interim educational plans, individualized education plans (IEPs), and Section 504 accommodations for these youth while waiting for records to arrive from another school (Sulkowski & Michael, 2014). Further, instead of subjecting youth from highly vulnerable populations to the same educational standards as youth from non-transient populations, it can be beneficial to offer flexible educational programming and grading options such as allowing them to recover credits that they may have been unable to receive because their educational programming was interrupted (Jozefowicz-Simbeni & Israel, 2006).

Fostering interdisciplinary communication and collaboration among school and community professionals is important for helping a range of students with risks and vulnerabilities (Sulkowski, Wingfield, Jones, & Coulter, 2011). In this vein, highly vulnerable students may need even greater support across settings and wraparound care to help them succeed. Therefore, it is important for educators to reach out to school-based mental health and health service providers as well as community-based case workers to work together to ensure that the physical, emotional, and behavioral health needs of highly vulnerable students are being adequately addressed. Collectively, these individuals can work together to provide psychoeducation to key stakeholders about students who are homeless, in foster care settings, and who have been in juvenile justice settings and reduce stigma and marginalization of these youth, ensure that appropriate special educational services are being provided, help manage any legal problems that may be affecting these students, and assess relevant family, community, and cultural factors that may influence service-delivery.

Conclusion

Despite displaying considerable risks and vulnerabilities, homeless students, students in foster care, and youth who have been in juvenile justice settings are students first and foremost and they display their own unique strengths, skills, and abilities. The most effective way that educators can help highly vulnerable students is to help recognize their "islands of competence" (i.e., special areas of personal strength and skill), celebrate their unique abilities, and provide as many opportunities as possible for them to demonstrate their talents to succeed. Additionally, they should be treated like any other student, which implies that they should have access to the full range of services, supports, and opportunities that all K-12 students receive, including opportunities for enriched instruction, accelerated learning, and extracurricular activities. Highly vulnerable students should be unencumbered to learn and grow in schools, which may be the most consistent and stable environments that they visit on a regular basis. These students should also be able to make friends, connect with teachers, and identify with adult role models at school and in the community. Ultimately, while helping to address their vulnerabilities, educators must enrich the school experience of highly at-risk and vulnerable students while also surrounding them with a community of support.

Note

1 The National Association for the Education of Homeless Children and Youth (NAECHY, 2008) defines "unaccompanied homeless youth" as youth experiencing homelessness while not in the physical custody of a parent or guardian.

References

Advocates for Children of New York (2000). Educational neglect: The delivery of educational services to children in New York City's foster care system. Retrieved at http://www.advocatesforchildren.org/sites/default/files/library/educational_neglect_2000.pdf?pt=1.

Ahrens, K. R., DuBois, D. L., Richardson, L. P., Fan, M. Y., & Lozano, P. (2008). Youth in foster care with adult mentors during adolescence have improved adult outcomes. *Pediatrics, 121,* e246-e252.

American Psychological Association Zero Tolerance Task Force. (2008). Are zero tolerance policies effective in the schools? An evidentiary review and recommendations. *American Psychologist, 63,* 852–862. doi: 10.1037/0003-066X.63.9.852

Amstutz, L., & Mullet, J. H. (2005). *The little book of restorative discipline for schools.* Intercourse, PA: Good Books.

Aviles de Bradley, A. M. (2011). Unaccompanied homeless youth: Intersections of homelessness, school experiences and educational policy. *Child & Youth Services, 32,* 155–172.

Balfanz, R., Spiridakis, K., Neild, R. C., & Legters, N. (2003). High-poverty secondary schools and the juvenile justice system: How neither helps the other and how that could change. *New Directions for Youth Development, 99,* 71–89.

Beebe, M. C., & Mueller, F. (1993). Categorical offenses of juvenile delinquents and the relationship to achievement. *Journal of Correctional Education, 44,* 193–198.

Berger, (2002). Expansion of police power in public schools and the vanishing rights of students. *Social Justice, 29,* 119–130.

Berlin, M., Vinnerljung, B., & Hjern, A. (2011). School performance in primary school and psychosocial problems in young adulthood among care leavers from long-term foster care. *Children and Youth Services Review, 33,* 2489–2497.

Braverman, P. K., & Murray, P. J. (2011). Health care for youth in the juvenile justice system. *Pediatrics, 128,* 1219–1235.

Britner, P. A., & Kraimer-Rickaby, L. I. S. A. (2005). Abused and neglected youth. In D. L. DuBois & M. J. Karcher (Eds.), *Handbook of youth mentoring* (pp. 482–492).Thousand Oaks, CA: Sage.

Buckner, J. C., Bassuk, E. L., & Weinreb, L. F. (2001). Predictors of academic achievement among homeless and low-income housed children. *Journal of School Psychology, 39,* 45–69.

Busen, N. H., & Engebretson, J. C. (2008). Facilitating risk reduction among homeless and street-involved youth. *Journal of the American Academy of Nurse Practitioners, 20,* 567–575.

Chamberlain, P., Price, J., Leve, L. D., Laurent, H., Landsverk, J. A., & Reid, J. B. (2008). Prevention of behavior problems for children in foster care: Outcomes and mediation effects. *Prevention Science, 9,* 17–27.

Cleverley, K., & Kidd, S. A. (2011). Resilience and suicidality among homeless youth. *Journal of Adolescence, 34,* 1049–1054.

Copeland, W. E., Keeler, G., Angold, A., & Costello, E. J. (2007). Traumatic events and posttraumatic stress in childhood. *Archives of General Psychiatry, 64,* 577–584.

Courtney, M. E., Terao, S., & Bost, N. (2004). *Midwest evaluation of the adult functioning of former foster youth: Conditions of youth preparing to leave state care.* Chapin Hall Center for Children at the University of Chicago.

Drewery, W. (2004). Conferencing in schools: Punishment, restorative justice, and the productive importance of the process of conversation. *Journal of Applied Social Psychology, 14,* 332–344.

Edidin, J. P., Ganim, Z., Hunter, S. J., & Karnik, N. S. (2012). The mental and physical health of homeless youth: A literature review. *Child Psychiatry & Human Development, 43,* 354–375.

Fields, B. A. (2003). Restitution and restorative justice. *Youth Studies Australia, 22,* 44–51.

Finkelhor, D., Turner, H., Ormrod, R., & Hamby, S. L. (2009). Violence, abuse, and crime exposure in a national sample of children and youth. *Pediatrics, 124,* 1411–1423.

Ginzler, J. A., Garrett, S. B., Baer, J. S., & Peterson, P. L. (2007). Measurement of negative consequences of substance use in street youth: An expanded use of the Rutgers Alcohol Problem Index. *Addictive Behaviors, 32,* 1519–1525.

Greene, J. M., & Ringwalt, C. L. (1996). Youth and familial substance use: Association with suicide attempts among runaway and homeless youth. *Substance Use & Misuse, 31,* 1041–1058.

Glueck, S., & Glueck, E. (1950). *Unraveling juvenile delinquency.* New York: The Commonwealth Fund.

Jozefowicz-Simbeni, D. M. H., & Israel, N. (2006). Services to homeless students and families: The McKinney-Vento Act and its implications for school social work practice. *Children & Schools, 28,* 37–44.

Julianelle, P. (2008). Using what we know: Supporting the education of unaccompanied homeless youth. *Seattle Journal of Social Justice, 7,* 477–536.

Karp, D. R., & Breslin, B. (2001). Restorative justice in school communities. *Youth & Society, 33,* 249–272.

Katsiyannis, A., Ryan, J. B., Zhang, D., & Spann, A. (2008). Juvenile delinquency and recidivism: The impact of academic achievement. *Reading & Writing Quarterly, 24,* 177–196.

Keeshin, B. R., & Campbell, K. (2011). Screening homeless youth for histories of abuse: Prevalence, enduring effects, and interest in treatment. *Child Abuse & Neglect, 35,* 401–407.

Kenrick, D. T., Griskevicius, V., Neuberg, S. L., & Schaller, M. (2010). Renovating the pyramid of needs: Contemporary extensions built upon ancient foundations. *Perspectives on Psychological Science, 5,* 292–314.

Kidd, S. A., Miner, S., Walker, D., & Davidson, L. (2007). Stories of working with homeless youth: On being "mind-boggling". *Children and Youth Services Review, 29,* 16–34.

Kidd, S., & Shahar, G. (2008). Resilience in homeless youth: The key role of self-esteem. *American Journal of Orthopsychiatry, 78,* 163–172. doi: 10.1037/0002-9432.78.2.163

King, R. A., Schwab-Stone, M., Flisher, A. J., Greenwald, S., Kramer, R. A., Goodman, S. H., . . . Gould, M. S. (2001). Psychosocial and risk behavior correlates of youth suicide attempts and suicidal ideation. *Journal of the American Academy of Child & Adolescent Psychiatry, 40,* 837–846.

Lawrence, C. R., Carlson, E. A., & Egeland, B. (2006). The impact of foster care on development. *Development and Psychopathology, 18,* 57–76.

Leslie, L. K., Gordon, J. N., Lambros, K., Premji, K., Peoples, J., & Gist, K. (2005). Addressing the developmental and mental health needs of young children in foster care. *Journal of Developmental and Behavioral Pediatrics, 26,* 140–151.

McCluskey, G., Lloyd, G., Kane, J., Riddell, S., Stead, J., & Weedon, E. (2008). Can restorative practices in schools make a difference? *Educational Review, 60,* 405–417.

McKinney–Vento Homeless Assistance Act, 42 U.S.C. §11431 et seq. (2007).

McKellar, N. (2007). Foster care for children: Information for teachers. *Communiqué, 36.* Retrieved from http://www.nasponline.org/publications/periodicals/communique/issues/volume-36-issue-4/foster-care-for-children-information-for-teachers.

McKellar, N., & Cowan, K. (2011). Supporting students in foster care. National Association of School Psychologists. Retrieved from www.nasponline.org/resources/principals/Foster_Children_Sept%202011.pdf.

McMillen, C., Auslander, W., Elze, D., White, T., & Thompson, R. (2002). Educational experiences and aspirations of older youth in foster care. *Child Welfare, 82,* 475–495.

Milburn, N., Liang, L. J., Lee, S. J., Rotheram-Borus, M. J., Rosenthal, D., Mallett, S., & Lester, P. (2009). Who is doing well? A typology of newly homeless adolescents. *Journal of Community Psychology, 37,* 135–147.

Miller, P. M. (2011). A critical analysis of the research on student homelessness. *Review of Educational Research, 81,* 308–337. doi: 10.3102/0034654311415120

Molnar, B. E., Shade, S. B., Kral, A. H., Booth, R. E., & Watters, J. K. (1998). Suicidal behavior and sexual/physical abuse among street youth. *Child Abuse and Neglect, 22,* 213–222. doi:10.1016/S0145-2134(97)00137-3.

National Association for the Education of Homeless Children and Youth. (2008). *Unaccompanied homeless youth: Intersections of homelessness, school experiences, and educational policy.* Retrieved from www.naehcy.org/educational-resources/youth.

National Association for the Education of Homeless Children and Youth (2014). *Education for homeless children and youths program data collection summary.* Retrieved from http://center.serve.org/nche/downloads/data-comp-0910-1112.pdf.

National Center on Family Homelessness (2009). *America's youngest outcasts: State report card on child homelessness.* Newton, MA: Author.

No Child Left Behind Act of 2001 (2001). 20 U.S.C. § 603

Nyamathi, A., Hudson, A., Greengold, B., Slagle, A., Marfisee, M., Khalilifard, F., & Leake, B. (2010). Correlates of substance use severity among homeless youth. *Journal of Child and Adolescent Psychiatric Nursing, 23,* 214–222.

Oosterman, M., Schuengel, C., Wim Slot, N., Bullens, R. A., & Doreleijers, T. A. (2007). Disruptions in foster care: A review and meta-analysis. *Children and Youth Services Review, 29,* 53–76.

Osher, D., Amos, L. B., & Gonsoulin, S. (2012). *Successfully transitioning youth who are delinquent between institutions and alternative and community schools.* American Institutes for Research. Retrieved from www.neglected-delinquent.org/sites/default/files/docs/successfully_transitioning_youth.pdf.

Osher, D., Sidana, A., & Kelly, P. (2008). *Improving conditions for learning for youth who are neglected or delinquent.* The National Evaluation and Technical Assistance Center for the Education of Children and Youth who are Neglected, Delinquent, or At Risk, Washington, DC.

Payne, A. A. & Welch, K. (2015). Restorative justice in schools: The influence of race on restorative discipline. *Youth & Society, 47,* 539–564.

Pecora, P. J. (2012). Maximizing educational achievement of youth in foster care and alumni: Factors associated with success. *Children and Youth Services Review, 34,* 1121–1129.

Pecora, P. J., Kessler, R. C., O'Brien, K., White, C. R., Williams, J., Hiripi, E., & Herrick, M. A. (2006). Educational and employment outcomes of adults formerly placed in foster care: Results from the Northwest Foster Care Alumni Study. *Children and Youth Services Review, 28,* 1459–1481.

Puzzanchera, C., & Kang, W. (2013). *Easy access to FBI arrest statistics 1994–2010.* Retrieved from www. ojjdp.gov/ojstatbb/ezaucr/.

Quest, A. D., Fullerton, A., Geenen, S., & Powers, L. (2012). Voices of youth in foster care and special education regarding their educational experiences and transition to adulthood. *Children and Youth Services Review, 34,* 1604–1615.

Quinn, M. M., Osher, D. M., Poirier, J. M., Rutherford, R. B., & Leone, P. E. (2005). Youth with disabilities in juvenile corrections: A national survey. *Exceptional Children, 71,* 339–345.

Rafferty, Y. (1995). The legal rights and educational problems of homeless children and youth. *Educational Evaluation and Policy Analysis, 17,* 39–61.

Rice, E., Milburn, N. G., & Rotheram-Borus, M. J. (2007). Pro-social and problematic social network influences on HIV/AIDS risk behaviors among newly homeless youth in Los Angeles. *AIDS Care, 19,* 697–704.

Riestenberg, N. (2012). *Circle in the square. Building community and repairing harm in school.* St. Paul, MN: Living Justice Press.

Rubin, D. M., O'Reilly, A. L., Luan, X., & Localio, A. R. (2007). The impact of placement stability on behavioral well-being for children in foster care. *Pediatrics, 119,* 336–344.

Scherr, T. (2008). Best practices in working with children living in foster care. In A. Thomas & J. Grimes (Eds.), *Best practices in school psychology V (pp. 1547–1563).* Bethesda, MD: National Association of School Psychologists.

Sickmund, M., Sladky, T.J., Kang, W., & Puzzanchera, C. (2011). *Easy access to the census of juveniles in residential placement.* Retrieved from www.ojjdp.gov/ojstatbb/ezacjrp/.

Skiba, R. J., Michael, R. S., Nardo, A. C., & Peterson, R. L. (2002). The color of discipline: Sources of racial and gender disproportionality in school punishment. *Urban Review, 34,* 317–342.

Skowyra, K. R., & Cocozza, J. J. (2007). *Blueprint for change: A comprehensive model for the identification and treatment of youth with mental health needs in contact with the juvenile justice system.* Delmar: National Centre for Mental Health and Juvenile Justice.

Sulkowski, M. L., & Joyce-Beaulieu, D. K. (2014). School-based service delivery for homeless students: Relevant laws and overcoming access barriers. *American Journal of Orthopsychiatry, 84,* 711–719. doi: 10.1037/ort0000033

Sulkowski, M. L., & Michael, K. (2014). Meeting the mental health needs of homeless students in schools: A multi-tiered system of support framework. *Children and Youth Services Review, 44,* 145–151. doi: 10.1016/j.childyouth.2014.06.014

Sulkowski, M. L., Wingfield, R. J., Jones, D., & Coulter, W. A. (2011). Response to intervention and interdisciplinary collaboration: Joining hands to support children and families. *Journal of Applied School Psychology, 27,* 1–16. doi: 10.1080/15377903.2011.565264

Teplin, L. A., Abram, K. M., McClelland, G. M., Dulcan, M. K., & Mericle, A. A. (2002). Psychiatric disorders in youth in juvenile detention. *Archives of General Psychiatry, 59,* 1133–1143.

Thompson, M. P., Ho, C. H., & Kingree, J. B. (2007). Prospective associations between delinquency and suicidal behaviors in a nationally representative sample. *Journal of Adolescent Health, 40,* 232–237.

Thompson, M. P., Kingree, J. B., & Ho, C. H. (2006). Associations between delinquency and suicidal behaviors in a nationally representative sample of adolescents. *Suicide and Life-Threatening Behavior, 36,* 57–64.

U.S. Department of Education, National Center for Homeless Education (2014). *Education for homeless children and youth program data collection summary from the school year 2011–12 federally required state data collection for the McKinney-Vento Education Assistance Improvements Act of 2001 and comparison of the SY 2009–10, SY 2010–11 and SY 2011–12 data collections.* Greensboro, NC. National Center for Homeless Education.

U.S. Department of Health and Human Services, Administration for Children and Families. (2012). The AFCARS report. Retrieved from www.acf.hhs.gov/programs/cb/stats_research/afcars/tar/report17. htm.

Walls, N. E., & Bell, S. (2011). Correlates of engaging in survival sex among homeless youth and young adults. *Journal of Sex Research, 48,* 423–436.

White, C. R., Havalchak, K., Jackson, L. J., O'Brien, K., Pecora, P. J. (2007). *Mental health, ethnicity, sexuality, and spirituality among youth in foster care: Findings from the Casey Field Office Mental Health Study.* Seattle, WA: Casey Family Programs. Retrieved from www.casey.org.

Yoder, K. A., Hoyt, D. R., & Whitbeck, L. B. (1998). Suicidal behavior among homeless and runaway adolescents. *Journal of Youth and Adolescence, 27,* 753–771.

Zamora, D. (2005). Levels of academic achievement and further delinquency among detained youth. *Southwest Journal of Criminal Justice, 2,* 42–53.

Zima, B. T., Bussing, R., Freeman, S., Yang, X., Belin, T. R., & Forness, S. R. (2000). Behavior problems, academic skill delays and school failure among school-aged children in foster care: Their relationship to placement characteristics. *Journal of Child and Family Studies, 9,* 87–103.

Part VI

Reducing School Violence and Preventing Suicide

15 Threat Assessment and Violence Prevention

School shootings and multiple victim attacks are exceedingly rare. However, they are extremely tragic and terrifying when they occur. Because of this, school shootings often affect an entire nation and they galvanize people toward wanting to prevent a similar event from occurring in the future. In response to school shootings, educators often worry that such a tragedy could occur in their own school and they may be concerned that harm could befall themselves and the students they serve (Borum, Cornell, Modzeleski, & Jimerson, 2010). This chapter discusses threats of violence to school communities as well as how educators can help with efforts to address these threats. Consistent with the expanded role of the educator, teachers, administrators, and other members of school communities are increasingly being recruited to help with strategies to reduce and mitigate school violence as well as maintain safe and supportive school environments. In particular, this chapter focuses on threat assessment procedures that have been found to be effective at addressing threats of violence and dispels misguided, ineffective, and even harmful approaches to reducing school violence and improving school safety. Lastly, this chapter concludes with suggestions on how educators should respond to threatening student behavior.

Reactions to Violent School Attacks

Because of the highly terrifying and devastating school attacks that have occurred in recent memory, it is not surprising that a range of options has been suggested to forestall such atrocities. Some of these options involve "target hardening" strategies, which aim to make schools harder to attack through implementing security technologies (e.g., metal detectors, automatic door locks, emergency call buttons, etc.), as well as increasing the number of armed law enforcement agents and school resource officers on site potentially to neutralize an attacker (Reddy et al., 2001). However, despite having positive intentions, many of these strategies are misguided and unlikely to thwart an attack before it occurs or quickly stop it once it does. In support of this position, most school shootings occur rapidly and are over in a matter of minutes, which makes it very hard for emergency response personnel to mitigate these attacks (Greenberg, 2007; Harnisch, 2008). In addition, because of the chaos, confusion, and incidents of miscommunication that occur during the "fog" of an attack, it is even difficult for trained emergency responders to identify an attacker, protect potential victims, and secure a school campus while an attack unfolds (Greenberg, 2007; Sulkowski & Lazarus, 2011). Therefore, in lieu of trying to stop an attack once it occurs, preventive strategies are needed to mitigate threats of violence to school communities (Cornell, 2003; Sulkowski, 2011). However, before delving into this subject, it is important to have a better understanding of the nature of these attacks as well as school violence more generally.

Threats of Violence to School Communities

Violent attacks at school are a major source of public concern, yet threats of violence far outpace the likelihood of these events actually occurring. For example, in one large study that included

35 different schools, 27 threats to kill another person and 24 threats to shoot someone were identified over the course of a school year. However, no actual acts of violence occurred in any of
these schools (Cornell et al., 2004). Furthermore, research on copycat threats that follow highly
publicized violent attacks indicates that threats are exceedingly more prevalent than actual incidents of violence. For example, research by Kotinsky, Bixler, and Kettl (2001) indicates that, in
the state of Pennsylvania alone, 354 threats of violence were reported in the 50 days that followed
the Columbine High School shootings in 1999, yet none of these threats materialized or resulted
in physical harm.

Because school attacks are highly publicized and aggressively investigated, a plethora of
data exists on these events and their frequency. According to research by Cornell and Nekvasil
(2012), 207 homicides occurred in U.S. schools between 1996 and 2006, which indicates that
an average of about 21 school-based homicides occur per year. Thus, if the country's 125,000
K-12 schools are divided by 21, the average school could expect to experience a student homicide about once every 6,000 years (Pollack, Modzeleski, & Rooney, 2008). Moreover, as further
evidence that school homicides are rare events, research by Modzeleski et al. (2008) indicates
that less than 1 percent of all homicides happen at school among youth (ages 5–18). Therefore, in
light of these findings, it is safe to conclude that the school environment is relatively safe. In fact,
research shows that most educational environments are safer than their surrounding communities
(Sulkowski & Lazarus, 2011).

Although multiple victim attacks in schools are rare, threats of violence are relatively common. According to research by the National Center for Education Statistics (NCES), almost half
of public schools (48 percent) experience a student-initiated threat of violence each year (Neiman
& DeVoe, 2009). Moreover, other studies indicate that about 5–10 percent of K-12 students have
been threatened by a peer with a weapon within the past year and that male students in middle
and high school are significantly more likely than females and their younger peers to be threatened (Nekvasil & Cornell, 2012; Roberts, Zhang, & Truman, 2010). In addition to overt threats,
many covert threats of violence also exist in school settings. According to the NCES, 6 percent
of students report having carried a weapon at school within the past year (Nieman & DeVoe,
2009). Thus, despite research indicating that this percentage is likely an overestimate (Cornell
& Nekvasil, 2012), even if a small proportion of youth who self-report that they carry weapons
at school actually do, all members of school communities ought to be concerned because of the
possibility that having access to weapons could result in lethal outcomes from regular student
conflicts that frequently occur, such as fights. However, it is important to note that most threats of
violence in school communities are not reported to adults, especially to adults at school. In support of this notion, one study found that only 22 percent of students who felt seriously threatened
by a peer reported this threat to an adult at school (Nekvasil & Cornell, 2012). Therefore, even
though mass acts of violence are rare, threats of violence in school communities are common and
many educators may be largely unaware of these threats.

Identifying Threats of Violence

Research indicates that someone usually has advanced knowledge of an ensuing violent attack at
school before it occurs. In this regard, results from the *U.S. Secret Service and U.S. Department
of Education (DOE) final report and findings of the safe school initiative* suggest that at least
one individual had prior knowledge of an attack before it occurred in the majority (81 percent) of
school shootings and often multiple people knew (Vossekuil, Fein, Reddy, Borum, & Modzeleski,
2002). Furthermore, another study that investigated nine U.S. school shootings found that all
school shooters had communicated their violent intentions to others before the attack and that
they even conveyed specific details about the future attack such as the time and place that they
expected it to occur (Verlinden, Hersen, & Thomas, 2000). However, it is important to note

that threatening statements vary in their specificity. Whereas some threats of violence might be directed toward specific individuals or environments, and indicate a planned time for an attack, others may be vague and devoid of precise details.

In a follow-up study to the *Final report and findings of the safe school initiative,* Pollack, Modzeleski, and Rooney (2008) investigated the relationships between informed bystanders (i.e., individuals with prior knowledge of attacks) and attackers, as well as how bystanders were informed of information pertaining to potential school attacks. Results of this study indicate that 34 percent of the informed bystanders were friends of attackers, 29 percent were peers (i.e., acquaintances, co-workers, classmates), 6 percent were family members, and 31 percent were other acquaintances (or they did not have close relationships with the attackers). Additionally, it was found that 82 percent of informed bystanders reported receiving information about an attack directly from an assailant (only 13 percent received this information secondhand), which suggests that most individuals who receive prior knowledge of school shootings often have close ties with attackers.

Characteristics of Potentially Threatening Students

To identify possible school shooters, profiles have been developed by law enforcement personal. An offender profile that was developed by the Federal Bureau of Investigation (FBI; Band & Harpold, 1999) and the "Classroom Avenger" profile, which was developed by McGee and DeBernardo (1999) are salient examples of this effort. However, the use of profiling techniques to identify future school shooters has been criticized, as concerns have been raised about their selectivity and specificity (Reddy et al., 2001). In other words, most individuals who fit a specified profile will not commit acts of violence and many school shooters do not embody characteristics that are described in the extant shooter profiles (e.g., having fascination with violence, being socially isolated; Fein et al., 2002; Reddy et al., 2001). Further, subsequent research by the FBI found that contrary to public perceptions, the characteristics displayed by school shooters could not be used for accurate profiling and that using the extant characteristics for this purpose would falsely identify and unfairly punish many students who pose no legitimate threat (O'Toole, 2000). For example, contrary to popular perceptions, few school shooters have histories of abuse (Langman, 2009), display psychotic symptoms (O'Toole, 2000), or are abnormally preoccupied with violent media sources such as violent video games (Ferguson, 2008). Thus, in light of these findings, the FBI's report cautions that "trying to draw up a catalogue or 'checklist' of warning signs to detect a potential school shooter can be shortsighted, even dangerous. Such lists, publicized by the media, can end up unfairly labeling many nonviolent students as potentially dangerous" (O'Toole, 2000, p. 2).

Even though surface characteristics cannot be used to profile or identify potentially threatening students, research by the U.S. Secret Service and the U.S. DOE found that several qualities are shared by the majority of school shooters (Vossekuil et al., 2002). Researchers in these organizations studied 37 attacks, involving 41 perpetrators, that took place in the U.S. between January 1974 and May 2000. Results of this investigation found that all school attackers were male, 98 percent had recently experienced or perceived a major personal loss (e.g., loss of family member, breaking up with a partner), 93 percent had planned the attack in advance of carrying it out, 83 percent had difficulty coping with a recent loss/perceived loss, 78 percent exhibited a history of suicidal thoughts/attempts, 73 percent had a grievance against at least one victim, and 71 percent felt persecuted, bullied, or vulnerable. In contrast, relatively few school shooters (17 percent) had been diagnosed with a psychiatric disorder, were motivated to attack to gain notoriety (24 percent), had previously received a mental health evaluation (34 percent), and demonstrated excessive interest with explosives (32 percent). Although no single one

Table 15.1 Percentages of School Shooters Displaying Specific Characteristics Prior to Carrying out Attacks

Characteristics of school shooters	Percentage of shooters with characteristic
Male	100
Recently experienced or perceived a major loss	98
Planned an attack in advance of carrying it out	93
Had difficulty coping with a recent loss/perceived loss	83
Exhibited a history of suicidal thoughts/attempts	78
Had a grievance against at least one victim	73
Felt persecuted, bullied, or vulnerable	71
Recently experienced a loss of social status or major failure	66
Had a history of feeling extremely depressed	61
Demonstrated excessive interest in violence	59
Experienced loss of a romantic relationship	51
Demonstrated excessive interest with weapons	44
Experienced a change in academic performance	44
Experienced a change in friendship patterns	41
Were frequently disciplined in school	37
Had previously received a mental health evaluation	34
Demonstrated excessive interest with explosives	32
Motive for attack included an attempt to gain notoriety	24
Had a diagnosis of a psychiatric disorder	17

Note: Data are reported by the U.S. Secret Service and U.S. Department of Education (Vossekuil et al., 2000)

of the aforementioned characteristics can be used to identify a possible school attacker with accuracy, these characteristics may best be used to identify students who display psychosocial adjustment issues and potentially could benefit from receiving mental health supports. Table 15.1 lists percentages of school shooters who displayed specific characteristics prior to carrying out attacks.

Threat Assessment

As previously noted, the great majority of school attackers convey threats to others before they perpetrate acts of violence (Pollack et al., 2008; Verlinden et al., 2000; Vossekuil et al., 2002). Therefore, it is important for all members of school communities to heed these important warnings. Consistent with this prerogative and with the goal of preventing future violent attacks at school, the *School shooter: A threat assessment perspective* (O'Toole, 2000) was created by the FBI's National Center for the Analysis of Violent Crime. The purpose of this document was to provide schools with a blueprint to evaluate and diffuse threats. To do this, schools are encouraged to use a multidisciplinary team of professionals to evaluate school threats using a four-pronged model. This model involves assessing and considering the following: (1) the personality and behavior of the student who made a threat; (2) the student's family dynamics; (3) the culture and climate of the school; and (4), the social dynamics of the larger community. However, despite these recommendations, this FBI report does not dictate how these assessments should be conducted.

To address this limitation, Cornell et al. (2004) refined and field tested the procedures outlined in the *School shooter*. During this process, 188 student threats were assessed in 35 primary (grades K-5) and secondary (grades 6–12) schools over the course of one school year. The study began with the organization of multidisciplinary threat response teams that consisted of school administrators (e.g., superintendent, principals), school psychologists, and school resource/law enforcement officers. However, preliminary meetings with school administrators revealed concerns about a lack of clear guidelines for evaluating threats. Additionally, school psychologists expressed concerns about their limited training on how to conduct psychological evaluations on students who had made threats of violence. To address these issues, a decision tree model was adopted to guide school-based professionals through the threat assessment process and school-based professionals were trained in following this process.

Results from the Cornell et al. (2004) study indicate that the use of the FBI's threat assessment guidelines allowed school administrators to resolve the majority (70 percent) of threats of violence quickly and efficiently without having to coordinate with multiple threat assessment team members. However, the remaining 30 percent of threats required a more extensive evaluation and intervention plan, including conducting a comprehensive psychological evaluation, designing interventions that involve caregivers or law enforcement officers, and notifying potential victims of targeted violence. It is impressive to note that only three students were expelled during the course of the study and no acts of violence were perpetrated. Collectively, results of the former study provide an impressive field test for the efficacy of threat assessment procedures. In addition, they suggest that these procedures can be applied in a diverse range of K-12 school settings.

The Virginia Student Threat Assessment Guidelines

In response to recommendations by the U.S. Secret Service and the FBI as well as early studies on the effective implementation of threat assessment procedures, researchers at the University of Virginia have developed, refined, and field tested threat assessment guidelines (Cornell, 2003; Cornell & Sheras, 2006). From previous research (e.g., Cornell et al., 2004), these guidelines— the Virginia Student Threat Assessment Guidelines (VSTAG)—use a decision tree format to allow members of school teams to comprehensively evaluate threats once they are made, categorize threats based on their severity and likelihood of being carried out, and inform educators on how to ensure the safety and security of school communities (see Cornell and Sheras, 2006, for the complete guidelines).

Figure 15.1 lists the VSTAG decision tree process for student threat assessment. Threats are categorized into transient threats (i.e., "a threat that could be resolved quickly and easily with an apology or explanation") and substantive threats (i.e., "lasting and enduring threats of causing serious harm to others"). Transient threats can be resolved easily and require few school resources, whereas substantive threats involve significant coordination among school team members to ensure that the threats are mitigated, potential victims are protected, and long-term supports are put in place to prevent the threatening student from harming members of the school community. Text Box 15.1 lists examples of transient and substantive threats.

Threat Assessment Teams

The VSTAG recommend for threat assessment teams to be comprised of school-based individuals as opposed to outsiders because these individuals will have a greater understanding of the needs of individual students and will likely be more nimble (Allen, Cornell, & Lorek, 2008). In addition, the inclusion of outside individuals such as community-based police officers is unnecessary because the majority of transient threats can be managed effectively by school-based professionals. Even further, the inclusion of outside professionals could magnify perceptions of threat and deplete needed resources from communities. However, with that said, it is important for school-based professionals to contact and cooperate with outside assistance when a substantive threat has been made and outside expertise is needed (Cornell & Nekvasil, 2012).

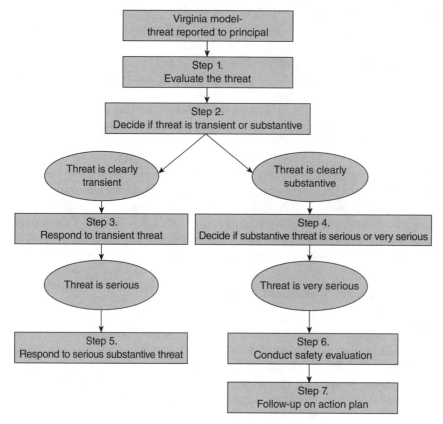

Figure 15.1 Decision Tree for Student Threat Assessment
Source: Cornell and Sheras (2006).

Text Box 15.1 Examples of Transient and Substantive Threats

Substantive threats

- I'm going to shoot people when they get off the bus in the morning.
- If I wanted to, I could off everyone.
- This place would be better off if I killed the principal.
- If I don't get on the team, I'm going to hurt the coach.

Transient threats

- I am going to pee on your leg if you don't quit bothering me.
- I am going to explode bombs in your pants.
- I am so angry we lost the soccer game, I feel like hurting someone.

The VSTAG specify that administrators should lead threat assessment teams because they have a primary responsibility to ensure school discipline and safety. In this role, school administrators first evaluate threats made by students through obtaining information about the threat via interviews, eyewitness accounts, and the presence of any potentially threatening physical evidence (e.g., weapons, illicit substances). During this process, administrators should carefully write down and record information that they are collecting to evaluate a threat and consider the context in which it occurred. Collectively, this information will allow for an assessment of the validity of the threat. For threats that convey little risk to members of the school community and are exceedingly unlikely to be carried out, the administrator usually can manage the incidents without the help of others. However, other threat assessment team members should be contacted if a threat is more concerning, complicated, or likely to be carried out and potentially cause harm.

Having law enforcement representatives who are familiar with educational practices, developmental issues that impact children and their behavior, student mental health concerns, and positive behavioral support practices is important for the development and coordination of threat assessment teams. See Chapter 10 for information on positive behavioral support practices. Ideally, these individuals will be school resource officers (SROs) who are members of the school environment (Cornell & Nekvasil, 2012). However, some schools may recruit law enforcement officers from the general community to fulfill this role, and if this is the case, it is important for members of the school community to ensure that these individuals have the previously mentioned knowledge and experience. As an integral team member, law enforcement officers can determine whether a particular student's behavior has violated the law and help the team to determine how to address illegal behaviors in schools. In addition, this individual can respond to violent conflicts among students, search potentially threatening students for weapons, and obtain a search warrant to investigate a student's home that may be harboring dangerous weapons.

School-based mental health professionals such as school psychologists, counselors, and social workers also should be included on threat assessment teams. These individuals can help administrators to evaluate a potentially threatening student's behavior and psychosocial functioning more generally. According to Cornell and Nekvasil (2012), evaluations conducted by school-based mental health professionals should aim to achieve two outcomes: (1) to screen a student for critical mental health issues such as homicidal thoughts, suicidality, psychosis, mania, derealization, and decomposition in functioning, and (2) to uncover why a particular student made a threat and what the student was trying to accomplish when he or she made the threat (e.g., obtain peer respect, retaliate against a bully, be suspended from school, etc.). In addition to these two aims, school-based mental health professionals should provide recommendations to other team members regarding a potentially threatening student's risk to him or herself and others as well as their overall psychosocial functioning.

Collectively, the aforementioned members of threat assessment teams should conduct a comprehensive interview to evaluate a potential threat. Team members should evaluate different aspects of the threat and the student's psychosocial functioning through collecting information from different data sources (e.g., students, caregivers, teachers) who may have witnessed concerning behavior in the student (Cornell, 2003). Overall, through this process, threat assessment team members will better understand the student in question, his or her behavior, and the risk that he or she poses to the school environment. However, this process will not allow for the perfect prediction of threats. Instead, team members should evaluate potential risks associated with including or removing the student from the school environment as based on his or her behavior. Again, research indicates that focusing on risk through employing a systematic threat assessment approach—although not a perfect procedure—allows for almost all threats of violence to school communities to be effectively managed (Cornell et al., 2004; Cornell, Gregory, & Fan, 2011; Cornell, Sheras, Gregory, & Fan, 2009; Strong & Cornell, 2008). In addition, the actual threat made in context can provide keen insight into a student's functioning. For example, telling a student "I am going to kill you" after being knocked down while going for the ball in a basketball game is a lot different than saying, "I am going to kill you with my Glock. You better be on the

Table 15.2 Assessments that School-based Mental Health Professionals Can Use to Augment Threat Assessments

Assessment	Number of Items	Major Constructs Measured	Ages (in Iears)
Behavioral Assessment Scale for Children, Second Edition (BASC-3)	60–75	Internalizing behavior problems, externalizing behavior problems, adaptive skills, school problems,	2–21
Child Behavior Checklist (CBCL)	120	internalizing behavior problems, externalizing behavior problems, social problems, thought problems, attention problems	6–18
Clinical Assessment of Behavior (CAB)	70	Internalizing behavior problems, externalizing behavior problems, adaptive skills, critical behaviors	2–18
The Conners-3	99–110	Externalizing behavior problems, learning problems, family/peer relations	6–18
Jesness Inventory-Revised	160	Antisocial behavior, delinquency	8–35
Hare Psychopathy Checklist, Youth Version	20	Antisocial behavior	12–18
Adolescent & Child Urgent Threat Evaluation (ACUTE)	27	Potentially homicidal behavior, suicidal behavior	8–18
Psychosocial Evaluation & Threat Risk Assessment	60	Threats of violence, psychosocial risk, suicide risk	11–18

lookout. You can never tell when I am going to go gunning for you." Table 15.2 details specific assessments that school-based mental health professionals can use to help augment the threat assessment process.

Aside from having specific competencies and professional backgrounds, it is important for members of threat assessment teams to display certain personal qualities. Evaluating threats of violence is inherently a stressful process that will produce a range of emotions among all who are involved. Therefore, members of threat assessment teams must possess a degree of equanimity that allows them to think clearly, objectively, and rationally when evaluating students and situations of concern. Their judgments must be based on accurately interpreting data that is collected through the threat assessment process. Moreover, they must do this in lieu of being swayed by preconceived notions regarding particular students, implicit or explicit biases that they may have, and their own history of being exposed to previous incidents of violence. Members must express sincere concern for the individual being evaluated, be empathetic, non-judgmental, and express a desire to problem solve rather than to punish. The mental health member of the team must also possess knowledge of psychopathology, psychopathy (i.e., a pattern of enduring anti-social behavior, diminished empathy and remorse, and disinhibited behavior), and be competent in suicide assessment. In light of these considerations, it is important for members of threat assessment teams to be highly trained and competent, sufficiently psychologically balanced, and to have the emotional fortitude to be up to the task. Further, it may be worthwhile to rotate positions on the team among equally skilled professionals to reduce potential emotional overload or burnout. Lastly, it also is crucially important to remove people from the team whose professional functioning is compromised for any reason.

The Threat Assessment Decision Tree

According to the VSTAG, threat assessment teams should follow a seven-step decision tree (see Cornell and Sheras (2006)). As a first step, a school administrator interviews a student who has made a threat using a standard set of questions. See Text Box 15.2 for a list of questions that have been adapted from the VSTAG and Text Box 15.3 for information on issues to focus on when conducting threat assessment interviews. As a general principle, these questions focus less on the verbal content of the threat than the overall context of the threat, which includes the student's intentions behind the threat, corroborating or disparate information from witnesses to the threat, the likelihood that the student in question could carry out the threat, and factors that would need to be considered to protect members of the school community from the threat.

Step two of the VSTAG involves determining whether a threat is transient or substantive. In general, transient threats do not convey a sustained desire to harm others whereas substantive threats do (Cornell & Nekvasil, 2012). Then, at step three, administrators take action to resolve transient threats. For example, this might involve having a student who made an unrealistic threat in a fit of anger apologize to another student or teacher. Conversely, if a threat is determined to be substantive (i.e., the threat conveys that a student intends to harm someone at some point in the future), then the administrator should coordinate with members of the threat assessment team to evaluate the seriousness of the treat. Thus, in summary, the first three steps of the VSTAG decision tree model involve quickly identifying a threat, determining whether it is transient or substantive, and deciding whether to involve a range of threat assessment team members to address the threat.

At step four, substantive threats (i.e., threats that convey that a student intends to harm someone at some point in the future) are determined to be either serious or very serious. A key distinguisher between serious and very serious threats is that serious threats might involve threatening to strike or beat up another person, whereas very serious threats involve an intention to kill, seriously injure, or sexually assault another person, (Cornell & Nekvasil, 2012; Cornell & Sheras, 2006).

Step five of the VSTAG involves coordinated effort by the threat assessment team to prevent a serious threat from being perpetrated, which can involve taking immediate protective actions such as warning the student about the consequences of his or her intentions, calling the student's parents and informing them of the threat, and suspending the student from school. Similarly, at step six, the team takes proactive actions to prevent a very serious substantive threat from occurring, which might involve calling law enforcement officers to intervene to protect the student and other individuals. At this point, a school resource officer or community-based police officer will need to determine whether a law has been broken and a school-based mental health professional should evaluate the student of concern using a structured assessment protocol. It is important to note that a landmark case decision from the *Tarasoff v. Regents of the University of California case* (17 Cal. 3d 425, 551 P.2d 334, 131 Cal. Rptr. 14) requires mental health professionals in many states to inform potential victims of homicide that they have been threatened. Thus, in these cases, even if the mental health professional and the potential perpetrator share a privileged relationship (i.e., a relationship such a therapeutic one that ensures the confidentiality of the information that is disclosed in therapy), the mental health professional is legally obliged to warn potential victims that the threatening individual names. However, even if no legal obligation exists within state statutes, it is highly recommended that all potential victims be warned and school districts can create a policy to this effect.

Lastly, step seven of the VSTAG involves creating a written safety plan with input from all threat assessment team members as well as information gleaned from individuals associated with and impacted by the threat. This plan often will stipulate important safety goals that must be met for school re-entry if a student is suspended or expelled and a plan for providing a student with important mental health supports such as counseling or therapy (Cornell & Nekvasil, 2012). The main goals of this plan are to protect the student who made a threat from undue harm and to ensure the safety of the school environment.

Text Box 15.2 11 Key Questions Provided by the U. S. Secret Service in Conducting a Threat Assessment

1. What are the student's motives or goals?
2. Any communications of intent to attack?
3. Any inappropriate interest in other attacks, weapons, or mass violence?
4. Any attack-related behaviors? Making a plan, acquiring weapons, casing sites, etc.
5. Does student have capacity to attack?
6. Is there hopelessness or despair?
7. Any trusting relationship with an adult?
8. Is violence regarded as way to solve a problem? Any peer influences?
9. Are student's words consistent with actions?
10. Are others concerned about student?
11. What circumstances might trigger violence?

Note that all of the Secret Service questions are oriented around determining if the student is on a behavioral pathway leading to an act of violence. There is considerable emphasis on situational and relationship factors and relatively little concern with personality factors or other individual characteristics that are often identified when profiling is used.

Text Box 15.3 Issues on Which to Focus When Conducting Threat Assessment Interviews

- Threat characteristics
  - estimated level of concern
  - involved a note
  - named a target
  - named a method of possible violence
  - access to weapons
  - evidence of planning
  - practice behaviors and history of making threats
  - how realistic
  - others are concerned.

- Person characteristics
  - suicidal behavior and intention (past and present)
  - conflict with other individuals
  - interest in death and violence
  - views violence as acceptable
  - has a violent motive
  - mental health and adjustment problems
  - recent personal loss
  - uncooperative during interview/assessment
  - few protective factors
  - little empathy for others
  - feels like a victim
  - experiencing relationship difficulties.

Expert Interview 15.1 features Dewey G. Cornell, Ph.D., who is an internationally known expert on threat assessment, particularly in school settings. In this interview, Dr. Cornell discusses the use of the VSTAG by members of school communities as well as how this approach is superior to others such as Zero Tolerance approaches to school discipline and safety. He also discusses what actions educators should take if they have been informed that a student has made a threat.

Expert Interview 15.1 with Dewey G. Cornell

University of Virginia

PJL. You have developed the Virginia Student Threat Assessment Guidelines for use in schools to help threat assessment teams evaluate students that may pose a threat. What are the most important things you have learned from school systems that have used your model? Has anything surprised you?

DGC. The positive response to this program has far exceeded my expectations. School-based teams have found it easy to apply the guidelines to their cases and feel confident that they are taking responsible and legally defensible actions to reduce the risk of violence. Schools have consistently been able to resolve student threats and keep almost all students in school. One of the most important things I have learned from school systems, however, is the need for central administration support and oversight to implement and maintain the threat assessment guidelines with fidelity. Especially when there is staff turnover in the principal's office, there can be a drop-off in a team-based approach. Nevertheless, I have been surprised to find that schools using the guidelines have sustained substantial reductions in school suspensions. It appears that schools are applying our approach to student threats to a wider variety of disciplinary situations and moving away from reliance on zero tolerance suspensions practices.

PJL. How does threat assessment differ from zero tolerance? And why do you think zero tolerance has not been effective?

DGC. Threat assessment is the antithesis of zero tolerance. In conducting a threat assessment you must always consider the student's intent and the context for the behavior, and you respond with consequences that are calibrated to the seriousness of the situation. In zero tolerance, you only consider whether the misbehavior occurred and you apply the same harsh consequences regardless of the circumstances or the student's intentions. It is a one-size-fits-all approach. It prevents administrators from using their good judgment and common sense. Zero tolerance sounds like a good idea to many educators, but empirically we find no evidence that it achieves its goals of deterring dangerous behavior and improving school safety. On the contrary, studies find that schools which make the greatest use of suspension have the worst student outcomes, including higher dropout rates and more juvenile court involvement. School removal has more negative effects than positive effects, because it fails to help students correct their behavior and causes them to fall further behind in their studies and return to school feeling alienated and frustrated, and so it is a failed experiment in school discipline that we need to put behind us.

PJL. Though your model has been shown to be highly effective in evaluating student threats, many school districts have not incorporated your model or developed specific well-defined procedures for their districts. What do you believe are the barriers to implementing the Virginia Model in schools? And can these barriers be reduced?

DGC. Schools are overwhelmed with the number of requirements they must meet and the number of programs pushed their way. School administrators, teachers, and mental health professionals are frequently understaffed and over-extended. There is a huge resource problem in education because of the way that schools are funded, largely because our legislators have an outmoded understanding of what schools must accomplish to prepare functioning citizens in the twenty-first century.

There is a lack of recognition of the diverse problems and needs of our student population. I believe that threat assessment will gradually become a standard practice in schools through legislative mandates, but it is important that schools receive the funding support they need to carry it out effectively.

PJL. One of the purposes of using the threat assessment model is to ensure that needed services are provided for troubled students. What types of services do most troubled students need?

DGC. Most student threats are transient threats that are not serious and can be resolved with brief counseling to clarify what the student meant and address an argument or dispute that might have precipitated strong language. In more serious, substantive cases, there may be a need for conflict resolution, anger control, social skills training, or an intervention around bullying. We also need mental health services focused on anger and alienation, in addition to the traditional problems of anxiety and depression. In cases involving a student who is receiving special education services, there may be a need to review the student's individual educational plan.

PJL. If a teacher hears a student making a threat toward another student or if a student informs the teacher that a student has made a threat, what should the teacher do, especially if there are no official guidelines in place?

DGC. Teachers should make sure that every student understands the difference between snitching for personal gain and seeking help to prevent someone from being hurt. Teachers and all other adults at school should let students know that they are available and receptive to hearing any concern about threatening behavior. Teachers should not be expected to make determinations about the seriousness of a threat, because that is the job of the threat assessment team. A threat assessment team will be able to gather the kind of information from multiple sources that is needed to assess the seriousness of a threat in a broader context. If there are no official guidelines in place, teachers nevertheless should report threats of violence and other behavioral concerns to the school administration. At appropriate times, teachers and other school staff members could make known the availability of threat assessment models that the school could adopt.

PJL. What are administrator's responsibilities related to threat assessment? How might they help ensure that every threat is taken seriously and adequately evaluated?

DGC. School administrators are key to the successful functioning of a threat assessment team. They should clarify the school's policy on threats, make sure that team members are trained, and provide leadership to the team. They should follow-up to make sure that threat cases are documented and individual plans for students are working.

PJL. Do you have evidence that shows that students are more likely to report a potential threat now than they were prior to Columbine? According to your knowledge what program, policies or procedures have been shown to be successful in getting students to report potential threats?

DGC. One controlled study found that students report greater willingness to seek help from school authorities and disclose a potential threat (such as a classmate with a gun) in schools that have adopted our threat assessment model. More generally, we have found that students are more willing to seek help for bullying and threats of violence in schools that have what we call an authoritative school climate, which means that students feel that school discipline is strict, but fair, and that teachers are supportive and concerned.

PJL. What is your opinion about permitting educators to carry concealed weapons on campus? Do you think this would help mitigate school shootings? Is this a potential solution?

DGC. There is far too much media attention to shootings in schools when in fact students are far more likely to be victims of shootings as well as other lethal violence outside of school. There are approximately 300 shootings in the United States every day, with only a tiny fraction occurring in or near a school. There are more shootings in restaurants than in schools, but no one has proposed that waitpersons and cooks be armed. The political debate over gun control has overshadowed a more objective look at school safety and gun violence.

PJL. What are the most important things you want educators to know about threat assessment in schools?

DGC. The term threat assessment is a bit of a misnomer that sounds ominous, but in fact threat assessment is a constructive, supportive, problem-solving approach to student concerns. The threat assessment team prevents violence by addressing student problems like bullying and peer conflicts before they escalate into more severe violence. Predicting violence is difficult, but identifying that someone needs assistance is not hard. There is a widespread misperception that we must be able to identify violent individuals and predict when they are going to attack in order to prevent violence. On the contrary, primary and secondary prevention methods address risk factors for violence in the general population without the need to predict the outcomes for specific individuals. We know how to prevent motor vehicle accidents even though accidents happen without warning, and we know how to prevent cancer by targeting risk factors long before the disease develops. We need a similar way of thinking about violence prevention. And in the rare cases where a student is actually planning and preparing to carry out a violent attack, an active threat assessment team is the most likely method of identification and intervention.

PJL. How can we find out more about threat assessment?

DGC. Visit our website at http://curry.virginia.edu/research/projects/threat-assessment

---

Zero Tolerance Approaches to School Discipline and Safety

Threat assessment protocols such as the VSTAG were designed to protect schools from violence as well as to reduce unnecessary suspensions. However, many other procedures have been adopted by many schools to accomplish the former aim (Skiba, Shure, Middelberg, & Baker, 2011). As the most salient example in this regard, zero tolerance policies toward school violence currently are in vogue and have been implemented widely across the U.S. However, a wealth of research indicates that zero tolerance policies are ineffective at mitigating school violence and are even harmful to certain groups of students. For example, a taskforce that was commissioned by the American Psychological Association (APA) reviewed research on the effects of implementing zero tolerance policies and found that no credible evidence existed that zero tolerance reduced school violence and that the policies tend to discriminate disproportionally against racial or ethnic minority students as well as students receiving special education services (American Psychological Association Zero Tolerance Task Force, 2008). However, as previously highlighted, the efficacy of threat assessment procedures is supported by research and the successful implementation of these procedures has been shown to reduce the number of students who are suspended each year, narrow the aforementioned disproportionate gap in suspensions, and effectively mitigate future threats of violence (Cornell et al., 2004; Cornell et al., 2011; Kaplan & Cornell, 2005). Thus, given the extant research, claims that threat assessment procedures are superior to Zero Tolerance policies are unquestionable. Lastly, as a final point that highlights the appeal of threat assessment procedures, research indicates that the use of these procedures reduces the need for overly aggressive disciplinary practices such as Zero Tolerance and makes these disciplinary practices less appealing among members of school communities (Allen et al., 2008; Cornell, Allen, & Fan, 2012; Cornell et al., 2011).

Responding to Threatening Student Behavior

Although previously noted, yet worth repeating, all members of school communities—including educators—should take all threats of violence seriously, even if they seem improbable or out-landish. This is because threats, even if they are unfounded, might be indicative of a severely distressed student who may struggle to ask for help in a more adaptive way (Cornell, 2003). In this vein, some students make threats because they feel desperate to improve their situation and because they lack conflict management skills. Because of this, it is important for educators to listen calmly to students who make threats and allow these youth to speak and communicate their concerns. While listening to students making a threat, it is important to pay attention to the content as well as the context of the threatening message. For example, whether a student is enraged and yelling in response to being provoked by a peer or is calm and delivering a threat in a deadpan tone of voice, a different degree of seriousness might be observed. Essentially, in addition to the threat content, contextual factors also help with quickly judging its seriousness.

Educators who encounter students making threats might benefit from employing active listening skills in the moment (i.e., listening without proffering judgment, guidance, or direction). Similarly, they also might benefit from reflecting and empathizing with the concerns that the student is expressing (e.g., "You look so mad right now. From what you just told me, I can understand why you feel angry and want to get back at the students who have been bullying you."). However, educators should not attempt to resolve most threats of violence to school communities on their own accord. In addition to the importance of protecting their own safety, because threats of violence usually are communicated to people who know the potential perpetrator well, educators who intimately know the students they interact with on a daily basis may lack a degree of separation that allows them to evaluate a threat objectively. In addition, most educators may lack the training or comfort level that is necessary to evaluate threats as well as the authority to sanction consequences for making threats and to protect potential victims. Therefore, in lieu of trying to address a threat directly, educators should quickly convey their concerns to a school administrator or whoever is leading the threat assessment team.

To report a threat accurately to the threat assessment team, educators must carefully attend to and record many salient threat-related details. At a minimum, they must record the who's, what's, where's, and possible why's of what exactly happened. In this regard, the who's involve the people that initiated and witnessed the threat; the what's involve the actual content of the threat (e.g., a violent verbal statement, a homicidal gesture); the where's involve detailing and describing the environment and context in which the threat was delivered; and the why's involve the putative functions behind why the student conveyed the threat. Upon documenting these important details, educators can convey them to a threat assessment team that operates within their respective local educational agency's (LEA) area. Text Box 15.4 is provided to help educators clearly document details and to help threat assessment teams collect information needed to evaluate the seriousness of the threat. It is also used to document disciplinary actions, interventions implemented, and safety precautions taken. However, in the absence of a LEA having an established threat assessment team, educators can still report threats to administrators and community-based mental health and law enforcement professionals. Regarding the previous point and beyond, every educator must identify the people in advance that he or she can contact to report a threat in order to prevent it from being carried out.

Text Box 15.4

This form should be used to document the threat assessment team's response to a student threat of violence. School administrators are advised to consult their division policy on recordkeeping for these forms.

General Information:

Your name: _____ Position: _____ School: _____

Name of student: _____

Date learned of threat: ____/____/____   Date threat occurred: ____/____/____

Type of threat: Transient   Serious Substantive   Very Serious Substantive

Who reported threat? _____   Location of Threat: _____

What student said or did to express a threat (quote student if possible):

_____

Student Who Made Threat	**Victim or Recipient of Threat**
Grade: _____	**Number of Victims:**
Gender: ☐ M ☐ F	☐ 1 ☐ 2 ☐ 3 ☐ 4 ☐ 5 or more
Race:	**Primary Recipient:**
☐ Caucasian ☐ African Am. ☐ Hispanic	☐ Student ☐ Teacher ☐ Parent
☐ Asian Am. ☐ Other: _____	☐ Administrator ☐ Other: _____
Special Education (if applicable):	**Grade (if applicable):** _____
☐ LD ☐ OHI ☐ MR	**Gender:** ☐ M ☐ F
☐ ED ☐ Other: _____	
Yes No – Had or sought accomplices	**Race:**
Yes No – Reported the threat as a specific plan	☐ Caucasian ☐ AfricanAm. ☐ Hispanic
Yes No – Wrote plans or list	☐ AsiaAm. ☐ Other: _____
Yes No – Repeated the threat over time	**Special Education (if applicable):**
Yes No – Mentioned weapon in the threat	☐ LD ☐ OHI ☐ MR
Yes No – Used weapon in the threat	☐ ED ☐ Other: _____

(continued)

(continued)

Yes   No – Had prior conflict with recipient (within 24 hours of threat)

Yes   No – Student previously bullied the recipient

Witness Interview

☐ Recipient (target) of threat   or   ☐ Witness to threat, but not recipient

Witness name and grade or title: _____

1.   What exactly happened today when you were (place of incident)?

    _____

    _____

    _____

    _____

    _____

    _____

2.   What exactly did (student who made the threat) say or do? (Write the witness's exact words.)

    _____

    _____

    _____

    _____

    _____

    _____

3.   What do you think he or she meant when saying or doing that?

    _____

    _____

    _____

    _____

    _____

    _____

4. How do you feel about what he or she said or did? (Gauge whether the person who observed or received the threat feels frightened or intimidates.) Are you concerned that he or she might actually do it?

_____

_____

_____

_____

_____

_____

5. Why did he or she say or do that? (Find out whether witness knows of any prior conflict or history behind threat.)

_____

_____

_____

_____

_____

_____

Threat Responses - Disciplinary Action

Yes　No – Reprimanded student

Yes　No – Parent Conference

Yes　No – In-school time-out

Yes　No – Detention (number of days): _____

Yes　No – Suspension (number of days): _____

Yes　No – Expulsion recommended

Yes　No – Other disciplinary actions: _____

Interventions and Safety Precautions

Yes　No – Interviewed and advised student who made threat

(continued)

(continued)

Yes   No – Interviewed and advised student's parents

Yes   No – Consulted with one or more school staff members

Yes   No – Interviewed and advised other students

Yes   No – Law enforcement consulted

Yes   No – Law enforcement contact with the student who made the threat, consequence of legal action (probations, detention, release into parent's custody, etc.):

_____

_____

Yes   No – Student might be eligible for special education services; referred for evaluation

Yes   No – Student already receiving special education services; referred to the IEP team for review

Yes   No – Student referred for a 504 plan

_____

_____

Yes   No – Mental health assessment conducted by school-base staff

Yes   No – Mental health assessment conducted by an outside agency (court, DSS, psychologist, etc.)

_____

Yes   No – Parents of the threat recipient notified of the threat

Yes   No – Conflict mediation

Yes   No – School-based counseling

Yes   No – Alter schedule of the student to increase supervision or minimize contact with the recipient

_____

_____

Yes   No – Alternative educational placement (alternative school, day treatment program, homebound, etc.)

Yes   No – Change in transportation (bus suspension, special transportation, etc.)

Yes   No – Inpatient mental health services

Yes   No – Outpatient mental health services (counseling or therapy with outside mental health provider)

Yes   No – Other safety precautions (please list):

_____

When conducting an investigation of a threat or dealing with a student who may be at risk for violence, there are a number of actions that a school team can take. Some of these actions will help the threat assessment team better understand the nature and seriousness of the threat, the rationale behind the threat, and the psychological makeup of the student. Other actions can be taken to provide support to the student and protect the safety of students and staff. A list of possible actions is provided in Text Box 15.5 and an example of thwarting the attack of a potential school shooter is provided in Text Box 15.6.

Text Box 15.5 Actions Educators Can Take to Address Potentially Violent Students

- Notify potential victims.
- Notify guardians.
- Notify law enforcement.
- Notify appropriate school staff.
- Conduct a threat assessment.
- Refer to a mental health facility.
- Recommend counseling or therapy.
- Recommend a psychiatric evaluation.
- Recommend an involuntary treatment order.
- Search students locker and possessions.
- Explore alternative educational placements.
- Consider homebound education.
- If suspended or hospitalized, develop a plan for school re-entry.
- Implement expulsion.
- Conduct a functional behavioral assessment (FBA).
- Implement a behavior intervention plan (BIP).
- Conduct a comprehensive psychological evaluation.
- Teach social skills.
- Provide increased supervision and positive behavior support at school.
- Implement check-in/check-out.
- Modify schedule.
- Recommend drug screening.

Text Box 15.6 Confronting a Potentially Violent Student

It was the heroic effort of two high school teachers who helped prevent a 14-year-old boy from engaging in a rampage school shooting at Philip Barbour High School in Philippi, West Virginia. On August 25, 2015, the student held 29 classmates and a teacher, Twila Smith, at gunpoint in a second floor classroom. According to Barbour County Superintendent, Jeff Wolker, "The teacher did a marvelous job of calming the student and maintaining order in the class." A little after 1 p.m., a new group of students was about to walk into the classroom, but Smith told them they weren't allowed in. Another teacher thought that seemed odd, so she went in. The 14-year-old pointed the gun at her.

The second teacher immediately ducked back out, slammed the door on the way out, went into her classroom, and buzzed the office at that time. An assistant principal put the school on lockdown and went classroom to classroom ensuring doors were closed and locked. Within a matter of minutes, dozens of officers arrived and every student not in that room was brought safely out to the football field. After the student held the class at gun-point for approximately an hour, Smith with the help of the police and the boy's pastor eventually convinced the 14-year-old to let everyone in the classroom

(continued)

(continued)

go, and a short time later, talked the boy into turning himself in. Fortunately, no shots were fired and no one was hurt. Smith, a veteran teacher of 30 years, later said, "I mean, when they walk in here, we're protecting, we're supposed to teach them and we're supposed to take care of them."

What prevented a tragic outcome was that the teacher had rapport with the student, listened to his concerns, and asked for his permission to let his classmates leave the class. Her calmness and control provided the support that enabled the boy to put the gun down and surrender to police. In addition, the school had a clear precise plan of action to deal with an ongoing threat that was followed with perfection.

Source: www.dailymail.co.uk/news/article-3210832/Boy-14-held-students-teacher-hostage-West-Virginia-high-school.html.
http://wchstv.com/news/local/wv-state-police-say-14-year-old-at-philip-barbour-high-school-held-students-teacher-hostage
http://abcnews.go.com/US/west-virginia-teacher-recalls-moment-student-drew-gun/story?id=33474988.

Expert Interview 15.2 with Jane Lazarus from Nova Southeastern University discusses the application of threat assessment procedures in the Broward County Public School System in Florida. She comments on the types of psychological services that students need after they have made a threat, training threat assessment teams, legal concerns, law enforcement issues, and how to reintegrate student into school after they have made a threat.

Expert Interview 15.2 with Jane Lazarus

Nova Southeastern University

PJL. You have responded to countless threats in schools where you have served as a school psychologist. What have you learned that would be helpful to teachers and administrators?

JML. From my experience working on school safety teams, the violence prevention process works best when teachers are involved in the initiative, schools use a step-by-step process to address threats, and all educators and staff are trained. Having district policies and previously established procedures enables the process to be more automatic and efficient. A school can have designated trained individuals (e.g. administrators, counselors, school psychologists, social workers, school resource officers, school nurses, etc.) to receive, document, and follow-up on all threats reported to them. The goal of the team is to take action before the end of the day. Someone must be willing to stay late (often an administrator) because problems can surface toward the end of the school day. A school administrator must always be made aware of the situation and be involved in taking action as soon as possible. Teachers need to know that they are obligated to report threats to one or more persons who are trained to follow-up; however, they should be reassured that they are not responsible to investigate or determine whether or not a threat is credible. In taking a threat report, teachers should document exactly what they hear or see and keep a copy of their report. By the end of the day, they should find out from the administration how the situation was handled and what is going to happen tomorrow. In order to increase the chances that students will report a dangerous situation to adults, adults should stand in the halls between classes, greet students by name, and listen. Students usually tell someone when they are planning to commit violence. In investigating threats, it is ideal if two adults work together when questioning a student. In my experience, I found it even better if one of the adults knew the student or had some knowledge of the student. Threats can be expressed orally, either directly or indirectly, or in writing. All potentially dangerous actions should be investigated in a timely manner.

PJL. What have been the most common threats you have encountered over the years?

JML. A few examples include:

- Student says, "I am going to do a Columbine."
- Student draws pictures of someone shooting a gun, exploding a bomb, or hanging from a noose
- Student writes in an assignment, "I am going to kill Mr. J. (the teacher)."
- Student verbally threatens to harm another student: "I am going to beat you up after school. I am going to bring my Dad's gun to school and kill you."
- Student leaves a note in the classroom or on the cafeteria floor that he/she is going to hurt him/herself or someone else.

PJL. How have parents responded when they learned their child has made a threat?

JML. Parent responses vary from "not my child" to "please help us; we have been worried about him/her" to anything in between. Parents are a great resource but need a lot of hand holding during the threat assessment process. They are afraid of repercussions and may be fearful of revealing information; their cooperation is important to put all the pieces together (e.g. weapons access) to determine a plan of action. Definitely involve parents and delegate someone on the team to support them through the process.

PJL. What types of psychological services do students need when they have made a threat?

JML. Depending on the results of the threat assessment and the lethality of the threat, a plan of care/supervision plan is developed. Parents are encouraged to participate. If the threat is considered low level, the student will be monitored by teachers and school mental health personnel. Sometimes, it is just a matter of helping the student understand that they cannot say the things they did and that their statements will be taken very seriously. However, counseling both in and out of school with family involvement may be necessary. When a threat is considered serious, immediate evaluation and treatment and/or law enforcement intervention is needed with an emphasis on 100 percent supervision and mental health and/or behavioral care. The goal, however, is to provide support prior to a violent situation. Medical consultation may be warranted. Be aware that many students who threaten targeted violence are often suicidal, are acting from the tunnel-vision of depression, and need mental health treatment.

PJL. What type of training has been given to threat assessment teams in your school district?

JML. Violence prevention in the Broward County, FL schools involves a three-pronged approach: Warning Signs Awareness, in which all school staff receive training in recognizing signs of potential violent behavior; Safe Zone Listeners, which involves having designated educators available to listen and take threat reports; and Threat Assessment Procedures, which entail investigating and making an informed team decision about the seriousness of a threat and how best to respond. All mental health professionals (school psychologists, social workers, counselors, etc.), administrators, and school resource officers are required to attend at least two days of training each year. They are provided with a manual outlining procedures and containing forms and materials. It is the responsibility of these professionals to train building personnel. The building administrator decides who receives training in the school. For example, in some schools, the principal determines that the entire staff receives training. In others, the support personnel receive comprehensive training, and the teachers/staff receive a modified version.

PJL. What have been some legal concerns that you have had to deal with in responding to students who have made threats?

JML. Questions about who can search a student's backpack and what are a teacher's rights with regard to asking that a student who has made a threat toward them not be allowed to return to their class are issues that have come up.

PJL. Under what circumstances does a threat become a law enforcement concern?

JML. When a student has done something clearly illegal such as bringing a weapon on campus, physically attacked someone, or posed imminent danger to others, law enforcement and school security should be immediately involved. They are a resource when information obtained from the threat assessment process reveals that there should be a search or check of the student's home for safety purposes. Law enforcement can follow up when a student has gone home for the day and may be in danger (e.g. suicidal). In our district, we consider suicidal behavior within the responsibility of the school safety team. For example, we had a situation in which we learned after a student had gone home on the bus that she had made comments related to self-harm. Consequently, we contacted our school resource officer who arranged a safety check of the student at home.

PJL. How has your school reintegrated students who have made threats in the past back into the school system?

JML. The school safety/threat assessment team is responsible for matching the interventions to the level of risk. The care plan/student supervision plan developed as a result of the threat assessment process should address the reintegration of the student back into school. Sometimes a schedule or school change is made. Counseling, peer mediation, academic support, check-ins, etc. may be warranted. Psychological evaluation and determination of need for special services can be considered. Security and monitoring issues are established. The situation should be tracked, and the student provided with adequate support and supervision until problems have diminished.

Conclusion

Although violent attacks that result in death are exceedingly rare in schools and educational environments generally are safe, at some point many members of school communities will experience a threat of violence. In addition to being scary, threats of violence pose significant challenges to school communities and require immediate attention. Thus, all threats of violence must be taken seriously. Schools can benefit by adopting a threat assessment approach that involves developing a threat assessment team to respond quickly and adroitly to threats. School administrators usually are in the best position to lead threat assessment teams, yet these teams should also include school-based mental health professionals and law enforcement officers who are familiar with members of the school community.

In contrast to overly punitive and ineffective discipline policies such as Zero Tolerance policies toward school violence, research supports the efficacy of threat assessment procedures such as the Virginia Student Threat Assessment Guidelines (VSTAG). The VSTAG allow for members of school communities to assess threats through the use of a structured protocol that aims to reduce over-reacting to transient threats while appropriately addressing substantive threats. Finally, an emerging body of research indicates that threat assessment procedures are effective at preventing incidents of school violence and they are valued by members of school communities.

References

Allen, K., Cornell, D., & Lorek, E. (2008). Response of school personnel to student threat assessment training. *School Effectiveness and School Improvement, 19*, 319–332. doi:10.1080/09243450802332184

American Psychological Association Zero Tolerance Task Force. (2008). Are zero tolerance policies effective in the schools? An evidentiary review and recommendations. *American Psychologist, 63,* 852–862. doi: 10.1037/0003-066X.63.9.852

Band, S. R., & Harpold, J. A. (1999). School violence: Lessons learned. *Law Enforcement Bulletin, 68,* 9–16.

Borum, R., Cornell, D. G., Modzeleski, W., & Jimerson, S. R. (2010). What can be done about school shootings? A review of the evidence. *Educational Researcher, 39,* 27–37. doi: 10.3102/0013189X 09357620

Cornell, D. (2003). Guidelines for responding to student threats of violence. *Journal of Educational Administration, 41,* 705–719.

Cornell, D., Allen, K., & Fan, X. (2012). A randomized controlled study of the Virginia Threat Assessment Guidelines in grades K-12. *School Psychology Review, 41,* 100–115.

Cornell, D., Gregory, A., & Fan, X. (2011). Reductions in long-term suspensions following the adoption of the Virginia Student Threat Assessment Guidelines. *Bulletin of the National Association of Secondary School Principals, 95,* 175–194.

Cornell, D., & Nekvasil, E. (2012). Violent thoughts and behaviors. In S. E. Brock and S. R. Jimerson (Eds.), *Best practices in school crisis prevention and intervention (2nd edn)* (pp. 485–502). Bethesda, MD. NASP Publications.

Cornell, D., & Sheras, P. (2006). *Guidelines for responding to student threats of violence.* Longmont, CO: Sopris West.

Cornell, D., Sheras, P., Gregory, A. & Fan, X. (2009). A retrospective study of school safety conditions in high schools using the Virginia Threat Assessment Guidelines versus alternative approaches. *School Psychology Quarterly, 24,* 119–129. doi:10.1037/a0016182

Cornell, D., Sheras, P., Kaplan, S., McConville, D., Douglass, J. Elkon. (2004). Guidelines for student threat assessment: Field-test findings. *School Psychology Review, 33,* 527–546.

Fein, R., Vossekuil, B., Pollack, W., Borum, R., Modzeleski, W. & Reddy, M. (2002). *Threat assessment in schools: A guide to managing threatening situations and to creating safe school climates.* Washington, DC: U.S. Secret Service and Department of Education.

Ferguson, C. J. (2008). The school shooting/violent video game link: Causal relationship or moral panic? *Journal of Investigative Psychology and Offender Profiling, 5,* 25–37. doi: 10.1002/jip.76

Greenberg, S. F. (2007). Active shooters on college campuses: Conflicting advice, roles of the individual and first responder, and the need to maintain perspective. *Disaster Medicine and Public Health Preparedness, 1,* 57–61.

Harnisch, T. L. (2008, November). *Concealed weapons on state college campuses: In pursuit of individual liberty and collective security.* A Higher Education Policy Brief. American Association of State Colleges and Universities.

Kaplan, S. & Cornell, D. (2005). Threats of violence by students in special education. *Behavioral Disorders, 31,* 107–119.

Kotinsky, S., Bixler, E., & Kettl, P. (2001). Threats of violence in Pennsylvania after coverage of the Columbine High School Massacre. *Archives of Pediatric and Adolescent Medicine, 155,* 994–1001.

Langman, P. (2009). Rampage school shooters: A typology. *Aggression and Violent Behavior, 14,* 79–86.

McGee, J. P., & DeBernardo, C. R. (1999). The Classroom Avenger. *Forensic Examiner, 8,* 16–28.

Modzeleski, W., Feucht, T., Rand M., Hall, J., Simon, T., Butler, L., . . . Hertz, M. (2008). School-associated student homicides–United States, 1992–2006. *Morbidity and Mortality Weekly Report, 57,* 33–36. Retrieved from www.cdc.gov/mmwr/.

Neiman, S., & Devoe, J. (2009). *Crime, violence, discipline, and safety in U.S. public schools: Findings from the School Survey on Crime and Safety: 2007–08.* (NCES 2009–326). Washington, DC: National Center for Education Statistics, Institute of Education Sciences and U.S. Department of Education.

Nekvasil, E., & Cornell, D. (2012). Student reports of peer threats of violence: Prevalence and outcomes. *Journal of School Violence, 11,* 357–375. doi: 10.1080/15388220.2012.706764

O'Toole, M. E. (2000). *The school shooter: A threat assessment perspective.* Quantico, VA: National Center for the Analysis of Violent Crime, Federal Bureau of Investigation.

Pollack, W. S., Modzeleski, W., & Rooney, G. (2008). *Prior knowledge of potential school-based violence: Information students learn may prevent a targeted attack.* Washington, DC: U.S. Secret Service and U.S. Department of Education.

Reddy, M., Borum, R., Berglund, J., Vossekuil, B., Fein, R. & Modzeleski, W. (2001). Evaluating risk for targeted violence in schools: Comparing risk assessment, threat assessment, and other approaches. *Psychology in the Schools, 38,* 157–172.

Roberts, S., Zhang, J., & Truman, J. (2010). *Indicators of school crime and safety: 2010 (NCES 2011-002/ NCJ 230812).* Washington, DC: National Center for Education Statistics, U.S. Department of Education, and Bureau of Justice Statistics, Office of Justice Programs, U.S. Department of Justice.

Skiba, R. J., Shure, L. A., Middelberg, L. V., & Baker, T. L. (2011). Reforming school discipline and reducing disproportionality in suspension and expulsion. In S. R. Jimerson, A. B. Nickerson, M. J. Mayer, M. J. Furlong (Eds.), *The Handbook of School Violence and School Safety: International Research and Practice (2nd edn.)* (pp. 515–528). New York: Routledge.

Strong, K., & Cornell, D. (2008). Student threat assessment in Memphis City Schools: A descriptive report. *Behavioral Disorders, 34,* 42–54.

Sulkowski, M. L. (2011). An investigation of students' willingness to report threats of violence in campus communities. *Psychology of Violence, 1,* 53–65. doi: 10.1037/a0021592

Sulkowski, M. L., & Lazarus, P. J. (2011). Contemporary responses to violent attacks on college campuses. *Journal of School Violence, 10,* 338–354. doi: 10.1080/15388220.2011.602601

Tarasoff v. The Regents of the University of California, 551 P.2d 334 (Cal. 1976)

Verlinden, S., Hersen, M., & Thomas, J. (2000). Risk factors in school shootings. *Clinical Psychology Review, 20,* 3–56.

Vossekuil, B., Fein, R. A., Reddy, M., Borum, R. & Modzeleski, W. (2002). *The final report and findings of the Safe School Initiative: Implications for the prevention of school attacks in the United States.* Washington, DC: U.S. Secret Service and U.S. Department of Education.

16 Suicide Assessment, Prevention, and Intervention

Few if any problems confronting our nation's schools are more urgent than suicidal behavior in students. Suicide is the third leading cause of death among youth in the U.S., trailing only behind accidents and homicides. Astoundingly, more teenagers have died by suicide than from influenza, cancer, birth defects, AIDS, pneumonia, and chronic lung disease combined (U.S. Centers for Disease Control (CDC), 2007). Further, it is tragic phenomenon that a young person dies by suicide every five hours in the U.S. and that the number of suicides has tripled since the 1950s, while rates of unintentional injury, congenital anomalies, and disease have decreased (Berman, Jobes, & Silverman, 2006; Wagner, 2009). Clearly, youth suicide is a pressing problem that warrants urgent action.

This chapter begins by describing the phenomenon of youth suicide and then it discusses why schools should engage in efforts to prevent tragic self-inflicted deaths in students. Additionally, content is provided on how schools can prevent suicide and how all educators can identify and help reduce suicide risks in students. Thus, this chapter covers suicide risk factors, warning signs, precipitants associated with suicide, and ways that potentially suicidal students can be supported. Lastly, this chapter concludes with strategies for transitioning students who have attempted suicide back to school as well as legal and ethical issues associated with supporting suicidal youth.

Scope of the Problem

Student suicide transcends all boundaries related to socioeconomic status, age, gender, ethnicity, geographical region, and sexual orientation (Lieberman, Poland, & Cassel, 2008). No particular family or community is immune to this phenomenon. The World Health Organization (WHO) estimates that globally over 800,000 people die by suicide each year (WHO, 2014), which is much higher than the annual number of deaths that are caused by war and homicide. According to the WHO, suicide is the second leading cause of death among young people ages 15–29 in the world and it has increased 60 percent during the past 50 years (Miller, 2011).

According to the 2013 Youth Risk Behavior Surveillance Survey, 17 percent of U.S. high school students report that they have seriously considered suicide, 14 percent made a suicide plan, 8 percent reported having made a suicide attempt, and 3 percent indicated that their suicide attempt required them to receive medical intervention (CDC, 2014). Thus, consistent with these findings, one out of every six high school students has seriously considered ending his or her life. Additionally, one out of every seven has developed a suicide plan and one out of every 12 has attempted suicide (CDC, 2014). Moreover, it is estimated that there are 100 to 200 suicide attempts for each completed case (Berman et al., 2006; Miller & Eckert, 2009). Considering the implication of these findings for school communities, within a typical high school classroom, it is likely that three students (one boy and two girls) have made some type of attempt to end their lives within the past year (American Association of Suicidology (AAS), 2014).

Considering the former, it is important to emphasize that suicidal behavior is highly problematic, even if this behavior does not result in death. Youth who attempt suicide, but do not complete, may suffer significantly as a result of their attempt as well as because of the factors that contributed to the attempt. This suffering may include experiencing serious bodily injuries such as broken bones, possible brain damage, or organ failure (Miller, 2011). Emotionally, youth who attempt suicide often suffer from serious mental health issues such as depression, which is inexorably linked with suicidal behavior. Research indicates that feelings of depression that include sadness, hopelessness, and helplessness are a major risk factor for suicide (Bearman & Moody, 2004; Brock, Sandoval & Hart, 2006). In support of this link, more than 90 percent of children and adolescents who complete suicide were suffering with a mental disorder prior to their death (U.S. Department of Health and Human Services, 1999).

How Schools Can Prevent Student Suicide

Members of school communities may wonder how they can help to prevent youth suicide. In response to this question, the Substance Abuse and Mental Health Services Administration (SAMHSA, 2012) has outlined four major reasons why schools should address student suicide and how they can help. These are listed in the document: *Preventing suicide: A toolkit for high schools*. A brief summary of each reason is listed below.

1. Maintaining a Safe School Environment is Part of a Schools Overall Mission

An implicit contract exists between schools and caregivers about ensuring the safety of children at school, and suicide prevention is consistent with this contract. Many activities designed to prevent violence, bullying, and substance abuse also can reduce suicide risk (Epstein & Spirito, 2009). In addition, programs that have been developed to improve school climate and promote connectedness have been found to help reduce risk of suicide, bullying, and substance abuse (Blum, McNeely, & Rinehart, 2002; Resnick et al., 1997). Further, efforts to promote safe schools and foster caring relationships between educators and students can help protect young people against suicidal ideation and attempts, especially among LGBTQ youth who display an elevated risk for engaging in suicidal behavior (Eisenberg & Resnick, 2006). Even further, some activities designed to prevent suicide and promote student mental health reinforce the benefits of student wellness programs and help ensure school safety. In support of this notion, research and findings from case studies indicate that the majority (78 percent) of targeted school shooters have been suicidal (Vossekuil, Fein, Reddy, Borum, & Modzeleski, 2002). Thus, if these homicidal and suicidal youth had been identified and effectively treated, some school shootings could have been prevented.

2. Students' Mental Health can Affect their Academic Performance

Depression and other mental health issues can interfere with students' ability to learn and be successful in school. Approximately half of students receiving grades of mostly Ds and Fs in high school report feeling sad or hopeless, yet only one out of five students excelling in school (receiving grades of mostly As and Bs) felt the same (CDC, 2010). Furthermore, in the same study, it was found that one out of five high school students receiving grades of mostly Ds and Fs attempted suicide, while only one out of 25 students who excelled in school engaged in the same behavior.

3. A Student Suicide can Significantly Impact Other Students and the Entire School Community

Knowing what to do following a suicide is critical to helping students cope with loss and prevent future tragedies such as contagion suicides. Contagion suicides are often referred to as the "copycat effect," which involves attempting suicide after the recent death of someone else. Research indicates that exposure to a completed suicide has been found to increase the risk that an individual will attempt suicide, and this risk is greatest in adolescence (de Leo & Heller, 2008; Hart, 2012). Although this phenomenon is rare, the possible contagion effect associated with suicide must be taken seriously. To help mitigate this risk, the American Academy of Suicidality (AAS; 1998); Hart (2012); and SAMHSA (2012) provide guidelines for managing the suicide postvention process.

4. Reducing Legal Risk can Help Protect Schools from Litigation

Schools can be liable for failing to take necessary steps to prevent student suicide. Essentially, if a school employee is informed that a student may be considering suicide, he or she has an obligation to address the risk and involve mental health professionals and emergency first responders who can help the at-risk student. In addition, as a primary step, they must contact a legal guardian of the student. Failure to notify parents if their child appears to be suicidal, failure to get assistance for a student at risk of suicide, and failure to adequately supervise a student at risk all open up a school to litigation (Doan, Roggenbaum, & Lazear, 2003; Juhnke, Granello & Granello, 2011; Lieberman, Poland & Cowan, 2006). Thus, in addition to having a moral prerogative to help prevent student suicide, compelling legal reasons also influence schools to help in this regard.

Myths, Misconceptions, and Realities about Youth Suicide

Many myths abound regarding the topic of youth suicide. Some of these are propagated in popular culture and others stem from lack of familiarity with the current research. Regardless of the origin of myths and misconceptions, it is important to clear these up. Consequently, the following section provides factual information that educators can use to understand and prevent youth suicide.

Myth 1: Talking about Suicide can Increase the Risk that Someone Will Attempt Suicide

Various studies indicate that this most basic myth about suicide has no validity (e.g., Gould et al., 2005; Mazza, 2006; Miller, 2012). Instead, talking to youth about suicide does not plant the idea in their mind. In fact, suicidal youth often appreciate the opportunity to talk about their feelings with an individual who is caring, non-judgmental, willing to listen, and not afraid to engage them in a difficult conversation that may involve highly personal and emotionally charged subjects that contribute to their thoughts about killing themselves.

Myth 2: People who Talk about Suicide Do Not Attempt Suicide

Students who talk about committing suicide are at-risk for engaging in suicidal behavior (Miller, 2011). Therefore, all threats of suicide must be taken seriously. Ignoring or dismissing suicidal statements as a means to obtain attention invalidates the suffering the student is experiencing as well as ignoring a crucial opportunity to support the student. The act of expressing suicidal thoughts should be viewed as a "cry for help" or a "cry of pain" rather than as a "cry for attention." Even if a student does not want to actually die, if he or she is making suicidal statements, the student is in a state of serious emotional pain that needs to be taken seriously. Moreover, if students' suicidal statements are not taken seriously, they might "up the ante" and engage in even more serious suicidal behavior, such as making an attempt.

Myth 3: Suicidal Youth Really Want to Die

Suicidal people typically do not want to die. Instead, they want to end the emotional pain they currently are experiencing. They want what Shneidman (1996) calls the "psychache" to end. According to Shneidman, a leading expert on suicide, individuals engage in suicidal behavior to end intense and intolerable psychological pain. Thus, many suicide attempts among youth are motivated by feelings of hopelessness about their current situation and a desire to end their suffering (Miller, 2011). It is important to understand that suicidal individuals are often in unbearable pain—pain from which they see no escape. In addition, suicidal individuals often have reduced cognitive flexibility and problem-solving abilities, which makes it hard for them to think of possible solutions to their problems (Linda, Marroquín, & Miranda, 2012). Therefore, in lieu of focusing on suicide itself (i.e., wanting to die), helping individuals to focus on treatment, problem-solving, and psychological pain reduction can help decrease or eliminate suicidal plans and actions (Williams, 2001). With support, a suicidal student can be prevented from engaging in a tragic solution to end temporary suffering.

Myth 4: When Depression Subsides, the Threat of Suicide is Over

Often, an individual who experiences a major depressive episode and is suicidal may not have the energy to act on a suicide plan. Episodes of major depression can be crippling and make daily tasks such as getting out of bed, showering, and getting dressed seem like insurmountable challenges. However, for most people, these episodes tend to lift after a few days or weeks and people then tend to regain their energy and stamina, even if they still feel depressed. Therefore, when the depression begins to lift, the individual may be at higher risk for actually planning and carrying out suicide. In addition, a recent study found that that "depressive mixed states," which involve feeling depressed yet also experiencing symptoms of excitation or mania, often preceded suicide attempts (Popovic et al., 2015). More specifically, individuals experiencing depressive mixed states were found to be 50 percent more likely to attempt suicide than were individuals with just depression. Therefore, it is important to support and reach out to people well after they seem to be rebounding from a particularly severe episode of depression with suicidal thoughts as well as to people who may not appear to be depressed in the way that this disorder is commonly understood.

Myth 5: Parents or Caretakers are Aware of their Child's Suicidal Behavior

Parents often are unaware that their child has had suicidal thoughts or has made an attempt and they may be totally surprised when they are informed that their child is suicidal. Adolescence is a period that is marked by distancing oneself from one's parents to develop a unique identity, and, subsequently, many adolescents hide information from their parents (Garbarino & deLara, 2002). Therefore, just asking parents about their child's previous suicidal attempts may result in obtaining incomplete information. Instead, it is best to ask the child or adolescent directly about their suicidal thoughts, intentions, or behaviors.

Myth 6: Those Who Attempt Suicide Usually Receive Medical Treatment

Only one out of three suicide attempts among youth ages 15–19 results in a youth receiving medical attention (Lieberman et al., 2008). Therefore, most (two out of every three) students who attempt suicide go to school the following day, which further highlights the need for educators to be aware of this phenomenon. Educators may be even more likely than medical professionals to encounter students who recently attempted to end their lives.

Myth 7: Nothing can be Done to Prevent a Suicide

Individuals who are suicidal are often in an acute crisis and feel overwhelmed by problems. It is not that the person cannot handle one crisis or setback; rather, they are beset by many crises that are occurring simultaneously. However, as feelings of being overwhelmed pass or are successfully managed, suicidal thoughts and intentions usually reduce. In a seminal study, Seiden (1978) examined 515 individuals who were restrained from attempting suicide from the Golden Gate Bridge from 1937 through 1971. Results of this investigation indicated that 94 percent of individuals did *not* later die by suicide. Further, researchers in Great Britain found a significant reduction in suicides (more than 50 percent) after a fence was installed on a local bridge where many individuals had jumped to their deaths (Benneworth, Nowers, & Gunnell, 2007). Additionally, no evidence of increased jumping from other sites in the region that did not have protective devices was found (Miller, 2011). This finding may best be explained by the fact that many suicidal individuals who have a plan to kill themselves do not have a contingency plan. Therefore, if their original plan is thwarted, they may not develop a second one. As a relevant example for educators that expands on the previous studies, not one suicidal student who was identified as being at "high risk" for suicide and who received interventions actually completed suicide during a five year period in Miami-Dade County Public Schools in Florida. Unfortunately, the students who completed suicide in the district never came to the attention of the school system (Zenere & Lazarus, 1997).

Myth 8: Once a Youth Attempts Suicide, He or She Should Always be Considered Suicidal

A considerable number of individuals who attempt suicide do so only once. Furthermore, for some individuals, a suicide attempt can be a wake-up call as well as a call to action to seek therapy or make important life changes (Bergmans, Langley, Links, & Lavery, 2009). Consequently, if an educator can refer a potentially suicidal student to a mental health professional for treatment, there is a good chance that the student will not attempt suicide.

Myth 9: Suicide is a Rational Response to Too Much Pain and Stress

Suicide is not a rational response—it is associated with mental health problems that cloud rational thinking and impair judgment (Linda et al., 2012). As foreshadowed above, the mental health problems most closely associated with suicidal behavior are major depression, dysthymic disorder, bipolar disorder, anxiety disorders, conduct disorder, borderline personality disorder, and substance abuse (Lieberman et al., 2008; Miller, 2012). Notice that all of these disorders involve having mood regulation problems. Yet, even though the symptoms and effects of the aforementioned disorders often endure without adequate treatment, suicidal thoughts and behaviors are often temporary. People generally are not suicidal all the time. With effective intervention and the passing of time, distress contributing to suicidal thoughts can be alleviated and painful feelings can dissipate.

Potential Risk Factors, Warning Signs, and Precipitants of Suicide

Risk Factors

Suicide is a complex and multidimensional behavior that is associated with many risk factors. However, the two most prominent risk factors are the presence of mental health disorders and previous suicidal behavior. In addition, many students who die by suicide have co-morbid disorders (i.e., more than one disorder), which establishes a link between suicide and experiencing multiple mental health problems (Mazza, 2006). See additional risk factors for suicide in Table 16.1. This table is based on the findings of American Foundation for Suicide Prevention (AFSP; 2014); CDC (2007); Kalafat & Lazarus (2002); and SAMHSA (2012).

Table 16.1 Risk Factors Associated with Suicide

- Previous suicide attempt (20% of those who kill themselves made a previous attempt).
- Current ideation, intent, and plan (resolve).
- Early childhood trauma/multiple adverse childhood experiences.
- A confluence of multiple stressors (discipline, rejection/humiliation, end of romantic relationship, conflict with family or peers, unmet school goals).
- Hopelessness and helplessness.
- Mental disorders—particularly mood disorders such as depression and Bipolar Disorder.
- Co-occurring mental and alcohol and substance abuse disorders.
- Personality disorders (most notably antisocial and borderline).
- Easy access to lethal methods, especially guns.
- Isolation, a feeling of being cut off from other people.
- Ineffective coping mechanisms and inadequate problem-solving skills.
- Exposure to suicide and/or family history of suicide.
- Influence of significant people—family members, celebrities, peers who have died by suicide—both through direct personal contact or inappropriate media representations.
- Local epidemics of suicide that have a contagious influence.
- Impulsive and/or aggressive tendencies.
- Barriers to accessing mental health treatment.
- Gender (males are four times more likely to die by suicide than females).
- LGBTQ individuals are more likely to attempt and to die by suicide, especially if there is family rejection, bullying, harassment, or lack of supportive resources.
- Relational, social, work, or financial loss.
- Trouble with the law.
- Chronic medical illnesses (e.g., HIV, traumatic brain injury).
- PTSD.
- Unwillingness to seek help because of stigma attached to mental and substance abuse disorders and/or suicidal thoughts.
- Cultural and religious beliefs—for instance, the belief that suicide is a noble resolution of a personal dilemma.

Warning Signs

In contrast to risk factors, warning signs are more variable and concerning. The presence of warning signs suggest the increased risk of suicidal behavior, yet they still do not mean that a student will complete suicide. The AAS has developed useful suicide warning signs and has created a mnemonic device to help remember them (available at www.suicidology.org/resources/warning-signs). This mnemonic is as follows: IS PATH WARM. Consistent with this mnemonic, Text Box 16.1 lists warning signs of suicide.

Text Box 16.1 Warning Signs Associated with Suicide

IS PATH WARM
Ideation
Substance Abuse
Purposelessness
Anxiety and Agitation
Trapped
Hopeless
Withdrawal
Anger
Recklessness
Mood Fluctuations

In addition to the listed warning signs, a person displaying a high risk for suicidal behavior may show these other notable warning signs: (a) threatening to hurt or kill him/herself, or talking of wanting to hurt or kill him/herself, and/or (b) looking for a way to kill him/herself by seeking access to firearms, available pills, or other means, and/or (c) talking or writing about death, dying, or suicide, when these actions are out of the ordinary. According to the AAS, additional warning signs include (a) increased substance (alcohol or drug) use; (b) feeling like there is no reason for living or no sense of purpose in life; (c) experiencing anxiety, agitation, being unable to sleep or sleeping all the time; (d) feeling trapped—as if there is no way out of one's current suffering; (e) feeling hopeless; (f) withdrawing from family, friends, and society; (g) experiencing rage or uncontrolled anger, seeking revenge; (h) acting recklessly or engaging in risky activities, seemingly without thinking; and (i) experiencing dramatic mood changes. Although no formula exists for aggregating the previously listed risk factors, a person's suicidal risk increases as they accumulate.

Potential Suicide Precipitants

Adverse life events can overwhelm students who already display risk factors and show evidence of potential suicide warning signs. Essentially, these types of events interfere with adaptive coping and make an individual more likely to consider suicide. Based on the findings of Kalafat & Lazarus (2002) and the U.S. Public Health Service (2001), these precipitants of suicide are listed in Table 16.2.

Protective Factors

In direct contrast to risk factors and adverse life experiences, protective factors buffer against risks and negative life experiences. Individuals who have a high number of risk factors yet do not engage in suicidal behavior are likely influenced by protective factors. Collectively, the triumph of protective over risk factors builds resiliency, which is the ability to endure adversity (See Chapter 6 for a more complete discussion of resilience). To date, less is known about protective factors than is known about risk factors (Gutierrez & Osman, 2008; Miller, 2012). Nonetheless, these factors are critically important for preventing student suicide and Table 16.3 lists important protective factors against suicide.

Table 16.2 Possible Precipitants of Suicide

- Getting into trouble with authorities (e.g., school or community, fear of the consequences).
- Romantic breakup.
- Death of a loved one or significant person.
- Disappointment and rejection such as a dispute with boy/girlfriend, failure to get a job, or rejection from college.
- Bullying or victimization.
- Conflict with family or family dysfunction.
- Disappointment with school results or school failure.
- High demands at school during examination periods.
- Unwanted pregnancy, abortion.
- Infection with HIV or other sexually transmitted diseases.
- The anniversary of a death of a friend or loved one.
- Knowing someone who committed suicide.
- Separation from friends, girlfriends/boyfriends.
- Real or perceived loss.
- Serious physical illness.
- Serious injury that may change the individual's life course.
- Feeling humiliated.

Table 16.3 Protective Factors that Mitigate Suicide Risk

- Effective problem-solving and interpersonal skills, including conflict resolution and nonviolent handling of disputes.
- Contact with a caring adult.
- A sense of involvement/belonging to one's school, based on opportunities to participate in school activities and contribute to the functioning of the school (effective school climate).
- Effective and appropriate clinical care for mental, physical, and substance abuse disorders.
- Easy access to a variety of clinical interventions and support for help seeking.
- Restricted access to highly lethal methods of suicide.
- Family and community support.
- Cultural and religious beliefs that discourage suicide and support self-preservation instincts.
- Positive self-esteem.
- Resilience and a sense of self-efficacy.
- A sense of purpose.
- Strong religious or spiritual connections.
- A strong network of caring friends.
- A positive and nurturing school climate.

School-based Suicide Prevention and Intervention

Identifying Potentially Suicidal Students

The following section will discuss the three main approaches to identifying and assessing potentially suicidal students. The first is to adopt a universal screening system that can be used to identify youth at risk for engaging in suicidal behavior. This method provides a suicide screening for *all* students in the school. The best known screening system has been developed by the SAMHSA and is called Signs of Suicide: The Brief Screen for Adolescent Depression (Aseltine, James, Schilling, & Glanovsky, 2007). This brief self-screening tool assesses depressive symptoms and suicidal ideation among students who are in the eighth grade and above (Lieberman, Poland, & Kornfeld, 2014). The second approach is to use selected assessments with students who display a higher risk for engaging in suicidal behavior (e.g., students who recently had a friend or family member die by suicide, students with substance abuse problems, students who are chronic victims of bullying). For example, Miami-Dade County Public Schools in Florida developed a Student Intervention Profile to identify students who may be at risk for serious emotional or behavioral problems—though not necessarily for suicide. Classroom teachers and other school professionals rate all students on their performance in the following areas: Academic achievement, effort, conduct, attendance, negative report card comments, code of conduct violations, and involvement with school resource officers. Students who show difficulty in three or more of these areas are referred to a school counselor. As a result, the counselor meets with the student and works with other school staff to help the student succeed in school and cope with serious emotional and behavioral problems (Zenere & Lazarus, 2009). The third approach is the one that will be discussed in the greatest detail and it involves assessing students who are referred to school-based mental health professionals by students, staff, or by self-referral.

Universal Approaches

Similar to efforts to improve students' mental health and behavior at school, a range of services and supports can be provided to reduce suicidal and related behaviors in students (Doll & Cummings, 2008; Hess, Short, & Hazel, 2012). According to research, universal prevention programs (i.e., those programs that target all students in the school) should focus on educating school professionals about suicide warning signs and risk factors; developing a district-wide school policy concerning suicide; encouraging collaboration among teachers, nurses, and mental health personnel; including suicide prevention education in the classroom curriculum; developing a peer assistance program; reducing the stigma of help-seeking behavior; and implementing activities aimed at increasing school connectedness (e.g., Kalafat, 2003; King, 2001; Mazza & Reynolds, 2008). Furthermore, such programs should also support school and family partnerships and establish a school-wide crisis team (Kalafat & Lazarus, 2002).

As part of a universal prevention approach, all districts need to have a policy regarding responding to suicidal behavior. In a presentation to school personnel, Brock (2014) provides one example of such a policy:

> It is the policy of the School District that all staff members learn how to recognize students at risk, to identify warning signs of suicide, to take preventative precautions, and to report suicide threats to the appropriate parental and professional authorities. Administration shall ensure that all staff members have been issued a copy of the District's suicide prevention policy and procedures. All staff members are responsible for knowing and acting upon them.

As a significant component of universal intervention, presentations to school personnel about suicide prevention and intervention should occur annually or at least every other year at a minimum. Knowledgeable school mental health professionals should deliver these presentations to all teaching, administrative, and support staff. Additionally, schools can also encourage volunteer coaches, bus drivers, after-school tutors, and other school personnel who interact with suicidal students to attend such presentations. Because adolescence is the time of greatest risk for student suicide, presentations on suicide prevention and intervention should be provided to all middle and high school students on a yearly basis. A key reason for delivering this information directly to students is that most suicidal youth talk about their intentions with peers yet not with adults (Kalafat, 2003). Unfortunately, a "code of silence" often exists between students and adults with regard to sharing important information such as suicidal statement made by a peer (Sulkowski, 2011). In one study, as few as 25 percent of peer confidents reported that they would tell an adult about a suicidal peer (Kalafat, 2003). Thus, a major goal of the aforementioned presentations is to increase students' willingness to report peers who can benefit from receiving professional help and support.

In all universal suicide prevention presentations, students should be provided information on where to get help if they or a peer are experiencing suicidal thoughts. In most cases, this involves first talking with a trusted adult at school. However, potentially suicidal students should be provided with multiple options for sharing their concerns. In other words, they should have a choice about with whom to share their painful thoughts and feelings.

Students can be taught that getting help for feeling sad and depressed is analogous to getting help for a physical health problem (Miller, 2011). Educators can emphasize that unless the student gets medical attention for a broken leg, diabetes, or an infected tooth, the problem will not get better and that the same is true for mental health problems. Reducing the stigma for seeking help for mental health issues is critically important for helping suicidal students. Also, students need to be taught that it is imperative that they not keep a secret about a friend feeling suicidal. Instead, they need to share the information with an adult who can help.

Presentations to school staff can occur in a large venue. However, when presenting to students, it may be better to hold these presentations in classrooms rather than in large assembly halls because of the sensitive nature of suicide. In some capacity, some students may have been impacted by suicide themselves so care and empathy is needed when broaching this topic. Moreover, time for questions, consultation, and follow-up with affected individuals may be needed that cannot be easily provided in a large group context (Poland, 1989). Underscoring the notion that many students have some experience with suicide, research indicates that 60 percent of adolescents report knowing a teenager who has attempted suicide and 20 percent report knowing a friend who has attempted suicide within the past year (Resnick et al., 1997). To those who lost a friend or family member to suicide, feelings run deep, and as a result a presentation on this topic can stir up strong emotions that need space, time, and empathy to be adequately processed.

Selected and Indicated Approaches

Proactively Responding

In selected and indicated approaches, educators and school- based mental health professionals respond to students at risk or at high risk for a particular problem, such as suicide. It is important to emphasize that it is not the responsibility of a classroom teacher to determine if a student is suicidal, but it is the educator's responsibility to inform a school-based mental health professional *immediately* who can help to make this assessment. In cases in which a mental health professional is not readily available on campus, the educator, in collaboration with the school principal or a member of the school crisis team, should immediately contact the mental health professional off campus and/or the district office and follow-up with them according to district policy. Tragedies can occur if an educator waits until the mental health professional is back on campus or if information related to suicide risk is not shared with those who can help mitigate this risk. As a prime example of this, in *Wyke v. Polk County* (1997), the U.S. Court of Appeals held a Florida junior high school responsible for the death of Shawn Wyke, 13, who died by suicide at home after he made two attempts to kill himself by hanging while in school. Rather than notifying parents after the first attempt, the assistant principal invited the boy into his office to read scripture. The court ruled, "We do not believe that a prudent person would have needed a crystal ball to see that Shawn needed help, and that if he didn't get it soon, he might attempt suicide again" (Poland & Chartrand, 2008). On appeal, the Eleventh Circuit court upheld financial damages awarded to Shawn's mother and ruled that when a child attempts suicide at school, and the school knows about the attempt, the school can be held liable for not notifying the parents (Fossey & Zirkel, 2011).

When encountering a student who expresses thoughts about dying, educators should remain calm, try to understand the student's plight, and be empathetic. This is the time for educators to listen genuinely using a non-judgmental approach. Show that anything that the student says will be respected and that all of the listed problems can have solutions. Essentially, during these critical moments, it is important not to ignore or dismiss the student's concerns or to sound shocked, which can inadvertently magnify these concerns. It is important that the educator ensures that the student knows that is okay to talk and that he or she is most concerned about the student's well-being. Often, just providing the student with the opportunity to vent painful feelings and be genuinely heard can help immensely (Poland, 1995).

In this role, it can be helpful to express to the student that it is not unusual for young people to think about self-harm and suicide and that with time and help, these thoughts and painful feelings can ease, even though it does not feel this way now. Moreover, it is important not to challenge the student's thoughts, negate their experiences, or argue with them. If appropriate, mention the family as a source of support (Lazarus, 2009). However, do not mention the shame or embarrassment this could bring to the family, as this could be a motivating factor. If the student is being indirect about his or her problems, and it becomes difficult to ascertain if the student is considering suicide, Brock (2014) recommends taking a direct approach and asking the following question: "Sometimes when people have had your experiences and feelings they have thoughts of ending their lives. Is this something you're thinking about?" If the student reveals that he or she has suicidal thoughts or shows warning signs, tell them that you will be walking with them to see someone at school who has experience with students who feel this way and knows what to do. Importantly, never promise confidentiality (Lazarus, 2009). Then, immediately take the student to a mental health professional at the school who can conduct a suicide risk assessment and follow up that same day (Lazarus, 2009).

Addressing Self-injury

Self-injury is not always the same as a suicidal gesture. In fact, many times self-injury is done for different reasons than wanting to die (Nock, Joiner, Gordon, Lloyd-Richardson, & Prinstein, 2006). However, it may be unclear at times if a student has suicidal or other intentions. This situation occurs when an educator finds out that a student is engaging in self-injurious behavior that involves cutting, scratching, burning or other forms of self-harm. This type of behavior is relatively common and has become increasingly more so during the past two decades. In one study, 28 percent of adolescents reported engaging in self-harm and 8 percent reported engaging in repetitive self-injurious behavior (Brunner et al., 2014). In contrast to students who engage in suicidal behavior with the intention of ending their own life, non-suicidal self-injury often is done to relieve emotional distress, dissociate from emotional pain, and as a help-seeking behavior without any intention of dying (Lieberman, Poland, & Kornfeld, 2014).

Nonetheless, self-injury is a risk factor for suicide and individuals who engage in self-injury are three times more likely to think about or attempt suicide (Whitlock et al., 2012). Moreover, if a student who engages in non-suicidal self-injury does become suicidal, then it may be easier for that individual to carry out an attempt due to possible desensitization to pain or blood. Overall, a student who is engaging in self-injury is experiencing deep pain and needs immediate mental health care. When encountering a student who engages in self-injurious behavior, educators should talk with the person with the same compassion and empathy as they would with a student who is in the midst of a suicidal crisis. Moreover, if an educator finds out that a student is engaging in self-injury, then a referral to a school-based mental health professional is recommended who can carry out a comprehensive evaluation.

In Expert Interview 16.1, Scott Poland, Ed.D., discusses self-injury, why students engage in this behavior, what school personnel can do to intervene, and the most effective treatment for this phenomenon. He also discusses the relationship between suicide and self-injury, common misconception regarding this behavior, and what school personnel can do to reach out to families of students who engage in self-injury.

Expert Interview 16.1 with Scott Poland

Nova Southeastern University

PJL. What is self-injury?

SP. Self-injury is defined as moderate superficial intentional wounds to the body that are not intended to cause permanent damage or result in suicide. The most common form of self-injury is cutting, followed by burning or scratching. Self-injurious behaviors most commonly occur during the teenage years. Self-injury was previously thought to begin and end in adolescence, but now upper elementary students are engaging in this behavior as well as many adults.

PJL. What are the latest statistics on teen self-injury?

SP. It is difficult to get exact figures about the incidence, as many teens are very good at hiding the behavior and deny that they engage in it. Research studies have consistently found that at least 10 to 15 percent of high school and college-age students engage in self-injury. The behavior is more prevalent for girls than boys.

PJL. Is a person who engages in self-injury necessarily suicidal? If not, why not?

SP. Self-injury is a coping mechanism utilized mostly by teenagers. Many have commented that they cut so that they will not kill themselves. Some professionals have thought that there are entirely separate groups of teenagers—those that engage in self-injury and those that are suicidal. There is actually a continuum and most teens who engage in self-injury are not suicidal, but some are. Often a suicide attempt is what alerts adults to a history of several months or even years of self-injury. The literature emphasizes that self-injurers who disassociate and who cut deeply are the most prone to suicidal behavior.

PJL. Why do teens engage in cutting and other self-injurious behavior?

S. P. Self-injury is most often engaged in after a stressful precipitating event. The most common stimuli are arguments with parents, difficulties with peers, disappointments, or a humiliation. Self-injury allows the teen to shut out the argument or stressful event and concentrate on the injury to their body. Many have commented that it feels good to experience physical pain when they are feeling overwhelmed by emotional pain.

PJL. Why has self-injury become popular among teens in recent years?

S. P. The behavior has been popularized through the media, and a number of celebrities admit to a history of self-injury. I was surprised by the prevalence and students' commitment to self-injury during my work in the schools. Self-injury is a learned coping behavior. Most teens learn about it from each other, either in person or online. Also, they sometimes engage in the behavior on a dare at an adolescent sleepover. They remember how it felt and engage in the behavior later on when they are feeling extreme stress or emotional pain.

PJL. What does self-injury do for the person who engages in this behavior?

SP. There are primarily three theories of why teens engage in self-injury. The most prevalent one is *biological* as the behavior releases endorphins immediately that help the teen feel better. These are the same endorphins that we wish that teens would release through exercise! The biological release can result in the behavior becoming addictive. I organized and created a video for the state of Florida entitled, *Self-injury: Testimony and critical issues*, where I interviewed two young women who received a national award for their willingness to talk about struggling with self-injury. They emphasized how addictive the behavior can become. The video is available on my university website under training materials. Please visit www.nova.edu/suicideprevention.

The second theory is *psychological regulation* as the teen is able to focus on their intentional injury instead of on the painful precipitating event. The third theory is *Freudian* and it posits that the teen is in a state of high or unbearable anxiety, and by engaging in self-injury the teen is experiencing catharsis and punishing themselves at the same time.

PJL. What are some common misconceptions and misunderstandings about self-injury?

SP. The most common misperceptions are that the behavior equates with suicide; that those that engage in it have extreme psychological problems; and that they hate their body image. There is a new breed of self-injurers and for the most part they are intelligent and likeable, but they break down under accumulated stress and engage in self-injury. This new breed is more amenable to treatment. Self-injurers are also often thought to be depressed or to have a borderline personality which may or may not be the case.

PJL. If a teacher, counselor or administrator finds out that a student is engaging in self-injury, what should they do and what are the legal issues involved in notifying parents?

SP. This has been a controversial issue as some of the professional literature cautions against telling parents as it may result in the teen not trusting key school personnel such as the counselor. I co-authored a chapter on self-injury for *NASP children's needs* and we stated that parents must be notified with one exception, and that is if the mental health professional believes that the parents are abusing their child and then child protective services needs to be contacted. I was an expert witness in a legal case filed against a school district where the plaintiffs claimed that the school counselor knew about the self-injurious behavior but did not tell the parents. The case went to court but no damages were assessed against the school district or the counselor, but the case did raise many questions about parent notification, created stress for the counselor, and resulted in legal costs for the district. The challenge is to get a supportive reaction from parents and refer the teen to the most effective treatment available. The best scenario is to have the teen tell their parents with key school personnel such as a counselor or school psychologist in the conference.

PJL. How can school personnel make a difference in the lives of children who are engaged in self-injury?

SP. School personnel need to be alert for signs of self-injury and work as a team to obtain the needed support and services for the student. Key personnel on the school team are teachers, counselors, nurses, and administrators who need to share information with each other and increase the circle of care for the student. Schools need to raise the awareness of the staff about self-injury through in-service; develop procedures for responding to self-injury; and keep up with the literature on the most effective treatments. The signs that would be most noticeable to school personnel include cuts, burns or bandages on the student's forearms. The most common places on the body where students self-injure are the forearms, thighs and stomach. School personnel should be alert when students always wear long sleeve shirts or sweatshirts even during the hottest months of the year. It is essential that school personnel respond with compassion and recognize the struggle and stress that the student is going through when they engage in self-injury. It is important not to be horrified about the behavior and to avoid demanding that the behavior be stopped immediately, but instead help the student engage in substitute strategies to help them reduce the behavior. It is also important to recognize that the treatment of self-injury will take some time, and that there is no quick fix.

PJL. What is the most effective treatment for self-injury?

SP. The most effective treatment has been a combination of medications such as anti-depressants and therapy. In particular the most effective therapy is Dialectical Behavior Therapy (DBT) which is a blend of cognitive therapy, relaxation and mindfulness. DBT therapy involves more than a weekly meeting, as the therapist needs to be available by phone to help the teen get through a few difficult moments when they have the urge to cut. In addition, the teen also attends group therapy weekly to develop more effective coping skills. To be honest, DBT is beyond what we could expect a school counselor or school psychologist to provide given ratios of one counselor to 700 students and two or three times that student number for the ratio of students to school psychologists. School personnel need to know the best treatment resources available in the community to treat self-injury and need to make a referral. They also should follow up with the teen and their parents and get a release of information so they can communicate with the community service provider.

Conducting a Suicide Risk Assessment

When a student engages in any form of self-injury, expresses a concern about suicide, or makes a suicidal gesture or threat, a mental health professional should be called upon immediately to determine the seriousness of the behavior. Also when educators, parents, or peers become concerned about a potentially suicidal youth, school staff will need to follow specific practices to protect the student, and a suicide risk assessment will need to be conducted. Brock (2014) and Lazarus (2015) have outlined specific practices that school staff should follow when a student has made a suicidal threat, and these are listed in Text Box 16.2. Ultimately, these practices should be built into a suicide risk assessment.

Text Box 16.2 Suicide Intervention Practices for School Staff

- Make sure the student is supervised at all times.
- Do not agree to keep a student's suicidal intention a secret.
- Do not allow the student to leave the school.
- Have the student speak to a school-based mental health professional.
- If the school-based mental health professional is not available then contact the school-based or district-based crisis team. In some districts staff may be directed to contact an outside mental health agency.
- If the student has the means to carry out the threatened suicide on his or her own person, determine if he or she will voluntarily relinquish it. Do not force the student to do so. Do not place yourself in danger. Call the police if they have a weapon and will not give it up.
- Inform the suicidal youth that professional help has been contacted and describe what the next steps will be.

Trained mental health professionals conduct suicide risk assessments. When conducting these assessments, it is imperative to convey empathy, support, and concern, and to explain why the assessment is being conducted. The mental health professional needs to communicate that the intention of the evaluation is to help ensure the immediate safety of the student. The student needs to understand that many people care about the student and want him or her to get the appropriate help they need. Poland (1989) provides further guidance during this process. Specifically, he recommends that the professional (a) use effective listening skills by reflecting feelings, remaining non-judgmental, and emphasizing the seriousness of the concerns; (b) respect developmental, cultural, and sexuality issues when gathering information; (c) be direct when questioning the student, staff, and parent; (d) use an assessment worksheet; (e) do not promise confidentiality to the student, and (f), ensure that the student is supervised at all times.

The task of actually talking with a student about suicide can be emotionally challenging to the mental health professional as well as potentially therapeutic for the student. Instead of suffering in silence, the student might feel heard and understood by a caring adult. Therefore, it is critically important to be open and empathetic when students share difficult subjects such as their suffering and thoughts about suicide and dying. In addition, students should be questioned in a conversational style (as opposed to in an overly formal style) in all areas of risk. Questions should focus on: (a) Is there a current suicide plan? (b) How much stress and pain is the student experiencing? (c) What resources are available to help the student? (d) Does the student have a prior history of suicidal behavior? and (e) What is the overall mental health of the student?

If a suicide plan has been developed, then the mental health professional can use the *SLAPT* acronym to understand the level of risk (e.g., Granello & Granello, 2007). This acronym is spelled out in the following: *S*pecific: How specific are the details of the plan? *L*ethality: How lethal is the proposed method? *A*vailability: What is the availability of the proposed method? *P*roximity: What is the proximity of helping resources? *T*imeline: How immediate is the timeline? (Note: The original acronym was SLAP and "T" was added to emphasize the timeline). See Text Box 16.3 for questions to ask a student who has a suicide plan.

Text Box 16.3 Questions to Ask a Student with a Potential Suicide Plan

Sometimes when people have dealt with similar things and felt the same way, they feel like they want to die or kill themselves. Every day, many people have these kinds of thoughts and it is not uncommon. Sometimes they even surprise friends and family members because they seem so happy and put together, yet they are struggling to deal with some heavy stuff. Anyway, you're not alone at all if you feel this way. Have you been thinking like this at all? If so, how often have you had these thoughts? (every day, a few times a week, a few times a month, etc.).

- If so, how would you harm yourself?
- Do you have a current plan?
- Do you have what you need to follow through on your plan?
- When are you planning on doing this?
- Have you ever attempted suicide before? If the answer is yes, then ask, Does anyone know?
- When was your last attempt and how did you go about it?
- What has been keeping you alive so far?
- What is your hurry? Why do it now?
- What do you think the future holds in store for you?

Securing Mental Health Treatment

Following a suicide risk assessment, some students will need acute mental health care. These are the individuals who display a legitimate risk of engaging in suicidal behavior or serious self-harm. In order to secure appropriate treatment, the answers to four critical questions are needed (Lieberman et al., 2008). These are: (a) Is the parent available? (b) Is the parent cooperative? (c) What information does the parent have that might help in assessing risk? (d) What health insurance does the student have?

If the parent is available and cooperative and the student is judged to be at high risk, then the mental health professional must provide parents with referral resources within the community based on their mental health insurance status. When suggesting community resources, school districts are obligated to suggest agencies that are nonproprietary, provide culturally responsive services, and treat children and adolescents. Some providers and clinics may offer sliding scale rates (Lieberman et al., 2014). The mental health professional needs to be aware of all local providers and keep a list of up-to-date mental health professionals who have expertise in dealing with suicidal youth. In addition, factors such as developmental level, language, culture, sexual orientation, gender, socioeconomic resources, and medical insurance status may need to be considered when making a referral. In some circumstances a male or female professional may be preferred. For example, if a female student had been sexually abused or assaulted by a male perpetrator, a female therapist would most likely be recommended.

With parental permission, or in tandem with the parent, the school-based mental health professional should contact the provider or community agency, provide pertinent referral information, and follow up to make sure the child arrived and was seen. It is highly recommended to get a parent's signature on a release of information form to ensure communication between the school and the provider or agency (Lieberman et al., 2008). Also SAMHSA (2012) recommends that the parents should be asked to sign an acknowledgment form confirming that they were notified of their child's risk and received referral for treatment. On another note, if the student needs to be hospitalized, it is important for the school staff to work with the parent to develop a plan for the student upon returning to school. As in every phase of assessment and intervention, all actions need to be documented and stored in a secure location.

Schools should have predetermined policies and procedures to guide crisis teams when a parent is not immediately available and these should be followed when a student is assessed to be at high risk. If there are no written policies or procedures, student safety should be the primary consideration. Perhaps, at the discretion of the school principal, two members of the school crisis team could take the student to the closest emergency mental health center and continue to try to contact a legal guardian of the student. Another alternative is to request that the local police, a school resource officer, or a mobile psychiatric response team assist in transporting the youth to a mental health center (Lieberman et al., 2008). In many states, such as in Florida (under the Baker Act), police can be contacted to secure and bring suicidal youth to the nearest treatment facility where the student will be further evaluated and can be held for treatment for up to 72 hours.

There are caveats regarding parental notification. Lieberman et al. (2014) recommend that if the team decides that it is more of a risk to inform a student's parents due to potential abuse, neglect, or retribution that could result from making a disclosure, then the school staff may directly contact child protective services without informing a caregiver. Or if parents do not take the suicide risk seriously, refuse to follow through with the intervention recommendations, or endanger the child by failing to remove or secure accessible weapons, dangerous objects or chemicals/potentially lethal medications in the home, then immediate notification of child protective services is warranted (Lieberman et al., 2008).

Responding to Parents of Suicidal Youth

As previously discussed, parents need to be contacted as soon as possible after a student has been identified as being at risk for suicide and provided with treatment options. The mental health professional working with the family needs to be sensitive toward the family's culture, including attitudes toward mental health, privacy, help seeking, and suicide. Most importantly, the parents and the student should not leave school that day without arrangements for appropriate mental health care or hospitalization (Lazarus, 2009). When communicating with parents about concerns for the suicidal student, it is important to convey specific information which is provided in Text Box 16.4.

Text Box 16.4 Key Points to Address when Talking to Parents about their Potentially Suicidal Child

When the parent or guardian arrives at school, the mental health professional will need to explain why he or she believes that the student is at high risk and emphasize these key points:

Thank you for coming to school right away to discuss something that happened today with your son, Robert. (Explain the incident and share any evidence related to the seriousness of the suicidal threat or concern.) It is important for us to recognize the significance of the problem and act quickly. This is the time to increase the amount of emotional support and supervision you provide. Show love and tolerance for Robert; this is not a time for tough love. Surround him with a circle of support. Keep the lines of communication open and avoid conflict for now. Immediately remove any potentially lethal instruments from your home such as knives and guns and lock up prescription medication. Be patient and offer to help him with "no strings attached." We can help you find a mental health professional that can provide the necessary support that Robert needs. It is imperative that you act on a referral to a mental health professional of your choice. If Robert refuses to see a mental health professional, then you must insist that he do so. Please take all suicide attempts seriously and accompany Robert to all appointments with mental health professionals. If you believe that his suicidal behavior is for attention, then you want to provide the attention and care that he wants and seems so desperately to need.

Following Up and Re-entry

School staff ought to maintain contact with the family and follow up on the student's progress after treatment for suicide has begun. Arranging for homebound instruction, coordinating for school work to be completed in an in-patient hospital, or making modifications to the student's academic program may be necessary. Essentially, maintaining a circle of care among the school, family, and mental health resources is key to helping students recover from suicidality and getting their lives back on track. Negligence in this regard can not only set a student back academically, but it also can have a negative impact on their social-emotional functioning.

Educators and school-based mental health professionals need to be prepared to facilitate school re-entry for students who have attempted suicide and were hospitalized. Returning to school can be difficult for these youth because they may have problems catching up academically and may worry about how their peers and teachers will treat them. Also, they may be taking medications that can interfere with their focus, energy, and concentration. Thus, these problems can create additional stress on students who are already feeling overwhelmed. To help assist students who are transitioning back to school after a suicide attempt or hospitalization, the SAMSHA recommends that a particular staff member be assigned the duty of facilitating the student's re-entry and aligning with parents throughout every step in the process (SAMSHA, 2012).

In Expert Interview 16.2, Richard Lieberman discusses his role as the former District Youth Suicide Prevention Coordinator in the Los Angeles Unified School District, the second largest public school district in the United States, and how suicide prevention, intervention and post-vention were addressed in the district. He also discusses the advantages and disadvantages of screening for depression and other suicide risk factors and how to access the district's website regarding policies, procedures and protocols, and other relevant material related to youth suicide.

Expert Interview 16.2 Richard Lieberman

Los Angeles Unified School District

PJL. How do you view the suicide rate of young people today? What have you been seeing in Los Angeles Unified School District (LAUSD)?

RL. After two decades of decline, there is some indication that suicide among youth is increasing. Every year, with its over 800,000 students, LAUSD suffers multiple student deaths by suicide. Despite the fact the suicide rate in Los Angeles and LAUSD is a fraction of the national suicide rate, news of one suicide is news too much and LAUSD will remain committed to doing everything it can to prevent youth suicide.

PJL. What has been your role as a suicide interventionist for LAUSD? And how do you help schools deal with this problem?

RL. My role has been to coordinate the Youth Suicide Prevention Program in place in the over 1100 schools of LAUSD. The program has a prevention component that involves training of school staff in knowing the risk factors and recognizing the warning signs of youth suicide. This is called a Gatekeeper approach where school staff, parents and students are educated on what to do when they are concerned about students or peers.

Crisis teams of administrators and mental health personnel are formed at each school and informed of the policies and procedures when intervening with a suicidal student. Perhaps the most difficult part of my job is reaching out to schools in the aftermath of a student or staff death by suicide. After a suicide occurs in a community, there is a greater chance of another occurring so all school personnel need to remain vigilant.

PJL. Describe how your school district responds to potentially suicidal youth.

R.L There are both general and specific guidelines for school personnel when a potentially suicidal student is identified. The student will be supervised throughout the entire process and escorted to a crisis team member who will assess the student for suicide risk. Based on that assessment, the crisis team member will follow district policies that will include making the appropriate notification to parents, guardians or Child Protective Services; they will make a plan and provide resources to both the student and family; and they will document all actions in a confidential file.

PJL . What would you say to administrators who would question whether or not suicide prevention efforts should be incorporated into the school curriculum? We know that schools already have so much on their plate.

RL. See me now or see me later. Suicide is preventable. Suicide prevention policies and procedures are an *essential* component to any school district's Safety Plan.

PJL. How can all members of school communities become involved in suicide prevention efforts?

RL. Schools can reach out to their parents and community agencies to come together and form a suicide prevention task force. This task force will provide a network of support for the schools to initiate suicide prevention policies and procedures. Suicide is not a school problem; it is a public health problem.

PJL. What are the advantages of screening young people for suicidal risk? Are there any disadvantages?

R.L. There are both advantages and disadvantages of screening students for depression and other suicide risk factors. The benefit is obvious, find students who are at risk *before* they hurt themselves. The disadvantage is also obvious, *Be careful what you ask for!* If you use depression screening as a universal approach and screen an entire school, be prepared to respond to somewhere between 10–20 percent of your student body who report a prolonged sense of sadness or hopelessness over the past year. If you cannot provide services on such a large scale, universal screening should be avoided. However, many schools have used a targeted approach to depression screening and only screen sixth or ninth graders so they can provide follow up services for possibly years after a student is identified.

PJL. Why don't more school districts use effective screening measures?

RL. They are afraid of identifying children and not being able to intervene.

PJL. What do you say to a parent that says, "My daughter (or son) is only doing this for attention and doesn't really mean it?"

RL. This is what is known as a "myth." For example, a parent might say, "a person who talks about it, never actually does it." They could not be more wrong! Youth, who talk about it, do it. I always agree with a parent who says their child is only doing this for attention. If a parent minimizes the danger and does nothing, I always say wait until you see what the child will come up with next. Sometimes a child says something, does something, writes or draws something that essentially says that they are thinking of killing themselves. We *must* intervene. The consequence of doing nothing can result in a preventable death.

PJL. What are the most important things that teachers or administrators can do to prevent suicide and help young people who are considering suicide or have already made an attempt?

RL. Supervise the student and take action immediately. Such actions can involve assessing the child for risk and taking appropriate action such as notifying parents or protective agencies; providing counseling or school and community resources; calling emergency services such a law enforcement or psychiatric mobile response teams.

PJL. Are there effective treatments for the risk factors of suicide? What are they?

RL. Yes! There are evidence-based treatments for the major risk factors of youth suicide, which include mental illness (most often depression), and alcohol and substance abuse. These treatments include cognitive, trauma focused, and dialectical behavioral therapies; medications; and firearm/means restrictions such as gunlocks or locked gun cases.

PJL. Please share information from your school district regarding suicide prevention, intervention and postvention.

RL. The district has information about policies, procedures, responsibilities of employees, suicide warning signs, self-injury, protocols for responding to students at risk for suicide and/or self injury, letters to parents, assessment checklists and protocols, release of information forms, sample letters to parents, a suicide risk assessment checklist, and much more. This information is available at http://notebook.lausd.net/pls/ptl/docs/PAGE/CA_LAUSD/ FLDR_ORGANIZATIONS/STUDENT_HEALTH_HUMAN_SERVICES/SHHS/MENTAL/ SMH_SUICIDE_PREVENTION/SUICIDE_PREVENTION_RESOURCE/BUL-2637.1_ SUICIDE_PREVENTION_INTERVENTION_POSTVENTION.PDF.

Legal Responsibilities of School Personnel

Several key issues influence a school's liability after the suicide of a student. These include *foreseeability*, *negligence*, and *state-created danger* (Erbacher, Singer& Poland, 2014). Regarding *foreseeability,* a school district could be held liable if it has been found that a reasonable person would have been able to recognize that a student was in such a state of emotional distress and that self-harm or danger should have been anticipated. Courts have allowed legal actions against school officials when a lack of appropriate school policies and procedures existed to respond to a suicidal student as well as when appropriate supervision of a suicidal student was not provided. In other words, schools have been found culpable for not taking adequate steps to prevent suicide if a student was in imminent danger or displaying acute signs of suicide risk (Erbacher et al., 2014).

The second issue that can result in a school being liable for a student suicide is *negligence*. Negligence involves "a breach of duty owed to the individual involving injury or damage that finds a causal connection between a student's suicide and an absence of duty to care for the student" (Erbacher et al., 2014, p. 52). Thus, schools that do not respond appropriately to address student suicide risk also can be found negligent. Finally, the third issue is *state-created danger*. In situations such as this, the plaintiffs have to present a highly compelling case, which can be challenging. Essentially, the plaintiffs must establish that (a) there was a foreseeable and direct harm, (b) a state actor (such as a school employee) acted with a degree of responsibility that shocks the conscience, (c) there existed a relationship between the plaintiff and the state actor such that the plaintiff was a foreseeable victim of the defendant's act, and (d) a state actor used authority to create danger for the citizen (Erbacher, et al., 2014, p. 52).

Fossey and Zirkel (2011) have reviewed almost two-dozen cases where a plaintiff sued educators and school-based mental health professionals for damages arising from a student's suicide. From this review, they concluded that under both common law and constitutional claims, in none of the cases reviewed, have school employees or school based-mental health professionals been held responsible for a damage award. Thus, the emotional burdens experienced by educators and school-based mental health professionals in the aftermath of student suicide likely far exceed financial risks and burdens.

For illustrative purposes two cases—one related to negligence and the other to constitutional claims—are briefly discussed in the following section. Both show the tremendous burden that is placed on plaintiffs to recover damages from a school district following the suicide of their child. By no means are these cases presented to reduce any vigilance among educators or others in identifying and treating suicidal students. Instead, they are presented to portray most relevant case law related to this issue as objectively as possible. See Fossey and Zirkel (2011) for a more extensive discussion of these issues.

Eisel v. Board of Education of Montgomery County (1991)

In this case, Nicole Eisel died as a result of an apparent murder suicide pact. According to her father's complaint, Nicole had told other students that she wanted to kill herself and her peers shared this information with school counselors. Reportedly, the counselors questioned Nicole about these concerns yet she denied having suicidal feelings or thoughts. Neither Nicole's parents nor school administrators were notified about suicidal statements that she was alleged to have made to her friends. Sadly, shortly after interviewing her, Nicole and her friend killed themselves.

The trial court dismissed the lawsuit. However upon appeal, Maryland's highest court reversed the decision and sent it back to the lower court for a trial. The appellate court listed six factors for determining whether school employees had a duty to warn Nicole's parents. These were:

(1) foreseeability of harm, (2) public policy considerations about the value of preventing future harm, (3) the close proximity in time between the actions of the school defendants and suicide, (4) moral blame, (5) the burden on the defendant that would be imposed if they assumed a duty to prevent Nicole's suicide, and (6) the defendant's ability to obtain insurance to cover the risk of liability for a student's suicide.

(Fossey & Zirkel, 2011, p.132)

According to the interpretation of the case, foreseeability was the most important determinant in deciding whether the school defendants had the legal duty to try to prevent Nicole from completing suicide. After deliberating, the jury determined that the counselors were not liable for Nicole's death. Though the court record does not explain why the jury made its decision, Fossey & Zirkel (2011) speculate that perhaps the jury believed that the counselors were not aware of Nicole's suicidal intent.

Sanford v Stiles (2006)

This case involved two constitutional claims. A 16-year-old student, Michael Sanford, gave a girl he once dated a disturbing note in which he brought up suicide. Although the student did not believe that Michael would complete suicide, she decided to tell her school counselor about the note. The counselor who was informed gave Michael's note to his own counselor, Ms. Stiles, who later brought Michael into her office and questioned him about suicide. Michael told Ms. Stiles that he was not suicidal and expressed to her that he had no plans to hurt himself. He is reported having said that he definitely would not do such a thing, yet Michael completed suicide by hanging himself a few days later. Michael's mother sued Ms. Stiles on the constitutional theory that Stiles had increased the danger that Michael would kill himself and also for negligence under Pennsylvania law (Fossey & Zirkel, 2011). However, the federal trial court dismissed the lawsuit and on appeal the Third Circuit affirmed the trial court's decision. They explained that the plaintiff could only prevail if they could

> prove these four elements: (1) the harm ultimately caused was foreseeable and fairly direct; (2) the state actor acted with a degree of culpability that shocks the conscience; (3) a relationship between the state and the plaintiff existed such that the plaintiff was a foreseeable victim of the defendant's acts, or a member of a discrete class of persons subjected to the potential harm brought about by the state's actions, as opposed to a member of the public in general; and (4) the state actor affirmatively used his or her authority in a way that created a danger to the citizen or rendered the citizen more vulnerable to danger than had the state not acted at all.
>
> (Fossey & Zirkel, 2011, p. 137)

The plaintiffs were unable to prove all the elements in the case, and in upholding the trial court's decision, the Third Circuit explained that Ms. Stiles had not ignored Michael's note and had determined that he was not suicidal as based upon her conversation with him.

Fossey and Zirkel (2011) conclude that courts tend to support the schools and their employees for a number of reasons in cases of a student's suicide. These include a refusal to recognize a claim that appears to be related to educational malpractice, statutory immunity, a lack of evidence that showed that school employees were a contributing cause of a student's death, or the doctrine that suicide is an intervening cause of death for which third parties cannot be held liable. Nevertheless, lawsuits are emotionally draining, time consuming, and expensive, and school districts need to engage in best practices to prevent these from occurring. Based on court rulings, Erbacher et al. (2014) admonish school personnel to protect themselves from suicide liability by (a) providing mandatory crisis training related to suicide prevention and intervention and documenting the dates and those in attendance; (b) keeping excellent records; (c) contacting parents whenever a student is at risk for suicide (in person, if possible); (d) maintaining constant supervision of suicidal students until the parents, the police, or child protective services has custody of the student; (e) maintaining liability insurance; and (f), following best practices (which are explained in this chapter or can be found in documents provided by AAS, AFSP, SAMHSA).

Conclusion

As expressed by former Surgeon General Satcher (U.S. Public Health Service, 1999), the impact of suicide is devastating to families, schools, and communities. Essentially, student suicide is a tragic national public health problem that concerns us all (Lazarus, Brock, Lieberman, Poland, Zenere, & Feinberg, 2009; Lazarus & Kalafat, 2001). It is an unfortunate fact that most school communities will be impacted by youth suicide at some point. Because of this, all school personnel must become involved with suicide prevention efforts.

Fortunately, however, educators and school-based mental health professionals can do a lot to prevent youth suicide. Most basically, they can pay attention to suicide risk factors, warning signs, and potential precipitants, and make referrals to professionals who can help potentially suicidal students. They can ensure that universal, selected, and indicated interventions are in place to prevent suicide and reduce its likelihood. As stated in the *NASP President's call to action to prevent suicide* (Lazarus et al., 2009), "Evidenced-based research suggests that if suicidal youth are identified by the schools and if appropriate treatment is provided, suicide can be dramatically reduced (Kalafat & Ryerson, 1999; Zenere & Lazarus, 1997, 2009). If this happens, lives will be saved" (p. 4).

References

American Association of Suicidology. (1998). *Suicide postvention guidelines: Suggestions for dealing with the aftermath of a suicide in the schools.* Washington, DC: Author.

American Association of Suicidology. (2014). *Youth suicide fact sheet.* Washington, DC: Author. Retrieved from www.suicidology.org/c/document_library/get_file?folderId=262&name=DLFE-627.pdf.

American Foundation for Suicide Prevention [AFSP]. (2014). Risk factors and warning signs. Retrieved from www.afsp.org/understanding-suicide/risk-factors-and-warning-signs.

Aseltine, R. H., James, A., Schilling, E. A., & Granovsky, J. (2007). Evaluating the SOS suicide prevention program. A replication and extension. *BMC Public Health, 7,* 161. Retrieved from www.biomedcentral.com/1471-2458/7/161.

Bearman, P. S. & Moody, J. (2004). Suicide and friendships among American adolescents. *American Journal of Public Health, 94,* 89–95.

Benneworth, O., Nowers, M., & Gunnell, D. (2007). Effects of barriers on the Clifton suspension bridge, England: Implications for prevention. *British Journal of Psychiatry, 190,* 266–267.

Bergmans, Y., Langley, J., Links, P., & Lavery, J. V. (2009). The perspectives of young adults on recovery from repeated suicide-related behavior. *Crisis, 30,* 120–127.

Berman, A. L., Jobes, D. A., & Silverman, M. M. (2006). *Adolescent suicide: Assessment and intervention.* Washington, DC: American Psychological Association.

Blum, R. W., McNeely, C., Rinehart, P. M. (2002). *Improving the odds: The untapped power of schools to improve the health of teens.* Minneapolis Center for Adolescent Health and Development, University of Minnesota. Retrieved from www.med.umn.edu/peds/ahm/prod/groups/med@pub@med/documents/asset/med_2 1771.pdf.

Brock, S. E. (2014, June). Suicide prevention. A PowerPoint presentation at Aptos High School in Pajaro Valley Unified School District, Aptos, CA.

Brock, S. E., Sandoval, J., & Hart, S. (2006). Suicidal ideation and behaviors. In G. G. Bear & K. M. Minke (Eds.), *Children's needs III: Development, prevention, and intervention* (pp. 225–238). Bethesda, MD: National Association of School Psychologists.

Brunner, R., Kaess, M., Parzer, P., Fischer, G., Carli, V., Hoven, C. W., & Wasserman, D. (2014). Lifetime prevalence and psychosocial correlates of adolescent direct self-injurious behavior: A comparative study of findings in 11 European countries. *Journal of Child Psychology and Psychiatry, 55,* 337–348.

Centers for Disease Control and Prevention (2007). *Suicide prevention scientific information: Consequences.* Retrieved from www.cdc.gov/ncipc/dvp/Suicide/Suicide-conque.htm.

Centers for Disease Control and Prevention (2010). *Youth risk behavior surveillance – United States, 2009.* Retrieved from www.cdc.gov/healthy/youth/health_and_academics/pdf/yrbs_slides_violence.ppt.

Centers for Disease Control and Prevention (2014). *Youth risk behavior surveillance – United States, 2013.* Retrieved from www.cdc.gov/mmwr/pdf/ss/ss6304.pdf?utm_source=rss&utm_medium=rss&utm_campaign=youth-risk-behavior-surveillance-united-states-2013-pdf.

de Leo, D., & Heller, T. (2008). Social modeling in the transmission of suicidality. *Crisis, 29,* 11–19.

Doan, J., Roggenbaum, S., & Lazear, K. (2003). *Youth suicide prevention school-based guide--Issue brief 4: Administrative issues.* Tampa, FL: Department of Child and Family Studies, Division of State and Local Support, Louis de la Parte Florida Mental Health Institute, University of South Florida. (FMHI Series Publication #218-4).

Doll, B., & Cummings, J. A. (2008). Why population-based services are essential for school mental health, and how to make them happen in your school. In B. Doll & J. A. Cummings (Eds.), *Transforming school mental health services: Population-based approaches to promoting the competency and wellness of children* (pp. 1–22; A joint publication with the National Association of School Psychologists). Thousand Oaks, CA: Corwin Press.

Eisel v. Board of Education of Montgomery County, 597 A.2d 447 (Md. 1991).

Eisenberg, M. E., & Resnick, M. D. (2006). Suicidality among gay, lesbian and bisexual youth: The role of protective factors. *Journal of Adolescent Health, 39,* 662–668. doi:101016/j.jadohealth.2006.04.023

Epstein, J. A. & Spirito, A. (2009). Risk factors for suicidality among a nationally representative sample of high school students. *Suicide and Life Threatening Behavior, 39,* 241–251.

Erbacher, T. A., Singer, J. B., & Poland, S. (2014). *Suicide in schools: A practitioner's guide to multi-level prevention, assessment, intervention and postvention.* New York: Routledge.

Fossey, R., & Zirkel, P. A. (2011). Student suicide case law in public schools. Appendix A. In D. Miller (pp. 131–137). *Child and adolescent suicidal behavior: School-based prevention, assessment and intervention.* New York: Guilford Press.

Garbarino, J., & deLara, E. (2002). *And words can hurt forever: How to protect adolescents from* bullying, harassment and emotional violence. London: The Free Press.

Gould, M. S., Marrocco, F. A., Kleinman, M., Thomas, J. G., Mostkoff, K., Cote, J., & Davies, M. (2005). Evaluating iatrogenic risk of youth suicide screening programs: A randomized control trial. *Journal of the American Medical Association, 293,* 1635–1643.

Granello, D. H., & Granello, P. F. (2007). *Suicide: An essential guide for helping professionals and educators.* Boston: Pearson.

Gutierrez, P.M., & Osman, A. (2008). *Adolescent suicide: An integrated approach to the assessment of risk and protective factors.* DeKalb, IL: Northern Illinois University Press.

Hess, R. S., Short, R. J., & Hazel, C. E. (2012). *Comprehensive children's mental health services in schools and communities: A public health problem-solving model.* New York: Routledge.

Hart, S. (2012). Student suicide: Suicide postvention. In S. E. Brock & S. R. Jimerson (Eds.), *Best practices in school crisis prevention and intervention* 2nd ed. (pp. 525–547). Bethesda, MD: National Association of School Psychologists Press.

Juhnke, G. A., Granello, D. H., & Granello, P. F. (2011). *Suicide, self-injury, and violence in the schools: Assessment, prevention and intervention strategies.* Hoboken, NJ: John Wiley & Sons.

Kalafat, J. (2003). School approaches to youth suicide prevention. *American Behavioral Scientist, 46,* 1211–1223.

Kalafat, J., & Lazarus, P. J. (2002). Suicide prevention in schools. In S. E. Brock, P. J. Lazarus & S. R. Jimerson, (Eds.), *Best practices in school crisis prevention and intervention* (pp. 211–223). Bethesda, MD: National Association of School Psychologists Press.

Kalafat, J. & Ryerson, D. M. (1999). The implementation and institutionalization of a school-based youth suicide prevention program. *Journal of Primary Prevention, 19,* 157–175.

King, K. (2001). Developing a comprehensive school suicide prevention program. *Journal of School Health, 71,* 132–137.

Lazarus, J. (2015, September 21). Personal communication.

Lazarus, P. J. (2009, February). The sustained reduction of youth suicidal behavior in a multicultural urban school system. Paper presented as part of a symposium entitled *School based suicide prevention: Research advances and practice implications* at the annual convention of the National Association of School Psychologists. Boston, MA.

Lazarus, P. J., Brock, S. E., Lieberman, R. , Poland, S. Zenere, F., & Feinberg, T. (2009*). NASP President's call to action to prevent suicide.* Available from www.nasponline.org/advocacy/suicide-calltoaction.aspx.

Lazarus, P. J., & Kalafat, J. (2001). Suicide prevention and youth: Recommendations for public policy. *International Journal of Sociology and Social Policy. 21,* 22–37.

Lieberman, R. A., Poland, S., & Cassel, R. (2008). Best practices in suicide intervention. In. A. Thomas & J. Grimes, (Eds.), *Best practices in school psychology V* (pp. 1457–1473). Bethesda, MD: National Association of School Psychologists.

Lieberman, R., Poland, S., & Cowan, K. (2006). Suicide prevention and intervention: Best practices for principals. *National Association of Secondary School Principals: Principal Leadership, 7*(2), 11–15.

Lieberman, R. A., Poland, S., & Kornfeld, C. (2014). Best practices in suicide prevention and intervention. In P. L. Harrison & A. Thomas (Eds.), *Best practices in school psychology: Systems-level services* (pp. 273–288). Bethesda, MD: National Association of School Psychologists.

Linda, W. P., Marroquín, B., & Miranda, R. (2012). Active and passive problem solving as moderators of the relation between negative life event stress and suicidal ideation among suicide attempters and non-attempters. *Archives of Suicide Research, 16,* 183–197.

Mazza, J. J. (2006). Youth suicidal behavior: A crisis in need of attention. In F. A. Villarruel & T. Luster (Eds.), *Adolescent mental health* (pp. 156–177). Westport, CT: Greenwood Publishing Group.

Mazza, J. J., & Reynolds, W. M. (2008). School-wide approaches to prevention of and treatment for depression and suicidal behaviors. In B. Doll & J. A. Cummings (Eds.), *Transforming school mental health services* (pp. 213–241). Thousand Oaks, CA: Corwin.

Miller, D. (2011). *Child and adolescent suicidal behavior: School-based prevention, assessment and intervention.* New York: Guilford Press

Miller, D. (2012). Preventing student suicide. In S. E. Brock & S. R. Jimerson (Eds.), *Best practices in school crisis prevention and intervention. 2nd Ed.* (pp. 203–222). Bethesda, MD. National Association of School Psychologists.

Miller, D. N., & Eckert, T. (2009). Youth suicidal behavior: An introduction and overview. *School Psychology Review, 38,* 153–167.

Nock, M. K., Joiner, T. E., Gordon, K. H., Lloyd-Richardson, E., & Prinstein, M. J. (2006). Non-suicidal self-injury among adolescents: Diagnostic correlates and relation to suicide attempts. *Psychiatry Research, 144,* 65–72.

Poland, S. (1989). *Suicide intervention in the schools.* New York: Guilford Press.

Poland, S. (1995). Best practices in suicide intervention. In A. Thomas & J. Grimes (Eds.), *Best practices in school psychology III* (pp. 155–166). Washington, DC: National Association of School Psychologists.

Poland, S., & Chartrand, D. (2008, April). *District Administration.* Available online at www.district administration.com/article/suicide-prevention-and-schools.

Popovic, D., Vieta, E., Azorin, J. Angst, J., Bowden, C. L., Mosolov, S. . . Perugi, G. (2015, August). *Suicidal behaviour in major depressive episode: evidence from the BRIDGE-II-MIX study.* European College of Neuropsychopharmacology Conference. Amsterdam, NL.

Resnick, M. D., Bearmen, P. S., Blum, R. W., Bauman, K. E., Harris, K. M., Jones., . . . Udry, J. R. (1997). Protecting adolescents from harm. Findings from the National Longitudinal Study on Adolescent Health. *Journal of the American Medical Association, 278*(10), 823–832.

Sanford v. Stiles, 456 F.3d 298 (3d Cir. 2006).

Substance Abuse and Mental Health Services Administration (2012). *Preventing suicide: A toolkit for high schools.* HHS Publication No. SMA-12-4669. Rockville, MD: Center for Mental Health Services, Substance Abuse and Mental Health Services Administration.

Sulkowski, M. L. (2011). An investigation of students' willingness to report threats of violence in campus communities. *Psychology of Violence, 1,* 53–65. doi: 10.1037/a0021592

Seiden, R. H. (1978). Where are they now? A follow up study of suicide attempters from the Golden Gate Bridge. *Suicide and Life-Threatening Behavior, 8,* 1–13.

Shneidman, E. S. (1996). *The suicidal mind.* New York: Oxford University Press. U. S. Department of Health & Human Services (1999). *The Surgeon General's call to action to prevent suicide.* Washington, DC: Available from www.surgeongeneral.gov/library/calltoaction/.

U.S. Public Health Service. (2001). *National strategy for suicide prevention. Goals and objectives for action.* Rockville, MD: U.S. Department of Health and Human Services.

Vossekuil, B., Fein, R. A., Reddy, M., Borum, R. & Modzeleski, W. (2002). *The final report and findings of the Safe School Initiative: Implications for the prevention of school attacks in the United States.* Washington, DC: U.S. Secret Service and U.S. Department of Education.

Wagner, B. M. (2009). *Suicidal behavior in children and adolscents.* New Haven, CT: Yale University Press.

Whitlock, J., Muehlenkamp, J., Eckenrode, J., Purington, A., Baral Abrams, G., Berreira, P., & Kress, V. (20120. Nonsuicidal self-injury as a gateway to suicide in young adults. *Journal of Adolescent Health, 52,* 486–492.

World Health Organization. (2014). *First WHO report on suicide prevention.* Retrieved from www.who.int/ mediacentre/news/releases/2014/suicide-prevention-report/en/.

Williams, M. (2001). *Suicide and attempted suicide.* London: Penguin Books.

Wyke v. Polk County School Board, 129 F.3d 560 (11th Cir. 1997)

Zenere, F. J., III, & Lazarus, P. J. (1997). The decline of youth suicidal behavior in an urban multicultural school system following the introduction of a suicide prevention and intervention program. *Suicide and Life-Threatening Behavior, 16,* 360–378.

Zenere, F. J. III, & Lazarus, P. J. (2009). The sustained reduction of youth suicidal behavior in an urban multicultural school district. *School Psychology Review, 38,* 189–199.

Part VII

Preventing and Responding to Crises in Schools

17 School Crisis Prevention

All schools must prepare for crisis events. Brock (2013) argues that "it is not a matter of if, but rather when a school will be required to respond to a crisis" (p.19). With this in mind all schools must plan for man-made and natural disasters as well as predictable and unpredictable crises (Lazarus, Jimerson, & Brock, 2002; Lazarus & Sulkowski, 2010). Although this task may seem daunting in that it is not possible to prevent some disasters, schools can develop plans and policies that reduce the devastation associated with these events as well as expedite healthy post-crisis recovery (Lazarus & Sulkowski, 2010; Sulkowski & Lazarus, 2013). Considering the importance of this task, school crisis prevention should be a central part of every school's plan for creating safe schools and fostering students' mental health.

Although some individuals and schools may never be the same following a major crisis, individuals may become wiser, more attuned to core values, and at times more resilient in the post-crisis period (Sulkowski, West & Lazarus, 2011). In fact, there is a line of research that examines posttraumatic growth (e.g., Hanley, Peterson, Canto, & Garland, 2014). This idea has been conceptualized as occurring within three major domains: personal growth, interpersonal relations, and life philosophy along five dimensions: (1) relating to others, (2) new possibilities, (3) personal strength, (4) spiritual change, and (5) appreciation of life (Tedeschi & Calhoun, 1996). Consistent with this assumption, the Chinese word for crisis is composed of two characters, "wei," which means danger, and "ji," which means opportunity. Wei describes the crisis event and ji predicts its potential impact. In concert, these symbols have also been defined as "opportunity blowing upon an ill wind." This particular focus does not diminish the pain and suffering associated with a crisis. Instead, it focuses on facilitating healthy recovery and healing. In this vein, this optimistic way of viewing crisis events is consistent with the intention of the concluding two chapters of this book, which deal with crisis prevention and management. In this chapter, school crisis prevention is discussed with a particular emphasis on understanding the impact of a crisis, establishing crisis response teams, developing crisis preparedness protocols and procedures, and planning for a culturally sensitive crisis response. In addition, research-based school crisis prevention strategies and curricula are covered. In the next chapter, effective strategies for crisis intervention and management are discussed.

A State of Crisis

Slaikeu (1990) describes a crisis state as a "temporary state of upset and disorganization, characterized chiefly by an individual's inability to cope with a particular situation using customary methods of problem solving, and by the potential for either a radically positive or negative outcome" (p. 15). Following this definition, the described state of disorganization results from the intense emotional, behavioral, physical, and cognitive effects associated with crisis exposure and how challenging it can be for individuals to manage these effects (Ager, Stark, Akesson, & Boothby, 2010). Because crisis events are outside of what individuals regularly experience at school or at home, they can overwhelm people's coping and problem- solving abilities. In this regard, crisis events may present problems that seem unsolvable to an individual who is struggling to cope (Brock, 2013). Lastly, consistent with the last part of the previous definition, outcomes following crises can be life changing. This is because crises impact affected individual's worldviews and crisis events may feel like a time to retreat in fear or to confront new challenges actively. Essentially, they are poignant and potentially life-altering events. Individuals who retreat may avoid situations or stimuli that trigger crisis-related thoughts and feelings; however, individuals who learn to cope with a crisis adaptively will learn how to solve problems better, become more resilient, and will be more likely to experience posttraumatic growth.

Similar to Slaikeu's (1990) definition of crisis, Brock et al. (2009) report that there are three core characteristics that define crisis events. First, crises occur suddenly, unexpectedly, and without warning. Second, crises have the potential to be extremely deleterious to the psychosocial functioning of individuals and to overwhelm their ability to cope with adversity; and third, crises often engender feelings of helplessness, powerlessness, or entrapment in those who are impacted (Brock, 2013).

Research indicates that highly unpredictable and sudden crises tend to be more distressing and traumatic than predictable and gradually unfolding events because if a crisis is more predictable, then there is more opportunity to prepare and make cognitive and emotional adjustments (Brock, 2002; Saylor, Belter, & Stokes, 1997). In other words, predictable and slowly unfolding crisis events allow for individuals to prepare psychologically and to take the necessary action to mitigate their impact. Research also indicates that human-caused crises such as school or public shootings tend to be more distressing than natural events such as floods, and crisis events that involve fatalities (or significant fear of death) tend to be more traumatic than those that do not (Charuvastra & Cloitre, 2009; Lazarus et al., 2002). Thus, crises that result in or could result in human-caused death tend to be particularly traumatic. Lastly, numerous studies suggest that the more severe the crisis event is (i.e., the intensity and duration), the greater the likelihood of victims being traumatized (Brock, 2002; Carlson, 1997; Lazarus, 1992; Lazarus, 1993).

While considering the previous findings, it is important to note that all crises have unique characteristics and affect individuals in different ways. Inevitably, some individuals will struggle to cope in the aftermath of a crisis, while others will be relatively unaffected. In support of this notion, research suggests that rates of Post-Traumatic Stress Disorder (PTSD) following crisis events are extremely variable (Saigh, Yasik, Sack, & Koplewicz, 1999). According to the most recent meta-analytic research that examined 72 peer-reviewed articles and involved 3,563 children and adolescents, the authors determined that 16 percent (or one out of every six youth) developed PTSD following a trauma (Alisic et al., 2014). The researchers also noted that interpersonal trauma provoked the highest risk for the development of PTSD.

The variability in developing PTSD following a trauma is due to the myriad of contextual factors that vary across crises. For example, the development of PTSD after a trauma is related to an individual's physical and/or the emotional proximity to the event, their trauma history, the amount and types of loss experienced, the extensiveness of the injuries sustained, and the actual experience of significant injury or death of friends or loved ones. It is also modulated by the fear of death or dying during the event and feeling of helplessness and horror. Moreover, research with children suggests that altered family functioning, separation from parents after the event, and ongoing maternal preoccupation with the trauma are more predictive of trauma symptomatology than is the level of exposure following a natural disaster (McFarlane, 1987). Moreover, the quality and the amount of support an individual receives is significantly related to experiencing PTSD symptoms. Thus, in light of this, even if individuals share similar characteristics, their experience of the event, their trauma history, the type of trauma experienced, their worldview, and the support they received in the aftermath all impact their post-trauma functioning. For example, students held hostage at gunpoint at Philip Barbour High School (see Chapter 15 on threat assessment and violence prevention), would be at much higher risk for developing acute stress disorder or PTSD than would other students in the building. This is because their lives were directly threatened. Moreover, because the trauma was perpetrated by an individual and students in Twila Smith's classroom were terrified of being killed, the probability of developing trauma symptomatology is significantly increased. Consequently, those individuals closest to the event (both physically and emotionally) need to be seen first. However, the needs of each affected person must be considered individually, as great variability exists in how people respond to traumatic and stressful events. When planning support for impacted youth, a good rule of thumb for schools to follow in the aftermath of a crisis is the 20/60/20 heuristic. This heuristic suggests that 20 percent of individuals will be seriously affected, 60 percent will be moderately affected, and 20 percent will be relatively unaffected (Lazarus, Zenere, & Feinberg, 2005).

Preparing for School Crisis Management

Current approaches to school crisis prevention have been shaped by both successful and unsuccessful crisis response efforts in the past. Thus, school crisis prevention strategies have largely been influenced by what has been learned from large-scale crisis response and management efforts. From this bank of knowledge, the U.S. Department of Homeland Security's Incident Command System (ICS; 2008) has structured crisis management strategies to include a number of different individuals who fulfill different roles. These individuals include command staff members, thinkers (i.e., planners), doers (i.e., operators), getters (i.e., logistics managers), payers (i.e., financers), and general staff such as medical support personnel (e.g., nurses), school-based mental health professionals (e.g., school psychologists, counselors, social workers), security personnel (e.g., school resource officers, school security officers), and school service/maintenance staff (e.g., food service staff, janitorial staff). Figure 17.1 presents the U.S. Department of Homeland Security's Incident Command System.

Ultimately, members of school crisis teams must be well prepared for a crisis so they can work quickly and efficiently to prevent any delays in the provision of crisis services (Brock, Sandoval, & Lewis, 2001). Therefore, members of these teams must be highly trained and knowledgeable of crisis management. Although no crisis management training programs have been empirically

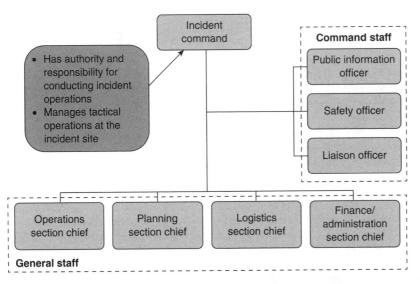

Figure 17.1 The U.S. Department of Homeland Security's Incident Command System

Note: Adopted from: http://emilms.fema.gov/IS800B/lesson1/is800b_Print.htm

validated in a randomized control trial (RCT) to date (the research gold standard) supportive evidence is mounting for the efficacy of the National Association of School Psychologists (NASP) PREPaRE School Crisis Prevention and Intervention Training Curriculum (Brock, Nickerson, Reeves, Jimerson, Feinberg, & Lieberman, 2009; Brock, Nickerson, Reeves, Savage, & Woitaszewski, 2011). The PREPaRE acronym stands for the following: *P*revent and prepare for psychological trauma; *R*eaffirm physical health and perceptions of safety and security; *E*valuate psychological trauma risk; *P*rovide interventions *and R*espond to psychological needs; and *E*xamine the effectiveness of crisis prevention and intervention.

As an integrated training program, the PREPaRE curriculum is divided into two workshops and it is designed to enhance the crisis management abilities of school-based mental health professionals, administrators, school safety personnel, and others. PREPaRE Workshop 1 is titled "Crisis prevention and preparedness: Comprehensive school safety planning" (Reeves et al., 2011) and it provides detailed information on the roles and responsibilities of school safety and crisis team members. Further, it emphasizes crisis preparedness and prevention as an ongoing process to which members of school crisis teams must adapt or adjust (Brock, 2013). See Text Box 17.1 for a review of the NASP PREPaRE curriculum.

Text Box 17.1 The NASP PREPaRE Curriculum

As an innovative curriculum, PREPaRE teaches school-based mental health professionals and educators to serve on school safety and crisis teams. The curriculum is based on the following assumptions:

- School-based mental health professionals and educators function more effectively when they are embedded within a multidisciplinary team that engages in the steps of crisis prevention, preparedness, response, and recovery.
- School crisis management is relatively unique and requires its own conceptual model that is sensitive to the needs of all members of school communities.
- School-based mental health professionals are best prepared to address the psychological impacts of school crises because of their hybrid training in psychology and education.

The PREPaRE model emphasizes that members of crisis response teams must be involved in the following specific hierarchical and sequential set of activities:

- **P—Prevent** and PREPaRE for psychological trauma
- **R—Reaffirm** physical health and perceptions of security and safety
- **E—Evaluate** psychological trauma risk
- **P—Provide** interventions
- **a—and**
- **R—Respond** to psychological needs
- **E—Examine** the effectiveness of crisis prevention and intervention.

The PREPaRE curriculum also incorporates foundational knowledge that is provided by the U.S. Departments of Education and Homeland Security. In this regard, the PREPaRE curriculum describes crisis response activities as occurring during the four states of a crisis: (a) prevention, (b) preparedness, (c) response, and (d) recovery. Further, it also incorporates the National Incident Management System's (NIMS) incident command structure (ISI).

Adapted from: www.nasponline.org/prepare/curriculum2.aspx.

Following PREPaRE Workshop 1, PREPaRE Workshop 2 focuses on crisis response and recovery. The official title for Workshop 2 is as follows: "Crisis intervention and recovery: The roles of school-based mental health professionals" (Brock, 2011). This workshop usually is delivered over the course of two days and it focuses on how school-based mental health professionals—and related professionals such as educators—can effectively engage in crisis management efforts. Overall, Workshop 2 focuses on mitigating deleterious impacts associated with crisis events, reaffirming the physical and psychological safety of students and other members of school communities, evaluating the degree of psychological trauma that was experienced by students, responding to the needs of students and other members of school communities, and examining the effectiveness of intervention and recovery efforts (Brock, 2011, 2013; Reeves et al., 2011). These crisis response and recovery strategies will be covered in Chapter 18 and they are critical to ensuring the success of overall crisis management.

Collectively, the PREPaRE curriculum covers school crisis prevention and intervention. The curriculum first covers content related to crisis prevention strategies (**P**revent) such as supporting students' natural resiliency, preventing school violence and suicide, and providing mental health services to at-risk students. In addition, the curriculum aims to teach educators and school-based mental health professionals effective strategies for preparing for crises such as developing crisis plans, establishing crisis response teams, and developing coordinated plans with local management agencies such as fire and police departments (Brock et al., 2009; Reeves, Conolly-Wilson, Pesce, Lazzaro, & Brock, 2012). Essentially, consistent with the curriculum, optimal crisis management involves efforts to prevent crises or mitigate their impact (if possible) before they occur. For example, even though it is impossible to prevent a tornado, a school could locate the safest place to shelter students and have them practice moving quickly to the shelter after immediate notice.

The PREPaRE curriculum then discusses ways to reaffirm the physical health of students and re-establish the safety (**R**eaffirm) and security of school settings. This involves evaluating (**E**valuating) and addressing the physical and psychological needs of affected students and other members of school communities such as teachers and administrators who also often are impacted by a crisis. To do this, schools will need to triage potentially affected individuals so that those who are most in need of support will receive it expeditiously while others who are coping well on their own are not burdened by having their healthy coping interrupted (Brock et al., 2009; Reeves et al., 2012). People have different styles of coping and forcing some people to talk about a crisis event or traumatic situation in some instances may interfere with healthy coping and may actually cause harm (Rose, Bisson, Churchill, & Wessley, 2009).

The next part of the PREPaRE curriculum covers ways to provide (**P**rovide) appropriate mental health interventions and (**a**nd) respond (**R**espond) to the psychological needs of affected students. Some of these interventions include holding classroom meetings to deliver factual information about a crisis, conducting psychoeducational groups, hosting caregiver trainings, conducting classroom-based group crisis interventions and individual interventions, and making appropriate referrals to community-based mental health professionals (Brock et al., 2009; Reeves et al., 2012). Lastly, the PREPaRE curriculum encourages members of crisis response teams (and crisis response efforts more generally) to examine (**E**xamine) the effectiveness of crisis prevention and response efforts through data collection and analysis. This process helps to understand the merits of the crisis management effort as well as highlight potential areas for refinement or improvement and continued mental health support (Brock et al., 2009; Reeves et al., 2012).

Expert Interview 17.1 with Dr. Melissa Louvar-Reeves, primary co-author of the PREPaRE curriculum and expert trainer, discusses the application of the curriculum in school settings. In addition, information is provided about allocating appropriate resources to crisis prevention and response efforts. Lastly, Dr. Louvar-Reeves discusses healthy recovery in the aftermath of large-scale crisis events.

Expert Interview 17.1 with Melissa A. Louvar-Reeves

Lecturer, Winthrop University

Co-Author and Developer of the PREPaRE Curriculum

PJL. As one of the key authors of the NASP PREPaRE Model, please tell us what the curriculum emphasizes and how it has helped school districts plan for crises and intervene in the aftermath.

ML-R. The PREPaRE curriculum has been developed by the National Association of School Psychologists (NASP) as part of decades-long leadership in supporting its school crisis prevention and response capabilities at the local level.

Developed specifically for the school context, PREPaRE:

- incorporates prevention, preparedness, response, and recovery
- provides for both physical and psychological safety
- builds on existing personnel, resources, and programs
- facilitates collaboration with community providers and first responders
- integrates with ongoing school safety efforts and multi-tiered systems of support
- develops skills important for coping with trauma
- provides for sustainability through a training of trainers model
- is adaptable to individual school needs and size
- aligns with federal emergency management guidelines
- supports legal compliance regarding crisis preparedness.

The PREPaRE model has been implemented by school districts across the country and also internationally. It has proven highly effective for schools committed to improving and strengthening their school safety and crisis management capacities. We believe that although school crisis response is not a choice, being prepared to respond effectively is.

PJL. Is PREPaRE training only available for mental health professionals or would it also be helpful for school administrators and educators to be trained in this model? What would be the benefits?

ML-R. PREPaRE is valuable to any and all school professionals, law enforcement professionals serving schools (e.g. SROs), district and school-level administrators, school mental health professionals, community mental health professionals, and selected teachers who are involved in overall safety, prevention and preparedness, and crisis response and recovery. School administrators have the responsibility to ensure plans are developed and staff members are trained. The PREPaRE workshops allow administrators to learn what they need to do to manage crisis events, the legal requirements supporting safety and crisis preparedness efforts, and also what supports, resources, materials, and training that their staff will need to respond effectively and efficiently to a crisis event.

PJL. What are the critical points that all educators should know about crisis management?

ML-R. Here are key points related to school crises:

- Schools play a critical prevention and response role in crises involving children.
- How schools respond to a crisis can shape the immediate and long-term effects on students and staff, thus impacting academic achievement.
- Effective crisis planning and response can help build students' resilience, facilitate a return to learning, and strengthen families and school communities.

- School crisis response presents unique issues that require specialized training and knowledge of schools, the learning process, mental health, and children's crisis reactions.
- Schools need the capacity to respond to a range of crises, (e.g., student deaths, suicides, school shootings, community tragedies, natural disasters, health epidemics, terrorism).
- Mental health is integral to crisis reactions and recovery; supporting children's mental health is essential.
- School psychologists and other school mental health professionals have extensive training in mental health and its impact on learning and the school environment.

School safety and crisis team members need formal training encompassing all aspects of crisis prevention, preparedness, response, and recovery. A strong emphasis on prevention programming helps prevent or at least mitigate a crisis event. However, if a crisis event occurs, how well the crisis response is delivered can have a direct impact on how well students, staff, and families cope with the event. If the crisis response and recovery supports are delivered well, healthy coping often ensues and a return to academic instruction can occur relatively quickly. On the other hand, if a school is unprepared, disorganized, or lacks crisis response skills, coping can be maladaptive and negative long-term consequences associated with the crisis may affect students academically, socially, and emotionally. School mental health professionals and administrators can be strong leaders in all aspects of crisis preparedness, response, and recovery. They are critical to help build resiliency beforehand that can serve as a protective factor in the event of a crisis.

PJL. Based on your work in the area of crisis preparation and response, do you recommend that every school have a crisis response team?

ML-R. Absolutely! Every school needs a leadership team that focuses on overall comprehensive safe school and prevention initiatives that establish a positive school climate. In addition, each school should have a crisis response team that is specifically trained to deliver crisis interventions based on their demonstrated need. In larger schools, these two teams may be comprised of different professionals with some overlap for continuity and planning. In smaller schools, the same professionals may perform duties associated with maintaining overall safety and prevention programming as well as crisis preparedness and response.

PJL. If a crisis such as a death of a student occurs, either on campus or off campus, what are some things that schools should consider in their response?

ML-R. School professionals must first address individuals' perceptions of physical safety and security. Students and staff must feel safe before they are able to begin to address their emotional needs. The level of traumatic impact then needs to be assessed to help determine the appropriate level of crisis interventions to be delivered. It is important to acknowledge that not all individuals will be equally affected by a crisis. Recovering from a crisis event is the norm for most people and there is a need to identify those who will recover relatively independently as un-needed crisis intervention may cause harm if it disrupts adaptive coping that an individual already employs.

Here are the variables to consider when assessing level of impact (psychological triage):

Variable 1:

(a) *Physical proximity*— Where were students when the crisis occurred (i.e., how close were they to the traumatic event)?
(b) *Emotional proximity*—Which individuals have/had close relationships with crisis victims? Those students/staff should be made crisis intervention treatment priorities.

Variable 2:

(a) *Internal Vulnerability Factors*—(e.g. pre-existing psychopathology, prior trauma history, lack of self-regulation).
(b) *External Vulnerability Factors*—(e.g. family resources and social supports or lack thereof).

Variable 3: *Threat Perceptions*—How threatening did the individual(s) perceive the event? Subjective impressions can be more important than actual crisis exposure. Adult reactions are important influences on student threat perceptions

Variable 4: *Crisis Reactions* that necessitate immediate mental health referral (e.g., PTSD symptoms, significant depression, homicidal/suicidal ideations, etc.).
   Based upon level of impact and demonstrated need, the following crisis interventions should then be delivered:

Reestablish Social Supports:

- Reunite students with their caregivers.
- Reunite students with their close friends, teachers, and classmates.
- Return to familiar school environments and routines.
- Facilitate community connections.
- Empower with care giving and recovery knowledge.

Provide Psychoeducation:

- Disseminate information.
- Hold classroom meetings.
- Conduct a student psychoeducational group.
- Host caregiver trainings.

Provide Directive Crisis Interventions*

- group/classroom-based
- individual.

*Involves actively exploring/processing the crisis event and must be led by mental health professional.

Long-term Psychotherapeutic Treatment Interventions

- Refer to mental health professionals outside of the school setting for more intensive and/or longer-term treatment interventions.

It is also important to emphasize that depending on the magnitude of the event and the nature of the impact, not all levels of crisis interventions may be needed; some students/staff may receive more directive crisis interventions than others.

PJL. *We have seen schools and communities that have been devastated by natural disasters. What are some key suggestions that schools can use to help students and faculty in the aftermath?*

ML-R. Establishing and maintaining social supports are critical in the aftermath of a natural disaster because of how many families are often impacted by these events. School professionals need to provide a forum for social supports to be activated (e.g., safe place for students to come together to support each other; activities to engage students to help rebuild the school and/or community; provide resources to parents). It is also important to remember that the initial recovery phase may mostly focus on physical needs (i.e., food, clothing, shelter), thus the psychological supports may often be delayed and offered at a later date. Moroever, it must be remembered that crisis reactions can be delayed, so assessing for traumatic impact (conducting psychological triage) is an ongoing process, not a one-time event.

Another unique feature of natural disasters is that often the caregivers (teachers, parents) and crisis responders are just as personally impacted as students are. Thus, care-for-the-caregiver support is critical to ensure their needs are also being met and they feel supported in their work with supporting students. Crisis responders from outside the school setting (e.g., district, community mental health) can be valuable resources to the school team as long as they have experience working with school-aged youth and there has been a pre-established relationship that outlines how they will support (not replace) the school team.

PJL. As a fellow Trainer of Trainers, I appreciate your responses. How should an administrator contact PREPaRE?

ML-R. For more information or to have your school district or organization arrange for PREPaRE training, https://www.nasponline.org/professional-development/prepare-training-curriculum/holding-a-prepare-workshop

Please note that Philip J. Lazarus, Melissa A. Louvar-Reeves, and Michael L. Sulkowski are all PREPaRE trainers.

Establishing Crisis Response Teams

It is important to get administrative support when establishing crisis response teams. According to Brock (2013), if administrators are involved in the process of developing crisis response teams, then the process will likely be straightforward. However, in the absence of administrative support, it behooves concerned educators to form a school safety or crisis response planning committee (Brock, 2000; Brock, 2013). This committee should include educators who know the school culture well and also have inroads to school and district administration. After forming and establishing an agenda to increase the school's crisis management potential, the team should engage school and district administrators to seek their buy-in and support.

For large-scale crises (e. g., tornados, floods, earthquakes, school shootings), crisis response teams should consider designating the roles and responsibilities of each team member in a way that follows the U.S. Department of Homeland Security's ICS. Thus, at a minimum, teams need to have an incident commander, an operations sections chief, a planning section chief, a logistics section chief, and a finance/administration section chief (Brock, 2013; Reeves et al., 2012). The incident commander is the person who ultimately is in charge and is most directly responsible for crisis response efforts. Thus, in addition to having advanced knowledge of school-based crisis management, this individual must have leadership skills and know how to manage people effectively under stressful settings. Under the ICS model, command staff members take orders from the incident commander, yet they also function somewhat autonomously in their respective roles. These individuals help with crisis response and management through ensuring school safety, coordinating effective resources, providing mental health services, and communicating accurate and reliable information to the public and members of the school community. Lastly, general staff members support the overall incident command structure and each other as the crisis unfolds, ends, and requires ongoing attention.

Integrating Crisis Response Teams into Extant Systems

Crisis management efforts should be developed for a range of crises that vary in their scope and magnitude. Following recommendations by Brock et al. (2009), planning efforts should determine who should be involved in crisis response at different hierarchical levels including at the school building level, the district level, and the regional level. Although large-scale disasters or crises can impact areas larger than a region and necessitate a state or federal level response, such as in the case of Hurricane Katrina, students likely will need to be evacuated during these major disasters and schools will be disrupted while the region recovers and is rebuilt. Therefore, members of school crisis response teams likely will defer to state and federal officials when responding to these crises.

School-level Response

It needs to be emphasized that the majority of school crises can be managed by school-based teams without the need for external support or an ICS (Brock, 2011, 2013). Members of these teams may include: administrators, general and special education teachers, school psychologists, counselors, social workers, school resource officers, behavior specialists, school nurses, and other support staff as necessary. These team members usually are well-known and familiar individuals in school communities, which can enhance their credibility and ability to elicit trust among members of the broader educational community. However, in the absence of having school-level crisis response personnel who are familiar to the broader school community, district personnel or others will have to step in to manage the crisis, which may cause some individuals to feel increased anxiety or distress. In this vein, school staff and students may jump to the conclusion that a crisis is more concerning than it is because new individuals, and not the people with whom they are used to communicating with at school, are disseminating information and directing the crisis response (Brock et al., 2001). Therefore, it is important for all members of school communities to support crisis management efforts even if they are not directly involved so that members of the broader school community can trust crisis responders and benefit from their help.

District-level Response

District-level resources and personnel will be needed in cases when a crisis cannot be adequately managed by school-building-level personnel. Some schools have access to district crisis response teams that can be quickly summoned during a crisis. Although these individuals may have more experience responding to crises, it still is important for school-level crisis response teams to remain engaged in the crisis response process, as they generally will have greater familiarity with victims and their families (Brock, 2011, 2013). In addition, particularly in tight-knit school communities, members of district-level crisis response teams may be seen as outsiders and it might take them some time to develop relationships with members of the school community. Consequently, it is helpful for district-level crisis responders to be introduced to the student body by current school personnel.

As foreshadowed above, it is important for school and district crisis team members to work together when discussing crisis management planning as well as to keep clear channels of communication open if a crisis does occur. District-level crisis response teams may follow the aforementioned ICS structure, which can help with coordinating roles and responsibilities between people on school and district teams that fulfill similar functions. Furthermore, members of these teams with experience in crisis management can educate school crisis response team members as well as consult with them on developing sound crisis prevention and response plans.

Regional-level Response

Although crises in school settings are common, extreme crises such as mass disasters that warrant a regional-level crisis response are relatively infrequent. These types of crises might include a school shooting, an accident that kills several members of the school community, or a large-scale natural disaster. Schools and districts can establish connections with other districts and community agencies to develop a crisis response coalition that can respond to a regional crisis. In this vein, school- and district-level crisis response team members can make agreements with members of other districts to share their time and resources in the event of a regional crisis (Brock et al., 2009). For example, prior to a devastating hurricane that partially destroyed school buildings in Hardee County, Florida, an arrangement had been made with the much larger and nearby Hillsborough County to share resources. Consequently, the entire maintenance department from Hillsborough was called up and employees were reassigned. Maintenance personnel even worked weekends to get all the Hardee County schools ready, and as a result, schools opened two to three weeks earlier than they would have otherwise.

Members of crisis management teams also should plan to contact specific national crisis response teams and resource providers if a school or district experiences a regional crisis. Local chapters of the American Red Cross can provide access to needed resources and shelter in the aftermath of a disaster that will be needed during the recovery process. Additionally, the National Association of School Psychologists (NASP) developed the National Emergency Assistance Team in 1996 (NEAT; this team has recently been renamed the National School Safety & Crisis Response Committee) to help schools recover from disasters and crises. This Committee is comprised of certified school psychologists who have had formal training in the PREPaRE curriculum and have direct experience with helping to manage school crises. Since 1996, members of NEAT have responded to many regional school crises and disasters such as high-profile school shootings, acts of terrorism (e.g., 9/11), suicide clusters, as well as technological, environmental, and natural disasters that inflicted damage on an entire region or community. They have also worked on developing documents for schools to help students, parents, and faculty deal with trauma. One example is found at http://www.nasponline.org/resources-and-publications/resources/school-safety-and-crisis/trauma/supporting-students-experiencing-childhood-trauma-tips-for-parents-and-educators.

Crisis Management Planning

Crisis Preparedness Protocols

As a first step toward developing crisis management plans, specific individuals should be educated about their respective roles within the aforementioned ICS framework. In other words, the specific roles and responsibilities of individuals should be delineated and the people fulfilling these roles should know what they are expected to do during a crisis. In addition, it is important for crisis management plans also to include alternates for each role on the crisis response team in case a team member is absent on a day that a crisis occurs or if a team member moves, is hurt, needs to take leave, or wishes to discontinue serving on the team unexpectedly (Brock et al., 2009).

It also is important for all members of crisis response teams to have easy access to the information and resources they will need to respond to a crisis. To help in this regard, schools can make crisis management toolkits and binders that are easy for members of the crisis response team to locate and utilize (Brock, 2011, 2013; Brock et al., 2009). Materials that may be included in these toolkits and binders can include school maps, master keys to the school, lists of emergency first responders and community agencies, phone directories, flashlights, tape, paper, writing instruments, walkie-talkies, portable computers, cell phone chargers, batteries, portable two-way radios, and an emergency power source. Information related to school crises response plans as well as school records can also be maintained in the cloud, in case of damage to local servers or schools. For example, during Hurricane Andrew, Miami-Dade County Public Schools lost countless student records when schools in south Florida were destroyed or damaged. Similarly, Hurricane Katrina wiped out thousands of school records in parishes throughout the greater New Orleans area.

Brock (2013) reports that crisis management plans must include several key preparedness protocols. These include visitor sign-in; crisis exercises and drills; student evacuation and assembly; student accounting and caregiver reunification; communications; and media relations. Because each crisis presents its own unique set of challenges, it is important for crisis response teams to establish each of these protocols and ensure that appropriate members of school communities know what they are expected to do in the event of a crisis. Each of these protocols is described in greater detail below.

Visitor Sign-in

As was discussed in Chapter 2 along with information on ensuring the physical safety of schools, it is important for schools to have sign-in procedures in place so that key members of the school staff or leadership can have a handle on who is in the building at any given time. Thus, sign-in procedures can provide information about unfamiliar individuals, why they are visiting the school, and how long they intend to be on campus. In addition to documenting the comings and goings of individuals, visitor sign-in procedures should describe how name badges will be disseminated and collected and what members of the school staff should do if they see an unfamiliar person without proper identification on school grounds (Brock et al., 2001).

Crisis Exercises and Drills

It is important for crisis response teams to have regularly scheduled meetings in which crisis response plans, related exercises, and drills are conducted. Brock et al. (2009) recommends for these meetings to include both discussion-based exercises, such as orientation seminars and tabletop exercises, and operations-based exercises such as emergency specific drills, functional exercises, and full-scale drills. The general purpose of these exercises is to train crisis response team members and others to ensure maximum readiness in the face of a crisis—not to cause anyone in the school community to experience distress. Currently, a small, yet significant, number of schools are implementing highly controversial drills and simulations that involve real police officers and weapons to help prepare members of school communities for rare events such as a school shooting. These practices—which have the potential to be highly distressing, especially to students with trauma histories—are not consistent with the aforementioned crisis exercises and drills that should be regularly conducted by crisis response teams. In addition, there is no evidence to suggest that they have any positive benefits (Frosch, 2014). Text Box 17.2 discusses practice considerations for schools in active shooter drills.

Text Box 17.2 Practice Considerations for Schools in Active Shooter Drills

The NASP and the National Association of School Resource Officers (NASRO) have partnered to provide this guidance on armed assailant training, with input from Safe and Sound: A Sandy Hook Initiative and the ALiCE Training Institute. Guidance from these experts on the important factors schools must take into account when considering and conducting armed assailant drills is listed below.

Overview

A.   Response to armed assailants has focused on implementing a school lockdown. Recently, discussion has emphasized options-based approaches, which sometimes include the "Run, Hide, Fight" model.

B.   Armed assailant drills have both benefits and concerns associated with their implementation.

- Armed assailants in schools account for only 1% of homicides among school-age youth; schools must balance costs and benefits when allocating crisis preparedness resources.
- Such drills have the potential to empower staff and save lives, but without proper caution, they can risk causing harm to participants.
- Available research supports the effectiveness of lockdown drills carried out according to best practices, but research is still needed on the effectiveness of armed assailant drills.

Drill approaches and planning

A. Traditional lockdowns should remain the foundation of an options-based approach to active assailant training, which allows participants to make independent decisions in evolving situations.
B. Exercises should be considered in a hierarchy with simple discussion-based exercises before complex operations-based drills are practiced.
C. Schools should keep simulation techniques appropriate to the participants' developmental maturity.

- Inform participants of the use and purpose of props and simulation aids prior to the drill.
- Using Airsoft guns as simulation aids requires careful safety measures and opt-out opportunities.

D. Regular practice helps participants develop readiness and quickly access and apply knowledge.

Developmental and mental health considerations

A. Children model their reactions on adult behavior, so effective drills should result in staff who inspire calm and confidence in students.
B. It is critical that participation in drills be appropriate to individual development levels, and take into consideration prior traumatic experiences, special needs, and personalities.
C. School-employed mental health professionals should be involved in every stage of preparation.

- Prior to the drill, staff should be trained to recognize common trauma reactions.
- Adults should monitor participants during the drill and remove anyone exhibiting signs of trauma.
- After completion, staff and students should have access to mental health support, if needed.

D. Participation should never be mandatory, and parental consent should be required for all students.
E. If staff choose to opt-out of intense drills, they should receive comparable, less intense instruction.

Steps for conducting safe, effective, and appropriate drills

1. Create a school safety team (including an administrator, a school mental health professional, a school nurse; security personnel, teachers, and parents) that also coordinates with local law enforcement and emergency responders.
2. Conduct a needs assessment of the school community.
3. Implement a cost–benefit analysis that considers all emergency preparedness needs and options.
4. Tailor drills to the context of the school environment.
5. Create a plan of progression that builds from simplest, lowest-cost training; identifies obstacles and goals; and establishes a timeline.
6. Prepare for drill logistics that ensure physical and psychological safety as well as skills and knowledge acquisition.
7. Develop a communications plan that gives all participants advance warning and the ability to opt out and/or provide feedback.
8. Establish a long-term follow-up plan to support sustainability that includes assessing ongoing and/or changing preparedness training needs.

Adapted from: NASP and NASRO. (2014). *Best practice considerations for schools in active shooter and other armed assailant drills [Brief]*. Bethesda, MD: National Association of School Psychologists.

Student Evacuation and Assembly

Depending on the nature of the crisis, different student evacuation and assembly plans will be needed. For example, a natural disaster such as a tornado may require that all students gather in a secure and safe part of a school that is away from exterior windows and walls. However, a man-made disaster such as a chemical spill or gas leak will require for all students to be evacuated to a different location where their safety can be guaranteed. Therefore, plans will need to be developed to coordinate the assembly and evacuation of students based on the nature of the crisis (Brock, 2011, 2013; Reeves et al., 2012). While doing so, it also is important to plan for assisting students with disabilities. These students may have mobility concerns that need to be considered and may be highly sensitive to confusing, loud, or chaotic environments. Lastly, while students are being moved or transported, it is important to make sure that resources that are needed to help manage the crisis can be transported as well. For example, as students are moved to a secondary location, attendance information also must be moved and updated as students are picked up.

Student Accounting and Caregiver Reunification

Because crises are inherently chaotic and can cause a state of confusion, plans must be established a priori for accounting for students and reunifying them with caregivers. Failure to plan in this regard can exacerbate chaos and stress associated with a crisis situation. To ensure accurate accounting of all students, attendance records will need to be accessible and educators will need to bring students to where they can be counted. In addition, clear communication will be needed between those who are attending to students who may have been injured during a crisis and others who may be looking for a student. Often, in the age of social media and the rapid flow of information, caregivers and other individuals will become aware of a situation shortly after it occurs and then come to school to check on the safety and well-being of their children (Griffin, Lazarus, Lieberman, Singh, & Diaz, 2015). Therefore, schools also will need to plan for the smooth reunification of students with their caregivers. This might involve managing traffic, setting up impromptu meeting places where students can be safely returned to the custody of their caregivers, and providing caregivers with accurate information about the crisis as it becomes available.

Communications

Crisis management plans must carefully consider how to address a range of different communication obstacles that may occur during a crisis. Within-building communication must hold up during a crisis so that educators and others will know how to move students safely or shelter them. Additionally, members of the crisis response team and school administrators will need to be able to communicate effectively with district-level administrators and members of the community such as directors of first response units. A breakdown in communication can exacerbate a crisis situation and forestall an effective crisis response (Sulkowski & Lazarus, 2011). Therefore, traditional communication systems such as phones and classroom-to-office PA systems should be backed up by other modes of communication such as emergency warning systems, text messaging, e-mail, landlines, walkie-talkies, and reverse 911 calling systems (Brock et al., 2009).

The role of social media has evolved rapidly in the past decade and it is now ubiquitous. Consequently, as a proactive strategy, schools are encouraged to have a Facebook and Twitter presence and to use social media and their school's website, Facebook, and Twitter to keep the community informed about the ongoing crisis and the school's response. These social media platforms can be updated instantaneously whereas websites and other ways to communicate take time to modify. However, because social media platforms can be modified so quickly, it is important to ensure that they do not spread misinformation while a crisis unfolds. Therefore, it is best for schools to develop a small team to maintain all the social media and to help ensure that information is accurate and provided in a timely manner. This will involve monitoring visitor's posts and comments in addition to the ones posted by members of the team. Overall, if schools adroitly manage their social media platforms, the likelihood of rumors and inaccurate information being disseminated is reduced (Flitsch, Magnesi, Brock, 2012; Griffin et al., 2015).

Another tool that schools can use to manage a crisis effectively is an electronic alert system. Systems such as K-12 Alerts that can rapidly send out emergency messages to faculty, parents, and members of the community can expediently provide everyone with the same message. Currently most U.S. universities use such systems and some states such as Arizona are using them statewide to help with important initiatives such as finding missing children. K-12 Alerts and other electronic alert systems use multiple social media outlets. They can send out e-mails and text messages, and update Facebook and Twitter with one click. As noted by Flitsch et al. (2012), messages sent by the school using this tool are authentic and leave less room for ambiguity or misinformation. It is also important that schools understand that traditional media will be monitoring the school's social media to get new leads and update their ongoing reporting of the crisis.

Schools should also develop templates for letters that they can use to communicate with parents and caregivers following a crisis. These templates can describe what has occurred, the school's present response, what will happen in the following day(s), the help that the school will provide, information on other available resources, and who to contact if their child experiences problems coping in the aftermath of the crisis. As previously noted, it is recommended that schools develop these templates prior to a crisis. It is much easier to modify existing templates, than develop new ones in the immediacy of a crisis.

Media Relations

Similar to concerned caregivers and community members, media personnel often come to campus shortly after a crisis or even while it is unfolding (Sulkowski & Lazarus, 2011). Also similar to caregivers, members of the media will attempt to solicit information from members of the school, which may even include students. However, because misinformation and rumors often accompany a crisis situation, it is important to ensure that accurate information is being presented to the media and that members of the media are not interviewing people who may misrepresent a crisis situation or have a distorted perspective because of distress they are feeling or inaccurate information that they have received from another party. Therefore, it is important for members of the crisis response team to determine how members of the school will communicate with the media proactively (Griffin et al., 2015: Sulkowski & Lazarus, 2013). In general, a school leader (e.g., superintendent, incident commander) with training in public and media relations can be designated as the main conduit to the media as well as the mouthpiece for presenting information to the public.

Additionally, as an important yet often overlooked aspect of crisis prevention and management, educators and other members of school communities should be coached on how to interact with the media as they may be approached in person or contacted via e-mail or phone. Although schools should not censor information or come across as being secretive, members of school communities—as well as the media—should respect the fact that the confusion and chaos accompanying a crisis can distort the accuracy and validity of information that any single person may have in the immediate aftermath of the crisis. Therefore, developing a specific protocol for interacting with the media is a key step toward ensuring the accuracy of information provided to the public during and following a crisis.

Schools can allocate a designated area near school grounds as a media staging area as a proactive strategy to ensure that the media receives accurate information in the wake of a crisis and to protect faculty and students from unwanted intrusion upon their privacy (Brock, 2013). In this area, designated members of the school community can provide press conferences or updates as needed. Meanwhile, by locating the media staging area away from the school grounds, regular school functions can be conducted as a school responds to or recovers from a crisis. Although most reporters behave responsibly and exercise sensitivity following a school crisis, having a designated staging area may protect students from insensitive reporters. With 24/7 news coverage, it has been painful to watch reporters stick microphones in front of distressed students and ask them to comment following a horrific tragedy. Consequently, students need to be informed that they are not required—nor is it recommended—that they talk to the media. As another proactive strategy, schools can develop templates for responding to various media outlets as a crisis unfolds. These may be similar to those designed for caregivers and members of the school community. These templates should encompass a range of natural and man-made disasters that can impact schools and they can be designed to be rapidly modified.

Crisis Response Procedures

Consistent with the goal of school crisis prevention, crisis response teams must also develop crisis response procedures in addition to preparedness tasks and activities. Over and beyond the aforementioned tasks and activities, developing these procedures often involves planning in order to (a) assess crisis situations; (b) identify and assist crisis victims; (c) implement crisis intervention services; (d) triage these services; (e) refer to outside agencies and providers as needed; and (f) debrief and evaluate the crisis response (Brock, 2013).

Accurately Assessing Crisis Situations

The first step in assessing a crisis situation is to determine who is immediately at risk, how pervasive the crisis impact will be, and how the crisis will impact the school community and beyond. The incident commander or the crisis team leader(s) must make an initial assessment of the crisis impact and then communicate the expected impact to other crisis response team members and district personnel. In addition to assessing the scope of a crisis, it also is important to determine the level of response that likely will be needed. Some crises can be managed effectively at the building level through utilizing members of the crisis response teams and school-building level personnel. However, additional mental health professionals or school resource officers from neighboring schools may be needed to respond effectively to crises of greater magnitude. Lastly, crises that are pervasive or impact a community or region will necessitate bringing in crisis response services from outside agencies or even state and federal organizations such as the American Red Cross or the Federal Emergency Management Agency (FEMA).

Identifying Crisis Victims

Members of crisis response teams and educators more generally need to be prepared to identify crisis victims in the immediate aftermath of a crisis. Although it is relatively easy to identify students who sustained physical injuries, it can be challenging to identify students who have been psychologically injured. According to Brock (2013), the most important factor that determines the degree of psychological distress or trauma that a student will experience in the wake of a crisis is their immediate proximity to the crisis event. In this regard, proximity might involve being personally close to the crisis and seeing victims or fearing for one's own security. However, it also might involve having close relationships to others who were impacted or threatened in a crisis. To ensure that crisis victims are accurately identified, members of the crisis team should educate all members of school communities on the signs that a student may be experiencing post-crisis distress. Table 17.1 lists vulnerability factors associated with high risk.

Table 17.1 Factors that Place Students at High Risk

Individual Crisis Experience Factors During the Event

Close to the crisis event
Long exposure to the crisis event
Close relationship with victim(s)
Individual was injured during the crisis
High perceived threat. That is, the individual thought he or she might die or be seriously injured during
   the crisis
Initial response was severe (e.g., panic, shock, disassociation)
Suffers significant losses

Individual Crisis Responses After the Event

Over time the individual does not emotionally self-regulate their feelings or thoughts
Has suicidal thoughts or engages in suicidal or self-destructive behaviors
Attempts self-medication (e.g., alcohol, drugs, or prescription medication)
Experiences symptoms related to depression, anxiety, PTSD
Significant negative changes in behavior
Withdrawal from social interaction

Vulnerability Factors within the Family

Not living with nuclear family
Parental mental illness
Parental incarceration
Family dysfunction
Ineffective or uncaring parenting
Child abuse or maltreatment
Lack of financial resources
Lack of social support or social resources
Family displacement following crisis
Family suffers significant losses

Vulnerability Factors within the Individual

History of prior traumatization
Previously suffered recent or multiple losses
Pre-existing mental illness
Low developmental level
Ineffective or avoidant coping skills
Poor emotional self-regulation
External locus of control
Low self-esteem

Source: Adapted from Brock (2002).

Implement Crisis Intervention Services

Important decisions must be made about what services will be delivered to crisis victims when they are identified. If there are a large number of victims, services will need to be triaged to support students who display the greatest need (Sulkowski, & Lazarus, 2013). In this regard, students who are experiencing shock, displaying signs of acute psychiatric symptoms, or feeling overwhelmed by severe anxiety and distress, should be assisted first. After that has occured, students who are experiencing more general and less severe adjustment problems in the aftermath of the crisis should then be assisted. Further, students who are significantly impacted may display problems that are more severe than many school-based mental health professionals are accustomed to handling and they may need to be referred to community-based specialists.

Debrief and Evaluate the Crisis Response

Crises, despite being negative and disruptive as defined, also provide opportunities for learning and growth. In light of this, members of crisis response teams should plan to meet and review crisis management plans and procedures following a crisis to determine areas for further refinement and improvement. During an ongoing crisis, a debriefing should occur every day. As part of this process, team members can discuss (a) what went well and what did not, (b) plans for the following day, (c) who is at high risk and needs to be seen or referred (which may also include faculty and staff), and (d) the emotional reactions of team members. A critical yet often overlooked aspect of crisis response involves making sure that crisis response team members feel emotionally supported throughout the crisis response process. Especially in crises of long duration, the processing of emotionally charged feelings by team members is important so that crisis responders are able to maintain their competence and not become so emotionally distressed that their effectiveness or well-being is compromised. In other words, it is important to care for the caregivers as part of the overall crisis management process.

Cultural Considerations in Crisis Prevention

Students and families are becoming increasingly diverse in the U.S. in terms of race/ethnicity, language, culture, religion, and customs. As a salient example of this trend, the percentage of children classified as Hispanic/Latino has increased to 23 percent in 2010 from 9 percent in 1980 (Federal Agency Forum on Children and Family Statistics, 2011). Further, by 2050, this percentage is expected to rise to 39 percent. A major contributing factor to the increase in diversity among U.S. students is related to immigration from Mexico and Central America. Immigrants from these regions often come from economically disadvantaged communities, conflict zones, or communities that have been impacted by violence. Thus, in light of this, they often have been exposed to crisis-like situations such as violent attacks, rape, or loss of a family member in their country of origin that may make them vulnerable when a crisis occurs at school (Sandoval, 2013).

Culture and Crisis

The majority of crisis responders and members of crisis response teams are part of the majority culture in the U.S., which is derived from White Anglo-Saxon and Protestant traditions (Sandoval, 2013; Spring, 2007). Values that are commonly espoused in these traditions include respect for individual rights, personal achievement, adherence to law, and belief in the democratic process. As major social institutions, schools also embody these values, and students from cultures that have a different set of values may feel disconnected at school and struggle to connect with crisis responders as well.

Part of the reason why some culturally diverse students struggle to connect with crisis responders results from different perspectives on what is a crisis and how someone should act in the aftermath of one. According to Sandoval (2013), events that influence an individual's response to a crisis in the majority U.S. culture may not cause the same reaction among students from minority cultures. In support of this notion, following a school shooting in Stockton, California, because the name of the shooter was Patrick, several Asian American individuals in the community were understandably upset by the public celebration of Saint Patrick's Day at school. Essentially, they misperceived that the school was glorifying the shooter and the motivations behind his actions. Fortunately, these misperceptions were disabused by providing information on how Saint Patrick's Day is a public holiday that is especially important to families with Irish roots and that the celebration had no relation to the school shooter.

Culture and Crisis Reaction

In Western societies, reactions to a crisis usually involve fear, confusion, re-experiencing of the traumatic event, emotional numbing, a range of sleep problems, and avoidant behavior (Sulkowski & Lazarus, 2013). However, in other cultures these reactions may be different or diminished. For example, among individuals from Asian and Hispanic/Latino cultures, somatic symptoms (e.g., stomach aches, headaches, etc.) also may commonly accompany (or even seem to supplant) the previously mentioned crisis reactions (Sandoval, 2013). Moreover, common coping strategies related to crisis exposure also vary across cultures. Whereas some coping strategies are perceived and understood as normal within their own cultural context, they may be perceived as deviant and pathological when viewed through a different cultural lens (Sulkowski & Lazarus, 2013). For example, in some Native American communities, it is common for bereaved family members to report communicating with lost loved ones as a source of comfort and it would be disrespectful to challenge the legitimacy of these experiences (Napoli, 1999).

Culturally Sensitive Crisis Management

Cultural considerations are particularly important in the development and composition of crisis teams. As such, team membership should represent the cultural, ethnic, and linguistic make-up of the school and community (Ortiz & Voutsinas, 2012). Moreover, all team members should examine and identify their cultural worldview and any potential biases they may harbor. This self-examination should help team members improve their work and cohesiveness as well as interact more effectively with students and families (Ortiz & Voutsinas, 2012).

According to Sandoval (2013), crisis plans and members of crisis response teams should emphasize specific, culturally sensitive crisis intervention planning strategies as well as response protocols as part of standard crisis management efforts. Thus, because of increases in the diversity of students and families in the U.S., as well as the importance of respecting the influence of important cultural factors that impact crisis management, all crisis response teams should plan in advance how they can support the needs of culturally diverse students and families in the schools they serve. Essentially, the following should be considered in culturally sensitive crisis planning: Assess the fit between the cultural norms of the majority group and minority groups; consider what culturally relevant external resources (e.g., family members, clergy, community leaders) would be available to people in a state of crisis; determine the capacity of students to utilize school, community, and other resources; anticipate and work toward clarifying incidents of miscommunication and misunderstanding; and identify appropriate referrals to culturally competent professionals and helpers. Collectively, engaging in these crisis intervention planning strategies can help ensure that crisis response efforts are well received by a diverse array of individuals in school settings.

In addition to the aforementioned strategies, school-based crisis management efforts should also involve engaging members of culturally diverse families on a regular basis in non-crisis related activities (Lazarus & Sulkowski, 2010). In other words, although crises often bring communities together and can reduce perceived differences among individuals, the best time to engage culturally diverse families is prior to a crisis through regular educational activities. To do this, educators should establish relationships with influential community leaders and mentors who can help members of the school community understand the values, norms, and traditions of culturally diverse groups of families that live in the area. Efforts to do this can also help with reducing the possibility for miscommunication and misunderstanding between members of majority and minority groups as well as help with identifying potential interpreters and translators.

Connecting with key community leaders also could help with identifying students and families that may be particularly vulnerable to a crisis as well as enable educators to understand the social issues that some of these individuals may be facing, such as discrimination, oppression, poverty, social isolation, trauma, and limited access to social services. Lastly, it is important for school documents to be translated into the languages that can be clearly understood by members of linguistically diverse families. Because this process takes time and documents might need to be checked to ensure accuracy, clarity, and readability, translating school documents—both usual school documents (e.g., handbooks, consent forms) and documents related to crisis response—must be done well before a crisis occurs on campus.

Conclusion

Responding to crises is insufficient. Instead, schools must be proactive and develop an integrated and comprehensive multilevel approach to crisis management. Therefore, schools need to prevent and prepare when possible, and crisis teams need to mitigate and respond when necessary. The National Association of School Psychologists has developed the research-based PREPaRE curriculum to help schools prepare for and respond to crises. This curriculum is based on the following acronym and principles: **P**revent and prepare for psychological trauma; **R**eaffirm physical health and perceptions of safety and security; **E**valuate psychological trauma risk; **P**rovide interventions <u>and</u> **R**espond to psychological needs; and **E**xamine the effectiveness of crisis prevention and intervention.

In addition to implementing research-based crisis prevention curricula, plans, and procedures, schools also must consider the impact of diversity in these initiatives. Therefore, it is important for schools to ensure that planning for crises addresses the unique needs of *all* the students and families they serve. Of course, this work must be done well in advance of an unforeseen crisis. Essentially, school crises are inevitable; consequently it behooves all educators to follow the Boy Scout motto: Be prepared!

References

Ager, A., Stark, L., Akesson, B., & Boothby, N. (2010). Defining best practice in care and protection of children in crisis-affected settings: A Delphi study. *Child Development, 81,* 1271–1286.

Alisic, E., Zalta, A. K., van Wesel, F., Larsen, S. E. Hafstad, G. S., Hassanpour, K., & Smid, G. E. (2014). Rates of post-traumatic stress disorder in trauma-exposed children and adolescents: Meta-analysis. *British Journal of Psychiatry, 204,* 335–340.

Brock, S. E. (2000). Development of a school district crisis intervention policy. *The California School Psychologist, 5,* 53–64.

Brock, S. E. (2002). Identifying individuals at risk for psychological trauma. In S. E. Brock, P. J. Lazarus & S. R. Jimerson (Eds.), *Best practices in school crisis prevention and intervention* (pp. 367–383). Bethesda, MD: National Association of School Psychologists.

Brock, S. E. (2011). *Crisis intervention and recovery: The roles of school-based mental health professionals (2nd edn).* Bethesda, MD: National Association of School Psychologists.

Brock, S. E. (2013). Preparing for the school crisis response. In J. Sandoval (Ed.), *Crisis counseling, intervention, and prevention in the schools, third edition* (pp. 19–30). New York, NY: Routledge.

Brock, S. E., Nickerson, A. B., Reeves, M. A., Jimerson, S. R., Feinberg, T. & Lieberman, R. (2009). *School crisis prevention and intervention: The PREPaRE model.* Bethesda, MD: National Association of School Psychologists.

Brock, S. E., Nickerson, A. B., Reeves, M. A., Savage, T. A., & Woitaszewski, S. A. (2011). Development, evaluation, and future directions of the PREPaRE school crisis prevention and intervention training curriculum. *Journal of School Violence, 10,* 34–52.

Brock, S. E., Sandoval, J., & Lewis, S. (2001). *Preparing for crises in the schools: A manual for building school crisis response teams.* New York, NY: John Wiley & Sons Inc.

Carlson, E. B. (1997). *Trauma assessments: A clinician's guide.* New York: Guilford Press.

Charuvastra, A., & Cloitre, M. (2009). Social bonds and posttraumatic stress disorder. *Annual Review of Psychology, 59,* 301–328.

Federal Agency Forum on Children and Family Statistics (2011). *America's children: Key national indicators of well-being 2011.* Retrieved from www.childstats.gov/pubs/

Flitsch, E., Magnesi, J., & Brock, S. E. (2012). Social media and crisis prevention and intervention. In S. E. Brock & S. R. Jimerson (Eds.), *Best practices in school crisis prevention and intervention 2nd ed. (pp. 287–304).* Bethesda, MD: National Association of School Psychologists.

Federal Emergency Management Agency (FEMA). (2010, August). *Introduction to the incident command system (ICS 100): Instructor guide.* Washington, DC: Author.

Frosch, D. (2014, September 14). "Active shooter" drills spark raft of legal complaints: Critics say simulation exercises can traumatize those taking part. *Wall Street Journal.* Retrieved from http://online.wsj.com/articles/active-shooter-drills-spark-raft-of-legal-complaints-1409760255.

Griffin, T. L., Lazarus, P. J., Lieberman, R. A., Singh, K., & Diaz, N. (2015, February). Social media's role in crisis: Prevention, intervention, postvention. Paper presented at the annual convention of the National Association of School Psychologists, Orlando, FL.

Hanley, A. W., Peterson, G. W., Canto, A. I., & Garland, E. L. (2015). The relationship between mindfulness and posttraumatic growth with respect to contemplative practice engagements. *Mindfulness, 6,* 654–662.

Lazarus, P. J. (1992). Hurricane Andrew and the aftermath. *NASP Communiqué, 21*(2), 1, 6–7.

Lazarus, P. J. (1993). When the walls come tumbling down: Crisis issues following hurricane disasters. *NASP Communique, 21*(7), 16–18.

Lazarus, P. J., Jimerson, S. R., & Brock, S. E. (2002). Natural disasters. In S. E. Brock, P. J. Lazarus & S. R. Jimerson (Eds.), *Best practices in school crisis prevention and intervention* (pp. 433–447). Bethesda, MD: National Association of School Psychologists.

Lazarus, P. J., & Sulkowski, M. L. (2010). Oil in the water, fire in the sky: Responding to technological/environmental disasters. *Communiqué, 39* (7), 16–17.

Lazarus, P. J., Zenere, F., & Feinberg, T. (2005, November). Helping students and faculty cope in the aftermath of Hurricane Katrina. Presentation to Plaquemines Parish Schools, New Orleans, LA.

McFarlane, A. C. (1987). Post traumatic phenomena in a longitudinal study of children following a natural disaster: The longitudinal effects of post-traumatic morbidity. *Australian New Zealand Journal of Psychiatry, 21,* 210–218.

Napoli, M. (1999). The non-Indian therapist working with American Indian clients: Transference-countertransference implications. *Psychoanalytic Social Work, 6,* 25–47.

Ortiz, S. O., & Voutsinas, M. (2012). Cultural considerations in crisis intervention. In S. E. Brock & S. R. Jimerson (Eds.), *Best practices in school crisis prevention and intervention 2nd edn* (pp. 337–357). Bethesda, MD: National Association of School Psychologists.

Reeves, M. A., Conolly-Wilson, C. N., Pesce, R. C., Lazzaro, B. R., & Brock, S. E. (2012). Preparing for comprehensive school crisis response. In S. E. Brock & S. R. Jimerson (Eds.), *Best practices in school crisis prevention and intervention, 2nd edn* (pp. 245–283). Bethesda, MD: National Association of School Psychologists.

Reeves, M. A., Nickerson, A. B., Conolly-Wilson, C. N., Susan, M. K., Lazzaaro, B. R., & Jimerson, S. R., & Pesce, R. C. (2011). *Crisis prevention and preparedness: Comprehensive school safety and planning (2nd edn).* Bethesda, MD: National Association of School Psychologists.

Rose, R., Bisson, J., Churchill, R., & Wessley, S. (2009). Psychological debriefing for preventing posttraumatic stress disorder (PTSD). *Cochrane Database of Systematic Reviews* (2). doi:10.1002/14651858.CD000560

Sandoval, J. (2013). Considering culture in crisis work. In J. Sandoval (Ed.), *Crisis counseling, intervention, and prevention in the schools, 3d edn* (pp. 31–45). New York: Routledge.

Saigh, P. A., Sack, W., Yasik, A., & Koplewicz, H. (1999). Child adolescent posttraumatic stress: Prevalence, comorbidity, and risk factors. In P. A. Saigh & J. D. Bremner (Eds.), *Posttraumatic stress disorder: A comprehensive approach to assessment and treatment.* Needham Heights, MA: Allyn & Bacon

Saylor, C. F., Belter, R., & Stokes, S. J. (1997). Children and families coping with disaster. In S. A. Wolchik & I. N. Sandler (Eds.), *Handbook of children's coping* (pp. 361–383). New York: Springer.

Slaikeu, K. A. (1990). *Crisis intervention: A handbook for practice and research.* Needham Heights, MA: Allyn & Bacon.

Spring, J. (2007). *The intersection of cultures (4th edn).* Boston, MA: McGraw-Hill.

Sulkowski, M. L., & Lazarus, P. J. (2011). Contemporary responses to violent attacks on college campuses. *Journal of School Violence, 10,* 338–354. doi: 10.1080/15388220.2011.602601

Sulkowski, M. L., & Lazarus, P. J. (2013). Five essential elements of crisis intervention to respond to technological/ecological disasters. *International Journal of School and Educational Psychology, 1,* 3–12. doi: 10.1080/21683603.2013.780192

Sulkowski, M. L., West, J., & Lazarus, P. J. (2011). It ain't easy livin' in the Big Easy: Down and dazed but not out. *NASP Communiqué, 39,* 1, 22–25.

Tedeschi, R. G., & Calhoun, L. G. (1996). The posttraumatic growth inventory: Measuring the positive legacy of growth. *Journal of Traumatic Stress, 9,* 455–471.

U.S. Department of Homeland Security (2008). *U.S. Department of Homeland Security. IS-800B-National response framework, An introduction.* Retrieved from https://emilms.fema.gov/IS800B/lesson1/is800b_Print.htm.

18 School Crisis Intervention

All schools need to be prepared to respond to crises such as violent attacks, natural and technological disasters, vehicle crashes, severe injuries, suicides, sudden deaths and other negative events that occur on or off school grounds that negatively impact members of school communities. With this in mind, the first step toward effective crisis response or intervention is proactive crisis preparation. Thus, Chapter 17 covered ways that educators can prepare for a range of crises. This chapter expands on crisis prevention to discuss how educators and other members of school communities can effectively respond to crises as they unfold, as well as how to help school communities recover in the aftermath. In particular, best-practice recommendations for assessment and triage, active outreach, and recovery are covered (Brymer, Pynoos, Vivrette, & Taylor, 2012). Additionally, the five empirically supported elements of crisis intervention that have been identified by Hobfoll et al. (2007) will structure this chapter as well as material covered in the PREPaRE school crisis intervention training curriculum by the National Association of School Psychologists (NASP). Moreover, discussion and suggestions in regard to how to deal with loss of life and how to help all impacted individuals cope with loss and grief in the aftermath of tragic events will be provided.

To illustrate much of the content discussed in this chapter, an interview is provided with Frank DeAngelis, the Principal of Columbine High School at the time of the tragic shootings that occurred there on April 20, 1999. During this rampage shooting, two perpetrators murdered 12 students and one teacher and injured 21 additional people before killing themselves. DeAngelis discusses lessons learned in the aftermath of this horrendous attack. He also discusses how schools can promote school safety and foster student and faculty mental health following a tragedy, how to understand and be sensitive to the reactions of students and staff, what additional supports need to be implemented following a tragedy, and how to facilitate school and community healing. Lastly, he discusses his own recovery process in the aftermath of the attack.

Expert Interview 18.1 Interview with Frank DeAngelis

Former Principal of Columbine High School

PJL. As the former Principal of Columbine High what lessons have you learned from the tragedy at your school where 12 students and one teacher were killed by two perpetrators in a rampage school shooting?

FD. If you had asked me prior to April 20, 1999, if a tragedy such as we experienced could have happened at Columbine High School, I would have said, "No" because I was under the impression that events like that do not happen in communities like Columbine. It is an urban community in which 93 percent of our students graduate within four years and over 85 percent go on to college. I think we learned that we are all vulnerable. Unfortunately, I had the opportunity to go to other places where school shootings occurred such as Virginia Tech, Sandy Hook, Chardon, etc. and one of the first comments they made was, "I can't believe it happened in this community." The biggest shock was that we are vulnerable and we need to be proactive. We need to unite, not only as a school but as a community, to prevent these tragedies.

PJL. Considering your experiences what do you want administrators, educators, and school-based mental health professionals to know about promoting school safety and fostering student mental health?

FD. You need to have systems in place, such as threat assessment procedures at each individual school. Depending on the outcomes of the threat assessment, you need district-level support and programs to support students at risk. The other message I share is that you need to know all of your students. I was naïve in thinking that all students were buying into the Columbine family. I think it is only human nature that you are going to talk to people who tell you what you want to hear. That creates a sense of false security. For example, I often spoke with students who were doing well academically and who were involved in co-curricular and extracurricular activities. They would say, "Mr. D., Columbine is great; we are Columbine!" But what I failed to do was go out to the smoking pits where students were hanging out or go to the mall where they were cutting class. I did not go to the skate park. After the tragedy, I tried to contact as many students as possible and find out what it would it take for them to feel part of the school.

It was initially portrayed in some of the media that the perpetrators were outcasts, students who did not feel connected with the school. What their teachers, their friends, and I saw were students who were actively involved. These students were enrolled in advanced classes. Over break, one perpetrator went on a college visit to Arizona State because he planned to go to college. He, along with his date and four couples, attended our prom three days prior to the killings in a stretch limo. So, it seems he was actively involved. However, we know that there are always at-risk students who are crying out for help. We need to identify these troubled students and give them the help that they need.

PJL. Tell me about what happened to your staff in the aftermath and how they reacted over the years.

FD. I remember my opening comments the day after the tragedy. I said we needed to remain strong and stick together; the road would be tough but we did not have to travel it alone. The majority of the staff made a commitment to stay until the freshmen graduated in 2002. Even though every student and teacher had the opportunity to transfer, most of our staff stayed until 2002 and honored their pledge. After 2002, we saw a large turnover. As of my retirement, in June 2014, there were about 17 of us left out of 150 who were there on the day of the shooting. People in similar situations have told me this is typical. About 75 percent of the staff leaves because it is so difficult to enter the building day after day and relive what they saw on that day.

PJL. What happened to your student body? How did they react immediately and over the years?

FD. Immediately afterwards, many students left Columbine. I think parents were concerned with their well-being. We had a lot of students switching to home schooling. Some came to school part-time and completed the rest of their instruction at home. No one had anticipated they would start high school and be dealing with post-traumatic stress. Common situations such as fire alarms created extreme tension. When we planned a fire drill, hundreds of students stayed out because they were traumatized. There were many triggers that reminded us of the event such as the food we served. We could not serve Chinese food because that was served on the day of the shooting. Ketchup left on the table reminded students of blood. On our first day back at Chatfield High School, the neighboring school that opened their arms to us, a group of parents welcomed us with an archway of balloons. When some balloons popped, students dove to the ground. This was all new to us. Teachers had to change their curriculum. They could no longer show a movie clip of a World War II battle because of the gunfire. References to violence had to be omitted.

As expected after trauma, students were not in a good frame of mind to retain information. It was fortunate for the students who returned because we provided help for them. We brought in additional mental health workers, counselors, and people who were knowledgeable in dealing with grief. I was extremely concerned about the students graduating the following month. Many of them were going to college in August and I was afraid they would not get the support they needed to understand and deal with their emotions. I could imagine that all of a sudden memories would be triggered and they could have a meltdown. Or they might not understand why they were having so much difficulty concentrating and retaining information. I thought about the students who left the state to go to out-of-state schools. I now realize that one size does not fit all. We had students and staff who seemed to be doing well and felt that if they survived a year, they were okay and if they survived three years, they were out of the woods. But all of a sudden, seven, eight, nine, and ten years out they were starting to feel things they never felt before. Unfortunately, for many of our students, the money to provide the help they needed ran out about three years after the tragedy. Recognizing this, there are groups still fund raising to provide help for former students who are adults in their thirties and still suffering. It is important when providing care for people who have experienced severe trauma not to be short-sighted; you must look five, ten, and 15 years out for the impact it is going to have on the community and plan accordingly.

PJL. What was your personal experience like after the tragedy?

FD. For me personally, several things saved me. My mom worked for a chiropractor who was a Vietnam veteran. He called me a day after the tragedy with some of the best advice I received. He said, "You can't help anyone else if you don't help yourself." So I got into intense counseling early. Not that it made it easy but it gave me the skills to carry on. I knew that seeking counseling carried a stigma and could be considered a weakness, especially for guys. However, by getting counseling, I was able to share the knowledge I learned and also be a role model. I could then deal with comments from others such as: "If you show that you are weak you cannot lead this school; if you cry and you are emotional, you can't lead this community." Through counseling, I learned about post-traumatic stress and how to cope and help others.

I still go for counseling. I call it maintenance because, for example, when the tragedy at Sandy Hook occurred, I had a meltdown. Even though it was a different community and almost 14 years later, I relived my experiences. I know this is something I will need to deal with, but when I start feeling these feelings, I know what is going on and I can get through it. I have been in six car accidents in the month of April and I know when April comes around each year, I have to concentrate because I am going to go through difficult times. It may be other things that trigger emotions such as a song, a book, or driving down the street. I have driven by the school and seen snow on the ground which takes me back to 1999. The good thing about it is that I have learned skills that allow me to cope. My faith has had a great deal to do with my survival. I wear two religious medals around my neck. When I feel these feelings that take me back, I grab the medals and say "this is not 1999, it is 2015."

PJL. What changes did you make to your school physically to help deal with the aftermath of the crisis?

FD. We formed a group called HOPE (Helping Our People Everywhere) comprised of parents, including parents of the deceased and injured students, school staff, students, and community members to help decide what needed to be done. We concluded that we needed to go back into the building and utilize the existing building while making some changes. In Sandy Hook, they made the decision not to use the building. In fact, they wanted me to give them advice about that and I said it was important for them to do what was best for their community. But for Columbine High, we felt the need to go back into the school. We felt that if we did not go back into the building then the two killers had won. It was very similar to what happened on 9/11. The terrorists aimed to create terror in future generations; they wanted to make sure every time someone got on a plane there was fear of another 9/11. It was the same for our community. We felt that if we did not go back into the building then the killers would have haunted us for the rest of our lives. As we considered our return to Columbine, we felt we could not use the area of the library where many of our students were killed. We restructured where the library was located, took out the floor of the old library, which was the ceiling of the cafeteria or the commons, and created an atrium. The new library was opened two years after the tragedy. We also made simple changes to the décor and changed the paint to tranquil colors.

We made additional changes to the building to address safety. We have surveillance cameras and all that, but we have many windows. Although we have a lockdown system that activates immediately when the alarm sounds, what is going to stop a gunman from entering the building by breaking through the glass? Sandy Hook Elementary is a prime example. They had a secure entry but did not anticipate a gunman shooting through the glass to get in. Research shows that the longer you deter a gunman from entering the building, the better chance you have of stopping them. Now we are working with the state of Colorado and Jeffco Schools to find glass that is more difficult to penetrate. With the additional physical changes, we are probably one of the safest schools in the nation.

PJL. What changes did you make to the school culture, school climate and the social environment? What programs or supports did you initiate?

FD. I am a big proponent of the "mental detector" aspect of prevention and of helping students who are crying out for help. One thing we did was to try to make everyone feel a part of the Columbine family. We wanted every student to have at least one adult or several adults they could talk to. It was not just teachers and administrators but it could be non-instructional staff, such as a maintenance personnel, secretaries, or bus drivers. One of the things I believed in was family. We used the Links Program in which we linked our juniors and seniors with incoming freshmen to help them transition to high school. I met with students and families aiming to provide an environment that was welcoming to all.

There are several things you can do to help ensure every student is connected to an adult in the school in a meaningful way. We have what we call an Access Period. It is a homeroom where teachers or staff members are assigned five or six students over the four years. Students are there so they can develop special connections, not only with their peers but with adults. The adults check in with students to see how they are doing academically, check on their attendance, and monitor how they are doing socially.

I initiated an anonymous tip box that I would check every day. We wanted a culture that gave students permission to share what they felt was not right at Columbine. I think many times there are situations where students are not being treated properly. You have victims, you have bullies but the key to a successful school is creating a climate where students and staff will not fear retaliation and will say to someone who is bothering a student, "Hey knock it off." If you create a system where information is shared with administrators and adults and they deal with it effectively, then you create a climate that is conducive for learning.

I promised the students that if they signed the tip, I would call them in and have a conversation. It could be something like, "Mr. D. I feel this would make the school better." Whether it was about an assembly or testing, I sat down with them and we had a one-to-one talk like adults. The students appreciated the open-door policy. I think at times students would make comments such as "you probably will not read this" and they were shocked when I called them into my office to talk. I have faults as an administrator, but I think that if you speak with most of the students who attended Columbine, one of my strengths is the relationship I had with my students. I think it is so important that they trusted me. Being there for such a long period of time and getting ready to retire, at nearly 60 years old, I still have that positive relationship with the students. The fact that the students and parents had faith in me is another reason that I was able to stay 15 years after the tragedy. Not that people always agreed with me but they knew I treated them fairly and I looked at all the information before making a decision. The bottom line is they knew that what I did was hopefully in the best interest of their child.

One of the best programs we have in Colorado is Safe2Tell, a 24/7 hotline. If a student or parent feels threatened or perceives a serious school problem, they notify the hotline and the information immediately goes to the law enforcement agency associated with the school. The response might be a wellness check. For example. I cannot tell you the number of lives that were saved because students reported concerns about a friend who was making comments that implied they were thinking about harming themselves or others. Probably 99 percent of the Safe2Tell messages are legitimate. Having a way to report potential dangers gives students and parents tools to help establish a safe environment. I am on the board which includes personnel from law enforcement and the state attorney general's office. For more information, go to www.safe2tell.org.

PJL. Do you have any other advice for administrators who have experienced the death of a student on campus or a school shooting?

FD. During a tragic incident, I think people often think that administrators know more than they are letting on. That is not necessarily so; however, there are times when they are being directed by the police or investigative team not to share information. This dilemma makes it challenging because it is so important to keep people updated. When the Columbine tragedy happened and we wanted to send a mass e-mail or voicemail to all parents, it would have taken eight hours. Now, due to advanced communication techniques, we can update parents quickly.

I can't emphasize enough the importance of having an emergency plan. You cannot predict how people will respond in an emergency, so it is important to train, train, and train. In Jeffco Schools, we work with the executive director of security who does an excellent job meeting with schools and conducting emergency drills. Soon, I am going to serve as a consultant with him and we will go into schools, conduct drills, debrief students and teachers, and make recommendations.

In our drills, we are careful not to traumatize students unnecessarily. But we do simulate various lockdown situations and teach students why they should not open the door even if they know the person knocking. We teach them to make sure that their cell phones are put away because the lights from their phones can signal a perpetrator that there are students in a room. One of the worst situations we actually had was when we received a threat of a potential bomb in the building but at the same time, there were snipers outside. So what do you do? We problem-solve these various scenarios and always look at "what if, what if, what if." We talk about protecting as many people as possible. We are always reminding and encouraging staff and students to report suspicious people and situations immediately.

PJL. What suggestions do you have on how to facilitate the healing process after a tragedy?

FD. Providing grief counseling and support is key. People are in different places in the healing process. We cannot assume that everyone is feeling the same way at the same time. Reassurance that everyone grieves in a personal way is important. I remember once we returned to school at Chatsfield, there were teachers on the first day back attempting to collect homework. Other teachers wanted their students to journal, journal, journal. You have to find the happy medium and give people some latitude.

I believe that teachers are caregivers and our teachers were also hurting. As I learned earlier, if you don't take care of yourself, you can't take care of the students. Now all of the sudden, we put these teachers in front of the class and if they were not ready, they could be doing a disservice to the students and themselves. I am always amazed that when police officers are involved in a shooting, they are required to talk to a mental health professional before going back to work. Yet after school shootings, there is no requirement for teachers and staff to talk to someone to find out if they need help before they go back to work with students; I think that is something that needs to be done. I know that if I had not received the help I needed, I am not sure I could have led our community. People think that after a tragedy they are going to wake up one day and everything will be back to normal. Now, I tell people we had to redefine normal. When a community goes through a tragedy such as Columbine, Sandy Hook, Chardon, or Virginia Tech, it's not that they can't heal, but things are never going to be the same as they were before the tragedy. So the healing process involves providing as much support as possible for everyone and respecting people for where they are in the process. It is a marathon, not a sprint.

Looking back, I think we need to give staff members permission to leave the school if it is best for them. Earlier, I told you that for us, there was an allegiance to stay with the students; staff made a promise to be there until that last student graduated. But, I think it should be a number one priority for staff members to take care of themselves. If walking in the building daily created intense anxiety or high blood pressure, they should be allowed to transfer. If the administrator believes someone is being negatively impacted emotionally or physically, he or she needs to reassure them that to leave would not be letting people down; it is vital that they take care of themselves.

For me, personally I had a difficult time coping when I was allowed back into the building. I can't tell you the number of times I walked out of my office into that hallway that I would relive the event. I became nauseous and would start crying. I had to keep coming out each day to try to get a little bit further and further down the hallway. That's when I knew I was messed up. What my counselor said was, "I had to decide how that recording would play back in my mind." She said "If every time I walked out of the office, if I envisioned the gunman coming towards me and the students standing behind me and I hear the shots being fired, I will never truly heal and I will never be able to stay here." What I needed to do was to retrain or re-tape that image in my head. That reprogramming of my brain allowed me to stay at Columbine 15 years after the tragedy.

PJL. Speaking about armed gunmen, what is your opinion about having educators carry weapons in school?

FD. I don't know if I could have pulled the trigger if I was one of the staff members to be armed. The gunmen were students of mine. Law enforcement officers who are trained to do this go through extensive training and it is much more than just doing target practice; it requires a whole different mental set. Also, the perpetrators are moving and there are other students around. Being able to hit someone without hitting innocent bystanders is extremely difficult. I can't imagine how devastating it would have been for me if I was armed and shot an innocent student accidently. Just think of the potential dangers and lawsuits resulting from injuring or killing an innocent student in friendly fire. I am not sure how many educators would sign up for that.

Yet, I do believe having School Resource Officers (SROs) in schools who are highly trained in weapon use is a good idea. We do have SROs in Jefferson County schools who are sheriffs. However, their function is to talk to students, go to classes, teach students, and ensure a safe environment. At Arapahoe High School in Colorado, their SRO was instrumental in stopping a school shooter from committing further rampage after he had killed one student. The SRO responded quickly and engaged the gunman, so that rather than being shot or apprehended, the perpetrator took his own life.

PJL. Do you have any final words you would like to share with educators and administrators from your perspective at 15 years post-trauma?

FD. I hope that no one becomes a member of this club; I refer to it as a club when I call administrators after a shooting. I say now we are members of a club that no one wants to join. But, unfortunately there will be shootings and the membership will grow. But Columbine High represents hope. Though it seems you go through the darkest times of your life, there is a light at the end. You never go it alone; no matter how tough times are, you will have support. I look at Michelle Gay, a mother who lost her daughter in the Sandy Hook shooting, and how she has handled everything; she is one of my heroes. I got to know her and befriend her. I saw her speak at a conference and I am thinking, this woman has such a passion for what she is doing. She loved her child so much and now, she helps others heal from similar tragedies. I made a vow after the Columbine tragedy that I was not going to allow those students and teachers to die in vain, and I was not going to allow all the students and people who were physically injured to go unnoticed. I was going to continue until the day I died to speak on their behalf to help prevent shootings. There was a plaque in my office that signified the message I would like to send. It says, "In our lives we cannot determine what happens to us but we can determine how we respond to what happens to us."

A Multitiered Model of Differentiated Services

Before educators consider how best to respond during and after a crisis, it is important to understand that the primary goal of crisis intervention is to "help restore the crisis exposed student's basic problem solving abilities and in doing so to return the student to his or her pre-crisis levels of functioning" (Brock, Reeves, & Nickerson, 2014, p. 214). Moreover, a crisis event may prompt a need to provide crisis intervention services, yet the mere occurrence of a crisis may not justify the provision of extensive services. Instead, it is the consequences that the crisis event has on the school, students, and staff that determine whether crisis intervention services are needed as well as the amount and intensity of these services.

As discussed in previous chapters, using a multi-tiered system of support (MTSS) framework is consistent with best practices in intervention service delivery. In this regard, providing differentiated or multi-tiered services is especially important during and after a school crisis. As Brock et al. (2014) note, the selection of specific crisis interventions depends on different considerations. For example, intervention selection often is based on proximity—both physical and psychological—to the crisis event. As such, some interventions will need to be provided immediately, whereas others can be offered days or weeks later. Also, not all individuals will require the same type of intervention. In general, individuals who are more emotionally or physically impacted by a crisis may require more intensive and comprehensive supports.

At the Tier 1 level, crisis intervention services are offered to all individuals who have been exposed to the crisis. The purpose of doing so is to ensure the perceptions of safety and security, to prevent or lessen psychological trauma, and to reaffirm physical and mental health. As will be further discussed, Tier 1 interventions may include disseminating information, providing psychological education to both teachers and caregivers on how to help students cope with trauma, and facilitating classroom meetings that enable students to understand crisis facts and reactions (Brock et al., 2009, Brock et al., 2014). Also at the Tier 1 level, students can be evaluated for psychological trauma risk, which then allows for decisions to be made about subsequent service delivery.

At the Tier 2 level, services are offered to students who are moderately and severely traumatized. However, following a highly traumatic crisis, selected Tier 2 level services may need to be offered to an entire school population. These interventions typically include classroom-based crisis interventions that help students to process and normalize their crisis experiences and reactions and one-on-one crisis interventions that aim to help more severely impacted students cope more effectively. Finally at the Tier 3 level, recommendations and referrals are made for more long-term and intensive mental health treatment for those most severely impacted members of school communities. Fortunately, Tier 3 interventions are typically needed to be received only by a minority of youth in schools following a crisis (Brock et al., 2009, Brock et al., 2014).

Level of Response

In addition, to providing universal (Tier 1), selected (Tier 2), and indicated (Tier 3) interventions, it is important for schools to gauge the level of response that will be needed to respond to a crisis accurately. First, it is important not to underreact and fail to meet the needs of students. Second, schools also should not overreact and potentially make a "mountain out of a mole hill" (Brock, 2011, p. 42). In other words, it is important for crisis intervention to be tailored to the needs of those who have been adversely impacted.

Crisis response can be divided into the following four levels: *minimal response, building-level response, district-level response*, and *community or regional-level response*. Crises that require *minimal response* are not highly traumatic and can be effectively managed by school personnel as they serve in their current roles. Essentially, the school is capable of functioning normally during these crises and members of school crisis teams do not need to clear their calendars to help with response efforts. A crisis that may require minimal response might include a non-intentional student injury that is not caused by others, such as a student being injured on the playground and then needing medical attention. Crises that require a *building-level response* are those that that have the potential to be traumatic yet the school possesses the resources and personnel needed to respond effectively without having to rely on external supports. These crises require some school personnel to adjust their calendars and assist with the response. An example would be a serious accidental injury caused by another person (Brock, 2011).

Crises that require a *district-level response* have the potential to be highly traumatic to a number of victims. These crises require members of the school community to rely on supports and personnel from the school district because the event has impacted a large number of individuals in an adverse way and the number of students that require attention cannot be effectively served by a smaller school crisis response team. In some incidents that require a district-level response, members of the crisis team may have been personally impacted, feel too personally close to the event to be effective, or feel overwhelmed. These crises might include events that have resulted in fatalities, caused serious damage to the school, and occurred with little or no warning. In addition, these crises present victims with ongoing challenges to coping and recovery (Brock, 2011). Lastly, crises that require a *community or regional-level response* are highly traumatic and have impacted many victims. These crises require school personnel to get significant help from emergency responders, the community, and outside agencies. During community or regional crises, school functioning is disrupted and school personnel have to leave their respective roles. Similar to district-level crises, these crises could include situations in which human life was lost and a school was seriously damaged or destroyed or the community was severely impacted (e.g., floods, fires, hurricanes, tornadoes, mass shootings). Because of their potential to impact students and school staff, these crises significantly challenge post-crisis coping. In the next section, best-practice recommendations are provided to help with managing district, community, or regional-level crises, which require intensive and comprehensive responses and services.

Best Practice Recommendations

Reunification

Following a serious school crisis (e.g. violent attack, natural disaster that damages the school, technological disaster), students often will have to be reunited with family (or other caregivers) at a safe location off campus. In these cases, law enforcement officials may need to carry out an investigation at the school or inspectors may need to test whether the school is safe to reoccupy. Therefore, school crisis response teams must designate a safe location for families to pick up their children in advance of a crisis and figure out how to coordinate student and staff transfers to this location as well as to respond to unique problems that may present during this process.

Often a safe reunification location is a neighboring school in a district, if it is within walking distance. However, some schools also coordinate with local fire stations, churches, or other locations to plan a reunification site. In general, a reunification site must be easily accessed by caregivers yet also allow school staff and crisis responders the ability to coordinate the reunification process efficiently. Therefore, school administrators will need resources to be able to document students coming to and leaving the site as well as to vet all individuals who are part of the reunification process. A complete set of the necessary school documents for student dismissal should be available at the reunification site. In addition, basic necessities may be needed to support students and staff who may have to wait hours for full reunification to occur. With this in mind, the reunification site will need ample food, water, and clothing supplies. It also must be accessible and equipped to provide students with disabilities and health problems with the care they need and receive on a regular basis. For example, students with pediatric diabetes will need to receive continued medical care (e.g., blood glucose monitoring, insulin) as a crisis unfolds and during the reunification process.

Reunification with family members is an important part of the crisis intervention response. During this process, members of the school community and emergency first responders can help students re-establish a sense of safety and support. Further, reunification may be the only part of the crisis intervention process that many children and adolescents need in order to recover, as families typically are the most potent forms of support for students (Barenbaum, Ruchkin, & Schwab-Stone, 2004; Horowitz, McKay, & Marshall, 2005). Crepeau-Hobson, Sievering, Armstrong, and Stonis (2012) report that the post-crisis reunification process usually takes between two to ten hours depending on the context of the crisis. In general, the speed and efficiency of the reunification process depends on the scope of the crisis (e.g., the number of individuals impacted; the level of disruption to the school environment; the type and extent of the threat to the student body; the number of individuals injured, killed, hospitalized or unaccounted for; and available resources). Moreover, it also depends on the strength of the crisis prevention and preparation plans made by the school crisis response team prior to the event and the coordination between the school and community during the event (Reeves et al., 2011).

Triage

Triage, or determining who will receive what types of interventions and supports, is an essential component of effective crisis intervention planning (Brock et al., 2009). This process involves identifying which students, caregivers, and school personnel have been most impacted and need immediate crisis intervention as well as which individuals may need intervention or support at some point in the future. Although people's response to crises are highly variable, research indicates that proximity—both physical and psychological or emotional—to a crisis is a strong risk factor for trauma and impaired coping (Brock & Davis, 2008). Thus, individuals who have directly experienced or witnessed a crisis event or knew people who were directly impacted should be the first to receive assistance.

In the aftermath of a serious crisis, law enforcement officials often interview individuals who may have been impacted by or directly witnessed the event. In light of this, members of the school crisis response team should pay extra close attention to these individuals, as they have an elevated risk for experiencing trauma. The identities of these individuals should then be made known to school administrators, school-based mental health professionals, and others who can help with the recovery process. This will prevent a potential delay in providing individuals at higher risk with the appropriate level of support that they may need. It is important to note that if a student or school staff member seems to be coping well in the wake of a crisis, they should not be overlooked and they may need to be seen later—even though they might not be designated as a high priority. At times, individuals impacted by a crisis may be able to maintain composure in social settings and may not open up and disclose their suffering until they see a mental health professional. This frequently occurs when teachers and administrators do their best to maintain a sense of calm and self-control, and suppress their own feelings in order "to be there for their students." Also, as noted by DeAngeles (this chapter), it is important to note that trauma-related symptoms may not occur immediately.

Beyond students and staff that are in proximity to a crisis event, Crepeau-Hobson et al. (2012) report that triage for the general school community works well if school-based mental health professionals and administrators greet everyone when they enter the school. Individuals who are noticeably distressed can be offered the option of meeting with a mental health professional in a private location where the impact of the crisis on them can be assessed. The PREPaRE school crisis intervention training curriculum includes a range of materials for evaluating individuals that may be struggling to adjust in the aftermath of a crisis. This curriculum focuses on both internal and external risk factors as well as early warning and enduring crisis reaction warning signs. Table 18.1 lists some general signs that an individual may have been adversely impacted by a crisis event.

Table 18.1 Signs that an Individual may have been Adversely Impacted by a Crisis Event

- Re-experiencing symptoms in one's mind

  - Having flashbacks related to the crisis
  - Engaging in play related to the crisis (e.g., acting out a school shooting)
  - Excessively drawing stimuli related to the trauma

- Hyper-arousal and reactivity

  - Irritable behavior and outbursts (with little or no provocation)
  - Reckless, impulsive, and self-destructive behavior
  - Hypervigilance (i.e., an exaggerated state of sensory sensitivity accompanied by intense worry that a threat is present)
  - Exaggerated startle response
  - Difficulty concentrating because of rumination about the crisis event
  - Impaired sleep and nightmares related to the crisis event or threats more generally

- Dissociative symptoms

  - Derealization (e.g., feeling like one is in a dream, feeling like reality is not real)
  - Depersonalization (e.g., feeling like one is outside of one's body, feeling like one's body does not belong to oneself)

- Behavioral avoidance and change

  - Avoidance of people, places, interactions, conversations, and stimuli that trigger thoughts about the crisis
  - Marked increases in negative emotional states (e.g., fear, sadness, guilt, shame, rage, confusion)

- ○ Diminished interest in previously enjoyed activities such as play and socializing
- ○ Social withdrawal and school refusal
- ○ A reduction in the display of positive affect or emotions

- Increases in anxiety post-crisis

  - ○ Feelings of panic and worry about having a panic attack
  - ○ Generalized fears about the world not being a safe place and that bad things will happen to oneself or important others (e.g., family members, friends, classmates)
  - ○ The development of new phobias and avoidant behavior related to these phobias
  - ○ Difficulty separating from caregivers and support people and difficulty being alone
  - ○ Carrying safety objects around (e.g., a favorite toy, a stuffed animal, a religious object) that make someone feel safer and more in control of the environment
  - ○ The development of obsessive thoughts and compulsive behaviors that reduce anxiety associated with these thoughts

- Increases in depression post-crisis

  - ○ Feelings of hopelessness and worthlessness
  - ○ Loss of interest in most academic, social, and family activities
  - ○ Persistent fatigue
  - ○ Increased somatic complaints
  - ○ Reductions in engagement and motivation

- Maladaptive coping

  - ○ Excessive substance use or self-medication
  - ○ Taking excessive precautions (e.g., sleeping only with the lights on, sleeping with access to a real or perceived defensive weapon)
  - ○ Having revenge-related delusions or delusions of having been able to avert the crisis

---

Creating a Safe Space

To help with the immediate and long-term recovery process following a crisis, schools can designate a safe space or a location that is open to students, family, and staff members. In this space, individuals can congregate, provide each other with social support, receive credible information, and receive mental health support. Thus, according to Reeves, Kanan, and Plog (2010), creating a safe space or haven is a crucial step in re-establishing psychological safety and facilitating the overall recovery process.

A range of issues must be considered prior to designating and setting up a safe space. If it is located on a school campus, it is important that the safe space is able to integrate well with regular school functioning while still providing crisis victims with the privacy and support that they need. Conversely, if the safe space site is located off campus (e.g., a fire station, church) it should be in proximity to the school to allow for accessible transportation and easy access. In general, safe spaces should be shielded from the media and allow for crisis victims to feel like they can communicate freely and not be interfered with by bystanders.

In the aftermath of a school shooting in Colorado, Crepeau-Hobson et al. (2012) report that about 75 percent of parents brought their students to a safe space shortly after the shooting and the families stayed for about one to two hours afterward on average. Further, they report that the high number of members of the school community who utilized the safe space highlights the importance of having such a supportive gathering place during the recovery process. While members of the school community utilize the safe space, their attendance can be tracked—not to make these individuals feel like they are being monitored unnecessarily—but rather so that the school can follow-up with them to ensure that they receive adequate support throughout the crisis recovery process. Lastly, it is important to ensure that interpreters are present or can be accessed to communicate with families at safe spaces so that linguistically diverse students and families do not feel disconnected from the school (Annandale, Allen-Heath, Dean, Kemple, & Takino, 2011).

Psychological First Aid

Psychological first aid involves providing acute interventions to assist individuals who are experiencing post-crisis distress to help them regain a sense of healthy coping and adaptive functioning. In addition, it can involve linking these individuals with long-term service providers who can assist them throughout the duration of the crisis recovery process. The provision of psychological first aid differs from counseling or therapy in that it is a short-term approach that does not involve the disclosure or processing of traumatic experiences, especially if individuals are reluctant to share these experiences (Brock et al., 2009).

According to established provision models (e.g., Brymer et al., 2006), psychological first aid is intended to be delivered by a range of school personnel, regardless of whether they have had mental health training. Thus, educators of diverse backgrounds can serve as psychological first aid providers or at least help to contribute to this process as long as they have been adequately exposed to and mastered curricula such as *Psychological first aid: Field operations guide, second edition* offered by the National Child Traumatic Stress Network's and National Center for Posttraumatic Stress Disorder (Brymer et al., 2006). Thus, contingent on following these curricular aims regarding psychological first aid, educators can assume crucial roles in crisis intervention. Table 18.2 lists goals associated with providing psychological first aid.

Stabilization

After a crisis, a number of victims may need to be stabilized. According to Schoenwald, Ward, Henggeler, and Rowland (2000), crisis stabilization involves assisting individuals to prevent psychiatric hospitalization or further mental health problems. This probably will be a small number of individuals in most crisis events. However, large-scale crises that have a profound impact on many individuals will require mental health professionals to triage and stabilize a large number of individuals in a short amount of time. Therefore, crisis stabilization efforts should match the degree of psychological distress that has been caused by the crisis event.

In general, individuals who display previous vulnerabilities (e.g., have a trauma history, engage in maladaptive coping, have limited social support) are most likely to become overwhelmed in the aftermath of a crisis and may need to be stabilized. These are the individuals whose needs should be prioritized by members of school crisis teams and school-based mental health professionals. However, there is no one-size-fits-all approach to accomplishing this important aim. Similar to crisis reactions, the degree of stabilization needed by crisis victims is variable. Some victims can be stabilized by therapeutic grounding, whereas others may

Table 18.2 Goals of Psychological First Aid

Psychological first aid is a powerful approach and when used appropriately it can accomplish the following goals:

- Provide a sense of comfort, calm, reassurance and support
- Provide an accurate account of the individual's experience
- Show respect to individuals that decline the opportunity to discuss their experience
- Promote acceptance and validation of reactions and feelings
- Emphasize the importance of social support connections
- Enhance problem-solving ability
- Address fears and anxieties
- Reduce stigma and shame
- Disseminate information important to the recovery process
- Emphasize that help is available (Litz and Gray, 2004)

---

need acute psychiatric care and long-term, evidence-based psychotherapy afterward. Text Box 18.1 discusses therapeutic grounding and how it can be applied as part of the school crisis intervention process.

Text Box 18.1   Strategies for Achieving Therapeutic Grounding

Therapeutic grounding involves staying present with negative emotions and thoughts with the support of a therapist or therapeutic materials. Essentially, it involves a set of skills, techniques, and strategies one uses to prevent oneself from feeling overwhelmed, detached, or flooded with anxiety while coping with trauma-related distress. Below are some strategies that can be used during therapeutic grounding:

Strategies for Immediate Relief

- Use diaphragmatic breathing or breath slowly and steadily while taking exaggeratedly deep breaths
- Focus on appealing or beautiful natural phenomena (e.g. the clouds, leaves on trees, currents in a stream, the reflection of the sun on water, patterns in the bark of a tree, contours of hills/mountains, etc.).
- Eat or drink tasty food or drink and focus intently on the sensation.
- Lie down and imagine relaxation coming and going through one's body like waves washing across a beach shore.
- Take a shower or bath and notice the sensations of the water.
- Light candles and pay attention to the pleasant smells and warm glow.

Strategies for Relief Maintenance

- Read positive or uplifting reading materials, comics, or internet memes.
- "Pay-it-forward": Do something nice for someone else, even if the act is as simple as holding the door for a stranger.
- Send someone a kind email or make a kind phone call.
- List five really positive things that exist in your life.
- Write about things for which you are grateful.
- In a stream of consciousness, write as much as you can in five minutes.
- Think about times in your life when you overcame stressful and painful experiences.

Enhanced Support

Prior to providing enhanced support for impacted students, caregiver training is recommended. Typically, members of the school or district crisis response team provide the necessary information to enable teachers to share the facts about the crisis, prepare teachers as to what reactions they may expect from their students, provide strategies that caregivers can use to help students cope in the aftermath of a crisis, ensure that caregivers can potentially identify students that show severe and concerning reactions, and know how to make a referral for mental health assistance. Generally these trainings are brief and occur before school starts or at the end of the school day prior to meeting with the students the following day.

Enhanced support for victims of school crisis events often involves the following: re-establishing social support, providing psychological education, conducting classroom meetings, providing classroom-based intervention, providing individual crisis intervention, and referring and connecting those most severely impacted to mental health professionals.

Re-establishing social support involves connecting affected students with primary support systems such as important peers, teachers, administrators, counselors, staff members, and coaches. School communities often come together after crisis events; however, these bonds may become strained over time. Therefore, it is important to ensure that continued social support is provided to students who have been impacted by a crisis during the entire recovery process.

Providing psychological education to students and caregivers and *conducting classroom-based meetings* are Tier 1 interventions that aim to dispel myths and rumors as well as provide students with factual information that can help with understanding a crisis and its impact. Additionally, psychological education helps students who have been affected by a crisis understand the types of emotional reactions that they can expect to experience post-crisis. Psychological education can often be accomplished by disseminating informational material. In addition, information can be shared with parents via community meetings, handouts, the internet, a school's website, or on a school's Facebook page. Most often the information provided during psychological education relates to the specific crisis, the school's actions, typical crisis reactions of children and adolescents, strategies to help students cope, and when and how to refer children for professional care.

Classroom meetings are typically led by a classroom teacher who has been provided with a fact sheet about the crisis and they help students understand and share crisis reactions (Brock et al., 2014). In addition, classroom meetings allow students who may be confused about a crisis or feel overwhelmed to ask questions and get factual answers. These meetings also provide a teacher with an opportunity to determine how students in the classroom are coping in the aftermath of a crisis and identify students who may require additional help.

A *classroom-based crisis intervention* is often provided in the aftermath of a large-scale disaster in which the number of impacted students tends to overwhelm the available crisis team members. This is considered a Tier 2 crisis intervention. Classroom-based crisis intervention is similar to the classroom meeting but it typically lasts much longer than the latter and is led by a school psychologist or other experienced mental health professional (Brock et al., 2014). During classroom-based crisis intervention, students actively explore and process their individual crisis experiences and reactions as well as discuss proactive coping strategies.

Considering the diversity in students' responses to crises, it is important for students to be able to choose if they want to participate in discussions about a crisis and how it impacted them and others. This approach has been used in classrooms following crises and the results of doing so have been promising according to anecdotal evidence. Brock (2002) writes that the classroom-based crisis intervention model has treatment advantages that: (a) help students feel less alone and more connected to classmates, (b) build group cohesion which may enable students to deal with the emotional after-effects of the crisis, (c) promote the idea that trauma responses are normal, (d) enable students to regain a sense of optimism and hope which may then help them see their reactions as manageable, and (e) provide crisis team members with an efficient and practical way to identify students who need more intensive support. Unfortunately, empirical research using controlled clinical trials on this classroom-based approach is needed. Thus, as a caveat, in the absence of supportive research and because highly traumatized students could experience severe psychological distress, this approach is contraindicated for these students, who could become highly distressed and re-trigger their peers (Everly, 2003). Essentially, seriously traumatized youth require individual attention over and beyond Tier 2 intervention.

Individual school-crisis intervention, a Tier 2 intervention, involves working one-on-one with a school-based mental health provider to determine a student's needs in the aftermath of a crisis. Although this form or intervention is not psychotherapy, it can provide students with important emotional support. Essentially, the crux of individual school-crisis intervention involves providing students with the supports they need to cope independently with crisis-related problems. Of course, some students may need more support and help than is provided with this intervention approach. In these cases, it is important to provide these students with a Tier 3 intervention and *refer and connect* them with community-based mental health professionals and specialized providers.

Linking with Collaborative Service Agencies and Service Providers

Schools should develop lists of community services that might be needed post-crisis as well as a range of service providers who can be relied on in the immediate aftermath of a crisis. Developing such a list is a fluid rather than a static task, as turnover often is high at community-based mental health agencies and there may be fluctuations in the ability of various agencies and providers to help with a crisis response. Therefore, it behooves members of school crisis teams to check regularly and follow-up to ensure that providers and agencies are still accepting new clients that can be supported during the crisis recovery process.

Although educators usually are not the primary people who coordinate efforts to link crisis victims with collaborative service agencies and service providers, they can play an important role in this process. Teachers, administrators, and educational support staff spend a lot of their time getting to know and understand the students they see on a daily basis—much more than is possible for members of school crisis teams or school-based mental health professionals who are typically understaffed in school systems (Cowen, Vaillancourt, Rossen, & Pollitt, 2013). Therefore, because of their proximity to students—both physically and emotionally—educators can be the first link in a chain that connects crisis victims to the services they need to recover. Table 18.3 lists several key actions that educators can perform to help link students to services as well as support the provision of psychological first aid more generally.

Table 18.3 Key Actions that Educators can take to Link Students to Services and Support Students'
  Mental Health

- Know all of the school psychologists, counselors, social workers, and other school-based mental health professionals in the building.
- Adopt a pro-mental health and anti-stigma attitude.
- Learn signs that students may be suffering with mental health problems.
- Communicate to educators about the importance of supporting student mental health.
- Become involved in school-building-level committees that address student mental health.
- Get to know the name of every student in class and arrange regular check-in times in which they can share what they are thinking and feeling.
- Advocate for multi-tiered systems of support (MTSS) for mental health.
- Proactively address student bullying and school violence.
- Integrate social-emotional learning into the curriculum and into lesson plans.

Skills for Psychological Recovery

A range of cognitive, behavioral, emotional, and adaptive skills are needed for optimal psychological recovery post-crisis. Currently, trauma-focused cognitive-behavioral therapy (TF-CBT), a Tier 3 intervention, is the best established treatment for individuals who have been exposed to trauma and crisis events. Because TF-CBT usually is provided by specialized and highly trained mental health professionals that are few in number, many crisis victims never have access to this evidence-based form of treatment, especially students who have limited access to community-based mental health specialists more generally (Sulkowski, Joyce, & Storch, 2013).

Empirically Supported Elements of Crisis Intervention

Currently, five elements of crisis intervention related to responding to natural disasters, technological disasters (i.e., disasters that are caused by an interaction between human behavior and industry), and mass acts of violence have been rigorously studied and validated as evidence-based practices. These include (1) promoting a sense of safety, (2) calming and supporting fearful individuals, (3) engendering a sense of self- and collective efficacy in affected individuals and communities, (4) increasing feelings of connectedness with others, and (5), instilling and inspiring hope in victims (Hobfoll et al., 2007; Lazarus & Sulkowski, 2010; Sulkowski & Lazarus, 2013). Although much of the research on crisis intervention has occurred outside of school settings, each of the aforementioned elements can be flexibly applied to treat affected schools and communities. Essentially, schools, as relatively well-organized institutions within larger communities, can utilize existing organizational structures, crisis teams, and a variety of supports to promote the recovery process.

Promoting Safety

Crises shake people's fundamental sense of safety and this is even truer for students. Children's beliefs that the world is a safe place and that they are protected by their teachers and parents often are challenged by a crisis situation. Thus, the first step of crisis intervention is to end the crisis (if possible) and provide a foundation for students' sense of physical and psychological safety to be rebuilt. Essentially, the crisis must stop—and students must believe that the crisis has ended—for healthy stabilization and recovery. To encourage this process, educators can communicate that a crisis has passed (if it has) and that students are safe (if they are).

Promoting safety involves providing accurate messages about risks and the efforts that important adults are taking to ensure a safe school environment. This process involves providing all members of school communities with accurate and balanced information so that they can realistically appraise threats and risks. Furthermore, ways to minimize risk should be provided to mitigate feelings of panic, helplessness, and hopelessness. In the absence of credible information during a crisis, "horror stories," rumors, and conspiracy theories can abound that cause students to feel unsafe and thus need to be dispelled (Brock et al., 2009). In order to promote a sense of safety, educators need to get ahead of a crisis by providing reliable information.

In the immediate aftermath of a crisis, usual behavioral expectations and school rules can become compromised as schools re-establish new norms and members of the school communities adjust. As such, schools must be both flexible and realistic and make the necessary adjustments to campus and classroom operational protocol in the aftermath of disaster. For example, in August 2004, Hurricane Charlie, a category 4 hurricane, hit Southwest Florida and impacted a number of schools in Hardee County School District in Wauchula, Florida. As a result, the school system was shut down for weeks. Several days prior to reopening, Dennis Jones, the District Superintendent addressed his entire instructional staff of nearly 800 individuals. Excerpts of his heartfelt message follow:

> Until further notice, I am instituting the following measures. No homework will be given, for many of our students have no home in which to complete it. Attendance will be taken, but all absences and late arrivals will be excused. Cafeteria lunches will be free of charge for students and employees. There will be no fundraising activities, since our community has been financially depleted. Lastly, I want each of you to focus on the social and emotional healing of our students at this critical time, not on preparing for high stakes testing.
>
> (Zenere, 2005)

Moreover, the dress code was relaxed for both students and faculty because many individuals had lost all their clothing in the wake of the hurricane. Also, the schools became centers for increased community activities as many of the other sources of support were destroyed and were yet to be rebuilt (Lazarus & Zenere, 2005).

The tendency to change school functioning in the wake of a crisis is understandable and can be beneficial, as demonstrated by the overwhelming support of the community for the reordered priorities of the Hardee County School District. However, research also indicates that returning to normal or usual school functioning is an important element of ensuring safety and crisis recovery (Brock et al., 2009; Reeves et al., 2011). Therefore, a fine balance needs to be achieved between making the necessary adjustments and returning to so-called "regular school functioning," which typically is a process rather than an event. Returning to regular school functioning at an appropriate time after a crisis imparts the message that adults are in control and will take care of students as well as that it is important for students to continue learning and re-engage in other educational activities.

Lastly, in the age of social media and instant communication, a reduction of post-event crises and adversities often involves reducing students' exposure to re-triggering or anxiety provoking media and messages (Sulkowski & Lazarus, 2011). Research indicates that excessive exposure to the media following a crisis can exacerbate crisis-related stress by those who experienced the event. In addition, it can induce trauma in individuals who vicariously witnessed the event. For example, several studies have found that children who excessively viewed the 9/11 attacks on television displayed elevated levels of trauma as well as disruptions in their psychosocial functioning post-disaster (Ahern et al., 2002; Otto, Henin, Hirshfeld-Becker, Pollack, Biederman, & Rosenbaum, 2007). Therefore, it is important for adults to filter the amount and type of information students are exposed to in the wake of a crisis.

Calming and Supporting Fearful Individuals

People cope with stress and trauma differently and there is no "right way" to feel after a crisis. Because of this, educators should respect individual differences in the way that students respond to crisis situations. Immediately after a crisis, some students will want to talk about their experiences while other students will feel safer and calmer by keeping their thoughts and feelings private. Students who do not wish to talk about the crisis event may instead feel better simply by reuniting with their families, peers, and teachers. Consistent with recommendations by Sulkowski and Lazarus (2013), members of school communities can use therapeutic grounding techniques (i.e., exercises that encourage individuals to feel safe and supported in the present moment regardless of previous trauma) to help victims feel calmer and less fearful. In general, techniques that promote calming in the aftermath of a crisis reduce anxiety, fear, grief, and emotional arousal. Research indicates that teaching diaphragmatic breathing and progressive muscle relaxation techniques helps students manage their stress better (Joyce-Beaulieu & Sulkowski, 2015). More specifically, these techniques have been shown to help decease anxiety, hyperventilation, disassociation, and anxious thoughts and they can be taught to individuals and groups in therapy or seminars (Jaycox et al., 2010; Joyce-Beaulieu & Sulkowski, 2015; Rolfsnes & Idsoe, 2011). Although it may seem counterintuitive, exposure and response prevention (ERP) therapy has been established as an effective treatment for overcoming traumatic stress (Foa, Keane, & Friedman, 2000). This form of therapy involves having individuals systematically face feared stimuli and situations so that they gradually habituate to these anxiety triggers. Lastly, although not as much research has been conducted on these approaches as they pertain to crisis intervention, mindfulness techniques such as meditation and yoga display promise for helping students feel calm in the aftermath of a crisis (Brymer et al., 2012; Meiklejohn et al., 2012). However, supportive yet not targeted forms of psychotherapy such as play therapy and art therapy have not yet been validated as effective stand-alone treatments for trauma (Brymer et al., 2012; Rolfsnes & Idsoe, 2011). Therefore, play and art therapy should be used in conjunction with evidence-based treatments if they are used as part of the therapeutic process.

Engendering a Sense of self- and Collective Efficacy

Self-efficacy is the belief that the regulation of thoughts, emotions, and behaviors can solve problems and lead to desirable outcomes. With this in mind, the concept of "collective efficacy" relates to the belief that one belongs to a group that can accomplish desired outcomes through the work of its members (Benight, 2004). Unfortunately, during and after a crisis, some individuals may struggle to make decisions that they could normally do when not under duress (Reeves et al., 2011). This effectively can keep people stuck and struggling in the wake of a crisis. However, research indicates that the belief that one can cope with trauma has been found to predict adaptive functioning in the aftermath of acts of mass violence and natural disasters (Basoglu, Salcioglu, Livanou, Kalender, & Acar, 2005; Bleich, Gelkopf, & Solomon, 2003). Therefore, it is important for educators to support efforts to increase self- and collective efficacy.

To facilitate efficacy beliefs in individuals and communities that have been impacted by a crisis, educators can model leadership and adaptive coping. This process often involves re-establishing regular routines, coordinating needed services (e.g., food, clothing, water), and engaging key community members and agencies to help with recovery efforts (Chen & Bliese, 2002). The more that crisis victims feel supported and empowered, the more likely they are to recover quickly and readjust to normal life (Benight, 2004). After a disaster or crisis, individuals from recovery and relief organizations come into the community to support victims and members of communities come together to support each other in unprecedented ways (Crepeau-Hobson et al., 2012). Therefore, educators can capitalize on this phenomenon to help increase a sense of collective efficacy among crisis victims. Table 18.4 lists specific strategies that educators can use to help support self- and collective efficacy.

Table 18.4 Strategies that Educators Can Use to Help Support Self- and Collective Efficacy

---

- Map out community resources that victims can utilize.
- Create a safe space in the school.
- Have regular meetings and forums at school where members of the community can be informed of what is being done to address a crisis.
- Provide regular, clear, and consistent communication through different channels (e.g., letters home, social media, public meetings) to all members of school communities.
- Ensure that all communication is translated into appropriate languages for non-English speaking families. Also ensure that interpreters are present at meetings at school.
- Institute and communicate that an "open door" policy exists for students in need of mental health support or someone to talk to.
- Make sure school-based mental health professionals go into classrooms rather than wait in their office for referrals.
- Provide a variety of ways for key community members to engage and support students.
- Reach out to nearby school districts to cover personnel who may need to take a leave.
- Consider bringing in recently retired school personnel who may be able to offer additional support.
- Reach out to national agencies and organizations such as the National Association of School Psychologists www.nasponline.org/resources/crisis_safety/neat.aspx.
- Coordinate with local law enforcement officers to arrange for extra security on or near campus if needed
- Increase opportunities for support before and after school for families that may be struggling to adjust to normal routines.
- Designate and support a mental health incident commander (MHIC) in addition to the incident commander (IC).
- Coordinate appropriate referrals for students and caregivers who are engaging in maladaptive forms of coping.
- Reach out to medical centers and health care professionals in the community to coordinate care as crisis victims often experience both physical health and mental health problems.
- Create official school-supported social media pages (e.g., commemoration page on Facebook) that can be monitored and refereed by school personnel to ensure respectful content.

Increasing Feelings of Connectedness

Chapter 8 discusses ways that educators can help students feel more supported socially and connected to others in the school community. In the aftermath of a crisis, it is especially important to redouble these efforts (Weems et al., 2007). In general, feeling socially supported and bonded to the school community is associated with improvements in students' emotional well-being and recovery following traumatic experiences (Norris & Elrod, 2006; Openshaw, 2011). In addition, efforts to engage students who have been impacted by a crisis can help with identifying who is most at-risk for negative outcomes and allow for effective triage for supportive services. Therefore, it is important for educators and school-based mental health professionals to work together to connect with each and every student who may have been impacted by a crisis. As emphasized by Frank DeAngelis in the chapter interview, it is especially important for educators to reach out to students who are less connected to the school and may be perceived as outliers.

Instilling and Inspiring Hope

Students and other members of school communities that have favorable outcomes after experiencing a crisis tend to be optimistic, expect a positive future, and feel like they have the skills they need to cope with the crisis (Brymer et al., 2012). In other words, they are hopeful about the future and their ability to handle adversity. In a study of protective factors in war-affected students, Kasler, Dahan, and Elias (2008) found a negative correlation between a sense of hope and the development of Post-Traumatic Stress Disorder (PTSD). Therefore, consistent with this finding, hope can even protect against the development of trauma in students who have been impacted by recurrent and severe crises.

Although an important protective factor, hope is not a homogenous construct and it is described differently across cultures. For example, hope often is described as being action-oriented and goal-driven in Western middle-class societies (Haase, Britt, Coward, Leidy, & Penn, 1992). However, in other cultures, hope may be associated with holding specific beliefs, maintaining a connection to a higher power, feeling trust in a responsible government/society, and even with believing in superstitions (Hobfoll, Briggs-Phillips, & Stines, 2003; Smith, Pargament, Brant, & Oliver, 2000). Considering the marked differences in the perception of hope, educators must be sensitive to the unique cultural values and beliefs embraced by crisis victims that influence their feelings of hope and optimism.

While trying to instill hope in crisis victims, educators must walk a fine line between fatuously promoting hopeful messages and failing to highlight potential opportunities for emotional, personal, and spiritual growth that can be derived post-crisis (Sulkowski & Lazarus, 2013). In this vein, prematurely trying to highlight "silver linings" may feel insensitive and invalidating to victims and it may minimize the distress they are experiencing. Nonetheless, experiencing a sense of hope about the future is integral to healthy post-crisis adjustment and recovery (King & Miner, 2000). Thus, even if students are not yet ready to start feeling hopeful again, educators can project an optimistic view of crisis recovery that students can embrace after their trauma and pain have diminished in intensity. This can occur over time and as students feel safer, calmer, more in control, more socially connected and supported, and as they adjust to their new reality.

Responding to Death and Grief in the School Community

Schools are well-positioned to help students and faculty after a death occurs in the school community. In the aftermath of a death, schools can provide supports to a large number of students and monitor those who are most at risk and need intensive support (Poland, Samuel-Barrett & Waguespack, 2014). In addition, teachers, who often know their students better than any other adult at school, can play a vital role by helping students come to terms with a death. Unfortunately, however, many educators report that they are ill-prepared to respond to the death of a student or faculty member (Adamson & Peacock, 2007). For example, in a recent survey of more than 1,200 teachers, 93 percent never received training related to bereavement and 92 percent reported that grief is a serious problem that deserves more attention in schools. In this survey, the greatest barrier that prevented teachers from providing support was found to be insufficient training and/or professional development (Demaria, 2015). Therefore, it is necessary to improve education and training for all pre-service and current school personnel on grief and bereavement issues.

In 2015, the Coalition to Support Grieving Students (http://grievingstudents.scholastic.com/) was established to help educators deal with issues related to children's grief and bereavement. Its founding members include major organizations representing educators, school administrators, school nurses, elementary and secondary school principals, school psychologists, school counselors, and school social workers. Modules, PowerPoint presentations, pdf files, videos, and other resources are available on the Coalition's website to help school personnel understand and respond effectively to student grief.

The National Center for School Crisis and Bereavement (n.d.) (https://sowkweb.usc.edu/about/centers-affiliations/national-center-school-crisis-and-bereavement) estimates that 40 percent of students will experience the death of a peer prior to graduating high school and most children experience the death of a family member or a friend during the same time frame. In addition, between 4 percent and 7 percent will experience the death of a parent before age 18 (Social Security Administration, 2000). Based on these statistics, the experience of loss, death, and grief although emotionally jarring, is common among students. With that said, educators can expect to have students in their classes who are in the midst of grieving.

Children who experience the loss of a loved one grieve internally but not all children exhibit outward signs of grief. As noted by Worden (1996), although most youth display a normal adjustment to loss, as many as 15–20 percent can be expected to experience significant difficulties following the loss of an important person in their lives. If educators do not address the needs of these students, then they display increased risk for experiencing behavioral and emotional challenges as well as a significant decline in academic performance (Poland et al., 2014). In fact, it is not unusual for a student who suffered the loss of a parent or sibling to become so overwhelmed by the death that they begin to fail in school. Another concern related to bereavement is that students or their caregivers do not always tell teachers about a death in their family. Therefore, teachers may not be able to support or make reasonable accommodations to help these students. Moreover, as students navigate grief and bereavement, their behavior may be misperceived as being malicious, manipulative, or deliberately disruptive. Consequently, schools need to help students and caregivers feel comfortable informing school personnel that a death has occurred to someone close to the family.

Understanding Death: Developmental Considerations

One of the most common misconceptions about death is that children understand this concept in the same way that adults do (Pfhol, Jimerson, & Lazarus, 2002). However, the way that children understand death depends on the their developmental level, which encompasses their social-emotional and cognitive developmental functioning as well as their past experiences (Bertoia & Allen, 1988). In this regard, research has yielded four important concepts regarding a child's understanding of death: (1) *universality*, (2) *irreversibility*, (3) *nonfunctionality*, and (4) *causality* (Jimerson, Stine & Rime, 2012; Schonfeld, 1993; Speece & Brent, 1984)

Universality, as it relates to death, refers to the understanding that all living things eventually will die. The concept of universality related to death includes three interconnected components. These are inclusiveness (i.e., every living thing will die), inevitability (i.e., each living thing will die eventually), and unpredictability (i.e., death may occur to any living thing at any moment in time). During the first five years of life, children do not understand the concept of universality (within the context of death and more generally). For most children, the notion that death is universal begins to coalesce between the ages of seven and nine.

Irreversibility refers to the concept that dead bodies will not live again. Many young children believe that death can be reversed spontaneously by praying, wishful thinking, magic or medical interventions. A child's belief regarding the irreversibly of death influences grief reactions and coping in the aftermath. As an example, a school psychologist went to a first grade class to explain that Willie, a classmate, had died over the weekend in a traffic accident. She provided an opportunity for the children to talk about the deceased student, process their emotions, and ask any questions. Just as the school psychologist was leaving one of the students raised his hand and asked, "Will Willie be coming to school tomorrow?" As illustrated in this example, some students in the first grade class may understand the concept of irreversibility whereas others may not.

Nonfunctionality refers to the understanding that once a living thing dies, the internal (e.g., thinking, feeling) and external (e.g., walking, eating) life functions cease to exist. When they do not understand this notion, it is not unusual for young children to ask how will the deceased be fed or be kept warm (Schonfeld, 1993). *Causality* refers to an understanding of the internal and external causes of death. For example, a young child might believe that exhibiting bad behavior or wishing someone dead could cause an individual to die. In contrast, adults display greater awareness of true causes of death such as an individual died as result of a traffic accident or from a medical problem. As children grow and enter the formal operations period of cognitive development (Piaget, 1952) they develop a more mature understanding of death. However, it is important to be cautious about the use of specific age references. Students in the same class may have very different understandings of death. Therefore, it is best to listen to each child when supporting him or her through the grieving process (Pfhol et al., 2002).

Understanding the Grieving Process

People tend to use the terms "grief" and "mourning" interchangeably; however, an important distinction exists between these terms. *Grief* represents the feelings and thoughts experienced by children when someone they love dies. Grief may best be understood as the internal meaning given to the experience of bereavement. In contrast, *mourning* refers to the outward expression of feelings of grief with others (Wolfelt, 2002).

Although death is a common and universal experience, multiple factors influence the way that children and adolescents respond to death. These include age and developmental level, emotional maturity, personality, gender, cultural and religious beliefs, experiences with death, relationship to the deceased, concurrent stressful events, adverse childhood experiences, and the availability of social support (Poland et al., 2014). Bereaved children typically experience a number of grief reactions such as shock, sadness, anxiety, fear, guilt, crying, denial, longing for the deceased, somatic complaints, difficulty focusing and concentrating, sleep disturbances, irritability, regressive behavior, and a decline in academic performance (Fiorelli, 2010; Pfhol et al., 2002; Poland et al., 2014).

In the past, individuals were believed to work through the grieving process in distinct stages. People have used the term "stages of grief" to try to make sense of a process that is not as predictable or orderly as previously envisioned. However, this view has been replaced with an understanding that bereavement is more cyclical in nature, implying that grief reactions may come and go and individuals may revisit different aspects of the grieving process in response to changes in life circumstances (Poland et al., 2014; Wolfelt, 2002).

Consistent with the cyclical nature of bereavement, grief and mourning are best understood as processes (not events). After the death of a loved one (especially a parent) a return to normalcy is not always possible, and the bereaved child is changed forever by the experience (Wolfelt, 2002). Children do not heal quickly and some may never get over feelings of grief (Webb, 1993). Consequently, adults should avoid using specific timetables for a child to overcome their grief completely. Instead, with time and support, a child can become reconciled to the loss and integrate it into the fabric of his or her life.

It has been theorized that if a child does not experience healthy mourning and is unable to be supported throughout the grieving process then subsequent development may be compromised (Jimerson, Brown, & Stewart, 2012). Some mental health concerns related to disordered mourning may include severe anxiety, desire to die, hopes of reunion with the deceased on Earth, aggressive and destructive outbursts, persistent blame and guilt, and compulsive caregiving (Bowlby, 1982). Clearly, the degree to which a child copes with loss is dependent on developmental, personal, family, and situational factors (Jimerson et al., 2012). Moreover, with the support of family, friends, the faith community, and the school, the bereaved child can work through the tasks of mourning. Table 18.5 outlines helpful ways educators can support grieving students.

Table 18.5 Helpful Ways that Educators can Support Grieving Students

- Tell students the facts regarding the death. Make sure to avoid euphemisms such as "gone to sleep."
- Clear up any rumors or misinformation regarding the death.
- Let students ask any questions they want. Provide brief truthful answers without giving unnecessary details. It is okay to say you do not know if you do not know the answer. Focus more attention on the students' reactions and feelings rather than on the specifics of the death.
- Acknowledge the intensity of the loss.
- Let students reminisce and share their memories of the deceased. Allow students to express feelings of loss, sadness, and grief. Acknowledge that not all children will need to discuss their feelings or reactions and this is perfectly acceptable.
- Help normalize that all feelings are okay. Let students know that every child grieves in their own way. Some children feel the need to talk about the death, whereas others may prefer to keep their feelings to themselves.
- Give students permission to cry as necessary. Some students may believe that it is not acceptable to cry or express strong emotions in public, and some boys may have been told that it is unmanly to cry.
- Educate students about the expected reactions to grief and loss. Let them know that at times they may feel a cascade of strong emotions, whereas at other times, they may be able to go on with their day without thinking of the deceased.
- Be available to all the students and listen in a caring, supportive, and non-judgmental manner.
- Expect that some students, especially younger children, may experience regressive behaviors and somatic complaints. Some may also find it difficult to focus, concentrate, and complete schoolwork.
- Refrain from sharing your own religious or personal beliefs with students.
- Validate students' reactions and feelings and do not minimize the impact of the death on their lives. No one can truly understand exactly what the student is going through. Consequently, these statements would *not* be appropriate to say, "I know what you are going through." "You must be very angry." "This is hard but it is important to remember the good things in life." "You will need to be strong now for your family. It is important to get a handle on your feelings." "My cat died last year. I know how you must be feeling."
- Provide coaching to students on how to cope with strong emotions. Let them know that some good strategies are to talk with trusted adults and friends. Ask students what has worked in the past to make them feel better after some sad event had occurred.
- For students who may feel uncomfortable talking about death or the deceased, provide them with alternative ways to express their feelings, such as by writing, drawing, or listening to music.
- Model effective coping strategies. Share strategies that have worked with others. Again, let students know that there is no one strategy that will work with everyone.
- Encourage students to be especially supportive of one another at this time. Explain that this does not mean that they have to sit around and express how sorry they feel for a student who experienced a significant loss. Just make sure that the grieving student feels supported and included.

- Tell students that it is not necessary that they say the "right thing" when a student experiences a death in the family as there is no one right thing to say. The most important thing is to acknowledge the death and express sympathy. It is especially critical not to ignore the grieving student because they don't know what to say or do.
- Understand that students who may have had a recent conflict or a troubling relationship with the deceased may be may particularly affected.
- Temporarily adjust academic demands on students who are going through the grieving process. This is especially important for those students who lost a family member or close friend. For example, teachers can choose to change or eliminate an assignment, change the focus or timing or a lesson, or reschedule or adapt tests.
- If a student in the classroom has died, then do not immediately eliminate the student's presence in the classroom such as by removing the student's work or desk. It may be best to seek students' input regarding how they would like to deal with the student's presence. Some teachers have maintained the student's desk for a brief time, then rearranged the seating configuration at an appropriate and agreed upon time.
- Maintain regular classroom routines whenever possible in order to establish a sense of safety and security.
- Monitor students' emotions and behavior following a death, and refer students who demonstrate intense and long-lasting reactions to a school-based mental health professional.
- Recognize that some students who barely knew the deceased may have especially strong reactions due to the impact of a prior death in their lives.
- Understand that there will be a range of reactions following a death. Some students will be significantly impacted, some will be moderately impacted, and some will go about their lives as if nothing much has happened. Do not expect all students to have strong reactions.
- Recognize that holidays, birthdays, anniversaries, and special events may be difficult for some students and they may require extra attention and support. Therefore, make an effort to reach out to grieving students at school events where the absence of a loved one may be especially noticeable.
- Consider the culture and the traditions of the victims and their families when providing care.

Source: Based on information from the Coalition to Support Grieving Students, the National Center for School Crisis and Bereavement, and Poland et al., 2014.

Specific Tasks for Schools to Initiate in the Immediate Aftermath of a Death

Mourning the death of a student, faculty member, or a staff member often is overwhelming to the entire school community. Therefore, it is important to plan and prepare in advance so that the school can ensure that (a) grieving students receive requisite support; (b) that the psychological equilibrium of the students, faculty, and staff is restored as quickly as possible; and (c) that individuals who require additional support that the school is unable to provide are identified and referred. Below are specific tasks that schools should undertake as soon as it is known that a death has occurred in the school community. Information for this section is gleaned from the suggestions of various authors and our personal experiences (e.g., Jimerson et al., 2012; Jimerson & Huff, 2002; Poland et al., 2014; Poland & Poland, 2004; the National Center for School Crisis & Bereavement, n.d.).

1. Verify the facts.

It is extremely important to verify the facts of the death either from the family, the coroner's office, or from law enforcement agencies. After the death has been verified, determine what information the family would like to share or what information has already been publically released from a reliable source. Because of the rapid flow of information via social media and texting, this needs to be done as quickly as possible to prevent any inaccuracies and to dispel any rumors.

2. Notify the school crisis team and develop a plan.

If the death occurred outside of school hours, this may require initiating a phone tree to help organize school staff and to plan a meeting before school begins. At this time, faculty and other staff can be provided with the known facts and a faculty meeting can be planned to help coordinate a unified response.

3. Prepare an announcement to be distributed to the faculty.

After faculty and staff have been notified of the death, it is important to develop a fact sheet and a written statement to ensure that everyone is provided with the same information.

4. Notify teachers and staff first at a faculty meeting.

At this time teachers and staff can be provided with the fact sheet and the written statement. They can be given the opportunity to ask any questions and prepare themselves to discuss the death with their students. Mental health personnel should be present at this meeting to help support the teachers, staff, and administrators. There may be some teachers who may be too impacted to provide grief support and may need a school-based mental health professional to accompany them or serve in their place. In some circumstances the principal may also be so distraught by the death of a student or faculty member that they may extra support to help lead the school. In these cases, principles will need support from members of central office or the superintendent's office.

5. Notify students face to face.

If possible, teachers should announce the death in their homeroom or their first class of the day. In this way students can ask questions, express their feelings, and grieve with a familiar and trusted adult. When notifying students it may be best to have a prepared statement to read. Information can be provided about the availability of mental health support services, and where students can go to receive these services. The use of large group assemblies or the public address system to announce the death of any student, faculty member, or staff member needs to be avoided. The rationale for this is that announcing a death in a large scale meeting offers little opportunity to gauge students' personal reactions or to provide individual support and may create confusion or panic. In the case of a student's death, it may be beneficial to have a school-based mental health professional follow the deceased student's class schedule and share details of the death with those classes most impacted. If a teacher has died, then consider having a counselor or a teacher from the same grade or from a lower grade who is highly familiar with the deceased teacher's students notify the class. If necessary have this teacher remain with the most impacted class for the next few days and have a substitute teacher cover the less impacted class.

6. Notify parents.

Draft a letter to send to parents/caregivers to notify them of a death of a member of the school community and inform them of the services that are being offered to students and families. This letter can provide a brief explanation of the death, what students have been told, typical emotional responses that might be expected of children and youth, how parents/caregivers can best support their children and what resources are being made available in the school and community.

The suicide of a student or faculty or staff member creates additional complications for the school. See Text Box 18.2 for special consideration in the aftermath of a suicide.

Text Box 18.2 Unique Considerations Related to Suicide

The suicide of a student of faculty member creates unique issues for school personnel. As noted by Poland et al. (2014), the grief response following a suicide is complex. Because of the traumatic nature of suicide, many individuals are at an increased risk for experiencing complicated grief. Close friends and siblings and those with complex or even troubling relationships with the deceased may be especially vulnerable. Some survivors may feel intense anger, regret, guilt, or self-blame following a suicide. In other instances, survivors may blame the death on other students in the school (e.g. a girl who broke up with the suicidal student, three teenagers who bullied the deceased student) or on themselves (e.g. if only I had responded to Jenny's last text, she might be alive right now). Consequently, it is especially important to be aware of particular circumstances that may impact students' grief response and ensure that the students that are the most in need of help get it.

In terms of actions to take, clarify with the family the information they wish to disclose about the cause of the death and respect their wishes. If the family is willing to acknowledge that the cause of the death was suicide, then tell the truth about the suicide without providing explicit details. While being sure to acknowledge the individual who died, avoid romanticizing or glamorizing suicide—instead focus on helping students grieve. The aftermath of a death by suicide can be a time to educate the entire school community on warning signs of distress and symptoms of depression and distribute information about hotlines, crisis centers, and school supports. During this time, it is important to encourage students who are experiencing suicidal thoughts and feelings to seek mental health services.

In the following interview Frank Zenere, offers his advice regarding mourning and coping in the aftermath of tragedies and death that impact the school community. He describes what happens to communities in the aftermath of school shootings and emphasizes the long-term impact of large-scale tragedies after the national media has moved on. He emphasizes the critical task of identifying students who suffer from mental illness and the importance of providing necessary support. He also discusses strategies to help caregivers help themselves when caring for others.

Expert Interview 18.2 with Frank Zenere

Miami-Dade County Public Schools

PJL: I know you have responded to countless tragedies impacting communities. You assisted in Newtown where 20 children and six adults were ruthlessly murdered. What can you tell us about the recovery process?

FZ: Recovery from a tragic event is not a sprint, it is a marathon; it is not a destination, it is a journey; it is not linear, but consists of emotional peaks and valleys of despair. Likewise, recovery cannot be placed on a calendar, as each individual and community follows its own unique path moving forward.

Betsy Thompson, Student Services Director of Jefferson County Schools, made the following comment regarding the handling of the Columbine High School tragedy: "It was an exhausting process, and yet the power of the people to come together and support one another in the deepest, dreariest days is absolutely incredible. The resiliency of the human spirit is second to none." If tragedy brings us into darkness, it is resiliency that brings us into the light. Resilient individuals and communities may experience temporary and sporadic difficulties following a tragedy, but generally exhibit stable and healthy functioning. Resiliency is actually quite common.

PJL. You have led numerous crisis responses teams in the aftermath of targeted school shootings. Moreover, you have responded to different cultures and communities. One of them was the Red Lake community which is located on a Native American reservation. Please share what happens after an event such as this occurs.

FZ. In March, 2005, I lead a team of school psychologists from NASP in responding to the tragic shooting at Red Lake High School in Red Lake, Minnesota. During this horrific event the 16-year-old perpetrator shot and killed seven people at the school and wounded five others. The dead included a teacher, an unarmed security guard, and five students. When the police arrived, the perpetrator exchanged gunfire with them. During this shoot-out, the rampage killer was wounded and completed suicide in a vacant classroom. The following events occurred during the immediate to intermediate time frame following the tragedy.

- Long after the national media had left the scene of the school community, a series of negative cascading events continued to impact survivors:

   o The Superintendent took a three-week leave of absence as a result of emotional distress;
   o The school's principal suffered a heart attack one month after the tragedy.
   o There was an increase in depression among students and staff.
   o An increase in student suicides and attempts was observed.
   o A dozen members of the faculty developed PTSD and resigned and most never taught again.
   o School staff that was heavily impacted by the tragedy who did not initially seek counseling support suffered in many ways later. They were so concerned for the well-being of the children that they compartmentalized and neglected their own needs. This phenomenon was also observed among staff of Miami-Dade County Public Schools following Hurricane Andrew in 1992, as between 12–18 months after the storm, the Employee Assistance Program observed significant referrals of staff reporting depression, anxiety disorders, alcohol and substance abuse, domestic violence, and extreme absenteeism.
   o Red Lake High School was closed for three weeks following the tragedy. Once classes resumed, only 30 percent of the students returned for the remainder of the school year.

PJL. It can be seen that any tragedy such as occurred at Red Lake High School have both immediate and long-term impacts. Consequently, what might be some lessons that you have learned responding to campus homicides?

FZ. The following recommendations are offered from my experiences in responding to several school shootings and other campus homicides:

- During the summer of 1999, my colleagues and you and I of the NASP National Emergency Assistance Team, hosted a multi-day training for educators and school mental health professionals representing school communities across the nation that had experienced school shootings. During the gathering, the Superintendent of Jefferson County Schools in Littleton, Colorado, made the following statement:

   As we prepare to reopen Columbine High School, I know that I could arrange to surround the school with law enforcement officers and even the National Guard, and by taking such action, our students, staff and parents would feel physically safe. However, it will take years for them to experience psychological safety.

Physical safety measures are not by themselves sufficient to protect our students and staff. We need to balance physical safety and psychological safety. Ideally, we need more mental detectors than metal detectors; more heart-ware than hardware. We need to expand the emotional safety net for all children and adolescents to ensure that we can do what we can to develop mentally healthy youth; to identify youth that suffer mental illness early on (50 percent of lifetime mental illness develops by age 14) and provide necessary intervention; and to provide long-term surveillance and support for these youth and their families

- Target psychological interventions toward students, staff, families and caregivers that are at high risk for post-event trauma. Not everyone is equally impacted by tragedies, nor is everyone traumatized by such incidents. To evaluate who needs services we must look at the following factors: proximity to the event (physical and emotional), pre-existing vulnerabilities, threat perceptions and crisis reactions. Providing mental health interventions for those who don't need them is not only an inefficient use of resources, it may be harmful in some cases.
- Schedule stress management activities for faculty and support staff to include: meditation, therapeutic massage, pet therapy, yoga, dance, exercise and additional relaxation techniques.
- Create additional extracurricular activities for students so that they may make and/or maintain positive and healthy connections to the school and caring adults (e.g., mentors, coaches, clergy, clubs, organizations, athletics, and other community-based activities). Social support plays a critical role in aiding recovery and strengthening resiliency. Therefore, students who are isolated or have withdrawn from such support require attention.
- Community-based activities and counseling services should remain available for students, families and staff throughout the summer following the tragedy. Many in the Red Lake community felt abandoned when government sponsored mental health providers left the community to work with Hurricane Katrina survivors.
- Provide outreach support and monitoring for students that have dropped out, been suspended, and/or expelled from school. We cannot afford to let them and their needs drop off the radar.
- Increase collaboration between school mental health professionals, community-based mental health professionals, and families. Wraparound services are essential to providing effective treatment and support.

This interview was adapted from a personal email and a later publication in the NASP Communiqué.

Caring for the Educator

Crises exert a heavy emotional toll on all who are affected. In particular, educators and school-based mental health professionals involved in the crisis intervention process may experience considerable emotional upheaval and feel burned out as they continue to be surrounded by distressed students, families, and colleagues. Therefore, it is important for all school professionals who are providing care to others to exercise self-care and seek support when necessary.

To help crisis responders and educators remain resilient through the crisis intervention and recovery process, it is important for these individuals to engage in physical, spiritual, and psychological self-care (Brock, 2011; Lazarus, Cash & Pitts, 2005). This involves getting adequate rest and relaxation, avoiding extended periods of work, eating well and leading a balanced lifestyle, getting adequate exercise, engaging in spiritual or religious activities, regularly applying stress management strategies/techniques, becoming more assertive about one's own needs, using effective time management strategies, forgiving oneself for not being omnipotent or able to help everyone, monitoring one's own psychological response to a crisis, processing feelings with trusted friends and loved ones, and seeking help if one feels overwhelmed or highly distressed.

Yet in the midst of enduring crises and/or when lives have been lost, it is not unusual for caregivers to feel over-extended or burned out. Signs that caregivers need significant support include experiencing compassion fatigue; feeling numb and depersonalized; harboring signifi-cant and disproportionate anger at co-workers and others; feeling depressed, hopeless, and/or having suicidal thoughts; and experiencing sudden and significant disruptions in interpersonal relationships. Simply put, individuals experiencing these symptoms need to be excused from their crisis intervention duties and provided with the space and supports needed to stabilize and recover. In the midst of large-scale crises, it is often the adults at school who do not get req-uisite emotional support and feel that their needs are being overlooked or ignored. Therefore, as emphasized by both Frank DeAngelis and Frank Zenere, before symptoms get out of hand, school professionals need to be proactive by exercising self-care and getting psychological help when their coping capacities have been overwhelmed. Only then can the helper sustainably assist others who need their help.

Conclusion

Consistent with best practices, a MTSS framework helps guide school personnel with responding to crises and provides flexibility in service-delivery. In order to deliver high-quality crisis inter-vention services, schools need to have a well-developed crisis plan that considers issues related to establishing reunification procedures, facilitating triage, creating a safe space, delivering psy-chological first aid, maintaining stabilization, enhancing support, and linking severely impacted students with collaborative service agencies and providers.

Five elements of crisis intervention have been validated in the empirical literature which can all be flexibly applied in school settings using a MTSS service delivery framework.

These include (1) promoting a sense of safety, (2) calming and supporting fearful individuals, (3) engendering a sense of self- and collective efficacy in affected individuals and communities, (4) increasing feelings of connectedness with others, and (5), instilling and inspiring hope in vic-tims (Hobfoll et al., 2007; Lazarus & Sulkowski, 2010; Sulkowski & Lazarus, 2013).

A critical part of crisis intervention is to help support grieving students and those who suffered other types of losses. In order to do so, school personnel need to understand the grieving and bereavement process in youth and initiate critical and specific actions. Armed with this under-standing, educators can help mitigate the emotional pain that students feel following death and loss. Moreover, to maintain healthy functioning, educators and mental health professionals need to exercise self-care in the aftermath of a school crisis.

References

Adamson, A. D. & Peacock, G. G. (2007). Crisis response in the public schools. A survey of school psy-chologists' experiences and perceptions. *Psychology in the Schools, 44,* 749–764.
Ahern, J., Galea, S., Resnick, H., Kilpatrick, D., Bucuvalas, M., Gold, J., & Vlahov, D. (2002). Television images and psychological symptoms after the September 11 terrorist attacks. *Psychiatry, 65,* 289–300.
Annandale, N. O., Heath, M. A., Dean, B., Kemple, A., & Takino, Y. (2011). Assessing cultural compe-tency in school crisis plans. *Journal of School Violence, 10,* 16–33.
Barenbaum, J., Ruchkin, V., & Schwab-Stone, M. (2004). The psychosocial aspects of children exposed to war: Practice and policy initiatives. *Journal of Child Psychology and Psychiatry, 45,* 41–62.
Başoğlu, M., Şalcıoğlu, E., Livanou, M., Kalender, D., & Acar, G. (2005). Single-session behavioral treat-ment of earthquake-related posttraumatic stress disorder: A randomized waiting list controlled trial. *Journal of Traumatic Stress, 18,* 1–11.
Benight, C. C. (2004). Collective efficacy following a series of natural disasters. *Anxiety, Stress & Coping, 17,* 401–420.
Bertoia, J. & Allen, J. (1988). School management of the bereaved child. *Elementary School Guidance and Counseling, 23,* 30–38.
Bowlby, J. (1982). *Attachment and loss: Attachment.* New York: Basic Books.

Bleich, A., Gelkopf, M., & Solomon, Z. (2003). Exposure to terrorism, stress-related mental health symptoms, and coping behaviors among a nationally representative sample in Israel. *JAMA, 290,* 612–620.

Brock, S. E. (2002). Group crisis intervention. In S. E. Brock, P. J. Lazarus, & S. R. Jimerson (Eds.), *Best practices in school crisis prevention and intervention* (pp. 385–403). Bethesda, MD: NASP.

Brock, S. E. (2011). *PREPaRE Workshop 2, Second edition. Crisis intervention and recovery: The roles of school-based mental health professionals.* Bethesda, MD: NASP.

Brock, S. E., & Davis, J. (2008). Best practices in school crisis intervention. In A. Thomas & J. Grimes (Eds.), *Best practices in school psychology* V (pp. 781–798). Bethesda, MD: NASP.

Brock, S. E., Louvar Reeves, M. A., & Nickerson, A. B. (2014). Best practices in school crisis intervention. In P. L. Harrison & A. Thomas (Eds.), *Best practices in school psychology: System-level services* (pp. 211–230). Bethesda, MD: NASP.

Brock, S. E., Nickerson, A. B., Reeves, M. A., Jimerson, S. R., Feinberg, T., & Lieberman, R. (2009). *School crisis prevention and intervention: The PREPaRE model.* Bethesda, MD: NASP.

Brymer, M., Layne, C., Jacobs, A., Pynoos, R., Ruzek, J., Steinberg, A., & Watson, P. (2006). *Psychological first aid field operations guide.* Los Angeles, CA: National Child Traumatic Stress Network.

Brymer, M. J., Pynoos, R. S., Vivrette, R. S., & Taylor, M. A. (2012). Providing school crisis interventions. In S. E. Brock & S. R. Jimerson (Eds.), *Best practices in school crisis prevention and intervention* (2nd edn) (pp. 317–336). Bethesda, MD: NASP.

Chen, G., & Bliese, P. D. (2002). The role of different levels of leadership in predicting self-and collective efficacy: Evidence for discontinuity. *Journal of Applied Psychology, 87,* 549–556.

Coalition to Support Grieving Students (n.d.). Retrieved from http://grievingstudents.scholastic.com/.

Cowan, K. C., Vaillancourt, K., Rossen, E., & Pollitt, K. (2013). *A framework for safe and successful schools [Brief].* Bethesda, MD: NASP.

Crepeau-Hobson, F., Sievering, K. S., Armstrong, C., & Stonis, J. (2012). A coordinated mental health crisis response: Lessons learned from three Colorado school shootings. *Journal of School Violence, 11,* 207–225.

Demaria, T. (2015, February). Coalition to support grieving students: The launch of a new dedicated online resource. A presentation at the National Association of School Psychologists annual convention. Orlando, FL.

Everly, G. S. (2003). Early psychological intervention: A word of caution. *International Journal of Emergency Mental Health, 16,* 621–634.

Foa, E. B., Keane, T. M., & Friedman, M. J. (2000). Guidelines for treatment of PTSD. *Journal of Traumatic Stress, 13,* 539–588.

Fiorelli, R. (2010). Grief and bereavement in children. In N. Kinzbrunner & J. Policzer (Eds.), *End of life care: A practical guide* (2nd edn) (pp. 635–665). New York: McGraw-Hill.

Haase, J. E., Britt, T., Coward, D. D., Leidy, N. K., & Penn, P. E. (1992). Simultaneous concept analysis of spiritual perspective: Hope, acceptance, and self-transcendence. *Journal of Nursing Scholarship, 24,* 141–147.

Hobfoll, S. E., Briggs-Phillips, M., & Stines, L. R. (2003). Fact or artifact: The relationship of hope to a caravan of resources. In R. Jacoby, & G. Keinan (Eds.), *Between stress and hope: From a disease–centered to a health–centered perspective* (pp. 81–104). Westport, CT: Praeger.

Hobfoll, S. E., Watson, P., Bell, C. C., Bryant, R. A., Brymer, M. J., Friedman, M. J., . . . & Ursano, R. J. (2007). Five essential elements of immediate and mid–term mass trauma interventions: Empirical evidence. *Psychiatry, 70,* 283–315.

Horowitz, K., McKay, M., & Marshall, R. (2005). Community violence and urban families: Experiences, effects, and directions for intervention. *American Journal of Orthopsychiatry, 75,* 356–368.

Jaycox, L. H., Cohen, J. A., Mannarino, A. P., Walker, D. W., Langley, A. K., Gegenheimer, K. L., . . . & Schonlau, M. (2010). Children's mental health care following Hurricane Katrina: A field trial of trauma-focused psychotherapies. *Journal of Traumatic Stress, 23,* 223–231.

Jimerson, S. & Huff, L. (2002). Responding to a sudden unexpected death in school: Chance favors the prepared professional. In S. E. Brock, P. J. Lazarus, & S. R. Jimerson (Eds.), *Best practices in school crisis prevention and intervention* (pp. 451–488). Bethesda, MD: National Association of School Psychologists.

Jimerson, S. R., Brown, J. A. & Stewart, K. T. (2012). Sudden and unexpected death: Preparing and responding to the unpredictable. In S. E. Brock & S. R. Jimerson (Eds.), *Best practices in school crisis prevention and intervention* (2nd edn) (pp. 469–483). Bethesda, MD: National Association of School Psychologists.

Jimerson, S. R., Stine, R. & Rime, J. (2012). Developmental considerations regarding psychological trauma and grief. In S. E. Brock & S. R. Jimerson (Eds.), *Best practices in school crisis prevention and intervention* (2nd edn) (pp. 377–399). Bethesda, MD: National Association of School Psychologists.

Joyce-Beaulieu, D., & Sulkowski, M. L. (2015). *Cognitive behavioral therapy in K-12 school settings: A practitioner's toolkit.* New York, NY: Springer.

Kasler, J., Dahan, J., & Elias, M. J. (2008). The relationship between sense of hope, family support and post-traumatic stress disorder among children: The case of young victims of rocket attacks in Israel. *Vulnerable Children and Youth Studies, 3,* 182–191.

King, L. A., & Miner, K. N. (2000). Writing about the perceived benefits of traumatic events: Implications for physical health. *Personality and Social Psychology Bulletin, 26,* 220–230.

Lazarus, P. J., Cash, G., & Pitts, S. (2005, September). *Coping in the aftermath of Hurricane Katrina.* A series of workshops presented in Mississippi in the aftermath of Hurricane Katrina. Sponsored by the National Association of School Psychologists.

Lazarus, P. J., & Sulkowski, M. L. (2010). Oil in the water, fire in the sky: Responding to technological/environmental disasters. *Communiqué, 39*(1), 1, 16–17.

Lazarus, P. J., & Zenere, F. (2005, March). *Tropical trauma: Implications for responding to natural disasters in the school community.* An invited presentation at the annual convention of the National Association of School Psychologists. Atlanta, GA.

Litz, B. T. & Gray, M. J. (2004). Early intervention for trauma in adults: A framework for first aid and secondary prevention. In B.T. Litz (Ed.), *Early intervention for trauma and traumatic loss* (pp. 87–111). New York: Guilford.

Meiklejohn, J., Phillips, C., Freedman, M. L., Griffin, M. L., Biegel, G., Roach, A., & Saltzman, A. (2012). Integrating mindfulness training into K-12 education: Fostering the resilience of teachers and students. *Mindfulness, 3,* 291–307.

National Center for School Crisis and Bereavement, (n.d.). *Guidelines for responding to the death of a student or school staff.* Cincinnati, OH: Author. Retrieved from www.nctsnet.org/nctsn_assets/pdf/CBITSfactsheet.pdf.

Norris, F. H., & Elrod, C. L. (2006). Psychosocial consequences of disaster: A review of past research. In F. H. Norris, S. Galea, M. J. Friedman, & P. J. Watson (Eds.), *Methods for disaster mental health research* (pp. 20–42). New York: Guilford.

Pfhol, W. Jimerson, S. R. & Lazarus, P. J. (2002). Developmental aspects of psychological trauma and grief. In S. E. Brock, P. J. Lazarus & S. R. Jimerson (Eds.), *Best practices in school crisis prevention and intervention* (pp. 451–488). Bethesda, MD: National Association of School Psychologists.

Piaget, J. (1952). *The origins of intelligence in children.* Translated by Margaret Cook. New York: International Universities Press.

Openshaw, L. L. (2011). School-based support groups for traumatized students. *School Psychology International, 32,* 163–178.

Otto, M. W., Henin, A., Hirshfeld-Becker, D. R., Pollack, M. H., Biederman, J., & Rosenbaum, J. F. (2007). Posttraumatic stress disorder symptoms following media exposure to tragic events: Impact of 9/11 on children at risk for anxiety disorders. *Journal of Anxiety Disorders, 21,* 888–902.

Poland, S. & Poland, D. (2004). Dealing with death at school. *Principal Leadership, 4*(8), 8–12.

Poland, S., Samuel-Barrett, C. & Waguespack, A. (2014). Best practices in responding to death in the school community. In P. L. Harrison & A. Thomas (Eds.), *Best practices in school psychology: Systems-level services* (pp. 303–320). Bethesda, MD: National Association of School Psychologists.

Reeves, M. A., Kanan, L. M., & Plog, A. E. (2010). *Comprehensive planning for safe learning environments: A school professional's guide to integrating physical and psychological safety – Prevention through recovery.* New York: Routledge.

Reeves, M. A., Nickerson, A. B., Conolly-Wilson, C. N., Susan, M. K., Lazzaro, B. R., Jimerson, S. N., & Pesce, R. C. (2011). *PREPaRE WS #1, 2nd edition. Crisis prevention and preparedness: Comprehensive school safety planning.* Bethesda, MD: NASP.

Rolfsnes, E. S., & Idsoe, T. (2011). School-based intervention programs for PTSD symptoms: A review and meta-analysis. *Journal of Traumatic Stress, 24,* 155–165.

Schoenwald, S. K., Ward, D. M., Henggeler, S. W., & Rowland, M. D. (2000). Multisystemic therapy versus hospitalization for crisis stabilization of youth: Placement outcomes 4 months postreferral. *Mental Health Services Research, 2,* 3–12.

Schonfeld, D. J. (1993). *Talking with children about death. Journal of Pediatric Health Care, 7,* 269–274.

Smith, B. W., Pargament, K. I., Brant, C., & Oliver, J. M. (2000). Noah revisited: Religious coping by church members and the impact of the 1993 Midwest flood. *Journal of Community Psychology, 28,* 169–186.

Social Security Administration, (2000). *Intermediate assumptions of the 2000 trustees report.* Washington, DC: Author.

Speece, M. W. & Brent, S. (1984). Children's understanding of death: A review of three components of a death concept. *Child Development, 55,* 1671–1686.

Sulkowski, M. L., Joyce, D. K., & Storch, E. A. (2013). Treating childhood anxiety in schools: Service delivery in a response to intervention paradigm. *Journal of Child and Family Studies, 21,* 1–10. doi:10.1007/s10826-011-9553-1

Sulkowski, M. L., & Lazarus, P. J. (2011). Contemporary responses to violent attacks on college campuses. *Journal of School Violence, 10,* 338–354.

Sulkowski, M. L., & Lazarus, P. J. (2013). Five essential elements of crisis intervention for communities and schools when responding to technological disasters. *International Journal of School & Educational Psychology, 1,* 3–12.

Webb, N. B. (1993). *Helping bereaved children: A handbook for practitioners.* New York: Guilford Press.

Weems, C. F., Watts, S. E., Marsee, M. A., Taylor, L. K., Costa, N. M., Cannon, M. F., & Pina, A. A. (2007). The psychosocial impact of Hurricane Katrina: Contextual differences in psychological symptoms, social support, and discrimination. *Behaviour Research and Therapy, 45,* 2295–2306.

Wolfelt, (2002). Children's grief. In S. E. Brock, P. J. Lazarus & S. R. Jimerson (Eds.), *Best practices in school crisis prevention and intervention* (pp. 653–673). Bethesda, MD: National Association of School Psychologists.

Worden, J. W. (1996). *Children and grief: When a parent dies.* New York, NY: Guilford Press.

Zenere, F. (2005). Hurricane experiences provide lessons for the future. *Communiqué, 35*(3). Retrieved from www.nasponline.org/publications/cq/cq335flhurricane.aspx.

Afterword

This afterword was written on the third anniversary of the Sandy Hook mass shooting. This horrific event focused national attention on two interrelated issues: school safety and mental health. It also served as the impetus for writing this book. Our purpose was to help educators prevent future tragedies as well as provide information to help schools become safer and more supportive.

In the aftermath of the Sandy Hook massacre, as an antidote to the brutality of this act, many schools responded to this tragedy with acts of compassion and loving kindness. As a salient example, students at Notre Dame Catholic High School in Fairfield, CT established the 26 Days of Kindness campaign to honor the six adults and 20 children killed in nearby Newtown, CT. Each day, for 26 days, students involved in this effort aspire toward doing something good for their school, classmates, or community. These efforts might include writing letters of gratitude to first responders and teachers, donating essential goods to homeless individuals, and volunteering to help those less fortunate. The school principal, Chris Cipriano, believes that the world would be a better place if we could live our lives like this every day. Kindness has become part of the school curriculum and the 26 Days of Kindness movement has spread to other schools across the nation (see www.nbcnews.com/nightly-news/video/26-days-of-kindness-honors-sandhook-elementary-school-victims-585359427715).

We know from research that doing regular acts of kindness makes people happier and more fulfilled (See Chapter 9). These acts are gifts to ourselves and others. They bring people together to recognize their shared humanity and form bonds that can last a lifetime. The 26 Days of Kindness movement is a prime example of school spirit, character education, and science melding together to foster the emotional well-being of students to create a better world.

Schools such as Notre Dame Catholic High School understand that mental health, good character, and social-emotional skills are force multipliers. That is, students with these qualities do better in all facets of life. They understand that teaching academics is simply not enough; they also understand that it is important to develop programs, policies, and strategies that support the whole child.

Through decades of research (See Chapter 4) we now know that students with effective social-emotional skills do better academically and have better mental health outcomes than their peers who lack these skills. For our children to thrive in a global and interconnected economy that values diversity, communication, and interpersonal problem-solving, students need to develop social-emotional competence and good character more so than ever. As evidenced by the countless school shootings that have occurred over the past two decades, President Teddy Roosevelt's words ring as true today as when they were first spoken more than a century ago: "To educate a person in mind and not morals is to educate a menace to society."

Research also indicates that schools that have an authoritative school climate and adequate social supports, and that allow for the forging of important social connections also are force multipliers (See Chapters 7 and 8). A positive school climate that fosters kindness and school connectedness is positively related to healthy self-esteem, self-efficacy, optimism, and positive peer relationships; it is also negatively related to the development of conduct problems, antisocial behavior, depression, anxiety, emotional distress, and suicidality. Additionally, a positive school climate has a significant impact on children's educational performance and long-term success in school and beyond.

In our efforts to ensure students' success—not just in the classroom, but in life—we believe a serious national discussion on how to create safe and supportive schools and to foster the emotional well-being of our youth is necessary. As contributors to this discussion, we don't have all the answers, nor even all the questions, but we do know we can do a number of things to nurture our children and help them thrive in all aspects of life.

We can reduce our students' anxiety by making schools more nurturing and less stressful and competitive places. We can provide more mental health services in the schools by hiring more school psychologists, school social workers, and counselors. We can ensure that our schools implement a multi-tiered model for mental health care. We can provide universal prevention services that teach children resiliency and problem solving and give them coping strategies so they can function in the twenty-first century.

We can adopt new approaches such as School-wide Positive Behavior Supports and public health models that aim to challenge the current culture of the classroom and the environment rather than focus on trying to change each child one by one. We can make sure that all children are connected to at least one adult at school in a meaningful way. We can ensure that our children are safe and secure by implementing bully prevention, threat assessment, and other violence prevention programs including suicide prevention. In addition, we can advocate for highly effective preschool programs for all students so every child has the opportunity to achieve the American dream.

We also believe that creating safe and supportive schools rests in the hands of concerned educators. When educators begin to implement the aforementioned supports, programs, and policies, children are more likely to succeed in school, home, and life. After reading this text, you are now better prepared for this task. You can become a force multiplier. Although the information contained in the previous 18 chapters is not a substitute for rigorous mental health or law enforcement training, it does provide a foundation and an appropriate starting place. Consequently, we encourage you to continue learning and updating your knowledge of the topics covered in this book.

However, while learning, we also encourage you to do the little things each day that make students feel safer, more secure, and supported. We encourage you to practice little acts of kindness. We encourage you to take time to get to know a student. And we encourage you to spend a few extra minutes to ask, "Is everything okay?" and to reach out to caregivers to make them feel welcome at school. These efforts can make a world of difference. These efforts do not cost millions of dollars or make schools look more like correctional facilities, and they benefit everyone involved. They are simple, pure, and necessary.

We can do little things today that can lead to big changes tomorrow—and years from now. To drive this point home, the words of Edward Everett Hale are apt: "I am only one, but I am one. I cannot do everything, but I can do something. And I will not let what I cannot do interfere with what I can do." Similarly, the words of Malala Yousafzai, the youngest-ever Nobel Prize laureate resonate: "Let us make our future now, and let us make our dreams tomorrow's reality."

About the Authors

Michael L. Sulkowski, Ph.D., NCSP, is an Assistant Professor in the School Psychology Program, a Clinical Assistant Professor in the Department of Psychiatry, and an affiliate faculty member in Family Studies at the University of Arizona. He teaches classes on law and ethics in psychology, crisis management, mental health service delivery, behavior modification, research methods and design, and personality/social-emotional assessment. Dr. Sulkowski's research focuses on how risk and resiliency factors influence the academic and psychosocial outcomes of youth who have been victimized or are socially disenfranchised more generally. In addition, Dr. Sulkowski is interested in exploring how contextual factors influence various outcomes of at-risk youth as well as in efforts to support student mental health, to reduce school violence, and to foster nurturing learning environments for all students.

To date, Dr. Sulkowski has published over 50 journal articles and book chapters and he is a co-author on the 2015 book: *"Cognitive behavioral therapy in k-12 schools: A practitioner's workbook."* For research and scholarship, Dr. Sulkowski has received awards from the Melissa Institute for Violence Prevention, the National Association of School Psychologists (NASP), the American Academy of School Psychology, the Florida Association of School Psychologists, the University of Florida Alumni Association, the College of Education at the University of Florida, the American Society for the Advancement of Pharmacotherapy (APA Division 55), and the Society for General Psychology (APA Division 1).

Dr. Sulkowski is a licensed psychologist and credentialed school psychologist in Arizona. He also is a Nationally Certified School Psychologist and the Chair of the NASP Early Career Committee. Lastly, in addition to his academic appointments, Dr. Sulkowski has a private practice in Tucson, AZ where he primarily treats individuals and families affected by anxiety and obsessive-compulsive disorders.

For fun, Dr. Sulkowski enjoys playing guitar, long-distance running, reading novels, exploring new restaurants, cooking vegetarian cuisine, and hanging out with his dog Bodhi.

Philip J. Lazarus, Ph.D. is an Associate Professor and the Director of the School Psychology Training Program at Florida International University and has served in this position for more than 30 years. He is a graduate of Tulane University, the University of Miami, and the University of Florida. Dr. Lazarus is the co-editor of the texts, *Psychoeducational evaluation of children and adolescents with low-incidence handicaps* and *Best practices in school crisis prevention and intervention.* He has written more than a dozen book chapters and over three-dozen scholarly articles. Dr. Lazarus has given more than 200 presentations and keynote addresses both nationally and internationally.

Dr. Lazarus is a licensed psychologist and licensed school psychologist with a family practice. He has served the profession of psychology as the President of the National Association of School Psychologists (NASP), the President of the Florida Association of School Psychologists, founder and Vice President of FASP Children's Services Fund, Inc., Chairperson of the Florida

Council of Trainers and Supervisors, founder and Chairperson of the Florida Board of Examiners in School Psychology. He is also a founder of Camp Kadima, a camp for physically and mentally challenged youth that began with 12 youth and now serves more than 140 youngsters. Dr. Lazarus is also a founder and Past-Chairperson of the National Emergency Assistance Team of NASP. This team has provided direct crisis assistance in the aftermath of the tragic school shootings and natural disasters and he has led crisis teams in response to Hurricane Katrina and the Gulf Oil Spill and multiple natural disasters. He has received numerous state and national awards including the Willard Nelson Lifetime Achievement Award from the Florida Association of School Psychologists.

Dr. Lazarus has been interviewed by a number of media sources such as the CNBC, CNN, the Glenn Beck Show, Newsweek, Seventeen Magazine, Washington Post, Reader's Digest, Men's Health, National Public Radio dealing with such topics as anxiety and depression in children and adolescents, responding to natural disasters, coping with trauma following school shootings, school violence, helping children deal with grief and trauma following 9-11, bullying in schools, threat assessment, and identifying troubled students.

For fun, Dr. Lazarus enjoys traveling with his wife Jane, reading books on Audible, going scuba diving, exercising, practicing yoga, and taking long walks with their family dog, Riley.

About the Experts

Dr. Dewey G. Cornell is a forensic clinical psychologist and Bunker Professor of Education in the Curry School of Education at the University of Virginia. He was the principal developer of the Virginia Student Threat Assessment Guidelines and has authored more than 200 publications in psychology and education, including studies of juvenile homicide, school safety, bullying, and threat assessment.

Frank DeAngelis was the Principal of Columbine High School at the time of the school massacre on April 20, 1999 and was later selected as Colorado High School Principal of the Year. He retired in 2014 after serving for 18 years as principal. He currently works part-time as a school safety expert for the Jefferson County School District. He has lectured and consulted nationally with school districts regarding school safety and coping with school tragedies.

Dr. Beth Doll is the Associate Dean for Academic Affairs and Professor of School Psychology, College of Education and Human Sciences, University of Nebraska Lincoln. She served on the editorial board of major school psychology journals, as officer for three state associations, and as president and council representative for the American Psychological Association's Division 16. She researches models of school mental health that foster resilience and enhance the well-being of students and has authored numerous books on these topics.

Kevin Dwyer is a National Association of School Psychologist Past President, Distinguished and Lifetime Achievement Awardee, with 30 years working in Maryland schools. He continues supporting public policies using the early prevention and intensive intervention paradigm. Under Secretary Riley and President Clinton, Mr. Dwyer led development of *Early Warning Timely Response: A Guide to Safe Schools* a cornerstone for school violence prevention science. In 2000 he received the Tipper Gore "Advocacy award for improving the lives and mental health of America's children."

Dr. Katie Eklund is an Assistant Professor in the School Psychology Program at the University of Missouri and a licensed psychologist. She has served as a school psychologist at Fountain Fort Carson School District where she provided comprehensive school-based mental health supports to military children and their families at Fort Carson Army Base.

Dr. Maurice J. Elias is a Professor and the Director of Clinical Training in the Department of Psychology, Rutgers University and Director of Rutgers Social Emotional Learning Lab. He has been elected a fellow in five divisions of the American Psychological Association. He is the author of numerous books such as *The Educator's Guide to Emotional Intelligence and Academic Achievement: Social Emotional Learning in the Classroom*, and *School Climate: Building Safe, Supportive and Engaging Classrooms and Schools*.

Michele Gay is the Co-founder and Executive Director of Safe and Sound Schools: A Sandy Hook Initiative. Following the tragic loss of her daughter, Josephine, in the Sandy Hook School tragedy, Michele joined Sandy Hook mother Alissa Parker to establish Safe and Sound Schools as a national resource for school safety. Michele travels across the country sharing her message of inspiration, recovery, and school safety education and advocacy. She provides workshops and seminars to facilitate school safety development.

Dr. Sam Goldstein is an Adjunct Assistant Professor at the University of Utah School of Medicine and on staff at the University Neuropsychiatric Institute. He is Clinical Director of the Neurology Learning and Behavior Center. Dr. Goldstein has authored fifty trade and science texts as well as over three dozen science-based book chapters and thirty peer reviewed research articles. He has also co-authored six psychological test instruments. Two of his recent books include *Handbook of Resilience – 2nd Edition, Raising Resilient Children with Autism Spectrum Disorder.*

Dr. Ross Greene is a clinical psychologist and author of these influential books, *The Explosive Child, Lost at School, Lost and Found,* and *Raising Human Beings.* He is the originator of the Collaborative and Proactive Solutions (CPS) approach to dealing with behaviorally challenged youth. Dr. Greene was on the faculty at Harvard Medical School for over 20 years and is now founding director of the non-profit Lives in the Balance which offers free web-based resources on CPS.

Dr. Robert Horner is a Professor of Special Education at the University of Oregon. His research has focused on applied behavior analysis, positive behavior support, instructional strategies for learners with severe disabilities, and implementation science. Dr. Horner has been the co-editor of the *Journal of Positive Behavior Interventions,* and associate editor for the *Journal of Applied Behavior Analysis.*

Jane M. Lazarus, Ed.S. is a Florida licensed school psychologist and a former Florida School Psychologist of the Year. She is the Fort Lauderdale Site Manager for the School Psychology Program at Nova Southeastern University's College of Psychology. A nationally certified school psychologist, Mrs. Lazarus has over 30 years' experience in Broward County, Florida schools and has guided the student support team at the middle school level in threat assessment and student care plan development.

Richard Lieberman, MA, NCSP is a lecturer in the Graduate School of Education at Loyola Marymount University and from 1986-2011 he coordinated Suicide Prevention Services for Los Angeles Unified School District. Mr. Lieberman is co-author of *School Crisis Prevention: the PREPaRE Model* and *Best Practices in Suicide Intervention (2014, 2008 & 2002)* for the National Association of School Psychologists.

Dr. Troy Loker is a school psychologist in the Honolulu District of Hawaii and a former Co-Chair of Tampa Bay's Gay, Lesbian, and Straight Education Network; a former District Coordinator for Positive Behavioral Interventions & Supports in Hillsborough County Public Schools, FL and a Past-President of the Florida Association of School Psychologists. He earned national research awards for his dissertation on inclusive school-based supports for LGBTQ youth and trains professionals on this topic.

Dr. Melissa Louvar-Reeves is a nationally certified school psychologist and licensed professional counselor and special education teacher. She is an adjunct instructor at Winthrop University, school psychologist at a pre-K-12th grade school, and a Crisis Management and

Psychological Recovery expert. Dr. Louvar-Reeves is a co-author of the NASP PREPaRE School Crisis Prevention and Intervention curriculum and 2016-17 President of the National Association of School Psychologists.

Dr. Terry Molony is a School Psychologist in Cherry Hill, NJ where she spearheads several initiatives related to positive behavior supports and positive psychology. She serves as an adjunct faculty member in the School Psychology Program and an Assistant Clinical Professor in the Clinical Psychology Programs at the Philadelphia College of Osteopathic Medicine. Dr. Molony was selected by National Association of School Psychologists as the 2014 National School Psychologist of the Year.

Shamika Patton, Ed.S. has worked with the Florida Department of Children and Families as a caseworker and supervisor working with abused and neglected children and those in foster care. She is also a certified school psychologist and presently serves as the Program Manager overseeing child welfare programs for the Seminole Tribe of Florida.

Dr. Donna Poland is the former Director of the Middle School at the Nova Southeastern University School. She has worked as a teacher, coordinator, and administrator in Texas and Florida in both public and private schools. She offers training in school and community engagement.

Dr. Scott Poland is a Professor and Co-Director of the Suicide and Violence Prevention Office at Nova Southeastern University and a Past President of the National Association of School Psychologists. He is an internationally recognized expert on school crisis and youth suicide. He has authored five books on these subjects. He has assisted many schools after tragedies including school shootings, suicides, terrorism and natural disasters. He has testified before the U.S. Congress on four occasions.

Dr. Eric Rossen is a Nationally Certified School Psychologist and licensed psychologist. He has experience working in public schools and independent practice, and is currently the Director of Professional Development and Standards for the National Association of School Psychologists. Dr. Rossen has published several manuscripts and books, and he has presented nationally on issues related to school safety, psychological trauma, and school psychological practices. He also served as adjunct faculty at the University of Missouri and Prince George's Community College.

Dr. Susan Swearer is the Willa Cather Professor of Educational Psychology at the University of Nebraska – Lincoln. She co-directs the Bullying Research Network, directs the Empowerment Initiative, and is coauthor/coeditor of the books: *Bullying Prevention and Intervention: Realistic Strategies for Schools*, *Handbook of Bullying in Schools* and *Bullying in North American Schools*. Dr. Swearer has authored over 100 chapters and articles on bullying, depression, and anxiety.

Kenneth S. Trump, M.P.A. is President of National School Safety and Security Services specializing in school security, emergency preparedness, safety communications and litigation consulting. He is the author of three books and more than 400 articles on school safety issues. Mr. Trump is a four-time Congressional witness and has testified before the U.S. Commission on Civil Rights. (For more see www.schoolsecurity.org)

Frank Zenere, Ed.S. is a crisis specialist for Miami-Dade County Public Schools. He has served on the National Association of School Psychologists' National Emergency Assistance Team. He has responded to multiple school shooting incidents, cluster suicides, earthquakes, hurricanes, floods and acts of terrorism. He led crisis teams for the National Organization for Victim Assistance following 9/11, earthquakes in Turkey and the tsunami in Malaysia. He has trained countless responders nationally and internationally on crisis prevention and intervention.

Index